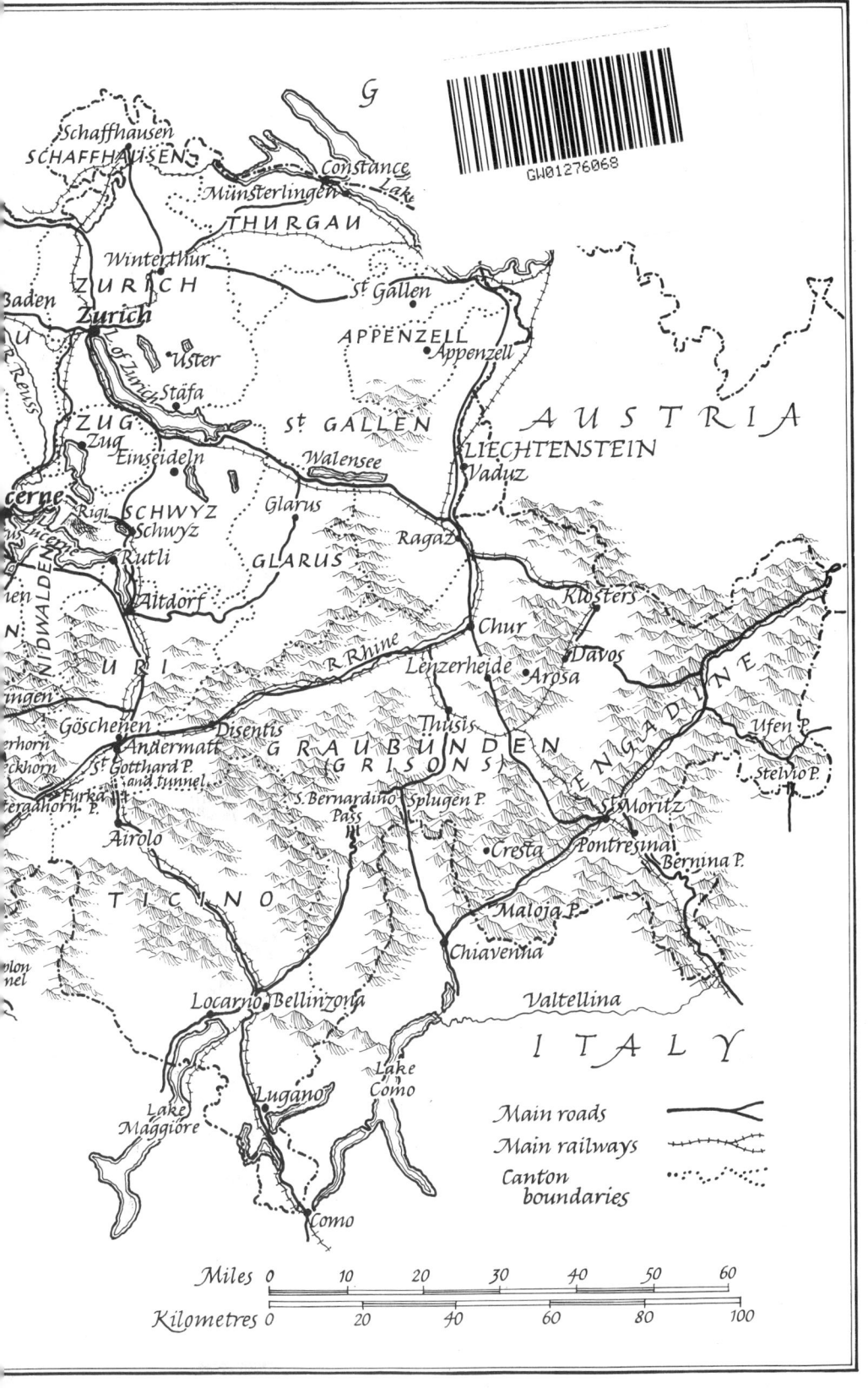

THE SWISS
AND THE BRITISH

The Town Hall, Berne

THE SWISS
AND THE BRITISH

JOHN WRAIGHT

MICHAEL RUSSELL

First published in Great Britain 1987
by Michael Russell (Publishing) Ltd,
The Chantry, Wilton, Salisbury, Wiltshire

Endpaper map by Denys R. Baker

Printed and bound in Great Britain
by Robert Hartnoll, Bodmin, Cornwall

All rights reserved
ISBN 0 85955 143 1

TO MY WIFE
WITHOUT WHOSE ENCOURAGEMENT
AND FORBEARANCE THIS BOOK
COULD NOT HAVE BEEN WRITTEN,
IN RECOLLECTION OF OUR YEARS OF
PARTNERSHIP AT THE BRITISH EMBASSY
IN BERNE.

Contents

Acknowledgements	ix
Author's Note	xiii
Introduction	1
Chronology	89
Notes	367
Bibliography	369
Appendix A	431
Envoys between the Countries	
Appendix B	435
Foreign Trade and Exchange Rates	
Index	437

Acknowledgements

I should like to acknowledge my debt to the late ambassasor Beat de Fischer and Sir Arnold Lunn, both of whose enthusiasm for the history of the Anglo-Swiss relationship inspired me to research the subject further.

To list the name of everyone who has in some way helped me this book would be an almost impossible task. However, I must record my deep gratitude to the Swiss Ambassador in London, M. François-Charles Pictet and to his Cultural Attaché, Dr Hans Kunz, in particular, and also to his Minister (Economic and Financial) M. Milan Lusser, together with (in alphabetical order) Richard Amstad, Dr Walter Amstutz, Patricia Barnes, Dame Gillian Brown and Peter Tangemann, for their great kindness in reading through my draft and in giving me so many valuable suggestions and so much helpful advice.

I should equally like to express my sincere thanks to the following individuals (again in alphabetical order), all of whom have contributed particularly useful additions to my text, or have given me especial help in connexion with the preparation of this book: Allan Allbeury, Peter Arengo-Jones, Franz Blum, Mungo Campbell, John Chick, Sandra de Laszlo, Dr R. Dietrich, Dr P. Fellner, Lewis Foreman, Anne Furrer, Dr Rosemary Gordon, Dr Clive Grey, Martin Hayman, Grace Holmes, Elizabeth Hussey, Nicky James, Jean-Pierre Jelmini, Dr Dorothy Johnson, Patricia Johnson, Struky Kalev, Wing Commander Timothy King, Albert Kunz, Robert Lawford, W. Leuch, Dr Michael Lynch, Hugh McAndrew, Alison Macdonald, Dr Theophile von Mandach, Sir Peter Marshall, Vicki Martineau, Guy de Meuron, Clemens Moser, Michael Moss, Gillian Newman, the Ven. Anthony Nind, Dennis Paravicini, C. J. Pennington, David Pimlott, John Powell-Jones, Jimmy Reeve, John Rich, Renate Riedl, Canon T. Roberts, Sandy Rowe, Colonel H. Rüesch, Margaret Savill, the Rt Revd John Satterthwaite, Bishop of Gibraltar in Europe, Douglas Simmons, Robert Smart, Frank Solari, Professor

x *Acknowledgements*

Dr Hans Stark, Patrick Stobart, Dr B. Stüdeli, Carl Ulmer, Pauline Wickham, R. A. R. Wilson.

I wish also to thank the following institutions and companies who have willingly answered my questions, or undertaken research for me, or have kindly provided additional material: Aberdeen University; The Alpine Club, London; The Anglo-Swiss Society, London; Bank of England; BBC – Brown Boveri, & Cie A.G, Baden; British Aerospace plc, Stevenage; British Airways plc, Historical Aviation Service; British Brown-Boveri Ltd, Knutsford; British Consulate-General, Geneva; British Consulate-General, Zurich; The British Council; British Embassy, Berne; British Manufacturing & Research Co. Ltd, Grantham; British-Swiss Chamber of Commerce, Zurich; British Telecom plc, London; British Tourist Authority; *Der Bund*, Berne; Cadbury-Schweppes plc, London; CIBA-Geigy A.G, Basel; CIBA-Geigy plc, London; Thomas Cook Ltd, London and Peterborough; Courtaulds plc, London; Credit Suisse; The Dreyfus Foundation, New York; Edinburgh University; Eisenbibliothek and Georg Fischer A.G, Schaffhausen; Foreign and Commonwealth Office; Glasgow University; Imperial Chemical Industries plc, London; Kümmerly & Frey, Berne; Montres Rolex S.A., Geneva; Musée d'Art et d'Histoire, Neuchâtel; Musée Militaire de Colombier; Museum zu Allerheiligen, Schaffhausen; National Galleries of Scotland, Edinburgh; Nestlé S.A, Vevey; The Nestlé Company Ltd, Croydon; Phillips & Drew, London; Pro Helvetia, Zurich; Roche Products Ltd, Welwyn Garden City; The Royal Institute of International Affairs, London; St Andrews University; Sandoz A.G, Basel; The Ski Club of Great Britain, London; The Society of Analytical Psychology, London; Spink & Son Ltd, London; Sulzer Bros A.G., Winterthur; Swissair, London; Swiss Bank Corporation; The Swiss-British Society, Basel; The Swiss-British Society, Berne; Swiss Life & Pension Co. Ltd, London; Swiss National Tourist Office; Swiss Volksbank; Three Kings Hotel, Basel; Union Bank of Switzerland; Wander Ltd, King's Langley; Watches of Switzerland Ltd.

LIBRARIES

Of the various libraries whose services I have called upon in the compilation of this book, I should like to thank in particular the Guildhall Library, City of London, always unfailingly helpful, quick and efficient, the Alpine Club Library, a treasure-house of books on Switzerland, the British Library with its incomparable wealth of printed sources, the London Library, the Bodleian Library, Oxford, the Foreign and Commonwealth Office Library, Chatham House Library, the Swiss Embassy Library, the libraries of the Ski Club of Great Britain, of the Order of St John of Jerusalem, and of the Overseas Trade Board, and of course the Public Record Office both in London and in Kew.

PERMISSIONS TO QUOTE

Finally, it is a pleasure to acknowledge the permission kindly granted by the following publishers and authors or their agents, to quote extracts from works published by them: Geo. Allen & Unwin (Sir Arnold Lunn, *Unkilled for So Long*, 1968, and Michael Stewart, *Modern Forms of Government*, 1964); Edward Arnold (Walter Larden, *Recollections of an Old Mountaineer*, 1910); Ernest Benn (Christopher Hughes, *Switzerland*, 1973); Berg Publishers (J.R. de Salis, *Switzerland and Europe*, 1971); Chatham House (Sir Anthony Parsons, *International Affairs*, January 1985 issue); De Clivo Press, Zurich (John Russell and Andrew Wilton, *Turner in Switzerland*, 1976); Evans Brothers, by kind permission of Unwin Hyman (Monk Gibbons, *Swiss Enchantment*, 1950); Eyre & Spottiswoode (Sir Arnold Lunn, *The Story of Skiing*, 1952 and Sir Gavin de Beer, *Speaking of Switzerland*, 1952); T. Fisher Unwin (F.F. Roget, *Ski Runs in the High Alps*, 1913); Longmans (G.M. Trevelyan, *Clio, a Muse, and Other Essays*, 1913); Macmillan Publishers (R.F. Harrod, *The Life of John Maynard Keynes*, 1951); New Helvetic Society, Lenzburg (Eric Mettler in *Switzerland, Present and Future*, 1963); David Higham Associates/ Century (L.S. Amery, *Days of Fresh Air*, 1939); Oxford University Press (E.E. Reynolds, *Baden-Powell*, 1942); A.D. Peters & Co. on behalf of the Estate of Hilaire Belloc (Hilaire Belloc, *The Path to Rome*, 1902); SPCK (Karl Barth, *A Letter to Great Britain from Switzerland*, 1941); Swiss Volksbank, Berne (Hans Christoph von Tavel, *Un siècle d'art suisse*, 1969); A.P. Watt Ltd on behalf of the Royal Literary Fund (Somerset Maugham, *Ashenden*, 1928).

ILLUSTRATION SOURCES

Alpine Club Library, pp. 35, 90, 98, 99, 123, 220, 249 (a-f), 256, 257, 263, 324; Dr Walter Amstutz, p. 354; Atlantis Musikbuch Verlag, Zurich, p. 57; Bibliothèque Publique et Universitaire de Genève, pp. 75, 215; City of Birmingham Art Gallery, p. 217; British Aerospace, p. 341(a); British Airways Historical Archives, p. 314; British Library, pp. 50, 119; Brown Boveri & Co. Ltd, p. 274; Burgerbibliothek, Berne, p. 100; Cadbury Schweppes plc, p. 72;

xii *Acknowledgements*

Crown Copyright (from original in Public Record Office), London, pp. 26, 27; Galerie George, Kensington, p. 283; Guildhall Library, City of London, pp. 47, 52, 141, 158, 163, 247; Historisches Museum, Basel, p. 253; Historisches Museum, Berne, pp. 103, 147; I.C.I. plc, p. 265; Kandahar Ski Club/Ski Club of Great Britain, pp. 303, 305, 306, 309, 310; Keystone-Press AG, Zurich, pp. 325, 356; Kümmerly & Frey, Berne, p. 88; Kunstmuseum, Berne, pp. 13 (Gottfried Keller-Stiftung), 166; Ministry of Defence, p. 340 (b); Montres Rolex, Geneva, p. 300; Musée d'Art et d'Histoire, Neuchâtel, p. 172; Musée Militaire de Colombier, p. 196; Museum zu Allerheiligen, Schaffhausen, p. 136; National Galleries of Scotland, pp. 108, 117, 180; National Portrait Gallery, London, pp. 20, 24, 39, 56, 61, 64 (a & b), 128, 134, 152, 173, 184, 211, 212, 234, 237, 240, 267, 307, 312, 339; Phillips & Drew, p. 78; The Photo Source, London, p. 363; Royal Ordnance plc, p. 341 (b); Spink & Son Ltd, London, p. 182; Staatsarchiv, Basel, p. 201; Sulzer Bros, Winterthur, p. 206; Swiss Air Force, p. 340 (a); Swissair, London, p. 316; Swiss National Library, Berne, p. 223; Swiss National Museum, Zurich, pp. 4, 80; Swiss National Tourist Office, frontispiece, pp. 6, 37, 66, 83, 96, 114, 132, 149, 170, 175, 228, 229, 259, 261, 270, 276, 278, 286, 293, 328, 351; Tate Gallery, London (copyright ADAGP, 1986), pp. 334, 348; courtesy of the Board of Trustees of the Victoria and Albert Museum, London, pp. 44, 46, 94, 179, 204; Wander Ltd, King's Langley, Herts, p. 290; Zentralbibliothek, Zurich, pp. 110, 138.

Author's Note

The Swiss Confederation in its present form has been built up gradually over seven centuries. In 1291 the three founding cantons of Uri, Schwyz and Unterwalden formed an everlasting league to frustrate the ambitions of the Dukes of Habsburg to control the approaches to the St Gotthard Pass. Lucerne joined them in 1332, then Zurich and Berne. By 1353 there was a confederation of eight cantons. Fribourg and Solothurn acceded in 1481 and Basel in 1501, and the Confederation had grown to thirteen cantons by 1513. Napoleon imposed a new constitution on Switzerland in 1803, and a confederation of nineteen cantons which now included the Grisons, Ticino and Vaud. After the French defeat, the Valais, Neuchâtel and Geneva joined and a new, loose confederation was formed with twenty-two cantons in all. On 1 January 1979 a new canton, the Jura, was added, made from part of the canton of Berne. Today Switzerland is a federal state of twenty-three cantons of which three are divided into half cantons, making twenty-six sovereign units, autonomous save where rights have been ceded to the Confederation. However, for the purposes of this book reference to Switzerland, or Swiss, in the context of the earlier stages of Swiss history means territory, or the inhabitants of territory, later to become part of the present-day Swiss Confederation.

The story of the British-Swiss connexion that follows is in two main parts. There is an introductory survey of the subject, followed by a Chronology of events year by year from earliest times. There is a detailed index for those who may wish to follow particular aspects or themes. There is, too, a statistical appendix giving figures of Anglo-Swiss trade over the years and exchange rates, and a historical list of British envoys to Switzerland and of Swiss envoys to Britain. Finally, there is a fairly extensive bibliography of existing works on Anglo-Swiss relations.

Introduction

A Unique Relationship

'I have often wonder'd that a Country situated almost in the Middle of Europe, as Switzerland is, should be as little known' wrote Abraham Stanyan, a former British envoy to Berne, in *An Account of Switzerland Written in the Year 1714*. Stanyan's book, one of the best English studies of the country up to then, was written before the British discovered the Swiss Alps and Switzerland's attractions as a holiday centre. However, Stanyan's remarks were not about the physical aspects of the country but about its history, its system of government and its people; and, despite the great improvement in communications and in the flow of information, his comments remain largely true today. As Jonathan Steinberg wrote in his excellent *Why Switzerland?* (1976), 'No country is more frequently visited but less known.'

Perhaps one reason for this is that there have never been any wars between the British and the Swiss, adding a martial detachment to the physical detachment of no adjoining frontiers. Indeed Switzerland is the only European nation which Britain has never fought against as an enemy nor alongside as an ally. Both nations have, by and large, been able to choose the degree of their relations with each other based on a reasoned assessment of each other's qualities, faults, achievements and place in the world. Moreover, the Swiss have never posed a threat to Britain's interests as each of Switzerland's neighbours has at one time or another. Nor has Britain ever posed a serious threat to Switzerland.

Yet each country has had a deep influence on the other in a number of ways. There have been periods of close amity and periods of controversy and tension. On several occasions Britain has risked war in Europe to uphold Switzerland's independence. Few peoples have sent a higher proportion of their sons to Britain to find their fortunes than the Swiss. And while in more recent times, hardly any country has inspired in the British such a love and enthusiasm for its scenery than has Switzerland, and no nation has been more responsible for the birth of the Swiss tourist industry than Britain, over many centuries Switzerland has meant to the British many different things – a recruiting ground for some of the finest soldiers in Europe, a place of refuge, a source of religious guidance, a centre for education, a country of literary inspiration; to some a safe haven for their funds. Turner chose to lavish more of his talents on Swiss scenes than on those of any other foreign country. Churchill chose Switzerland as the place from which to make his first grand appeal for European unity after the Second World War. Today, when economics have supplanted tourism as the most important Anglo-Swiss connexion, Switzerland, now one of the wealthiest countries in the world, generally imports more from Britain per head than the Germans and the French combined. And there is no country, except America, that has invested more money in Britain than Switzerland.

THE NATURE OF RELATIONS BETWEEN COUNTRIES

Relations between Britain and Switzerland, as indeed between any two countries, take several forms. There are the official, or political, relations between the two governments, conducted at the diplomatic level, the responsible ministry in London being the Foreign and Commonwealth Office, usually working through the British Embassy in Berne, while the responsible ministry in Switzerland is the Federal Department of External Affairs in Berne, usually working through the Swiss Embassy in London.

These official relations include not only political questions, but military and defence matters, the government aspects of commercial and economic questions and of some cultural, scientific and social matters too. In addition, each embassy has a number of consular posts reporting to it. Concerned primarily with the protection of their nationals and with the promotion of trade, they are generally located in the more important centres of the country.

Then there are the normal trade and financial relations between British and Swiss business firms, between manufacturers and merchants, banks and insurance companies in each country. There are cultural relations, covering the whole range of the arts and sciences, medicine, education, philosophy and religion, built up of innumerable contacts, visits and exchanges between individuals, artists and writers, lecturers, teachers; and through learned societies, exhibitions, theatre groups, orchestras, opera companies; and manifested also in less concrete form through the effects which books and publications in one country have on cultural groups in the other – exchanges of thought and ideas. Again, there are social relations, which include tourism and sports, and in the case of Britain and Switzerland, the groups of young people who go to work as 'au pairs' in the other country. In addition, mostly arising from one or other of the types of relations described, supplementing and often reinforcing the other relations, are the myriad of personal relationships between individuals.

Although government policies clearly dominate relations between countries, economic realities (in a free society at least) also play an important part – the need, or the opportunities, for trade and investment. Today, too, the attitude for the time being of the media – the press, radio and television – can have a strong influence on one nation's attitude towards another. Again, historical, and often emotional, factors play a significant part. Essentially, however, the way that one nation regards another stems from the character of the people themselves, from the similarities and from the differences they see between them, from the traits they may admire or dislike in each other, from the general perceptions they may hold of one another.

HOW ONE NATION PERCEIVES ANOTHER

These judgements and opinions which nations form of each other are made up of a multitude of factors. The majority of first impressions probably come from childhood stories – perhaps *Heidi* or *William Tell* in the case of the British about the Swiss, or *Robinson Crusoe* or a novel by Robert Louis Stevenson in the case of the Swiss about the British. Then come gleanings from history books at school, information probably already thirty years or so out of date but which many people tend not to update consciously for the rest of their lives. To this is added a variety of *ad hoc* impressions gained over the years from what the press and television choose to show about 'newsworthy' aspects of the country concerned, from chance encounters with nationals of that country, and from visits made to it in the course of holidays or business.

In all, the image that one nation has of another is often quite heavily weighted towards the past, or towards somewhat superficial or inconsequential aspects of its real character or identity. Thus, for many in Britain, their image of Switzerland might be, at its simplest, Swiss chalets and mountains, cheese, clocks the Red Cross, banks and perhaps muesli; while for many in Switzerland, their image of Britain might be, again at its simplest, roast beef, seafarers, Mr Pickwick, sport, pageantry, fair play and perhaps London and its policemen.

A milkmaid making butter near Lucerne: sketch by Georg Ludwig Vogel (1788-1879).

The Swiss and British Compared

On the face of it, there might seem to be little in common between the Swiss and the British. Switzerland is a small republican confederation of twenty-six cantons. With a total of 16,000 square miles, it is less than two-thirds the area of Scotland. The most mountainous country in Europe, its position in the central Alps makes it the fountain-head of four of the major rivers of the Continent – the Rhine, Rhône, Po and Danube. It is at the intersection of four main climatic regions of Europe, and at the meeting point of three of the main cultural and linguistic areas. Of its 6½ million population, some two-thirds are German-Swiss speaking, one-fifth French, one-tenth Italian, while about one per cent are remnants of a fourth linguistic group – Romansch (a debased form of Latin), which survives among the high valleys of the Grisons. Nearly half the people are Protestant, nearly half Roman Catholic. Over 900,000 of the population are foreigners.

By contrast, Britain – the United Kingdom of Great Britain and Northern Ireland – is six times as big as Switzerland, with nearly ten times its population. Five hundred miles away from Switzerland, an island off the mainland of Europe, for centuries pursuing a maritime way of life, English-speaking (plus a little Welsh and Gaelic), having an Established Church which is Protestant, a hereditary monarchy, and, until the middle of this century, constituting the rich and powerful centre of a vast overseas empire.

The Swiss character has, in large part, been formed by the mountains, while the British character has been much influenced by the sea (and by the weather resulting from it). But although these very different environments have bred a number of differences between the Swiss and the British, they have also produced some common traits – a certain impermeability, a sense of self-sufficiency, a desire to be one's own master, and a strong love of freedom. This latter common characteristic has been well expressed in Wordsworth's poem 'Thoughts of a Briton on the Subjugation of Switzerland', written at the time of the Napoleonic Wars:

> Two Voices are there; one is of the sea,
> One of the mountains; each a mighty Voice:
> In both from age to age thou didst rejoice,
> They were thy chosen music, Liberty!

A Landsgemeinde in the old town square of Glarus, with the peaks of Wiggis and Rautisputz behind.

Professor F. F. Roget of Geneva has put it another way. He wrote in his book *Ski Runs in the High Alps* that he liked to regard the Swiss as navigators of the Alps and the English as mountaineers of the sea. 'There is some similarity in the risks incurred.'

REGARD FOR LIBERTY

Ils jouissent d'une liberté qui élève l'esprit
Beat Ludwig de Muralt – of the English

A mutual attachment to liberty has long provided the strongest bond between the Swiss and the British. Muralt's comment, made of his visit in 1725, that the English enjoyed a liberty that exalts the mind, was echoed by many other Swiss observers. In 1789 Jakob Heinrich Meister, fresh from witnessing the French Revolution, remarked that he had not taken fifty steps on British soil before he sensed a spirit of liberty that he had never experienced before. The British have similarly admired Swiss liberty. After a visit to Switzerland in 1776, Archdeacon William Coxe wrote: 'A general spirit of liberty pervades and activates the several constitutions.' And Lord Bryce used similar words in his *Modern Democracies* (1921): '. . . They are all imbued with a spirit of liberty.'

In both countries this regard for liberty has produced strong democratic institutions: in the field of political affairs and of civic tradition the Swiss have more in common with the British than with virtually any other country in Europe. The British are proud to regard Westminster as the Mother of Parliaments, but in fact the Landsgemeinde (the annual meeting of all the citizens who vote directly on issues of the day) in the small founding cantons of Switzerland dates back to before Simon de Montfort's Parliament of 1265. And while this ancient method of open voting has become impracticable with the growth of population in most of Switzerland today, the contemporary Swiss political system with its proportional representation, its frequent referendums and its people's initiatives (enabling citizens to oppose a new law or to propose an amendment to the constitution) is still much more of a direct democracy than the representative system in force in Britain. Indeed, the referendum is a logical and practical expansion of the old Landsgemeinde. As Lord Bryce concluded: 'Among the modern democracies which are true democracies, Switzerland has the highest claim to be studied.'

SWISS DIFFERENCES FROM THEIR NEIGHBOURS

The Swiss might seem to have much more in common with their German, French and Italian neighbours than with the British. The Swiss Confederation, after all, is comprised of three of the main cultures of the Continent, while the British, be they English, Scots, Welsh or Northern Irish, are comprised by and large of one rather more homogeneous Anglo-Saxon culture. But while the Swiss do have many common bonds with their neighbours, they also have several very important differences. Unlike the Germans, they are not susceptible to regimentation. Unlike the French, they dislike brilliance and cleverness. Unlike the Italians they abhor ostentation and histrionics. And these Swiss attitudes are all ones which, in greater or lesser degree, find sympathy with the British.

There is another sphere in which the Swiss differ from their German and French neighbours and come closer to the British. Like the

British they tend to be empirical and practical; and this has shown itself, among other ways, in the number of eminent scientists and mathematicians which both countries have produced. The corollary of this is a dislike in general of abstract thought. It is no coincidence that both the Swiss and the British tend to feel uncomfortable when culture in the national context is mentioned, and to play down their considerable cultural achievements. C. F. Ramuz perhaps expressed the Swiss attitude when he remarked of his fellow countrymen: 'Ils sont peut-être poètes, mais avant tout électeurs.'

REGIONAL CHARACTERISTICS

Each nation, predictably, has its different regional characteristics. The Swiss have in them not only Germanic and Romanic, but also Celtic blood like the Scots and the Welsh. And for the Scots and the Welsh, like the Swiss, mountains have played an important part in their history. To this day every Swiss keeps his rifle at home for the defence of his country, as did the Scots their personal arms until at least the middle of the eighteenth century. Perhaps the Scots are, of all the British, the most akin to the Swiss.

Through John Knox they not only have absorbed Calvinism as the basis of the Scottish Church; with it they accepted the basic teaching that all men are equal in the sight of God – that the poorest peasant is as good as the richest laird. And whereas in Switzerland this tenet of Calvin's faith was soon embraced by all Swiss, in Britain its dissemination stopped for centuries at the Scottish border. The Scots have another trait, too, in common with the Swiss. A shared experience of hard soil and years of enforced frugality has made both races conscious of the need for insurance and good money management. (The Swiss have the biggest savings per head of any country in the world.) Again, many of the more adventurous Scots, like many Swiss, went abroad to seek a living, first as soldiers in foreign armies on the Continent and later extending into wider fields – in trade and commerce, and the professions.

In the eighteenth and nineteenth centuries many Swiss, like the Scots, served in the British forces or settled in outposts of the British Empire.

ANGLO-SWISS DIFFERENCES

There are naturally many traits which distinguish the Swiss from the British, some resulting from different ways of life, some caused by deeper influences. Thus the Swiss are more solid, serious, and perhaps stiffer and more methodical than the British. They tend, too, to be a little combative compared with the more easy-going British (or at least the English). The British, though they like their privacy, live generally in an essentially open way, with open house and with an attachment to clubs and pubs. The Swiss live in a more closed society, with a strong attachment to the family. While the British are grumblers, the Swiss are worriers. The British have an open sense of humour; the Swiss have a more private one.

The British are usually slow starters but strong finishers. The Swiss are slow in accepting new ideas and often slow in reaching decisions (both because of an innate caution and because all must be consulted), but once a decision has been made they are meticulous in implementing it. For the British, many Swiss may on occasion seem a little stuffy, smug or obstinate, and to have a rather narrow horizon. But, equally, they are not an impressionable people; they are shrewd, and are not taken in by loud claims. For the Swiss, many British often seem somewhat hypocritical, lazy, improvident and short-sighted (it may have been a Swiss who remarked that the British cannot see the writing on the wall until they have their backs to it). They consider that the British give far too much attention to sport. And the time and money that many British trade unionists are prepared to lose on protracted strikes are, to the thrifty Swiss, who have not had a real strike for fifty years, beyond belief.

Another aspect of the British character which has often puzzled the Swiss is the inability of many Englishmen to express their feelings. A visitor from Berne in 1767, Charles Victor de Bonstetten, a friend of the poet Gray, wrote home: 'It is only in England that people know how to be silent; I have seen fifteen people, men and women, sitting in a circle and saying nothing to each other for a quarter of an hour.'

The Swiss find difficulty, too, in understanding English class-consciousness. Every Swiss considers himself as good as the next man. He strongly resents anyone who puts on airs. He thinks it quite right, for example, that Swiss cabinet ministers should travel to their offices on the bus, or be served last in a restaurant. And in industry, Swiss management knows better than to flaunt its difference in wealth or status in front of the employees.

Notwithstanding their strong individuality, the Swiss are more disciplined than the British in many ways. Most of them still consider cleanliness to be next to godliness. Their streets are tidy, their public transport the cleanest, and probably the most efficient, in Europe. They are fond of precision – witness not only the development of the

Swiss watch industry, but also the small intricate designs in their peasant art and the quiet but detailed black and white frescoes seen in their churches. They are early risers and hard workers. They are peaceful and strongly law-abiding. Indeed, while they dislike being told by politicians what to do, they freely impose on themselves innumerable rules and by-laws in the interests of civilised living and orderliness. At the same time they seem to enjoy pursuing petty feuds with their neighbours; and they can be litigious, sometimes quick to resort to their lawyers.

While both nations have a strong civic sense, the average Swiss generally has a rather more balanced view of the political situation in his country than the average Englishman has in his. This has something to do with Swiss education, with the stability which proportional representation gives to Swiss politics, and to the fact that there is less political partisanship. It has also to do with the attitude of the Swiss informational media. It is important that the Swiss should be well-informed when they are expected to vote in frequent local and national referendums.

SWISS CALMNESS . . .

Swiss calm and tranquillity has been favourably noted by British travellers for many years. The diarist John Evelyn, on a visit to Switzerland in 1646, commented on the Swiss: '. . . neither envied nor envying . . . they live in great simplicity and tranquillity . . .'

And in 1701, Joseph Addison, founder with Richard Steele of *The Spectator,* wrote: 'I have often considered with a great deal of pleasure the profound peace and tranquillity that reigns in Switzerland.'

Samuel Johnson never visited Switzerland, but that did not prevent him from giving his opinion (1742):

Let those who despise the capacity of the Swiss, tell us by what wonderful policy, or by what happy conciliation of interests, it is brought to pass, that in a body made up of different communities and different religions, there should be no civil commotions, though the people are so warlike that to nominate and raise an army is the same.

. . . AND HONESTY

Swiss honesty, too, has been remarked upon by many British observers. In *The Wealth of Nations* Adam Smith cited the example of the Swiss attitude towards taxation:

[In] the Canton of Unterwald . . . the people assemble and everyone is said to declare with the greatest frankness what he is worth in order to be taxed accordingly. At Zurich the law orders that . . . everyone should be taxed in proportion to his revenue, the amount of which he is obliged to declare on oath. They have no suspicion . . . that any of their fellow-citizens will deceive them. At Basil . . . all the citizens make oath that they will pay every three months all the taxes imposed by law . . .

BRITISH QUALITY OF LIFE

If the British have admired Swiss tranquillity, the Swiss have, for just as long, admired the quality of life in Britain. The Bernese, Beat Louis de Muralt, in his *Lettres sur les Anglais,* wrote:

The English have neither the avidity of the French in amassing wealth, nor the niggardliness of the Dutch in keeping it . . . After having accumulated riches, some of them give up trade and become country gentlemen, that is they know how to stop and enjoy the fruits of their labour.

In 1786 the author Benjamin Constant, born in Lausanne, on a return visit to Britain (he had earlier studied at Edinburgh University) commented on 'the impression of happiness, good sense and orderliness which the natives convey'. And in 1813 Benjamin Constant's companion of many years, Mme de Staël (whose Swiss father, Jacques Necker, had been French Minister of Finance), wrote:

One of the marvels of English liberty is the great number of men who give up their time to public works in every town and county, whose mind and character are formed by the occupation and duties of a citizen.

CHARACTERISTICS IN COMMON

Despite their differences and occasional misunderstandings, the Swiss and the British have, over the centuries, developed a mutual esteem for each other. While times and moral attitudes may be changing now, a common Puritan belief in the Bible long helped both Swiss and British to give their national life its sobriety, its sincerity and its fixed trust in character. Each admires the other's love of freedom, straightforward approach to affairs, level-headedness, stability, undemonstrativeness, determination and integrity. In the early seventeenth century Francis Bacon, in his essay *On Nobility,* wrote: 'We see the Switzers last well, notwithstanding their diversity of religion and of cantons. For utility is their bond, and not respects.' De Muralt, again, thought that the English had plenty of common sense. Another percipient Swiss observer, César de Saussure, considered that the Englishman would sacrifice everything to retain his liberty. John Ruskin, writing of the Swiss, declared:

You will find among them . . . no suble wit nor high enthusiasm, only an undeceivable common sense, and an obstinate rectitude . . . They use no phrases of friendship, but they do not fail you at your need.

Regard for each other has been particularly strong in some periods. The years following the Napoleonic Wars was one. Johann Georg Bodmer, the Swiss inventor, on a visit to England in 1816, found everywhere the English 'prepossessed in favour of the Swiss'; while a writer in Geneva in 1834 called the English 'the model people from whom emanates all that is noble, beautiful and laudable'.

Perhaps Castlereagh summed up best the feelings of the British for the Swiss and of the Swiss for the British when, as Foreign Secretary in a speech in Parliament in 1821, he referred to

. . . the mutual attachment of the people of each country arising from similarity of character and political institutions, [and] of their extraordinary respect for each other.

The Military Connexion

Stettono Roma e Sparta multi secoli armate e liberi;
gli Svizzeri sono armatissimi e liberissimi.
Niccolo Machiavelli

There is yet another bond which links the Swiss and the British. Each has, over the centuries, admired the other's determination to defend its freedom. The Swiss military reputation is of long standing. Detachments of *gaesati* (javelin throwers) from the Grisons were brought to England by the Romans to help defend Hadrian's Wall. After the birth of the Swiss Confederation (1291), in the fourteenth and fifteenth centuries Swiss arms beat in succession three of the greatest powers on the Continent. After their defeat at Marignano in 1515 the Swiss adopted a policy of neutrality, but Swiss troops offered their services abroad, and were much sought after by the monarchs of Europe. Henry VIII's attempt to win the Swiss to the British side against the French, the raising of Swiss troops by successive British monarchs from William III to George III and the recruitment of Swiss volunteers for the Crimean War, are described in the Chronology.

Over the years, largely because of Switzerland's strategic situation in the centre of Europe and the pressures upon it from its powerful surrounding neighbours, Swiss neutrality has become indissolubly linked with Swiss independence. But the Swiss have long held that if

The Swiss and the British Compared

The Retreat from Marignano, *by Ferdinand Hodler, 1899.*

their neutrality is to be credible they must be able to defend themselves. 'Permanent armed neutrality' is a basic principle of Swiss policy. This has meant continuing compulsory annual military service for ages twenty to fifty, and a militia army which is twice the size of the professional British one. It was successful in keeping the peace for Switzerland for nearly three centuries until the Napoleonic Wars, and has been afterwards until the present day.

The close link that the Swiss have always kept between the maintenance of liberty and a strong defence was recognised as far back as the sixteenth century by Machiavelli when he wrote: 'Rome and Sparta were for many centuries armed and free; the Swiss are the most highly armed and the most free.' Successive British visitors to Switzerland, too, have remarked on this connexion. John Evelyn, on his visit in 1646, commented:

Every man goes with a sword by his side, the whole country well-disciplined, and indeed impregnable, which made the Romans have such ill success against them . . . I look upon this country to be the safest spot in all Europe.

In *An Account of Switzerland Written in the Year 1714* Abraham Stanyan wrote: 'There is no one quality so universally allowed to the Switzers as that of valour . . .' Another observer, William Coxe, wrote of the Swiss in 1779:

The youth are diligently trained in all martial exercises . . . and the whole people are enrolled and regularly exercised in their respective militia . . . While most of the other states upon the continent are tending towards a military government, Swisserland alone has no standing armies and yet . . . it is more secure from invasion than any other European power . . .

In 1854, Robert Ferguson, in his *Swiss Men and Swiss Mountains,* commented: 'There is probably, for its size, no more efficient army in Europe than the Swiss'; while *The Times,* in 1860, said: 'Our correspondent, who knows what campaigning is . . . ranks them for strength, endurance, and skill in the management of their weapons, with any *corps d'élite* of any European army.'

Some fifty years later the British military attaché in Berne reported to London:

There can be no doubt that the Swiss army, notwithstanding its militia character and the shortness of its training, has reached a degree of efficiency which would make any of its neighbours more anxious to respect the neutrality of the country than to violate it.

In fact, when the British Army reforms were being drawn up in 1906, a British commission was sent to Switzerland to study the organisation of the Swiss army and its suitability for Britain. At that time General Sir Douglas Haig wrote: 'The Swiss system seems to be exactly what is wanted to root the army in the people.' Though Haig's recommendation was not accepted, the Swiss militia system had many British admirers and has continued to have them since.

On the other side, the Swiss have at various periods in history, had a high esteem for British military strength. This was particularly so during the time of Henry VIII, of Elizabeth and of Cromwell, and again during the Anglo-French wars. In the seventeenth, eighteenth and nineteenth centuries many Swiss were attracted into the British military service, first for the wars against France in the Low Countries, then in different parts of the growing British Empire. William III had a Swiss bodyguard which he brought with him from Holland. (Incidentally, tradition has it that they marched into London to the strains of a *Bernermarsch* which had been composed by one of Cromwell's former generals, Edmund Ludlow, the regicide who spent a lifetime of exile in Switzerland after Charles II came to the throne.) Swiss troops almost certainly saved Marlborough's life at the Battle of Ramillies. Swiss troops from Holland were brought over to Scotland to help counter the 1715 rebellion of the Old Pretender. And in 1745 Swiss Protestant residents in London formed a battalion to help fight against Charles Stuart's uprising. There were Swiss military tutors in the households of the first three Georges, Swiss generals and colonels in the British forces in Northern America, Swiss commanders in India.

In 1756, at the beginning of the Seven Years' War, Swiss officers played a leading part in the formation of George II's Royal American Regiment, later to become the King's Royal Rifle Corps or 60th Rifles. Under Henri Bouquet, the 1st Battalion were the first regular unit in the British Army to change their red coats for inconspicuous clothing when on operations (well before the introduction of khaki). During the Regency, another Swiss, Heinrich Clias (formerly Käslin), introduced a systematic programme of physical training into the British Army and Navy.

In those periods when the British have lost sight of the vital connexion between liberty and national defence, Swiss respect for Britain has declined. In the time of Edward III, the victories of the English bowmen over the French in the early stages of the Hundred Years' War had been due to the far-sightedness of Edward I who, by the Statute of Winchester, had made it compulsory for every male between the ages of fifteen and sixty to provide himself with arms according to his quality. (Perhaps it is no coincidence that Edward I's secretary and adviser was a member of the Swiss Grandson family – see, the Chronology.) However, by 1363 a proclamation had to be issued forbidding ball games and cockfighting, or 'suchlike vain plays which hath no profit in them', and again instructing all men strong in body to exercise the art of shooting in their leisure time. In 1512 the Statute of Winchester had to be invoked once more. Every man under sixty was required always to keep and use a bow and arrows and every boy had to be taught archery from the age of seven; this was followed by a prohibition on the playing of tennis and bowls.

Unlike the Swiss, an ambivalence towards the need for military training has been a trait of the British throughout history. Although they have risen magnificently to the occasion when the threat was imminent, time and again they have displayed a lack of preparedness for war. In the early years of this century when the war clouds in Europe were already gathering but the British defence forces were weak, the British military attaché in Berne reported: 'Clearly, Swiss officers do not regard ours as a serious army at all.' Again, before the

Second World War, the complacency of the British government and its policy of appeasement seriously worried the Swiss, as it did many British followers of Winston Churchill. Switzerland's apprehension and scepticism at Neville Chamberlain's ill-fated visits to Hitler at Berchtesgaden and Godesberg were expressed by a member of the Swiss Federal Council, Herman Obrecht: 'We Swiss will not start making pilgrimages abroad.' A percipient Swiss observer, Eric Mettler, in an article on Switzerland and the English-speaking world written in 1963, remarked; 'We are severely critical of the British only when it looks occasionally as if Sir Winston's cigar might be replaced again by Chamberlain's umbrella'.[1]

The Swiss have few heroes, but Winston Churchill is one of them. In 1940, when Belgium and Holland, Denmark, Norway and France had all fallen, when Switzerland herself was surrounded by the Axis Powers and many Swiss were preparing fearfully to accept Hitler's 'New Order' in Europe, Churchill epitomised the spirit of resistance and independence, and encouraged those who supported the Swiss Supreme Commander, General Guisan, in his policy of positive defence and a fight to the end in the mountain redoubt. There is a Churchill Foundation in Switzerland and a Churchill memorial has been erected on the lakeside at Oberhofen, near Thun. The writer Charles Graves, visiting Switzerland at the end of the war, wrote: 'The respect for Great Britain in 1940 will last for centuries.'[2]

Today political alignments in Europe have changed. The Swiss occupy the geographical gap in NATO's defence line which runs north to south across the Continent. They still maintain a fully equipped militia army which is among the largest in Western Europe; and over the past forty years much of its equipment has been bought from Britain – Centurion tanks and tank ammunition, Vampire, Venom and Hunter jet fighters, Bloodhound and Rapier missiles and armoured recovery vehicles. Moreover, every Swiss of military age still leaves his business once a year for continued army training. And Switzerland is still as determined as ever to defend its neutrality and its independence.

The Historical Perspective

PERIODS OF CLOSE CONTACT

While Great Britain has never fought with or against Switzerland, there were brief periods, in 1516 and again during the Hundred Days in 1815, when she very nearly did so. Moreover, groups of British mercenaries have, on at least two occasions, fought on Swiss soil under foreign commanders. And, as has already been seen, Swiss troops have a long record of service in British employ in Britain's own wars.

There have been several periods of close contact and considerable activity. As the Chronology shows, in the thirteenth century, before the formal beginnings of the Swiss Confederation itself, the England of Henry III and of Edward I had close feudal relations with the House of Savoy, who then controlled the Vaud, Fribourg and part of the Canton of Berne. In 1246 Amadeus IV of Savoy transferred to Henry the fief of St Maurice in the Valais. And in 1257 Henry's brother, Richard of Cornwall, became overlord of Gümmenen, then a strong-point between Berne and Morat (Murten), by reason of his election as King of the Germans.

The early sixteenth century saw the culmination of two hundred years of Swiss military ascendancy on the Continent. In 1513 a Swiss, Cardinal Matthias Schinner of Sion, a friend of Cardinal Wolsey, having forged an alliance between the Pope, the Emperor Maximilian and the Swiss Confederation, tried to bring England into the struggle to drive the French out of Italy. Swiss envoys came to London that year, and English envoys continued the negotiations in Zurich in 1514. An agreement was reached in principle under which Henry VIII was to give the Swiss 15,000 crowns in time of peace and 40,000 crowns in time of war. The Swiss undertook to make war on France whenever Henry chose, with at least 18,000 foot; and neither party would make peace with France without the knowledge of the other. But when the English envoys returned to London, Henry decided to marry his sister to the King of France, and left further discussion in abeyance. (It is indeed possible that Henry knew that he would make peace with France before he sent his ambassadors to Switzerland, and only did this to frighten the French.) However, when Louis XII died suddenly and the ambitious François I succeeded him, Henry reopened discussions with the Swiss. But the latter, chastened by their first military defeat by François I at the Battle of Marignano, were now hesitant. Long and tortuous negotiations followed. The French king, impressed by the military prowess of the Swiss, sought, with offers of large subsidies, to win them onto his side. The Swiss concluded with the French a treaty of perpetual peace and neutrality.

Even so, several of the cantons were reluctant to ratify the treaty, and the English envoy, Richard Pace, together with Cardinal Schinner, continued negotiations with them. They succeeded in raising 17,000 Swiss troops to fight on the Emperor's side, and Pace and Schinner marched with these troops to the outskirts of Milan. But Maximilian's last-minute withdrawal of his own army wrecked the enterprise and the Swiss returned home.

Unwilling to admit defeat, Cardinal Schinner himself came to London in 1516 and succeeded in negotiating a formal alliance between Henry VIII, the Emperor Maximilian, and the King of Spain, in which the Swiss Confederation was included. Schinner suggested that if England attacked France in Picardy the following spring, a Swiss army could be put under the command of the Duke of Suffolk and attack in Burgundy. Another body of Swiss could be made available for operations in Italy. Under the treaty which was signed, the Swiss were to provide 20,000 men, to be paid by England for a three months' campaign against the French. Henry VIII ratified the treaty in November of that year, only to have it nullified soon afterwards when Maximilian made his own agreement with the French.

CONTACTS DURING THE REFORMATION

Another period of close contact was during the era of the Reformation. Already, in the 1520s, the teachings of Swiss reformer Huldrych Zwingli had begun to attract English divines. Henry VIII himself sought Zwingli's opinion, among others, when he wished to divorce Catherine of Aragon. Zurich soon became a centre for English theological students. In 1546 John Hooper, later to become Bishop of Gloucester and Worcester, fled to Switzerland to escape persecution for embracing Zwingli's Protestantism; and when he returned home it was due to Bishop Hooper's influence that Zwingli's leading followers were welcomed in England. Meanwhile, that other great reformer in Switzerland, the Frenchman Jean Calvin, had also begun to attract the attention of the English who in the 1550s came in increasing numbers to Calvin's Academy in Geneva. Henry VIII's successor, Edward VI, was not only personally influenced by the Zwinglian theology, but he and his chief councillor, the Protector

OPPOSITE *Cardinal Matthias Schinner of Sion: portrait by Raphael. After his visit in 1516, Schinner remained a good friend of England. He supported Cardinal Wolsey's candidature in the election in Rome for the new Pope.*

Lady Jane Grey: painting c. 1545 attributed to Master John.

Somerset, and his Archbishop, Thomas Cranmer, were all in relations also with Calvin. Edward's successor, Lady Jane Grey, the queen of nine days, on the scaffold took off her gloves and asked for them to be sent to her religious friends in Switzerland. When Mary came to the throne, and the Marian persecutions began, large groups of churchmen fled to the Continent, and many came to Zurich and Geneva, and also to Basel. As the Chronology shows, they included some of the greatest names in the English church. The group in Geneva were led by the Scottish reformer John Knox who, attracted by the teachings of Calvin, spent several years there. (He was made a citizen of Geneva.) It was to the work of some of these British exiles in Switzerland that we owe, *inter alia,* the Zurich Bible of 1535, Foxe's *Book of Martyrs* of 1559, and the famous Geneva Bible of 1560.

Later, during the English Settlement under Elizabeth I, the Swiss reformists exerted a strong influence on the changes in the Church in Britain. Jean Calvin and his successor Theodore Beza (or de Bèze) in Geneva, largely through John Knox and, later, Andrew Melville, played a significant part in the development of the rites and organisation of the Scottish Church, including its fight to abolish the episcopacy and establish Presbyterian government. Zwingli's religious successor in Zurich, Heinrich Bullinger, partly through those members of the English clergy who had formerly been exiled there, exerted a considerable influence on Elizabeth in the somewhat different development of the English Church (eventually to become Episcopalianism). For long afterwards, Bullinger's books and sermons were required reading for English priests.

Elizabeth's regard for the Swiss and for the Genevan Republic was demonstrated several times during her reign. In the years leading up to the night attack on Geneva by the Duke of Savoy, known as the Escalade (see 1602), the city found itself isolated and under threat from both Savoy and Spain, and sought financial and diplomatic help from England, to which Elizabeth responded quickly and positively. In 1589 she even suggested to the Swiss Diet that Geneva should be invited to join the Swiss Confederation, but without success. (Geneva eventually became a canton only in 1815.) James I continued to protect Geneva's independence. The Duke of Savoy tried to place an economic blockade round the city, and James intervened with him several times to allow shipments through. Indeed it can also be said that it was due largely to England's diplomacy that Geneva was not drawn by Savoy into the Thirty Years' War.

THE SEVENTEENTH CENTURY

> I do conclude that the correspondence of his Majestie
> in Helvetia and Rhetia is not onley good but necessary.
> *Sir Isaac Wake,* recommending the appointment of
> a British envoy to Switzerland in 1626.

At the beginning of the seventeenth century diplomatic contacts between England and Switzerland centred largely on England's efforts to counter growing Spanish influence in the Swiss cantons and in the Grisons (Rhaetia). England's ambassador to Venice, Sir Henry Wotton (who had received part of his education in Geneva), even urged the formation of a secret defensive league between Venice, England, France and the Swiss Protestant cantons and perhaps a German principality as well; but this came to nothing. However, the strategic importance of Switzerland and the Grisons, which then also controlled the Valtellina, began to be increasingly recognised in London, particularly in the context of the great struggle between the Protestant and Catholic powers of Europe which soon developed into war. As the Chronology shows, it was in 1629, in the reign of Charles I, that – following a strong recommendation from Sir Isaac Wake – a permanent British diplomatic agent, Oliver Fleming, was appointed to Switzerland.

Although Fleming's main immediate task was to watch the activities in and around Switzerland of the Catholic powers of Europe, a task in which he needed to maintain close liaison with the Swiss Protestant cantons, he was specifically instructed not to neglect his relations with the Catholic cantons (who had had a separate league since 1586, with a Diet of their own in Lucerne):

Concerning the Catholique cantons, you are to take fitt tymes and occasions to assure them in like manner of our sincere intentions towards theyr preservacion, and restoring the publique liberty of Christendome; and you are to exhort them to keepe an indissoluble union with theyr confederates and brethren, the Protestant cantons, without which union there will be no subsisting against the common ennemy of theyr liberties.

Fleming held his post in Switzerland for some fifteen years. However, although Fleming had his diplomatic successes and was knighted in 1639, the developing constitutional struggle between the king and Parliament, the failure to help the Huguenots in France, the revolt of the Covenanters in Scotland and finally the Civil War, caused the alienation of the Protestant cantons from the England of

Charles I. Even in 1632, the Venetian agent in Zurich reported home that 'the Swiss pay little attention to any proposals from that pompous and ease-loving court since the loss of La Rochelle'.

Following the execution of Charles I and the establishment of the Commonwealth, a close affinity was soon forged between the Protestant cantons of Switzerland and Cromwell. In 1653 the Protestant cantons sent their special representative, Johann Jakob Stockar, to London. During the Anglo-Dutch war, through Stockar they expressed their anxiety at this strife between two Protestant powers and offered their services as mediators. The following year Cromwell sent his own agent, John Pell, to Zurich, primarily to try to detach the Protestant cantons from their alliance with the French and to draw them into the great Continental Protestant League headed by England that Cromwell envisaged. When in 1654 the Swiss entreated England to help stop the persecution by the Duke of Savoy of the Protestant Waldensians living in the valleys of Piedmont, Cromwell responded quickly and obtained redress. (This event, incidentally, inspired perhaps the finest sonnet ever to be written by a State Secretary – 'On the Late Massacher in Piemont'. John Milton not only knew Switzerland quite well, but his best childhood friend, Charles Diodati, was a Genevan.) Cromwell later helped the Protestant cantons with the costs of the first Villmergen War, in which they were defeated by the Swiss Catholics.

In fact, Cromwell's admiration for all things Swiss (or, at least, Protestant Swiss) was several times exploited by his Royalist opponents. In 1655, when Cromwell, fearing an uprising, strengthened his military government, dividing England and Wales into eleven districts each under a major-general and each with power to raise money independently of Parliament, the Royalists accused him of 'cantonising' the kingdom. They also spread rumours that Cromwell was negotiating to raise a bodyguard of 3,000 Swiss troops because he could not trust his own army, and that to conceal this design Swiss families were being brought over to London in large numbers. They claimed further that part of the money which had been raised in the churches for the relief of the Protestant Waldensians (see above) was being diverted to help pay for the project. When the Swiss force did not materialise, it was said that the scheme had been dropped because some of Cromwell's generals had found out about it.

On the restoration of the monarchy in England, when the judges who had condemned Charles I to death were declared regicides, the Swiss granted sanctuary to Ludlow and to several of his fellow

Oliver Cromwell, 1656. Portrait after S. Cooper.

fugitives (though even so one of them was assassinated in Lausanne by an agent of the avenging Charles II). Understandably, relations between the government of Charles II and the Protestant cantons were at a particularly low ebb. The Bernese refused to receive a representative of the king in Berne. Charles tried several times to persuade them to withdraw their protection from the regicides, even offering them an alliance, and inviting them to appoint an agent in London, but they rejected his overtures.

THE TREATY OF 1690

When William III arrived in England, contacts with the Swiss grew close again. The crushing of the revolt in Ireland led by the deposed James II was a first priority before England could turn its attention to the war which was beginning against the French (the War of the League of Augsburg). But this tied down troops that were needed on the Continent. William III turned to Switzerland for help. In 1690 William signed a Treaty of Defensive Union (see illustration overleaf) with the Protestant cantons under which the Swiss agreed to supply 4,000 troops for the king's service in the Low Countries. He could not expect any help from the Catholic cantons since these, strongly pro-French, recognised James Edward Stuart, the Old Pretender, as the legitimate king of Britain, and they continued to do so until after the accession of George I. The treaty with the Protestant cantons was a cultural and trade agreement too. William would provide twenty-four places in the royal colleges for Swiss students, and reciprocal freedom of trade was allowed between the Protestant cantons and England, Scotland and Ireland, with import duties on any goods not to exceed two per cent. However, the Swiss, under strong pressure from the French (who, having Swiss troops in their own service did not want them on the opposing side too), raised numerous difficulties over the interpretation of the treaty. They suspected also – not without some foundation, though nothing of this was suggested in the treaty – that William had plans to involve Berne and Zurich in an attack on France from the south-east.

It was not until 1694 that a full regiment (Colonel Sacconay's) was raised. Thereafter, for over a hundred years, Swiss soldiers were from time to time recruited for the British service – often against considerable French opposition – either directly or by transfer from the service of the Netherlands. The States General made a treaty with Berne in 1712, and under article 2 of this the Dutch were at liberty to make use of the Swiss in their pay for the defence of 'the dominions belonging

Traité d'Union
Entre Sa Majesté Britannique et Les Cantons Evangeliques du Corps Helvetique.

Au Nom de la Tres-Sainte Trinité. Amen.

A tous soit notoire, comme ainsi que de tems en tems, et principalement depuis l'an 1514. il y a eu bonne amitié et intelligence entre les Serenissimes Roys de la grande Bretagne, et les Magnifiques Seigneurs des Cantons Evangeliques du Corps Helvetique; à cette cause, Nous Guillaume Troisieme, par la Grace de Dieu, Roy d'Angleterre, d'Ecosse, de France, et d'Irlande, d'une; et Nous les Bourgmaistres, Advoyers, Land Ammans, Grands et petits Conseils des Villes et Cantons de Zurich, Berne et Glarus de la religion Evangelique, comme membres des anciennes Ligues de la Haute Allemagne, d'autre part; Ayant fait meure reflexion sur les conjonctures presentes, Nous ledit Roy Guillaume avons deliberé des expediens, par lesquels cette ancienne bonne amitié entre Nostre Couronne et ledits Cantons pût être disposée à une union plus etroite; et pour cet effet, en qualité d'Envoyé Extraordinaire auprés d'Eux, Nous avons chargé Nôtre feal et amé Thomas Coxe, Ecuyer, qu'à la gloire et honneur du Dieu tout-puissant et eternel, et à la consolation, defense, sureté, Repos et prosperité reciproque de Nos Terres et Sujets,

il

renvoyer le Tiers de leurs officiers, sur la demande qu'ils Luy en feront. Fait, comme dessus à Arau le vingt-troisieme jour d'Aoust, mil six cent quatre-vingts dix vieux Style.

[signatures with wax seals]

Andreas Meyer Stadthalter v. Zürich.
Johannes Caspar Landolt Seckelmeister v. Zürich.

Axelhoffer Landerat

[signature]

Fridolin [...]

Conrad [...] Bürgermeister zu Schafhausen

Johan Conrad Weytzer Seckelmeister.

[signature] Landtman

Tobias Schobinger Boursier de la Ville de St. Gall

to the king of Great Britain'. For example, when John Burnaby, the new British Minister to Switzerland, found it impossible in 1744 to obtain the troops he was instructed to seek directly for the British service, he switched his efforts to helping his Dutch colleague raise more for the Low Countries so that transfers to Britain could be arranged from there.

THE EIGHTEENTH CENTURY

Up to the end of the eighteenth century Britain was not averse, from time to time, to trying to persuade the Swiss to abandon their neutrality in support of wider British interests in Europe. Following the outbreak of the War of the Spanish Succession, Savoy's changeover to the Allied side against France caused the British government to regard with renewed interest the strategic importance of Switzerland. The Protestant cantons were well disposed towards Britain; and there was even talk of Britain and Holland reviving Cromwell's idea of building a great Continental Protestant league to include the Protestant Swiss. Marlborough set great store by a strong British presence in Berne. D.B. Horn in his *Great Britain and Europe in the Eighteenth Century* quotes the Duke as saying that 'an active stirring minister in Switzerland would be capable of doing more service than anywhere else, both in supporting and encouraging the Protestant cantons, and in furnishing the quickest intelligence from all parts'. In 1702 William Aglionby was appointed with instructions to try to 'compasse an allyance with the cantons and an offensive league against France'. But he found that the Swiss 'still avoyd disobliging France unnecessarily' and that 'their circumstances would noe wayes allow them to depart from an exact neutrality'. However, Aglionby's successor, Abraham Stanyan, proved himself an able envoy. Thanks largely to his efforts more Swiss troops were recruited, not only for the Low Countries but also to help defend Savoy and some Austrian territories in southern Germany.

When Britain became an ally of France in 1716, her interest in Switzerland waned for a while; but in 1734, after the formation of a Franco-Spanish-Sardinian coalition to attack Austria in Italy, Sir Robert Walpole revived the idea of a defensive alliance with the Swiss – without success. By this time Britain had become thoroughly concerned at the extent of French influence in the cantons, and successive British envoys were charged with trying to diminish it. Newcastle had a scheme to neutralise Savoy and link it with the Swiss Confederation in order to provide a barrier to France in the south-east; but he underestimated the distrust of Savoy that had built up in Protestant Switzerland over so many years. He had earlier, at the beginning of the War of the Austrian Succession, offered an alliance to the Grisons leagues as part of which the Grisons were to provide troops for the British side in the war. But the Grisons declared their neutrality. In 1765 the new British minister, William Norton, was asked to see if an alliance with the Protestant cantons was then a possibility, but it was not. From then until the outbreak of the French Revolution Britain's interest in the Confederation once more declined.

THE NAPOLEONIC WARS

In 1790 Professor Cleghorn, who sometimes acted as a secret agent for the British government and who later arranged for the recruitment into the British service of the de Meuron regiment from Neuchâtel (see 1795), made a visit to Switzerland. On his return he strongly recommended that Britain should seek an alliance with the Swiss. At first this met with a lukewarm response, as did formal appeals for assistance from both Berne and Geneva. But soon the realisation that the Swiss Confederation might indeed play a key rôle in the growing struggle against France caused the government to appoint Lord Robert Fitzgerald to Berne with instructions to do everything he could to encourage Switzerland to join the European crusade against the Revolution. When it became clear that it was now too late for this, Pitt himself picked a new envoy to Switzerland, William Wickham, a man who already had many contacts there. As British Minister Wickham not only organised, with the aquiescence of the Berne government, an intelligence service against the French but also established arms depots along the Jura frontier to aid the French resistance. Wickham was forced by French pressure to leave in 1797, just before the French invaded Switzerland. In 1799, however, he was back – unofficially – in eastern Switzerland where Britain financed, and British officers helped to organise, the assembly of a Swiss army in readiness for operations against the French as soon as the advancing Austrians and Russians were in a position to attack. But the defeat at Zurich of General Korsakov's Russian army by the French caused the abandonment of these plans.

In 1802, when the Swiss Federal Government appealed to the Powers in Europe for help in the face of a new invasion by Napoleon, determined to impose his own political solution on Switzerland, Britain alone responded. The British, enjoying the brief cessation of hostilities which resulted from the Peace of Amiens, risked a renewal of the war with the French by protesting strongly to Napoleon on the Swiss behalf, and sending an agent to Zurich to encourage resistance. In the event the Swiss yielded to Napoleon and further British intervention was deemed useless.

In 1815, however, after Napoleon had escaped from Elba, Britain and her allies did in fact persuade Switzerland to accede to their new treaty of alliance. The Swiss agreed but considered that this did not prejudice their neutrality since it was on condition that their army should be used solely for the defence of Swiss frontiers. The British minister, Stratford Canning, did his best to get them to go further but, reporting on the signing of the agreement to London, wrote that 'it would have been fruitless to insist upon offensive operations'. Moreover, although the Swiss army did engage in some skirmishes with the French, notably around the French fortress of Hüningen near Basel, Switzerland's accession to the treaty did not, in the event, come into force until after Waterloo had been won and the war was over.

THE NINETEENTH CENTURY

England ist zwar nicht der einzige,
aber der zuverlässigste Freund der Schweiz.
Carl Spitteler

In the years after the Napoleonic Wars, British influence was fairly consistently directed towards encouraging, and protecting, the development of a strong, unified and neutral Switzerland. Cogent evidence of this is the British record over the threat of foreign intervention in the civil war in 1847 between the Swiss Protestant cantons and the Catholic cantons of the Sonderbund, when Palmerston's diplomacy delayed joint action by the Powers until the Sonderbund had been defeated and it was too late. So, too, is the way in which British diplomacy helped to head off outside interference in Switzerland during Swiss efforts at political and constitutional reform in the period known as the Regeneration, again over the recurrent Neuchâtel question, and again over the problem of political refugees. The story of these events is recounted in the Chronology.

There is no doubt that by the middle of the nineteenth century a special Anglo-Swiss relationship had been established. In the Swiss Federal Council's report for 1850 to the Federal Assembly, Britain was the only country in Europe for whom the Swiss had a good word. Another sign of this Anglo-Swiss affinity was the founding in

1850, by a group of Swiss Anglophiles, of the Bernese newspaper *Der Bund,* which they modelled on *The Times* of London, whose independence and objectivity they admired. On the British side, some indication of how Switzerland was regarded in the Foreign Office in those days can be learnt from this extract from Stratford Canning's memorandum to Palmerston written during the Sonderbund crisis:

> The importance of Switzerland is not to be measured by the extent of its territory, the resources of its industry, or the amount of its population. Its position in the heart of civilised Europe, its command of the main channels of communication between Italy, France and Germany, the hardy character of its inhabitants, and its capacity for defensive operations would alone make it an object of deep interest even if the features of the country were less remarkable, its institutions less free, and its early records less glorious and affecting. It cannot long suffer even by its own fault without enlisting the sympathies of every kindred state and generous mind. It cannot be enfeebled, convulsed, or mutilated without imparting a shock to the present system of peace – without suggesting dangerous fears or guilty hopes to the great military monarchies which nearly surround it.

British policy towards the Swiss Confederation was of course not a wholly disinterested one. England's first interest was the peace and stability of Europe, and a strong and independent Switzerland acting as a buffer between France, Germany and Austria was important to that peace and stability. Nonetheless, as the eminent Swiss writer Carl Spitteler pointed out at the beginning of the First World War, when many of his compatriots were openly pro-German:

> We have reason to be especially grateful to England; for more than once has she protected us from great danger. England is indeed not the only but the most dependable friend of Switzerland.

THE TWENTIETH CENTURY

There have of course been periods of misunderstanding. The virulent anti-British campaign in the Swiss press at the time of the Boer War was a particularly unhappy incident in Anglo-Swiss relations. In the current century those relations have gone through the changing fortunes of two world wars, when Britain was fighting for her life and Switzerland was determined to defend her independence despite pressures from both sides. There were trials and tensions but, through it all, understanding. On the Swiss side this was manifested by the great theologian Karl Barth when in 1941, in his *Letter to Great Britain from Switzerland* he wrote:

> When the British government declared war on Adolf Hitler's Germany . . .

it acted as the government of a righteous state according to Christian standards. And I believe this was true of Switzerland when she resolved, at the same time, on the armed defence of her neutrality, the maintenance of which is her historic mission.

On the British side it has never been so well expressed as in Winston Churchill's famous wartime minute in 1944:

> I put this down for the record. Of all the neutrals, Switzerland has the greatest right to distinction . . . she has been a democratic state, standing for freedom in self-defence among her mountains, and in thought, in spite of race, largely on our side.[3]

Since the Second World War the main area of development in Anglo-Swiss relations has been in trade and investment. Inter-governmental contacts have grown too. From 1959 Britain and Switzerland became partners in EFTA, the European Free Trade Association. However, when the United Kingdom left EFTA to join the European Community (the E.E.C.) the frequent opportunities for Anglo-Swiss contact in the EFTA forum were no longer available. A conscious effort was therefore made in succeeding years to increase the number of bilateral meetings between Britain and Switzerland. The first exchange of visits between Swiss and British foreign ministers took place in 1972/3, to be followed by visits by other ministers and by senior officials, and by the respective chiefs of the general staff in 1975/6. Such exchanges now take place on a fairly regular basis. Many of the leading personalities in British political life and senior members of the Swiss Parliament know each other well, often through working together in Council of Europe committees or in the International Parliamentary Union. A special occasion for informal contact is the annual British-Swiss inter-parliamentary ski race at Davos. The Prime Minister, Mrs Thatcher, has spent several holidays in Switzerland during which she met all of the then members of the Federal Council. In 1980 the Queen made the first ever state visit of a British sovereign to the Confederation. She received a magnificent welcome from the people of a democracy as old as that of her own country. And it was appropriate that, in her address to the Federal Parliament, she should compare the compact made by the first Swiss Confederates on Rütli meadow in 1291 with the signing of the Magna Carta on another meadow in Runnymede in 1215.

While Switzerland maintains her neutrality, she is an integral part of the Western heritage and adheres firmly to Western values. Switzerland and Britain nowadays have much in common. Both countries are highly industrialised but depend increasingly on services to help earn their living. Both depend largely on foreign trade; both are important centres of international finance; both have extensive investments abroad. They share many common interests: among them, the maintenance of confidence and security in Europe, in developing a world-wide multilateral trading system, in helping the poorer countries to improve their prosperity, in combating the threats of drugs, subversion and terrorism. The British government values highly the Swiss role as protecting power of British interests in countries with whom diplomatic relations have been broken off – in past years, for example, in Nazi Germany, in Iran, in Egypt, Guatemala and more recently in Argentina. Today, at the end of the 1980s, Anglo-Swiss relations have not been so warm for many years.

Travellers and Visitors

THE BRITISH IN SWITZERLAND

> Come the shortest possible way to this delicious country . . . the finest mountains – the greenest hills – the richest plains – the neatest houses – the best inns – the most limpid streams . . .
> *Stratford Canning,* on the attractions of Switzerland (1814).

Throughout history the flow of travellers and visitors between Britain and Switzerland has continued, not only of traders and diplomats, religious leaders, businessmen and engineers, but of statesmen and politicians, writers, artists, scientists, students, sportsmen and tourists, and this flow has grown rapidly in recent years.

In medieval times, many of the British travellers passed through Switzerland simply to get to Rome or to other places further south. King Canute was one of the most notable; Edward I was another; others included successive Archbishops of Canterbury, monks, knights and travelling merchants. Several accounts of these early crossings of the Alps are included in the Chronology.

In the days of the European Grand Tour, most travellers still used Switzerland as only a staging post on the way to or from Italy. However, there were always some who as part of their tour made long stops at Lausanne or Geneva, and quite a few who came to see more of Switzerland itself. Among the former were Sir Henry Wotton, Lord Chesterfield's son Philip Stanhope, John Milton, Dr Charles Burney, and Adam Smith as tutor accompanying the young Duke of Buccleuch. Among the latter were Fynes Morryson, John

Evelyn, Sir John Reresby, Gilbert Burnet (afterwards Bishop of Salisbury), James Boswell and Archdeacon William Coxe. Another was Frederick Hervey, fifth Earl of Bristol, an inveterate traveller whose reputation for good living and for staying at the best hotels in town explains why there are so many hotels named 'Bristol' both in Switzerland and elsewhere in Europe.

It was not until near the end of the eighteenth century that wider British interest began to awaken in Switzerland for its own sake. Descriptions of the country in the works of Wordsworth, Shelley and Byron and later of Ruskin, among others, caused more of their countrymen to come and see for themselves, among them the politicians Fox, Disraeli and Cobden. (Of Ruskin it was said that no man, and no mountaineer, ever loved the Alps with a more absorbing passion.) It was the Victorians, with their newly-found wealth, who were the first real tourists in Switzerland, although as early as 1816, when the first inn on the summit of the Rigi was built, the first names in the visitors' book were those of three Englishmen. In 1818 a Mr Emery of Charing Cross had begun to organise group tours to Switzerland by stage-coach. Thomas Cook began his first tour in 1863. Five years later Queen Victoria spent a holiday in Lucerne, stimulating more Britons to follow her example.

The British were by then already popularising mountain climbing, assisted by splendid Swiss guides. A few British had been climbing in Switzerland since the 1770s, and books like Horace-Bénédict de Saussure's *Voyages dans les Alpes* encouraged more to do so. But it was in the 1840s that they began in earnest (by then several peaks had already been scaled by the Swiss). The year 1857, and the founding of the Alpine Club, marked the beginning of systematic British mountaineering. Whymper's ascent of the Matterhorn was but one in dozens of British 'firsts'. Names such as Ball, Barrington, Malkin, Speer, Wills, Smythe, Forbes, Tyndall, Stephen, Conway, Schuster and Winthrop Young have earned a special place in the history of British climbers in Switzerland. Many of the climbers were ladies. In twenty-one years Lucy Walker made ninety-eight Swiss mountain expeditions.

In the 1860s the British were the first foreigners to discover the attractions of Switzerland in winter, and they played a major role in the introduction and development of winter sports – first skating and tobogganing (the British inaugurated the Cresta Run), then skiing, followed by ski mountaineering and ski racing. Arnold Lunn was the first to develop downhill ski racing and invented the modern slalom.

The Walker family, friends and guides. Lucy Walker, third from left in back row, was the first woman to climb the Matterhorn.

    The Swiss, with their incomparable ability for turning their scenery into money, were quick to encourage these trends by building a superb range of travel facilities – the grand hotels and, in addition to the railways, more lake steamers, then funiculars and later ski-lifts and cable cars. At the same time the large numbers of British in Switzerland, both tourists and residents, brought the opening of more British consulates and, in particular, the building of more English churches. By the early years of this century a remarkable total of more than sixty English churches had been opened in Switzerland.

    Sir Arnold Lunn maintained that Swiss and British climbers and skiers had done more for Anglo-Swiss relations than any other single group of people; and for the hundred years from about 1840, which saw the heyday of both mountaineering and skiing, that was doubtless perfectly true. Right up until the early 1920s British tourists in Switzerland usually outnumbered those of any other nationality. As late as 1929 they still provided about one third of all Swiss earnings from tourism. In the 1970s, the decline in the value of the pound against the Swiss franc led to a sharp reduction in the number of Britons who holidayed in the Confederation, and they nowadays take fourth place after the Germans, the Dutch and the French. Even so, in 1983 there were some 695,000 British visitors in Switzerland.

BRITISH RESIDENTS

Among the visitors to Switzerland from the British Isles there have always been those who came to stay. Some of the earliest, in the seventh century AD, were a group of Irish monks under the leadership of the scholar-saint Columbanus. One of his followers, Gallus, built his cell near Lake Constance on the site of which the Abbey of St Gallen was later founded. On the site of the cell of another Irish monk, Sigisbert, the Abbey of Disentis in the Grisons was established.

A second wave of Irish monks came to St Gallen and to neighbouring monasteries in the ninth century; and there is evidence of quite a considerable inflow of religious travellers from Britain in Anglo-Saxon times. In the tenth century King Athelstan sent envoys to several Swiss monasteries, including St Gallen. Athelstan's brother, Gregory, was probably the Gregory who was Abbot of Einsiedeln in the last half of the tenth century. His sister, Aldgitha (or Adela), may have founded the convent of Münsterlingen. Old documents in several religious centres in Switzerland are in Anglo-Saxon characters. St Guillaume of Neuchâtel was an Anglo-Saxon monk; and up to the end of the twelfth century there are reports of more Irish monks in Swiss monasteries and of their reputation for music and painting.[4]

During the Reformation there were significant British colonies of theological students and religious refugees in Zurich, Geneva and Basel among other centres. In 1555 John Knox became the first pastor of the British community in Geneva, while Thomas Lever became minister to a substantial English congregation in Aarau. When the religious exiles returned home, Geneva in particular, with Calvin's Academy, retained its attraction for the British as a place both for study and for residence, and it remained so for over four hundred years. In the sixteenth, seventeenth and eighteenth centuries many prominent British families sent sons to finish their education in Geneva, among them the Richmonds, Hamiltons, Stanhopes, Clarendons and Mannerses. Anthony Bacon, the brother of Sir Francis, lodged

The Abbey of St Gallen.

there with Beza himself. Robert Devereux, son of Elizabeth's favourite the Earl of Essex, spent several years in Geneva, as did Robert Boyle, the future scientist, George Keith, fifth Earl Marischal of Scotland (whose descendant, the tenth Earl, became Governor of Neuchâtel), and the Duke of Kent, father of Queen Victoria. As late as 1821 a British travel writer remarked of Geneva that 'many young English are sent there for education', and another in 1833 wrote that English students sent to learn French were on the increase.

Lausanne, too, soon became an important centre for the British in

Switzerland. Several other of the regicides in addition to Ludlow fled there when Charles II came to the throne. James Boswell remarked on the English colony when he visited Lausanne in 1764; and in 1770 Dr Burney noted that it had at that time become more fashionable for the English than Geneva. Later it became so full of British officers retired from outposts of empire that in some ways it resembled a mini-Cheltenham. The first double-taxation agreement that the Swiss government ever made was with the British government for the benefit of the British residents in the Canton of Vaud (of which Lausanne is the capital).

The beginning of the railway era saw a new influx of British into Switzerland – engineers and contractors and labourers this time, The expansion of Anglo-Swiss trade in the following century brought more new arrivals – businessmen and industrial specialists, particularly into Zurich and Basel. From around 5,000 in the 1880s, the size of the British colony had approximately doubled by the turn of the century, and it is probably over 20,000 today.

THE SWISS IN THE UNITED KINGDOM

> Here in England the trees and the meadows are greener than in Switzerland, and there is more variety in the fields, the meadows, and the charming woods. *Hans Caspar Escher* (1814)

In the other direction there has been a steady flow of Swiss visitors to Britain. A Swiss, Bishop Ermenfried of Sion, was one of the Papal Legates who officially crowned William the Conqueror. In the thirteenth century Peter of Savoy (whose family ruled much of south-western Switzerland) married his niece to Henry III. He was made Earl of Richmond and for twenty years played an important part in shaping English foreign policy. Among the estates he received was the land in London upon which the Savoy Hotel is now built. One of Peter's companions from Grandson in Neuchâtel founded the Grandison family in Britain, and in the next hundred years several of its members attained high offices of state.

Some Swiss came as merchants and traders, some to find their fortune, others to study at Oxford or Cambridge or Edinburgh. A few came simply to see the country. Thomas Platter, whose visit in 1599 is recorded in the Chronology, and Jakob Heinrich Meister who came in 1789 and 1792, were two of these. They displayed an approach remarkably similar to that of the tourist of today.

From early times a sizeable Swiss colony had developed in England. The first recorded meeting of Swiss residents took place in

Painting of Madame Tussaud, aged eighty-nine: attributed to F. Tussaud.

London in 1574. In the next two hundred years the flow accelerated. Particularly after about 1690, Protestants arrived in some numbers – merchants and bankers, doctors and scientists, engineers, artists and writers. By the second half of the eighteenth century the Swiss colony in Britain has become an important and established group of society. In 1762 a permanent Swiss church was built in London.

The colony was augmented from time to time by political refugees. Jean-Jacques Rousseau came in 1767 at the invitation of the philosopher David Hume. J. C. de Sismondi, the eminent historian and economist, came in 1792. The Swiss Madame Tussaud arrived from revolutionary France in 1802 to set up her waxworks in London.

Many of the Swiss who came to Britain soon began to take part in

British affairs. It is particularly interesting to note the number who were employed in the service of the Hanoverian kings in England in the eighteenth century. Swiss in the royal employ of the first three Georges, or under their royal patronage (indeed of William III and Anne, too), included secretaries, tutors, readers, drawing masters, military instructors, aides-de-camp, advisors, physicians, painters, goldsmiths and enamellers, clock- and watchmakers, medallists, jewellers, musical instrument makers and theatre managers. There were Swiss generals in George III's army, Swiss ambassadors in his diplomatic service, and Swiss governors in his colonial services.

Indeed it is remarkable how many Swiss immigrants reached eminent positions in British public life. As the Chronology shows, the Swiss have provided Britain with at least ten generals (several more in the second generation), twelve colonial governors, several ambassadors and other diplomats, a secretary of the Treasury, several members of Parliament, three Governors of the Bank of England, and numerous distinguished members of the Royal Society, the Royal Academy, the Royal Society of Arts and several other learned or professional bodies.

In 1337 Admiral Sir Otho de Grandison became commander of the Western Fleet, while John Grandison was Bishop of Exeter. Philip Burlamaqui of Geneva, the former London merchant and government financier, in 1637 became Head of the Royal Posts and Postmaster of England and Scotland. Andrew Schalch from Schaffhausen became known as 'the father of Woolwich Arsenal' where he was master founder for fifty years. Charles Labelye of Vevey was the architect for the first Westminster Bridge, opened in 1750. Joseph Planta from the Grisons was Principal Librarian of the British Museum. Several generations of the Vulliamy family were among the most famed of clockmakers in England. Vincent Perronet from the Vaud became John Wesley's most intimate friend and adviser, and was known as the 'Archbishop of Methodism'. The Swiss bankers Haldiman & Sons financed and organised the building of Belgrave Square for the Earl of Grosvenor. Arriving as poor immigrants from the Ticino, the Gatti family, by the 1880s, owned much of the Strand, and amongst other charitable acts, gave the land for the construction of part of Charing Cross Hospital. César Ritz, from Niederwald, when he opened his hotel in London, was called by Edward VII 'the hotelier of kings and king of hoteliers'.

During the present century the Swiss colony in the United Kingdom has changed somewhat in its composition. The widening of trade and financial links with Britain and the establishment there of an increasing number of Swiss-owned manufacturing and service companies, has led to its becoming more heavily weighted towards businessmen. In the 1960s just under 14,000 Swiss nationals were registered as living in the United Kingdom though no doubt this is less than the real figure. To help look after their needs there were thirty-five Swiss societies, clubs and institutes.

Cultural Relations

> If you are thoroughly familiar with someone else's language and literature, if you know and love the country, its cities, its arts, its people, you will be instinctively disposed, all other things being equal or nearly equal, to buy goods from him . . . to support him actively when you consider him to be right, and to avoid punishing him too fiercely when you consider him as being in the wrong.
> *Sir Anthony Parsons*

While Britain and Switzerland may both play down their interest in culture, in fact cultural exchanges between the two countries constitute a significant part of Anglo-Swiss relations. Like Britain, Switzerland has probably contributed rather more than her fair share to the Western heritage. A people accounting for less than 1½% of the population of Europe has, over the years, provided some of the leading figures in several important cultural spheres. But Swiss artists, and particularly writers, start with a special disadvantage. Not only does their own country provide a very small market for their work; its division into three main cultural and linguistic areas (four, with Romansch) makes the primary market even smaller. On top of this, some Swiss are so parochial that they consider even fellow Swiss in the next canton to be 'foreigners'. Small wonder that a good many aspiring architects, writers, painters, sculptors, musicians and scientists have long sought their recognition abroad; and in consequence have tended to become identified with their country of adoption – Borromini, Rousseau, Mme de Staël, Le Corbusier, Alberto Giacometti, Arthur Honegger and Professor Piccard are only a few.

At the same time, Switzerland has long attracted thinkers and writers and artists from all over the world. It is not only that the Swiss climate of liberty and tolerance has made the country a haven for political and religious refugees; Switzerland's scenic beauty, and its atmosphere of calm and tranquillity, has been enough in itself to inspire many foreign creative spirits.

SWISS ARTISTS IN BRITAIN

L'art suisse? Cette notion n'a jusqu'ici réussi ni à réveiller la fierté du citoyen helvétique, ni à meubler son imagination d'images exaltantes . . .
Hans Christoph von Tavel

There have been a surprisingly large number of Swiss artists who came to Britain and of British artists who went to Switzerland. From the seventeenth century onwards, the main attraction of Britain for many Swiss painters was the chance of finding patronage and a good market for their work. At first the main demand was for portraits, partly at least the result of the Englishman's growing sense of his individual importance deriving from the Reformation, and from his strong regard for character. Since these traits were Swiss ones too, most Swiss artists were on familiar ground. But Heinrich Füssli was made in a different mould. One of the most brilliant of Swiss artists who came to Britain, Füssli declared there was 'little hope of Practical painting finding encouragement in England. The People are not prepared for it. Portrait with them is everything. Their taste and feelings all go to realities.'

One of the most famous portraitists of the sixteenth century, Hans Holbein the younger, the son of a German father, became a citizen of Basel in 1520. From 1526 he spent much of the rest of his life in England and became court painter to Henry VIII. Holbein had a strong influence on a number of English painters, particularly on the miniaturist Nicholas Hilliard. In the seventeenth century a Genevan artist, Jean Petitot, was much favoured by Charles I, as also was Matthias Merian the younger, a follower of Van Dyck. Jean Louis Petitot and Jacques and Pierre Bordier had many connexions at the court of Charles II. Johann Schmutz of Zurich was attracted to England by the work of Sir Godfrey Kneller, in whose style he painted very successfully. Jean Etienne Liotard stayed several years in London in the time of George II and painted most of the royal princes and princessess. Liotard had a formative influence on the most accomplished British pastellist of the eighteenth century, Francis Cotes.

George Michael Moser from Schaffhausen was one of the founders of the Royal Academy, and his daughter, Mary, was much patronised by Queen Charlotte. Mary Moser became a Royal Academician, a distinction she shared for many years with only one other woman, her compatriot from Chur, Angelica Kauffmann. Angelica Kauffmann was a close friend of Sir Joshua Reynolds. She also worked with the brothers Adam. Samuel Hieronymus Grimm, who arrived in England in 1768, the same year as the Mosers, was employed by the naturalist Gilbert White to make drawings for *The Natural History of Selborne*. Johann Wäber, known as John Webber, and the son of a Swiss sculptor in London, accompanied Captain Cook on his last voyage to the South Seas as official artist to the expedition.

Heinrich Füssli of Zurich, becoming Henry Fuseli, was a familiar figure at the Royal Academy and was Keeper in 1804. He introduced a style and a tension unique in English painting at the time, and inspired William Blake to develop this into what Nikolaus Pevsner has called 'the flaming line'. Blake was a lifelong admirer of Fuseli's work. When one of Fuseli's paintings had been slammed by the London critics, Blake wrote to the press commenting on the suggestion that Fuseli was a hundred years in front of his time. 'I hope contemporary taste will shorten the hundred years into as many hours'; he said, 'for I am sure that any person consulting his own eyes must prefer what is so super-eminent'.

A painter of a different type was Sir Peter Bourgeois, son of a Swiss watchmaker in London. Encouraged by both Reynolds and Gainsborough, he was appointed landscape painter to George III; and he bequeathed the several hundred pictures which formed the basis of the Dulwich Gallery's collection. Bourgeois was buried in the chapel of Dulwich College.

In the nineteenth century, the brothers Jean-Jacques and Alfred-Edouard Chalon were well established in London, and Alfred was painter in watercolours to Queen Victoria. Jacques Laurent Agasse, 'the Swiss Stubbs', was an elegant and highly regarded animal painter in England. Born in Geneva, his family was said to be of Scottish origin. He spent fifty years in London and died there in 1849. Frank Buchser from Solothurn had considerable success among the fashionable London society of the 1850s. Buchser returned to England in 1862 and was responsible for the Swiss section of the International Exhibition of painting held in London in that year, where over fifty Swiss artists were represented.

Some of the most eminent of Swiss painters never came to Britain; but in many cases their reputations did. To take only one example, it is interesting that when the English composer Edward Elgar took up painting as a hobby in 1905, his wife compared his style with – out of all the other artists in Europe – that of two Swiss painters and an Englishman who had been much influenced by a Swiss. In a letter to Elgar's music publisher (who was holidaying in Davos) Lady Elgar

ABOVE *Tiriel, on the shoulders of Ivim, addresses his daughters; illustration by William Blake for one of his unpublished poems. It is perhaps influenced by Henry Fuseli's study* (BELOW) *for Saul and the Witch of Endor. Blake was a lifelong admirer of Fuseli's work.*

wrote '... he paints strange symbolical pictures à la Böcklin and Segantini and Blake!'[5]

The names of many other Swiss artists in Britain are given in the Chronology.

BRITISH ARTISTS IN SWITZERLAND

Paradise is in the slopes of the meadows, orchards and corn-fields on the sides of a great Alp, with its purple rocks and eternal snows above.
John Ruskin

It had been in 1444, when Konrad Witz painted his *Miraculous Draught of Fishes* with its setting on Lake Geneva, that a Swiss had become the first in European art to produce a landscape portrait with a recognisable setting. It was not until the second half of the eighteenth century, however, when the art of landscape was gaining importance in England, that British artists began to take an interest in Switzerland and its delightful scenery. And as the use of watercolour came into its own, Swiss and British painters discovered a special affinity. In Switzerland, as in Britain, the changeable weather gave effects of light and atmosphere, and delicate gradations of colour, which were often similar.

The watercolourist William Pars travelled through Switzerland with Lord Palmerston and showed his Swiss drawings in London in 1771. John Robert Cozens, the greatest of all precursors of Turner and Girtin, went in 1776 and made fifty-four watercolour drawings. In 1781 Francis Towne spent some months there with his colleague John 'Warwick' Smith. Sir George Beaumont, who helped Constable to recognition, came two years later. During this time Abraham-Louis-Rudolphe Ducros, with other members of the Swiss school, had by use of a new technique been making watercolour compete in strength and depth with oil, and their example caused several British watercolour painters, including probably Cozens and Turner, to adopt their method.

In 1802 William Turner made the first of six extended visits to Switzerland. Turner was much attracted to the Swiss scenery, and tended, consciously or unconsciously, to echo Rousseau in his feeling of oneness with nature, expressing in magnificent colours what the Swiss philosopher had expressed in words. Andrew Wilton, in *Turner in Switzerland,* says that Turner's interpretation of the Swiss atmosphere is 'so vivid, so strong and expressive that the broad foundations of his classically-based compositions seem to be disintegrated by it: it is the air itself that expresses the monumentality of the landscape'.

La Place du Molard, Geneva, *by Richard Parkes Bonington.*

And John Russell, in the same book, says that while other countries – Italy, France, Germany, his native England – fired Turner's imagination, in his feelings for Switzerland there was always a special eagerness, and that 'we may wonder in fact whether any artist, before Turner or after him, has been more ardent or all-comprehending in his devotion to the Swiss scene'.

One of the first exponents of the Romantic school, Richard Parkes Bonington, spent some time in Switzerland in 1825. The few paintings he made there are notable in their naturalness and delicacy. Francis Danby and Thomas Hartley Cromek followed shortly afterwards. By this time, inspired by the Romantic movement and the growing interest in mountains as objects of beauty, a school of Alpine painting had been fast developing. In the 1770s Casper Wolf had been the first great Swiss exponent. Following in his school were Gabriel Lory and his son, and Jean Antoine Linck and his brother Jean Philippe. British artists soon caught up and, for a time, overtook them. In 1825 the Genevan painter Adam Wolfgang Töpffer, on a visit to England, wrote to his wife: 'It is very useful to see the paintings in London. We are prodigiously behind in Alpine painting.' Later the Swiss came again into their own. Alexandre Calame, the distinguished artist from Vevey, made his name as an Alpine painter with his *Handegg Falls* in the Bernese Oberland, a painting which had been commissioned in England by Lady Osborne.

John Ruskin first saw the Swiss mountains as a boy of sixteen. In the 1850s appeared the successive volumes of his *Modern Painters* which, with their frequent allusions to Switzerland, heightened the interest in that country of a new generation of artists. British painters

One of John Ruskin's studies of cloud effects over Berne Minster.

were now pouring into Switzerland – William Callow, James Holland, Edward Lear, William Leighton Leitch, William James Muller, and many others. By the 1870s photography was becoming a practicality, and began to reduce demand for artists' landscapes and for the coloured prints which had been made from them. Thomas Wedgwood, the "first photographer", had visited Switzerland in 1796. But it was William Henry Fox Talbot who in 1833, baffled in his attempt to draw accurately the Swiss mountains, was led to devise the first real camera. But Switzerland continued strongly to attract the pure artists and does so to this day.

THE TWENTIETH CENTURY

In the twentieth century the facility with which exhibitions can now be mounted and transported has enabled Britain and Switzerland to keep in touch more easily with the work of some of each other's major artists. Barbara Hepworth and Henry Moore have been the subject of major exhibitions in Switzerland as have Paul Klee and Alberto Giacometti in Britain. Other artists who have had shows of their work in the other country include, on the British side, Eduardo Paolozzi, Graham Sutherland, David Hockney, Bridget Riley, Anthony Caro and Ben Nicholson (who went to live in Switzerland); and Sophie Taeuber-Arp, Max Bill, Richard P. Lohse and Jean Charles Tinguely, among others, on the Swiss.

LITERARY RELATIONS
Books as Ambassadors
Title of an essay by John Galsworthy

Literary relations between Britain and Switzerland are made up of many activities and influences. Among them are the books which have been written about travel in the other country, or its history, character or manners. Some examples of these have been quoted already; many more are given in the Chronology and in the Bibliography. The sheer quantity of travel, tourist, mountaineering and winter sports literature on Switzerland which has been published in Britain over the years is indicative of the special place Switzerland has enjoyed with so many British. (Another phenomenon, the number of poems and essays about Switzerland, is referred to later.) In quite a different field are the important books written by Swiss in Britain and by Britons in Switzerland. And, most important of all, there are the exchanges of thought and ideas which have been made over the centuries through books – the effects which books by British authors have had on the Swiss, and those by Swiss authors on the British – 'books as ambassadors'.

In a special category are those Swiss and British books for the young which have been widely read in both our countries. They include Daniel Defoe's *Robinson Crusoe*, which has had its influence on many generations of Swiss children (a new edition was even published in Switzerland in the middle of the Second World War) and Johann David Wyss's *Der Schweizerische Robinson* which from 1814 to date, as *The Swiss Family Robinson,* has gone through more than 200

English editions. Another is Johanna Spyri's *Heidi* which has seen an average of one new English edition a year for the past hundred years.

Over the centuries some aspects of Anglo-Swiss relations have been reflected in works by British or Swiss authors who otherwise had little or no connexion with the other country. The Swiss doctor Paracelsus was a well-known name in sixteenth-century England and references to him are to be found in works by Shakespeare, Ben Jonson and John Fletcher. Several of Shakespeare's plays also contain allusions to the reputation of the Swiss soldiers in foreign armies; and other references to Swiss soldiers were made in Sir Thomas More's *Utopia* and in Thomas Nash's *Tears over Jerusalem*. In the last century, Sir Walter Scott wrote a fine 'Swiss' novel, *Anne of Geierstein,* with its references to the Battle of Buttisholz and to those of Grandson and Morat (Murten).

Some of the earliest evidence of literary relations between Britain and Switzerland is to be found in the monasteries of St Gallen and of Einsiedeln, which contain inter alia ninth-century manuscripts of works by the Venerable Bede, the 'Father of English History', and of his pupil Cuthbert. Books by Alcuin, Charlemagne's educational adviser from York, were carefully studied by the monks of St Gallen. Basel, which was one of the early centres of printing to be established on the Continent, published a number of books by British authors in the fifteenth and sixteenth centuries (including incidentally an eight-volume edition of Bede's works in 1563).

During the Reformation Anglo-Swiss literary relations were close. More's *Utopia* and other books by the Oxford reformers were eagerly read in Switzerland. Zwingli's chief mentor was Erasmus, and he wrote several of his major works while he was in England. The second edition of *Utopia* was printed in Basel. It was in Basel also that John Foxe wrote his *Book of Martyrs* and, as has been said earlier, the great Zurich and Geneva Bibles were prepared by British scholars exiled in Switzerland. The theological works of the Swiss reformers, Zwingli and Bullinger, Calvin and Beza, had much influence in Britain. Some twenty of Bullinger's works were translated into English and published in England. Indeed one English admirer of Bullinger wrote to him 'The booksellers here get rich on the sale of your books alone.'

In England at that time a Swiss printer, Reginald Wolf, was himself the author of a *Universal History of Cosmography*. From this, Holinshed, who was in Wolf's employ, drew part of his *Chronicles,* which

DE SCRIPTV-
RAE SANCTAE AVTHORITA-
TE, CERTITVDINE, FIRMITATE ET ABSOLVTA
perfectione, deçque Episcoporum, qui uerbi dei mini-
stri sunt, institutione & functione, contra su-
perstitionis tyrannidisque Romanæ anti
stites, ad Sereniss. Angliæ Regem
HEINRYCHVM VIII.
Heinrychi Bullin-
geri Libri
duo.

IESVS.
Hic est filius meus dilectus in quo placata
est anima mea, Ipsum audite.
Matth. XVII.

TIGVRI IN OFFICINA FROSCHOVIANA
MENSE MARTIO, ANNO
M. D. XXXVIII.

*POTENTISS. REGI ANGLIAE, DO-
MINO SVO CLEMENTISS. H.
BVLLINGERVS, D.D.*

Title page of a special presentation copy of De Scripturae Sanctae . . . *by Heinrich Bullinger, 1533, addressed to Henry VIII; with an autograph by the author.*

in turn provided Shakespeare with the historical background for several of his plays. A Genevan in England, the Protestant scholar Isaac Casaubon, wrote a work, *De Rebus Sacris*, which played a major part in opposing the efforts of Cardinal Baronius to give back to the Catholics the pre-eminence of theological learning in Europe.

In the sixteenth, seventeenth and eighteenth centuries theologians and philosophers in both countries strongly influenced one another through their writings. The Swiss reformers in Zurich affirmed the belief that the Church and the State should be considered as two arms of the same Christian body, and this concept was developed later by Richard Hooker (a protégé of Bishop Jewell, who had spent several years as one of the Marian refugees in Zurich) in his *Laws of Ecclesiastical Polity*.

The works of Hooker, Hobbes, Shaftesbury and particularly Locke were widely read in Switzerland. The influence of Hooker's *Laws* can be seen in Rousseau's *Du contrat social*. Ideas in Locke's *Treatises on Government* are also reflected in Rousseau's work, while Locke's idealisation of the state of nature was developed in Rousseau's *Discours sur l'inégalité*. Adam Smith's *The Wealth of Nations* had immense influence on Swiss thinkers, including J. C. de Sismondi whose *La richesse commerciale* shows clearly its debt to Smith. Jeremy Bentham had his Swiss disciple in Etienne Dumont who for many years edited and published Bentham's writings, and acted as a kind of official interpreter between Bentham and the world at large.

Rousseau's works, in turn, had many admirers in Britain. His *Émile* inspired the Edgeworths to write their classic *Practical Education*, while even a hundred years later Herbert Spencer's *Education, Intellectual, Moral and Physical* has been called 'largely Rousseau's *Émile* in nineteenth-century disguise'. Daniel Malthus was a passionate admirer of Rousseau and spent much time with him when David Hume invited Rousseau to take refuge in England. Malthus's son, Robert, whose theories on population caused much controversy in Switzerland as elsewhere, became Rousseau's literary executor.

It was in the eighteenth century that the influence of English literature began to grow in Switzerland, thanks largely to the efforts of Johann Jakob Bodmer, professor of Swiss history at the Academy in Zurich. Bodmer translated much of Milton, Butler, Pope and Percy, and sponsored the first German translation of Shakespeare. He and his colleague Breitinger in 1721 launched a periodical *Die Discourse der Mahlern*, based on Joseph Addison's *Spectator*. 1730 saw the publication of the Scottish poet James Thomson's *The Seasons*, a

In the Cottage of Semira: *illustration for Salomon Gessner, drawn by Thomas Stothard, engraved by Robert Cromek, 1802.*

poem which had a tremendous effect not only on Swiss writers but throughout the Continent. Montesquieu claimed that it contributed to the 'rural delirium' of Rousseau. It much affected, too, the Swiss writer Albrecht von Haller, whose notable poem *The Alps* followed soon after. Among others, Samuel Richardson was also much read in Switzerland. Haller translated Richardson's *Clarissa* into German, while Rousseau made *Clarissa* a model for his *La nouvelle Héloïse*.

In the other direction, the Swiss Salomon Gessner's poem *Der Tod Abels*, an affecting tale of the sad end of an idyllic way of life, when translated into English had a considerable influence on contemporary British poetry. Later, Gessner's essay on 'Landscape' was eagerly read by the young John Constable, who became the father of modern British landscape painting. In 1758 a book by a Swiss author which was destined to become a classic in its field was first published in London. This was Emmerich de Vattel's *Les droits des gens, ou,*

Principes de la loi naturelle. According to Professor Brierly, Vattel has probably exercised a greater influence than any other writer on international law, and his work is still cited as an authority in international controversies. Soon after it was published, George II complained (of William Pitt) that a man who had never read Vattel should presume to undertake the direction of Britain's foreign affairs. Two other admired books in eighteenth-century England were Johann Caspar Lavater's *Essays on Physiognomy* which appeared in three different translations between 1789 and 1798, and his *Aphorisms on Man*. Albrecht von Haller's *Die Alpen* was translated into English in 1794.

At the end of the century British literature received a further boost in Switzerland through the foundation in Geneva by the brothers Pictet of the *Bibliothèque Britannique*. This review of British thought and ideas was published throughout the French occupation of Switzerland and attained an important international reputation. During that occupation Sismondi remarked that Geneva had become a city 'where men speak and write in French but read and think in English'.

In Britain, during the French Revolutionary wars, Joseph Planta, who had become Principal Librarian at the British Museum, was the author of a major work on the history of the Swiss Confederation. A little earlier John Louis de Lolme had written his important *Constitution of England*, while in 1787 Francis Grose had published his massive *Antiquities of England and Wales*. The first edition of Benjamin Constant's *Adolphe* was printed in London in 1816. In 1852 Peter Mark Roget, the son of a Swiss pastor, published the first edition of his *Thesaurus of English Words and Phrases*. Roget also wrote articles for the *Encylopedia Britannica* and took an active interest in the development of popular education in England.

Apart from Thomas Lovell Beddoes, who settled in Zurich in 1835, most British writers who went to Switzerland stayed only for some months or years at most. But the Swiss atmosphere, its scenery and tranquillity, has been as conducive to creativity for the British as it has been for many other foreign artists. Indeed, the number of writers who have been attracted to Switzerland is remarkable.

Edward Gibbon worked for some years on his *Decline and Fall of the Roman Empire* during his residence at Lausanne. William Beckford finished *Vathek* at La Tour de Peilz. Wordsworth and Tennyson both composed several poems in Switzerland. In 1816 Shelley wrote 'Hymn to Intellectual Beauty', and Mary Shelley wrote *Frankenstein* while staying with Byron at Cologny. Byron composed the third canto of *Childe Harold* there. He wrote *Manfred* while on a visit to Wengernalp, and *The Prisoner of Chillon* at Ouchy. Dickens wrote *Dombey and Son* and *The Battle of Life* during several months at Lausanne. Matthew Arnold made Switzerland the scene of the only love-episode in his poetry. Thackeray wrote part of *The Newcomes* in Vevey, where Arnold Bennett wrote his novel *The Card*. Mrs Gaskell wrote *Mothers and Daughters* at Pontresina. Samuel Butler took his description of the descent into *Erewhon* from the descent into the Ticino from the mountains around Airolo. Sir Arthur Conan Doyle set the 'death' of his hero Sherlock Holmes at the Reichenbach Falls at Meiringen (Bernese Oberland). Robert Louis Stevenson finished *Treasure Island* and James Elroy Flecker *Hassan* while they were convalescing in Davos. T. S. Eliot wrote part of *The Waste Land* at Lausanne. Other British writers to spend time in Switzerland include John Milton, Joseph Addison, Thomas Gray, William Hazlitt, Robert Southey, George Eliot, Robert and Elizabeth Barrett Browning, Alfred Tennyson, Wilfrid Scawen Blunt, Gerard Manley Hopkins, John Addington Symonds, George Meredith, Thomas Hardy, Christina Rossetti, Henry James, Oscar Wilde, Edmund Gosse, Joseph Conrad, Hilaire Belloc, D. H. Lawrence, and Somerset Maugham; and the list continues into today.

Perhaps one of the most striking aspects of Anglo-Swiss literary relations is the very large number of British writers who have been inspired to write poems or essays about Switzerland itself. The names of Milton, Wordsworth, Byron, Shelley, Beddoes, Browning and Arnold have already been mentioned. But the roll also includes Goldsmith, Coleridge, Ruskin, Richard Glover, William Collins, George Keate, William Lisle Bowles, Samuel Rogers, Helen Maria Williams, James Montgomery, Thomas Campbell, James Sheridan Knowles, Felicia Dorothea Hemans, Letitia Elizabeth Landon, William Liddiard, Samuel Miller Waring, Stopford Brooke and Llewelyn Powys. Even the famous diplomat Stratford Canning wrote several poems on Switzerland. His 'Lines to the Swiss', written in 1814, occupy the first page in his *Shadows of the Past,* published in 1866.

In more recent years English books in increasing number have been translated and published in Switzerland. Nowhere better was this trend manifested than at the important *Books of Switzerland* exhibition which was held in London in 1946, soon after the end of the Second World War. In the introduction to the catalogue of that exhibition, Dr Martin Hürliman of Zurich wrote: 'Never have English authors – including first and foremost, Winston Churchill – and the British attitude of mind been more popular in Switzerland than during the years when a German invasion hung as a constant menace over the country.'

Since then Anglo-Swiss literary relations have continued to flourish. After forty years of peace in Europe, which has allowed the development of a substantial increase in the volume of personal and business contacts between the two countries, English has become for many Swiss almost a fifth national language; and the number of books read, and indeed published, in Switzerland in the original English is now greater than ever before.

MUSIC

*We speak a loftier language than mere human speech,
in the wondrous accents of Music.*
E.T.A. Hoffmann

Some sources claim that Irish monks introduced the Gregorian Chant into the monastery of St Gallen in the ninth century. There seems no doubt that the Irish scholar Moengal at St Gallen taught music to one of Switzerland's greatest early composers, Notker Balbulus. Notker's sequences were sung in England for centuries, and one of them, J. M. Neale's version, 'The Strain Upraise of Joy and Praise, Alleluia!', is still in many Anglican hymn books today.

Anglo-Swiss relations in music are less well documented than for the visual arts. But the Chronology records an intriguing possibility. In 1603, at a banquet in Geneva celebrating the first anniversary of the Escalade, a patois song was introduced – 'Cé qu'é laîno, le Maître de Bataille' ('He who is there on high, the Lord of Battle'), which later became a quasi-national hymn of the canton. Several phrases of the tune are common to that of the British national anthem, 'God Save the Queen', the origins of which are unclear but which some attribute to a keyboard piece by John Bull. John Bull travelled in 'France and Germany' between 1601 and 1606, and it is conceivable that his travels included a stay in Geneva. If so, Bull may have taken his tune from there. His composition has been identified by some researchers as the hymn, 'God Save Great James Our King', which he composed, in 1607, the year after his return to England, for a banquet for James I and Prince Henry of Wales to celebrate the discovery of the Gunpowder Plot. What is incontrovertible, however, is that the Swiss later took the whole tune of 'God Save the Queen' for their national hymn, 'Rufst Du, Mein Vaterland', and that this was in use for over a century until displaced by another hymn in 1961.

The Tschudi Family, *c. 1744*, by Karl Marcus Tuscher.

Among Swiss who came to Britain in the seventeenth century was Johann Jacob Heidegger, who became manager of the Opera House in the Haymarket, London. Patronised by George II, Heidegger was known as the 'Swiss Count'. Pope called him, in his *Dunciad*, 'a strange bird from Switzerland'. For several years he was in operatic partnership with Handel, in 1737 offering him £1,000 for two new operas. Another Swiss friend of Handel was Burckhard Tschudi, who became a famous harpsichord maker in London. John Broadwood, founder of the piano manufacturers of that name, married Tschudi's daughter. Other Swiss harpsichord makers in London at that time included Hans Zopfi and Samuel Blumer, both like Tschudi, from Glarus. Xavier Stalder, who came to England from Lucerne in the mid-eighteenth century was one of the most sought-after professors of music in London and amassed a small fortune. Joseph Elouis from Geneva, who arrived a little later, composed some variations for harp on a Welsh air and set for the piano a selection of Scottish songs. Among English musicians who went to Switzerland later that century was Dr Charles Burney. He adapted Jean-Jacques Rousseau's opera *Le devin du village*, which was produced at Drury Lane as *The Cunning Man*.

In the nineteenth century the music of Joachim Raff was very popular in Britain; and the pianoforte virtuoso Sigismond Thalberg played to capacity audiences. A scholarship in his memory was established at the Royal Academy of Music. But although both were born in Switzerland, Raff of German parents, Thalberg of Austrian, perhaps neither was sufficiently identified with their country of birth to be called Swiss.

Several Swiss composers of opera have taken literary themes from Britain as the basis for their libretti. The libretto of Frank Martin's *Der Sturm*, first produced in 1956, was taken from Shakespeare's *The Tempest*. In the other direction, the British composer Frederick Delius's opera *A Village Romeo and Juliet* has a libretto based on Gottrfried Keller's story *Romeo und Julia auf dem Dorf*.

Arnold Dolmetsch of Zurich, who gave splendid concerts in England at the turn of the century, made a distinguished career in the field of early music. He restored many old instruments in the British Museum and elsewhere. In 1925 he created the Haslemere Festival and in 1928 the Dolmetsch Foundation. His son, Dr Carl Dolmetsch, carries on his work.

Today Anglo-Swiss musical relations are quite close. British composers, such as William Walton, Lennox Berkeley, Michael Tippett and particularly Benjamin Britten, have had many of their new works performed in Switzerland very soon after they first appeared in Britain. Britten was commissioned by Basel University to compose a Cantata Academica for it 500th anniversary celebrations. Paul Sacher, the eminent Swiss conductor and musicologist, has both encouraged and performed the work of a number of contemporary British composers. Sir Yehudi Menuhin has founded a music festival near Gstaad.

Paul Sacher, conductor and musicologist.

Swiss composers, except perhaps Ernest Bloch, Frank Martin and Arthur Honegger, may not have had quite the same recognition in Britain, though Ralph Vaughan-Williams strongly defended Willy Burkhard from the London critics. However, Swiss executants have had considerable success, both in personal appearances and in sales of their records in Britain. The conductors Ernest Ansermet, Peter Maag, Charles Dutoit and, latterly, Matthias Bamert (principal guest conductor of the Scottish National Orchestra), the singers Sophie Wyss, Hugues Cuenod and Lisa Della Casa, the pianists Edwin Fischer and Clara Haskil and the oboist Heinz Holliger, among others, follow in the tradition of Otto Hegner, who gave numerous English concerts and who, in the 1880s, was hailed by the London critics as a boy prodigy.

One other feature of Anglo-Swiss musical relations which is worth mentioning is the remarkable number of British orchestras and musical groups that have been welcomed by Swiss audiences in recent years. They include the New Philharmonia, the Royal Philharmonic, the London Symphony, the London Philharmonic, the Hallé Orchestra, the BBC Symphony, the National Youth Orchestra, the English Chamber Orchestra, the Amadeus Quartet, the Melos Ensemble, the Royal Ballet, Welsh National Opera, and the Monteverdi Choir.

Education

*With the matter of education, the Swiss
people manifest a veritable passion.*
Sir Horace Rumbold (1866)

The challenge which the Swiss have experienced in the need to mould a cohesive and viable and democratic state, faced both by ethnic diversity and lack of natural resources, has produced a remarkable response in the careful development of a high standard of education, geared to practical needs. British visitors to Switzerland have long remarked upon this; and many have taken advantage of it themselves. The British religious exiles who studied in Zurich and Geneva in the sixteenth century have already been mentioned, as also has the continuing attraction thereafter, for generations of British students, of Calvin's Genevan Academy.

In the second half of the sixteenth century there were numerous Scots, in particular, not only studying but also teaching at the Academy, among them Henry Scrimgeour, Alexander Brisson and

Andrew Melville. Melville returned to Scotland intent on remoulding and revitalising teaching in the Scottish universities along the lines he had come to admire in Geneva. In the years that followed, the recovery of Glasgow University in particular was largely the result of Melville's work there as principal. St Andrews, too, later came under Melville's influence (where the second master in St Mary's College in 1593, John Johnston, had also been in Geneva). At King's College, Aberdeen the principal, Alexander Arbuthnot, was a friend and associate of Melville and followed his example at Glasgow and St Andrews, amongst other things giving emphasis to theological learning. The founder of Marischal College, Aberdeen's other university (before both institutions were amalgamated), George Keith, had also been educated at the Genevan Academy, while its first principal, Robert Howie (who incidentally became Melville's successor at St Andrews), had studied at Basel. In 1583, when the University of Edinburgh was founded, Melvillian enthusiasts proposed to mould it upon the lines of Calvin's Academy but were overruled by those on the Edinburgh town council who preferred a more traditional type of establishment. But even in Edinburgh the Genevan influence was still felt indirectly.

Through the centuries Switzerland's reputation for good education has increased. In 1611 an English traveller, Thomas Coryat, wrote of the chapter school (the Carolinum) which Zwingli had reorganised in Zurich (and which much later became the cantonal university), 'It hath bred more singular learned writers than any one of the famous Universities of all Christendome.' Coryat added that Oxford and Cambridge 'do yield as many learned men as any in the world: but for the quantity, not the quality, of writing, the Tigurines [the people of Zurich] without doubt have the superiority of our English men'. In the succeeding years William III and Anne, and the first three Georges, all had Swiss teachers in their households, as did many of the leading families of England of the time.

It is, however, the great Swiss educationalists of the eighteenth and nineteenth centuries who have perhaps had the biggest impact on Anglo-Swiss relations in this field. Rousseau had many British disciples of the educational system he expounded in his *Émile* (the Edgeworths have been mentioned in this connexion). Later, Heinrich Pestalozzi at his institute at Yverdon, and Emmanuel von Fellenberg at Hofwyl, both had numerous British visitors and admirers including, in addition to the Edgeworths, Robert Owen, Robert Southey, Elizabeth Fry, and Lord Brougham. J.P. Greaves, the future secretary of the London Infant School Society, stayed with Pestalozzi seven years, while Charles Mayo, who founded Cheam School on Pestalozzi's principles, was there for three. Père Girard had not quite the reputation in Britain of Pestalozzi and Fellenberg, but several English schools were run on his methods.

Largely as a result of the work of these great educationalists, universal compulsory schooling was introduced into Switzerland in the first half of the nineteenth century (though Geneva had had it since 1536). In England, however, universal primary education did not become a reality until Gladstone's Bill of 1870. By the end of the century little was still being done for secondary education. In 1899 the amount of public money spent per head on secondary education in England was about 0.3p, or about one eighteenth of the 5.5p spent per head in Switzerland.

It is small wonder therefore that Swiss regard for English (as opposed to Scottish) education has never been very high. Marc-Auguste Pictet, the co-founder in Geneva of the famous *Bibliothèque Britannique,* after a tour of Britain in 1787, wrote of the old 'public' (actually private) school system then in force:

[As regards] English education . . . I have reason to believe it to be pretty bad. Boys are sent as boarders to public schools such as Harrow, Westminster and Eton. There are a great number of boys together, virtually unsupervised, and restrained only by fear of a flogging . . . Instruction is purely classical . . . It is only at Edinburgh that one finds being taught the variety of practical sciences which tend to form a man to be of use to society.

It was not only the Swiss who criticised English public schools at that time. Many English did so themselves. Two years before Pictet came to his conclusion the poet William Cowper had written in his 'Tirocinium':

> Would you your son be a sot or a dunce,
> Lascivious, headstrong, or all at once,
> Train him in public with a mob of boys . . .

And, even after the public school reforms introduced by Dr Arnold of Rugby, the doctor's own son, Matthew Arnold, branded the English system of secondary education as 'the worst in the world'.

Matthew Arnold visited many Swiss schools. In his report on *Schools and Universities on the Continent* he wrote:

The grand merit of Swiss industrialisation, even though it may not rise to the conception of 'La Grande Culture', is that it has already seen that, for genuine

Matthew Arnold in 1861: portrait by Camille Silvy.

and secure industrial prosperity, more is required than capital, abundant labour and manufactures, it is necessary to have a well-instructed population. So far as instruction and the intelligence developed by instruction are valuable commodities, the Swiss have thoroughly appreciated their market worth and are thoroughly employing them. They seem to me in this respect to resemble the Scotch.

Many improvements have been made to English education since Arnold's day; and the percentage of students who go on to higher education is now larger in England than in Switzerland. But, making full allowance for our different history and for differing economic and social conditions, the English system still seems to lack the solid attachment to practical needs which is the hallmark of the Swiss.

There is, however, at least one branch of education in which the English have made a useful contribution to Anglo-Swiss relations and that is in the number of English finishing schools which have been established in Switzerland, and which have attracted young people from all over the world. Another positive influence, unquantifiable but perhaps underestimated, has been the effect which the British nanny has had on several generations of many Swiss families. From about the middle of the last century until the middle of this, the flow of British nannies into Switzerland was at least as great as that to many other parts of the world.

Science

> Science is nothing but trained and organised common sense.
> *T.H. Huxley*
>
> The whole of science is nothing more than a refinement of everyday thinking.
> *Albert Einstein*

If in their approach to education, their attitudes have often been different, Britain and Switzerland have long had a common attachment to scientific learning and a mutual regard for scientific achievement. As has been indicated earlier, this stems, in part at least, from a shared attraction for the empirical and for the practical approach. It also has some connexion with another area in which Britain and Switzerland have much in common – that of civic tradition. For, as Karl Pearson has pointed out in his *Grammar of Science,* the scientific method of examining facts is applicable to social as well as to physical problems; and this frame of mind is also an essential of good citizenship.

Some of the earliest scientific contacts between Britain and Switzerland were in the field of medicine. The reputation in Britain of the Swiss doctor Paracelsus has already been mentioned. Conrad Gesner of Zurich, who first used belladonna in 1540, had a more durable standing here. Successive British sovereigns had a tradition of seeking specialised medical advice from Switzerland. Paulus Lentulus of Berne was for some years personal physician to Elizabeth I. Sir Theodore Turquet de Mayerne was physician to both James I and Charles I, while Sir John Colladon from Geneva and his son Theodore, who was also knighted, long served both the Stuarts and William and Mary. Another Swiss doctor highly regarded by the English court was Theodore Diodati, whose son Charles was John Milton's best friend. The first three Georges all retained numerous Swiss medical men on their staffs. Even the distinguished Swiss scientist and poet Albrecht von Haller was court physician to George II. (Haller was, incidentally, so well regarded by the king that the Bernese Government sought to appoint him as their minister to London, but George felt that he could do better work where he was as a professor at Göttingen University.)

Medical contacts have been numerous since then. In the first half of the nineteenth century the Zurich professor Christian Albert Theodore Billroth, known as the founder of abdominal surgery, studied in England as a young man. He was a keen follower of Lister's methods, and without Lister's work Billroth's advances in surgery would not have been possible. A little earlier the work of Franz Anton Mesmer on the physical state of trance was being studied, and his methods introduced into Britain, by John Elliotson in London and by James Braid in Manchester. As a result the terms mesmerism and hypnotism entered the English language. Then, in 1946, the Society of Analytical Psychology was founded in London, to study and discuss the teachings and methods of the Swiss psychologist Carl Gustav Jung. The same year a British C.G. Jung Institute was opened.

The high tide of Anglo-Swiss scientific contacts was probably during the seventeenth and eighteenth centuries. The Chronology gives some interesting insights into the nature of some of those relationships. In the early seventeenth century the Swiss mathematician Jost Bürgi and his Scottish counterpart, John Napier, were working contemporaneously on the logarithmic principle. Unfortunately Bürgi delayed publishing his book *Progress Tabulen* until a few years after Napier had announced the same discovery.

The scientist Robert Boyle spent several of his most formative

LEFT *The Hon. Robert Boyle FRS: portrait after Friedrich Kerseboom, c. 1689.* RIGHT *Sir Theodore Turquet de Mayerne, c. 1630, after Rubens. He was buried in the church of St Martin-in-the-Fields, London.*

years in Geneva, perfecting his French. He later had many contacts among his Swiss scientific contemporaries, including the famous Bernoulli family. Jakob Bernoulli was in England in 1676 making himself familiar with the work of, amongst others, John Wallis and Isaac Barrow. Jakob's two sons, Nicolas and Daniel, were also visitors and both became Fellows of the Royal Society of London. His brother Johann Bernoulli became involved in the great Newton-Leibnitz controversy over which of them really invented the calculus, a controversy which another Swiss living in England, Nicolas Fatio de Duillier, had been responsible for starting. Fatio was a great supporter of Newton, but Johann Bernoulli was the author of two anonymous attacks on him.

Yet another Swiss got caught up in the Newton-Leibnitz quarrel. Firmin Abauzit from Geneva, who came to England in 1698, was a friend and correspondent of several eminent British scientists and philosophers. 'You are the only man', wrote Newton, 'whom I recognise as a judge between Leibnitz and myself.' William III tried to get Abauzit to come and teach at Cambridge, but he preferred to stay in Geneva.

Several other outstanding Swiss mathematicians had strong links with England. Gabriel Cramer spent some years at Cambridge and studied astronomy with Edmund Halley. Leonhard Euler, the star pupil of Johann Bernoulli, received an award of £300 from the British government for his development of the theorems useful in navigation. Amongst several other outstanding achievements, Euler also discovered the achromatic lens, which made possible the construction of the first modern telescopes. He had his lens made in England by the Huguenot optician Dollond, who thought that the attempt would fail after Sir Isaac Newton had declared it impossible. Euler, too, became a Fellow of the Royal Society (FRS).

One English mathematician who spent several years in Switzerland was Dr John Pell, but he was there as Cromwell's political agent to the Protestant cantons.

The eighteenth century in particular saw close relations between British and Swiss naturalists and geologists. Johann Jakob Scheuchzer, author of a famous early map of Switzerland 'Nova Helvetiae Tabula Geographica', made several visits to England and had many friends among the leading scientists. He dedicated his *Itinera Alpina*, a record of extensive journeys throughout the Alps, to the Royal Society. Some of the plates for the illustrations were made at the expense of English scientific colleagues, including Newton and Sir Hans Sloane. Scheuchzer's son, Johann Caspar, settled in England and became librarian to Sloane. He was one of the pioneers in advocating inoculation against smallpox.

The geologist and meteorologist who had perfected the barometer, Jean André de Luc, came to England in 1773. He became an FRS and was appointed Reader to Queen Charlotte. Another, Horace-Bénédict de Saussure, was known in England amongst other things for his classic book *Voyages dans les Alpes*, a pioneering work of mountain literature which dealt with scientific observations and travel alike. Several of de Saussure's scientific friends, including M.-A. Pictet and Abraham Trembley, also had close connexions with England; de Saussure, Pictet and Trembley were all fellows of the Royal Society. Trembley was made an FRS for his work on the freshwater polyp. Indeed, it is a remarkable fact that between the founding of the Royal Society in 1660 and 1791, no fewer than thirty Swiss became fellows.

The Swiss mountains began to interest British scientists well before they did the climbers and the tourists, principally because of their glaciers but also because of their wild flowers. Encouraged by the works of Gesner, Scheuchzer, de Saussure, Bourrit, Agassiz and others, a small but steady stream of naturalists and geologists visited Switzerland. Amongst them were John Ray, the 'father' of English

Melchior Füsslinus Tigur. pinx.   Jos. Nutting Lond. Sc.

Johann Jacob Scheuchzer: by Melchior Füssli, engraved by Jos. Nutting, 1672.

natural history, in 1665, the botanists Thomas Blaikie in 1775 and Sir Thomas Constable in 1784, Sir William Hooker, creator and director of Kew Gardens, in 1814, and in later years, J.D. Forbes, John Tyndall and Professor T.H. Huxley. Tyndall and Huxley wrote a joint study on glaciers for the Royal Society.

One British naturalist who had an especial influence on Swiss scientific thinking – indeed on scientific thinking everywhere – was Charles Darwin. Darwin's *Origin of Species* probably had every bit as much impact in Switzerland as, in a very different sphere, had Newton's *Principia* some two hundred years earlier. Interestingly, the *Origin of Species* contains many references to the work and ideas of, among others, the Swiss scientists Louis Agassiz, Alphonse and Augustin Pyrame de Candolle, Oswald Heer, Nägeli, François Jules Pictet and Rütimeyer. Agassiz was all his life a strong opponent of Darwin's theory.

One or two other scientific connexions are worth noting. In 1806, a young geologist from Geneva, Louis Albert Necker, came to study at Edinburgh. Two years later he completed the earliest known geological map of Scotland. In 1814 the eminent chemist Sir Humphry Davy came to Geneva, accompanied by his new assistant, the future physicist Michael Faraday. Davy was the guest of several leading Genevan families. He experimented on iodine in the de Saussures' house and on the solar spectrum in the Pictets' house. Davy later died on another visit to Geneva and was given a public funeral there. Michael Faraday returned to Switzerland several times. With Jean-Daniel Colladon of Geneva, and the Frenchman André Ampère, he opened the way to the electric motor.

Science has always been very much of an international concern. This is more than ever the case today. International – rather than bilateral – exchanges now go on virtually unnoticed at all levels. The cost and complexities of modern research necessitate international cooperation often on a very large scale. The setting up of the European Organisation for Nuclear Research (CERN) in Geneva is but one example. However, three events this century of particular interest to bilateral relations may be mentioned. When in 1920 the Ramsay Memorial Fellowship Trust was founded to perpetuate the memory of the British chemist Sir William Ramsay, one of the first acts of the trustees was to sign an accord with the Swiss Government establishing a special fellowship in the United Kingdom for Swiss researchers, financed mainly from a bourse provided by Swiss Government and industry. Later, in 1949, the CIBA Foundation was set up in

London with funds provided by the Swiss CIBA group (with several leading British scientists among the trustees) to offer research facilities and accommodation to students in chemistry, medicine and surgery, and, among other things, to award bourses for special studies. Again, in 1981, the Sandoz Institute for Medical Research was founded as a result of cooperation between Sandoz Products Ltd and University College, London.

Economic Relations

Economic relations between Britain and Switzerland have generally been important but particularly so in the past three hundred years. Today they are the dominant factor in the relationship. In some periods, e.g. in the eighteenth century, it was financial relations which were strongest; in others, in the early years of the nineteenth, it was industrial contacts that were of particular importance. But for most of our history the continuous economic link has been trade.

ANGLO-SWISS TRADE

*In democracies, nothing is more great
or more brilliant than commerce
Alexis de Tocqueville*

As early as 1398, English goods were recorded in the accounts of the Receiver of Tolls in Neuchâtel. By the end of the fifteenth century linen from St Gallen and books from newly established printing-presses in Basel were being sent to England. There were English cloth merchants in Geneva in the 1550s. Some indication of the goods exchanged by early traders in the sixteenth century is given in the Chronology. They included wooden long-bow staves from Glarus, ships' masts from Berne, shoes, paper and books from Zurich, and woollen goods, pewter ware and even English cheese from Britain. Silk goods were first exported from Switzerland to England in 1593. In the seventeenth century slate slabs and tiles were sent down the Rhine to Britain from Glarus, which also exported fine grained woods for furniture until deforestation caused the authorities to stop these sales.

By the early seventeenth century Britain was already making conscious efforts to improve trading relations with Switzerland. In 1628 Charles Emmanuel, Duke of Savoy, offered special trade privileges for British merchants who would use his free port facilities at Nice/

Villefranche. Britain proposed to send goods imported from the Levant and other places via Nice to Geneva for the Swiss market and via Schaffhausen and St Gallen to southern Germany. She persuaded the Duke to accord the same privileges to Genevan and Swiss traders as for the British. But the project died with Charles Emmanuel's death. However, soon after, trade promotion was included in the instructions sent to Sir Oliver Fleming, Britain's first permanent envoy to Geneva and the Swiss Cantons:

> Next Government and religions, wee advise them to consider how to increase their wealth by trade which by reason of general application to the warres is not so much improved as it might bee. The example of their late neighbour, that politique Duke of Savoy, may direct them, that as hee included at Villa Franca, so they may set up in fit places, free scales of trade for al merchants to resort unto. And to further them therein (if they wil give convenient privileges) wee wil send unto them some of our Adventurers, to begin the trade with our cloth, and other staple commodities and with manufactures of all kinds . . .

Though statistics are not available, it is reasonable to suppose that trade with the Protestant cantons was encouraged by the Anglo-Swiss treaty of 1690 which *inter alia* set a maximum 2% duty on imports both ways. Britain's trade with Geneva had begun to take off in the middle of the seventeenth century. By 1716 it had reached several hundreds of thousands of pounds sterling a year, but was practically all one way. Britain sold textiles, hats, hosiery and colonial goods to Geneva but bought only a few watch parts in return. Significant trade between both countries began to build up from the days of the Industrial Revolution, but the real increase came in the middle of the nineteenth century, when the new Swiss Confederation had unified its currency and customs regimes and an era of freer trade was beginning in the United Kingdom and on the Continent. The Anglo-Swiss Trade Agreement of 1855, with its most favoured nation clause (although not always seemingly observed), gave a boost to commercial relations.

Thereafter Anglo-Swiss trade has gone through several vicissitudes which can be followed in the Chronology. (The trade figures used in much of the Chronology and in the Appendix table are in Swiss francs, since this currency has remained considerably more stable than sterling.) In the last quarter of the nineteenth century increasing Swiss protectionism helped to cause a growing trade imbalance. In 1885 the value of Switzerland's exports to the United Kingdom (part of them admittedly in transit to British colonial territories) was twice that of United Kingdom imports into Switzerland; in 1899 it had trebled; by 1901 it was four times. This state of affairs was not of course unique to Britain's trade with Switzerland – hence the growing campaign for the introduction of protection led by Joseph Chamberlain. During the last fifteen years of the nineteenth century the value of United Kingdom exports to Switzerland hardly rose at all, though part of this was due to the general decline in prices which Great Britain suffered during that time.

Because of the special conditions in force during the First World War, Anglo-Swiss trade in both directions reached record heights. And although British exports to Switzerland dropped back somewhat thereafter, Swiss exports to Britain maintained their levels. In the first half of the 1920s, the United Kingdom was Switzerland's biggest export market. It was not until higher duties were introduced by the United Kingdom in 1925 that Swiss exports began to be affected. With the world slump of the 1930s Anglo-Swiss trade sank to very low levels, although for the first time it was roughly in balance. In the Second World War, trade was minimal: Switzerland was entirely surrounded by the Axis powers. When trade built up again afterwards the balance began to swing into Britain's favour and has remained so, with occasional years of rough balance, until today.

The rapid increase of Anglo-Swiss trade since the late 1950s was helped greatly by the dismantling of tariffs following Britain's and Switzerland's entry into the European Free Trade Area. Then, when the United Kingdom joined the European Economic Community and Switzerland negotiated a special agreement with that organisation, the free trade benefits were retained. From the late 1960s the continuing increase in value terms was a result in part of inflation, in part of the decline in the value of the pound sterling. In 1966 one Swiss franc was worth just over 8p. In 1986, it cost about 40p, or five times as much. But despite this, even in terms of Swiss francs, the value of total visible trade (imports plus exports) has in the same period more than quadrupled. Nowadays the large value of movements of precious metals and precious and semi-precious stones tends to distort the pure merchandise figures; but in the five years to 1984 alone, the cumulative value of Anglo-Swiss trade was about Sw.fr. 38bn or, in sterling terms, over £15bn. Today this trade is running at an average rate of over £75m a week. For her part, Britian exports more to Switzerland than to all the Latin American countries together.

INDUSTRIAL RELATIONS

Apart from trade, Britain and Switzerland have long had important relations in the field of manufacturing and industry. Quickly following Britain's Industrial Revolution, Swiss industry had by 1836 become the most efficient on the Continent. Switzerland was then, after England, the most important producer of cotton goods in the world.

This position was not achieved easily, for the export of the newly invented textile machinery from England was at first banned and the Swiss had to resort to extraordinary measures to obtain examples. Moreover, many nascent Swiss enterprises went bankrupt before success was achieved. The historian, Jean-François Bergier, in his *Histoire économique de la Suisse*, questions why Switzerland ever decided to develop its cotton industry in the face of the opposition of, and strong competition from, Britain. He puts it down to an evident affinity with Britain; but maintains that the business and financial relations, and the intellectual ties between the two countries which then existed, were not in themselves enough to explain this phenomenon. It seems, he says, rather that the industrial upsurge in England had 'produced a kind of fascination in its Swiss victims'.

The affinity certainly existed, and in several important areas British processes and British engineers played a not insignificant part in the early development of Swiss industry. The founders of several of Switzerland's greatest companies, including Sulzer Bros., Georg Fischer, and Escher-Wyss, spent much time in Britain studying new trends and new types of machinery. British consultants and engineers, including Robert Stephenson, Charles Vignolles and Thomas Brassey, helped with the layout and construction of some of the first Swiss railways. A British engineer, Charles Brown, founded the Swiss Locomotive and Machine Works in Winterthur. His son pioneered some early industrial achievements for the Swiss Oerlikon works, and was co-founder of Brown Boveri of Baden. His oil-filled transformer, which made it possible to transmit electric current over long distances, helped to open up Swiss water resources to exploitation by the power companies. Britons were in charge of the first lake steamship construction department of Escher-Wyss. Later, two British companies developed tar deposits near Neuchâtel, as a result of which many of the streets of London and other cities were paved with Val de Travers asphalt.

In 1855 the British chemist Sir William Perkin discovered the first synthetic dyestuff derived from mauvine, a process which, a few

Jacob Schweppe: portrait based on a description of him during his stay in London.

years later, the industrialist Alexandre Clavel began to exploit in Basel, thus laying the foundation of the Swiss chemical industry. Later, during the First World War the Geigy and Sandoz chemical companies in Basel saved Britain from a critical shortage of dyestuffs when supplies were cut off from Germany.

At the same time, the Swiss have founded, or have been associated with the founding of, several well-known British companies. J.G. Bodmer, an early Swiss inventor, set up in business in Manchester for twenty years and designed engines and rolling mills for British industry. In 1865 the bank in Birmingham which Jean Louis Moilliet had built up (he had come to England from Geneva as a boy of sixteen) merged with Lloyds & Co. to become Lloyds Banking Co., now Lloyds Bank plc. A Swiss chemist whose father came from Zurich, John Brunner, with his partner, Mond, formed Brunner Mond, later to become part of I.C.I. George Matthey was taken into partnership by Mr Johnson to form Johnson Matthey. Jacob Schweppe brought the secret of his carbonated water to Britain from Geneva. Another Swiss, Albert Eugster, created the British Syphon Manufacturing Co. In 1901 Nestlé, with their compatriots the Anglo-Swiss Condensed Milk Company, established the first tinned milk factory in England. And, in 1916 the Clavel-Dreyfus group of Basel set up in England, at the invitation of the British government, a chemical plant which became known as the British Celanese Company, later to be merged with Courtaulds. Hans Renold of Aarau founded Renold Chains, now Renold plc; and William de Vigier of Solothurn built up the Acrow group. Ferdinand Hurter set up the first real industrial research laboratory in Britain, while Hans Wilsdorf originated his famous Rolex watches in England, moving only later to Geneva.

Since the end of the nineteenth century, as trade has increased, or sometimes because trade has been frustrated by high tariffs, British industrial companies have set up subsidiaries in Switzerland and Swiss companies in Britain. Fixed investment in each other's country has grown rapidly. In 1981 British investment in Switzerland was approximately £600m while Swiss fixed investment in Britain was estimated to total some £1.4bn. Today Switzerland is the second largest investor in the United Kingdom after the United States. In addition to Nestlé, the chemical firms of CIBA-Geigy, Sandoz and Hoffmann-La Roche all manufacture in the United Kingdom, as do Sulzer Bros, Brown Boveri, Oerlikon-Bührle, Georg Fischer, Alusuisse, Schindler, Landis & Gyr and many smaller firms too. Swiss-owned products made in Britain range from Ovaltine and Crosse & Blackwell's soups, through Ilford films, Bally shoes, chocolate, perfumes, vitamin tablets, pharmaceuticals, and aluminium foil, to electronic control systems, bearings, precision tools, printing ink, metal castings, electric pumps and motors, refrigeration equipment, lifts, Kent instruments and Sulzer diesels.

FINANCIAL RELATIONS

> If you see a Genevan banker jump out of
> the window, be sure to follow him for
> there is money to be made.
> *Voltaire*

Genevan bankers and merchants in particular had been established in London well before the eighteenth century. Philip Burlamaqui, who has been mentioned earlier, was one of the leading financiers in the City from the early days of the Thirty Years' War. Calendrini & Co., also from Geneva, were particularly active in the middle of the seventeenth century and benefited from Cromwell's close affinity with the Protestant cantons. In 1703, during the War of the Spanish Succession, a group of Genevan bankers invested £300,000 in British stock.

A few years later the Bernese Government began to buy British securities, and in 1710 lent £150,000 at 6% to the British Government. But in 1720 two Bernese banks in London, Müller & Co. and Malacrida & Co., together with the Bernese government and many Swiss private investors, suffered heavily in the crash of the South Sea Company – the South Sea Bubble. The Berne government in fact saw the crash coming and were one of the first overseas investors to give orders to sell, making a large profit at the time; but their London agents went on to invest much of this in other ventures which failed. Most, if not all, of the loss was however later recouped, and by the 1770s Berne had some £440,000 invested in London. Some other Swiss cantons were investing on a smaller scale. Zurich had in 1727, put 100,000 guilders into English government stock and had bought 20 shares in the reconstituted South Sea Company. Later, investing through the bank Leu, Zurich had, by about 1790, some £50,000 in British securities. At about the same time the Grisons had £4,000 – its sole investment abroad. The English East India Company at that time had quite a few Swiss stockholders, particularly from Neuchâtel, Berne, Lausanne and Geneva. Genevan bankers had by then become expecially numerous in England. Their names included Gaussen, Cazenove, Sellon, Pictet, Lullin, Thellusson and Achard. A frequent visitor to London in the last half of the eighteenth century was Jacques-Louis Pourtalès of the powerful banking and commercial house of Pourtalès & Cie in Neuchâtel. Pourtalès made a fortune of several millions but lost most of it during the French Revolution.

When the French invaded Switzerland during the Napoleonic

Caricature of a Genevan banker, c. 1770; by Louis Arlaud.

Wars, the assets in London of Berne and Zurich were sequestrated, but released in 1816. At that time bankers in Basel took part in a £30m British loan marketed in Europe by Baring Bros. During the rest of the nineteenth century, Haldimand and Prevost, among others, were well-known Swiss names in the City, as well as Moilliet in Birmingham.

In the railway era of the mid-nineteenth century it was the turn of British capital in Switzerland. The British were heavy investors in the new Swiss railway companies (and it is said that Lord Palmerston himself was a shareholder). Later, the increasing number of British tourists to Switzerland encouraged the growth of Anglo-Swiss banking facilities. From the beginning of this century both banking and insurance links have expanded considerably. The Swiss Bank Corporation was the first of the large all-purpose Swiss banks to open in London in 1898, to be followed by Crédit Suisse in 1954, the Union Bank of Switzerland in 1967 and the Swiss Volksbank in 1977. In the other direction, Lloyds Bank established itself in Switzerland in 1919, the National Provincial Bank in 1920, and Barclays in 1935. In the last twenty-five years alone some fifteen British banks have opened branches or offices in Switzerland, while at least ten Swiss banks and insurance companies have established similar bases in Britain.

As Anglo-Swiss trade has grown and economic relations have become more complex, more and more firms of all kinds have found it desirable to set up a physical presence in the other country. This includes not only manufacturers, bankers and insurance houses, but travel companies, retailers, merchants, accountants, management consultants, advertising agents, and a host of others. By 1976 the number of British companies of all kinds which then had either branches or subsidiaries in Switzerland totalled approximately 400, while at least 130 Swiss firms had branches in Britain. This extensive development of economic relations has been accompanied, on the government level, by the negotiation of a whole network of bilateral agreements on trade and payments, double taxation, trademarks, social insurance, arbitration, air services and a number of other subjects important to contemporary relations between states.

CHANGING ECONOMIC CONDITIONS

Money alone does not buy happiness.
You must also have it in Switzerland.
German dictum

Over the years the swings in trade and investment – both fixed and portfolio – between Britain and Switzerland have largely reflected the changing economic background against which they have taken place. In the early days the main reason for the flow of Swiss money into Britain was the lack of suitable domestic opportunities – just as today the lack of a big enough home market, however rich, is one of the reasons that has caused many Swiss firms to develop manufacturing abroad. For several centuries much of Switzerland was desperately poor. The main export was Swiss manpower, soldiering for foreign monarchs. Berne was long the richest canton, but even there, only 170 years or so ago one in ten of the population was a pauper. Britain on the other hand, with vast trading resources, became one of the wealthiest nations in history.

Today, Switzerland is one of the richest countries in the world. It has the highest GDP per head in Europe. Despite the periodic attractions of the dollar, the DM, and the yen, the Swiss franc is probably the most consistently sought-after currency. Switzerland has the highest gold and foreign-exchange reserves *per capita* in the Western world. Unemployment is only 1% of the work force. There is hardly ever a strike. It has the most stable government in western Europe. No wonder the money pours in. At the same time, in Britain, after two world wars and the loss of an empire, economic conditions have become considerably harder. The strain of this on Anglo-Swiss relations was particularly evident in 1964 when a British minister was constrained to speak of the 'Gnomes of Zurich'.

Since then, North Sea oil has assisted British recovery and, with Britain's entry into the European Economic Community and the lifting of foreign exchange controls, the attraction of London as a world financial centre, and the United Kingdom in general as a worthwhile place to invest in, has again increased. Indeed, the Swiss banks have not been slow to recognise London as a key market in the rapidly changing international investment scene that has been taking place since the late 1970s (just as, earlier, they recognised the potential of the developing Eurobond market and took a leading rôle in this). And with the opening up of the London Stock Exchange to overseas securities houses, the Swiss 'big three' and several of the more important private Swiss banks have already greatly strengthened their own securities operations there, mainly by the purchase of leading firms of established London stockbrokers. The Union Bank of Switzerland have linked with Phillips & Drew, Crédit Suisse with Buckmaster & Moore, and the Swiss Bank Corporation with Savory Milln.

THE FORMULA FOR SWISS SUCCESS

It may be useful at this point to consider how the Swiss, from such unpromising beginnings, have achieved the economic success they enjoy today. How do they do it, and are there any lessons for the British?

First, two myths. It is sometimes said that the Swiss, being neutral

A dealing room at City of London stockbrokers Phillips & Drew.

in all recent European wars have had an unfair advantage – no war damage, no great costs in manpower, money or armaments; and that because of their laws on banking secrecy, they have become the bankers of the world. The Swiss get rich on other people's money.

As regards the first allegation, the Swiss are indeed neutral; but, as we have seen, they believe strongly that if their neutrality is to be credible they must be able to defend themselves. About 20% of the Federal Budget goes on civil and military defence. The Swiss army was mobilised throughout both world wars. No factories were destroyed, but often, as we have found, this can be a handicap, not an advantage (witness Germany's and Japan's post-war industrial resurgence with brand new factories). Neutrality has however brought the Swiss one big advantage: that is, stability, which has enabled economic enterprise to thrive and has encouraged investment.

As regards the second allegation – that banking secrecy has helped the Swiss to get rich – the Swiss laws on banking secrecy date only from the 1930s. And they were passed for very good humanitarian reasons – to protect the money of Jewish and other refugees from the attentions of the Nazi and Fascist regimes of that time. Of course, illegal funds do come into Switzerland, taking advantage of the secrecy laws, but the Swiss authorities and the Swiss banks certainly do not want them, and cooperate fully with other countries in uncovering them (that is, unless the crimes committed in those countries were, in Swiss eyes, only fiscal misdemeanours). Indeed, any large, continuing inflow of funds from abroad tends to undermine the government control of the domestic money supply. The reason for most of the ordinary inflow is not so much the attraction of banking secrecy (though this is a factor) as the wish to find a safe, stable and low-inflationary haven in periods of world uncertainty. In other words, it is a consequence, rather than a cause, of Switzerland's success.

THE KEY FACTORS

In fact, Swiss success has been due to a combination of factors: to the character of the Swiss themselves; to the way they have reacted to their geographical situation and to their lack of natural resources; to the influence upon them of Swiss history and of their political and social institutions.

We have discussed earlier the Swiss character and have compared it with that of the British. Put briefly, those aspects which have contributed ingredients to economic success are a truly democratic outlook, a level-headedness, a love of precision, and a strong regard for the law, for orderliness, hard work and thrift.

The Swiss reaction to geography and resources has been the classic one of challenge and response. The origin of their prosperity derives from the hardships of the past. Lacking indigenous raw materials, the Swiss could make a living only by getting the maximum added-value from the expensive materials they had to import. When the Industrial Revolution spread through Europe, the first textile mills began to appear in Switzerland. They needed water for power, and this was one thing the Swiss had. One way of adding value to cotton cloth was to embroider it, and much of this could be done cheaply at home. By the years just before the First World War, embroideries headed the list of all Swiss exports.

From the textile industry grew a need for dyes, and this was the basis of the chemical factories established in Basel – a convenient centre for the import of raw materials up the Rhine. The Swiss market soon became too small for their production, so they began exporting. Thus begun the growth of CIBA-Geigy, Hoffmann-La Roche and Sandoz. Today Basel is the biggest centre for pharmaceuticals production in Europe; and Hoffmann-La Roche have perhaps nearly half of the total world market for vitamins.

Embroiderers at work in the home at Appenzell, c. 1830.

From the textile industry grew also the need for textile machinery. We have seen how Britain's early ban on exports caused the Swiss to make their own. Sulzer Brothers soon became famous for looms. They then launched out into oil engines (with the help of a young German named Diesel). Today Sulzers still make excellent looms which sell, despite the strength of the Swiss franc, on their reliability. On the same principle of reliability, Sulzer marine engines now power some 40% of the world's shipping.

Another company, started about this time, was Oerlikon. It began with electric machinery, then locomotives for the first railways, and armaments for Swiss defence needs. Then came Brown Boveri, also specialising early on in electrical equipment. They soon found a ready market in the development of the new Swiss hydro-electric stations. Today they make some of the biggest generators in the world and most of their business is abroad. In another field, the brothers Bühler began to build milling machinery to treat the grain that had to be imported to feed the Swiss. Today perhaps one quarter of the world's flour mills contain machinery made by Bühler Bros.

The origins of Swiss watchmaking go back to the sixteenth century. As has been mentioned, the art grew out of Swiss love for, and skill at, intricate work; and until fairly recently many of the watch parts were made in Swiss homes. However, watchmaking is one industry where the Swiss have lost some of their supremacy. Switzerland had half of the world market for watches in 1970. By 1978 American and Japanese competition had reduced this to one quarter, and the industry has been making fundamental structural changes.

The food industry, which developed out of the processing of Alpine dairy products, goes from strength to strength. Nestlé is now the biggest company in Switzerland, with over 95% of its business done overseas. In a different area again, Alusuisse is one of the world's largest aluminium companies; and Holderbank one of the largest international cement groups, with plants in nineteen countries. Other Swiss manufacturers who have built up a significant international reputation include Georg Fischer, Schindler Holdings, Landis & Gyr, Bally and Jacobs-Suchard among numerous others. Switzerland is also a world market leader in the production of machine tools.

THE DEVELOPMENT OF THE SERVICE INDUSTRIES

It is in the field of services that the Swiss have made even more of their geography and their circumstances than in manufacturing. The service industries now employ over half of the total Swiss work force, and the percentage continues to grow.

In no area have the Swiss responded more clearly to the challenge of their environment than that of communications. The area now occupied by Switzerland, with the long water stretches on the Alpine routes provided by its lakes and rivers, had been an important transit country at least from the time of the Etruscans. The birth of the Swiss Confederation itself stemmed from the struggle to control the approaches to the Gotthard Pass, when the first three cantons of Uri Schwyz and Unterwalden, along Lake Lucerne, combined to frustrate the ambitions of the Dukes of Habsburg in that area. By the fourteenth century the leading political families in the Alpine cantons were drawing much of their income from the organisation of transport over the passes. Steamers began to enliven the Swiss lakes in the 1830s, while the building of the railways in the mid-1800s, and the opening of a rail tunnel through the Gotthard in 1882, gave a spur to the nascent tourist industry. In 1844 the first Baedeker guide had already acclaimed the Swiss inns of those days as 'the best in the world'. But the Swiss now began to build the hotels for which they have become rightly renowned; and some, like César Ritz, went abroad to become leaders in the hotel industry overseas. Today, 6%

of the working population are employed in tourism, and tourism accounts for some 10% of Swiss foreign income. With the advent of air travel, the Swiss were again able to exploit Switzerland's strategic position in the centre of Europe. Swissair is one of the few world airlines that has nearly always made a profit (and without any subsidies from the state).

BANKING AND INSURANCE

Swiss banking has its origins in the Middle Ages. Zurich, Geneva and Basel were all centres on the old trade routes across Europe, where goods were sold and money exchanged. The deep-rooted respect the Swiss have for saving contributed early on to the strong development of Swiss banking expertise, and to a flourishing banking industry. At the same time, the lack of sufficient investment opportunities at home led to the setting up of Swiss banking houses abroad.

With the foundation of the Federal State in 1848, a unified monetary system was introduced, paving the way for a modern banking system. (Before then, there had been over twenty different currencies circulating in the various cantons). Following the establishment thereafter of the 'Big Three' all purpose banks – the Union Bank of Switzerland, the Swiss Bank Corporation and the Crédit Suisse, the Swiss reputation for banking grew internationally. The 'Big Three' now have balance sheets which, together, are roughly half as large again as the whole of the Swiss gross national product. And despite the great inflow of foreign money into Switzerland in recent years, the 'motor' of the Swiss banking system is still the Swiss themselves. Swiss nationals and companies own probably twice as many foreign assets as foreigners hold in Switzerland.

The Swiss attraction to insurance derived initially from Swiss poverty, from an age-old need to 'cover' against misfortune. A bad harvest, or an avalanche, could spell disaster to a village of meagre resources. Today, the Swiss spend four Swiss francs a day to insure themselves, and Switzerland has some 110 insurance companies, twelve specialising in reinsurance. Switzerland as an international insurance centre ranks behind only the United States and the United Kingdom. Premium income in 1984 was well over Sw.fr. 26bn. The investment portfolio of the country's three leading life companies – Swiss Life, Winterthur Life, and Vita – alone total at least Sw.fr. 39bn.

INDUSTRIAL POLICY

Most of the big Swiss industries began by filling a local need, then, to

Tourists in the Bernese Oberland, *1870; drawing by A. Class.*

maintain growth, they were forced to find markets abroad. Today, nine-tenths of their business – and that of many of the smaller companies too – is done internationally; and this despite the handicap they have suffered from the strength of the Swiss franc. The Swiss formula for exporting success can be summed up as: concentration on specialisation, technical expertise, quality, and reliability; avoiding price-sensitive, mass-produced goods where international competition is strong (e.g. motor cars); and while investing heavily in research and development, avoiding costly 'prestige' products, in favour of perfecting existing technologies, and the production of well-proven, dependable goods, delivered on time.

So far as investment in research is concerned, Switzerland is among the leading countries of the world (allocating an average of 2.3% of GNP a year between 1970 and 1980). And since they have spread their research effort overseas, like their manufacturing, the big Swiss internationals can call on a worldwide network of researchers.

GOOD LABOUR RELATIONS

In addition, Swiss industry enjoys the inestimable benefit of good labour relations. Since the pact made in 1937 between the engineering and metalworking unions and the employers there have been virtually no strikes. It was a historic agreement and one of which both labour and management have become particularly proud. The unions in Switzerland are generally reasonable and sensible. They have evolved in a different socio-historical background from those in Britain with, for exmple, no concentrations of heavy industry. The fact that a good deal of early Swiss manufacturing, such as embroidery, straw-plait making and watch making, was decentralised and done in the home also helped. Moreover, Swiss workers do not like to lose money by stoppages. The large number of foreign workers (more than one in four of the work force) on tightly controlled work permits is an additional factor.

RESPONSIBLE MANAGEMENT

Swiss management is also generally sensible and reasonable. Most companies make a point of maintaining a continuing dialogue with their workers about conditions – how the company is doing. They do not wait for the formal, periodic wage negotiations. The employers also take care to be seen to be working as hard, if not harder than, their employees. They generally arrive in advance of their work force (just as, in government, Swiss ministers usually arrive before most of their civil servants). They often share the same canteen and drive modest cars.

THE INFLUENCE OF MILITARY SERVICE

Compulsory military service also helps labour relations. Swiss conscription is a deliberate social, as well as a defence, policy. In the process, Swiss of different ethnic and social backgrounds are mixed up; and the foreman in a factory may have a higher military rank than a manager in the same company.

THE EDUCATIONAL SYSTEM

Again, the Swiss educational system plays a part. Swiss education, as we have seen, is consistently geared to solid, practical training for everyday life, and particularly for business and industry. There are ten educational institutions of university status in Switzerland; and it is significant that the prestige of education at the Federal Institute of Technology (E.T.H.) in Zurich is probably higher than that of one at any of Switzerland's conventional universities.

SOUND MONEY

The poverty of the past and the inborn tendency of the Swiss to save has made them place a particular importance on money. They not only like to ensure that they get every penny's worth of what they spend; they value highly a sound currency. The government and the National Bank devote primary attention to the protection of the Swiss franc from excessive pressure both internal and external. They ensure that, so far as possible, it is not undermined by lax fiscal or credit policies, or by inflation. Years of low inflation have brought low rates of interest and lower costs for industry. Comparatively low taxation gives more scope for incentive and helps capital formation. All this is eminently favourable to a spirit of free enterprise.

POLITICAL MODERATION

Behind all this is a background of political tolerance and stability which permeates all aspects of Swiss life. Switzerland is not a country in the sense that we understand most nation states. In its ethnic, linguistic, religious, economic and geographic diversity it is probably unique. It has suffered many threats to its unity in the past. Despite enjoying long periods of tranquillity, the country was shaken by religious wars in the sixteenth and seventeenth centuries. In 1798 a revolution in the French-speaking canton of Vaud was the pretext for the French invasion of Switzerland. Years of tension between Catholics and Protestants culminated in civil war in 1847. There was widespread internal dissention at the end of the First World War, and a brief general strike. There is today great disparity in size and wealth between the big industrialised cantons such as Zurich and Basel and the tiny forest cantons, some of whom were the proud founders of the nation. The Italian-speaking canton of Ticino is virtually cut off from the rest of the country by the mountains.

To keep the Confederation together in the face of so many potentially centrifugal influences has needed special restraint on the part of everyone in authority. The Swiss have learnt by experience that a spirit of compromise is essential to their existence. Their political institutions have been developed to facilitate this end.

THE SWISS SYSTEM OF GOVERNMENT

Government in the Swiss Confederation is based primarily on the twenty-six cantons (actually twenty-three, but three are divided into half-cantons). They have all the powers not specifically reserved to the federal government in the Constitution; and additions to the central power are always fiercely resisted. The practice of local self-government has taught the Swiss to associate duties with rights and to respect one another's convictions. The Referendum and the Popular Initiative which have already been mentioned are widely used on both a national and a cantonal basis. Proportional representation was introduced in 1918 after two earlier attempts had failed. (Incidentally, when the first attempt was made in 1909 the British Minister in Berne reported to London that: 'the sober-minded citizen views with some distrust this proposed alteration to the electoral system'.) Proportional representation has, for many years, produced a stable and moderate coalition government of the four main parties (Radicals, Christian-Democrats and People's Party on the centre-right, and Social-Democrats on the centre-left. They represent the vast majority of the people; only the extremes of either side are excluded. The government consists of only seven ministers (federal councillors), elected by both houses of Parliament every four years, and chosen always to represent a balance between not only the parties, but also the main linguistic groups and the bigger cantons. The civil service is relatively small, but of high calibre.

The Swiss system may slow down decision-making (it took until 1971 before women were given the vote) but the government can act swiftly on occasion when Swiss vital interests are at stake. Moreover, the Referendum and the Initiative provide the people with an important counter-balance to the power of a virtually permanent coalition, and a Federal Council which cannot be forced to resign. And while the Swiss electorate can be notoriously 'cussed' and frustrate desirable reform on occasion, both devices work well. Indeed it can be argued that the virtues of Swiss government have not received the attention of other countries that they rightly deserve.

Montesquieu wrote that 'rulers establish institutions, and afterwards the institutions mould the rulers'. Switzerland is an excellent example of this dictum; for much of the reason why it is such a successful democracy lies in its general way of life, which has grown out of its democratic institutions. Its main features are: a special consideration for minorities; a readiness to compromise; an abhorrence of direct confrontation; a continuous effort to maintain a social concensus; attachment to the principle that everyone must be consulted. This all makes for calm and stability; and with the reputation for hard work, for correctness and intregrity, it is understandable that the country thrives.

Admission to the confederation	1351 Zurich	1481 Solothurn	1803 Ticino
	1353 Berne	1501 Basle-Town	1803 Vaud (LIBERTÉ ET PATRIE)
	1332 Lucerne	1501 Basle-Country	1815 Valais
	1291 Uri	1501 Schaffhausen	1815 Neuchâtel
	1291 Schwyz	1513 Appenzell-Outer-Rhodes	1815 Geneva
	1291 Obwalden	1513 Appenzell Inner-Rhodes	1979 Jura
	1291 Nidwalden	1803 St. Gall	
	1352 Glarus	1803 Grisons	
	1352 Zug	1803 Aargovia	
	1481 Fribourg	1803 Thurgovia	

The arms of the Swiss cantons and their date of entry into the Swiss Confederation.

A Chronology of Anglo-Swiss Relations

A SELECTION OF EVENTS WHICH HAVE INFLUENCED OR HAVE BEEN OF INTEREST TO POLITICAL, ECONOMIC, CULTURAL, SOCIAL AND SPORTING RELATIONS BETWEEN BRITAIN AND SWITZERLAND

Introduction

Relations between countries are made up of a complex of contacts, exchanges, negotiations, transactions, issues, impressions and influences, which take place against a background of differing political, economic, cultural and social conditions. The history books pick out the main threads and weave them into a coherent story. But, in reality, day by day, year by year, a multitude of different events are happening.

This Chronology of Anglo-Swiss Relations, by presenting the story as it happened, aims to give, in as succinct a form as possible, something of the tenor of affairs between the two countries, in a little of the full variety of their aspects, as they unfolded. Of necessity, it is a selective and, to some extent, arbitrary summary of the many hundreds of contacts which took place in the earlier centuries, and of the many hundreds of thousands of more recent times as links became more comprehensive and more complex. But it includes as many as possible of the most interesting and important events and developments.

Since this is a story of bilateral associations, relations between Switzerland and Britain in the multilateral context (for example, in the international organisations which have become increasingly numerous in this last century) are not included, except in a few instances where the Anglo-Swiss element was particularly important.

The Chronology is designed to be read through from beginning to end. However, the index will assist the reader who wishes to follow in more detail some of the separate themes or subjects.

Although the record that follows begins from medieval times, the history of Anglo-Swiss relations goes back at least 2,000 years. This is evidenced by the vestiges of the decorative La Tène art found in Britain, named after the Celtic Iron Age settlements at La Tène on Lake Neuchâtel in Switzerland, and by other Helvetic artefacts discovered earlier this century on the South Downs. There may have been Helvetic officers among the Roman forces in the later stages of the Roman occupation of Britain. Certainly, we know from Roman altars to Jupiter found at Risingham in Northumberland that there were detachments of javelin throwers or spearmen from Rhaetia – basically the present-day Swiss canton of the Grisons – amongst the Roman troops fighting the Caledonians (Scots) along Hadrian's Wall. These Rhaetians had adopted the language of the Romans; and the language spoken today in some parts of the Grisons is still a debased form of Latin called Romansch (or Ladin). Again, one of the best known Roman silver ingots found in Britain bears the stamp of the Emperor Magentius and is known to have come from the fourth-century fort at Kaiseraugst in Switzerland. However, facts are scarce until we get to the Middle Ages, and even then some are mixed with legend.

A dragon in the Alps, from J.J. Scheuchzer's Itinera Alpina, *1723.*

Medieval Times

Irish monks in Switzerland – Bishop Ermenfried and William the Conqueror – Travellers over the Great St Bernard – Henry III and Edward I and the Counts of Savoy – the Grandsons – the 'Guglers' and the Hundred Years' War

At least one source has it that the legendary English King Arthur waged a victorious campaign against a Roman Emperor near the St Gotthard. According to Huchoun of the Awle Ryale, a Scottish or northern English poet of the fourteenth century, in the poem 'Morte Arthure' ascribed to him, King Arthur went first to Lucerne: 5th C

> . . . on the Lammen-day to Lucerne he wendez,
> Lengez thare at laysere with lykynge inowe,

and then 'ouere mowntes so hye. . .' attacked the emperor on the 'Goddarde'.[6] (See also c.1195.)

The first British travellers to the Bernese Oberland were, according to local legend, Beatus and Justus, monks who reached Lake Thun via the Brünig Pass at the end of the fifth century or the beginning of the sixth. A cave at Beatenbucht which they chose as their habitat was occupied by a dragon, who disappeared when Beatus made the sign of the Cross. (Dragons featured strongly in early Alpine literature.) Beatus preached the Gospel all round the Thunersee, and is said to have crossed the water on more than one occasion by floating on his cloak. 6th C

Among other early visitors to Switzerland from the British Isles was a group of Irish monks under the leadership of the scholar-saint Columbanus. As a result of his influence, stemming from an earlier sojourn in Burgundy, monasteries were established in the Jura mountains at Romainmôtier, Ste Ursanne and Moutier-Grandval (see also 1979). From AD 610 Columbanus with a group of twelve companions came to Switzerland itself. He was active in Alemanian territory around the Lake of Constance, probably having travelled down the Rhine. When he later left for Italy, his follower Gallus (who, tradition has it, shared his meals with a bear) remained behind with two 7th C assistants, Magnoald and Theodore. They first established themselves in Arbon and then moved a few miles south. On the site of Gallus's cell the Abbey of St Gallen was afterwards (AD 720) built.

c. 614 Another follower of Columbanus, Sigisbert, journeyed into Rhaetia. On the site of his cell the Abbey of Disentis (Grisons) was founded.

c. 650 Yet another Irish monk, Fridolin, is said to have founded a monastery and a school for boys at Säckingen, on the Rhine. Fridolin is also reputed to have built a chapel consecrated to St Hilarius in a remote valley of the Alps, near the source of the Linth, which sanctuary afterwards may have given its name to the canton of Glarus (a corruption of Hilarius).

c. 689 Ceduald, King of the West Saxons, made a pilgrimage to Rome by way either of the Great St Bernard pass or the Mont Cenis. He died in Rome in 689.

800 When Charlemagne was crowned Emperor of the West, he invited the Anglo-Saxon scholar Alcuin (735 – 804) from Northumbria to his court to act as his counsellor on education and to make a revision of the Bible. A copy of Alcuin's Bible was presented to the church of Zurich. Alcuin became a great friend of Remedius, Bishop of Chur (Rhaetia), who was one of Charlemagne's chief supporters. He was also the teacher of Abbot Grimwald of St Gallen.

c. 850 By the ninth century the Abbey of St Gallen was well established, and a new flow of Irish monks to the area began. Among those who came to St Gallen were Eusebius, the scholar-monk Moengal, and Bishop Marcus (who was born in Wales).

929 The Anglo-Saxon King Athelstan sent an envoy, Bishop Cenwald of Worcester, to visit several religious establishments in Germany and Switzerland. At St Gallen, where Cenwald stayed four days, prayers were said for the king, and the names of Athelstan, Cenwald and several other dignitaries of the English church were entered on the Roll of the Fraternity of St Gallen. Cenwald probably also visited the monastery of Pfäfers.

949 St Gregory, an Anglo-Saxon monk (and probably a brother of King Athelstan), joined the community at Einsiedeln Abbey, where he

became abbot. His rule coincided with the period of greatest monastic splendour of the abbey. He died in 996.

Sigeric, one of a number of successive Archbishops of Canterbury who made the pilgrimage to Rome, crossed the Great St Bernard pass on his return journey, staying in Martigny, Lausanne, Yverdon and Vallorbe. The whole journey took eighty overnight stops. 990

King Canute, of England, Denmark, Norway and the Hebrides, made a pilgrimage to Rome, crossing the mountains by the Great St Bernard. He found that pilgrims and merchants on the route were being robbed and held to ransom by brigands in the approaches to the Alps. He is said to have come to an agreement with the local raiders whereby Anglo-Saxons and Scandinavians would not be molested. (The brigands were evidently still there when Bernard de Menthon established the hospice on the pass in about 1048.) 1027

Bishop Ermenfried of Sion in the Valais came to England as envoy of Pope Alexander II to Edward the Confessor, 'in order to enlighten the king's private conscience' and to forward the foundation, or development, of Westminster Abbey. 1062

Bishop Ermenfried of Sion came again to England as one of three papal legates invited by William the Conqueror to help bring the Church up to Norman standards, and to replace English clergy with Normans. At the official coronation of William at Winchester (he had had himself crowned first at Westminster in 1066), Bishop Ermenfried placed the crown on the royal head with the Pope's blessing. Later that year, Ermenfried, at William's request, journeyed to France with William's queen, Matilda, and her son Robert, to urge Lanfranc, Abbot of Caen, to accept William's invitation to him to become Archbishop of Canterbury. Lanfranc agreed. 1070

In the Domesday Book, which was drawn up on William the Conqueror's instructions to make an inventory of all properties in England, a Robert de Watteville is listed as farming an estate at what is now Malden in Surrey. However, whether this de Watteville was of the Swiss branch of the family or from an earlier Bavarian line seems uncertain. 1086

In common with many other pilgrims from the British Isles at that 1188

The Sion Gospels cover, dating from about AD 1000. Some authorities link it with the Gospels of Charlemagne, a book which belonged to the abbey of St Maurice d'Agaune in the Valais.

time, John de Bremble of Canterbury made the journey over the Great St Bernard pass on his way to Rome. His ink froze in its bottle, and he wrote; 'Feeling myself so much nearer to heaven that I was more sure that my prayer would be heard, "Lord," I said, "restore me to my brethren, that I may tell them that they come not to this place of torment."'

c. 1195 Ulrich von Zatzikhofen of Thurgau, in his poem 'Lanzelot', was the first poet writing in German to treat of the subject of the English King Arthur and his knights.

Swiss 'undesirables' in England? In the Magna Carta, assented to by King John, one of the undertakings he gave his barons was that 'we will remove completely from office the relations of Gerard d'Athée, so that in future they shall have no office in England, namely . . . Geoffrey de Martigny and his brother . . . and their unsavoury tribe. . . .'

1215

Death of Guillaume, or William, an Anglo-Saxon saint who had established himself at Neuchâtel.

1234

Peter of Savoy, whose family at that time ruled most of the Vaud, married his niece Eleanor of Provence to Henry III of England. Peter himself came to England and Henry made him the Earl of Richmond (1241). For twenty years Peter played an important part in the constitutional debates in England and in shaping English foreign policy. He carried out several diplomatic missions for Henry. One of his brothers, Boniface, was made Archbishop of Canterbury (1245). Another, William, became Bishop of Winchester.

1236

Peter of Savoy's brother, Amadeus IV (1197–1253) who was then Count of Savoy, made an agreement with Henry III. In return for a sum of £1,000 and an annual pension, Amadeus gave his allegiance and homage to Henry and made over to him the fiefs of Saint Maurice d'Agaune in the Valais, and, on the other side of the Great St Bernard pass, the castle of Bard and two other strong points now in Italy, Avigliana and Susa.

1246

In Berne, the most common coin was the pfennig, of which 12 made a schilling, and 20 schillings, or 240 pfennigs, made 1 pfund.

c. 1250

In the years that followed Peter of Savoy's establishment at the English court, numerous relations and friends of Peter's from Savoy, the Vaud and Berne, came to England too, many of whom obtained favours, land or religious livings through Peter's good offices. Amongst them were Ebel de Mont who in 1256 became Steward of Henry III's household, Pierre de Champvent who became Sheriff of Gloucester, and Jean de Grilly who became Seneschal of Gascony.

1256

Another of Peter's friends was William, Seigneur de Grandson, of Lake Neuchâtel, who was married to Blanche of Savoy. William's two sons, Otes and William, both had distinguished careers in Eng-

The Château of Grandson, Lake Neuchâtel.

land (see 1270 and 1300). The English branch of the family prospered, changing its name to Grandison. (The family were also known, in early documents, by the name of Grauncon, Graunzon, and Grandissono.) By the fourteenth century they owned estates in London, Wales, Ireland and the Channel Islands.

1259 When Peter of Savoy returned home from England he received many favours from Henry III. Together with his nephew, Boniface, now Count of Savoy, he became one of the most important seigneurs in the region. In 1256 the towns of Fribourg, Berne and Morat (Murten), and the Haslital, had placed themselves under Peter's protection, in view of the threat to them posed by the Dukes of Habsburg. A year afterwards, Henry III's brother, Richard, Earl of Cornwall, and a close associate of Peter, obtained election to the imperial crown as King of the Romans (the Electors not having been able to agree on a German prince). In this capacity Richard acquired recognition up the Rhine as far as Basel. As German king he also had the overlordship of Gümmenen, a strongpoint disputed by Savoy and the Habsburgs, which commanded the road from Berne to Morat. In 1259 Richard gave Gümmenen to Peter of Savoy

1260 Among the English retainers whom Peter had brought back with him from England was a master builder who became known as Master James of St George. James helped to build Peter of Savoy's castle and new town at Yverdon on Lake Neuchâtel (see also 1286).

Another Swiss friend of Peter, William de Champvent, was made Dean of St Martin-le-Grand in London. In 1273 he returned to the Vaud and became Bishop of Lausanne. — 1262

A member of the Grandson family (see 1256), Sir Otes de Grandson, accompanied Prince Edward to the Holy Land (where he is said to have saved the Prince's life by sucking the poison from a stab wound). When in 1272 the Prince became King Edward, Sir Otes became his secretary. He later retired to Switzerland. He founded the altar of St George in the cathedral of Lausanne in 1317, and was buried in the cathedral in 1328. (See also 1282.) — 1270

On his way home from Italy, Edward I stayed with Philip I of Savoy (c. 1207–85), who had succeeded his brother Peter as count (Peter became count in 1263 and died in 1268). Edward received Philip's homage as his vassal. — 1273

In response to an appeal from Philip of Savoy for help against Rudolf of Habsburg who was preparing to attack him, King Edward sent his secretary and friend Sir Otes de Grandson, together with the dean of Lichfield to try to find a peaceful solution to the dispute. (In 1283, Philip gave back Morat and Gümmenen to Rudolf.) — 1282

After Philip's death, his nephews Amadeus and Louis quarrelled over the succession to the Savoy possessions. King Edward and his mother (the former Peter of Savoy's niece), together with the Pope and the King of France, Philip the Fair, acted as arbitrators between them, allocating Savoy to Amadeus and the Vaud as a fief to Louis. — 1285

When Edward I had stopped in Switzerland in 1273 to receive the homage of Philip of Savoy, the work of the English castle-builder at Yverdon, Master James of St George, had attracted his attention. Edward had him brought home, and by 1286 James was Master of the King's Works in Wales, building a string of castles which Edward had planned as part of his settlement of Wales. Several of James's castles in North Wales bear a strong resemblance to that at Yverdon. James later became Constable of Harlech Castle. — 1286

A Swiss from Berne, Johann de Strätlingen (1260–94), a nephew of Sir Otes de Grandson, received from his uncle a royal fiefdom in Ireland, later confirmed by Edward I. — c.1289

1290 Girard de Viuppens, from the Vaud in Switzerland, was made a canon at York Cathedral. He undertook a diplomatic mission to the Pope, Boniface VIII, for Edward I. In 1302 he returned to Switzerland and succeeded William de Champvent (see 1262) as Bishop of Lausanne.

13th C The Order of St Bernard reputedly owned some eighty estates in England and elsewhere, gifts of kings, princes and knights for services rendered to travellers by the Hospice of St Bernard throughout the Middle Ages. Among the British properties were the Hospice of St Nicholas and St Bernard at Hornchurch, Essex, as well as Priors Inn and the site of the present Savoy Hotel in London. The latter came to the Order on the death of Peter of Savoy (see 1236), who had received it from his niece Eleanor, queen of Henry III. Eleanor bought it back from the Order in 1270.

1300 A brother of Sir Otes de Grandson, William de Grandson, was engaged on the side of the king in the war in Scotland. In 1326 he became prior of the Hospital of St John of Jerusalem in England.

The Lake of Great St Bernard from the Hospice: *from William Brockedon's* Passes of the Alps, *1828*.

Edward III, by an unknown artist.

A son of William de Grandson, John de Grandison, became Bishop of Exeter, a post he held for forty-two years. John transformed Exeter Cathedral from the former austere Norman structure into today's richly decorative Gothic style. — 1327

Yet another member of the Grandison family, Admiral Sir Otho de Grandison, became Commander of the Western Fleet. He had previously been Governor of the Channel Islands. — 1337

William de Grandson's sister, Catherine, who became the Countess of Salisbury, was possibly the lady reputed to have dropped her garter — 1344

The battle with the Guglers at Fraubrunnen, 1375: from Diebold Schilling's Spiezer Chronicle, *1484-5.*

and inspired Edward III's creation of the Order of the Garter. (Another contender for the honour was the Fair Maid of Kent.) The order was formally established some four years later.

A member of the Swiss branch of the Grandson family, Otto de Grandson (d. 1397), fled to England accused of complicity in a political murder. One of the most remarkable poets of his time, Otto entered the services of Edward III and of his successor Richard II. Chaucer called him 'the flower of the French poets', and wrote English versions of one of Otto de Grandson's poems which he called 'The Compleynt of Mars' and 'The Compleynt of Venus' (c. 1394).   c. 1370

A French noble, Enguerrand de Coucy, Count of Soissons and Earl of Bedford, a son-in-law of Edward III of England, acted in support of his claim to an inheritance from the Habsburgs which was located in Swiss territory. He led a horde of some 40,000 largely English and Welsh unemployed mercenaries from the Hundred Years' War by way of Basel to plunder and ravage into western and central Switzerland and Aargau. The Welsh freebooters were led by Evan Griffith ab Einion and by Evan Llewellyn. They were known to the Swiss as the 'Guglers', because of the pointed shape of their helmets. The men of Berne, Schwyz. Lucerne and Unterwalden mobilised and came to Basel's defence. Berne also was threatened, and made a temporary alliance with Duke Leopold III of Austria to help repel the invaders. Some 3,000 'Guglers' were defeated at Buttisholz by a much smaller Swiss force from the Entlebuch (Lucerne); and after two other battles, at Fraubrunnen and Ins, the rest of the insurgents were thrown out of the country. The remains of those freebooters killed at Buttisholz were buried in a mound there, later called the English Barrow.[7]   1375

Later, de Coucy relinquished his membership of the Order of the Garter which had been conferred on him by Edward III. And several of the more prominent Welsh leaders of the expedition were assassinated in France by secret orders of Edward's successor, Richard II.

One of the earliest indications of Anglo-Swiss trade was an item in the accounts of the Receiver of Tolls in Neuchâtel showing dues paid on 130 bales of English merchandise. At around this time, too, English cloth was being sold at fairs in Geneva.   1398

Crossing the Gotthard at the beginning of the fifteenth century, Adam of Usk wrote that he was drawn in an ox-wagon, 'half dead   1402 with cold, and with mine eyes blindfold lest I should see the dangers of the pass'.

1444 At the end of the Hundred Years' War 'free companies' of ex-soldiers looted and pillaged throughout France. When they began to menace Savoy, a force of 1,700 Switzers went to the aid of their ally, the Count of Savoy, and annihilated several bands of English pillagers.

c. 1465 A chief magistrate of the Republic of Berne, Conrad de Scharnachtal (d. 1472), came to England in the course of a journey round Europe and was received by Edward IV who gave him a letter of protection. Another Bernese who arrived in England a little later was Nicholas de Diesbach (1430–75). He was also received by the king.

1476 After his defeat at the hands of the Swiss at Grandson, Charles the Bold of Burgundy gathered a fresh army at Lausanne, and strengthened it with several thousand English archers recruited from the English army of Edward IV that was at Calais. (Edward had brought over his army the year before as part of a plan to attack Louis XI of France, in concert with Charles the Bold; but Edward had made peace with Louis before the army was needed.) However, Charles was again defeated by the Swiss at the Battle of Morat (Murten). Some sources say that the Duke of Somerset was amongst Charles's retinue at that battle. Of this battle the historian G.M. Trevelyan wrote in his *Clio, a Muse* of 1913:

There, over that green hill beneath the lowland firwood, the mountainers from alp and glacier-foot swept on with thundering feet and bellowing war-horns, and at the sight of their levelled pikes the Burgundian chivalry, arrayed in all the gorgeous trappings of the Renaissance armourers, fled headlong into Morat lake down there. From that day forward the Swiss democracy, thrusting aside the Duke of Savoy, planted itself on the Genevan shore, and Europe, therefore in the fulness of time, got Calvin and Rousseau.

1485 Some relics of King Oswald, seventh-century English King of Northumbria, were reputedly brought to the parish church of St Oswald in Zug, Switzerland. (St Oswald's body was originally given to the monastery at Bardney in Windsey, but most of the relics disappeared during the Danish invasions of Britain and were carried off by devout persons.)

1487 According to the Bernese chronicler Valerius Anshelm, a Martin

Schwarz of Augsburg engaged a number of Swiss troops to fight in England on the side of Lambert Simnel during the latter's uprising against Henry VII.

The long line of victories by the Swiss, over the Habsburgs, the Burgundians and the French, had by the end of the fifteenth century found a reflection in English dress. In their search for brighter and more fanciful clothes the young men of England sought to emulate the costumes of the victorious Swiss soldiery.

c. 1498

Swiss man-at-arms: by Hans Rudolf Manuel

The Sixteenth Century

Efforts to reach an Anglo-Swiss alliance – Cardinal Schinner and Richard Pace – some early traders – contacts during the Reformation – British religious refugees in Switzerland – Zurich's and Geneva's influence on the English and Scottish churches – Geneva seeks British support – and a modern tourist

1503   Newly printed in Basel, the writings of Duns Scotus (1265 – 1308) much influenced the young Swiss reformer Huldrych Zwingli (1484 – 1531), then studying at Basel University.

1513   Cardinal Matthias Schinner of Sion (1465 – 1522), an able churchman and a skilful diplomat, had succeeded in putting together an alliance between the Pope and the Swiss Confederation. He had then enlisted the Emperor Maximilian of Austria's aid in the Pope's struggle to drive the French out of Italy. In 1513 Schinner tried to bring England, too, into his alliance. He wrote to his friend Cardinal Wolsey, and to Henry VIII, warmly sponsoring an embassy that the Swiss cantons were sending to England at his suggestion, headed by Mauritz Hurus of Zurich and Johann Stolz of Basel. Hurus and Stolz were well received by Henry and were given presents, but no agreement was reached.

1514   When the Swiss emissaries returned home, Henry VIII had Wolsey send two diplomatists, Richard Pace and Dr William Knight, together with William Rynk (probably of the Hansa merchants Hermann Rynk, who were to help find the funds needed), to Zurich and Berne to continue negotiations with the Swiss cantons. They too had a good reception. The Milanese envoy in Zurich reported home: 'The Swiss lords have shown the English ambassadors more honour than have ever been shown to any others, doubling the quantity of wine that is usually given to ambassadors . . .' With Cardinal Schinner's help, in August of that year, they finally reached an agreement in principle with the Swiss under which the Swiss were to put 18,000 troops into the field against the French whenever Henry VIII chose, in return for both wartime and peacetime subsidies. But with a change of policy, Henry married his sister to Louis XII of France and made an alliance with him. The Swiss negotiations were left in abeyance.

When Louis XII died suddenly and François I came to the throne of France, Henry VIII instructed Pace to renew discussions with the Swiss. At Schinner's suggestion, Michael Abbate, secretary of Maximilian Sforza, the deposed ruler of Milan, went to London with a plan. The aim was a full alliance to eject the French from Milan, with the Swiss to serve the Emperor Maximilian of Austria but to be paid by England. Henry was to pay 100,000 crowns for 20,000 Swiss when they were in the field. If the Swiss defeated the French in Italy, they were to be kept in pay for an invasion of France itself. Pace re-opened negotiations.

1515

After the Battle of Marignano in September 1515, when François I defeated the Swiss and their allies (ending 200 years of Swiss military ascendancy in Europe), some of the Swiss cantons were already favouring a future policy of neutrality. At the same time France sought to woo the Swiss, who had been such redoubtable opponents, on to the French side. While British subsidies arrived slowly, through the agency of the merchants Rynk and of the Banquiers Fugger of Augsburg, French gold was used widely in the cantons for pensions and presents. After intense French diplomatic pressure the Swiss in November concluded with France a pact of perpetual peace and neutrality, the Treaty of Fribourg.[8] However, by the end of the year only eight of the then thirteen cantons had ratified the French treaty.

In January, Zurich and the four other cantons who had not ratified the treaty offered a strong force to Pace if the English payment was raised to 120,000 crowns. This was agreed, and 17,000 Swiss assembled at Chur. Joining the Emperor Maximilian and his troops at Trento, they marched into Italy accompanied by Pace and Cardinal Schinner. They raised the siege of Brescia and advanced to the outskirts of Milan. When English funds were again slow in arriving, Maximilian's support turned lukewarm: he finally withdrew from the campaign and his own troops followed him, leaving the Swiss in an impossible position. They, too, abandoned the expedition.

1516

Richard Pace's negotiations with the Swiss led more than once to his imprisonment, notwithstanding the diplomatic nature of his mission. During his stay he found time to compose his moral treatise *De Fructu*, which he said was written in the public baths at Constance.

Determined not to give up, and with the five cantons still favouring the English, Richard Pace got a Swiss Diet held in October. Cardinal Schinner himself came to England as emissary of the Emperor Maximilian, who was now worried about the French becoming supreme in Italy. Schinner quickly negotiated a treaty of peace, friendship and mutual defence between Henry VIII, Maximilian and Spain. The Pope (Leo X) was to be included in the pact, if he wished, as Principal Member. A special clause stated that the Swiss Confederation was included in this alliance and that a pension would be paid to the Swiss.

Cardinal Schinner said that the Swiss would provide 20,000 men if Henry VIII would give them security for three months' pay, but the money must be ready at hand or the Swiss 'would lose confidence in England'. Henry said he was ready to pay the money – 180,000 crowns, for a three months' campaign, but this would be reduced pro rata if it took less time, and to nothing if the Swiss did not give battle. (The King of Spain was asked to contribute 80,000 of the 180,000 crowns that was offered.)

Henry ratified the treaty in November 1516. However, the alliance was soon nullified when Maximilian made his own agreement with the French. When Cardinal Schinner left England he was given 3,000 ducats by Henry VIII and 1,000 by Cardinal Wolsey. He asked in addition for an annual pension to be paid to him for his services to England.

Sir Thomas More's *Utopia* was first published (in Latin). It contained a veiled attack on the Swiss mercenary system, no doubt influenced by the tortuous negotiations undertaken by More's friend Richard Pace to win the Swiss on to England's side after Marignano, and by the further negotiations with Cardinal Schinner. In referring to the imaginary Zapolites,[9] More wrote:

> They go forth of their country in great companies together, and whosoever lacketh soldiers, there they proffer their service for small wages. This is the only craft they have to get their living by. They maintain their life by seeking their death. For them, whomsoever they be in wages they fight hardily, fiercely and faithfully. But they bind themselves for no certain time. But upon this condition they enter into bonds, that the next day they will take part with the other side for greater wages, and the next day after that they will be ready to come back again for a little more money.

The printer Johannes Froben of Basel published the first Greek text of the New Testament, which had been collated by Erasmus in 1512 while he was living in Cambridge. Erasmus was (with Colet, that other early reformer) one of More's best friends and shared the same Christian ideals. Born in Rotterdam, Erasmus lived mainly in England during the earlier part of his life and in Basel during the later part (he died there in 1536).

1517 Having heard no more from Henry, Cardinal Schinner sent his nephew to England to claim his pension, which was granted. When Richard Pace returned to London from Zurich later that year, he arranged for Schinner's pension to be increased.

1518 Erasmus sent a copy of *Utopia* (see 1516) to Froben of Basel, who published a new version in March 1518 and another in November of that year. This important work of moral philosophy was eagerly read in Switzerland, as in the rest of Europe. The Swiss reformer Huldrych Zwingli must have approved of the passage on the Zapolites since his own views were turning against the mercenary system (see 1519).

c. 1518 The Swiss physician and alchemist Paracelsus (1493-1541), whose real name was Theophrastus Bombastus von Hohenheim, came to England in the course of one of his many travels through Europe. From London, he went to Oxford. He also visited the lead mines in Cumberland and the tin mines in Cornwall, to examine the minerals which he was convinced held curative properties.

Many of Paracelsus's contemporaries claimed that he was charlatan hiding behind a mask of genius. But his reputation certainly survived him as is evidenced by references, direct or indirect, to him in Shakespeare's play *All's Well That Ends Well*, in Ben Jonson's *Volpone* and *The Alchemist* and in John Fletcher's *Fair Maid of the Inn*.

1519 When Huldrych Zwingli began to preach at the Grossmünster in Zurich, his views on the true course of the Church were studied carefully in England. But he also preached against the Swiss system of mercenaries, urging the young to find work rather than turn to soldiering (advice which was easier to follow in the big towns like Zurich and Berne than in poor mountain cantons, who remained true to their Catholic traditions).

For labour (said Zwingli) is verily a thing divine. It wards off wantonness and vice, brings forth goodly fruits upon which man may feast deeply with

Theophrastus Paracelsus (left) and Huldrych Zwingli: portrait after Hans Asper.

serenity, without fear that he is consuming the blood of the innocent and thereby polluting himself. Labour makes the body young and strong, and devours the ills that stem from idleness.

1523 Following the Treaty of Windsor (June 1522) between Henry VIII and the new Emperor Charles V, renewed efforts were made to persuade the Swiss to join the alliance against France. The Emperor sent ambassadors with money to the Swiss to try at least to divide them, so that the French, who now 'paid badly,' would be unable to obtain any substantial help from them. Richard Pace, then British Ambassador to Venice, went again to Switzerland with the same object, though he declared he had no great hope as the Swiss character was 'full of inconsistency'. He was joined by William Knight from London. The attempt failed.

1529 When Henry VIII wished to divorce Catherine of Aragon, he submitted his case to the universities of several countries for their opinions. Professor Simon Grynaeus, the successor to Erasmus at Basel University, was in England at the time, and was chosen by the King as correspondent for consulting the leading German and Swiss divines. Zwingli in Zurich gave his opinion that 'if the marriage be against the laws of God it ought to be dissolved, but the Queen should be put away honourably, and still used as a Queen'.

Oecolampadius of Basel, for his part, considered that a royal union lasting eighteen years could not be considered inexistent. 'We shall not say what the king wishes to hear,' he wrote, 'but that which our duty tells us.'

Theological students from England began to come to Zurich to learn at first hand more of Zwingli's teachings.   1530

The Zurich Bible was published, translated into English by 'Thomas Matthew' (a pseudonym for John Rogers, an assistant of Tyndale) and inspired by the texts of Tyndale and Coverdale. Printed by Christopher Froschauer, it may have been a second edition of Coverdale's Bible itself (see also 1555).   1535

Two theological students from Britain, John Burcher and William Peterson (described as 'a destitute Scotsman'), who had been studying in Zurich, decided to set up in business there. They obtained permission to cut timber in the forests south of Zurich, which they had converted into longbow staves by a Swiss partner, Schentius of Glarus. They then began exporting the staves to England.   1536

Another English theological student, Nicholas Partridge, came with several colleagues to study in Zurich, at the express wish of Archbishop Cranmer. They lodged with Zwingli's religious successor, Heinrich Bullinger (1504-75). Partridge went back to England on a short visit taking with him Bullinger's foster-son, Rudolf Gualter. They returned to Zurich later in the year, bringing with them two more students, Nicholas Eliot and Bartholomew Traheron.   1537

An early English merchant, Richard Hilles, established himself in Zurich where he was a friend of Heinrich Bullinger. He did business with numerous Swiss merchants including Falckner, Ebli, Rappenstein, Michael Adam and Peter Hürzel. Hilles had an agency in Basel and in several other European cities including Frankfurt, Strasbourg and Antwerp.   1541

Among imports from England at that time appear to have been woollen cloth, pewter ware and English cheese, while the Swiss sent back timber products, carved wooden articles, shoes, and paper and

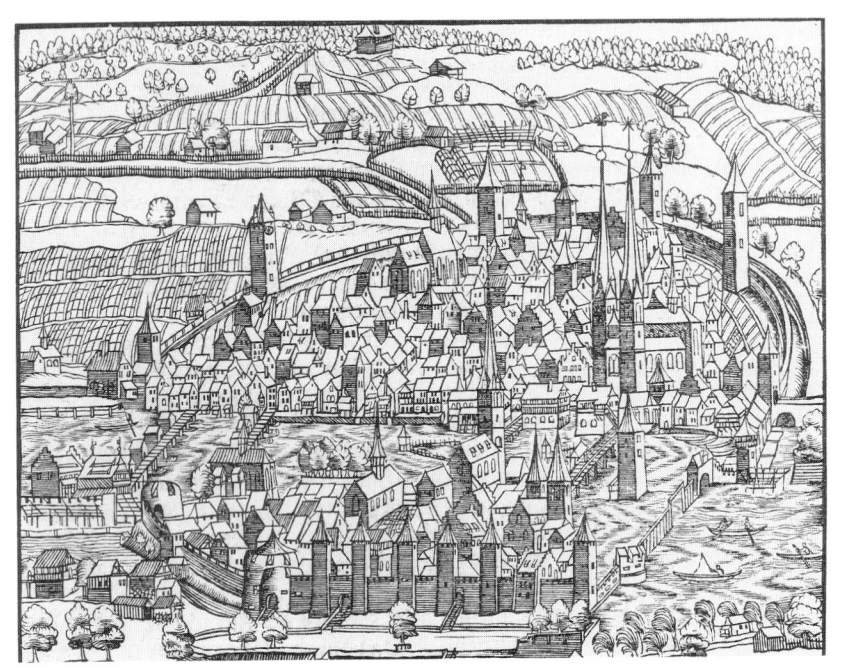

Engraving of Zurich from J. Stumpf's Chronicle, *1548. View taken from the west – the Grossmünster is right centre.*

books from the Zurich printer Christopher Froschauer. John Burcher (see 1536) joined forces with Hilles and undertook frequent business trips for him on the Continent.

1542   The English merchants in Zurich, Richard Hilles and John Burcher, ran into difficulties when some 8,000 of their wooden longbows destined for Henry VIII were held up at Mainz at the instigation of trade competitors in Nuremberg, who claimed the monopoly of deliveries down the Rhine. Diplomatic intervention and several appeals to the Archbishop of Mainz were needed to release the cargo.

Hilles and Burcher also offered the king between two and three hundred masts for ships for his navy, cut from trees in the forests around Berne, and delivered to Dordrecht, Holland, within three years. The masts were sold at 120 crowns each.

1543   Hans Holbein the Younger, court painter to Henry VIII, died in London of the plague. Holbein, son of a German father, became a citizen of Basel in 1520. He came to England in 1526 and, with occasional spells on the Continent, lived there until his death.

Before the English Reformation, the works of Huldrych Zwingli, the Swiss reformer, had caused several of the English clergy to embrace Protestantism. Following the passage of Henry VIII's Act of the Six Articles for enforcing religious unity, one of these, John Hooper, later to become Bishop of Gloucester and Worcester, fled to the Continent to escape prosecution for heresy. After marrying in Basel in 1546, he moved to Zurich, where he took a course in Zwinglian theology and became friends with Heinrich Bullinger. He returned to England to participate in the Reformation, but when Mary came to the throne he suffered the fate of his colleagues Latimer and Ridley (see 1555).

1547

It was due to Bishop Hooper's influence that some of Zwingli's leading followers were welcomed in England. Peter Martyr came to Oxford, and Fagius and Bucer to Cambridge. Martyr later returned to Zurich, but Bucer died in England. In the reign of Queen Mary his remains were dug up and burnt by the hangman.

Bartholomew Traheron, who had stayed with Bullinger in Zurich (see 1537), also gave many Swiss theologians the kindest reception in England. One of them, Johannes ab Ulmis, became tutor to Lady Jane Grey (1537-54) – who after Edward VI's death became queen for nine days (see also 1555).

1548

Richard Hilles (see 1541) returned to England, leaving his Swiss business in the hands first of John Burcher, and then of his son Barnaby Hilles. In London, Hilles represented the Zurich printer Froschauer, who in turn acted as Hilles's financial agent in Switzerland.

c.1548

Letters at this time between England and Switzerland were usually sent via forwarding agents. Those from London to Zurich went via Frankfurt while, from Zurich to London, the route was generally via Basel, Strasbourg and Antwerp. In London one of the forwarding agents, who sometimes acted also as courier, was Reyner (Reginald) Wolf, a Swiss printer who was a colleague of Christopher Froschauer in Zurich. Edward VI appointed him royal printer and 'His Majesty's book seller'. One of the founding members of the Stationers' Company in London, he was Master of the Company in 1559.

c.1549

1550　Reginald Wolf was himself the author of a *Universal History of Cosmography* from which Holinshed, who was in Wolf's employ, drew part of his *Chronicles* (1577). These in turn provided Shakespeare with the historical background for several of his plays.

Christopher Froschauer (see c.1548) paid a visit to England and received a particularly warm welcome from friends in Oxford. Later, when the Marian refugees came to Zurich, Froschauer proved a most generous host to several of them.

1551　Swiss theological students continued to come to England in some numbers, for England was still then, for a short time, the light and hope of the religious reformers on the Continent. Among them was Josua Maler, or Mahler (1529-99), whose studies at Oxford were sponsored by Heinrich Bullinger and the Zurich City Council. Maler and some Swiss friends called on Bishop Hooper (see 1547) in Gloucester, who lent them 45 English crowns. Hooper subsequently asked Bullinger if he could have repayment of this sum in the form of books printed in Zurich, 'particularly those which include your works'.

A teacher from Geneva, Antoine-Rodolphe Chevalier, went to England and became Professor of Hebrew at Cambridge under Edward VI. For some time he also acted as French tutor to the future Queen Elizabeth.

1552　Edward VI's second Prayer Book in three years was published, with revisions mainly to accommodate the views of Bishop Hooper and his friends of the Zwinglian party in the English Church (see 1547). The young Edward VI and his chief advisers all had close relations with religious circles in both Zurich and Geneva.

1553　Bullinger had for some years maintained correspondence with many contacts in England. One of his admirers (to whom he dedicated his treatise on *Christian Marriage*) was Lady Jane Grey. She described his letters and sermons as 'most precious flowers from a garden'.

1555　When Mary Tudor came to the throne there was an immediate return to Catholicism in England; and Latimer, Ridley, Cranmer and seventy fellow martyrs were burnt at the stake for their beliefs. A group of English and Scottish refugees went to live in Geneva where Jean Calvin (1509-64) ruled. The community of some 200 included John

1555 – 1556 Chronology 113

Scorye, later Bishop of Rochester, Miles Coverdale, translator of the first completely printed edition of the Bible in English, William Kethe, author of the hymn 'All People That on Earth Do Dwell', and John Bodley and his family – including his eldest son Thomas Bodley (from whom the Bodleian Library takes its name). Among others who came were Sir William Stafford (who died there), Anthony Gilby, Christopher Goodman, Sir John Borthwick, David Lindsay, later minister at Leith and a John Davidson who may have been the Principal of Glasgow University (see also 1556).

Another group of British religious refugees (among them Edwin Sandys, later Archbishop of York, Robert Horne, later Bishop of Winchester, John Parkhurst, later Bishop of Norwich, and John Jewell, later Bishop of Salisbury) went to live in Zurich where Zwingli's successor, Heinrich Bullinger, made them welcome. There were eventually so many young Englishmen studying in Zurich that a special seminary was opened for them.

Yet another group of British refugees was in Basel. They included John Bale, James Pilkington later Bishop of Durham, Richard Turner and Thomas Bentham, all preachers who also read lectures at the University. Another of them, John Foxe (1516-87), found employment as a reader with the publisher Oporinus (Johann Herbst). Others at Basel were Lady Dorothy Stafford, who went there after her husband had died in Geneva, Sir Francis Walsingham and Sir Francis Knollys.

John Knox (1505-72), attracted by the teachings of Jean Calvin, came to Geneva, to join the other British exiles there. Obliged to leave Britain in 1554, he had first come to Geneva the following year, but had left soon afterwards at Calvin's request to give help to the English refugees who had settled in Frankfurt. In Geneva Knox preached at the Church of Notre Dame-La Neuve, later to be known as the Temple de l'Auditoire. For Knox, Calvin's Geneva was 'the most perfect school of Christ that ever was in the earth since the day of the Apostles'. It was in Geneva that he wrote his famous tract *The First Blast of the Trumpet against the Monstrous Regiment of Women* (1558), which, though intended for Queen Mary, did not endear him to Elizabeth I either. When Knox returned to Scotland, William Whittingham succeeded him as Minister in Geneva. Whittingham later became Dean of Durham (see also 1560).

1556

The Reformers' Wall, Geneva: left to right, Farel, Calvin, Beza and Knox.

Thomas Lever (1521-77), another English refugee from the Marian persecutions, who had supported Lady Jane Grey, and escaped first to Zurich, became Minister to the English congregation at Aarau (Aargau). He lived in the house of Hans Dür. Some twenty-five English families were established there until 1559, and the local authorities put a church at their disposal.

1558   During the religious settlement under Elizabeth I, the Swiss reformists exerted a strong influence on the changes in the Church in Britain. *The Helvetic Confession of Faith,* which had been adopted and proclaimed at a great synod held in Berne in 1532, had already been approved of by the Church in Scotland. Thereafter, Jean Calvin and Theodore Beza (or de Bèze), Calvin's successor in Geneva, largely through John Knox and Andrew Melville, played a significant part in the development of the rites and organisation of the Scottish Church, eventually to become Presbyterianism, and the *Book of Geneva* (Knox's liturgy) became the fixed standard of worship (see also 1576). Heinrich Bullinger in Zurich, with the help of his English friends formerly exiled there, many of them now bishops, exerted a considerable influence on Elizabeth in the somewhat different development of the English Church, eventually to become Episcopalianism.[10] Elizabeth, in thanks for the hospitality that Bullinger had shown to the English during the Marian persecutions, sent him a silver goblet, now in the Swiss National Museum.

At this time, Johann Georg Grob, from Zurich, was Professor of Hebrew at Oxford.

One English religious refugee who, after living in Basel, went to Zurich, was John Bale (1495-1563), Bishop of Ossory. On his return to England, Bale wrote his own letter to Bullinger, whom he called 'as it were the Oracle of the Christian World': c. 1558

> I must mention what Zurich has done for us Englishmen. When I was with you and enjoyed your hospitality, Bullinger, and the good wishes of others, I saw with what love you took unto yourselves those of us who were, and are, with you.

After the death of Latimer and Ridley at the stake, John Foxe in Basel (see 1555) had begun work on his *Book of Martyrs*, his very remarkable history of the persecutions of reformers in England. It was published in 1559, in Latin, by Oporinus of Basel, Foxe's employer. Foxe's projected work on a second part, the persecutions of reformers on the Continent, was abandoned and taken over by Heinrich Pantaleoni of Zurich. (In Foxe's time, Pantaleoni was a professor at Basel University.) When the *Book of Martyrs* was issued, Pope Paul IV announced that he had prohibited Oporinus from publishing any further books. An English edition appeared in 1563. 1559

The third Earl of Arran (1530-1609), eldest son of James Hamilton, Governor of Scotland, fled to Geneva from France where he had embraced the Protestant faith and where his arrest had been ordered. Probably on the advice of John Knox, Sir Robert Cecil sent an envoy to bring Arran back to England.

The Geneva Bible was published, an important English translation made by William Whittingham, with Anthony Gilby and Thomas Sampson, religious exiles in Geneva. It was printed by Rouland Hall, another member of the refugee community. It was popularly known as the 'Breeches Bible' for its rendering of Genesis iii, 7: 'The eyes of them bothe were opened . . . and they sewed figge-tree leaves 1560 together and made themselves breeches'. The Geneva Bible was immensely popular, and some 200 editions of it are known.

1563 That year in Basel appeared an eight-volume edition in Latin of the works of the Venerable Bede (673-735), 'the Father of English History'. It was the fruit of five years of editorial research and preparation there.

Two sixteenth-century travellers, Sir Edward Unton and Richard Smith, visited Zwechary, as they called Switzerland. They crossed the Gotthard pass, where Richard Smith

ffound extrem cold uppon this hill. [He was impressed with the construction of the route, and noted in his diary]: Our way lay amongst mountains marvelous straite in dyvers places . . . and made for the most parte with men's hands forced with stones . . . hewed out of the great rocks . . so that in many places two horses may not well mete without danger, very stony.

1564 While most of the British refugees in Geneva from the Marian persecutions had by now returned home, other theologians came out to study, or to teach, at Calvin's Academy. One of the first Scots to enrol in the Academy's register had been Peter Young, 'Scotus Dundonensis', in 1559. Another Scot, Henry Scrimgeour, of Dundee, was a professor of civil law there. He had built up a distinguished reputation in Europe before coming to Geneva: and the Genevan magistrates conferred on him the freedom of the city. Scrimgeour witnessed Calvin's last will and was present at his death in 1564.

1569 Andrew Melville (1545-1622), Scottish Presbyterian leader and scholar, arrived in Geneva having come on foot from Poitiers in France. Recognising his ability, Theodore Beza secured his appointment as a teacher of humanity at the Schola Privata. Melville spent five years in Geneva studying theology with Beza, and Greek, Chaldaic and Syriac with other teachers. He had an insatiable thirst for learning and was particularly interested in the methods and scope of the teaching at Calvin's Academy, knowledge which he used later in his years as Principal at Glasgow University and then at St. Andrews. In 1570 Melville attended the lectures that the French philosopher and theologist Petrus Ramus was giving in Lausanne (see also 1576).

Andrew Kingsmill (1538-69), Puritan divine and Fellow of All Souls, died in Lausanne. He had spent the three previous years in Geneva studying the Calvinist doctrine.

Andrew Melville

1570 During the development of the English Settlement (see 1558) a trend towards Puritanism caused for some time increasing strains among the religious establishment in England. Thomas Cartwright, a young professor of divinity at Cambridge, and Walter Travers, another Puritan divine, strongly influenced by the doctrines of Beza in Geneva and by the Genevan system of Church government, went into exile there for several years. However, the more moderate view of Bullinger, friend of the English bishops, eventually prevailed in England; and as late as 1586 English clergy were required to peruse Bullinger's sermons (*The Decades*).

1572 Two grandsons of Huldrych Zwingli, Rudolf Zwingli, and his cousin Rudolf Gualter (the younger), arrived in England to study English at Cambridge. They visited Bishop Parkhurst at Norwich and Bishop Sandys in London, both of whom had sheltered in Zurich during the Marian persecutions (see 1555). Rudolf Zwingli fell ill and died in London at the house of the Bishop of Ely. Gualter went on to Oxford and took his M.A. before returning to Switzerland.

Elizabeth I had for some years been under strong pressure from Rome as regards the changes which were being introduced into the Church of England, and Pope Pius V had issued a Bull strongly criticising Elizabeth for her attitude. Heinrich Bullinger in Zurich went to her defence and his reply was printed in England in 1572: *A Confutation of the Pope's Bull Published More than Two Yeres Agœ against Elizabeth the Most Gracious Queene of England, Fraunce and Ireland, and against the Noble Realme of England: together with a Defence of the Sayd True Christian Queene, and of the Whole Realme of England.*

The Swiss writer Ludwig Lavater's book *De Spectris et Lemuribus* was translated into English as *Of Ghostes and Spirites Walking by Night*. One of its readers was William Shakespeare, who, shortly afterwards, began work on *Hamlet*.

c. 1573 George Keith, later to become fifth Earl Marischal of Scotland, and his brother, William Keith, were sent to Geneva to study under Theodore Beza. William Keith was killed while on an excursion into the country. George Keith later (1593) founded Marischal College, Aberdeen, which, with King's College, became Aberdeen University.

OPPOSITE *Title page of* Sermonum Decades *by Heinrich Bullinger, with a personal dedication to an English friend.*

SERMONVM
Decades duæ.

De potissimis ueræ religionis capitibus, quorū catalogū uersa pagella exhibebit, authore Heinrycho Bullingero.

ACCESSIT operi Præfatio de certa ratione qua possit iratus peccatis nostris Deus placari. Accesserunt item uetustissimorum Conciliorum & antiquissimorum orthodoxorum patrum symbola.

TOMVS PRIMVS.

IESVS.

HIC est filius meus dilectus: in quo placata est anima mea. Ipsum audite. Matth. 17.

TIGVRI APVD FROSCHOVERVM,
ANNO M. D. XLIX.

Among other Scots who went to study at Geneva in the 1570s were George Gillespie and William Collace, both from St Andrews University, and James Lindsay, son of the Earl of Crawford.

1574   The first recorded meeting of Swiss residents took place in London. It was called at the house of engraver, Christopher Schwyzer, at St Andrew Undershaft.

1576   In Scotland, the future system of Church government was still evolving. James, the Regent, was unsympathetic to the Reformation and official policy remained conformity with England. But the return of Andrew Melville from Geneva (see 1569), bringing with him 'his new opinions and oversea dreams, his imitation of the Geneva discipline and laws', caused renewed controversy and doubt, particularly over the retention of the episcopacy. The Lord Chancellor decided to consult Melville's teacher in Geneva, Theodore Beza, as to whether *inter alia* it was necessary to have the office of bishops. Beza's reply (known as *De Triplici Episcopatu* because he referred to three types of bishop – of God, of man, and of the devil), came down decisively against 'the sitting of bishops' which, he wrote, 'is to our mind to be utterly abolished'.

c. 1579   The influence of the new creed from Geneva in the Scottish Church had, in the years that followed, a remarkable effect on the attitude of the people. A correspondent wrote to Lord Burghley in London:

> You would be astonished to see how men are changed here. There is little of that submission to those above them which there used to be. The poor think and act for themselves. They are growing strong, confident, independent.

1580   The Scottish historian and poet David Hume (c. 1560-1630) made a stay, for study, in Geneva.

The same year, Alexander Brisson (or Bryson), from Edinburgh, became Professor of Philosophy at Geneva. He left after several years, when the Consistory opposed his marrying the mother of his deceased fiancée.

A notable Englishman who arrived to study at Geneva in 1580 was Anthony Bacon (1558-1601), the future diplomatist and brother of Sir Francis. He lodged in the house of Theodore Beza. Beza esteemed Bacon so highly that, 'out of respect for him', he dedicated his *Meditations* to Anthony's mother, Lady Bacon.

1582 Geneva's independence had for some years been under intermittent threat from both the Duke of Savoy and the King of Spain. At the same time, her natural allies, the cantons of Switzerland, had become estranged, leaving Geneva in somewhat dangerous isolation. In 1582 the Republic of Geneva sent to Britain Councillor Jean Maillet, the first of three envoys over twenty years, to seek financial help from Elizabeth I. Maillet had previously lived in Britain for some years, partly as teacher to the Duke of Lennox in Scotland. He was received by the queen's secretary, Sir Francis Walsingham, who spoke first of the queen's anger that John Knox's pamphlet against women (see 1556) should have been allowed to be published in Geneva. However, Maillet was allowed to collect funds among the Protestant community around the country. John Bodley, who had been a refugee in Geneva during the Marian persecutions (see 1555) was appointed to supervise the collections. Some £6,000 was raised, which was equal to about a third of the republic's revenue at that time.

1583 The Melvillian party led by the Edinburgh minister James Lawson proposed to model the newly founded Edinburgh University on the lines of Calvin's Academy in Geneva. But the scheme was changed at the last moment by the Court party in the Edinburgh town council, who preferred the safer option of a conventional university, teaching a traditional curriculum. However, the Genevan influence became indirectly apparent when a divinity faculty was subsequently opened.[11]

1584 The Council of the Republic of Geneva wrote to Eliabeth I to congratulate her on escaping the attempted assassination by John Somerville. A little later Geneva received a gift from England of 800 écus for poor foreigners in the city and 200 écus for theological students there.

1588 A number of Scottish students studied at Basel as well as Geneva during the second half of the sixteenth century. Robert Howie (1568-1645), who arrived at the University in Basel in 1588, was the most outstanding of them. His teacher and patron was Professor Grynaeus, to whom Howie dedicated his theological tract, published in Basel in 1591, *De Reconciliatione Hominis cum Deo*.

1589 Geneva sent another emissary to Britain, Jacques Lect. He had a long audience with Elizabeth, who charged the Archbishop of Canterbury to make a collection on behalf of the Republic. Lect brought back £15,000, together with a friendly letter from the queen.

That year Berne made an agreement with the Duke of Savoy that they would stand neutral if the Duke should attack Geneva. The agreement raised protests from several of the Protestant cantons; and after Lect's visit Elizabeth wrote a letter to the 'Magnifiques et Illustres Seigneurs' of the thirteen cantons of Switzerland to recommend to them in pressing terms the protection of the city of Calvin. Berne's agreement with Savoy was not ratified.

1590   Among other Scots who were in Switzerland that year was John Johnston (c.1565-1611). He went first to Zurich and then to Berne where Benedict ab Erlach engaged him as his son's tutor. With the young Erlach he travelled to Geneva to meet Theodore Beza and the leading men at the Academy. When the situation in Geneva again became tense Johnston spent some months with his charge at Nyon.

1592   The English traveller Fynes Moryson visited Baden (Aargau) where, in the sixteenth century, the baths from the warm springs were much more popular with visitors than the mountains. He remarked that 'many have no disease but that of love, howsoever they faine sickness of body, come hither for remedy, and many times find it.'

c. 1592   Paulus Lentulus (1560-1613), a Swiss doctor from Berne, was for several years personal physician to Elizabeth I.

1593   The future British diplomat Sir Henry Wotton, on the Grand Tour, stayed in Geneva to improve his French. He lodged with the Professor of Greek at Calvin's Academy, Isaac Casaubon (1559-1614) – later a great favourite of James I (see also 1614).

The brothers Wertmuller in Zurich began exporting silk products, some of them to England.

1594   Richard Hooker (c. 1553-1600) published his *Four Books of the Lawes of Ecclesiastical Polity*. He influenced Rousseau's *Du contrat social*.

Swiss mercenaries were still very much in the news in England. In his book *Christ's Tears over Jerusalem*, published that year, the satirist Thomas Nash (1567-1601) wrote: 'Law, Logicke and the Switzers can be hired to fight for anybody.'

Mineral springs in the Alps, from Josias Simmler's Die Alpen, *1574.*

Shakespeare, too, alluded to them in several of his plays, including *Hamlet, King John, Richard II, Henry V, The Tempest* and *Macbeth*.

1596 Roger Manners (1576-1612), the future fifth Earl of Rutland, was in Geneva to finish his education.

A Swiss politician from Glarus, Michael Bäldi, came to England on a diplomatic mission on behalf of the Protestant cantons. Bäldi who had been many years a colonel in the French service, probably came at French instigation, too. He drew the attention of the Earl of Essex and of Elizabeth to the increasing Spanish influence in Switzerland and in the Grisons, and of Spain's efforts to obtain rights for the passage of her troops over the Alpine passes to reinforce the Spanish Netherlands – a development which would be welcome neither to England or France (who were then in alliance against Spain). Bäldi urged Elizabeth to be more active in securing the friendship of the Swiss Confederation and to support France's efforts there, which were not making much progress, in combating Spanish designs.

1597 Bäldi's representations received support from Paulus Lentulus in Berne (see c.1592) who wrote to Sir Henry Wotton (see 1593) saying that the Swiss had become disillusioned with the French and that the King of Spain was wooing them.

1599 A modern tourist? Thomas Platter (1574-1628) of Basel (later to become a distinguished professor at Basel University) visited England. At Dover officials asked him why he had come; he replied, 'Out of curiosity.' He was much interested in the wrecks of the Spanish Armada he saw at Dover; and he went to a new play, *Julius Ceasar,* by a young English dramatist, William Shakespeare. He saw Elizabeth I at Richmond and wrote home 'No one may ask if she is still a virgin, for they consider her too holy to admit to doubt.' At an interview with the queen's secretary, he asked him to petition Elizabeth for a scholarship for a Swiss compatriot, Caspar Thoman of Zurich, who wanted to study in England – a petition afterwards granted.

Platter was struck by the pride and confidence of the English in themselves. He wrote:

> They believe that no nation can compare with the English for virtue or comeliness. So soon as they see a handsome man they say he is an Englishman, or if they believe him a foreigner they say it is a pity he is not English.

The Seventeenth Century

Relations with Geneva – the first permanent British envoy to Switzerland – formal recognition of Swiss neutrality at the Peace of Westphalia – Cromwell and the Protestant cantons – English regicides in Switzerland – a Swiss begins the Newton-Leibnitz controversy – Genevans in London – a Treaty of Defensive Union – the Neuchâtel Question.

Following the repulse of an attack on Geneva, when troops of Charles Emmanuel, the Duke of Savoy, tried to take the city by scaling the walls at night (known as the Escalade), the Genevans again sought financial assistance from England (and from several other countries), this time to equip a force to make a retaliatory attack on Savoy. The veteran Theodore Beza himself wrote to Elizabeth on behalf of the pastors of the Church of Geneva, telling her 'in what anguish' the city found itself 'having just escaped the jaws of the tiger'. Elizabeth sent Henry Lock, a former student at the Academy there, to Geneva to discover the true state of affairs. When she received Lock's report, she remarked: 'I begin to have a good opinion of the Genevans.' And when Jacques Anjorrant was subsequently despatched by Geneva to collect funds, Elizabeth exhorted her bishops and all other Protestants to give generously to such a worthy cause. Politically, too, Elizabeth did what she could to counter Savoy's claims to Geneva.

1602

At a banquet in Geneva celebrating the first anniversary of the Escalade, a patois song was introduced, 'Cé qu'é laîno, le Maître de Bataille', which from then on became a kind of national hymn of Geneva. Several phrases of the tune are common to that of 'God Save the Queen', which some attribute to a keyboard piece by John Bull (?1563-1628). John Bull was travelling in 'France and Germany' for some years at around this time and it is possible that he visited Geneva (for, though an independent republic, Geneva was often then loosely considered part of France). If so, Bull may have heard the song and taken his tune from there.

1603

Theodore Beza of Geneva wrote to James I after his succession to the

1604

throne following Elizabeth's death. James's reply was read to the assembly of pastors in Geneva.

1606 A Swiss pastor from Basel, Johann Jakob Grasser, on a visit to England, was much impressed by James I's military strength. In his *Italienische, Französische und Englische Schatzkammer*, Grasser put this at 100,000 foot, 20,000 horse and 100 ships. 'The inhabitants', he wrote, 'are skilled on the sea beyond all other peoples, and ply their commerce to the farthest parts of the earth.' During his visit Grasser witnessed the quartering of a Jesuit for his part in the Gunpowder Plot of the year before. He was invited to a Lord Mayor's banquet in the City of London.

1607 A group of Bernese participated in the foundation by English settlers of Jamestown (Virginia).

Among other young Englishmen in Geneva for educational purposes was Robert Devereux (1591-1646), later third Earl of Essex.

1609 A Genevan, Stephen Le Sieur, who had come to England as a young man and had undertaken a number of diplomatic missions for the Crown, was appointed by James I ambassador to the German Protestant Princes. He was later knighted.

1610 Following rumours of renewed military preparations by Charles Emmanuel of Savoy against Geneva, the Republic wrote to James I as well as to Henry IV of France and to the German Protestant states. James made representations on Geneva's behalf to the Duke of Savoy.

1611 An English traveller, Thomas Coryat (1577-1617), visited Zurich in the course of a walking tour in Europe. He inspected the Carolinum or chapter school of the Fraumünster there, which had in the previous century been reorganised by Zwingli.

A Genevan, Theodore Turquet de Mayerne, Baron d'Aubonne (1573-1655), a godson of Theodore Beza, came to London and was appointed physician to James I, and later to Charles I. He was instrumental in founding the Society of Apothecaries. Mayerne was also a painter of note, and a friend of Van Dyck. He was later knighted. Turquet de Mayerne also acted as a kind of unofficial ambassador in London for the Republic of Geneva and kept the king informed of events there.

John Parkhurst (a relative of the Bishop of Norwich – see 1555) was 1613
secretary to the British Minister to Savoy, at Turin, Sir Henry
Wotton.[12] He was sent by Charles Emmanuel, Duke of Savoy, to
negotiate for him with the Swiss Protestants in Geneva. With
memories of the Escalade in mind (see 1602), the Swiss were somewhat alarmed as to how this unusual conduct by a British diplomat
might reflect the policy of James I. (In fact James was hoping for the
Duke's support of James's son-in-law's candidature for the crown of
Bohemia.) It was hurriedly explained that the visit was a personal
favour on the part of Parkhurst for the Duke of Savoy, an act in
which James was in no way concerned.

Around the beginning of the seventeenth century the great Roman 1614
Catholic researcher Cardinal Baronius had produced his *Annale Eccle-
siastici,* which gave back to the Catholics in Europe pre-eminence in
theological learning. Protestant scholarship devoted itself to refuting
Baronius, the most notable effort coming from a distinguished Genevan scholar in England, Isaac Casaubon (see 1593). Casaubon's work
De Rebus Sacris Ecclesiasticis Exercitationes XVI AD Baronii Annales was
published in 1614, the same year as he died, a prebendary of Canterbury Cathedral.

Having received overtures from the Duke of Savoy, the Government 1615
of Berne sent an emissary to London, Hans Rudolf von Erlach, to
ascertain England's views on a possible agreement between Berne and
Savoy. James I gave Erlach every encouragement, since this would,
inter alia, help to contain Spanish influence in northern Italy. (This
may have been the same Erlach who had studied in Switzerland under
John Johnston – see 1590.)

With the consent of James I, the new British Minister to Savoy, Sir 1617
Isaac Wake (1580?-1632), went to Berne at the request of Charles
Emmanuel, Duke of Savoy, to mediate an alliance between Savoy
and the Swiss cantons. However, he also visited Geneva and assured
the council there that James had the interests of the Republic at heart.
On his return to Turin he several times urged the Duke of Savoy to
respect the treaty of peace he had signed with Geneva.

As a result of Sir Isaac Wake's diplomacy in Berne, the Bernese 1618
agreed to put at the Duke of Savoy's disposal 4,000 troops, paid for

James I: artist unknown.

three months. In return, the Duke gave up, finally and totally, all his claims to sovereignty over the Vaud.

In addition, at James I's request, the Bernese agreed to lodge for four months in the Vaud the mercenary army under Count Mansfield which was then in Piedmont in the service of the Duke of Savoy. Later that year, at the beginning of the Thirty Years' War, Mansfield's army of 20,000 men was used by James's son-in-law, the Elector Palatine, to take the Catholic stronghold of Pilsen.

In pursuit of an English plan to try to convert the people of the State of Venice to Anglicanism, James then asked permission of the Grisons government to establish at Sondrio, in Grisons' territory in the Valtellina, a seminary where English priests could learn Italian and be prepared for work in northern Italy. The project was warmly supported by the head of the Venetian party in the Grisons, Hercules von Salis. Permission was granted, and some buildings were obtained; but the project foundered two years later when the Valtellina was invaded by Spanish forces based in Milan.

1620 When the Pilgrim Fathers landed at Plymouth, Massachusetts, after their voyage from England, they carried with them the Geneva Bible (see 1560).

1621 The Duke of Savoy again began to adopt an aggressive attitude towards Geneva. James I made firm diplomatic representations to him enjoining him to leave the Republic in peace.

1622 The following year Savoy put obstacles in the way of the transit of wheat from France for Geneva. The British Minister in Turin was instructed to ask the Duke of Savoy to withdraw them.

When the Grisons was invaded by the Austrians who were supporting their Spanish allies occupying the Valtellina, the Venetian government, on behalf of the Grisons, sent a plea for help to James I through Sir Henry Wotton (British Minister to both Venice and Savoy). James did not respond.

1624 Philip Burlamaqui (or Burlamachi), a Genevan who had come to London, found favour with James I and been granted a licence to trade in 1617, had by this time become one of the biggest financiers and merchants in the City of London. He had correspondents in all the major financial centres of Europe, and was also closely connected with the East India Company. In the five years from 1624 he made some very large loans to the British government, and he frequently acted as paymaster to the British forces operating on the Continent. However, the financial retrenchment in the early 1630s brought about his bankruptcy in 1633. (But see 1637.)

1626 Sir Isaac Wake undertook a mission to Berne and Zurich on behalf of the canton of the Grisons. After his visit Wake urged London to appoint a permanent British mission to Switzerland, arguing that an official representative there could give powerful support to the Protestant cantons and could obtain first-hand information about the designs of hostile Catholic powers.

Wake's full reasons for having a British representative in Switzerland were later published in part 1 of his book *A Threefold Help to Political Observations: i, concerning the Thirteen Cantons of the Helviticall League* (London, 1655). He cited the strategic importance of Switzerland, controlling the passes on the routes between Germany and Italy, and the usefulness of having an envoy there who, among other things, could on occasion intercede for, or be of help to, 'our good friends Venice and Savoy'.

I do conclude [he wrote] that the correspondence of his Majestie in Helvetia and Rhetia is not onley good but necessary, having found by expecting that the Pope, the Emperor, France and Spain, have expressed displeasure at the appearing of any Minister of his Majestie's in those parts, upon whatever occasion.

1627 Cardinal Richelieu's policies in France had caused England to sever relations; and the Duke of Savoy, too, felt threatened. The new British Minister to Turin, Sir Walter Montagu, visited Geneva to try to disperse Genevan mistrust of the Duke and to discredit France.

1628 On the way home from his embassy to Constantinople, Sir Thomas Roe, then England's leading negotiator on international trade, called at Geneva to discuss the Duke of Savoy's project for free port facilities at Nice and Villefranche and England's plans to send goods imported under those arrangements via the Mont Cenis route and Geneva.

The same year, as part of a general diplomatic and military offensive against France, Sir James Hay, Viscount Doncaster (later to become the Earl of Carlisle), visited the Swiss Protestant cantons and Geneva in order to gain support for English policies and to explain Buckingham's efforts to relieve the French Huguenots beseiged at La Rochelle. In Basel, Hay was joined by Sir Thomas Roe from Geneva.

Wake's advice to London (see 1626) was accepted, and a British Agent in Switzerland, Sir Oliver Fleming, was appointed. Fleming was also accredited to the Republic of Geneva, and presented his credentials there before proceeding to Zurich and Berne. — 1629

The Genevan painter Jean Petitot the Elder (1607-91), in England on a visit, was introduced by his fellow countryman Sir Theodore Turquet de Mayerne (see 1611) to Charles I. The king took to him and gave him apartments in Whitehall. Petitot painted portraits of the king and his family. He was also an enameller and, assisted by Mayerne, was the first artist in England to bring enamel painting to technical perfection. On Charles's death Petitot fled to Paris. Twenty years later his son, Jean Louis Petitot, came to London to live. — 1630

Another Genevan friend of Sir Theodore de Mayerne, John Colladon, also through Sir Theodore's introduction, was appointed a physician in ordinary to the king and queen. He was later knighted. Colladon, too, acted on occasion as spokesman for Geneva at court. — 1631

Jost Bürgi (born 1552), an early Swiss mathematician, died. One of his great achievements was the discovery of the logarithmic principle. Unfortunately he delayed publicising it and his book *Progress Tabulen* eventually appeared (in Prague) a few years after his Scottish contemporary John Napier had announced the same discovery. — 1632

Yet another Swiss doctor in England, Theodore Diodati (1573-1650), was a court physician. His son, Charles, until the latter's death in 1638, was John Milton's best friend (see also 1639). — 1633

On his way to take up his new post as British Ambassador to Venice, Sir Basil Fielding stopped in Geneva to proffer Charles I's greetings and to enquire into the source of a rumour said to be prevalent there that 'the king would go to mass'. He assured the city that the king 'was not failing in the true faith'. — 1634

The former financier Philip Burlamaqui (see 1624) became head of the Royal Posts and Postmaster of England and Scotland. — 1637

Swiss travel in the seventeenth century

1639   The poet John Milton travelled through Switzerland on his return from Italy, via the Simplon pass, stopping at Brig, Martigny and Geneva. In Geneva he stayed at the house of the theologian Jean Diodati, whose nephew, Charles, had been Milton's best friend.

Another visitor who stayed with Jean Diodati for a time was the young Hon. Robert Boyle (1627-91), son of the Earl of Cork, later a distinguished scientist. He spent two years with his brother in Geneva, to perfect his French and to learn Greek and Hebrew. His tutor in Geneva, Isaac Marcombes, had been recommended to Boyle's father by both Sir Henry Wotton (who had stayed in Geneva himself as a young man) and the banker Philip Burlamaqui. Apart from Marcombes, Jean Diodati had a formative influence in the development of Boyle's deeply religious outlook throughout life. Boyle returned to Geneva from 1642 to 1644 for a second spell with Marcombes.

Following the revolt in Scotland against Charles I, the signature of the National Covenant and the declaration by the Church Assembly at Glasgow that the Episcopacy was abolished and full Presbyterian government restored, Scotland and England began preparing for war.

Worried at these events, the pastors and divines of Zurich, Berne, Basel and Schaffhausen sent a joint letter to Archbishop Laud of Canterbury in support of the Scottish Church. They drew attention to the menaces that the Church was suffering and urged restraint. They also corresponded with the Scottish Church and were preparing to write again both to the king and to Laud, when they heard that terms of peace had been agreed and the Episcopacy in Scotland overthrown.

When popular attack on Charles I was growing in England, Johann Heinrich Hummel, a Bernese chaplain in London, met two of his compatriots, Sigismund and Albrecht von Erlach, at the Royal Exchange and 'proceeded to church with them to celebrate the happy event'. (See also 1660.) 1640

A Swiss artist who came to London that year, attracted by the paintings of Charles I's court painter, Van Dyck, was Matthias Merian the younger (1621-87). His English portraits closely followed Van Dyck's style.

Another Genevan artist who arrived in England at this time was Jacques Bordier (1616-84). He was a friend of Jean Petitot (see 1630). He stayed many years, becoming a well-known portrait painter and miniaturist with many connexions at the court of Charles II. His cousin, Pierre Bordier, who had been Jean Petitot's first teacher, also came to England, where he became a distinguished goldsmith and enameller. 1641

When the British Agent in Switzerland, Sir Oliver Fleming, returned to England, he left some large debts at Zurich, Berne and Basel. These provoked claims from creditors which were not settled until 1655, when Hans-Ulrich Gessner was sent to London to obtain payment from Cromwell's government. 1645

The diarist John Evelyn (1620-1702), on a visit to Switzerland, noted down his opinion of the Swiss. He saw in their dress: 1646

... little variety of distinction betwixt the gentleman and the common sort, by a law of their country being exceedingly frugal. Add to this their great honesty and fidelity, though exacting enough for what they part with. I saw not one beggar ... I look upon this country to be the safest spot of all Europe, neither envied nor envying; nor are any of them rich or poor; they

John Evelyn in 1648: portrait by R. Walker.

live in great simplicity and tranquillity; and although of the fourteen cantons, half be Roman Catholic, the rest Reformed, yet they mutually agree, and are confederate with Geneva.

1648 At the Peace of Westphalia, at the end of the Thirty Years' War, Britain, together with the other contracting powers, formally recognised the sovereignty and independence of the Swiss Confederation.

Sir Kenelm Digby (1603-65), Chancellor of Charles I's queen, Henrietta Maria, returning from Rome to Paris, passed through Chur and

Zurich where he was entertained with great ceremony by the burgomasters of those towns.

Jean Louis Petitot the younger, an enamellist like his father (see 1630), came to settle in London. After the Restoration, Petitot became a court painter to Charles II. He died in London in 1695.

1650

Genevans, and Swiss from the Protestant cantons, had for some time been coming into England to live. Many of them retained close relations with their country of origin. These close associations called for the services of bankers who had offices or agencies in both England and Switzerland.

1652

In 1652 the Genevan banking house of Calendrini opened an office in London, and soon became well established. Several members of the Calendrini family had been living in England for many years – a Philip Calendrini, brother-in-law of Philip Burlamaqui (see 1624), had taken part in a consortium to buy pepper from the Dutch East India Company in 1630. Jean Louis Calendrini became a friend of John Milton, then Latin secretary to Oliver Cromwell, which helped the bank's relations with the British authorities.

Private banks in England were now multiplying. Other Swiss bankers who opened offices in London in the second half of the seventeenth century included François Turrettini from Geneva, Louis Guiguer from Bürglen (Thurgau) and Samuel Müller from Berne.

Following the execution in England of Charles I and the establishment of the Commonwealth, an affinity was soon forged between the Protestant cantons of Switzerland and Cromwell. At about this time Cromwell evolved an idea to unite in one great Protestant league all the Protestant countries and communities of Europe. The Protestant cantons sent as Envoy-Extraordinary to Cromwell's government Johann Jakob Stockar (1615-81), the Stadtschreiber (town clerk) of Schaffhausen. (Stockar was also accredited as Swiss envoy to the Low Countries.) Calendrini & Co. (see 1652) were responsible for transmitting Stockar's funds from Switzerland and his correspondence to and from that country.

1653

During the Anglo-Dutch War Stockar was instructed to express to Cromwell Swiss anxiety at this conflict between two Protestant countries and to propose mediation. In the Peace Treaty of 1654 the

Johann Jacob Stockar: artist unknown.

good offices of the Protestant cantons were recognised, and they were named as arbitrators for disputed points.

One of the disputes referred to the Protestant cantons was the case of two English ships, *Buena Esperanza* and *Buena Avventura*, belonging to the East India Company, which had been seized and confiscated by the Dutch.

At one of his meetings with Stockar, Cromwell asked him to brief him on the history of Switzerland. Stockar presented the Lord Protector with copies of the *Chronicon Helveticum* by Aegidius Tschudi (1505-72), known as the Father of Swiss History, and of *De Republica Helvetiorum* by Josias Simmler, a godson of Heinrich Bullinger.

Stockar was accorded privileges in England which far exceeded those bestowed on many other diplomatic representatives. Among other things, he asked permission of Cromwell's government to import some wine duty free. He was given authorisation for twenty tuns (one tun was the equivalent of two pipes or 252 old wine gallons) – which should have been enough to see him through his mission in England. (At the same time, the Portuguese Ambassador received permission to import two pipes of wine.)

Another Swiss who was in London at that time, and who had come to England originally from the Grisons to be the pastor of the Huguenot church in Threadneedle Street, was Jean-Baptiste Stuppa (1606-72). A polyglot theologian, Stuppa became a favourite political counsellor of Cromwell, advising him, *inter alia,* on the Protector's plan for a European-wide Protestant League. Stuppa was sent by Cromwell on several diplomatic missions (see 1655 and 1656). Later he incurred the dislike of Secretary of State Thurloe, and on the restoration of the monarchy he had to leave the country.

Also during the Anglo-Dutch War, the Swiss merchants Zollikofer of St Gallen had their ship *Peter Matthias* seized by Cromwell's navy and brought to Plymouth while on its way to Hamburg with a cargo of spices, almonds and raisins. After much argument, the ship was released but the cargo held until Zollikofer were able to prove that it was destined for a neutral port.

The usual time, in summer, for letters to go from London to Zurich was now twenty days. 1654

Cromwell appointed John Pell (1611-85), linguist and mathematician, as his political agent to the Protestant cantons. Residing in Zurich, Pell was given a salary of £600 a year. His instructions included the encouragement of trade and the exchange of students. But the real object of his mission was to detach the cantons from their alliance with France and draw them into the Continental Protestant League, headed by England, that Cromwell envisaged. There were prolonged negotiations which in the end led nowhere. In 1656 Pell reported to London from Baden where the Diet was being held,

The Diet at Baden, 1653. Foreign envoys sat on the left of the table in the centre.

'They move so slowly here that it is hard to discern whether they go forward or backward.' Pell was recalled in 1658.

An English traveller, Sir John Reresby, who was visiting Switzerland at the time, wrote of the Swiss:

They are believed to be very faithful and trusty, which reputation (with that of their courage) prefers them before others to the service of the Pope, the King of France and many other princes as guards to their persons and soldiers in their wars . . . What gentlemen may expect from democracy sufficiently appears in this, where there is none left that dare pretend to a better quality, one than the other.

A massacre of members of the Waldensian sect living in the valleys of Piedmont, by troops of the Duke of Savoy during a quarrel between the Duke and his Protestant subjects, aroused deep resentment in England. The Duke of Savoy was called the 'Man of Sin'. A day of solemn mourning, 'humiliation and fasting' on behalf of the Waldensians was declared, and collections for them were ordered in all the churches.

1655 At that time a Protestant divine, John Durie, was visiting Switzerland, with the approbation of Cromwell, to enlist support for his scheme for Christian unity. Having presented letters from Cromwell to the Swiss Protestant divines assembled at Aarau, Durie wrote the following despatch, which he sent to John Pell in Zurich:

> Sir, I am spoken to by the Lords of Zurich who are here (at Aarau), to entreat you to help, by your letters to his Highness, to second their representations to the Duke of Savoy, on behalf of the poor distressed Protestants of the Piedmont, who are commanded to be gone out of their native country (where they have lived so many hundred years) if they will not go to mass.

Cromwell sent an envoy, Sir Samuel Morland, to the Duke of Savoy's court with demands for redress. To reinforce his case he persuaded, with an offer of subsidies, Geneva and the Protestant cantons of Switzerland to promise a force of 10,000 men for an attack on Savoy. Cardinal Mazarin of France, fearing a widening of the conflict, forced the Duke of Savoy to grant the English demands.

While Morland went to see the Duke of Savoy, Jean-Baptiste Stuppa (see 1653) was charged to go and assure the Waldensians of the Piedmont of Cromwell's support for them.

Since the Swiss troops were no longer needed against Savoy, Cromwell asked the Genevans to pass on the subsidies he had given them to the families of the victims of the massacre. Sir Samuel Morland, who had stayed on in Geneva as English Resident, then assisted John Pell, Cromwell's agent to the Protestant cantons, to distribute money sent by charitable bodies in England for the relief of the Waldensians. (The money was transmitted to Geneva by Calendrini & Co. – see 1652.) It totalled in all about £38,000.

In August, Morland was able to announce that the Duke of Savoy, at the request of the King of France, had granted an amnesty to the Waldensians and had confirmed their ancient privileges.

The same year Milton published his sonnet 'On the Late Massacher in Piemont':

> Avenge, O Lord, thy slaughter'd Saints, whose bones
> Lie scatter'd on the Alpine mountains cold;
> ...
> Slayn by the bloody Piemontese that roll'd
> Mother with Infant down the Rocks . . .

The British scholar and mathematician John Wallis (1616-1703) published his *Arithmetica Infinitorum*. It was later studied by the distinguished Swiss mathematician Jakob Bernoulli (1654-1705) when forming his own mathematical theories. (See also 1676.)

1656 Cromwell promised funds to Berne and Zurich to help them with the costs of the first Villmergen War, when the Protestant cantons were badly defeated by the Swiss Catholics. Here again, Stuppa (see 1653) was employed by Cromwell to transmit to the cantons his assurances of financial support.

1658 Now back in England, Sir Samuel Morland published his *History of the Evangelical Churches of the Valleys of Piedmont. Together with the Most Naked and Punctual Relation of the Late Bloody Massacre, 1655, and a Narrative of the Following Transactions to the Year of Our Lord 1658*. It was illustrated with sensational prints of the Waldensians' sufferings.

On the death of the Protector, Oliver Cromwell, the Council of Geneva sent his son and successor Richard Cromwell, by the hand of John Colladon (see 1631), a letter of condolences about his father and congratulations about his succession. Richard in reply suggested that the Council should appoint Colladon as Resident for the Genevan Republic in London. The Council, afraid of offending France who considered herself the protector of Geneva, avoided replying.

1660 On the restoration of the monarchy in England, the judges before whom Charles I had been tried and condemned to death in 1649 were declared regicides, and some fled to Switzerland. Thanks partly to the influence of Pastor Johann Heinrich Hummel (see 1640), now back in Berne, the Bernese authorities granted Ludlow and his fellow fugitives, Lisle, Cawley, Love, Phelps and Broughton, an Act of Protection, permitting them to reside anywhere in their territories. Phelps set up in business in Geneva. Several others settled in Vevey; and they are commemorated by mural monuments in St Martin's Church there.

1662 The theologian Samuel Chappuzeau of Geneva (1625-1701) was tutor at the court of William of Orange to the future King of England, William III (see also 1667).

1663 John Lisle, one of the regicides (see 1660), wrote to Pastor Hummel thanking him and 'their Excellencies in Berne' for preserving their lives. But the following year Lisle was assassinated in Lausanne by an agent of Charles II, Thomas MacDonnell, an Irishman.

1664 The Swiss satirical poet Johann Grob of Toggenburg made a stay in London.

Lieutenant-General Edmund Ludlow.

The naturalist John Ray (1627-1705) travelled through Switzerland. 1665
In his *Observations . . . Made in a Journey through the Low Countries, Germany, Italy and France* he wrote that

all the Switzers in general are very honest people, kind and civil to strangers. One may travel their country securely with a bag of gold in his hand. When we came to our inns they would be troubled if we distrusted them so far as to take our portmanteaus into our lodging chambers and not leave them in the common dining room.

Of the people of Zurich, Ray commented:

The Zurichers who anciently had the reputation for valour, are now much given to merchandise and to accumulate riches, and so taken off from martial studies and exercises.

That year at Vevey, Edmund Ludlow (see 1660) composed a military march for the Bernese forces, the 'Bernermarsch', which was later used by Bernese troops in the service of William III in England.

1667　Death of Francesco Borromini (b. 1599) from the Ticino, eminent architect of the Roman high baroque. Borromini's complex spatial unities and innovative embellishments had a strong influence on Sir Christopher Wren, Sir John Vanbrugh, Nicholas Hawksmoor and several other English architects. Some of the effects can be seen in St Paul's Cathedral and in the Painted Hall of Greenwich Hospital.

L'Europe vivante; ou, Relation nouvelle historique et politique de tous ses estats, by Samuel Chappuzeau (see 1662) was published in Geneva. Dedicated to Charles II, it was a kind of *Inside Europe Today*. Chappuzeau described the English as liking their ease, eating much meat and little bread, and being great smokers. The Scots were generous and brave, and stood the rigours of war better than the English; but they were a little inclined to vengeance. The Irish were generally handsome people, constant in their friendships but emotional and irreconcilable in their hatreds. Chappuzeau noted that rebuilding was already under way in London after the Great Fire of 1666.

1668　In the years after the English regicides fled to Switzerland (see 1660), Charles II and his government made several attempts to persuade the Bernese to deliver them up. At one time the king offered an alliance with Berne if they would do so, but the Bernese refused even to receive an envoy. In 1668 an agent of the British government, Claude Roux, a Frenchman, met a representative of the Bernese government in Geneva. He said that Charles wanted to improve his relations with the Protestant cantons and with Berne in particular, and would welcome the appointment of a Bernese representative in London if only Berne would withdraw its protection from those who had judged and condemned his father to death. Roux's approach was reinforced by a letter from Charles's government to the Council of Geneva asking that its contents should be communicated to the rulers of Berne. However, the Bernese replied that it was not the custom of the Swiss to betray those who had put themselves under their protection.

A group of Swiss from Fribourg settled in Canada in the region of Quebec.

1670　At around this date, or a little earlier, the watchmaking industry is said to have been introduced into the Neuchâtel region. An English merchant brought a London-made pocket watch to a locksmith in a remote village and asked if he knew anyone who could repair it. The locksmith's son, Daniel Jean Richard, succeeded in doing so. He also made a note of the mechanism and then began to make copies. By 1705 Richard had established himself as a watchmaker with a flourishing business in Le Locle.

1676 Jakob Bernoulli, eldest member of the Basel family of mathematicians and brother of Johann (see 1748), visited England. He made himself familiar with the work of John Wallis and Isaac Barrow and met Robert Boyle and other leading scientists. He then decided to devote himself to science.

1679 The son of Sir John Colladon of Geneva (see 1631), Theodore Colladon (d. 1712), was court physician to Charles II. He too was knighted and remained through the reigns of James II and William III (he signed William's death certificate in 1702). His daughter, Anne, became a teacher of the royal children.

Death of Thomas Hobbes (b. 1588), whose philosophical works, particularly *Leviathan*, had a marked influence on Jean-Jacques Rousseau and on other Swiss thinkers.

1681 An early entrepreneur from Canton Glarus, Melchior Jenny, was the first Swiss to export slate down the Rhine to England and to Scotland, where he cut it on site into tiles and slabs. His seven brothers were continually en route keeping him supplied with material.

1682 Edward Hyde, Lord Cornbury, son of the Earl of Clarendon and nephew of James II's queen, who had been studying in Geneva since 1680, realised his ambition to become the first Englishman to win, in a musket competition, the title of 'King' of Switzerland's oldest military society. This, dating from 1474, was the Exercice de l'Arquebuse. After Cornbury's return to England, he was given command of a regiment in James II's army. During the Revolution of 1688, he defected and brought his regiment over to the side of William III.

1684 This year saw the publication of the first real Swiss guidebook, by J.J. Wagner (1641-95), a Zurich naturalist, under the title *Index Memorabilium Helvetiae*.

1685 After the Revocation of the Edict of Nantes, relations between Geneva and England were strengthened still further. Protestant refugees from France, having first settled in Geneva, began to arrive in England. Genevan Protestants also came in some numbers; and the Société des Genevois was formed in London (see also 1703).

Gilbert Burnet, afterwards Bishop of Salisbury, journeyed through Switzerland. On his return he published *Some Letters Containing What Seemed Most Remarkable in Switzerland, Italy, etc.* In Chur he found that the cathedral was dedicated to St Lucius, believed locally to have been a King of Britain who left to preach Christianity and who came to the Grisons in AD 176. Lucius was said to have been executed by the Roman Governor, and his sister Eremita burnt at the stake. Burnet assured the Bishop of Chur that this legend was false.[13].

In Geneva, where it seemed that the facilities for worship which John Knox and William Whittingham and their flock had enjoyed (see 1556) no longer applied, Bishop Burnet wrote:

Before I left Geneva, the number of English there was such that I found we could make a small congregation . . . so I addressed myself to the Council of Twenty Five for liberty to have our worship in our own language . . . This was immediately granted.

The Bishop was told that when the congregation was large enough they could have a church, as in the time of Queen Mary. Until then, they could hold their services as they thought fit. (See also 1853.)

Visiting Berne, at that time the richest canton in Switzerland, Bishop Burnet found the inhabitants serious and hard-working.

The men are generally sincere, but heavy . . . The women are generally employed in their domestic affairs; and the wives, even of the chief magistrates of Bern, look into all the concerns of the house and kitchen as much as the wives of the meanest peasants. Men and women do not converse promiscuously together; and the women are so much amused with the management at home . . . that . . . as an eminent physician there told me . . . that made them sleep well . . . nor did they know what amours were.

1686   A young Swiss scientist, Nicolas Fatio de Duillier (1664-1753), came to England and the following year was made a Fellow of the Royal Society at the age of twenty-three. He was a friend of Sir Isaac Newton (1642-1727).

1687   Sir Isaac Newton's *Principia* was published. It had a tremendous influence on scientists both in Switzerland and on the rest of the Continent.

When William III arrived in England, following the revolution to depose James II, he was accompanied by a Swiss personal guard. Two of the officers were the captains Emmanuel Kirschberger and Sigismund d'Erlach. The Swiss troops, halberdiers, had been raised originally by the Prince of Orange in 1672. They were mostly of Bernese and Vaudoise origin. There were also Swiss officers with some of the troops William brought with him to join the operations against James's army, before James fled to France.

1688

Philibert de Hervart, Baron de Heunniguen, was appointed British Envoy Extraordinary to the Republic of Geneva. Hervart resided in Geneva from 1690 to 1692 but, perhaps because of a fear of French reaction, was not acknowledged officially as Envoy Extraordinary by the magistrates there. When Thomas Coxe (see 1690) left Berne on transfer to another post, Hervart went to Berne from Geneva and took charge, later receiving formal appointment as envoy to the Swiss Confederation.

1689

Nicholas Fatio (see 1686) published in England a scientific tract in which he used a form of calculus that he had devised himself. He also attacked Leibnitz, claiming that neither he nor Leibnitz were the true inventors of the calculus, but Newton, whom Leibnitz had plagiarised. Later, Fatio's compatriot, Johann Bernoulli (see 1748), went to Leibnitz's defence. The controversy continued for over twenty years.

During his campaign in Ireland against the deposed James II, who, with French backing, had rallied his Catholic supporters there, William III again employed several Swiss officers among his troops. Most of them were Bernese, and included the names of Erlach, Bonstetten, Vischer, and de Steiger.

A Treaty of 'Defensive Union' was signed in Aarau (Aargau), then the seat of the Protestant Swiss Diet, between the five Protestant cantons of Switzerland – Zurich, Berne, Glarus, Schauffhausen and Appenzell (Ausser-Rhoden), and the town of St Gallen, and Thomas Coxe, British Minister to Switzerland, on behalf of William III. Under this treaty the Swiss agreed to supply 4,000 men (two regiments) for the king's service in the Low Countries. The soldiers were to be paid 7 *écus* (of 58 French sous each) per month, and colonels 1,160 *livres tournois* (about £97 per month). The Swiss had the right to withdraw their troops if their territory was attacked during the validity of the agreement (which was the length of the war – the War of the League of Augsburg – or four years).

1690

The Swiss inserted a clause which stated that the treaty did not contravene their treaties with Austria and France. William III was given the right to choose and nominate the colonels and the captains of the troops raised. And provision was made for arbitration of any disputed points.

The treaty was a cultural and trade agreement too. As a gesture of his goodwill, William offered to provide twenty-four places in the royal colleges for students of the participating towns and cantons. In addition, under Article 27 of the treaty, reciprocal freedom of trade was to be allowed between the Protestant cantons and England, Scotland and Ireland. All goods made in those countries, and authentically attested as such, would pay no more than 2% for all taxes and dues on entry into the country of the other.

The same year, the British Minister to Switzerland, Thomas Coxe, and his wife made an 'official visit' to Interlaken and Grindelwald, where they saw the glaciers. Their travelling suite included a train of thirty horses, and the Governor of Interlaken incurred expenses amounting to 120 crowns in entertaining the party.

1691   The Bernese patrician Beat de Fischer established a Swiss transalpine postal service with a direct link between London and Berne, passing along the left bank of the Rhine so as to be independent of France.

1692   The treaty of 1690 had been ratified by William III in November of the same year: but, following intensive pressure on them by the French, the Swiss began to raise innumerable difficulties over the interpretation of many of its clauses. Coxe asked London for money to help counter the French intrigues against Britain in the cantons, and for permission to ask the Swiss call a Protestant Diet to thrash things out. But French influence was strong. Some private recruiting of Swiss troops was made in Berne and elsewhere by Swiss and German officers already in William III's service in operations against the French in Piedmont. However, the French had agents to watch the bridge of St Maurice in the Valais on the route over the Alps through which the men passed to reach Piedmont. (But see 1694.)

1693   Guy Miège, who was born in Lausanne and who had spent several years in England as a French teacher, published some of his observations in London in a book, *The New State of England:*

Jean de Sacconay

The dampness of the air, the perpetual hurry of the carts and coaches, with the want of a common sewer in many places . . . are a great obstruction to the cleanliness of this place.

But he thought that there was no other city of its size where murders and outrages were so seldom heard of. He noted that the English venison pasties were 'the best in the world'.

The previous year William III had sent Lord Galloway to Switzerland to find an old friend Colonel Jean de Sacconay (1646-1729) in retirement, and asked him to raise a regiment for England, initially to help the Duke of Savoy who was being menaced by Louis XIV. Saconnay immediately accepted and the regiment was signed up in January 1694. It came to be known as Lord Saxony's Regiment. Composed mostly of Vaudois, it also included two companies of men from Berne (commanded by Captains May and Bonstetten) and four companies of men from Zurich. Some of the latter had already had three years of English service in Piedmont. The regiment later rendered distinguished service on the allied side in the forces of the Duke of Marlborough (see also 1706.)

1695 The Swiss painter Johann Schmutz of Regensberg (Zurich) came to England, attracted by the work of portraitist Sir Godfrey Kneller, then at the height of his reputation. Schmutz painted very successfully in Kneller's style. He died in London in 1715.

c. 1696 Towards the end of the seventeenth century relations between Geneva and England were close. This was largely because of their history of religious ties, which in turn had led to Geneva's becoming, in the eyes of many English, a desirable place for general educational studies too. But both Geneva and London had become great rival centres for clock-making. By about this time Geneva was reputedly producing some 5,000 clocks a year, while London probably had already exceeded that figure.

1697 The brilliant Swiss mathematician Johann Bernoulli challenged Sir Isaac Newton to solve two mathematical problems. Newton did so in a period of twelve hours, by working through the night from when he arrived home at 4 p.m. (see also 1748.)

1698 The Genevan scholar Firmin Abauzit (1679-1767) visited England. He was a friend and correspondent of several eminent British scientists and philosophers, including Newton.

The memoirs of the regicide Edmund Ludlow (see 1660) were published in Vevey, where he had lived after his escape from England. They were dedicated to 'Their excellencies the Lords of the Council for the canton of Bern: Having been the protectors of the author . . . during the many years of exile . . .'

1699 In Neuchâtel (which enjoyed co-citizenship with several Swiss cantons but was still an independent principality) the male line of the ruling family had become extinct. There were several claimants. Louis XIV of France nominated his cousin, the Prince de Conti, while Berne, fearing a French fiefdom on its border, supported, with other cantons, the Duchess of Nemours. In 1699 Louis menaced the Swiss and forced the withdrawal of Swiss troops that had entered Neuchâtel. Then Hervart, the British Minister to the Swiss Confederation, announced that William III had claims to Neuchâtel (by his relationship to the House of Orange-Nassau which had formerly ruled the principality.) Unwilling to risk a conflict, Louis withdrew his support of Conti in favour of the Duchess of Nemours, whom all accepted.

The collegiate church of Notre Dame and the castle, Neuchâtel.

The Eighteenth Century

Swiss investments in London – the South Sea Bubble – Swiss troops save Marlborough's life – increasing cultural contacts – a Scotsman in Neuchâtel – the growth of travellers – and some candid comments – the French Revolutionary Wars – William Wickham in Switzerland.

1701 Joseph Addison (1672-1719), founder with Richard Steele of *The Spectator,* visited Switzerland. He wrote:

It is very wonderful to see such a knot of governments, which are so divided among themselves in matters of religion, maintain so uninterrupted an union and correspondence, that no one of them is for invading the rights of another . . . This I think must be chiefly ascribed to the nature of the people, and the constitution of their governments.

He also commented on the dislikes of the Swiss for pretension and show: 'It is the great endeavour of the several cantons to banish from among them everything that looks like pomp or superfluity.'

1702 With the decline of Holland, the City of London soon became the world's major money centre. The technique of the money market was being perfected; and the British government, needing funds to finance the new war (the War of the Spanish Succession), was a strong competitor in borrowing.

More foreign banks set up in London, among them the Bernese banking house of Malacrida & Co. – which subsequently joined forces with Samuel Müller (see 1652) and formed a new London banking house called Müller & Co.

During the War of the Spanish Succession, a ship belonging to the Swiss merchants Locher of St Gallen was seized by the British navy and its cargo held until proof was furnished that it was destined for a neutral country.

Geneva, too, was becoming one of the great money centres of Europe. A group of Genevan bankers, including Marcet, Buisson, Saladin, Lullin, Perdriau and Favre, formed a syndicate to invest

£300,000 in British government stock, producing an annual interest of £20,000.

Apart from Genevans, Swiss from other cantons were increasingly coming to live in London, and the Société des Suisses was founded. It was later (1718) united with the Société des Genevois.

1704 Death of the philosopher John Locke (b.1632), whose works had a strong influence in Switzerland, and particularly on Jean-Jacques Rousseau (see 1762). Locke's idealisation of the state of nature was developed in Rousseau's *Discourse on Inequality* (1754).

Among other Swiss visitors to England that year was the naturalist Johann Jakob Scheuchzer (1672-1733), who was making his third visit in three years. He had many friends among the leading scientists in Britain, including Sir Isaac Newton. When he read Woodward's *Essay towards a Natural History of the Earth,* Scheuchzer was so impressed with the idea that fossils could be treated as evidence of the Flood that he both translated the essay into Latin and made his own publications 'witness of the Deluge'. (See also 1713.)

1705 Abraham Stanyan (1669-1732) was appointed British Envoy Extraordinary to the Swiss cantons. His instructions were to detect and neutralise the artifices of the French Minister in Switzerland, and to try to obtain free passage for the allied troops in Italy through the Alpine passes. Stanyan was also made Envoy Extraordinary to the Grisons from 1707 to 1714.

1706 At the Battle of Ramillies, during a skirmish with the French cavalry, the Duke of Marlborough was thrown from his horse. Seeing him in danger, two Swiss battalions led by General Murray marched quickly up to save him. The Duke ran towards them and was able to resume control of the battle from behind the Swiss bayonets.[14]

1707 The ruler of Neuchâtel, the Duchess of Nemours (see 1699) died, throwing open once more the question of succession, with ten additional contenders raising claims. Before his death, William III had assigned his claim to the principality to his cousin, Frederick I of Prussia. Britain, the Netherlands and Austria (already at war with France in the War of the Spanish Succession), together with the Swiss, now supported Frederick's claim. The British Minister in

Abraham Stanyan, c. 1710: by Sir Godfrey Kneller.

Berne, Abraham Stanyan, and the Dutch envoy, hastened to Neuchâtel and succeeded in obtaining the investiture for Frederick. However, Louis XIV revived the cause of the Prince de Conti, and moved troops to the frontier. The Swiss, in turn, mobilised against him. Stanyan proposed to London that they should let the French attack; then the Bernese would be obliged to go to the aid of their friends in Neuchâtel, bringing the Swiss on to the side of the Allied Powers in the general war against France. The British Cabinet were in favour. However, Berne proposed to Louis that the Swiss regime of perpetual peace under their treaty with France should be applied to Neuchâtel as well. Louis accepted, and recognised Frederick of Prussia as ruler of the principality.

After the death the previous year of the queen's physician, Sir Theodore Colladon (see 1679), another Genevan was appointed as his successor, Etienne Rougeat. 1708

The canton of the Grisons sent a diplomatic envoy to London, Peter de Salis (1675-1749), who eventually stayed on and founded the English branch of the de Salis family. In 1713 de Salis rendered personal service to Queen Anne in connexion with negotiations for the Treaty of Utrecht. 1709

The Berne Treasury began to invest in British stock. It already had some large loans outstanding to English borrowers, secured against property. Müller & Co. and Malacrida & Co. were jointly responsible for transmitting to Switzerland the interest earned on these Bernese investments.

At the Battle of Malplaquet a Bernese mercenary regiment under the command of Colonel de May fought with Prince Eugene's forces on the side of Marlborough, while another Bernese regiment, commanded by a member of the same de May family, fought on the other side.

The canton of Berne made a loan of £150,000 at 6% interest to the British government. The British Minister in Berne, Abraham Stanyan, received from the Bernese authorities the first quarterly instalment of interest as consideration for his part in arranging the loan agreement. 1710

A group of Bernese, led by Christophe de Graffenried (1661-1743), founded New Berne in North Carolina in America, having first received the approval of Queen Anne.

Publication of *Characteristics of Men, Manners, Opinions, Times* by Anthony Ashley Cooper, third Earl of Shaftesbury. Shaftesbury's works, and those of other English moral philosphers around this time, were keenly read in Switzerland and stimulated such Swiss writers as Albrecht von Haller (see 1739). 1711

1713 Johann Jakob Scheuchzer (see 1704) published his 'Nova Helvetiae Tabula Geographica', the most complete map of Switzerland of the eighteenth century, which became one of the influences that encouraged men of art and letters to visit that country and which later led to the development of Swiss tourism. He followed this in 1723 with *Itinera Alpina,* a record of nine extensive journeys through the Alps which he dedicated to the Royal Society of London of which he was a Fellow. It included several illustrations of dragons alleged to have been seen by travellers in the Alps. Scheuchzer's other great work was his *Natural History of Switzerland.*

Johann Jakob Heidegger (1666-1749), the son of a Zurich clergyman, became manager of the Opera House in the Haymarket, London. Known as 'the Swiss count', he was patronised by George II and became his Master of Revels. Henry Fielding characterised Heidegger in his *Author's Farce and the Pleasures of the Town* (1730), as Count Ugly, who called himself the 'surindendent des plaisirs d'Angleterre'. Pope also satirised him in the *Dunciad.* In 1729 Heidegger went into partnership with Handel at the King's Theatre, and they opened the season with Handel's *Lotario.* The partnership lasted for several years. He died in Richmond in 1749.

1714 Publication in London of *An Account of Switzerland Written in the Year 1714* by Abraham Stanyan, former British Minister in Berne. It was considered to be an acute and generally accurate study and was used later by William Coxe when he wrote his Swiss narrative (see 1776). In his book Stanyan commented on the character of the Swiss:

> There is no one quality so universally allowed to the Switzers as that of valour . . . Livy and Caesar speak of them in their writings as a brave, warlike people; and they have ever since kept up that character in the world.

And again:

> I have nowhere met with men of more sound and clear judgement, of greater dexterity in the management of affairs, nor of more lively conversation, with true wit and genuine humour, than are to be found of that nation who have had the advantage of a good education improved by travel.

Remarking on the paucity of good investment opportunities in Switzerland at that time, Stanyan wrote:

> the want of conveniences in placing money at interest upon good security . . . forces the people to put it into foreign banks, and so the country is deprived of the use of it.

And on the wealth of the Berne Treasury:

Berne . . . has at this time 300,000 pounds sterling at interest, yet that sum, as I am credibly informed, makes not a sixth part of what remains in the treasury.

As part of the English military operations against the rebellion that year of James Edward, the Old Pretender, six battalions drawn from Swiss regiments in the Netherlands were sent to Scotland (see also 1719).

1715

The colonel and proprietor of one of the Swiss regiments, George Goumoëns, who particularly distinguished himself in the Scottish campaign (he was wounded seven times), was in 1719 made an honorary citizen of Stirling and of Glasgow.

The Genevan George-Louis le Sage (1676-1759) published his *Remarques sur l'état présent d'Angleterre*. During the years he was in England he was a much sought after teacher.

Since the deposing of James II in the Glorious Revolution of 1688, the Catholic cantons of Switzerland had refused to recognise his successors, William III and Queen Anne. Under French influence, they continued to regard the House of Stuart as the legitimate rulers of Britain. However, following the failure of the 1715 Jacobite rebellion, and the alliance which Britain made the next year with France, the Catholic cantons finally changed their attitude and recognised the new regime of George I.

1716

Andrew Schalch, born in Schaffhausen in 1692, arrived in England where he was engaged to build furnaces for the new government brass gun foundry at Woolwich. Master founder there for fifty years, Schalch became known as 'the father of Woolwich Arsenal'.

Trade between Britain and Geneva was growing fast, and Geneva had developed a flourishing *entrepôt* trade in some British goods, particularly textiles and colonial goods. Some estimates put the total value per annum at several hundred thousand pounds a year. But it was nearly all one way. Britain bought little from Geneva.

Vincent Perronet (1693-1785), a Swiss from Château d'Oex, came to England and was naturalised. He took holy orders, embraced Methodism, and became John Wesley's most intimate friend and

1717

adviser. Perronet became known as 'the Archbishop of Methodism' (see also 1752).

Armand-Louis de St Georges, Count de Marsay, a Hanoverian, became British Minister in Geneva. Count Marsay remained in this post until 1734 when he was made British Minister Resident to the Helvetic Republic and to the Grisons Leagues. From 1739 he returned to Geneva and represented Britain there until his death in 1762.

1718 The first complete translation of the Bible into the Romansch language appeared in Chur (Grisons) and was dedicated to George I's son, the Prince of Wales. The king acknowledged the compliment with a gift of fifty guineas.

Sir François de Pesme de Saint Saphorin (1668-1737), a Swiss, became George I's ambassador in Vienna. He gave long service to the British crown. Amongst other things, he became known for the length of his diplomatic despatches; and for some time afterwards any excessively lengthy report received in the Foreign Office was known as a 'Saint Saphorin'.

1719 Daniel Defoe's (c. 1661-1731) novel *Robinson Crusoe* was first published. Translated into German and French, for many generations of Swiss children it played a significant part in forming ideas about the British.

For some time the Churches in Geneva and in Switzerland had been at variance among themselves about some abstract points of theology in Church doctrine. The Archbishop of Canterbury, William Wake, thereupon wrote several letters to the pastors and professors of Geneva and Berne recommending a spirit of mutual tolerance and forbearance in their subscription to the Articles of Faith. He proposed to them the example of the Church of England as worthy of imitation in this respect. (See also 1723.)

James Stuart, the Old Pretender, made another effort to recapture the English throne. His main expedition, with Spanish troops, was dispersed by a storm before reaching England but a small force landed in the Highlands. This was led by George Keith (1693-1778), who later became Governor of Neuchâtel (see 1754). Keith's troops, and a handful of Highlanders who had joined them, were met by government troops consisting mainly of Swiss and of Dutch from regiments in the Netherlands. The Pretender's troops surrendered at Glenshiel. Keith was wounded but escaped; and was exiled from Britain.

When the British government repaid its £150,000 indebtedness to Berne (see 1710), the Bernese reinvested most of the proceeds in South Sea Company stock. They had begun to buy this stock in 1719, and between April and November, through Müller & Co., they bought 1,300 shares in the company at an average price of £113. But the Bernese government were not the only Swiss buyers. Altogether, there were over 200 Swiss investors holding over £560,000 in South Sea stock. 1719/20

By 1 January 1720 the stock was quoted at 123. In the following months it doubled and tripled. Excitement and speculation increased daily. The Bernese government was one of the first large overseas investors to read the danger signs correctly. They ordered Müller & Co. to sell 450 shares, from which they recovered their original capital sum of £150,000, and they had this repatriated to Berne. By early June the price of the stock was over 900. The Bernese government sold another 350 shares. On 24 June the stock touched 1,050. The Bernese sold their remaining 500 shares. From the last two transactions they cleared three quarters of a million pounds. But speculative fever in London continued. Müller & Co. made further investments with this money in other companies which had been floated on the boom, apparently not all with Berne's approval. In August the British government suddenly tightened its control on speculative dealings in stock. Just at the same time, many investors decided to sell their holdings and realise their gains. The crash began; and other stocks fell too. 1720

The bursting of the 'South Sea Bubble' caused a financial crisis in Berne as well as in London (where the Chancellor of the Exchequer went to the Tower). The banking house of Malacrida & Co. failed, owing 406,000 thalers to the Bernese government, and owed in turn large sums from the failure of the famous Bank Law, the largest bank in Paris, which had been built up by the Scot John Law. (The Bank Law disaster also caused severe losses among investors in the canton of Vaud.) The government of Berne lost £268,000 in all. 1721

In London Müller & Co. lost much of their own money too in the South Sea crash. The Bernese authorities sent a committee of inves-

The South Sea Bubble: contemporary cartoon.

tigation to London and over the following years Müller & Co. were required to make enough reparation to leave the Bernese Treasury eventually in profit.

Sir Luke Schaub, born in Basel, was appointed British Ambassador in Paris. He had previously served in the British Diplomatic Service in Vienna, Madrid and Hanover. He was at one time private secretary to George I and was a favourite companion of George II. He was said to have been a protégé of Abraham Stanyan (see 1705).

A Swiss painter of miniatures, Jacques-Antoine Arlaud (1668-1746), arrived for a stay in England, where he made the acquaintance of Sir Isaac Newton.

At about this time a Swiss Church was formed in London. Known as the Church of the Switzers, the congregation met for some years, sometimes in a rented room, sometimes in a chapel in Glasshouse Street, near Piccadilly, holding services in both German and French. George I accorded the Swiss some land on which to construct a permanent building, but this offer was not used. (However, see 1762.)

1723 When the Bernese government tried to force the canton of Vaud to accept the rigid 'Formula Consensus' in religious practice, the ecclesiastics of the Vaud appealed to George I. The king joined with his Archbishop of Canterbury in exhorting Berne to be indulgent towards the recalcitrants.

1724 Johann Caspar Scheuchzer (1702-29), son of Johann Jakob (see 1713), came to England and became librarian to Sir Hans Sloane. In a short but distinguished career he was elected a Fellow of the Royal Society and a Licentiate of the Royal College of Physicians. He was buried in Chelsea Old Church in London.

1725 Johann Jakob Bodmer (1698-1783), the eminent promoter of English literature in German-speaking Switzerland, became Professor of Swiss History at the Academy in Zurich. Bodmer had first become interested in England through reading some copies of *The Spectator* (see 1701). He then gave currency to English ideas in a periodical he founded with some friends, *Die Discourse der Mahlern.* He translated the whole of Milton's *Paradise Lost,* Butler's *Hudibras,* and Pope's *Dunciad,* and later some of Thomas Percy's *Reliques of Ancient Poetry.* He also sponsored the first German translation of Shakespeare (see

1762). It was largely owing to the work of Bodmer, and of his colleague J. J. Breitinger (1702-76), that the influence of English literature in German-speaking Switzerland began to overtake that of the French.

The Bernese Beat Louis de Muralt published his *Lettres sur les Anglais* – an early study in comparative national psychology, based on a visit he had made to England in 1695. Muralt compared the English with their dogs – both were 'taciturn, obstinate, lazy, intrepid, and stubborn in fight'.

The Englishman has plenty of commonsense, he neglects manners but cultivates reason . . . He has the courage to defy fashion and public opinion . . . He is not courting royal favours: in a word he is the free-est man in the world.

The English, he suggested, had taken several of their traits from the nations that had subdued them:

They drink like the Saxons; they love hunting like the Danes; the Normands have left them chicanery and quarrelsomeness; they have retained from the Romans a love of bloody spectacles and a contempt for death. They are kind but they can be cruel . . . They usually despise foreigners but sometimes admire them too much . . . Their government is gentle; they enjoy a liberty that exalts the mind.

Muralt was one of the first foreign observers to record his appreciation of Shakespeare. 'England', he wrote, 'is a country that affords a large scene of passions and catastrophes, and Shakespeare, one of the best of their late poets, has put a great part of their history into his tragedies.'

c. 1726 The celebrated Swiss mathematician Gabriel Cramer (1704-83) was studying astronomy at Cambridge. He later became a Fellow of the Royal Society.

1726 Another Swiss observer of the British character, César de Saussure, who had arrived in England the previous year, wrote to his mother:

Politics in this country seems to interest everyone, I suppose this taste is cultivated by the liberty which the government affords, and in which the Englishmen take great pride, for they value this gift more than all the joys of life, and would sacrifice everything to retain it . . . There is no country in the world where such perfect freedom may be enjoyed as in England . . . Their soldiers fight with the greatest valour. This has been sufficiently proved in the latest wars.

In another letter de Saussure wrote:

> I have found many people very interested in money matters, and one might use the celebrated phrase 'point d'argent, point de Suisses' as much with regard to them as to my own countrymen . . . English workmen are everywhere renowned and that justly. They work to perfection and, though not inventive, are capable of improving and of finishing most admirably what the French and Germans have invented.

(See also 1729.)

1727 — Death of Johann Conrad Brunner, a Swiss physician of world renown, and originator of the term 'Brunner's glands'. His medical advice was sought by George I.

1728 — The Swiss mercenary system came under attack from the poet Alexander Pope. In his satirical poem *The Dunciad* he wrote:

> Around him wide a sable army stand,
> A low-born, cell-bred, selfish, servile band.
> Prompt to guard, or stab, to saint or damn,
> Heav'ns Swiss, who fight for any God or man.

1729 — The young Genevan César de Saussure (see 1726) accompanied the British Ambassador, Lord Kinnoull, to Constantinople and was appointed by him first secretary at the embassy. He left in 1733.

1730 — The Bernese government began to appoint official agents in London to represent their financial interests there. They continued to invest large sums in Bank of England stock and, later, in 3% Bank Annuities of 1745 and 4% Annuities of 1762. (See also 1763.)

Publication of the Scottish poet James Thomson's (1700-48) *The Seasons*, a poem which had a considerable influence on both Swiss and other Continental writers. The libretto of Haydn's oratorio *The Seasons* is based on it. Several editions of Thomson's poem were published in Switzerland.

1731 — David Pury (1709-86) of Neuchâtel was sent to London to work in the City. He specialised in diamonds and in property and, after a number of years also in Portugal, amassed a fortune which he spent on funding orphanages and schools in Switzerland. His father, Jean-Pierre Pury (1675-1736), had been an inveterate wanderer. Among other things, he introduced the vine to the Cape Province of South Africa, bringing with him some plants from Neuchâtel; he submitted to the British government a project for the colonisation of Australia; he became an officer, successively, in the British army and the British navy; and he founded a town in America, Purysberg in South Carolina.

Jean Dassier (1676-1763), medallist, who had come to England from Geneva in 1728, began to produce his notable series of medals of the Sovereigns of England.

c. 1732 Another Genevan banker in London, François Pictet, left correspondence written around this time about stock exchange investments he was making for his client, Jean Alphonse Turrettini, Professor of Theology in Geneva. Alphonse Turrettini had spent some years studying at Oxford and was priest to the British community in Geneva.

1732 Anti-British riots in the Valais. In 1730 the Valaisan government, looking for experts to exploit the iron mines in the valley of Binn, had appointed two Englishmen, Mandel and Aston. They were given a ten-year contract, and work began the following year. Not long afterwards local agitation against the Valaisan government began, on the grounds that the Englishmen were Protestants to whom good Catholic ore was being sold. Meetings of protest at Stalden led to a threat to march on Sion, the capital. Bowing to the storm, the Valaisan government rescinded the contract and paid Mandel and Aston compensation on the understanding that they would leave without any trouble.

1733 One acute – and cynical – observer of the banking community in both Geneva and London was Voltaire (1694-1778). Although French, Voltaire spent three years in Britain and the last years of his life as a refugee in Geneva. He once wrote; 'Geneva imitates England as the frog imitates the bull' (a reference to La Fontaine's fable). In his *Letters concerning the English Nation,* published in London in 1733, he commented on the trust established between different faiths in the City of London:

Go into the London Stock Exchange . . . Here Jew, Mohammedan and Christian deal with each other as though they were all of the same faith, and only apply the word infidel to people who go bankrupt.

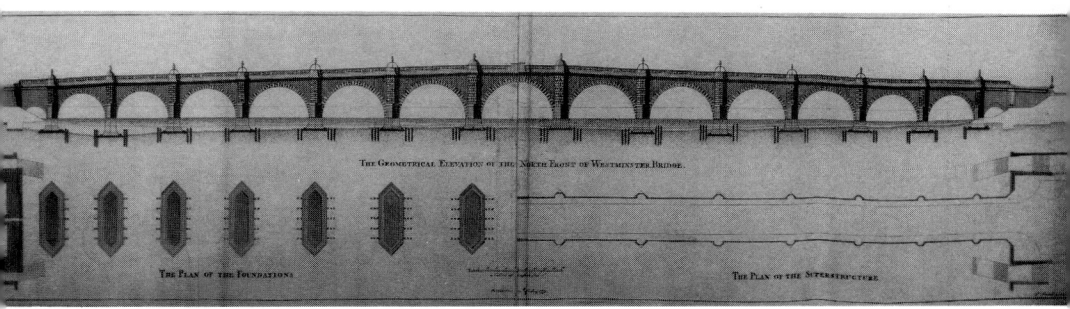

Labelye's plan for Old Westminster Bridge, with ABOVE *a view of the completed bridge.*

A Swiss, Charles Labelye (1705-81) of Vevey, was appointed architect of the first Westminster Bridge. Labelye had come to England about 1725 and had for some years been employed as a draughtsman in Nicholas Hawksmoor's office. In 1735 he undertook a survey of the Kent coast near Sandwich. Labelye obtained the commission for Westminster Bridge against considerable competition. The authorities had at first wanted a wooden bridge on stone piers, but Labelye said the public would be disgusted at the thought of a timber bridge in the 'metropolis of the British Empire'. He was proved right. Public opinion forced the authorities to change their minds and Labelye's design for a stone bridge was accepted.

1738

Another Swiss, François Gaussen, set up a merchant's business in Nicholas Lane, London. His son, Peter Gaussen (born 1723), in 1777 became the first Swiss Governor of the Bank of England. Another descendant became Governor in 1877.

Another member of the famous Swiss Bernoulli family, Daniel Bernoulli (1700-82), published his magnum opus *Hydrodynamica*. In this, *inter alia*, he developed hydrostatics and hydrodynamics using Isaac Newton's laws of force.

1739 The celebrated scientist, philosopher and poet Albrecht von Haller (1708-77) of Berne was appointed physician to George II. The same year he was elected a Fellow of the Royal Society. Haller, in his poem *The Alps*, is said to have been much influenced by two British poets, James Thomson (see 1730) and Edward Young (1683- 1765). Haller also made a study of the English constitution, which in a book entitled *Alfred, King of the Saxons* he praised as the most perfect. It may be no coincidence that James Thomson also wrote, with David Mallet, a masque, *Alfred* (in which appeared the song 'Rule Britannia'). (See also 1749.)

Horace Walpole (1717-97), younger son of Sir Robert Walpole, on one of his visits to Switzerland, wrote of the Alps, 'I hope I shall never see them again.'

Le Sieur & Jacquier's edition of Isaac Newton's *Principia* was published in Geneva.

The English poet Thomas Gray (1716-71), travelling through the Alps to Italy, made a stay in Geneva. He was delighted with the

> happy and lively countenances of its inhabitants . . . not a beggar and hardly a disconsolate face to be seen . . . Numerous and well-dressed people swarming the ramparts, drums beating, soldiers well-clothed and exercising; and folks, with business in their looks, hurrying to and fro . . . I do not wonder [Gray wrote to his father] so many English choose it for their residence.

1740 Burckhardt Tschudi (1718-73), from Schwanden (Glarus), became established in London as a famous harpsichord maker, providing instruments for the Prince of Wales, the Empress Maria Theresa, Frederick the Great, Haydn and Clementi, among others. Handel was a frequent guest at the Tschudis' house. John Broadwood, founder of the family of piano manufacturers, joined Tschudi as an apprentice and married his daughter. Tschudi's son and John Broadwood made their first 'grand pianoforte' in 1794.

Another Swiss medallist, Jacques Antoine Dassier (1715-59), the son of Jean Dassier (see 1731), came to London to try his luck. His work attracted many patrons, and among his clients were George II, Prince Frederick of Wales, Lord Chesterfield and Sir Robert Walpole.

1741 William Windham (the father of William Windham who was William Pitt's close colleague - see 1788), in Geneva as part of his Grand Tour, led a group of seven other British residents there on an early expedition to Chamonix, the glacier and the slopes of Mont Blanc.

Having remained about half an hour on the glacière, and having drank there in ceremony Admiral Vernon's health and success to British arms, we climbed to the summit . . . with incredible difficulty, the earth giving way at every step we set. From thence, after having rested ourselves a few minutes, we began to descend and arrived at Chamonix just about sunset.

In the reign of George II, the fife, or 'Swiss pipe', was brought into use in military bands of the British Army. Originally introduced from Switzerland in the sixteenth century, it had been discarded in 1685 in favour of the oboe.

1742 The Swiss watchmaker Justin Vulliamy (fl. 1730-90) came to London to study the construction of English clocks and watches. He later succeeded to his master's business in Pall Mall, and was appointed clockmaker to the Crown in 1747 (see also 1781).

George II sent on a diplomatic mission to the canton of the Grisons Jerome de Salis (1709-85), son of Peter de Salis who had been that canton's emissary to London in 1709. He stayed there for seven years.

1743 A new British Minister to Switzerland, John Burnaby, was appointed. His instructions were to try to destroy the 'overgrown credit' of the House of Bourbon in the Swiss cantons and to raise a body of Swiss troops for the king's service. Burnaby's efforts were later turned towards persuading the Bernese government to allow more troops to be raised for the Netherlands service (see also 1744).

A Bernese artist, David Morier (1705-70), came to settle in England. The Duke of Cumberland, who became one of his patrons, later gave him a pension. Morier painted many equestrian studies, including portraits of George II and George III.

John Burnaby, British Minister in Berne, 1748: portrait by Emanuel Handmann.

A rising Genevan scientist, Abraham Trembley (1710-84), was made a Fellow of the Royal Society in London for his work on the freshwater polyp. However, his interest in such lowly organisms was derided by a number of prominent British writers, including Fielding, Smollett and Goldsmith (see also 1747 and 1750).

In 1744, partly as a result of Burnaby's efforts, the Bernese Council of Two Hundred agreed to the provision of additional troops for the Dutch service; and in the following years at least twelve new companies were formed – not only from Bernese territories but from Zurich too.

1744

In a list of authors recommended by Johann Jakob Bodmer (see 1725) as 'suitable for the library of a Swiss lady', were Joseph Addison's *Cato*, Samuel Richardson's *Pamela*, Henry Fielding's *Joseph Andrews*, the Earl of Shaftesbury's *Characteristics of Men*, James Thomson's *The Seasons*, Alexander Pope's *Essay on Man*, and Archbishop Tillotson's *Sermons*.

Following the Scottish uprising of the Young Pretender, the Swiss colony in England put a battalion of several hundred men at the disposition of the king. The volunteers were recruited by Sir Luke Schaub (see 1721). The king, in gratitude, presented the Swiss colony with a standard.

1745

The eighteenth century was the era of the Grand Tour, and one young Englishman who was undertaking it, and had just arrived in Switzerland for a year's stay at Lausanne University, was Philip Stanhope, son of the Earl of Chesterfield. In one of his famous letters to his son, Lord Chesterfield drew a moral from the difficult travelling conditions of the time:

1746

Your distress in your journey from Heidelberg to Schaffhausen, your lying upon straw, your black bread, and your broken Berline, are proper seasonings for the greater fatigues and distresses which you must expect in the course of your travels; and if one had a mind to moralise, one might call them the samples of the accidents, rules and difficulties, which every man meets with in his journey through life.

In another letter Lord Chesterfield urged his son to take full advantage of his stay and to study carefully the country he was in:

1747

Bishop Burnet has wrote his travels through Switzerland; and Mr Stanyan, from a long residence there, has written the best account, yet extant, of the thirteen cantons; but those books will be read no more. I presume, after you shall have published your accounts of that country. I hope you will favour me with one of the first copies. To be serious, though I do not desire that you shall immediately turn author and oblige the world with your travels, yet, wherever you go, I would have you as curious and inquisitive as if you did intend to write them.

Samuel Richardson (1689-1761) published the first two volumes of his novel *Clarissa,* which was soon translated into French. Rousseau made *Clarissa* a model for his *La nouvelle Héloïse* (1760). In a letter to D'Alembert, Rousseau said that there was in no language a romance equal to, or approaching, *Clarissa* (see also 1753).

Towards the end of the War of the Austrian Succession, the Swiss Abraham Trembley (see 1743), now living in England, was sent to aid the British negotiators, Lord Sandwich and Sir Thomas Robinson, drawing up the peace treaty at Aix-la-Chapelle. He was rewarded by George II with a pension of £300 a year for life.

1748 Death of the Swiss jurist Jean-Jacques Burlamaqui (b. 1694). Inspired partly by John Locke, Burlamaqui wrote a classic work, *Principes du droit naturel et du droit public,* which went through eleven English editions between 1748 and 1817.

Death also of the Swiss scientist and mathematician Johann Bernoulli. At thirty-two he was already a member of the Academy of Sciences in Paris, together with an English genius who was in some fields his rival – Isaac Newton (see 1689). Bernoulli's work with Leibnitz on calculus, continued by his pupil Euler (see 1783), laid the foundations for the system which Britain eventually adopted in 1820.

James Hutton (1715-95), founder of the Moravian missions in England, who was married to a Swiss member of the Moravian sect, a Louise Brandt from Neuchâtel, made a tour of Switzerland. He wrote: 'The Lord loves Switzerland and will save many who might not be suitable for the congregation.' Perhaps he was thinking of his wife who apparently did not always come up to his high standards. In a letter to John Wesley, Hutton apologised for 'the uncongregation-like fashion' of his wife's gown. (Hutton eventually broke with John Wesley, and Wesley noted in his journal, after Hutton had paid him a visit, that he believed Hutton would be saved – 'but as by fire'.)

Another Englishman who was in Switzerland that year was Thomas

Hollis (1720-74). Hollis described himself as a republican and a 'true Whig', and he gave numerous books on his ideas to libraries in Berne and Zurich. In his memoirs, he wrote of the Swiss:

> Upon the whole in all our travels, Holland not excepted which has many things similar to this country, we nowhere saw so general an ease through all the ranks, and so much seeming content and happiness.

Among other Swiss who joined the British forces in America was Denys-Guerard Burnand (1707-65). He was later a captain in the Royal American Regiment (see 1756). A British descendant, Sir Francis Burnand (1836-1917), became editor of *Punch*.

1749

Albrecht von Haller (see 1739) was now so well regarded by George II that the government of Berne planned to appoint him as their representative to London. But the British Minister at Berne received the following instructions:

> As the King has been informed that the Republic of Berne has some intention of sending M. Haller, Counsellor to His Majesty and Professor of Physick in the University of Göttingen, to reside at this Court in the quality of their Minister, His Majesty would have you inform their Excellencies that although he approves entirely of the choice their Excellencies have made of so good and great a man, yet as his presence is very necessary at Göttingen towards the perfecting of that plan which His Majesty has so wisely countenanced for the encouragement of the study of all useful learning in that university, it would be a satisfaction to His Majesty to have his Mission to England deferred for some time.

Abraham Trembley (see 1747) was appointed tutor to the third Duke of Richmond and accompanied him on a Grand Tour of the Continent. They spent the first two years in Geneva.

1750

Charles Labelye's Westminster Bridge (see 1738) was finished. It soon became a favourite promenade. *The Gentleman's Magazine* commented:

> The surprising echo in the arches brings much company with French horns to entertain themselves under it in summer; and with the upper part, for an agreeable airing, none of the public walks or gardens can compare with it.

The Bernese Vincent Bernard de Tscharner, on a visit to England, met the English poet Edward Young (see 1739). Tscharner translated into German Young's masterpiece, *The Complaint, or Night Thoughts*.

1751

Sir Luke Schaub (see 1721), with the aid of his friend Gaspard Sellon,

Albrecht von Haller, by F.W. Städer. Haller spent seventeen years at Göttingen as professor of anatomy, surgery and botany at the new university there. He was possibly the greatest universalist of his century.

a Genevan banker established in London, recruited from Switzerland four companies of infantry and a company of artillery, on behalf of the British East India Company. They were soon incorporated into Clive's forces in India. One of the Swiss who was designated to command a company, Colonel Antoine Polier, was brought before the Bernese authorities for having been concerned in the recruitment outside the territories belonging to the canton; and the British Minister, Arthur Villettes, was asked to intercede on Polier's behalf (see also c. 1784).

A number of emigrating Swiss entered the service of the British East India Company. One of these, Daniel Frischmann of Basel (1728-1808), became commandant of Cape Comorin province in 1766 and colonel and commandant of Madras in 1769.

Another Swiss who joined the East India Company was Louis Beat   1752
Braun (1718-92), a son-in-law of Albrecht von Haller. He became a
colonel and was then made Governor of Chittagong. In 1776, after
his retirement and return to Berne, he was appointed chargé d'affaires
at the British Legation there, a post he retained until his death in
1792.

Joseph Planta, a Swiss pastor from Castegna (Grisons) came to settle
in London as minister to the German Reformed Church. He became a
Fellow of the Royal Society. From 1758 he was Assistant Librarian at
the British Museum; and he was appointed a reader to Queen Charlotte. (See also 1776.)

Also coming to England that year was Jean Guillaume de la Fléchère
(1729-85) of Nyon (Vaud). Like Perronet (see 1717), he met John
and Charles Wesley, and was soon ordained in the Church of England. Changing his name to John Fletcher, he became vicar of
Madeley in the Shropshire coalfields during the Industrial Revolution. He was one of the Evangelical Revival's most powerful thinkers
and John Wesley thought of him at one time as his spiritual successor;
but he died before Wesley.

Samuel Richardson, author of *Clarissa* (see 1747), received from   1753
Albrecht von Haller of Berne a translation which Haller had made of
his novel into German.

The Genevan painter Jean Etienne Liotard (1702-89) came to England
for several years. He made a celebrated series of portraits in pastels of
the Princess of Wales, and of the young princes and princesses. He
returned for a second stay in 1772, exhibited at the Royal Academy,
and found a large clientele for his paintings.

Another arrival in England was the Swiss composer and teacher
Josef-Franz-Xavier Stalder of Lucerne (1725-65). He had much suc-
cess with his compositions and an opera of his was performed in
London. He remained in England for several years.

Lord Keith, tenth hereditary Earl Marischal of Scotland, who had   1754
been outlawed as a young man for his attachment to the House of
Stuart (see 1719), was made Governor of the principality of
Neuchâtel for the King of Prussia. (Only in 1857 did Neuchâtel,
although nominally a Swiss canton from 1815, cease to be a Prussian
principality.) Keith was known locally as 'Milord Maréchal'. He

Lord Keith, Governor of Neuchâtel: by an unknown artist, probably in Rome in the 1720s or 1730s when Keith was at the court in exile of James Stuart, the Old Pretender.

retired in 1760 but continued to live for a time in Neuchâtel. He later went to England to receive the king's pardon and redeem his property which had been confiscated.

Bonnie Prince Charlie, the Young Pretender, visited Basel and stayed at the hotel Drei Könige under the name of Mr Thompson. He was travelling with Miss Walkinshaw and their daughter (the future Duchess of Albany). Their stay in Switzerland was the subject of anxious confidential dispatches from the British Minister to Switzerland to the Foreign Office. (Miss Walkinshaw died in 1802 in Fribourg.)

The city of Zurich set up a state-controlled bank, the Investment Commission, soon to be called Leu & Co., to invest public and private funds abroad. The first year the bank appointed agents in London and invested 30% of their initial portfolio in £2,000 sterling 3% consolidated annuities. From 1762, for some years all new money received by the bank was used to buy securities in London, and by 1770 its holding of English annuities had reached £34,700, or nearly 300,000 florins. (In 1798, during the French occupation of Switzerland, Leu & Co. became a privately-owned bank.)

In Turin Savoy and Sardinia signed a treaty with Geneva, the result of skilful negotiations by Sir Luke Schaub (see 1721). This gave some assurance that Geneva's independence would be maintained, as indeed it was until the French Revolution.

Edward Gibbon (1737-94), sent by his father to Protestant Lausanne   1755

Edward Gibbon: artist unknown.

174 Chronology 1755 – 1756

to rid him of his Catholic leanings, made his first tour of Switzerland, after two years of study there. He wrote:

The fashion of climbing the mountains and viewing the glaciers had not yet been introduced by foreign travellers who seek the sublime beauties of nature. But . . . I contemplated with pleasure the new prospects of man and manners: though my conversation with the natives would have been more free and instructive had I possessed the German as well as the French language.

Among other places Gibbon visited was the Benedictine abbey of Einsiedeln, where he went 'not out of devotion but of curiosity'.

I was astonished by the profuse ostentation of riches in the poorest corner of Europe; amidst a savage scene of woods and mountains, a palace appears to have been erected by magic.

In Lausanne Gibbon fell in love with Suzanne Curchod, the daughter of a Protestant pastor, but his father vetoed the marriage and Gibbon obeyed. Suzanne Curchod later married the future stateman Jacques Necker, their daughter becoming the celebrated Mme de Staël. Gibbon went back to England in 1758 but returned to Lausanne some years later.

1756 At the beginning of the Seven Years' War a new British regiment was founded in North America – the Royal American, in which Swiss officers played a leading part (a special bill had been passed allowing the granting of commissions to foreigners provided they were Protestants). Jacques Prevost (later to become a major-general) raised the regiment and was colonel-commandant, while Henri Bouquet (see 1765) and Frederic Haldimand both commanded battalions. Jacques Prevost's brother Augustin (see 1778) was a major and his other brother Jean Marc was a captain. Under Henri Bouquet, the 1st Battalion were the first regular British unit to drop their red coats and adopt inconspicuous clothing on operations. The regiment later became the King's Royal Rifle Corps or 60th Rifles (now the Green Jackets).

Oliver Goldsmith (1728-74) made Voltaire's acquaintance in Lausanne. While in Switzerland, Goldsmith wrote the first sketch of his poem *The Traveller* (1764):

OPPOSITE *The Abbey of Einsiedeln.*

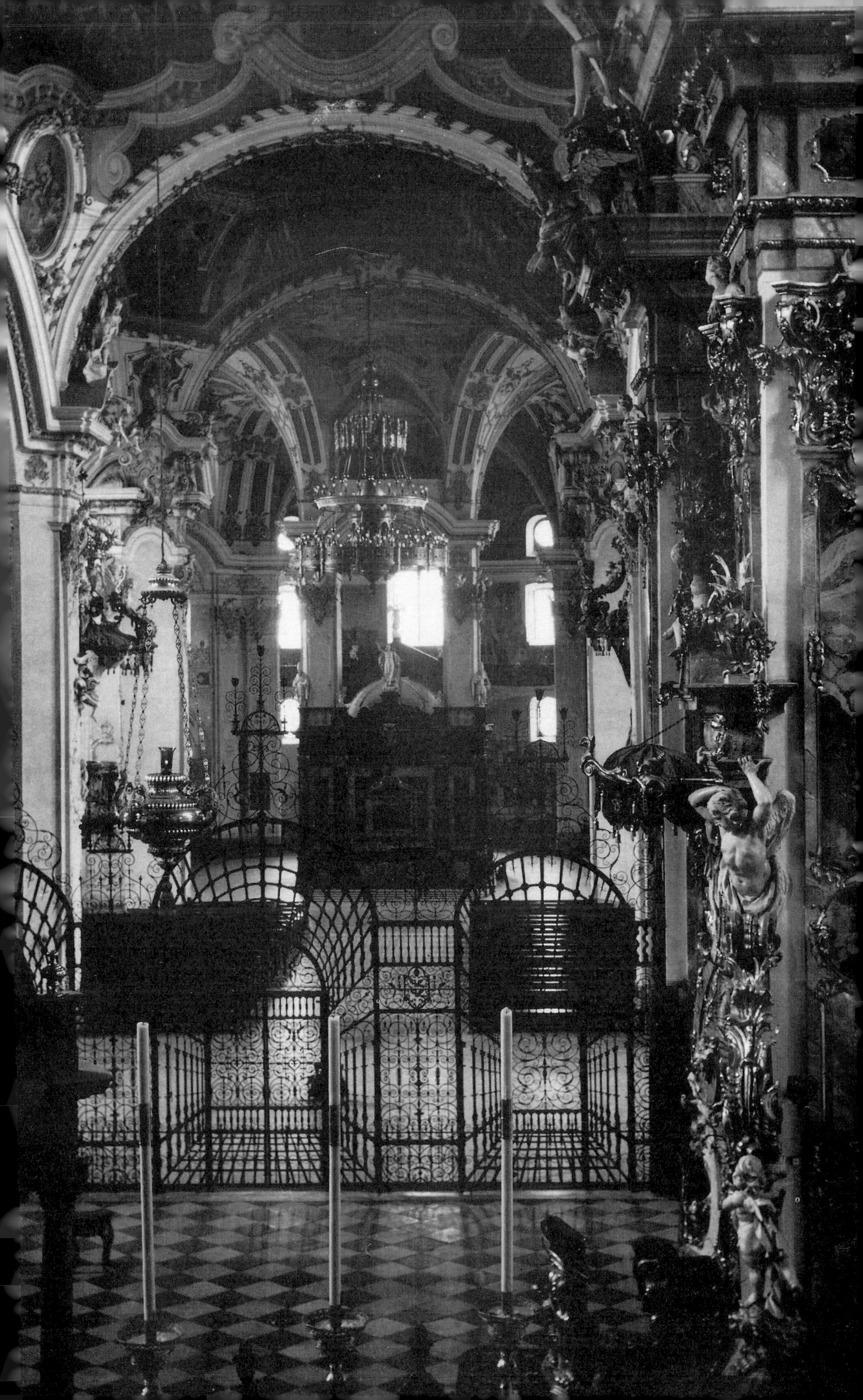

> ... Where rougher climes a nobler race display,
> Where the bleak Swiss their stormy mansions tread,
> And force a churlish soil for scanty bread;
> No product here the barren hills afford,
> But man and steel, the soldier and his sword.

George Keate, on a tour of Switzerland, wrote *The Helvetiade – Verses Occasioned by Visiting a Small Chapel on the Lake of Lucerne in the Canton of Uri, Erected to the Memory of the Famous William Tell.*

1757 During Colonel Clive's campaign in India, a Swiss Captain Jean-François Paschoup of Lutry commanded the English artillery at the Battle of Plassey.

1758 Publication of the Zurich poet Salomon Gessner's (1730-1788) poem *Der Tod Abels* ('The Death of Abel') which, translated into English, was widely read in Britain where it had much influence on contemporary poetry. Among Gessner's admirers were Byron, Scott, Wordsworth and Hood. (See also 1797.) The whole of Gessner's works were later published in Britain.

1759 A translated edition of the works of Jonathan Swift (1667-1745), *Satyrische und Ernsthafte Schriften,* with a preface by J. von Breitenfels, began to be published (in eight volumes) in Zurich.

1760 The Genevan Jean Mussard (b. 1707), an enamellist, was working in London.

1761 Simon Matthey, a Swiss from Le Locle (Neuchâtel), arrived to set up in business in London. His business prospered and he settled in England for good. His grandson, George Matthey, joined the precious metals firm of Johnson & Cock in Hatton Garden in 1838 as apprentice to P.N. Johnson, the founder. Another brother, Edward, joined in 1850. George Matthey was taken into partnership in 1851 and the current style of Johnson, Matthey was then adopted.

1762 By the first half of the eighteenth century the Swiss merchants in London had become an important and established group of society. Royal Assent was given to the erection of a permanent Swiss church, and l'Eglise Helvétique was inaugurated.

Peter Thellusson, a scion of the Swiss banking house established in

Geneva and Paris, arrived in London and took British nationality. He became partner in J. & A. Fonblanque & Thellusson and later set up on his own. (It is likely that Dickens, in describing the banking house of 'Tellson' in *A Tale of Two Cities,* had Thellusson in mind). Several members of the Thellusson family in England became Members of Parliament.

Lord Keith (see 1754) gave Jean-Jacques Rousseau (1712-78) help and protection when the latter fled to Neuchâtel from France, where an order for his arrest had been issued. When he received back his Scottish property, Keith settled an annuity on Rousseau.

The same year Rousseau's *Du contrat social* was first published. In writing it Rousseau had been much influenced by the works of the English philosopher Thomas Hobbes and by John Locke's *Treatises on Government.*

The first German translation of Shakespeare's plays, by Christoph Wieland, the German poet then living in Zurich, was published by Orell Gesner & Co. of Zurich. Sponsored by Johann Jakob Bodmer (see 1725), a total of twenty-two of Shakespeare's plays in eight volumes appeared over the next four years.

One Swiss reader of Shakespeare's plays in translation was a peasant in Toggenburg, Ulrich Bräker, who wrote a remarkable essay on them – 'A few words about William Shakespeare's plays, by a poor ignorant citizen of the world who had the good fortune to read him' (see Bibliography).

Colonel Jacques Pictet, known by the English as James, Count Pictet, was appointed for four years British Representative in Geneva by George III. Since Pictet was a member of the City's Council of Two Hundred, he was instructed to be uncontroversial in his diplomatic post. However, he became publicly identified with the Opposition and was told his attitude was 'highly disapproved of by the king'.

1763

The same year the agent of the Bernese government in London, Louis de Muralt, was recalled apparently because of his bad management of Berne's investments on the London market. The bank of Van Neck & Co. then took over the representation of Bernese financial interests in London. After putting up guarantees, Van Neck & Co. received an annual fee of £200 for their services; and de Muralt was condemned to pay this annuity himself for the first two years.

1764 After the Peace of Paris had ended the Seven Years' War, the way was open again to many Britons to travel to the Continent. A Swiss observer estimated that of twenty guests in a Swiss inn at that time, it was usual to find that fourteen were British.

One of these travellers was James Boswell (Dr Johnson's biographer). He visited Lord Keith in Neuchâtel, made six calls on Rousseau at Motiers, and spent time with Voltaire at Ferney, near Geneva. He also stayed at the Hôtel de la Couronne in Solothurn. From there he wrote to a friend:

You are shivering with cold in Edinburgh, while I bid defiance to winter in Solothurn. You are probably thoughtful and gloomy. I am thoughtful and gay. And whence comes this mighty difference between two men who in many hours of their existence have differed less than most men? Why, from no other cause but position. You are in a Scots town. I am in a Swiss town. You are in a dirty town. I am in a clean town. You have passed the day in uniformity. I have passed the day in variety . . . I have kissed (but no more) a comely healthy maid at my inn . . .

Charles (later third Earl) Stanhope (1753-1816) came with the whole of his family to Geneva where he pursued his studies. In 1766 he spent two months with Adam Smith when the latter was in Geneva as tutor to the young Duke of Buccleuch. Stanhope later enrolled for some years in the militia of the Republic. He returned to England in 1774.

Another British traveller in Switzerland that year was Daniel Malthus, father of the economist (see also 1767).

1765 Anthony Francis Haldimand (1741-1817), of Yverdon, came to London and became a partner in Zachary, Long & Haldimand, general merchants and operators in exchange. Later he set up his own merchant banking business which in 1805 became A.F. Haldimand & Sons (see also 1809).

General Henri Bouquet (1719-65), a Swiss who had been for many years in the British military service in North America, died in Florida. The year before, he had been appointed Commander of all British troops in the Southern counties of British America.

John Wilkes (1727-97), the Whig politician, stayed in Geneva.

1766 The Swiss artist from Chur (Grisons), Angelica Kauffmann (1741-1807), came to live in England. She became one of the founder

Angelica Kauffmann's design for a ceiling decoration at Burlington House, London.

members of the Royal Academy in 1769 and exhibited there every year until 1782. She was a particular friend of Sir Joshua Reynolds, and had admirers also in Goldsmith, Garrick and Henry Fuseli (see 1779). She also knew the brothers Adam and painted some of their ceilings and other decorations. She went to live in Italy in 1782.

The economist and philosopher Adam Smith (1723-90) made a stay in Geneva accompanying, as travelling tutor, the young Duke of Buccleuch. He met Voltaire at Ferney; and he worked in Geneva on his *Wealth of Nations,* which he had begun during his earlier stay in Toulouse.

Jean-Jacques Rousseau, now in Bernese territory, accepted an invitation from the Scottish philosopher David Hume (a friend of Keith) to come and live in England.

Jean-Jacques Rousseau: portrait by Allan Ramsay, 1766, at the request of Ramsay's friend David Hume.

Dr Charles Burney (see 1770) adapted Rousseau's opera *Le devin du village,* which was produced at Drury Lane, London that year as *The Cunning Man.*

Rousseau, now in England, was, as a result of David Hume's intercession, given a pension of £100 by George III. Through Hume, too, he met his admirer Daniel Malthus (father of Robert – see 1802). Rousseau and Malthus became close friends. Rousseau thought at one time of settling in Wales, which he said reminded him of Switzerland. However, after several bitter arguments with Hume, he left England for France.

1767

The political writer Edmund Burke (1729-97) was one Briton who was not such an admirer of Rousseau. He remarked:

> We have just had the great professor and founder of the philosophy of Vanity in England. As I had good opportunities of knowing his proceedings almost from day to day, he left no doubt in my mind that he entertained no principle either to influence his heart or to guide his understanding but vanity: with this vice he was possessed to a degree little short of madness.

Dr Johnson, too, disliked Rousseau. 'I think him one of the worst of men: a rascal who ought to be hunted out of society.' But these feelings were not all on one side. Rousseau later wrote in his *Confessions* (which he had begun during his stay in England): 'I have always disliked England and the English.'

The son of a Bernese patrician family, Charles Victor de Bonstetten (1745-1832) came to study in England. He became a friend of the poet Gray (see 1739) and spent many hours with him at Cambridge. When the young Bonstetten returned to Switzerland, Gray wrote to him:

> I did not conceive till now, I own, what it was to lose you, nor felt the solitude and insipidity of my own condition before I possessed the happiness of your friendship.

Publication of *Mémoires littéraires de la Grande Bretagne pour l'an 1767,* a joint work by the Swiss Jacques-Georges Deyverdun (1734-1789) and his friend Edward Gibbon. Helped by Deyverdun, Gibbon also projected a *History of the Liberty of the Swiss* (in which, incidentally, he showed strong scepticism about the William Tell legend). But he abandoned the work after the first few chapters had been written.

George Michael Moser (1704-83) of Schaffhausen, goldsmith and

1768

Caernarvon Castle: *painted by Samuel Hieronymus Grimm during his tour of Wales.*

enameller, became one of the founders of the Royal Academy, and Keeper in 1769. He had been drawing master to George III during the latter's boyhood. His daughter, Mary Moser, a distinguished flower painter and much patronised by Queen Charlotte, consort of George III, also became a Royal Academician, a distinction as a woman she shared for many years only with her compatriot Angelica Kauffmann (see 1766).

The Swiss artist Samuel Hieronymus Grimm (1734-94), of Burgdorf (Berne), arrived in England. He exhibited at the Royal Academy's first exhibition in 1769. In 1776 Gilbert White, the naturalist, employed him to make drawings for the book he was then contemplating (but which did not appear until some years later), the famous *Natural History of Selborne*. The following year Grimm was commissioned by H.P. Wyndham to tour Wales for an enlarged edition of his *Gentleman's Tour through Monmouthshire and Wales*.

1769　John Louis Delolme (1741-1806), a Genevan, attracted by the political system in the United Kingdom, came to live in England. He wrote several works on the constitution, his major work being *The Constitution of England* (1775). This was later translated into several languages. An English edition was published in Basel by J. J. Tourneisen in 1792.

Death in Richmond of Francis Grose, a jeweller of Berne, who had come to England early in his life, and who, *inter alia,* had prepared the coronation crown of George III. His son became a well-known antiquarian and topographer (see 1789).

Louis Pictet, a son of Jacques (see 1763), entered the service of the British East India Company. He occupied several important offices in the Company and became known as Pictet of Bengal.

The Irish painter Edmund Garvey exhibited a watercolour of a *Waterfall in the Alps* at the Royal Academy, one of the first Alpine paintings to be shown in Britain.

The English painter William Pars (1742-82) was engaged by the second Lord Palmerston to accompany him on a tour of Switzerland to 'make drawings of the most remarkable views and antiquities'. With four companions they visited most of the country. Horace-Bénédict de Saussure (see 1779) joined them for part of their tour. When Pars exhibited some of his Swiss drawings in London the following year they played a significant part in making the untravelled Englishman aware of the high Alps.

1770

Frederick Hervey (1730-1803), Bishop of Derry and fourth Earl of Bristol, made one of his several visits to Switzerland. The Bishop travelled widely on the Continent, and his reputation for good living and for staying at the best hotel explains the number of hotels named 'Bristol', both in Switzerland and elsewhere in Europe.

Pierre Jean Grosley, lawyer and man of letters, published his *Londres* in Lausanne, a book which remained the best guide to London in French for thirty or forty years afterwards. Grosely praised the English inns but was not too keen on the food. He drew attention to the smog, which he said might soon prevent the Londoner from seeing the sun at all. Because of the smoke, London swarmed with cleaners' shops. He recommended viewing the monuments in Westminster Abbey where he had 'seen the vulgar weep at the sight of Shakespeare's beautiful statue'. Hell, he reported, was the favourite topic of the Methodist preachers in London.

Dr Charles Burney (1726-1814), the musician and author, made a tour of France, Switzerland and Italy. He produced an account of his travels the following year, parts of which were subsequently incorporated into his *History of Music*. During his stay in Geneva, Burney met the Swiss composer Gaspard Fritz (1716-82).

Fanny Burney, Madame d'Arblay: by her cousin Edward Francis Burney, c. 1784.

Dr Burney was enchanted with Geneva, He wrote: 'The weather is fine and I am in love with this place . . . Cleanliness, industry and plenty appear wherever one turns one's eyes'; but noted:

> The great number of your foreign strangers sent here from the Protestant countries of Europe, but chiefly English, is much diminished and it now becomes the fashion to prefer Lausanne.

1771 Charles Stanhope (see 1764), still in Geneva, became a Commandeur of the ancient Swiss company of the Exercice de l'Arquebuse. Stanhope also founded an English-language debating club there.

Jacques Pictet's son Isaac (see 1763) went to London and secured from the king the post of British Chargé d'Affaires in Geneva. His public attitude soon brought him into trouble with the Genevan authorities, and his mission ended in 1774. He became known by the local wags as the 'Déchargé d'Affaires d'Angleterre'. However, the official reason given for revoking his commission was that 'it was by no means consistent with the king's dignity to keep a minister in Geneva, or at any other state, who is not admitted to every honour and privilege to which he is justly entitled'.

1772

Another Genevan, Jean André de Luc, distinguished geologist and meteorologist, who had perfected the barometer, came to settle in England. He became a Fellow of the Royal Society, and was appointed reader to Queen Charlotte. He was in almost daily attendance on the queen at Windsor for many years. (No doubt his reading was mainly in German and French, for Fanny Burney claimed in her diary – perhaps with some exaggeration – that having heard him read her own novel, *Cecilia*, to the queen, he could 'hardly speak four words of English'.)

1773

The eighth Duke of Hamilton arrived in Geneva on the Grand Tour, accompanied by his tutor, John Moore. They found a large British colony studying or living there, among them Lord Mahon, Lord Clive, Lord Grenville, Lord St Leger and the diplomatist Sir Richard Neville.

It was another period of excellent relations between Britain and Geneva. John Moore wrote: 'Our countryman were never on so friendly and sociable a footing with the citizens of this republic as at present.'

James Watt, son of the scientist who developed the steam engine, came to Geneva 'to perfect his French without risk to his Protestantism'.

c. 1773

An Englishman, Charles Greville, was the first person to negotiate the Gotthard pass in a wheeled carriage. It cost him eighteen louis to employ a gang of men to help the vehicle over the most difficult parts.

1775

Thomas Blaikie, the botanist, made a long tour of Switzerland, visiting fellow botanists. He narrowly escaped being murdered near Champéry.

The Swiss watch- and clockmaker, Jaquet-Droz of Le Locle, established a branch in London, managed first by Henri-Louis Jaquet-Droz (1752-91), son of the founder.

On the outbreak of the War of American Independence a group of Swiss Protestant officers offered their services to Lord North in London. Their intermediary was a Scottish visitor to Switzerland, James Francis Erskine.

1776 Johann Wäber (1750-93), known as John Webber, was the son of Abraham Wäber, a Swiss sculptor working in London. He accompanied Captain Cook on his last voyage to the South Seas as official artist to the expedition.

The young Swiss historian Johannes von Müller (1752-1809) went on a trip to Schinznach with several of his British friends living in Geneva, including Lord Clive (1754-1839), son of Clive of India.

Archdeacon William Coxe (1747-1828) made his first visit to Switzerland, described later in his *Sketches of the Natural, Civil and Political State of Swisserland* (1779), the celebrated Swiss physiognomist and writer. Coxe was enchanted by the vivacity of Lavater's conversation, 'the amenity of his manners and the singularity and animation of his style'. Coxe also called on the poet Salomon Gessner (see 1758), whom he found 'plain in his manners, open, affable and obliging in his address, and of singular modesty'.

Of his visit to Schaffhausen, Coxe commented:

Here every person has the mien of content and satisfaction. The cleanliness of the homes and of the people is peculiarly striking, and I can trace in all their manners, behaviour, and dress, some strong outlines that distinguish this happy people from neighbouring nations. Perhaps it may be prejudice, but I am the more pleased because their first appearance reminds me of my own countryman, and I could almost think for a moment that I am in England.

Of the Swiss as a whole, William Coxe wrote:

Perhaps there is not a similar instance in ancient or modern history of a warlike people divided into little independent republics . . . having continued during so long a period in an almost uninterrupted state of tranquillity.

He attributed this to the diligent training of their respective militia.

Joseph Planta (1744-1827) of Castegna (Grisons), son of a Swiss pastor who came to settle in London (see 1752), was made Secretary of the Royal Society. He had been secretary to the British Minister in Brussels for several years up to 1773. He later became Principal Librarian at the British Museum (from 1799 until his death). At the turn of the century he published his *History of the Helvetic Confederation*, dedicated to George III.

The British artist John Robert Cozens (1752-97) visited Switzerland to paint. He spent his time mainly in the Bernese Oberland and around Lake Lucerne. The sketches he made were later studied and copied by William Turner and may have helped to arouse Turner's great interest in Swiss scenery (see 1802). Cozens went from Switzerland to Italy where, in Rome, he came into contact with the Swiss artist Louis Ducros. He was probably influenced by Ducros's new method of watercolour and gouache painting (see 1810).

An early *Map of Switzerland* was published in English in London by William Faden, geographer to the king. It was based on the great map of the Confederation by Johann Jakob Scheuchzer.

Mr Sherlock, librarian to the Earl of Bristol (see 1770), fulfilled a lifelong ambition and called on Voltaire at Ferney. His excitement at the interview made him forget much of what passed between them; but, when he got back to his inn, he recalled that the old man had 'said some shocking things against Moses and Shakespeare'.

1778 Lieutenant-General Sir Frederick Haldimand (1718-91), a Swiss from Yverdon, became Governor and Commander-in-Chief, Canada. Haldimand spent much of his career in the British army, becoming a colonel in 1758, when he distinguished himself at the British attack on Ticonderoga. (He was the uncle of Anthony Francis Haldimand – see 1765.)

Major-General Augustin Prevost (1723-86), a Swiss who had served under General Wolfe in Canada, was made Governor of East Florida.

1779 One of the most brilliant of Swiss artists, Heinrich Füssli (1741-1825), came to London to settle. Known as Henry Fuseli, he was a familiar figure, and lecturer, at the Royal Academy, becoming Keeper in 1804. He was a friend of John Constable, and was particularly known as the friend and mentor of William Blake. He found many of his subjects in the works of Pope, Milton and Shakespeare.

Other Swiss artists who travelled to London in that year included Johann Heinrich Hurter (1734-99), a miniaturist from Schaffhausen, who came at the invitation of Lord Dartrey. He stayed for five years.

Publication of Horace-Bénédict de Saussure's *Voyages dans les Alpes*, the pioneer of mountaineering literature. It was sufficiently well known half a century later for John Ruskin (1819-1900) to choose it as a present for his fifteenth birthday.

1780   Major John André, son of a Genevan merchant settled in London, became Adjutant-General in General Clinton's forces in the American War. He was captured by the colonists while on a secret mission to try to obtain the surrender of West Point. George Washington had him shot as a spy.

1781   Among the Swiss who were in the household of George III and Queen Charlotte at about this time were Miss Planta, the sister of Joseph Planta (see 1776), who was in charge of the princesses, and General Jacob Budé of Geneva, who was military tutor to the princes. The Revd Charles de la Guiffardière was a teacher of French. Paul Mallet was a history tutor. Miss Julie de Montmollin of Neuchâtel dealt with some of the queen's correspondence and also taught French and needlework to the princesses. She was a cousin of General Charles Daniel de Meuron whose regiment was later in the British service in India (see 1795).

Benjamin Vulliamy (*fl.* 1775-1829), famous son of Justin Vulliamy, was clockmaker to George III. (See also 1854.)

Francis Towne (1740-1816), watercolourist, went to Switzerland to paint, together with his friend John 'Warwick' Smith (1749-1831). John 'Warwick' Smith made a return visit in 1786.

c. 1781   The Swiss composer and harpist Joseph Élouis (b. 1752) came to Britain and spent several years in the service of Prince Edward. Amongst the compositions he wrote during his stay were a 'Welsh Air' for harp and a selection of Scots songs with pianoforte accompaniment.

1782   When political strife broke out in Geneva between the aristrocratic and democratic parties, it seemed that the French would intervene. A young Genevan, Francis d'Ivernois, through the intermediary of James and Isaac Pictet (see 1763 and 1772), asked Lord Mount Stuart, the British Ambassador at Turin, and Charles James Fox in London to intervene with the Continental powers in favour of preserving Genevan independence. But the British government preferred to remain neutral.

Later, after a revolution in Geneva, 1,000 fugitive Genevans, through the initiative of d'Ivernois, sought asylum in Ireland, and were granted permission to settle there by Earl Temple, George III's Lord Lieutenant. The Irish Parliament helped with money and bought them land near Waterford. An advance party of settlers began building a new town, which they called New Geneva. However, numerous difficulties arose; there were disputes between the prospective immigrants and in 1784 the scheme was finally abandoned. (See also 1794.)

The Duke of Gloucester, brother of George III, came to Switzerland to live for several years. After an argument with an innkeeper at Stäfa on Lake Zurich, where the Duke considered he had been grossly overcharged (and the innkeeper had thrown down and stamped upon the smaller amount of money offered), the British Chargé d'Affaires in Berne, Louis Beat Braun, had to write to the 'Magnifiques et Puissants Seigneurs, les Seigneurs Bourgmaîtres, et Conseil de la République de Zurich', complaining of the treatment His Royal Highness had received. He asked them to adjudicate and pay the innkeeper on the Duke's behalf whatever they considered fair.

Death of Leonhard Euler (b. 1707), the distinguished Swiss scientist and mathematician. One of his discoveries was the achromatic lens which made possible the construction of the first modern telescopes. Euler had his lens made in England by the optician John Dollond (1706-61). (John Dollond later patented his own version of the achromatic lens.) 1783

Edward Gibbon (see 1755) came back to settle in Lausanne while he worked on his masterpiece, *The Decline and Fall of the Roman Empire*. In his *Memoirs* he later wrote:

Lausanne is peopled by a numerous gentry whose companionable idleness is seldom disturbed by the pursuits of avarice or ambition . . . I shall add as a misfortune rather than a merit that the situation and beauty of the Pays de

Vaud, the long habits of the English ... and the fashion of viewing the mountains and glaciers have opened us on all sides to the incursions of foreigners.

Sir George Beaumont, Bt. (1753-1827), watercolourist, came to paint in Switzerland.

The Swiss writer and journalist Jacques Mallet du Pan (1749-1800) was forced to seek refuge from the French in England, where he soon launched his periodical review, the *Mercure Britannique*. The first number was devoted to the destruction of Swiss liberty by the French. Mallet's son, John Lewis, became a British subject, and he and numerous members of the Mallet family in Britain subsequently served in high offices of state.

c. 1784 Another Swiss in the service of the British East India Company, Antoine Louis Polier (see 1751), became Commandant of Calcutta. On his return to Switzerland he gave an important collection of oriental works to the British Museum.

1784 Sir Thomas Constable (1762-1823), topographer and botanist, travelled on foot through Switzerland pursuing his botanical studies.

1785 The English writer William Beckford fled to Switzerland to escape a scandal and settled in La Tour-de-Peilz, near Vevey. While there he put the final touches to his novel *Vathek*. He later bought Gibbon's library at Lausanne (see 1787).

Among other English visitors, Sir Richard Colt Hoare (1758-1838) was sketching and painting in Switzerland. Hoare was a great patron of the Swiss painter Louis Ducros (see 1810).

Swiss weavers in Appenzell and Zurich began to buy English cotton thread.

1786 The writer Benjamin Constant (1767-1830), who had earlier spent several years at Edinburgh University (and liked to surprise people by speaking English with a Scottish accent), returned to Britain from Switzerland. He wrote of his journey back to Scotland:

The beauty of the countryside ... the magnificence of the roads, the cleanliness of the inns, the impression of happiness, good sense and orderliness which the natives convey – all these are a source of continuous enjoyment for any observant traveller.

Edward Gibbon completed *The Decline and Fall of the Roman Empire* in Lausanne. He later wrote:

1787

> It was on the day, or rather the night of the 27th of June, between the hours of eleven and twelve that I wrote the last lines of the last page in a summerhouse in my garden. After laying down my pen, I took several turns in a covered walk of acacias . . . I will not dissemble the first emotions of joy on the recovery of my freedom and perhaps the establishment of my fame . . . But . . . a sober melancholy was spread over my mind by the idea that I had taken my everlasting leave of an old and agreeable companion. . .

Gibbon returned to England in 1793). (Some thirty years later Lord Byron sent a sprig of acacia from Gibbon's former garden in Lausanne to his publisher in London, John Murray, with the words 'The garden and summer house where he composed are neglected, and the last utterly decayed; but they still . . . seem perfectly aware of his memory.'

The Genevans Charles Pictet de Rochemont (b.1755), his brother Marc-Auguste Pictet (1752-1825) and friend Prévost-Dassier made a visit to England. A compatriot of theirs living in England, Jean de Luc (see 1773), took them to the Royal Society and the Houses of Parliament; another, Jacquet-Droz (see 1775), gave them an itinerary for a provincial tour; and they made the acquaintance of the philosopher Adam Smith.

Some forty to fifty Englishmen were imprisoned in Geneva following a scuffle with the guard while trying to get out of the city after the gates were shut. They were released after a week by the intercession of the Duke of Gloucester (see 1782), then in Geneva; but they were banished for life from the Republic.

An English climber, Colonel Mark Beaufoy, ascended Mont Blanc soon after it had been climbed by Horace-Bénédict de Saussure.

Charles James Fox (1749-1806), William Pitt's most formidable Parliamentary opponent, visited Bienne, Berne and Lausanne. William Windham, who met Fox at Berne, wrote:

1788

> Among the observations Fox was making, one was the extreme mildness of the government of this canton, and at the same time the great power lodged in the aristocracy, and again the sample given here lately of the greater prudence sometimes of people in the administration of public money than in that of their own.

Daniel Beat Christin of Payerne, a Swiss who had been some twenty years in the service of the British East India Company, came to England, changing his name to Christie. His descendant John Christie (1882-1962) was the founder of the Glyndbourne Opera.

An English landscape painter visiting Switzerland at this time was George Augustus Wallis (1760-1847).

1789 A Swiss, Jakob Heinrich Meister (1744-1826), made the first of two visits to England. In his *Letters Written during a Residence in England* he remarked upon the propensity of the English for talking about the weather. 'A sky in which no cloud is to be seen takes the place of all other news.' Of the smog in London at that time, he wrote: 'To breathe the fresh air of the morning is a sort of luxury which is not to be enjoyed in this noble large city.' As regards the inns:

> I did not approve of the large table-cloths which covered the dining tables, and were used to wipe your mouths and fingers in the place of napkins: I did not like the linen the better for smelling so strongly of smoke; nor do I relish that heady strong porter . . . nor the rich muddy port. However, I make no doubt but I shall soon be reconciled to English cookery; for I know nothing more nourishing, or that I could eat more frequently without being cloyed, than a good beefsteak with potatoes, plum-pudding, and good Cheshire cheese.

Alexandre Marcet (1770-1822) from Geneva came to study at Edinburgh University. He became a doctor at Guy's Hospital in London and later founded the Medico-Surgical Society.

Among books published in Basel that year were English editions of Edward Gibbon's *Decline and Fall of the Roman Empire* and of David Hume's *History of England*.

Archdeacon William Coxe (see 1776) published his second book on Switzerland, *Travels in Switzerland*. He had visited Switzerland in 1776, 1779, 1785 and 1786. Of his stay in the Grisons, he mentioned that the only investment that canton had was £4,000, all in English stock.

Prince Edward, Duke of Kent and father of Queen Victoria, sent to complete his education for three years in Geneva, paid a visit to the Jura where, in Bienne, he called on Sir Philip de Loutherbourg, the distinguished artist.[15] The same year he joined the Masonic Lodge of Geneva (twenty years later he became Grand Master of the Masonic Order in England). Prince Edward had many friends in Switzerland, including Count Pictet, Dr Louis Odier and Jean de Tournes-Rilliet.

Francis Grose, son of Francis Grose of Berne (see 1769) and author of *The Antiquities of England and Wales* (1787), toured Scotland to study the antiquities there. He met Robert Burns, and is the 'chield amang you takin' notes' of Burns's poem 'On the Late Captain Grose's Peregrinations through Switzerland'.

While the revolutionary fervour in France at this time was greeted with satisfaction by many Swiss intellectuals, it caused much concern among the established governments of the Swiss cantons. Berne and Geneva addressed a plea for support to the British Foreign Secretary, the Marquess of Carmarthen (later to become the Duke of Leeds). Professor Hugh Cleghorn, Professor of Political Economy at St Andrew's University, who had just visited both France and Switzerland, strongly recommended that Britain should seek an alliance with Switzerland. When the new British minister, Lord Robert Fitzgerald, was appointed to Berne, his instructions were to try to gain the cantons to the European coalition that Britain had organised.

1790

A Swiss portraitist and miniaturist, Louis Arlaud (1751-1829), who had studied at Liotard's school in Geneva (see 1753), came to England where he worked for twelve years.

William Wordsworth (1770-1850) made his first extended visit to Switzerland. It produced an outstanding Alpine poem – his description of the Simplon Pass:

> The immeasurable height
> Of woods decaying, never to be decayed,
> The stationary blasts of waterfalls,
> And in the narrow rent at every turn
> Winds thwarting winds, bewildered and forlorn,
> The torrents shooting from the clear blue sky,
> . . .
> The unfettered clouds and region of the Heavens
> Torment and peace, the darkness and the light . . .

Members of the Genevan banking families of Lullin and Pictet were established in London around this period. Other Swiss bankers in the City included Jacques Achard and Pierre Chauvet. Yet another, Antoine de Roveray, came to London from Geneva as a refugee to escape the guillotine. He joined several of his family who were already established there.

The amount invested by the canton of Berne in British government stocks now amounted to £440,960, estimated to be the equivalent of Sw.fr. 18m. at that date. Zurich also retained investments in British securities (see 1754), including £50,500 in Bank of England stock.

1791 Prince Augustus, Duke of Sussex and brother of Prince Edward (see 1789), came to Lausanne, where he lived in the house that had been the regicide Ludlow's (see 1660).

The Genevan Marc-Auguste Pictet (see 1787) was made a Fellow of the Royal Society in London.

Joshua Wilkinson, an Englishman on a tour of Switzerland, was arrested at Rolle (between Geneva and Lausanne) on suspicion of being the escaped Louis XVI.

1792 The Genevan historian Jean Charles Léonard de Sismondi (1773-1842) and his family took refuge in England for two years when revolution broke out in his native city. (See also 1803.)

Another arrival in London from Geneva that year was Jacob Schweppe (1740-1821), inventor of carbonated water. He had been selling his products there since 1783. Among his British customers in Geneva had been the Duke of Gloucester (see 1787) and the Duke of Kent (see 1789). Schweppe came to England with a letter of introduction from Marc-Auguste Pictet (see 1787). He soon set up in business in Drury Lane, and was the first to use the term 'soda water'. Some years later, after successfully launching J. Schweppe & Co.'s products in England, he revealed 'The Whole Art, Mystery and Process of Making and Composing Artificial Mineral Waters' to three partners from Jersey, and returned to Switzerland. His company later merged with Cadbury's to become Cadbury-Schweppes plc. (See also 1816.)[16]

Yet another Genevan, François-Pierre Pictet (1728-98), arrived in England and became a teacher of French in Reading. The following year William Pitt charged him with a diplomatic mission to Berne.

On his second visit to England, Jakob Heinrich Meister (see 1789) commented on the sympathy still shown by many people for the French Revolution. 'They talk, read and dream of nothing but revolution here as well as in France.' Of the graffiti, he wrote:

... those horrible words, 'no King, no Parliament' have more than once been found written in large characters on the walls at street corners, and have been read without any great degree of indignation and astonishment.

Events in France (see 1790) and the massacre of Louis XVI's Swiss bodyguard in the Tuileries had made the governments of the Swiss cantons even more concerned. When France declared war on England, the British Minister in Berne, Lord Robert Fitzgerald, asked the cantons to supply troops in return for British subsidies. However, the Swiss still had an alliance with France. While the Bernese, and particularly the statesman Niklaus de Steiger, were in favour of joining the European crusade against the Revolution, those led by Zurich in favour of maintaining Swiss neutrality prevailed. Nevertheless the allied powers of Sardinia, Spain and England were allowed to recruit some troops in 1793 and 1795.

1793

When the British Minister published a pamphlet appealing directly to the people of Switzerland to break with France, he met with opposition in prominent quarters, but was allowed to carry on his political activities unmolested.

Sir Peter Francis Bourgeois (1756-1811), artist son of a Swiss watchmaker working in London, was made a member of the Royal Academy. In his youth he had been encouraged by both Reynolds and Gainsborough. In 1794 he was appointed landscape painter to George III. On his death, he bequeathed 370 pictures (including 22 of his own paintings) to Dulwich College. They formed the basis of the Dulwich Gallery's collection.

Mme de Staël (1766-1817), whose father Jacques Necker was Genevan Minister to France and then French Minister of Finance, was in England again. She had come as a child with her parents in 1776. When she was seventeen her mother conceived a match for her with 'one of the most eligible Protestant bachelors in Europe', William Pitt the younger. This came to nothing, but Mme de Staël, in 1794, dedicated to Pitt her *Réflexions sur la paix*. She came once more to England in 1813.

In the early stages of the war with France, William Wickham, another British envoy, was sent to Switzerland on a special mission. Wickham, who had studied at Geneva University and who had a Swiss wife, was charged by the Foreign Secretary, Lord Grenville, with organising a secret service against France. At first his task was concealed from the Foreign Office itself; but after the recall of the British Minister in Berne, Lord Robert Fitzgerald, Wickham was appointed in his place. On special instructions from the Prime Minister, William

1794

Pitt, Wickham worked hand in hand with royalist agencies in Paris and Lyons, established arms depots along the Jura frontier and introduced counter-revolutionary material into France. When the French Directory eventually demanded his expulsion from Switzerland, Wickham left on his own accord in 1797 to save the Swiss government embarrassment.[17] (Switzerland was invaded by the French in 1798.)

Since there was no official Swiss representation in London, the Swiss Church there (see 1762) was authorised to furnish passports to Swiss wishing to travel from Britain to France, or through France to Switzerland.

Following the fall of the aristocratic government in Geneva, Francis d'Ivernois (see 1782) came to England to settle. He took an active part in current affairs and was knighted by George III.

Johann-Jakob Iselin (1768-1828) of Basel arrived in England and set up as a merchant. He founded the English branch of that family.

Albrecht von Haller's great poem *Die Alpen* (see 1739) was published in London in an English translation by Mrs Howorth.

1795 The British government had officially begun the recruitment of Swiss troops. These included complete regiments commanded by de Watteville of Berne, de Salis of the Grisons and Louis de Rolle of Solothurn. Between them they served in Malta, Corsica, Elba, Portugal, Gibraltar, Sicily, Corfu, Egypt and Canada, amongst other places.

Another Swiss regiment enrolled in the British service that year was the regiment de Meuron from Neuchâtel. Under its colonel-proprietor, Charles Daniel de Meuron (1738-1806), the regiment had been in the service of the Dutch East India Company; but following secret negotiations in Neuchâtel between de Meuron and an old Scottish friend of his, Hugh Cleghorn (see 1790), it was transferred to the service of George III. (See also 1797 and 1799.)[18]

A Swiss banker, Jacques-Louis Pourtalès (1722-1814) from Neuchâtel, made his eighty-fifth visit to England. He had been coming to London, where he had extensive business interests, since his bank, Pourtalès & Cie, had been established in 1753. In the second

OPPOSITE *Lieutenant-General Charles-Daniel de Meuron.*

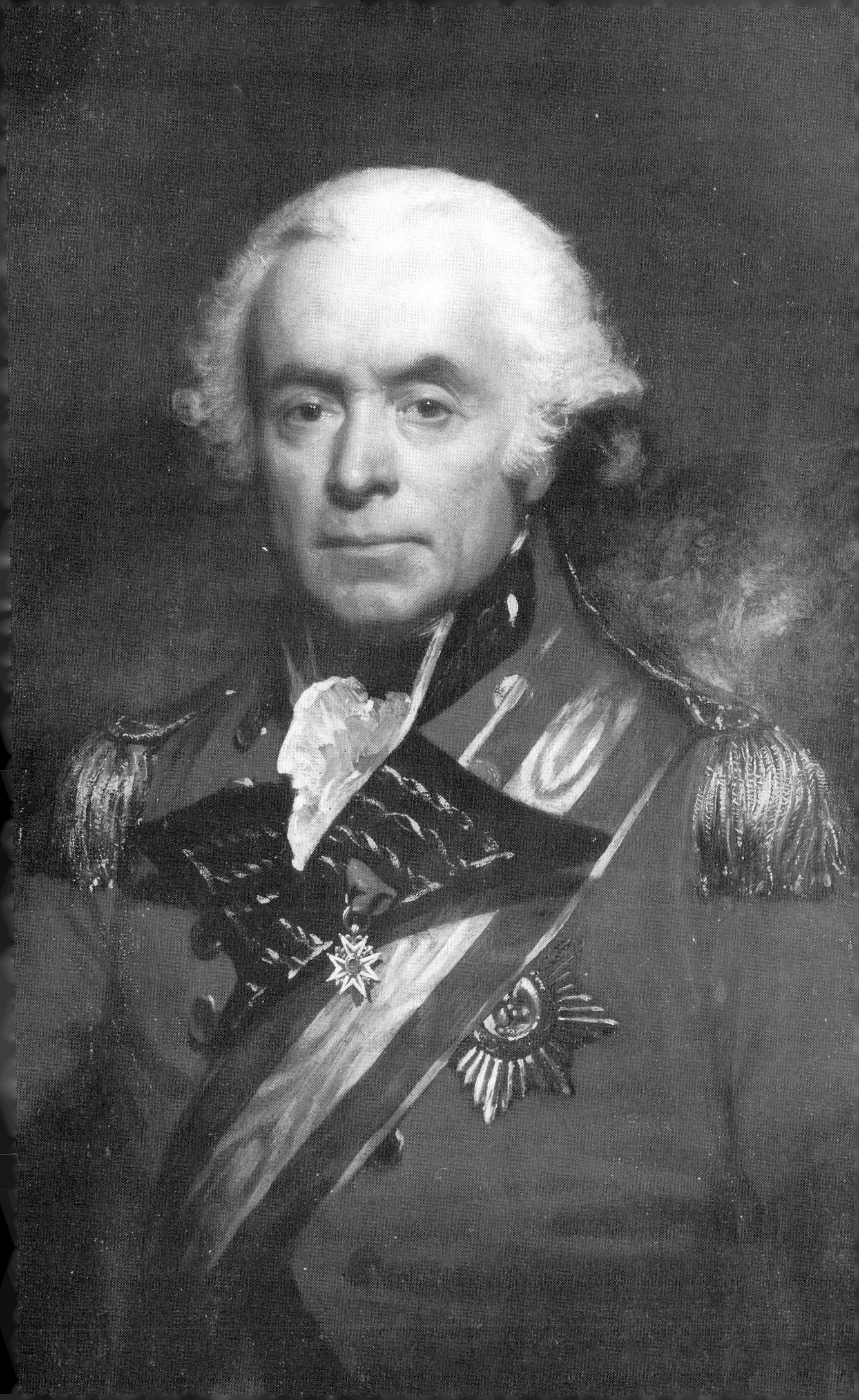

half of the eighteenth century Pourtalès & Cie became perhaps the leading international banking and commercial house in Switzerland. It was said of Jacques-Louis that it was he rather than the King of Prussia who really ruled Neuchâtel.

1796 Two young Swiss painters, Jean-Jacques Chalon (1778-1854) and his brother, Alfred-Edouard (d. 1860), came to live in London. Both became Royal Academicians. Jean specialised in landscapes; Alfred-Eduard was later appointed portrait painter in watercolour to Queen Victoria. Both became friends of John Constable.

Marc-Auguste Pictet (see 1791), and his brother Pictet de Rochemont, founded in Geneva the *Bibliothèque Britannique,* a review of British thought and affairs. The first issue was devoted to a detailed review of British agriculture.

Thomas Wedgwood (1771-1805), a son of Josiah Wedgwood, and the 'first photographer', visited Lucerne, the Rigi, the Brünig pass and Meiringen. He was acccompanied by Sir John Leslie. Another visitor that year was Thomas Smith (*fl.* 1780-1822) on a painting expedition.

The last volumes appeared of Horace-Bénédict de Saussure's *Voyages dans les Alpes,* which inspired many English to go and see them for themselves.

1797 The young John Constable (1776-1837), later to become the father of modern British landscape painting, read Salomon Gessner's *Essay on Landscape,* of which a new edition had just been published in English translation. Gessner, known mainly as a Swiss poet (see 1758), was also a painter. Later in life Constable read all of Gessner's works.

Salomon Gessner's artist son Hans-Konrad (1764-1826), who painted horse and genre themes, had arrived in England the year before (to stay eight years). It is possible that he drew Constable's attention to his father's work.

Major-General Pierre Frédéric de Meuron (1747-1812), brother of the colonel-proprietor of the Swiss regiment that helped to take Seringapatam (see 1799), became military commander of Ceylon. He was also appointed head of a committee to investigate the state of the revenues in Ceylon.

Soon after William Wickham left Berne (see 1794), diplomatic relations between Britain and Switzerland were suspended until 1814.

On their invasion of Switzerland, the French confiscated the wealth of the richer cantons, one particularly rich catch being the Bernese treasury, with the equivalent of some Sw.fr. 10m in securities, almost entirely British. The money was immediately sent to Toulon to finance Napoleon's forthcoming Egyptian campaign. The French flagship, *L'Orient,* in which the Swiss money was carried, was sunk by Nelson in Aboukir Bay during the Battle of the Nile.

1798

At the Battle of Aboukir Bay, one of Nelson's frigates, *Fly,* was commanded by a Swiss, Thomas Duval of Geneva. (Several members of the Duval family in England became successive directors of the French hospital in London.)

In view of the French occupation of Switzerland the British government sequestrated the property in England of the Swiss cantons. Later (in 1805), the Court of Chancery refused a plea for the release of blocked Swiss funds, including £85,449 in 3% Consols, £158,383 in South Sea stock and about £34,000 in Bank of England stock. The moneys were finally released (see 1816) after the Congress of Vienna.

The British educationalists Richard Edgeworth (1744-1819) and his daughter Maria Edgeworth (1767-1849) published their classic *Practical Education,* which, in essence, was a modification of the educational theories expressed in Rousseau's *Émile* of 1762. Richard Edgeworth had brought up his son on Rousseau's system, and in 1771 had travelled to Paris to show him to Rousseau as an illustration of *Émile*.

The Edgeworths' book was translated into French by Marc-Auguste Pictet and published in Geneva in his *Bibliothèque Britannique*. Pictet also published Maria Edgeworth's *Moral Tales* of 1801.

Neuchâtel, which at that time had been able to remain neutral, became a rallying point for refugees from France and for escaped prisoners. These formed a nucleus for anti-French agitation and activities organised by Colonel Pillichody, who operated with British subsidies.

1799

Meanwhile, an appeal to Britain from the Grisons for support in their efforts to maintain their independence was sent to London through John de Salis, a member of the English branch of this distinguished

Grisons family (see 1709). The Grisons asked for a loan of £8,000, which was readily granted, and de Salis undertook to take the first £3,000 personally to Chur, with authority to draw the remainder whenever circumstances required.

In June, when the prospects were bright for a speedy deliverance of Switzerland from the French, William Wickham was sent by Lord Grenville, British Foreign Secretary, on a special confidential mission to the Swiss cantons and the allied armies fighting the French in Europe. He was to hold himself ready to take over the British legation again as soon as there was a government willing to receive and recognise him. The British plan was for the Bernese statesman de Steiger (see 1793) to be invited to form a new provisional government as soon as the French had left.

Wickham was joined in Switzerland by Lieutenant-Colonel Robert Craufurd who had first been attached to the headquarters of the Austrian army with authority, and finance, to maintain a Swiss army which was in the course of being raised to assist in 'the delivery of Switzerland'. Craufurd was instructed to seek confidential advice should he need it from de Steiger. By July, Craufurd reported from Zurich that an army of 3,700 had been assembled, under the command of the Swiss General Bachmann. It included regiments commanded by Colonels Roverea and de Salis and contingents from Zurich, Glarus, Schwyz, Uri, Einsiedeln and the Valais.

Further British officers were sent to Zurich: Major-General Lord Mulgrave, Lieutenant-Colonel John Ramsay and Lieutenant-Colonel H. Clinton. (Clinton later joined Wickham at General Suvorov's headquarters in Italy, and both were with Suvorov during his epic Alpine crossings, just after he had defeated a division of the French army near the Gotthard pass.) Another British officer, Lieutenant-Colonel Williams, equipped a small flotilla on the Bodensee and on Lake Zurich. But the French victory at the second Battle of Zurich in September 1799, over General Korsakov's Russian forces, put an end for the time being to British influence in Switzerland. In a bitter report to London on the disaster at Zurich, Colonel Craufurd wrote: 'Korsakov has neither the knowledge nor decision to . . . fight this campaign . . . We might soon expect to see the Swiss consider the French as not the worst of their enemies.'

Meanwhile, in the British operations in India, the Swiss regiment from Neuchâtel under Charles Daniel de Meuron played a distinguished part in the capture of Seringapatam when the French-backed Tipoo Sultan was killed. The year before, de Meuron's regiment had become His Majesty's Regiment de Meuron, all ranks enjoying the same privileges as British troops. De Meuron himself retained proprietorship of the regiment and received £20,000 and a pension of £3,000 a year for ten years. In 1802 he was promoted to lieutenant-general in the British Army list. However, his claims for large arrears of pay and expenses for his regiment, incurred in the service of both the Dutch and the British governments, were never met in full (see also 1813).

That year in London, Georgiana Cavendish, Duchess of Devonshire, and a daughter of Frederick Hervey, Earl of Bristol (see 1770), published her *Memorandums of the Face of the Country in Switzerland*, an early English travel book. Of the attractions of Swiss valleys she wrote:

It is difficult to express the cheerful calm and tranquillity the mind feels in travelling through them.[Of Lake Thun] There was a fine morning scene. Nature seemed not yet fully awake; a dripping cloud, that had lingered after all the rest had departed with the night, drooped between the folds of the mountain at that part where there is a small creek. Upon the whole it appeared to be more beautiful than I had before thought it.

View of Basel, c. 1747, by Emanuel Büchell.

The Nineteenth Century

The Napoleonic Wars – Stratford Canning in Switzerland – painters and writers – Swiss unrest, and civil war – the Neuchâtel question solved – railways – Swiss and British engineers – a trade agreement – the Victorians in Switzerland – and in the mountains – the beginnings of tourism – and of winter sports – tariff problems – and strains over the Boer War.

1800 Despite an early prohibition on exports of textile machinery from Britain, the first textile mills in Switzerland were equipped with British machinery. But as the Napoleonic Wars continued, supplies became even more difficult to obtain. Several Swiss entrepreneurs imported used British machinery from France, and then began to make copies. Another Swiss, Marc-Antoine Conod, called Pellis, had been working in Bordeaux where he had met two English engineers, John Heywood and James Longworth. In 1800 Pellis set up a factory in St Gallen (General Sozietät der Englischen Baumwollspinnerei) with machines made largely by Heywood and Longworth.

1801 Pellis succeeded in getting the Swiss government to issue patents for his key machines, including those made by Heywood and Longworth.

Three other Swiss companies, located in Winterthur, engaged an English engineer named Travies and set up a spinning factory at Wulflingen near Winterthur, with machines made by Travies.

Isaac Morier (1750-1817), a Swiss merchant living in Smyrna, joined the British Levant company and took British nationality. He became British Consul-General in Constantinople. Several of his descendants joined the British Diplomatic Service. His son David Richard (1784-1877) was made British Minister at Berne in 1832. Another, William Morier (1790-1864), became a vice-admiral.

1802 The Peace of Amiens in March brought a cessation of hostilities between France and Britain; and the flow of visitors between Britain and Switzerland was able to begin again. For several years, however, there had been political confusion in Switzerland and a series of coups d'état in Berne, some with French collusion, some without. In October, after the Federalists under Aloys Reding had regained power in Berne, Napoleon ordered General Ney into Switzerland with 30,000 men to crush all opposition. The Swiss federal government sent appeals for help to Britain, Austria and Prussia. Only Britain responded. The British government protested strongly to Napoleon and, fearing that as a result war with France might again be inevitable, called up more troops and sent secret instructions to Lord Wellesley in India to delay evacuation of French territories that were to have been returned to the French under the Peace of Amiens. They also let the French know that the planned British evacuation of Malta would depend on the result of negotiations relating to Switzerland.

The British government also sent an agent to Zurich with funds, to see what opposition to Napoleon could be encouraged. By the time the agent arrived, however, Ney's army was in complete control and there was nothing to be done.

Following the Peace of Amiens, the English artist J.M.W. Turner (1775-1851) made the first of six extended visits to paint in Switzerland. His tour took him via Geneva, the Great St Bernard, Martigny, Vevey, Saanen, Thun, Lauterbrunnen, Grindelwald, Reichenbach, Lucerne, St Gotthard, Zurich, Schaffhausen and Basel.

In the reverse direction, the Genevan Jacques-Laurent Agasse (1766-1849) came to England and made a reputation as an animal painter, becoming known as 'the Swiss Stubbs'. His style much appealed to the British taste and he exhibited for many years at the Royal Academy.

Amongst other Swiss artists that Agasse found working in England at that time was François Ferrière (1752-1829), who had several patrons amongst the court of George III.

Another Swiss, Heinrich Webber, a brother of Johann (see 1776), became an artist at the Wedgwood pottery factory at Stoke-on-Trent and produced some of their best-known pieces of that time.

The Revd Robert Malthus (1766-1834), whose theories on population had aroused considerable controversy on the Continent, took advantage of the peace in Europe to visit Switzerland. For some years he had been in correspondence with Voltaire, and also with his own father's friend Jean-Jacques Rousseau (see 1767). On Rousseau's death Malthus became his literary executor.

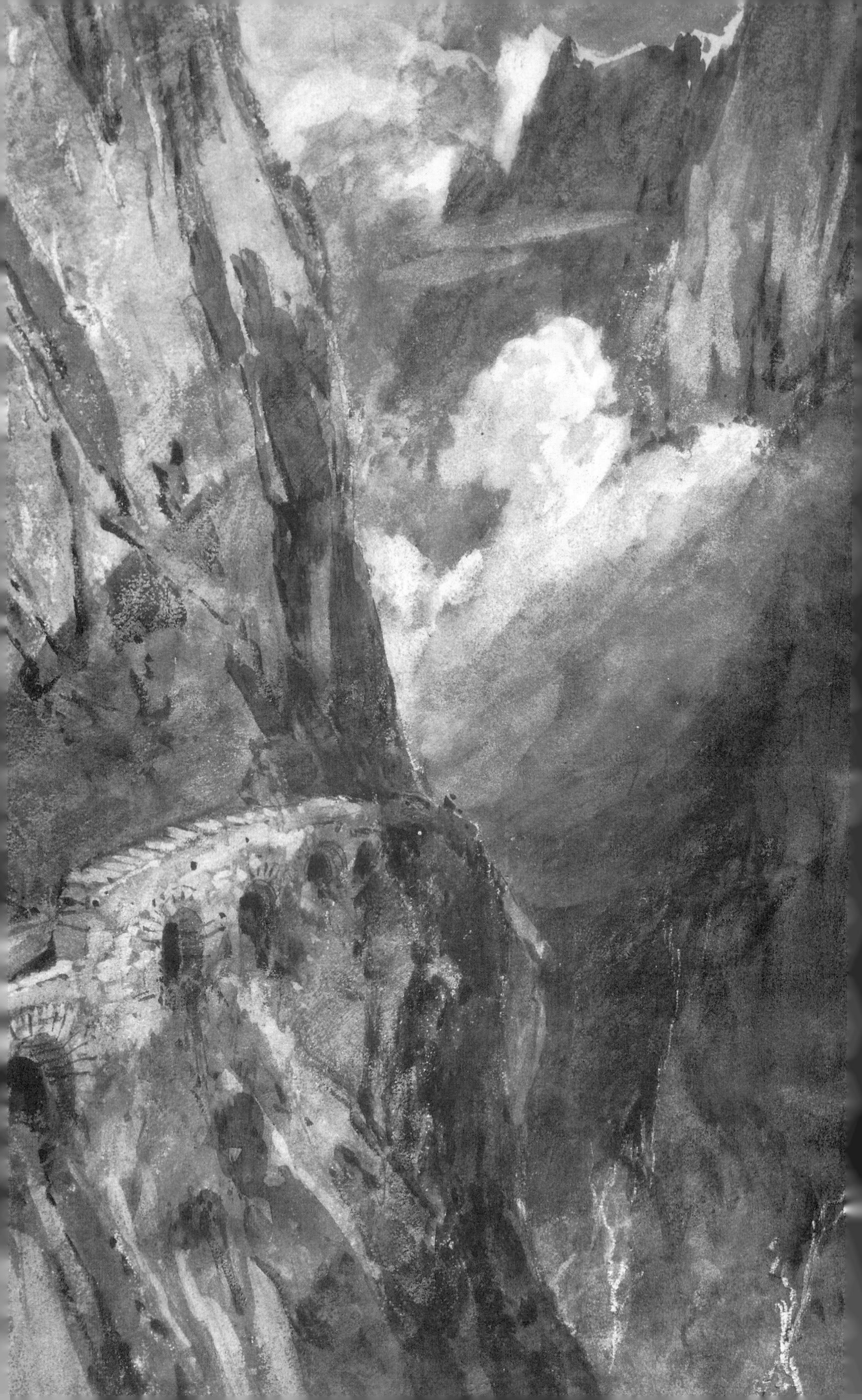

That year also, Madame Tussaud (1760-1850) came to London to establish her waxworks museum. Born Marie Grossholz, 6f Bernese parents, she was taken to Paris as a child by her uncle and taught how to mould wax. There she modelled the main personalities of the French Revolution, including Marat and Robespierre, and the heads of many victims of the guillotine. She chose the brief period of peace after Amiens to escape to England.

In January, when Napoleon received a consultative assembly of Swiss delegates in Paris, he told them that if the British government made further representations to him about Switzerland he would annex the country outright. In February the Swiss delegates accepted Napoleon's Act of Mediation, which imposed a new constitution upon Switzerland, replacing the Helvetic Republic by a Swiss Confederation of nineteen cantons. The Act of Mediation brought Switzerland completely under the control of Napoleon, and the British Cabinet deemed further intervention useless.

1803

In Geneva, despite the French occupation, Marc-Auguste Pictet and his brother Pictet de Rochemont continued to publish the *Bibliothèque Britannique,* the literary review which they had founded in 1796. The *Bibliothèque Britannique* now began to attain an important international reputation. Its influence on the Continent during the French occupation is shown by the remark of Talleyrand who, at the Congress of Vienna, observed to Pictet de Rochement: 'Your review had behind it such a weight of public opinion that its suppression would have amounted to a coup d'état.' (The name of the review was changed in 1816 to the *Bibliothèque Universelle*.)

Jean de Sismondi had now returned from London. As well as being a historian, Sismondi was an important economist. In 1803 he published *La richesse commerciale* which reflects the influence of Adam Smith, of whom Sismondi was for most of his life a faithful disciple.

Among other British artists who came to Switzerland to paint that year was Thomas Sutherland (1744-1828), a watercolourist and a pupil of J.R. Cozens.

Johann Conrad Fischer (1773-1854), an eminent Swiss metallurgist and founder of the Schaffhausen steel and engineering works later to

1804

OPPOSITE The Devil's Bridge, St Gotthard Pass, *by J.M.W. Turner.*

Hans Caspar Escher (1775-1859).

become Georg Fischer, had been making many trips to Britain to study industrial developments. On one such trip he had met Benjamin Huntsman, the inventor of cast steel. In 1804 Fischer succeeded in making in his workshop at Mühletal steel of superior quality that had up to then remained an English speciality. Fischer's father had earlier been to Britain and had worked at the foundry in Woolwich Arsenal which at that time was run by his compatriot from Schaffhausen, Andrew Schalch – see 1716.

John Owen (1766-1822) founded the British and Foreign Bible Society. It soon had branches in Basel, Berne, Chur, Geneva, Lausanne, St Gallen, Schaffhausen and Zurich. Owen went to visit them in 1818.

Death of Thomas Pitt, second Baron Camelford, a colourful Cornishman who had spent a year of his youth on the Isle of St Pierre in the Lake of Bienne, where Rousseau had at one time been in exile. Camelford directed that he should be buried there and deposited £1,000 with a Bernese banker to buy him a plot of land. Because of the war in Europe his instructions could not be carried out immediately and his remains were temporarily deposited in London in St Anne's Church, Soho.

Another Swiss entrepreneur, Hans Caspar Escher (1775-1859), who had also been to England to inform himself of new industrial developments, joined with financier Salomon Wyss to found the textile machinery company of Escher-Wyss, later to become part of Sulzer Brothers. Escher-Wyss made, at first, machines adapted from British models. (See also 1824.)

1805

The Swiss educational reformer Johann Heinrich Pestalozzi (1746-1827) opened his famous institute in Yverdon. His teaching methods were far in advance of his time. The British educationalist Richard Edgeworth, who devised the term 'secondary schools' and whose works, written with his daughter Maria (see 1798), marked a significant advance in English educational thinking, came to Yverdon to see Pestalozzi and study his methods. Other British visitors included the social reformer Robert Owen (1771-1858), who *inter alia* established the infant school in England, Robert Southey (1774-1843) and Henry Brougham, the future Lord Chancellor. Later there was a sizeable colony of English students at the Institute (see also 1817 and 1819).

Louis Albert Necker of Geneva (1786-1861) came to Edinburgh as a young geology student to continue his studies at the university there. In 1808 he completed the earliest known geological map of the whole of Scotland, which he presented to the newly formed Geological Society of London. After returning to Geneva to occupy the chair of geology at the Academy, he later returned to Scotland and settled in Portree, Isle of Skye, where he died.

1806

When Napoleon decreed his economic blockade of England, he accused Basel of being one of the main centres from which English goods were smuggled into France. Large quantities of merchandise belonging to Basel merchants were seized by the French, and their owners sent to prison.

The Scottish poet James Montgomery (1771-1854) published *The*

Wanderer of Switzerland, a work treating of the French aggression against Switzerland. It touched the British public and quickly went through three editions.

1807 William Wordsworth (1770-1859), originally a supporter of the French Revolution but now disillusioned, published his sonnet 'Thoughts of a Briton on the Subjugation of Switzerland'. Coleridge (1772-1834) had also had a change of heart. In his 'France, an Ode', he had written:

> Forgive me, Freedom! O forgive those dreams!
> I hear thy voice, I hear thy loud lament,
> From bleak Helvetia's icy caverns sent . . .

The Swiss painter Michel-Vincent Brandoin (b. 1733) died in Morges (Vaud). He was called 'l'Anglais', after he had studied watercolour in England with Paul Sandby.

1808 Meuron's regiment (see 1799) was now stationed with the British forces in Malta. Towards the end of the Napoleonic Wars, when the Ionian Isles came under British control, one of its former officers, Charles-Philippe de Bosset (1773-1845) from Neuchâtel, was made Governor of Cephalonia.

1809 Franz-Friedrich de Watteville (1753-1838), colonel-proprietor of another Swiss regiment in the British service, was made a major-general on the British List. He later gave command of his regiment to his nephew (see 1813) and retired to Berne.

William Haldimand, a son of Anthony Francis (see 1765), after first entering his father's bank of A.F. Haldimand & Sons, became a member of the Court of the Bank of England at the age of twenty-five, and remained on the Court for thirteen years. In 1820 he was elected MP for Ipswich, but retired to Lausanne in 1828. He was a friend of Dickens (see also 1846).

1810 In trying to tighten his Continental System against Britain, Napoleon imposed a complete blockade of Switzerland, claiming that Switzerland was at the heart of English smuggling in Europe. The Valais was annexed and Napoleon's troops occupied the Ticino and the Alpine passes. Though the blockade was relaxed a little afterwards, the Swiss economy was severely damaged, causing bankruptcies in the cotton trade and mass unemployment.

Death in Lausanne of the Swiss painter Abraham-Louis-Rudolphe Ducros (b. 1748) who, with other artists of the Swiss School born in the mid-1700s, influenced a generation of British artists with their technique of making watercolour compete in strength and depth of tone with oil. Ducros had many English patrons, including Lord Breadalbane, the Earl of Bristol, Sir William Hamilton (the British Ambassador in Naples), Sir John Acton and, particularly, Sir Richard Colt Hoare.

General Sir George Prevost (1767-1816), elder son of Augustin Prevost (see 1778), became Governor of British North America. He was made a baronet. Thirty years in the British Army in America, he had been Governor of St Lucia in 1798. After a controversial engagement against the American colonists on Lake Champlain where he was accused of not pursuing the attack strongly enough, he was recalled in 1814 to London. 1811

George Prevost's brother, Thomas Jacques (1771-1855), became an admiral in the British Navy.

Johann Ludwig Burckhardt (1784-1817) of Basel, one of the notable explorers and orientalists of the time, was employed by the African Association in England to lead several expeditions. His perfect knowledge of Arabic enabled him to visit Mecca disguised as a pilgrim; and amongst other exploits he rediscovered Petra in 1812. He died in 1817 in Cairo when organising an expedition to go up the Nile. He left some 800 oriental manuscripts to Cambridge University (where he had earlier studied). 1812

De Meuron's Swiss regiment (see 1799), now commanded by François-Henry de Meuron, was sent to Canada. They took part in the campaign on Lake Champlain when the British forces were commanded by the Swiss general Sir George Prevost (see 1811); and they covered the retreat of Prevost's army at Plattsburg. 1813

Another Swiss regiment sent to Canada at this time was one commanded by Abraham-Ludwig-Karl de Watteville (1776-1830). De Watteville was made a major-general and became military governor of Quebec.

Alexandre Louis Prevost, who had come to London from Geneva in 1807, set up the financial and merchanting business of A.L. Prevost.

In 1818 this became Morris, Prevost & Co., at the time with Alexandre's brother Jean Louis Prevost as a partner. In 1828 Morris, Prevost & Co. took over the firm of A.F. Haldimand & Sons (see 1809).

1814 The British Foreign Secretary, Lord Castlereagh, sent Stratford Canning as British Envoy Extraordinary and Minister Plenipotentiary to the Swiss republic. A cousin of George Canning and later created Viscount Stratford de Redcliffe, he was Britain's most celebrated nineteenth-century diplomat. He went first to Zurich where the special Swiss Diet had been convened. His instructions were to encourage the reorganisation of a federal Switzerland after the Napoleonic Wars. When, after several months, the Diet had drawn up a draft of a federal structure to put to the Powers at the Congress of Vienna, Canning transferred his activities towards encouraging the various cantons to support the plan.

Later that year Castlereagh passed through Switzerland on his way to the Congress of Vienna. He appointed Stratford Canning to the British delegation to the Congress, and Canning became British member and chairman of the drafting committee of the commission formed to draw up the frontiers and constitution of the Swiss Confederation. Working closely with Pictet de Rochement of Geneva and the other Swiss representatives, Canning also contributed largely towards the successful negotiation of the guarantee of permanent neutrality which the Swiss obtained at Vienna (see 1815).

In view of the importance for Switzerland of Britain's part in the international negotiations leading to the agreement at Vienna, the Republic of Berne sent an envoy extraordinary, C.F. de Freudenreich, on a limited mission to London for one year. When de Freudenreich left London, his counsellor of legation, A.E. de Haller, was appointed in his place as envoy of both Zurich and Berne, again for one year.

Percy Bysshe Shelley (1792-1822) eloped with Mary Godwin and, together with Mary's stepsister Claire Clairmont, travelled to Switzerland, arriving at Lucerne and Brunnen via Neuchâtel. They walked most of the way across France. After several weeks they ran into financial difficulties and returned to England. (See also 1816-17.)

Sir William Hooker (1785-1865), creator and director of Kew Gardens, spent several months on a botanical tour in Switzerland making contact with Swiss botanists.

Stratford Canning, Viscount Stratford de Redcliffe, in 1853: portrait by C. Richmond.

Sir Humphry Davy: after Sir Thomas Lawrence.

Sir Humphry Davy (1778-1829), the distinguished chemist, who had been travelling on the Continent during the war by special permission of Napoleon, arrived in Geneva accompanied by Michael Faraday. He was the guest of the De la Rive family. (See also 1829.)

Among other British visitors to Switzerland that year were Caroline, Princess of Wales, who made an extended tour, and Sir Arthur Wellesley, later to become the Duke of Wellington.

After the fall of Napoleon, the Swiss Church in London appealed to the Foreign Office for the release of Swiss prisoners of war who had been fighting on the French side and who were now in British hands. The Foreign Office replied the same day promising their immediate release.

In Vienna on 20 March, by a 'Declaration of the Eight Powers on the affairs of the Swiss Confederation', the allies gave Switzerland a guarantee of perpetual neutrality. On 27 May Switzerland acceded to the treaty, which then came into force immediately. However, in March Napoleon had escaped from Elba and landed in France, and the allies hastily put together a new alliance on 25 March. The Swiss cantons split on whether to support the allies or Bonaparte, with Vaud and Aargau Bonapartist, Basel and Geneva neutral and Berne for the allies. Under the combined efforts of Stratford Canning and other allied representatives, the Swiss Diet agreed to join the alliance.

1815

The Swiss signed a Treaty of Accesssion to the alliance on 20 May, agreeing to keep in readiness for the defence of the Swiss frontier the force of 30,000 men plus reserves that they had already under arms. By the time ratifications had been exchanged on 27 June, Waterloo had been won.

After the Swiss signed the treaty, a British liaison officer, Colonel William Leake, was attached to the Swiss army then assembled near the French frontier. A topographer in private life, Leake sent home reports on the line of the frontier and on the state of readiness of the Swiss troops. When the news of Waterloo was received in Switzerland, Leake reported to Lord Castlereagh that it had been announced by the C.-in-C. Swiss Army, General Bachmann, with a salute of 100 guns. 'This incident I have thought worthy of being mentioned to your Lordship', he wrote, 'considering the existing neutrality of this country and that it has taken place without any instruction from the Diet.'

On 20 November a new act, recognising and guaranteeing the permanent neutrality of Switzerland and the inviolability of her territory, was signed by the Allied Powers in Paris.

Johann Conrad Fischer (see 1804) came again to Britain to study industrial developments. He wrote in his diary

... although it is twenty years since I was last in London ... I cannot honestly say that things have improved in this time. The great difference is that now everything is fantastically expensive. Many prices, even those of daily necessities, are from 20% to 50% higher . . . presumably the result of the war economy . . . The gold coins which were formerly in general circulation have been replaced by paper money.

The war left Switzerland in even worse economic shape. Moreover, there was a severe famine in 1816/7; in the canton of St Gallen, for example, some 4% of the population died of hunger.

Swiss bankers in Basel took part in a £30m British loan marketed in Continental Europe by Baring Bros. during the Hundred Days. Part of the proceeds were to be remitted as a subsidy to those countries subscribing who had been allies of Britain.

A Swiss, Jean Louis Moilliet (1770-1845), who had come to England from Geneva at the age of sixteen, joined Robert Coale's Bank in Birmingham. He soon came to dominate the partnership, and the name was changed in 1840 to J.L. Moilliet & Sons (see also 1865).

1816 Stratford Canning, now in Berne, drew up a memorandum which he submitted to the confederate commission for military reform, advocating the setting up of a standing military authority, a Swiss military academy and a national war fund. Canning's initiative gave impetus to the Swiss federal army reform of 1817. He left Switzerland in 1819. (His wife had died in Lausanne.)

The investments which the cantons of Berne and Zurich had had in London at the time of the French occupation of Switzerland, and which had been blocked by the British Government in 1798, were finally released. With accumulated interest, the amounts handed over (in gold) were £416,978 to Berne and £53,500 to Zurich.

Shelley, together with Mary Godwin and her stepsister Claire Clairmont, came again to Switzerland and met in Geneva Lord Byron (1788-1824) and his companion-physician John Polidori. Together they settled down for the summer at Cologny. Byron lived at the Villa Diodati, and Shelley in a house nearby. Their stay was productive in several ways. Shelley wrote 'Hymn to Intellectual Beauty' and Mary Godwin wrote *Frankenstein*, a classic Gothic novel. Byron composed the third canto of *Childe Harold* in Cologny. He also wrote *Manfred* while on a visit to Wengernalp, and *The Prisoner of Chillon* at Ouchy. And Claire Clairmont had a child by Byron. The Genevan bankers Hentsch & Cie received and forwarded Byron's letters.

The Villa Diodati, Cologny, where Byron stayed in 1816: by Alexandre Calame.

The Shelley and Byron ménages caused considerable scandal in Geneva. The proprietor of the Hôtel d'Angleterre, where they had all stayed before moving to Cologny, found that you could see directly across the lake from the hotel to the Villa Diodati. He erected a telescope trained on Byron's window and allowed his guests to view for a small charge.

For many Englishmen 1816 was the first time since the ending of hostilities that they could travel freely again on the Continent. A contributor to the *Bibliothèque Universelle* (see 1803), commenting on Byron's arrival in Geneva, went on: 'It is raining English at present.' A month later he wrote: 'The English continue to arrive by the dozen; it is a real invasion.' And the *Gazette de Lausanne* commented: 'The number of Englishmen who are now living at, or passing through Geneva is immense.'

The former British Minister to Switzerland, William Wickham (see 1794 and 1799), was back in Geneva. He was taken to visit Jacob Schweppe (see 1792) at Sacconex by Charles de Constant, one of Schweppe's neighbours. De Constant noted in his diary that Jacob Schweppe had brought back 'une jolie fortune' from England.

Gilbert Elliot, second Earl of Minto (1789-1854), was also in Geneva with his family. The whole party, with servants, numbered thirty-one, and they took up residence in the village of Chambésy. Minto returned to Switzerland during the Sonderbund crisis on a mission for Lord Palmerston (see 1847).

Other visitors to Switzerland that year included the Revd John Swete (1752-1821), topographer and watercolourist, and Major James Cockburn (1799-1847), who was probably the first to use a camera lucida in making his drawings and sketches in the Alps (see also 1820).

In Canada, when the de Meuron and Watteville regiments (see 1813) were de-commissioned, a group of officers and men joined an expedition to protect the Red River colony which Lord Selkirk was establishing for the Hudson Bay Company. They included Protais d'Odet d'Orsonnens of Fribourg, Frédéric Matthey of Neuchâtel and Frédéric de Graffenried of Berne.

Benjamin Constant (see 1786) was again in Britain. He gave readings from the manuscript of his (largely autobiographical) novel *Adolphe* in London, where the first edition (in the original French) was published that June.

The Swiss inventor Johann Georg Bodmer (1786-1864) came to England to try to sell his breech-loading rifled cannon to the British government. He failed; but he wrote in his dairy: 'I have everywhere found the English people prepossessed in favour of the Swiss.'

1817 Returned to Switzerland, Bodmer made the first attempt to put a steam-powered ship on a Swiss lake. He ordered the engine from Britain but, when he ran into financial difficulties, the manufacturers stopped delivery and the craft lay for some years derelict beside the Lake of Constance.

Among other Swiss industrialists who were in England at that time was J.J. Römer, a textile manufacturer who stayed six years.

Shelley published in London his *History of a Six Weeks' Tour*, describing his visit to Switzerland in 1814. He wrote:

On passing the French barrier, a surprising difference may be observed between the opposite nations that inhabit either side. Swiss cottages are much cleaner and neater, and the inhabitants exhibit the same constraint.

After leaving Neuchâtel, Shelley described his first view of the Alps from the Jura in words which were uncannily echoed by Hilaire Belloc nearly a century later (see 1902):

> ... range after range of black mountains ... and, towering above every feature of the scene, the snowy Alps. They ... reach so high in the heavens that they look like those accumulated clouds of dazzling white that arrange themselves on the horizon during summer. Their immensity staggers the imagination ... it requires an effort of the understanding to believe that they indeed form part of the earth.

Among British visitors to Switzerland that year was Robert Southey (1774-1843), who wrote: 'Were I to settle anywhere on the Continent, Switzerland should be the country, and probably Lausanne the place.'

Alexandre Louis Prevost (see 1813) became the first Swiss commercial agent and consul in London.

J.P. Greaves (1777-1842), future secretary of the London Infant School Society, came to Yverdon to study Pestalozzi's educational methods. He stayed with Pestalozzi for seven years.

Byron's dramatic poem *Manfred* was published. The description in it of Wengen, the Scheidegg and the Grindelwald glaciers helped to spread the fame of the Bernese Oberland throughout Britain and the rest of Europe.

Manfred on the Jungfrau: *watercolour by John Martin.*

218 *Chronology 1817 – 1819*

The third canto of Byron's *Childe Harold* had already appeared, with its unforgettable description of evening on Lake Geneva:

> It is the hush of the night, and all between
> Thy margin and the mountains, dusk, yet clear,
> Mellow'd and mingling, yet distinctly seen,
> Save darken'd Jura, whose capt heights appear
> Precipitously steep; and drawing near,
> There breathes a living fragrance from the shore,
> Of flowers yet fresh with childhood; on the ear
> Drops the light drip of the suspended oar,
> Of chirps the grasshopper one good-night carol more.

1818   After the Napoleonic Wars the Catholic monasteries were confirmed in their ancient rights and possessions, and the Jesuits became active. Partly in reaction to this, a vigorous evangelical movement arose in French-speaking Switzerland, in the promotion of which two Scotsmen, Robert Haldane (1764-1842) and Henry Drummond (1786-1860), played a conspicuous part. For two or three years Haldane, first in Geneva and then in Montauban, attracted round him many Swiss students for daily instruction. Drummond continued Haldane's work with zeal in Geneva. But when his activities were declared unwelcome by the Council of State, he withdrew across the frontier into French territory to carry on for some time from there.

Lord Brougham (see 1805) presented to Parliament a report on the institute at Hofwyl, near Berne, of another famous Swiss educationalist, Emmanuel von Fellenberg (1771-1844). Fellenberg's renown was not as high as that of his compatriot Pestalozzi, but he gained many English admirers, including Queen Victoria, with whom he maintained a correspondence, Robert Owen, Francis Duppa, Lady Shelley and Elizabeth Fry. Several schools in England were founded on Fellenberg's principles.

A predecessor of Thomas Cook, a Mr B. Emery of Charing Cross in London, began to organise tours to Switzerland by stage-coach. Each tour was limited to six persons, each of whom were allowed to take up to 1 cwt (50 kgs) of luggage. They had two days in Paris and fourteen days in Switzerland, stopping each night at a different place. The all-inclusive price was twenty guineas. The tours were continued for several years.

1819   A new guide book, *The Traveller's Guide through Switzerland* by

Daniel Wall, appeared in London. It contained some reassuring advice for its readers about boating on Lake Lucerne: 'Notwithstanding all that has been said to the contrary, the navigation is not dangerous, provided the steersman and rowers be not intoxicated.'

The English artist John Jackson (1778-1831), accompanying Sir Francis Chantry, visited Switzerland to paint.

Another visitor from England, Dr Charles Mayo (1792-1846), joined Pestalozzi's establishment at Yverdon, bringing with him some English pupils. After a stay of three years, he returned home resolved to devote his life to the introduction of Pestalozzi's principles into England. He founded Cheam School.

Publication in London of Samuel Miller Waring's *The Traveller's Fireside* – 'a series of papers on Switzerland, the Alps, etc, containing information and descriptions, original and selected from French and Swiss authors'.

Dorothy Wordworth's *'Journal of a Tour on the Continent,* was published in 1820. In it she described an encounter in an inn near Schwyz: 1820

A tall grave middle-aged woman entered . . . She ate her supper alone, being served with ceremony like a person of distinction . . . She seemed to be an adequate representative of the Helvetian matronage . . . and some of our party were reminded by her appearance and deportment of the complaint made by the French that, while stationed in this country, they could neither procure a mistress nor a spy.

Captain Edward Williams, RN (1793-1822) came to settle in Geneva. He moved to Pisa the next year to be near the Shelleys. He became Shelley's adviser and partner in the building of the *Don Juan,* the boat in which they were both drowned.

James Pattison Cockburn, later a major-general, published in London a volume of his drawings, *Swiss Scenery*. This book, together with his *Views to Illustrate the Simplon Route,* and *Views to Illustrate the Mont Cenis Route,* both published in 1822, supplied the Swiss scenes for illustrated editions, annuals and other works published in London for many years afterwards.

An English visitor to Switzerland that year, R. Bakewell, who later wrote a book on his *Travels in the Tarentaise . . . and in Switzerland and Auvergne in the Years 1820, 1821 and 1822* commented on the Bernese: 1821

The Château de Chillon, from Swiss Scenery from the Drawings of Major James Cockburn, *1820.*

The doctrine of the divine right of kings and governors, as maintained by the Tories in the time of the Stuarts, is still cherished here in its full extent. But however defective the theory of the Bernese government may be, the practice is excellent; for though the people are very imperfectly represented in the councils, the real power resides in them. They are all armed, and what may be thought strange in modern times, they pay no taxes, the public revenues arising from lands and forests being sufficient to defray the expenses of the state.

Bakewell also gave a description of conditions in Geneva, 'as this city is at present much resorted to by English families as a place of temporary residence and many young English are sent there for education.' He said:

A stranger who enters Geneva can scarcely fail to be prepossessed in favour of the people by their appearance . . . the men are sober and orderly, the females are plainly and neatly dressed . . . Perhaps there is no town in Europe of equal size, where the females are generally so well informed . . . The affection of children to parents is more durable, and I should say stronger, with the Genevans than with the English.

Sir John Herschel FRS (1792-1871) made the first recorded ascent of the Breithorn by way of Théodule (near Zermatt).

In a Parliamentary debate in London on the need for economies in the Diplomatic Service, the Opposition questioned in particular the need for a British minister in Switzerland. Castlereagh (now Lord Londonderry), in a spirited defence, pointed out the

1822

extraordinary respect of each nation for the other, besides the propriety of having a mission there on dry political and military considerations. It was at all times important for the preservation of the neutrality of the Cantons of Switzerland and for their protection from all the great powers of Europe . . . that we should have a minister there.

Moreover

. . . it formed no small proof of the importance attached to the preservation of that neutrality, and by that means the tranquillity of Europe, that persons of the highest consideration and importance had been appointed to that mission.

Heinrich Clias (1782-1854), son of a Swiss who had gone to America and changed his name from Käslin, came to England with the recommendation of the British minister in Berne. Clias had introduced gymnastics into the Swiss army. He was appointed Director of Physical Training at the military and naval training colleges at Sandhurst, Woolwich, Chelsea and Greenwich, and introduced his system into the British forces.

The tariff reforms which William Huskisson introduced in Britain that year had a beneficial effect on Anglo-Swiss trade. Among other things, imports of silk goods, hitherto prohibited, were allowed in at the maximum rate of duty – which was reduced to 30%; and exports of raw wool were now permitted. The repeal of the law which forbade the emigration of artisans abroad enabled Britons to travel freely to Switzerland to help in the build-up of some branches of Swiss industry.

1823

Rodolphe Töpffer (1799-1845), the son of Adam (see 1825), opened a school in Geneva which attracted many English students. He was also the author and illustrator of a number of humorous books. His illustrations owed a good deal to the style of the English caricaturists of that time.

John Philip Kemble (1757-1823), actor and London theatre manager, and brother of Mrs Siddons, died in Lausanne where he had been living for some years.

1824 Hans Caspar Escher (see 1805) was in England again. He brought his son Albert to be trained as an engineer in the Manchester workshops of Fairbairn and Lillie, from whom he also ordered two water-wheels for his Neumühle in Zurich. The Neumühle was by then one of the biggest cotton factories on the Continent. (Years later Albert Escher was taken ill on another visit to England and died in Manchester.)

Johann Georg Bodmer (see 1816) was also there again. A few years later he set up in business in Manchester and Bolton where he lived for nearly twenty years. Amongst his designs or inventions were steam valves, textile machinery, a screw-cutting machine, a travelling crane, rolling mills and engines. In 1845 he supplied locomotives to the Brighton and South East Railway.

Charles Joseph Latrobe (1801-75), a future Lieutenant-Governor of Victoria, Australia, made the first of several visits to Switzerland over the next three years. His book *The Alpenstock – or Sketches of Swiss Scenery and Manners,* published in 1829, was one of the best appreciated books on Switzerland of its time.

An English traveller across the Lake of Geneva, John Smith, found that the captain of the vessel in which he was travelling (the *Guillaume Tell*) was an Englishman named Errington. His engineer was English too, and so was the engine of the boat.

1825 William Hazlitt (1778-1830) made a literary pilgrimage to the scenes in Switzerland depicted by Rousseau in *La nouvelle Héloïse.*

Richard Parkes Bonington (1802-28), English watercolourist, visited Switzerland to paint. Two of his best known works of that period are *La Place du Molard, Geneva* (the final version of which he did in oils) and *The Bridge of St Maurice, Valais.*

At about this time the Swiss painter Adam-Wolfgang Töpffer (1766-1847) was on a visit to England.

'Switzerland in Miniature', a model of Switzerland by Professor M.A. Gaudin of Geneva, was exhibited at the Egyptian Hall in Piccadilly. Originally shown in Geneva, it was brought to London on the recommendation of several hundred English travellers who had seen it there.

The British poet Felicia Dorothea Hemans (1793-1835) published her *Tales of Many Lands,* which included several Swiss pieces, including

The Léman off Ouchy (Lausanne), where it was built in 1826 by British workers.

'The Switzer's Wife', 'On the Battle of Morgarten', and 'On a Flower from the Field of Grutli'.

Following the *Guillaume Tell* (see 1824), which had been built at Geneva, a new lake steamer, the *Léman* (280 tons) was built on the lake at Ouchy by British workers. It was equipped with two engines supplied by Boulton, Watt & Co. of Birmingham.

1826

The Swiss bankers in London A.F. Haldiman & Sons (see 1809) financed and organised the building of Belgrave Square for the Earl of Grosvenor.

Benjamin Disraeli, the future British Prime Minister, visited Geneva. A highlight of his visit was being rowed each night across the lake by Byron's old boatman and learning about Byron's activities when he stayed there in 1816.

The British climber Frank Walker succeeded in crossing the Oberaarjoch, while John Carne made what was probably the earliest winter visit by an Englishman to Lauterbrunnen.

Joseph Planta (1787-1847), born at the British Museum where his father was Principal Librarian (see 1776), became one of the Joint Secretaries of the Treasury. He had entered the Foreign Office at the age of fifteen. He was private secretary to Canning in 1807 and to Castlereagh in 1813. He accompanied Castlereagh to the Congress of Vienna. He later became MP for Hastings.

1827

On the death of the British Prime Minister, George Canning, the whole of the third page of the *Neue Zürcher Zeitung* was edged with black. His consistent opposition, when Foreign Secretary, to the policies of the Holy Alliance in Europe had earned the approval of many in Switzerland.

1828 The first Swiss consul (Emmanuel Zwilchenbart) was appointed in Liverpool.

By this time the first hotel in Montreux had been built. The proprietor conceived the idea when, a year or two previously, he had put up in his own house a party of English tourists who had been stranded there for the night after visiting the castle of Chillon.

1829 Thomas Arnold (1795-1842), the great headmaster of Rugby School, was visiting Switzerland and Northern Italy. Of Lugano he wrote:

> Immediately below our eyes, plunged into a depth of chestnut forest, varied as usual with meadows and villages, and beyond, embosomed amidst the nearer mountains, lay the lake of Lugano . . . If anyone wishes for the perfection of earthly beauty, he should see such a sunset as we saw this evening from the mountain above S. Maria del Monte.

Death of Pierre Etienne Dumont (b. 1759), Swiss scholar and disciple of Jeremy Bentham, the British reformer and economist, whose system he expounded in *Traité de la legislation* (1802) and other books. During the French Revolutionary wars, Dumont, who was then living in England, managed to publish parts of Bentham's *Manual of Political Economy* in the Geneva *Bibliothèque Britannique* (see 1803). For many years Dumont edited Bentham's writings and acted as a kind of official interpreter between Bentham and the world at large.

Sir Humphry Davy (b. 1778), British chemist and man of letters, died in Geneva, where he received a public funeral.

Sir Walter Scott (1771-1832) published his 'Swiss novel', *Anne of Geierstein*, with its references to the Battle of Buttisholz and to those of Grandson and Morat (Murten). Scott had earlier translated the *Sempacherlied* of Halbsuter.

1830 The English painter Francis Danby (1793-1861) left England to avoid his creditors and went to live near Geneva. He found some enthusiastic buyers for his paintings. He returned to England in 1841.

Another English artist who was painting in Switzerland in 1830 was Thomas Hartley Cromek (1809-73).

An English church was established at Pully, near Lausanne.

In London a new road from Marylebone to Finchley was being built. To help pay for its cost a toll system was introduced. One of the first buildings by the Junction Road toll-gate was a tavern designed as a Swiss chalet, a fashionable style in England at the time. This district of London soon became known as Swiss Cottage.

John Elliotson, a professor of medicine at New University College, London, took up the ideas of a Swiss doctor, Franz Anton Mesmer (1734-1815). At a time when anaesthesia was unknown, he discovered that wounds gave no pain in the state of trance that Mesmer had experimented with (which put the word 'mesmerism' into the vocabulary). However, when Elliotson tried to introduce his methods into University College Hospital, the reaction of the Governors was so violent that he had to resign his chair (see also 1843). 1831

The British writer William Liddiard (1773-1841) published his *Three Months' Tour in Switzerland and France*. Liddiard also wrote several poems about Switzerland, among them 'The Legend of Einsidlin', 'Stanzas upon Visiting Chillon', and 'To the Chapel of William Tell'. 1832

After the revolution in Paris in 1830, Switzerland was shaken by a succession of political and military struggles. In several cantons they threatened the patrician and other privileged groups who had regained power after 1815, and were aimed at introducing legislative and religious reforms. There were also other reasons for discontent – the problems caused by the structure of the Swiss state itself. The loose confederation of sovereign cantons that had been re-established in 1815 had left Switzerland with a multiplicity of currencies, customs duties, postal rates, weights and measures and even methods of military training.

When proposals were made by the Radicals in several Swiss cantons to amend the Constitution so as to unify these services and to create a limited central executive, the Austrian Chancellor, Metternich, reacted strongly against them. He recommended the Great Powers to take steps in common to prevent any changes. Prussia and Russia supported Austria in plans to intervene, but Britain, with France, thought that the Swiss proposals were reasonable, and Metternich had to give way. However, disagreement among the Swiss themselves caused the question of reform to be shelved (see 1844, 1847 and 1848).

An additional factor contributing to the discontent in Switzerland was industrial unrest. The early effects of mechanisation which had induced Luddism in England were reflected in Switzerland too. In 1832, in an anti-machine riot, weavers burnt down the Uster factory near Zurich.

1833   The scientist William Henry Fox Talbot (1800-77), on holiday in Switzerland and Italy, sketched the Swiss mountains from Lake Como with the help of a 'camera lucida'. He had previously tried with a 'camera obscura'. Dissatisfied with his attempts, he began to consider if it was possible to make permanent the pictures which his lens threw onto the paper, and developed the first real camera.

A visitor from England, L. Agassiz, who described himself as 'late of the Royal Navy and Royal Marines', and who used Mr Emery's travel service to Switzerland (see 1818), commented in his *A Journey to Switzerland*: 'The practice of sending young Englishmen to Geneva and the Pays de Vaud to acquire French is much on the increase: and it is a very good one.'

1834   The anti-machine agitation in Switzerland having to some extent subsided, Caspar Honegger (1804-83), one of the new Swiss entrepreneurs, started a mechanical cotton weaving mill in canton Schwyz, using fifty looms imported from England.

During the quarter of a century that followed Napoleon's downfall, fugitives from all parts of Europe sought the shelter that Switzerland afforded. Some 500 Polish exiles in Switzerland, however, marred their welcome by agreeing to a plan put forward by the Italian patriot Mazzini, then in Switzerland, and attempting an invasion of Savoy. The Swiss ultimately persuaded them to leave and they found a new haven in England, the sister-land of hospitality for political refugees.

Austria took advantage of the Savoy expedition to call a conference in Paris and put forward a proposal to surround Switzerland with a military cordon until she expelled all exiles. At the same time, Austria, the German states, Sardinia and Naples all sent Switzerland notes demanding action on the refugees. The British government showed its disapproval of the Austrian initiative, and France, too, gave support to Switzerland. The diplomatic storm died down.

Mrs Mary Somerville, after whom Somerville College, Oxford is named, was elected an honorary member of the Société de Physique et d'Histoire Naturelle de Genève for her work on 'The Mechanism of the Heavens'. She visited Switzerland several times.

In the years since the cessation of hostilities in Europe, Anglo-Swiss trade had been gradually expanding. By 1835, Swiss imports of British goods were, on one estimate, about £2.8m or the equivalent of some Sw.fr. 70m. They included cotton thread, raw cotton, cotton cloth, raw wool, woollen cloth and woollen goods, silk and cotton velvet, metal products, iron and steel plates and bars, cutlery, zinc, tin, porcelain, pottery, indigo and colonial products. Swiss exports to the United Kingdom were constrained by British tariffs, but included raw silk (in transit from Italy), goat skins, embroidered muslins, calico, silk ribbons and straw plaits and braid.

1835

John Ruskin (1819-1900) made his first visit to Switzerland at the age of sixteen. When he first stood on the Col de la Faucille, he said that 'the spectacle opened to me the Holy Land of my future work, and my true home in this world'.

Another early British mountaineer, Callender, succeeding in crossing the Old Strahlegg Pass, while Yeats Brown and Stanhope Templeton Speer made an unsuccessful attempt on the Jungfrau.

Mr Emery's tours to Switzerland (see 1818) were still being organised but the price had fallen to 20 pounds from 20 guineas. However, it still took a good ten days to get from London to Basel.

The American essayist and novelist Oliver Wendell Holmes, visiting Switzerland, remarked that it had become 'a thoroughfare of travelling Europe, and especially of the English, who swarm in it to the most outrageous extent'.

The author Thomas Lovell Beddoes (1803-49), who went abroad to study medicine, settled in Zurich. During his time there he undertook the first staging of Shakespearean plays in German in that city. Amongst his Swiss works were *Alpine Spirit's Song* and *Lines Written in Switzerland*. Beddoes was a nephew of Maria Edgeworth (see 1798).

The view from the Rigi

In England the young Robert Browning (1812-89) published his long poem *Paracelsus*, about the great Swiss doctor. It began to establish his reputation as a major poet.

1836   Swiss industry soon recovered from its depressed state at the end of the Napoleonic Wars, and then developed rapidly. Switzerland had become the second most important producer of cotton goods in the world: 58% of all cotton products came from England and 23% from Switzerland. In 1836 a British observer, Sir John Bowring (1792-1872), who had been to Switzerland on an official mission, stated in his report to the House of Commons that Swiss industry was the healthiest and most efficient on the Continent.

Richard Cobden (1804-65), the great advocate of free trade, also visited Switzerland at this time.

The Escher-Wyss factory in Switzerland (see 1824) had earlier ordered from England a lake steamer, the *Minerva*, for service on Lake Zurich. It had been imported in parts and assembled by Escher-Wyss. Soon afterwards Escher-Wyss designed their first steamship to be

Sunrise on the Rigi: *artist unknown*.

built in Switzerland without assistance from abroad, the *Escher-Linth*, for service on the Walensee. They employed to manage their new steam-boat department two Englishmen, Lloyd and Jackson.

George Grote (1794-1871), the English historian of ancient Greece, made a visit to Switzerland. He was attracted by similarities which he found between Swiss democracy and that of the classical Greeks (see also 1847).

1837

Prince Albert, later to marry Queen Victoria, made a long trip through Switzerland. Afterwards he sent the queen a small book containing views of most of the places he had visited, and a dried Alpen-rose from the top of the Rigi.

The English painter Thomas Miles Richardson junior (1813-90) published his *Sketches in Italy, Switzerland and France*.

A View of Mont Blanc and the surrounding mountains was exhibited at The Panorama, Leicester Square, London, by the English painter Robert Burford, who had made the drawings for his display in Switzerland in 1835.

1838 The French government nearly brought about a war with Switzerland through demanding the expulsion of Louis Napoleon, who had been named an honorary citizen of Thurgau (in his youth, he had done his military service in the Swiss army). The French moved 25,000 troops to the frontier, and the Swiss mobilised. Conflict was avoided only when the British government allowed Louis Napoleon to retire in Britain.

John Murray published *A Handbook for Travellers in Switzerland*, one of the earliest British tourist guides. It went through many later editions. Of Interlaken, he wrote that its beautiful position and closeness to numerous interesting sites, and its reputation of being inexpensive, had converted it into an English colony, 'two thirds of the summer visitors, on a moderate computation, being of our nation'.

Florence Nightingale (1820-1910) visited Geneva. Jean de Sismondi (see 1803) escorted the Nightingale party up the Salève.

1839 The Zurich painter J. Wolfensberger (1797-1850) came to England, where his patrons included the Duke of Sutherland and Lady Blessington.

The social reformer Elizabeth Fry (1780-1845) spent some time in Switzerland visiting prisons and other institutions. Seeing Dr Fellenberg's institute for boys at Hofwyl (see 1818), while impressed with his educational methods, she suggested there should be more teaching of the Holy Scriptures. Of her trip, she wrote:

> I . . . hope our circulation of books and tracts has been useful, and the establishment of at least one library at Brienz for the use of the labouring classes. We have travelled along gently and agreeably by Lucerne and through a delightful country.

A.T. Malkin climbed the Eggishorn and the Schilthorn in what were probably the first ascents of these Swiss mountains made by an Englishman. He also made the passage of the Tschingel Pass.

1840 Mary Shelley paid a nostalgic and sad visit to the shores of Lake Geneva where, as Mary Godwin, she and her stepsister and Shelley and Byron had spent many happy hours in 1816 (q.v.).

> At length I caught a glimpse of the scenes among which I had lived when I first stepped out from childhood into life. There on the shores of Bellerive, stood Diodati; and our humble dwelling, Maison Chapuis, rested close to the

lake below. There were the terraces, the vineyards, the upward path threading them, the little port where our boat lay moored; I could mark and recognise a thousand slight peculiarities, familiar objects then – forgotten since – now replete with recollections and associations. Was I the same person who had lived there, the companion of the dead? For all were gone now; even my young child, whom I had looked upon as the joy of future years, had died in infancy – not one hope, then in fair bud, had opened into maturity . . .

On a climbing tour John Ball, later Under-Secretary of State for the Colonies under Palmerston and first president of the Alpine Club (see 1857), made the first ascent of the Grauhaupt.

J.D. Forbes, a Scottish scientist and 'the father of British mountaineering', made the first ascent of the Stockhorn (Bernese Oberland). (Quite a number of Swiss peaks had already been climbed by then by the Swiss.) 1841

Death of Augustin Pyrame de Candolle of Geneva (b. 1778), the eminent botanist who became a Fellow of the Royal Society in London.

The physicist Michael Faraday (1791-1867) made a long tour of the Bernese Oberland. He was entranced by the falls at Giessbach:

The sun shone brightly and the rainbows seen from various points were very beautiful. One at the bottom of a fine but furious fall . . . remained motionless while gusts and clouds of spray swept furiously across its place and were dashed against the rock. It looked like a spirit strong in faith and steadfast in the midst of the storm of passions sweeping across it, and though it might fade and revive, still it held on to the rock as in hope and giving hope . . .

The gradual dismantling of the British protective import tariff from this date made it easier for Swiss exporters to gain a foothold in the British market. Moreover, more Swiss exports to third countries could be shipped via British ports. In the British budget of that year the reduction of import duties on 750 commodities did much to help Swiss trade with the United Kingdom. The duties, for instance, on silk and on cheese came down substantially. 1842

A group of English students from Fellenberg's school at Hofwyl (see 1818), including William Smith, a boy of fifteen, made the first ascent of the Riffelhorn.

J.M.W. Turner was in Switzerland again on his fourth painting visit.

Publication of *Essai sur la manifestation des convictions religieuses* by the Swiss critic and theologian Alexandre Vinet (1797-1847), which appeared in an English translation as *The Conscience of the State*.

1843 The removal, by Peel's government, of the prohibition on the export of machinery from Great Britain gave British exports to Switzerland a boost.

Jean Louis Prevost (see 1813) was now director of several British railway companies, including the London and Birmingham and its successor, the L.& N.W.R., as well as the South Eastern Railway for Dover and Tonbridge. He was also Agent and Consul-General of the Swiss Confederation in London. When the future Prime Minister of Italy, Count Cavour, came to England in 1843 to study the railways and the British industrial scene, it was Prevost who was his guide.

At roughly the same time that Professor Elliotson had been experimenting with mesmerism (see 1831), a Scottish surgeon in Manchester, James Braid, had also been studying Mesmer's ideas. In 1843 he published his *Nerypnology, or the Rationale of Nervous Sleep*, in which the terms 'hypnotism' and 'hypnotise' were first used.

1844 In the absence of any official trade statistics, the British Legation in Berne estimated the value of British exports to the three cantons of Berne, the Vaud and Geneva to be at least £327,000.

J.M.W. Turner made his last visit to Switzerland. Among the outstanding watercolours he made from his Swiss journeys were his views of Lucerne and the Rigi, the Lake of Zurich, Geneva, Fribourg and the Gotthard Pass.

Among numerous other British artists who painted in Switzerland around the mid-century or a little earlier, were William Roxby Beverley (1811-89), William Callow (1812-1908), James Holland (1800-70), Miles Birket Foster (1825-99), George Arthur Fripp (1813-96), Edward Lear (1813-88), William Leighton Leitch (1804-83), William James Muller (1812-45), Philip Phillips (*fl.* 1826-64) and George Price Boyce (1826-97).

In the other direction came to England the distinguished artist from Vevey, Alexandre Calame (1810-64). A little later, Calame was commissioned by Lady Osborne to paint a picture of the Handegg Falls in the Bernese Oberland, which made his name as an Alpine painter.

Queen Victoria's mother, Victoria, Duchess of Kent, went on holiday to Switzerland.

Death of the Scottish poet Thomas Campbell (b. 1777). His verses on Switzerland were quoted in William Beattie's classic guide (1836) to that country:

> The Switzer's Land! – Where grandeur is encompassed
> Impregnably in mountain-tents of snow;
> Realms that by human footprint ne'er were stamped,
> Where the eagle wheels, and glacial ramparts glow!
> Seek, Nature's worshipper, those landscapes! – Go,
> Where all her finest, fairest charms are joined,
> Go to the land where Tell drew freedom's bow;
> And in the patriot's country thou shalt find
> A semblance 'twixt the scene and his immortal mind.

When agitation among the Swiss cantons again assumed serious proportions (see 1832), the British Foreign Secretary, Lord Aberdeen, wrote a despatch to the British Minister in Berne which was subsequently published in its entirety in the Swiss and British press. In it Lord Aberdeen instructed David Morier to urge the Swiss government and the cantons against the use of violent means which could only invite foreign intervention.

The sincere and friendly interest which the British Government has always taken in the welfare of Switzerland and the relations which result from the position of Great Britain with regard to the Confederation, as one of the parties that took part in the act which guaranteed the independence of Switzerland . . . impose on it the duty to endeavour to call the serious attention of the Swiss, of all parties and all opinions, to the probable consequences of a further continuation of a such a state of affairs.

The industrialist Johann Conrad Fischer (see 1815) was on another of his periodic visits to England. Amongst old friends he saw was Michael Faraday. 1845

Stanhope Templeton Speer, with two Swiss guides, made the first ascent of the Mittelhorn (Bernese Oberland).

Returning from a stay in Italy with his family, Charles Dickens took the coach through the St Gotthard into central Switzerland. From Lucerne, he wrote to a friend:

The whole descent between Andermatt and Altdorf, William Tell's town, which we passed through yesterday afternoon, is the highest sublimation of

Charles Dickens in 1838: portrait by Samuel Laurence.

all you can imagine in the way of Swiss scenery. O God! What a beautiful country it is! How poor and shrunken, beside it, is Italy in its brightest aspect!

The trip decided Dickens to return to Switzerland (see 1846).

Peel's ministry in England had now revived the income tax and with its help had reduced or abolished import duties on a wide range of goods. The Swiss consul in London wrote to his government in Berne: 'It is evident that the reduction of the English tariff can only favour the commerce which already exists . . .' He suggested that new products such as cheese might be tried in the British market (a little Alpine cheese had been exported up to then). 1846

Since Britain had unrivalled overseas connexions, the Swiss also considered it beneficial to have British merchants, or Swiss merchants in Britain, handling some of their increasing foreign trade. One of these merchanting businesses was owned by the Swiss Imthurn family. In 1846 Johann Conrad Imthurn of Schaffhausen became head of the London office of his family's international merchant's business (later to become Czarnikow). One of his sons, Sir Edward Imthurn (1852-1932), had a distinguished career in the British Colonial Service. He was a Governor of Fiji, and later President of the Royal Anthropological Society.

Another member of the Pictet family, Armand-Jacques Pictet, became British Consular Agent in Geneva. In 1853 he was promoted to Consul-General.

Charles Dickens and his family rented the Villa Rosemont in Lausanne for a stay of several months, and Dickens wrote *Dombey and Son* and *The Battle of Life* there. He spent many hours with William Haldimand (see 1809). Amongst his literary visitors from Britain were Wilkie Collins, Henry Hallam and William Harrison Ainsworth. Alfred Tennyson, soon to become Poet Laureate, called in on his return from the Bernese Oberland. Tennyson (who indicated his attitude to Swiss scenery when he wrote 'I was satisfied with the size of crags, but mountains, great mountains disappointed me') left Dickens with the impression that the day had been a waste of time. On his return to England, Dickens wrote to a friend, 'I have never left so many friendly and cheerful recollections in any place.' (See also 1853.)

The Sonderbund War. Switzerland, affected by the revolutionary 1847 fervour still sweeping Europe, had become a country of national strife, between Conservatives and Radicals and between Catholics and Protestants. The Catholic cantons formed a separate defensive pact between themselves, the Sonderbund. The Protestant cantons, dominated by the Radicals, fearing for the unity of Switzerland, made preparations for civil war. For some years (see 1832) the Austrian Chancellor, Metternich, had been steadily urging a common intervention of the European Powers to 'rescue Switzerland from the throes of social dissolution'. The British government was the only one in Europe which had any sympathy for, or understanding of, the objects of the Swiss Radicals, so Lord Palmerston was averse to such a policy.

Since the British Minister in Berne, David Morier, appeared to have less than a full understanding of the aims of the Radical movement in Switzerland, and to be much influenced by Metternich's views, Palmerston had him withdrawn, leaving the attaché, Robert Peel (son of the Prime Minister), as chargé d'affaires at the British Legation in Berne.

In a speech in the Diet in July, the Swiss President, Ulrich Ochsenbein, was critical of the attitude of most of the Continental powers. Palmerston sent him his congratulations.

In September Palmerston charged the Earl of Minto (see 1816) with a special mission to Switzerland to urge moderation. Minto was instructed to warn the Swiss Diet not to give way to elements who wished to sweep away the separate sovereignty of the cantons and make the whole of Switzerland into a centralised republic, since this would be contrary to the fundamental principles upon which the Swiss Federal Compact had been drawn up under the Treaty of Vienna.

In mid-October the Swiss Diet decided to use force against the Sonderbund and appointed General Dufour to take charge of military operations. Under pressure from Austria and the other Powers, Palmerston had agreed to the principle of international diplomatic action, but continued to raise objections on details. As a result, joint action on the part of the Powers to intervene was delayed until it was too late. Before agreement on what to do had been reached, the Sonderbund were defeated and the civil war between the Protestant and Catholic cantons was over.'[19]

Lord Palmerston, 1858: by G. Vivian.

In December, at the end of the Sonderbund War, Palmerston sent the veteran diplomat Sir Stratford Canning to Switzerland once more (see also 1814) with instructions to encourage national reconciliation. Canning again urged respect for the principle of separate sovereignty of the cantons, and was assured by the Swiss President that this entirely accorded with his own views. Canning returned to London after some weeks in Berne.

Publication in *The Spectator* of George Grote's 'Seven Letters Concerning Politics in Switzerland', which did much to bring about a change in public opinion in Britain in favour of the victorious Swiss Radical party after the Sonderbund War. In his letters Grote explained in detail the background and history of the conflict. He added:

> There is so much of all that constitutes both the good man and the good citizen distributed throughout Switzerland that the previous dissensions which agitate that country cannot but inspire a profound and anxious interest. Industry, forethought, self-supporting energy, and reciprocal disposition to neighbourly help pervades a larger portion of the population than perhaps in any other country of Europe.

1848   When proposals were renewed to amend the Swiss Federal Pact of 1815 (see 1832), the Continental Powers, with the exception of Great Britain who did not associate herself with this initiative, once more attempted to block the way. Envoys were to be recalled, the Swiss frontier blockaded and, if needed, Austria, Prussia, France, the south German states and Sardinia were to occupy part of the country. But the February Revolution in Paris put an end to the project, and reforms to the Swiss constitution were finally carried through. A new Federal Constitution giving more authority to the federal government was adopted by a large majority. Britain, and all the other Powers except Russia, soon recognised the new government.

In Neuchâtel meanwhile, the Republicans overthrew the royalist government. The federal authorities did not challenge the change of government, and the new cantonal constitution omitted any reference to the King of Prussia (see 1707 and 1754). Prussia sent a sharp note of protest to the Swiss government. Palmerston warned King Frederick William against any intervention in the Confederation's affairs and sent Sir Stratford Canning to Prussia to appeal to the king to reconcile himself to the situation (but see 1852).

Another Swiss banking house was established in London, Rapp &

Coulon from Neuchâtel. It later changed its name to Coulon, Berthoud & Co. It closed down just before the First World War.

Matthew Arnold (1822-88) visited Thun in the Bernese Oberland and found romance. He went there on holiday for several years running. His cycle of lyric poems on Switzerland appeared in 1853. In the poem entitled 'Switzerland' he described his return to Thun:

> Again I see my bliss at hand,
> The town, the lake are here;
> My Marguerite smiles upon the strand,
> Unalter'd with the year . . .

The English author George Eliot (Mary Ann Evans, 1819-80) stayed six months in Geneva and witnessed the 'Fête de Navigation' on the Lake. She wrote home that she was becoming 'passionately attached to the mountains, the lakes and the streets'.

1849

The poet Elizabeth Barrett Browning (1806-61), staying at Interlaken, wondered who, 'with strength and opportunity, would pass into the world of spirits without a glance at the Jungfrau?'

A rising Swiss industrialist, Johann Jakob Sulzer (1806-83), visited a number of the newest factories in Britain, making notes on their methods and machines for the fast-developing Sulzer Brothers' industrial machine shops in Winterthur. Among other things, he was interested by a new machine invented in Manchester by his compatriot Johann Georg Bodmer (see 1824), and subsequently placed an order for it. To learn how to operate the machine, Sulzer's son Heinrich (1837-1906) was sent to England and worked for a time in the Manchester factory.

By now the Swiss Confederation was recognised as the most heavily industrialised country in Europe after Great Britain.

1850

Robert Stephenson (1803-59), the son of George Stephenson (inventor of *The Rocket*), went to Switzerland with Harold Swinburne, another British engineer, to help plan the layout of part of the future Swiss railway network. Their recommendation of strong federal control of railway development was turned down; but their proposal to make Olten the central railway junction of Switzerland was approved and their scheme for a main east-west line with branches implemented.

Robert Stephenson: portrait by John Lucas.

Death of Jean-Baptiste, Père Girard (b. 1765) of Fribourg, another famous Swiss educationalist. Girard's methods in the training of children were widely followed not only in Switzerland but in Great Britain and in several other countries in Europe.

Amongst other British climbers in Switzerland that year, Eardley Blackwell made the first passage of the Neue Weisstor.

For some time in the 1840s a number of Swiss had been admirers of the London newspaper, *The Times,* particularly its objectivity and independence. They thought to publish a similar journal in Switzerland, but their plans were interrupted by the Sonderbund War. After the introduction of the new Federal Constitution in 1848 and the choice of Berne as the permanent capital of the Confederation, National Councillor Andreas Rudolf von Planta revived the idea. Together with some parliamentary colleagues he launched the 'Swiss Times' – *Der Bund*.

The continued presence in Switzerland of political refugees from other European regimes led to the calling of another conference in Paris, where France, Prussia and Austria discussed sending an ultimatum to the Swiss government demanding the immediate expulsion of all refugees. Germany and France moved troops to the Swiss frontier, and the threat of attack became more serious than in 1847. The Swiss Federal Council tried to obtain amnesties for some refugees from their home countries, aand facilitated the emigration of others to England and America. By mid-1851 the refugees were reduced to a few hundred.

Britain's attitude over the refugee question earned a great deal of goodwill from the Swiss government. In the Federal Council's report for 1850 to the Swiss Federal Assembly, Britain was singled out for praise. Referring to the Paris conference, the report said:

England did not take part in this conference; it does not appear that she was invited to do so. However, England has not ceased to show great kindness towards the Confederation and the British Government has not failed to represent to the other Cabinets that there was no ground for measures against Switzerland. The testimony given afterwards in Parliament by Lord Palmerston as to the conduct pursued by Switzerland in international relations is confirmation of this declaration made in the face of the whole of Europe.

A high proportion of Swiss exports to overseas destinations was now being carried by British shipping. Swiss commercial agents abroad were instructed, with Foreign Office approval, to call on British consuls for help when needed.

1851

Another member of the Sulzer family, Gottlieb Hirzel, brother-in-law of Johann Sulzer (see 1849), came to England and worked for a time at Maudsley, Son & Field's machine shops in London. He met there a young fellow worker, Charles Brown (1827-1905). Through Hirzel, Brown was engaged as factory manager by Sulzer Brothers in Winterthur (see also 1871).

Another visitor to England was Colonel Denzler, superintending instructor of the Swiss Artillery, who was sent by the federal government to visit British arsenals and other military establishments.

At the Great Exhibition in London some 120 Swiss firms took part in showing their products, which included a wide range of textiles, embroideries, silk ribbons, straw-plaiting, clocks and watches, instruments, machinery and steel goods. During a visit to the Swiss section of the exhibition, Queen Victoria chose watches from Patek Philippe of Geneva for both herself and Prince Albert.

A young Swiss, Christian Albert Theodor Billroth (1829-96), was studying in England. At the age of thirty-one he became professor of surgery at Zurich. He was later known as the founder of abdominal surgery. He was a keen follower of Lister's methods of antiseptic treatment.

1852 Despite the ousting of the royalists from government in Neuchâtel (see 1848), the King of Prussia had not given up his claim to sovereignty over the canton. Amongst other things, he tried to get Britain to arrange a European conference on the question; but as long as Lord Palmerston was in office he could make no progress. In 1852, within a month of Palmerston's leaving the Foreign Office, Prussia again pressed Britain to arrange a conference. After some hesitation, and pressure from France, Britain agreed to a meeting at which the London Protocol was signed. Under it, however, Britain ensured that the King of Prussia agreed to renounce the use of force to re-establish his sovereignty over Neuchâtel.

The beginnings of Swiss railway development brought several British contractors and consultants to Switzerland, including Sir Charles Fox of Fox, Henderson & Co. Among British companies who were awarded construction contracts were Pickering & Co. and Williamson & Co. A number of British companies competed to build the Geneva-Basel line. Over the next few years there were British railway contractors working in, among other places, Lausanne, Solothurn, Olten and Ragaz (St Gallen). Many of them employed British workmen who came to Switzerland especially for these jobs.

The British government made representations to the Swiss authorities about alleged fraudulent imitations of British trade marks by watchmakers in the canton of Neuchâtel. Enquiries were instituted and instructions issued to try to prevent any recurrence.

First publication of Roget's *Thesaurus of English Words and Phrases*. Its author, Dr Peter Mark Roget (1779-1869), was the son of a Genevan pastor who had come to live in England. Roget also wrote articles for the *Encyclopedia Britannica,* gave courses at the Royal College of Physicians, and was a Fellow of the Royal Society – of which he later became Secretary for twenty years.

W.M. Thackeray (1811-63) visited Switzerland and wrote part of his novel *The Newcomes* in Vevey.

Albert Richard Smith (1816-60), having climbed Mont Blanc the year before, produced an entertainment in the Egyptian Hall, Piccadilly, London, describing the ascent. It became enormously popular and continued for five years. In 1854 Smith gave his performance before Queen Victoria and the Prince Consort at Osborne House.

Smith's success encouraged other ventures. A game of 'Mont Blanc' was sold in the shops, music publishers issued a 'Mont Blanc Quadrille' and a 'Chamonix Polka'; and St Bernard dogs were brought to London by one of Smith's former guides.

Robert Burford (see 1837) exhibited in Leicester Square a new panorama of Switzerland entitled *A View of the Bernese Alps,* constructed from drawings made by him on the spot earlier that year.

The British civil engineer Charles Vignoles (1793-1875), who was consulted on some of the earliest railway lines on the Continent, began – and over the next two years built – the first railway in western Switzerland. His son Henry, as resident engineer, constructed the line from Lausanne to Morges and Yverdon under his father's direction. 1853

Another British railway engineer, Thomas Brassey (1805-70), was responsible for building the Hauenstein tunnel, north of Olten. At that time it was the longest in Europe. Brassey was also responsible for some of the other works on the Basel-Olten line.

During the following decade British financiers were active in helping to promote the construction of not only the West of Switzerland Railway but also the Southeastern Swiss, the Lake Constance-Basel, and the Lausanne-Fribourg lines.

Charles Dickens (see 1846) made another visit to Switzerland. Other British visitors that year included the historian Thomas Babington Macaulay (1800-59) and the philosopher Herbert Spencer (see 1861).

A Swiss artist from Solothurn, Frank Buchser (1828-90), came for a stay in England, where his studio was much sought after by fashionable society.

The English community's own church, La Chapelle Anglaise, Holy Trinity, was founded in Geneva. (Since 1814, the Genevan authorities had granted them the use of the hospital church in the Bourg de Four.)

1854 The General Bank of Switzerland, newly founded in Geneva, opened a branch in London, much concerned with railway construction and property. It closed after eleven years.

The influx of British engineers and workers for various railway projects had increased the British resident community in Switzerland. But the attraction of the country as a haven for retirement was also already evident. In the fast-growing British colony in Lausanne, for example, there were some forty colonels in retirement from service in various parts of the Empire.

The British Legation in Berne proposed to London the idea of a treaty with the Swiss to help protect the position of British residents and of British trade with Switzerland. The British government agreed and a draft treaty was submitted to the Swiss government for negotiation in October.

On the outbreak of the Crimean War the Swiss Federal Council reminded the cantons of their strict neutrality. The Radicals, however, openly took the side of Britain. Under the eyes of the federal authorities, British officers illegally recruited from Switzerland some 3,000 men for service in the Crimea. In all, the British government raised from Switzerland two volunteer regiments of Swiss infantry (a total of 5,000 men). Apart from those recruited in Switzerland itself, another recruiting office was opened quite legally at Jougne in France, on the Swiss frontier. Those who wanted to emigrate after their service were offered a free passage and a plot of land in either North America or South Africa. Those willing to be employed for service in India were offered double pay. As training was completed in England during the following two years, the Swiss Brigade (commanded by a British colonel, Dickson, and a Swiss colonel, Jean Sulzberger) were sent to Smyrna in Turkey. But they had not gone into action by the time that peace was declared and they were returned to Britain and demobilised at the end of 1856.

During the Crimean War Swiss firms obtained large orders for equipment for the British army in the Crimea. These included 20,000 pairs of wooden-soled shoes, knitted woollen socks, jerseys, and other items of military uniform. Finance for the purchase of much of this equipment was provided by Banque Marcuard of Berne.

The electric telegraph between Britain and Switzerland was now in operation, and urgent messages from the British Legation in Berne to London were sent by 'telegraphic despatch'.

1854

Death in London of Benjamin Louis Vulliamy (b.1780), famous clockmaker and a descendant of Justin Vulliamy (see 1742). Vulliamy was five times Master of the Clockmakers' Company. In 1831, he had been made a Fellow of the Royal Astronomical Society.

The Jardin Anglais was constructed in Geneva.

The British mountaineer Alfred Wills (1828-1912) climbed the Wetterhorn in what he believed was the first ascent. In fact it had been climbed several times before by both British and Swiss. Two years later Wills published his book *Wanderings in the High Alps,* which gave a boost to mountaineering among the British. In it appeared a memorable description of the writer's feelings in the presence of a great mountain:

I am not ashamed to own that I experienced, as this sublime and wonderful prospect burst upon my view, a profound and almost irrepressible emotion . . . We felt as in the more immediate presence of Him who had reared this tremendous pinnacle, and beneath the 'majestical roof' of whose deep blue Heaven we stood, poised, as it seemed half-way between the earth and sky.

1855

With an era of freer trade beginning in the United Kingdom and on the Continent, the new Swiss Confederation of 1848, with its unified currency and customs regimes, was in a position to take full advantage of it. The total value of Swiss imports and exports was estimated to be about Sw.fr. 750m of which imports from, and exports to, the United Kingdom were some Sw.fr. 140m, or nearly 19% of Swiss total trade.

The value of Swiss watches and clocks sent to the United Kingdom was put at over Sw.fr. 7m.

Following a year's negotiations, a Treaty of Friendship, Commerce and Reciprocal Establishment between the Swiss Confederation and the British government was signed in Berne. It included a 'most favoured nation' clause. Among other things, the Swiss gained easier access to British colonial markets, while the British obtained more favourable treatment for British residents in Switzerland.

Sir William Perkin (1838-1907) discovered the first synthetic dyestuff derived from mauvine, a process which, ten years later, Alexandre Clavel began to exploit in Basel. In doing so he laid the foundations of the Swiss chemical industry (see also 1914). Clavel's factory eventually became the first works of the Society of Chemical Industry in Basel – later abbreviated to CIBA.

The Revd Charles Hudson (1828-65) made guideless ascents of the Klein Matterhorn and the Breithorn (Valais). He perished on the Matterhorn in 1865.

Alexander Seiler built the first hotel in Zermatt, the Monte Rosa, to be followed by several others. They were much frequented by British climbers, who were coming increasingly to the region.

A new Swiss church was consecrated in London, after an intensive fund-raising appeal lasting several years. Many English churches subscribed to this in recognition of the help which had been given in the past by Switzerland to British religious refugees.

1856 The Anglo-Swiss Treaty of Friendship, Commerce and Reciprocal Establishment of the previous year was ratified by both governments.

When conflict broke out between Swiss and British stockholders in the Swiss Southeastern Railway (British investors owned half of the capital), the Grisons government confiscated all the British shares. The British investors appealed to the Foreign Office for assistance and the British Legation in Berne raised the matter with the Swiss Federal Council. But before official intervention became necessary the matter was settled amicably.

The development of the railways in Switzerland led to an expansion in Swiss banking, and later insurance, because the previously existing forms of finance were not sufficient to cope with the new projects. At the same time the introduction of a unified monetary system after the reforms of 1848 had paved the way for a more modern banking system. The large all-purpose banks in Switzerland began to be established. The Credit Suisse was formed in 1856. The forerunner of

Fribourg: *sketch by John Ruskin from* Modern Painters.

the Union Bank of Switzerland, the Bank in Winterthur, was started in 1862 (to become the UBS in 1912). The Swiss Bank Corporation began operations in 1872.

British mountaineers were busy again. E.L. Ames scaled the Allalinhorn, John Ball the ridge of the Weisshorn range, and Robert Chapman the summit of the Jungfrau.

The City Swiss Club was founded in London by Swiss businessmen in England.

Publication of Volume 4 of John Ruskin's *Modern Painters,* in which appeared Ruskin's notable opinion of the Swiss:

> You will find among them . . . no subtle wit nor high enthusiasm, only an undeceivable common sense, and an obstinate rectitude . . . They use no phrases of friendship, but they do not fail you at your need.

The Neuchâtel question. At the Conference of London Frederick William IV of Prussia had obtained an express recognition of his rights to Neuchâtel (see 1852), though he at first took no steps to enforce them. But in the autumn of 1856 royalists in Neuchâtel, wishing to detach the canton from the Swiss Confederation, attempted a coup. This was defeated by republican troops and the rebels were imprisoned. Frederick sought the help of Napoleon III of France, broke off diplomatic relations with Switzerland and mobilised his troops. The Swiss government looked to Britain for support, which was forthcoming. Some British ministers sought the acquaintance of Swiss party leaders in order to learn at first hand the views of the most influential Confederate politicians. British public opinion showed itself unequivocally on the side of the Swiss and against the King of Prussia. The British Foreign Secretary, Lord Clarendon, warned the Prussian Prime Minister of the 'active part' in the defence of Switzerland that Britain might determine to take if Switzerland were to be attacked by Prussia. Queen Victoria and Albert, the Prince Consort, supported this diplomatic action in their correspondence with the Prussian royal family.

The British Minister in Berne, George John Gordon, received instructions from Lord Clarendon to inform the Swiss Federal Council that

the interests and honour of Switzerland are close to our hearts, and that we will consent to nothing which cannot be well accepted by the Federal Government. The behaviour of Switzerland and, I venture to say, of the Federal Executive, is admirable; and, happen what may, it will enormously increase the respect which all those feel for the Confederation whose views are not inspired by hatred of liberal institutions.

1857 After consultation with Britain and with France, the Swiss released and banished the rebel prisoners taken at Neuchâtel; and thanks largely to the firm line taken by Britain, the King of Prussia was finally persuaded to renounce his rights over the canton. In May a treaty was signed by which the complete independence of Neuchâtel was established.

Mountain climbing now had a fast-growing number of ardent devotees in Britain, and the first club for mountaineers was founded in London, the Alpine Club. Although they had not been the first in the field of climbing itself, it was the British, with the help of a splendid race of Swiss guides, who transformed mountaineering from the pursuit of a few enterprising individuals into a recognised sport.

The Finsteraarhorn was ascended by the Revd J. F. Hardy and party, and the Klein Schreckhorn by Eustace Anderson. The year marked the beginning of systematic mountaineering. During the next eight years, members or potential members of the Alpine Club made over eighty first ascents or first crossings of Alpine summits or passes.

T.W. Hinchliff's *Summer Months among the Alps* was published.

A holiday in Switzerland which the scientist T.H. Huxley (1825-95)

Some Presidents of the Alpine Club: TOP, LEFT TO RIGHT *John Ball, 1858-60; Edward Shirley Kennedy, 1861-3; Alfred Wills, 1864-5;* BELOW *William Martin Conway, 1902-4; Sir Claud Schuster, 1938-40; Geoffrey Winthrop Young, 1941-3.*

had with Professor John Tyndall (see 1858) led to their writing a joint paper for the Royal Society, 'On the Structure and Motion of Glaciers'.

British artists who were painting in Switzerland in 1858 included John Absolom (1815-95) and Samuel Philip Jackson (1830-1904) and his father, Samuel Jackson (1774-1869). Samuel Jackson had been to

1858

Switzerland before. In 1855 he painted a fine version of *The Fall of the Staubbach* in the valley of Lauterbrunnen, a favourite subject of generations of painters.

The poet and political writer Wilfrid Scawen Blunt (1840-1922), visiting Zermatt, was nearly killed by an avalanche of stones.

An Englishman, Richard Barrington, with Swiss guide Christian Almer, made the first ascent of the Eiger (Bernese Oberland), while Professor John Tyndall (1820-93) climbed the Finsteraarhorn and J. Llewelyn Davies scaled the Dom (Valais).

Matthew Arnold (see 1848) was in Switzerland again. In his poem 'The Terrace at Berne' he still remembered his romance at Thun:

> Ten years! – and to my waking eye
> Once more the roofs of Berne appear;
> The rocky banks, the terrace high,
> The stream! – and do I linger here?
>
> The clouds are on the Oberland,
> The Jungfrau snows look faint and far;
> But bright are those green fields at hand,
> And through those fields comes down the Aar;
>
> And from the blue twin-lakes it comes,
> Flows by the town, the churchyard fair;
> And 'neath the garden-walk it hums,
> The house! – and is my Marguerite there?

1859 The Victorians were now flocking to the Continent in their thousands, many to spend their newly earned wealth in exploring the mountains and flower meadows of Switzerland. John Ruskin, through his writings, did much to open the eyes of his countrymen in their journeys to the Alps.

The first volume of *Peaks, Passes and Glaciers,* an anthology of mountain literature, was published in England. Edited by John Ball, first president of the Alpine Club, it gave a further spur to wouldbe Alpine climbers.

British mountaineers were in Switzerland in earnest. F.F.Tuckett was first to climb the Aletschhorn, while William Mathews climbed the Eigerjoch and the Lysjoch. Leslie Stephen (1832-1904), also an early president of the Alpine Club, father of Virginia Woolf and later editor of the monumental *Dictionary of National Biography,* made the first ascent of the Bietschhorn (Valais).

The first edition was published of Charles Darwin's *Origin of Species*. French and German editions soon followed. The book had extensive influence on Swiss scientific thinking (as it did on scientific thinking everywhere).

The French annexation of Savoy caused a crisis in Switzerland. Napoleon III had spoken earlier of the possibility of a cession to Switzerland of Northern Savoy (a region which was included in the Swiss neutrality and which, if part of the Confederation, would not have left Geneva exposed). However, after a somewhat dubious plebiscite in the territory which went in favour of France, he declared it impossible. The Swiss appealed to the signatories of the Treaty of Vienna, and sent a special diplomatic representative, Auguste de la Rive, to London. Queen Victoria proposed to the British Cabinet that Britain should call a European conference to take the question out of Napoleon's hands, a suggestion repeated soon after by the Swiss. But none of the Powers were enthusiastic. Britain tried to rally support against France's intentions from Austria, Prussia and Russia, but without success. Robert Peel (see 1847), now in Parliament, made a series of passionate speeches in Switzerland's support. Palmerston, and his Foreign Secretary, Lord John Russell, were sympathetic to the Swiss case but indecisive, and unwilling to take any firm action. So the whole of Savoy went to France.[20]

1860

In Gladstone's budget of that year the process of dismantling the British tariff system was virtually completed. Duties were abolished on imports of paper and on almost all manufactured goods.

The Swiss Export Company, which had begun operations in Zurich in 1857, established branches in Manchester, London and Liverpool. (From about this time on, numerous Swiss companies began appointing agents for their products in Britain.)

Leslie Stephen (see 1859), with three Swiss guides, was the first to climb the Schreckhorn (Bernese Oberland). His other 'firsts' included the Blümlisalp, the Alphubel and the Oberaarhorn. Edward Whymper (see 1865) made the first of several attempts on the Matterhorn.

1861

The Revd J.F. Hardy (see 1857) and a large British party made the first ascent of the Lyskamm (Zermatt). Reaching the summit, Hardy later recorded how they sang the National Anthem:

> . . . as we sing with uncovered heads, the noble old anthem fills our English

hearts with happy thoughts of home and fatherland, and of the bright eyes that will sparkle, and the warm hearts that will rejoice, at our success . . .

John Ruskin discovered Switzerland in winter. 'I have made up my mind', he wrote, 'that the finest things one can see in summer are nothing compared to winter scenery among the Alps.'

The British educationalist and philosopher Herbert Spencer (1820-1903) published his *Education, Intellectual, Moral and Physical,* a work clearly influenced by Rousseau's *Émile.*

The novelist and poet. George Meredith (1825-1909) visited Basel and Zurich; and William Thackeray was again in Switzerland. He visited Chur (Grisons), and wrote his account of an episode there, 'On a Lazy, Idle Boy', which he published in his *Roundabout Papers.*

1862 Also in Switzerland again, Professor Tyndall made one of several attempts to climb the Matterhorn. A.W. Moore climbed the Jungfraujoch, the Gross Fiescherhorn and the Sesiajoch, and T.S. Kennedy with William Wigram made the first ascent of the Dent Blanche.

At the International Exhibition held in London, the Swiss section featured strong representation from the watch industry including Lang and Baume & Mercier from Geneva, Aubert and Audermars from the Vaud and Courvoisier and Gros-claude from La Chaux-de-Fonds. Among other exhibits were hand- and machine-made embroideries, silks, ribbons and metal manufactures.

The Swiss artist Frank Buchser (see 1853) was in England again and directed the Swiss participation in the International Exhibition of Painting held in London as part of the Exhibition. Over fifty Swiss artists were represented.

1863 The International Red Cross was founded in Geneva as a result of the initiative of the Swiss Henri Dunant. It was followed the next year by an international conference there, which resulted in the setting up of a British national aid society, later to become the British Red Cross. Charles Dickens did much to publicise Dunant's work in Britain and arouse sympathy for it. He published his own version of Dunant's book, *Souvenirs de Solférino,* describing the sufferings of the wounded on the battlefield.

The Swiss Re-insurance Company began operations in Zurich. In its first year it already had a contract with a British insurance company.

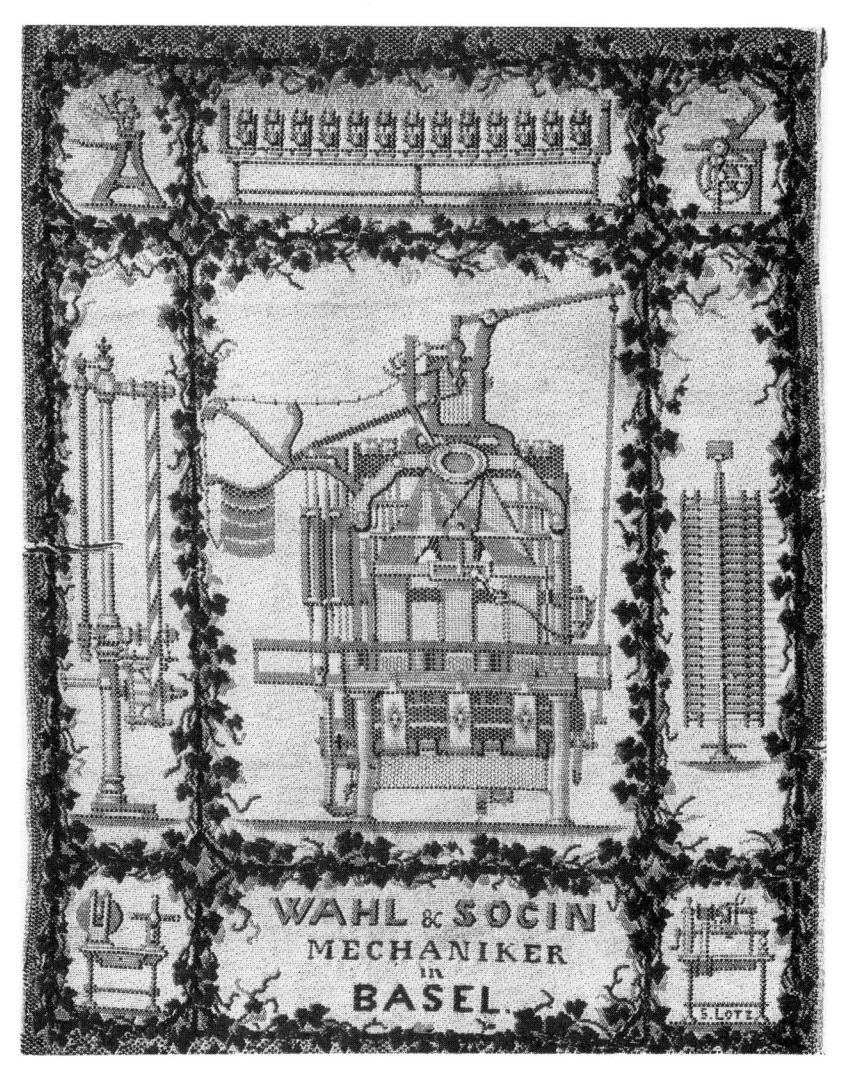

A Swiss exhibit at the London Exhibition of 1862. A piece of silk woven by the Jacquard method, showing some of the machines used at that time for silk weaving.

Thomas Cook organised his first tour to Switzerland. The route, via Paris, included Geneva, Sion, Martigny, Leukerbad, Kandersteg, Lauterbrunnen, Grindelwald, Interlaken, Brienz, Lucerne, the Rigi and Neuchâtel. One member of the tour afterwards noted in his diary: 'Account of a tour in Switzerland and France – June 26 to July 16, 1863, twenty-one days inclusive – £19.17.6.'

Thomas Cook, who organised his first tour to Switzerland in 1863.

The Swiss Alpine Club was founded. It soon had a number of British members. The same year the Alpine Club in London began to publish *The Alpine Journal*, the first periodical devoted entirely to mountains.

The Aletschhorn and the Jungfrau were climbed by Mr and Mrs Winkworth, both first ascents by an English lady.

1864 The first winter tourists in Switzerland. A group of British took up an offer by Swiss hotelier Johannes Badrutt of a free stay at his Kulm Hotel in St Moritz – to prove his assertion that winter in the mountains was survivable and even enjoyable. They found that it was.

Francis Walker and his daughter Lucy Walker were the first climbers to ascend the Balmhorn, together with the Swiss guide Melchior Anderegg.

The Duke of Connaught, son of Queen Victoria and Prince Albert, in one of his several visits to Switzerland, followed the exact route taken by his father in 1837.

The novelist Mrs Gaskell (1810-65) wrote *Mothers and Daughters* at Pontresina in the Grisons.

Jean Louis Moilliet's bank, J.L. Moilliet & Sons (see 1815), merged with the other important bank in Birmingham, Lloyds & Co., to become Lloyds Banking Co. Ltd. In 1889 the title was changed to Lloyds Bank Ltd, today Lloyds Bank plc.

1865

Swiss mountain climbing by the British continued unabated. Of forty-three ascents made that year, more than half were made by Englishmen.

Edward Whymper (1840-1911) climbed the Matterhorn. The descent ended in tragedy, three of his British companions, Lord Francis Douglas, the Revd Charles Hudson and Mr Hadow, together with one of the Swiss guides, Michel Croz, falling to their deaths. Afterwards Whymper described the accident in his book *Scrambles amongst the Alps*:

> ... For a few seconds we saw our unfortunate companions sliding downwards on their backs, and spreading out their hands, endeavouring to save themselves. They passed from our sight uninjured, disappeared one by one, and fell from precipice to precipice on to the Matterhorngletscher below, a distance of nearly 4,000 feet in height. From the moment the rope broke it was impossible to help them.

The English poet Christina Rossetti (1830-94) made a long tour through Switzerland. Among English painters there was Elijah Walton (1832-80) who specialised in mountain scenery. His books of reproductions of his Swiss paintings were very popular for some twenty years in England.

The Swiss violinist, conductor and composer, Jakob Zeugheer (b. 1808), died in Liverpool.

Albert Eugster, from Appenzell, came to London where he perfected his soda syphon, and later founded the British Syphon Manufacturing

c. 1865

MICHEL A. CROZ. — Hadow. — Charles Hudson 1828-1865 — Lord F. Douglas 1847

Peter Taugwalder Vater — Edward Whymper 1865 — 1865 (22) Peter Taugwalder Sohn

Edward Whymper and his party who made the ascent of the Matterhorn, 1865.

Co. Ltd. The project was financed partly by the Swiss banker Louis Falck of Lucerne. Several of Eugster's descendants in Britain enjoyed distinguished military careers (see also 1912).

1866   Sir George Grove (1820-1900), editor of the famous dictionary of music, made the first of several stays in Switzerland, visiting Lucerne, Altdorf and Andermatt.

Geld und Geist, a work by the Swiss author Albert Bitzius (1797-1854), known as 'Jeremias Gotthelf', was published in an English translation as *Wealth and Spirit*.

The forerunner of the Nestlé Group, the Anglo-Swiss Condensed

The Matterhorn, photographed by Edward Whymper and annotated by him.

Milk Co., was founded in Zurich. A Swiss company, its intention was to export largely to the United Kingdom. It opened its first factory in England in 1872. It merged with Nestlé in 1905.

The secretary of the British Legation in Berne, Horace Rumbold (later to return as Minister), wrote to London about the attachment of the Swiss to education:

> With the matter of education the Swiss people manifest a veritable passion and it is a thing worthy of sincere admiration, though but natural perhaps in the land that gave birth to Rousseau, Pestalozzi, Fellenberg and others, to note what heavy self-imposed pecuniary sacrifices they cheerfully make to the cause.

1867 Opening of the Mont Cenis route, linking Italy by rail with Switzerland and France, via the Mont Cenis tunnel into Savoy and Geneva. The British engineer Thomas Brassey built most of the line. Both British and Swiss capital had participated in this project with the French. Among the British bankers interested were Hambros, and among the Swiss were Lombard Odier of Geneva.

Ferdinand Hurter (1844-98), Swiss industrial chemist, came to England to work on the Leblanc soda process in Widnes, Lancashire. When the United Alkali Company was founded in 1890 by a merger of the major Leblanc manufacturers in the United Kingdom, Hurter was appointed chief chemist and set up the first real industrial research laboratories in Britain. In his spare time, Hurter carried out important photographic research with his friend V.C. Driffield, and for many years the speed of photographic plates and film was expressed in terms of their 'H & D' number.

Davos still remained to be discovered by the British. One visitor, R.H. Hutton, remarked that 'Davos is a primitive watering place inhabited almost solely by the Swiss.' (But see 1869, 1877 and 1891.)

The Revd J.J. Hornby, with Swiss guides, made the first ascent of the Gletscherhorn (Bernese Oberland). He also nearly achieved the first ascent (in 1865) of the Breithorn in the Oberland, but was just five minutes behind E. von Fellenberg.

No Thoroughfare, a play written jointly by Charles Dickens and his friend Wilkie Collins after the latter had accompanied Dickens on his second visit to Switzerland in 1853, was published in London. It included a striking description of the Swiss presence in London's Soho in the 1860s:

A curious colony of mountaineers has long been enclosed within that small flat London district of Soho. Swiss watchmakers, Swiss silver-chasers, Swiss jewellers, Swiss importers of Swiss musical boxes and Swiss toys of various kinds, draw close together there. Swiss professors of music, painting and languages; Swiss artificers in steady work; Swiss couriers, and other Swiss servants chronically out of place; industrious Swiss laundresses and clear-starchers; mysteriously existing Swiss of both sexes; Swiss creditable and Swiss discreditable; Swiss to be trusted by all means, and Swiss to be trusted by no means; these divers Swiss particles are attracted to a centre in the district of Soho. Shabby Swiss eating-houses, coffee-houses, and lodging houses, Swiss drinks and dishes, Swiss service for Sundays, and Swiss schools for weekdays, are all to be found there . . .

1868 Queen Victoria went on holiday to Switzerland. Together with Prince Arthur and Princess Louise, she stayed in a pension on a hill above Lucerne, near the present site of the Hotel Gütsch. Among other trips she made was one to the top of Mount Pilatus, escorted by

The view from Mount Pilatus.

her Highland attendants. She rode to the summit on her own pony which she had brought with her from England. For her journies on Lake Lucerne, the Swiss authorities put the steamer *Winkelried* at her disposal. A number of hotels and tea-rooms in Switzerland were subsequently named after her.

An Anglo-Swiss Postal Convention was signed in London.

The poet Gerard Manley Hopkins (1844-89) visited the Valais.

Professor John Tyndall was the first to traverse the Matterhorn from Breuil to Zermatt, while T.L. Murray Browne made a first ascent of the Eberfluh (Bernese Oberland).

The Alabama arbitration at Geneva. A new advance in the settlement of international disputes was made in Geneva as a result of the Alabama arbitration. Claims for damage done by Confederate cruisers equipped or harboured by British ports during the American Civil War had caused great strains between Britain and America. Their subsequent agreement to submit the dispute to an arbitration commission in Geneva was the first occasion when two great powers pledged themselves in advance to accept the results of international arbitration. Geneva's prestige as a centre for the resolution of international problems was much enhanced (and Geneva became the natural site for the League of Nations after the First World War).

However, the circumstances surrounding the appointment of the Swiss arbitrator, Jakob Stämpfli, and indeed the £3m damages he awarded against Great Britain, caused some displeasure in London. When the then British Minister to Switzerland, A.G. Bonar, retired from that post, the Foreign Office reduced the rank of the British representative from full envoy to Minister Resident, and the salary was cut by half, from £2,800 a year to £1,400. (See also 1881.)

1869 Queen Victoria's holiday in Switzerland stimulated more Britons to emulate her example. Mürren in the Bernese Oberland was already fashionable; and George Butler, one of the tourists there, complained that it was 'crowded to excess with English people'.

Davos received its first English winter visitor, Arthur William Waters.

Two British ladies, Miss Emmeline Lewis-Lloyd and Miss Stratton, made an attempt to climb the Matterhorn.

Skaters in Switzerland around 1870

John Ruskin, in Lugano, visited the church of Santa Maria degli Angeli and saw the frescoes of Bernardino Luini (1529). He wrote:

The crucifixion fails in colour, all its blue having changed . . . [but it is] the greatest rendering of the Catholic conception of the Passion existing in the world . . . and for my part, I would give the whole Sistine Chapel for the small upper corner of this, with the Infidelity of St Thomas and the Ascension.

During the Franco-Prussian War payments between Britain and Switzerland were suspended. Some debts were settled by couriers carrying gold sovereigns between the two countries.

1870

The year saw the publication in England of another book to become a classic in the literature of Alpine climbing, *The High Alps without Guides* by the Revd A.G. Girdlestone.

An English church, St Peter's, was opened in Zermatt.

1871 The British engineer Charles Brown (senior), who had begun building steam engines at Sulzer Bros works in 1851, founded the Swiss Locomotive and Machine Works in Winterthur. The first engines he built were four rack and pinion locomotives for the Rigi Railway. Later, in the 1880s, he joined the Oerlikon machine works, before eventually retiring to Basel where he practised as a consulting engineer. His son, Charles Eugene Brown, was also at Oerlikon and later became one of the founders of Brown Boveri & Co. Ltd (see 1885 and 1891).

Books on mountaineering were now becoming increasingly popular in England. In 1871 Leslie Stephen's book *The Playground of Europe* appeared, which aroused the interest of many more British in holidays in Switzerland. In describing a scene in the Bernese Oberland, he wrote:

> No earthly object that I have seen approaches in grandeur the stupendous mountain wall whose battlements overhang in mid-air the villages of Lauterbrunnen and Grindelwald; the lower hills that rise beneath it, like the long Atlantic rollers beaten back from the granite cliffs on our western coast, are a most effective contrast to its stern magnificence.

Death of Sigismond Thalberg (b. 1812), born in Geneva though of Austrian origin, the pianoforte virtuoso whose performances were compared to those of Liszt, Taussig and Rubinstein. Among his own compositions was a set of pianoforte variations on 'God Save the Queen'.

1872 The Swiss federal government signed with the British government its first double taxation agreement, on behalf of the canton of Vaud (for the benefit of British residents in that canton and covering the avoidance of double taxation on legacies).

The Swiss historian Jacob Burckhardt (1818-97) delivered an address to young Basel businessmen in which he forecast English as 'the future world language'.

Werner Munzinger (1832-75) of Olten, Swiss explorer and linguist, was made Governor-General of the Eastern Sudan. He had been British Consul at Massawa in 1865, and an assistant to Robert Napier during the Anglo-Abyssinian War (1868).

Sir H. Rider Haggard (1856-1925), the novelist, visited Flüelen, Altdorf and Andermatt, while the British artist Benjamin Williams

Leslie Stephen (right) with Swiss guide Melchior Anderegg

Leader (1831-1923) made the first of several visits to Switzerland to paint.

1873 A young Pole, Joseph Conrad (1857-1924), later to become a prominent English novelist; was on a six-weeks' tour of Switzerland. Near Andermatt he stayed at an inn which was full of English engineers who were working on the St Gotthard tunnel. Listening to them, he experienced his first sustained contact with spoken English. Shortly after, on the Furka pass, Conrad met 'an unforgettable Englishman' with red face, white moustache, and wearing knickerbockers, confidently leading a party of tourists. He seemed, Conrad wrote later, to be 'in the mystical ordering of common events, the ambassador of my future'. These two episodes determined Conrad to go to England and the sea.

John Brunner (1842-1919), son of the Revd John Brunner of Zurich, who had come to England and started a school, set up in business in Cheshire to produce alkali with his partner Ludwig Mond. The company prospered. Beginning with less than £20,000 capital in 1873 Brunner Mond & Co. showed capital employed of over £18m by 1926, when the company became one of the constituent companies of Imperial Chemical Industries (ICI). Brunner's output of soda ash rose from 800 tons in 1874 to 240,000 tons by 1903, by which time Britain was producing, thanks to Brunner, half of the world's supply. John Brunner went into Parliament as a Liberal. His father had been guided by the principles of the Swiss educationalist Pestalozzi (see 1805), which in turn influenced John Brunner's own campaigns in later life for educational and penitentiary reform.

Death in Cambridge (Massachusetts) of the Swiss scientist and zoologist Louis Agassiz (b. 1807), famous for his glacier exploration. He was an opponent of Darwin.

1874 British tourists in Switzerland were probably still the most numerous of all foreign visitors.

The first Anglo-Swiss extradition treaty was concluded.

The Unione Ticinese, a society of Swiss from the Ticino, was formed in London.

The Anglo-Swiss Condensed Milk Company, which had opened its first tinned milk factory in England in 1872, acquired the English

Sir John Brunner, joint founder of Brunner Mond & Co., which became one of the constituent companies of I.C.I.

Condensed Milk Co. of London with its additional manufacturing facilities.

British investors obtained a concession from the canton of Neuchâtel to exploit an asphalt mine in Presta, near Travers. They set up the Neuchâtel Asphalt Company to export to Britain and the Empire.

1875

The painter Edward Compton (b. 1849) was in Switzerland on one of several visits. He became a specialist in Alpine scenes, particularly of the Bernese Oberland.

One Victorian who was not enamoured of Alpine scenes was the writer and aesthete Walter Pater. He called the Alpine lakes that he had seen 'horrid pots of blue paint'.

1876   Sulzer Bros of Winterthur first began to export to the United Kingdom.

One of the earliest pioneers of winter sports in Switzerland, Franklin Adams, an Englishman who had learned to ski at St Petersburg, made a rough toboggan run at St Moritz.

1877   The historian John Addington Symonds (1840-93) went to live in Davos for health reasons. Two years later, with Christian Buol, a Swiss, he built a toboggan run there. In 1883, with four English friends, he founded the Davos Tobogganing Club. Later still, Symonds wrote:

Neither Rome nor the Riviera wins our hearts like Switzerland. We do not lie awake in London thinking of them; we do not long so intensely, as the year comes round, to re-visit them. Our affection is less a passion than that which we cherish for Switzerland.

1878   Proposals were made to Berne for an Anglo-Swiss treaty on the reciprocal protection of trade marks. Believing that such a treaty would place Switzerland at a disadvantage vis-à-vis Britain, the Swiss Parliament decided to defer the issue until a federal law on the subject had been passed (see 1880).

The novel which firmly established the fame of Henry James (1843-1916), *Daisy Miller,* first appeared in the London *Cornhill Magazine.* The opening chapter of the novel, set in Vevey, was derived from James's stay in Switzerland in 1872. (He was also there as a child.)

1879   A Swiss engineer, Hans Renold (1852-1943), came to Britain to set up in a small factory at Salford, Lancashire, making transmission chains. In 1903 he set up his own company, Hans Renold Ltd (see also 1930).

The British composer Sir Arthur Sullivan (1842-1900) was on holiday at Pontresina and St Moritz.

A society of German-speaking Swiss residents, the Schweizer-Bund, was formed in England.

Robert Louis Stevenson, 1887: by Sir William Blake Richmond.

From this date, from time to time the British War Office sent British observers to the Swiss military manoeuvres.

Robert Louis Stevenson (1850-94) convalesced at Davos for what was to be the first of several winters there. He finished writing his story *Treasure Island*, and composed several of his best essays. With his stepson he set up the Davos press, and cut blocks for his own illustrations. In the Hotel Belvedere, where he first stayed, he found 'eleven English parsons, all entirely inoffensive; four, true human beings . . .' Later he got his own house, and wrote to a friend:

1880

Now we have a fine, canny, twinkling, shrewd, auld . . . peasant body who gives us good food and keeps us in good spirits. If we could only understand what she says! But she speaks Davos language, which is to German what 'Aberdeen-awa' is to English, so it comes heavy.

The Genevan painter Albert Gos (b. 1852) exhibited his *Matterhorn* at the Royal Academy in London, where it won high praise.

An Anglo-Swiss declaration on trade marks protection was signed in Berne, and shortly afterwards a treaty for the mutual surrender of fugitive criminals, to replace the original extradition treaty signed in 1874.

The British market now occupied the first place among Switzerland's Western European customers for machine-made embroideries.

1881 The Foreign Office restored the British envoy's status in Berne to full Minister Plenipotentiary (see 1868). Lord Vivian, the Minister, reported to London:

'The President . . . expressed to me in the name of the whole Federal Council their warm and sincere satisfaction at the re-establishment of the British Legation in Switzerland on its former footing of rank. His Excellency said that this mark of the goodwill of England came at a peculiarly opportune moment, when a crusade was most unjustifiably preached against Switzerland for her alleged connivance at abuses of the asylum she gave to political refugees . . .

The author of *Erewhon*, Samuel Butler (1835-1902), who for several years running had spent two months each summer in the Ticino, published his *Alps and Sanctuaries of Piedmont and the Canton Ticino*.

William Martin Conway (1856-1937) published *The Zermatt Pocket Guide* to climbs in the Pennine Alps, the first real climbing guide as distinct from tourist guides.

1882 The British composer Dame Ethel Smyth (1858-1944) visited Berne, Thun, Interlaken, Altdorf and travelled through the St Gotthard to Bellinzona.

1883 The newly formed Salvation Army, which had found many adherents in Britain, its country of origin, staged an 'invasion' of Switzerland. The 'Army's' methods of conversion of sinners were much resented by the Swiss authorities. There were riots in some cities. In Neuchâtel, Miss Booth, the daughter of founder 'General' William

Booth, was first imprisoned and then expelled from the country. In 1888 a severe decree against the 'Army' was issued in Berne. (Today the Salvation Army has a handsome headquarters in Berne and enjoys considerable local financial support.)

A British chemist who had earlier tested in Switzerland the newly invented milk chocolate of the rising industrialist Daniel Peter, ordered 100 lb of the produce, giving Peter his first export order (see also 1903). Peter's company later became part of the Nestlé group.

For some years, in the British textile industry, over-production had been causing spinners to offer their cotton yarns on the Continental markets, and notably in Switzerland, at very low prices. Swiss manufacturers who were badly affected invoked anti-dumping legislation against these British imports.

The watercolourist Henry George Willink (1851-1938) was in Switzerland on one of his annual visits; and the writer Edmund Gosse (1849-1928) was on holiday at Villars.

1884

The new Swiss tariff of 1884 raised duties against imported yarns to some extent but, during the next few years, British yarns continued to be sold to the Swiss market at 'dumped' prices.

First publication in its English translation of *Heidi* by the Swiss children's writer Johanna Spyri (1829-1901). The book was read by several generations of English children, many of whom formed their ideas of Switzerland from it. More than 100 English editions have been published since 1884.

1885

The Englishman Charles Eugene Brown (1863-1924), the son of Charles Brown (see 1871), took over the management of the electrical engineering department at the Oerlikon works at the age of twenty-two. He pioneered in Switzerland some outstanding achievements, including the provision of the equipment for the first electric locomotive in Switzerland and, in 1891, the transmission of electricity (in Germany) at a voltage of 25,000 over a distance of 175 km, previously regarded as impossible (see 1891).

Official trade statistics began to be published regularly. Switzerland's (visible) trade with the United Kingdom (imports plus exports) totalled Sw.fr. 151m. Partly at least owing to the Swiss tariffs, Swiss imports from the United Kingdom at Sw.fr. 52m, were only just

Skeleton riders in 1891. The Cresta Run, opened in the winter season 1884/5, is rebuilt every year in December with soft snow.

over half the value of Swiss exports to the United Kingdom, at Sw.fr. 99m.

The possibilities for winter sports at Swiss mountain resorts were now coming to be realised. Tobogganing was increasingly popular. The Cresta Run was organised at St Moritz, on the initiative of a group of British sportsmen.

Johannes Badrutt, hotelier of St Moritz, imported into Switzerland the game of curling from Scotland.

Der Heilige, a historical novel by the Swiss writer Conrad Ferdinand Meyer (1825-1898) was published in an English translation as *Thomas à Becket the Saint.*

Death of August Corrodi (b. 1826), Swiss 'dialect writer' who made translations into Swiss-German of the songs of Robert Burns.

1886　While a British family, the Browns, were achieving success in Switzerland (see 1885 and 1891), a Swiss family, the Gattis, prospered in England. Arriving as poor immigrants from the Ticino, by the 1880s they owned the Charing Cross and Strand Electricity Supply Co., nine chocolate factories in and around London, some eighteen restaurants and ten theatres and music halls (see also 1911).

Carlo Gatti (1809-1878) founded the very successful United Carlo Gatti Co. to distribute ice throughout the capital. The ice was cut out in blocks from the fiords in Norway and transported in the company's ships to the Port of London. Agostino (1841-97) and Stefano Gatti (1848-1906) owned the prestigious Royal Adelaide Gallery Restaurant which occupied most of what is now the site of Coutts's bank in the Strand.[21]

The proprietor of the Schweizerhof Hotel at Neuhausen, near the Rhine Falls, built a small English church in the grounds of his hotel for the benefit of his English and American guests.

1887　The British Merchandise Marks Act of 1887 required all imported foreign goods to be stamped with their country of origin. In due course this had the effect of encouraging imports of Swiss watches into the colonies, as colonial buyers found that the best cheap watches were made in Switzerland.

In pursuance of its policy to give more protection to Swiss industry and agriculture, the federal government introduced the second increase in import duties in four years.

Some British artists who came to paint in Switzerland at around this time included John William Brooke (1854-1919), William Gershon Collingwood (1854-1932), Samuel Hodson (1836-1908), Emily Murray Paterson (1855-1934), John MacWhirter (1839-1911) and Sir Ernest Waterlow (1850-1919).

Bishop T.E. Wilkinson consecrated the new English church at Lausanne.

1888 The Swiss Mercantile Society was founded in London by the Schweizerischer Kaufmännischer Verein, to help young Swiss arriving in Britain. Today the Society's language school is used not only by Swiss but by other foreign nationalities as well.

Death of Ferdinand Schmidt (b. 1823) of Berne who, under the name of Dranmor, made some excellent German translations of the work of British poets.

The Swiss Geigy pharmaceuticals company appointed its first British agent (in Manchester).

There were estimated to be about 5,000 British residents living in Switzerland.

César Ritz (1850-1918), a Swiss hotelier from Niederwald in the Valais, was invited by Richard D'Oyly Carte (1844-1901) to take charge when the new Savoy Hotel was opened in London. Ritz at first refused but, encouraged by actress Lillie Langtry, D'Oyly Carte invited him to stay a few days as a guest. Ritz became interested in the possibilities and agreed to a contract (see also 1906).

The famous Swiss guide Melchior Anderegg came to Britain and was taken up Mount Snowdon by the English climber C.E. Mathews, who had employed Anderegg in Switzerland for many seasons.

Miss E.P. Jackson climbed to the summits of the Gross Lauteraarhorn, the Gross and Klein Fiescherhorn and the Jungfrau, all in the course of eleven days.

Colonel Napier was the first Englishman to ski at Davos.

1889 Quintin Hogg (1845-1903) organised his first Polytechnic Continental holiday to Switzerland. Conceived as an experiment to supplement school teaching in geography and history, the party consisted of sixty boys, three masters and a doctor. For twenty-seven days, the holiday cost £5.19s.0d. per head.

Among other British visitors to Switzerland that year, Thomas Henry Huxley was on holiday at Maloja, while Sir Hubert Parry, the composer, visited Lugano, Montreux and Berne.

The young Swiss pianist Otto Hegner gave a series of concerts in London. He was hailed as a boy prodigy. He returned to England several times in later years.

There were three British consulates in Switzerland at this time, at Zurich, Geneva and Lausanne. In 1889 the British vice-consul at Lausanne, Alfred Galland, founded the Banque Galland & Cie there. Later, the Banque Galland opened seasonal agencies at Zermatt and Grindelwald, partly to serve British tourists at those centres.

1890

By about 1890 there were over 2,000 Swiss from the Italian speaking canton of the Ticino living in Britain. Among some of the more notable restaurateurs there were (apart from the Gattis – see 1886) the Monico family and the Pagani family.

After an insurrection in the Ticino, Angelo Castoni, who was accused of murdering Councillor Rossi, a Ticinese minister, was arrested in London. His extradition was demanded by the Swiss but was refused by the Queen's Bench Division. The next year, following a reconciliation in the Ticino, a revised constitution was adopted and the revolters were acquitted.

An Englishman Edward Knocker was the first to introduce skiing into Meiringen (Bernese Oberland). Another, Wilson Smith, introduced the bob-sleigh into St Moritz.

The Swiss entrepreneur Julius Maggi set up a depot in London from which he began to sell his Maggi soups in the United Kingdom.

1891

After having had only commercial and consular representatives in London since 1817, the Swiss government upgraded the post, and Charles Bourcart was appointed the first diplomatic representative of the Swiss Confederation to the Court of St James's.

Charles Eugene Brown (see 1885) and Walter Boveri, a young German whom Brown had put in charge of project planning at Oerlikon, got together to found Brown Boveri & Co. at Baden. The first order was for the new Baden hydro-electric power station for which Charles Brown designed the generators.

One of Brown's and Boveri's several backers was Theodor Pfister of Baden, who had been a very successful merchant in London for over twenty years.

The Browns, father and son, Charles Brown (left) (1827-1905) founded the Swiss Locomotive and Machine Works in Winterthur; Charles Eugene Brown (1863-1924) was co-founder of Brown Boveri & Cie.

The author Sir Arthur Conan Doyle (1859-1930) chose the Reichenbach Falls, near Meiringen, as the setting apparently to kill off his hero, Sherlock Holmes, and end (for the time being) the famous detective series.

Gerald Fox, an Englishman, was the first to introduce skiing to Grindelwald. Skating there had for some time been popular among the British.

The 1890s saw the gradual expansion of British consular posts in Switzerland as the number of British residents and British tourists in that country grew apace. In 1891 British pro-consuls were appointed in Davos and St Moritz where, it was estimated, some 500 British lung patients were living.

The British pro-consul in Davos, W.G. Lockett, became a particularly well-known figure there for many years.

A military attaché's post was established at the British Legation in Berne.

1892   A new and disturbing element in Anglo-Swiss relations was the increasing number of anti-British articles which had begun to appear in the Swiss press. Influenced largely by the increasingly hostile attitude towards Britain of the German press, the Swiss newspapers were critical particularly of British policy in Africa and in some of the other colonies.

Some 17% of all Swiss exports went to the United Kingdom, while about 4.8% of all Swiss imports came from the United Kingdom. The figure included goods for onward transmission to other destinations via British ports. In terms of Swiss francs, Swiss imports from the United Kingdom were at their lowest for many years. This reflected, in part at least, the general decline in prices in the United Kingdom at that time.

The Swiss Bally Shoe Company opened an agency in London, to become the London Shoe Co. Ltd in 1899, and Bally Aarau Shoe Co. Ltd in 1908.

The 'cello concerto by the Swiss-born German composer Joachim Raff (1822-82) was performed in London (with Hugo Becker as soloist).

The English church in Grindelwald (among other buildings) was destroyed in the great fire there. The Bear Hotel, where the fire started, had only the Christmas before received its first group of winter visitors from Britain.

1893

British firms in Manchester had for long supplied large quantities of cheap grey cotton cloth ('Jacconets') to Swiss printers in Glarus which, when 'finished' were exported to the East as handkerchiefs. As a result of pressure from Swiss spinners and weavers, the federal government imposed prohibitive duties on this cloth, to the detriment not only of the British suppliers but also the small Glarus printers. The Manchester Chamber of Commerce protested to the Swiss government, claiming equal rights, under the Treaty of 1855, of duty-free temporary importation of their goods as were enjoyed by other Continental suppliers to Switzerland. The Swiss authorities maintained that free temporary admission could only be given to neighbouring states, and that the United Kingdom on account of its geographical position, was debarred. The British Minister in Berne suggested to London that a 10% duty should be imposed on Swiss watches in retaliation but the British government would do nothing which might seem like protection.

The Swiss federal railways opened an agency in London.

Early skiers in the Engadine, c. 1893.

The piano concerto by the Swiss composer Hans Huber (1852-1921) was first performed in London, with the Swiss virtuoso Otto Hegner as soloist.

A British consulate was opened in Berne, and a British pro-consul was appointed in Lucerne to help the increasing numbers of British tourists visiting central Switzerland.

1894   The young Winston Churchill, L.S. Amery and some other companions were holidaying near Zermatt. Amery wrote:

> Among those in whom our fame kindled the flame of ambition – short lived in this direction at least – was our old school fellow Winston Churchill who, in spite of our efforts to dissuade him from what we urged was a long and tiresome trudge unworthy of his prowess, insisted on climbing Monte Rosa because it was actually the highest mountain in Switzerland.[22]

The Swiss guide Melchior Anderegg made another visit to Britain and was honoured at a dinner of the Alpine Club where 260 people paid tribute to him.

The distinguished musician Arnold Dolmetsch of Zurich gave a series of concerts of early English music at his home in Dulwich (see also 1925).

1895 Anglo-Swiss trade was now slowly increasing. However, owing largely to the fact that most United Kingdom goods coming into Switzerland faced Swiss protective tariffs, while Swiss goods generally enjoyed entry free of duty into the United Kingdom there was a large imbalance in Switzerland's favour. The Swiss tariffs were a source of continual discontent among British exporters.

Publication of *Les roches blanches* by the Swiss novelist Edouard Rod (1857-1910), which appeared in an English translation as *White Rocks*.

Sir Arthur Conan Doyle was at Caux, where he finished the first of his 'Brigadier Gerard' series and began to write *Rodney Stone*.

1896 Another outburst of anti-British articles in the Swiss press was occassioned by the news of the Jameson Raid on the Transvaal and by the German Kaiser's telegram to President Kruger.

Among British artists painting in Switzerland at around this time were Harry William Adams (1868-1947), Sydney Lee (1866-1949), and James Lockhead (1866-1921).

British sportsmen at St Moritz played Davos at cricket on skates.

1897 Thomas Hardy (1840-1928) visited Switzerland. At Lausanne he wrote his poem of that name, on the anniversary of Gibbon's completion of *The Decline and Fall of the Roman Empire*. At Zermatt Hardy wrote his sonnet 'To the Matterhorn', about Whymper's triumph and tragedy:

> Thirty-two years since, up against the sun,
> Seven shapes, thin atomies to lower sight,
> Labouringly leapt and gained thy gabled height,
> And four lives paid for what seven had won.

The Swiss composer and inventor of eurhythmics, Jacques Dalcroze (see 1950), conducted a performance of his patriotic cantata 'Poème Alpestre' at St James's Hall in London. The final part included a rendering of the Swiss national hymn 'Rufst Du, Mein Vaterland' sung to the tune of 'God Save the Queen'.

An early bob-sleigh, St Moritz, 1893. The braker is the Revd Hofmann, former director of the St Moritz Tourist Office.

1898   The Swiss Bank Corporation was the first of the big Swiss banks to open an office in London. Probably one reason for the bank's decision was the steady increase of Swiss exports to the United Kingdom at this time.

Lever Bros of Liverpool established a Swiss company, Sunlight AG, at Olten.

The journey from Basel to London (595 miles) was now accomplished in 14 hours 35 minutes.

The first bob-sleigh race was held in St Moritz. It was won by an Englishman, Lord Hemsley.

At least six British climbers were killed in the Swiss mountains.

With the outbreak of the Boer War Swiss sympathies soon swung largely onto the side of the Boers. The Swiss press became increasingly hostile to Britain, publishing news and comments almost exclusively anti-British. Sir Frederick St John, then British Minister in Berne, wrote of this time in his memoirs: 'Great Britain had few friends on the Continent of Europe, and fewest of all, perhaps, in Switzerland.'

1899

The Quintet in F ('On Swiss themes') by the Swiss composer Joseph Lauber (b. 1864) received its first English performance at a South Place concert in London.

Oscar Wilde was in Geneva and Gland. He wrote: 'I don't like Switzerland. It has produced nothing but theologians and waiters.'

The Twentieth Century

British worries over German influence in Switzerland – the growth of winter sports – sixty English churches – a British military commission – the First World War – developing commercial relations – the great era of skiing – world depression – the Second World War – bilateral agreements – cultural contacts – the growth in trade and investment – closer economic cooperation – increased official contacts.

1900 In the face of the continuing hostile comment in Switzerland against the British conduct of the war against the Boers, a small group of Swiss in Zurich published a German translation of Sir Arthur Conan Doyle's reasoned pamphlet on the war. They commented:

> So much untruth has been published in the last two years about the causes of the South African conflict, the manner in which it has been conducted by the English . . . and so much has been distorted and misrepresented . . . that it is a relief to find a man like Conan Doyle, an Irishman, writing impartially, and on authentic data, the history of the war and the circumstances that led to it. Of all the charges brought against the British people, none is more astounding than that of barbarity and lack of human feelings. Has not England been ever the promoter of the cause of freedom and humanity?

A similar pamphlet was published in the French-speaking part of Switzerland by a group of thirty-six, including Edward Tallichet, editor of the *Bibliothèque Universelle* of Lausanne, who had already himself, despite opposition, written several articles in Britain's favour. The group reminded their compatriots:

> Not only has the British nation never evinced any hostility to our country, but the British Government has, on several occasions efficiently assisted us. In every [British] colony will be found numerous Swiss – some of them directing important industrial and commercial houses – all largely benefiting by a colonial system in which there is no impediment of any sort to activity and labour; and in which, in some points, there is even greater liberty than that of which we boast.

Reacting to the general attitude of the Swiss press, several British newspapers published scare stories about Swiss treatment of British tourists. The *Financial News* headed one report from Lucerne: 'Swiss violence for English tourists.'

The trade balance continued to be very much in Switzerland's favour, with Swiss exports to the United Kingdom nearly three times United Kingdom imports into Switzerland.

Brown Boveri & Co. Ltd of Baden (see 1891) obtained a licence to exploit the steam turbine invented by Parsons of the United Kingdom.

The Swiss colony in Britain was estimated to number approximately 20,000 and the British colony in Switzerland about 9,500.

The anti-British attitude of the Swiss press continued. An article in the *Journal de Genève* called the British Colonial Secretary, Joseph Chamberlain 'easily the most universally detested man in Europe'. The new British Minister in Berne, Sir W. Coyningham Greene, wrote to Lord Lansdowne:

1901

When I tell your Lordship that there are no fewer than seven hundred newspapers and periodicals circulating in this little country, it is easy to see what mischief may be wrought by this indiscriminate dissemination of falsehood among the ignorant population of the rural districts.

However, the anti-British articles in the *Journal de Genève* caused two members of its board of administration to resign in protest.

At a memorial service held in Berne Minster for Queen Victoria, some 4,000 people attended despite the general attitude of the Swiss press.

The imbalance in Anglo-Swiss trade became even greater. Swiss exports to the United Kingdom were four times the United Kingdom imports into Switzerland.

Sir Augustus Prevost (1837-1913), a partner in A.L. Prevost of London, Swiss financiers and merchants (see 1813), became Governor of the Bank of England. He had been a director of the Bank since 1881.

The British composer Frederick Delius (1862-1934) completed his opera *A Village Romeo and Juliet* with libretto based on the Swiss writer Gottfried Keller's story *Romeo und Julia auf dem Dorf*.

As a result of continuing pressure from Swiss industry and agriculture an ultra-protectionist general import tariff was announced by the

1902

federal government. It was accepted by a popular vote in the following year.

The political and trade problems which Switzerland posed for British policy had little effect on tourism. The founder of Lunn's tours, Sir Henry Lunn, was the first to popularise winter sports in the Bernese Oberland when he persuaded hoteliers in Adelboden to open for a winter tour from Britain.

Skiing was just beginning to become a popular sport. Sir Henry's son, Arnold Lunn, later wrote:

That first season Canon Savage, Percival Farrar, and a few others were the only visitors who ever attempted even the smallest tours on ski . . . I came back from the Elsighorn where I had scarcely skied for five minutes, drunk with the beauty of my first view from a winter summit.

Hilaire Belloc (1870-1953) published his account of a pilgrimage on foot across Europe, *The Path to Rome,* in which appeared his notable description of his first view of the Alps from the edge of the Jura:

I saw between the branches of the trees in front of me a sight in the sky that made me stop breathing, just as great danger at sea, or great surprise in love, or a great deliverance will make a man stop breathing . . . For there below me, thousands of feet below me, was what seemed an illimitable plain: at the end of that world was an horizon, and the dim bluish sky that overhangs an horizon . . . One saw the sky beyond the edge of the world setting purer as the vault rose. But right up – a belt in that empyrean – ran peak and field and needle of intense ice, remote, remote from the world. Sky beneath them and sky above them, a steadfast legion, they glittered as though with the armour of the immovable armies of Heaven.

The orientalist Gertrude Bell (1868-1926), holidaying in the Bernese Oberland, climbed up the face of the Finsteraarhorn with two guides in a blizzard. She had previously played cricket with Lady Mary Monkswell at Rosenlaui.

A British consulate was established in Lucerne and a vice-consulate in Montreux. The same year a new English church at Château d'Oex was consecrated by Bishop T.E. Wilkinson.

1903 Hans Wilsdorf (1881-1960), who had served his early years in the watch and clock industry in La Chaux-de-Fonds, came to Britain and set up the firm of Wilsdorf & Davis. At a time when most watches were made for the pocket, Wilsdorf ordered small Swiss movements from Aegeler of Bienne and launched his wrist watches in England,

Lucerne: *watercolour by Albert Goodwin, 1903.*

which he called by the trademark of Rolex. Wilsdorf later took British nationality. (See also 1920.)

Half of the Swiss manufacturer Daniel Peter's sales of Sw. fr. 6m of milk chocolate (see 1883) were now being bought by Britain.

One of the pioneers of skiing in Switzerland, E.C. Richardson, founded the Ski Club of Great Britain. The same year Richardson, together with his brother C.W.R. Richardson and two other enthusiasts, formed the Davos English Ski Club.

The English climber Walter Larden began to ski in Davos. 'Skiing at Davos I found myself among a new race of people. To them a mountain was a thing to come down; to me it still remained a thing to go up.'

Among other British artists working in Switzerland in 1903 were Sir Charles Holmes (1868-1936), a future director of the National Gallery in London, and the watercolourist Albert Goodwin (1845-1932), who was painting, among other places, in Thun and Lucerne.

Two more British vice-consulates were opened, one in Basel and another at St Galllen.

1904 An English church was opened in Arolla. British churches were now being established in increasing numbers at many mountain resorts. At one time there were over sixty Anglican churches or chapels in Switzerland, controlled mainly by two societies. The Colonial and Continental Church Society had churches at, besides Arolla, Adelboden, Andermatt, Les Avants, Ballaigues, Beatenberg, Bex, Champéry, Chandolin, Château d'Oex, Clarens, Davos, Les Diablerets, Eggishorn, Gletsch, Glion, Grindelwald, Interlaken, Loèche-les-Bains, Leysin, Locarno, Lucerne, Montreux-Clarens, Neuchâtel, Pully, Riffelalp, Saas-Fee, Samedan, Schinznach, Tarasp, Thun, Verbier, Vevey, Villars, Wengen and Zermatt. The Society for the Propagation of the Gospel in Foreign Parts had churches at Aigle, Arosa, Axenfels, Axenstein, Bad Ragaz, Belalp, Berne, Caux, Engelberg, Finhaut, Lugano, Maloja, Meiringen, Montana, Mürren, Neuhausen, Pontresina, Ragaz, Saas-Grund, St Moritz and Sierre. There were churches belonging to independent organisations at Geneva, Lausanne-Ouchy, Montcaux, Montreux-Territet, Spiez and Zurich. In addition Anglican services were conducted either in local Swiss Protestant churches or in hotels at, among other places, Basel, Champfèr, Chur, Gstaad, Gryon, Heiden, Kandersteg, Lauterbrunnen, Thusis and Vitznau (see also 1556).

Swiss tariffs were still an impediment to British trade. Owing to the high Swiss tariff on imports of their Sunlight soap, Lever Bros of Liverpool (see 1898) set up a factory to make it in Switzerland.

But, after nearly seven years of argument (see 1893), the Swiss government allowed 75,000 pieces per annum of grey cotton 'Jacconets' cloth to be imported from the United Kingdom duty-free, for treatment and re-export.

The Victoria Hall, Geneva's most important concert hall, was given to the city by a former British consul in Geneva, Daniel Barton, who had built the hall in 1894. Barton's wife, a granddaughter of the former British Prime Minister, Sir Robert Peel, who outlived her husband by twenty-eight years, became a celebrated hostess to League of Nations statesmen in Geneva in the 1920s and was known as the 'Queen of Geneva'.

1905 In Switzerland the Simplon tunnel under the Alps was completed and King Edward VII sent a telegram of congratulations to the Swiss Federal Council. The gesture was widely and warmly commented upon in the Swiss press. Reporting this to London, the British Minister in Berne, Sir W. Coyningham Greene, wrote:

It is also proof of the sound and rational sympathy which links at a distance the two European nations that were the first to know political liberty. The distance which separates them does not prevent them from understanding each other.

An Arbitration Treaty between Switzerland and the United Kingdom was ratified by the Swiss Federal Council.

Trade links were improving. Georg Fischer (see 1804), the large Schaffhausen steel company, established Le Bas Tube Co. Ltd in London, while the engineering company of Sulzer Bros (see 1876) opened a technical service office in London. Georges Dreyfuss, a son of the founder of Rotary Watches in La Chaux-de-Fonds, established a branch of the company in London. Moreover, modifications were made to the Swiss import tariff, bringing some alleviation for affected importers and for British and other suppliers.

The young Maynard Keynes (1883-1946), later to become the eminent economist, was taken by his former master at Eton, Geoffrey Winthrop Young, on a climbing tour of Switzerland, to get him away from the hothouse atmosphere of studies for his Cambridge Tripos. Keynes greatly enjoyed the challenge of several tough climbs, and wrote: 'I have seen the superbest views and the wildest and most desolate expanses of snow and ice. There was even danger . . . I liked the excitement.'

British tourists were still going to Switzerland in large numbers, and they were not all rich. A guide to economy holidays in Switzerland was published in England – *A Fortnight in Switzerland for Five Guineas* by E. Lamprell (see also 1956).

When plans for the British Army reforms were set afoot in England, the British War Minister, R.B. Haldane, asked General Douglas Haig to make a study and give his views. Haig wrote that 'the supposed situation' of military policy was 'a great war requiring the whole resources of the nation . . . The Swiss system seems to me to be exactly what is wanted to root the army in the people.'

1906

The new British military attaché in Berne, Colonel C. Delmé-Radcliffe, reported to London:

A point that very soon strikes the notice of a student of the Swiss army is the

César Ritz

influence of and sympathy for all things German . . . There can be no doubt that the Swiss army, notwithstanding its militia character and the shortness of its training, has reached a degree of efficiency which would make any of its neighbours more anxious to respect the neutrality of the country than to violate it . . .

E.C. Richardson (see 1903) and several British friends made one of the earliest mountain ski expeditions over the Strela pass and up the Brehmenbühl.

Anglo-Swiss trade began to pick up. After more than twenty years, United Kingdom exports to Switzerland began to show a significant increase.

The Swiss hotelier César Ritz (see 1888) had by this time earned a tremendous reputation in England. After having made the Savoy perhaps the best hotel in the country, he left to build the Ritz in Paris, and then the Carlton in London in 1899. In 1906 he gave his name to the Ritz Hotel in London. Edward VII declared: 'Where Ritz goes, we shall follow', and called him 'the hotelier of kings and king of hoteliers'. (Ritz is believed to be the first hotelier to have had the idea of an hotel with a bathroom for every bedroom.)

Brown Boveri & Co. Ltd (see 1891) opened an office in London and concluded later an agreement with Richardsons Westgarth & Co. Ltd for the construction of their steam turbines under licence. The number of Swiss-owned companies in the United Kingdom had now risen to about fifty.

In the opposite direction, the Royal Dutch Shell petroleum group opened an office in Switzerland, and Shell (Switzerland) was founded in Zurich.

1907 The British government asked permission of the Swiss Federal Council to send a Military Commission to study the Swiss army system and to observe the Swiss autumn manoeuvres. The Swiss willingly agreed and said that the Federal Council would be glad to take advantage of opportunities of doing something to efface unpleasant recollections of Swiss attitudes during the Boer War.

In September, a British commission of thirty, including Members of Parliament, officers, trade unionists and journalists, and led by Lord Ampthill, arrived in Basel. They spent a week in discussions and visits.

Another British vice-consulate was opened, this time in Lugano.

The Ladies Ski Club of Great Britain was founded in London by Mrs Aubry Le Blond.

1908 The visit of the British Military Commission to Switzerland unfortunately led to no firm results. The main objection of the Labour members of the mission to any army on the Swiss model appeared to be that it would serve the interests of the capitalists in the same way as a standing army.

Meanwhile the British military attaché at Berne, in his reports to London, continued to emphasise the German influence over the Swiss army and expressed strong doubts about continued Swiss neutrality in the event of war in Europe. He apparently did not however consult the British Minister in Berne about them. Sending his own annual report for 1908 to Sir Edward Grey at the Foreign Office, Sir George Bonham wrote: 'This year I have not had the advantage of seeing [Colonel Delmé-Radcliffe's] reports.' Radcliffe was also military attaché at Rome, where he normally resided.

British ski mountaineering now began in earnest (though Swiss skiers had been exploring the High Alps for some time). Scott Lindsay reached the Adler pass on ski, and C. Bracken the Blümlisalp. Cecil Wybergh crossed the Wildstrubel from Montana to Lenk, and in two more days skied across the passes to Villars. The Alpine Ski Club was founded in London by Sir Arnold Lunn.

The Swiss Re-insurance Company opened a London branch (see also 1969).

Hoffmann-La Roche Chemical Works Ltd was established in London by the Swiss pharmaceutical group, Hoffmann-La Roche of Basel. The group's founder, Fritz Hoffmann, made several visits to Britain in the following years (see also 1937).

The novelist Arnold Bennett (1867-1931) visited Vevey and commented: 'Really the scene is enchantingly beautiful.' He wrote his novel *The Card* in Vevey.

Frederic Harrison's *My Alpine Jubilee* was published. In it he wrote:

I hold, with Rousseau, Byron and Ruskin, that the highest and deepest charm the Alps can give is found in their combination of glories, as often as not in the lakes, their wooded valleys, their upland pastures – nay, even in their villages and towns – with their long record of memorable things in literature, science, history and art.

Charles Edouard Jeanneret (1887-1965), born at La Chaux-de-Fonds, known as Le Corbusier, Swiss pioneer of modern architecture, made a visit to England. As a young man, he was an admirer of the English Arts and Crafts movement; and the first houses he constructed in Switzerland (in 1906) contained decorative motifs partly based on the works of John Ruskin and Owen Jones. In his later life Le Corbusier's designs profoundly influenced a generation of British architects.

1909 Sir Henry Lunn (see 1902) opened up Mürren as a winter sports resort by organising, through his company Alpine Sports Ltd, a succession of tours of members of the Public Schools Alpine Sports

Club. Other centres that Lunn was the first to open up to winter tours from Britain included Villars, Morgins, Klosters and Lenzerheide.

The Swiss skier Professor F.F. Roget made an expedition from St Beatenberg through Interlaken and up into the Bernese Oberland via Kandersteg, the Lötschenlüke pass, the Finsteraarhorn, the Grimsel pass, and back to St Beatenberg. He wrote:

> This expedition, the first of its kind at such altitudes at that time of year [January], was an Anglo-Swiss piece of work. It was performed in company with Arnold Lunn.

W.A.M. Moore crossed the Col de la Dent Blanche and the Col d'Hérens from Zinal to Zermatt on ski.

The main categories of Swiss exports to the United Kingdom now included silk and wool products, clocks and watches, condensed milk, chocolate, chemicals and machinery. The United Kingdom's main exports to Switzerland were wool and linen goods, iron and steel, chemical products and semi-manufactures.

Following the Shell Company, the Anglo-Persian Oil Company formed a local company in Zurich, later to become BP (Schweiz).

Dr A. Wander SA of Berne set up A. Wander Ltd in Britain to import and sell their product 'Ovaltine'. They later opened a factory at King's Langley to make it there.

Increasing Swiss prosperity had led to a new rise in United Kingdom imports into Switzerland. These showed a 60% increase over five years previously, while Swiss exports to the United Kingdom were up 12½%.

1910

After the Swiss army manoeuvres, where two high-ranking officers of the German and Austrian general staffs had been present, the British military attaché in Berne wrote to London:

> The general impression . . . is that the Swiss, in everything but name, are the allies of the Austrians and Germans . . . From time to time one hears vague references to a 'Militarisches Ubereinkommen' (a military understanding) with Germany, which show that the idea is far from being a strange one even to the average regimental officer in Switzerland.

The number of British residents in Switzerland had increased to around 11,000.

Arnold Bennett (see 1908) was in Lausanne. He wrote part of his

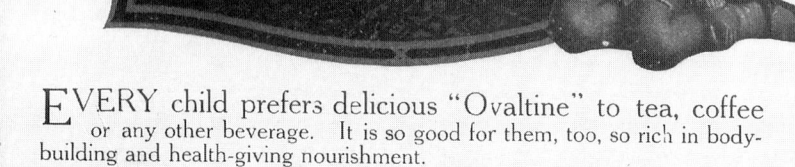

EVERY child prefers delicious "Ovaltine" to tea, coffee or any other beverage. It is so good for them, too, so rich in body-building and health-giving nourishment.

"Ovaltine" contains all the essential vitamins, and these are present in correct ratio; furthermore, it is emphasised that "Ovaltine" contains, also in correct ratio, all the other equally important factors of a complete and perfect food.

The constituents from which "Ovaltine" is made are Nature's foods which are richest in nutriment — ripe barley malt, creamy milk from England's richest pastures, fresh eggs and cocoa.

"Ovaltine" is digested with ease and completely absorbed. There is no waste material. Every particle passes immediately into the system — to give vitality and energy, to repair and restore the cells and tissues and to make good the deficiency in nutriment of all ordinary foods.

One cup of "Ovaltine" contains more nourishment than 7 cups of cocoa, 12 cups of beef extract or 3 eggs.

OVALTINE
TONIC FOOD BEVERAGE

Builds-up Brain, Nerve and Body

Sold by all Chemists throughout the British Empire.
Prices in Great Britain, 1/6, 2/6 and 4/6 per tin.

A. WANDER, Ltd., London, S.W.7.
Works: King's Langley.

P. 299.

'OVALTINE' RUSKS
More appetising, easily digested and much more nourishing than ordinary rusks or biscuits.
Price 1/6 and 2/6 per tin.

'OVALTINE' CHOCOLATE
Children — and adults, too — will enjoy this most delicious and very nourishing food-sweet.
Price 8d. and 1/3.

novel *Clayhanger* there. Another notable British visitor to Switzerland was Sir Oliver Lodge.

Vivian Caulfield's book, *How to Ski*, was published. This contained the first clear analysis of ski technique, which Caulfield had worked out on the slopes of the Bernese Oberland.

After failing to accept several invitations in previous years from the British War Office to send Swiss observers to the British manoeuvres, the Federal Council gave permission for the Swiss chief of staff, Commandant de Corps Wille, and another officer to attend the important British summer manoeuvres if asked. Instead, the War Office invited the Swiss to send an observer to the autumn exercises. The Swiss declined but said they could send two officers (unnamed) to the summer manoeuvres. The War Office, not knowing that the Swiss chief of staff himself would be available, regretted that no foreign officers were to be invited to the summer manoeuvres; and so an opportunity for closer military relations was lost. (However, Swiss officers attended British manoeuvres in 1911 and 1913.)

Skiing as a sport was now developing fast. British skiers organised the first downhill ski race in Switzerland (for the Kandahar Challenge Cup) at Montana (Valais).

1911

A curling club was formed in Wengen (Bernese Oberland).

Several Swiss companies were now giving particular attention to the British market. The Swiss CIBA chemical company acquired the Clayton Aniline Company in Manchester, while the Sandoz company of Basel established the Sandoz Chemical Company in the United Kingdom. (Its name was changed in 1945 to Sandoz Products.)

In addition, César and Emmanuel Trey, of Payerne, founded in London the firm of de Trey & Co., makers of dental supplies (to become the Amalgamated Dental Co. Ltd in 1924).

John Gatti (1871-1929), member of a Swiss family of restaurant and theatre owners in London (see 1886), became Mayor of Westminster. Gatti spent many years in local government, was knighted, and in 1926 became Chairman of the London County Council.

British fears about the pro-German attitude of the Swiss were growing. Austen Chamberlain, on holiday with his wife in Switzerland,

OPPOSITE *An early Ovaltine advertisement in England.*

wrote home after a talk with the British Consul-General in Zurich, Sir Henry Angst, that Angst had said that the Germans had it all their own way in German-speaking cantons. The newspapers were wholly dependent on them for news and comments on news, largely copying from the German papers so that their readers saw nothing but the German point of view. The people were wholly German in sympathy and Angst doubted whether, if a European war broke out, they would make more than a show of resistance. German Switzerland would be swallowed up in the German Empire.

1912 These British fears about the German influences in Switzerland were reinforced when the German Kaiser, Wilhelm II, arrived in Switzerland to see the Swiss army manoeuvres.

Partly as a result of this, the British military attaché in Berne continued to send home alarming reports on the Swiss attitude in case of war. He then assumed the truth of a rumour that a secret military agreement had been concluded between Switzerland and the Central Powers, especially Austria, a report which the Foreign Secretary, Sir Edward Grey, seemed disposed to believe. However, a categorical denial by the Swiss Foreign Minister that any secret alliance between Switzerland and Austria existed finally cleared the air.

An Anglo-Swiss telephone service was begun.

The Swiss hotelier Anton Sebastian Bon (1854-1915) went into partnership with his English friend Major Goldman, and built the Suvretta House hotel in St Moritz. Bon's eldest son, Anton, later became managing director of the Dorchester Hotel in London and also part-proprietor of Brown's Hotel.

More Swiss firms established a presence in the British market. Landis & Gyr of Switzerland set up Landis & Gyr Ltd in London, while the Tobler chocolate company opened an agency in Liverpool.

An association of British members of the Swiss Alpine Club was founded. They presented the Swiss club with the Britannia club hut above Saas Fee.

Lieutenant-Colonel Oscar Lewis Eugster (1880-1930), a descendant of Albert Eugster of Appenzell (see 1865), became Commander of 'A' Battery, Honourable Artillery Company, the oldest regiment in the British Army, and the approximate equivalent of Geneva's Exercice de l'Arquebuse (see 1682 and 1771).

The Lake of Lucerne from the air

The British-owned Neuchâtel Asphalt Company's concession in the Val de Travers was renewed for seventeen years. Production, though halted during the First World War, later reached between 30 and 50,000 tons a year.

Just prior to the outbreak of hostilities in Europe, the Swiss colony in the United Kingdom totalled, according to one estimate, approximately 12,000, of which more than half lived in London.

It was a good year for British visitors to Switzerland. The number of British tourists in Lucerne that summer exceeded 20,000.

1913

The novelist D.H. Lawrence (1885-1930) walked all the way from Schaffhausen to Zurich, Lucerne, and over the Gotthard to Bellinzona and Lugano. He wrote afterwards: 'I am cured of that little country for ever.'

Publication in London of Professor F.F. Roget of Geneva's book *Ski Runs in the High Alps* (see 1909). In it Professor Roget referred to the Swiss as navigators of the Alps and to the English as mountaineers of the sea.

There is some similarity in the risks incurred . . . It has hitherto been little realised how much Swiss neutrality and national integrity are one of the bulwarks of the freedom of Britain's movements in Europe.

While the German-Swiss press continued to publish the occasional anti-British article, the British Legation in Berne reported to London that relations with Switzerland were now 'uniformly good'.

1914 In March an amendment was made to the Anglo-Swiss Treaty of Friendship, Commerce and Reciprocal Establishment of 1855, to reflect the independent status of the new British Dominions and their right to determine their own economic relations with Switzerland.

Thomas Cook & Son opened a branch of its banking business in Lugano; and the merchant bankers Baring Brothers took over in London the formerly Swiss-owned bank of Morris, Prevost & Co. (see 1813).

In official circles at least, British fears about the Swiss will to resist German blandishments had subsided. In the tense days just before the outbreak of war in Europe, the British Minister to Switzerland, Sir Evelyn Grant-Duff, wrote to London:

There is, I think, no question that this country will strictly maintain her neutrality but any infringement of her frontier will be met with armed force.

On the outbreak of war, however, many Swiss were still openly pro-German. The writer Carl Spitteler made a famous speech warning his compatriots of the dangers for Swiss neutrality of this partisanship. He expressed understanding for all the belligerents. Of the British he said that England was Switzerland's most dependable friend.

Carl Spitteler's speech was published a day or two later in the *Neue Zürcher Zeitung*, evoking angry resentment from Germany.

Up to this time the United Kingdom had been dependent on Germany for about 90% of its imports of dyestuffs for the British textile industry. When war broke out, and this source was cut off, the Germans tried to prevent the Swiss chemical manufacturers from making up any of the deficiency. However, the British government were able to come to an agreement with the Geigy and Sandoz companies in Basel under which Britain procured, or allowed through the Allied blockade, necessary raw materials for the Swiss industry, in exchange for agreed quantities of dyestuffs made in Basel. Thus, exports of aniline dyes from Switzerland to the United Kingdom increased from Sw. fr. 3.3m in 1913 to Sw. fr. 38.2m in 1917, helping to relieve the British textile industry's acute shortage during the war. (See 1918.)

During the war the Swiss government took over the protection of German interests in Britain.

In September some British aeroplanes sent to bomb the Zeppelin workshops at Friedrichshafen in Germany, near the Swiss border, intruded into Swiss airspace. The British government expressed their regret to the Swiss Federal Council.

The arrest in Switzerland of five British journalists suspected of spying aroused considerable resentment in England, and questions were asked in the House of Commons. Four of the journalists were later released and the fifth expelled.

1915

In the special wartime conditions Swiss exports to Britain increased by 50% over the previous year. However, some trade suffered when the McKenna duties were introduced on some goods coming into Britain in order to restrict imports and save shipping space. One particularly important Swiss export, clocks and watches, was included in the list.

The need to regulate trade with the neutrals under the blockade which the Entente countries had imposed upon enemy Europe, led, in the case of Switzerland, to the formation of the Société Suisse de Surveillance Économique. The London office of this organisation was headed by Arthur Palliser. In Berne supervision was facilitated by weekly meetings between the Société Suisse and resident economic representatives of Britain, France and Italy.

The writer James Elroy Flecker (1884-1915) died in Davos. For several years he had been in the Swiss mountains working as hard as his health allowed to finish his play *Hassan*.

The Irish author James Joyce (1882-1941) arrived in Zurich where he worked on the early chapters of his *Ulysses*. During the Second World War, Joyce returned to Zurich and died there.

The Swiss government offered to take into Switzerland, for hospitalisation, a number of wounded prisoners of war from both sides. The British government accepted with gratitude.

1916 At the invitation of the British government, the Société de Cellonit Dreyfus et Cie, founded by the brothers Henri and Camille Dreyfus and Alexandre Clavel of Basel, established, together with some British industrialists, the British Cellulose and Chemical Manufacturing Co. Ltd, with a factory at Spondon, near Derby. The factory made a special varnish to the formula invented by Dreyfus which was used to protect the canvas-covered wings of Allied aircraft during the war. When hostilities ceased, the firm became British Celanese Ltd and, under the direction of Dreyfus, launched its first artificial silk products. British Celanese later merged with Courtaulds Ltd.

The first contingents of wounded British prisoners of war from Germany arrived in Switzerland for internment until the end of hostilities. They were put up in hotels and camps in Mürren, Interlaken, Château d'Oex, Leysin and elsewhere and looked after by the Red Cross, the YMCA and other voluntary organisations. By the end of the year there were 1,800 British prisoners of war in Switzerland.

A section of the New Helvetic Society was formed in London with Professor Arnold Lätt as secretary, largely in order to help explain Switzerland's position of neutrality during the war.

1917 In view of the growth of Anglo-Swiss trade, the Swiss Federal Council nominated Switzerland's first permanent commercial attaché at the Swiss Legation in London, Henri Martin of Geneva.

There were now Swiss consulates in the United Kingdom at Glasgow, Hull, Manchester and Liverpool.

A British vice-consulate was opened in Schaffhausen; but it was closed again after the war, in 1920. The British Consul-General in Zurich was Lord Acton.

A Swiss medical mission came to England to select German wounded and sick prisoners of war to be exchanged for British wounded and sick prisoners of war in Germany, under an agreement concluded in The Hague. The City Swiss Club entertained the mission at Gatti's restaurant in the Strand in the company of a number of other distinguished Swiss and British guests. During an air raid the Swiss sang patriotic songs.

Two novels of the Swiss writer Benjamin Vallotton were published in Britain in English translation – *Potterat and the War* and *In the Land of Death*.

Swiss trade with the United Kingdom continued at a high level. The United Kingdom's share of the Swiss market was roughly 10% compared with 6% in the years just before the war, while one sixth of all Swiss exports went to the United Kingdom. 1918

The repatriation of wounded British prisoners of war from Switzerland (see 1916) was completed. The King sent a warm letter of thanks to the President of the Swiss Confederation.

A Swiss Committee for Economic and Commercial Studies was formed in London to help develop postwar economic exchanges between Switzerland and the United Kingdom. The name was changed later to the Swiss Economic Council.

Within the framework of a community of interest agreement between Basel chemical companies, the Sandoz and Geigy companies each acquired an interest in the Clayton Aniline Co. Ltd (see 1911). This proved particularly timely when, in 1922, the British government introduced the Dyestuffs Act, obliging chemical producers to manufacture in the United Kingdom.

The novelist Somerset Maugham (1874-1963) spent the last year of the war in a sanatorium in Switzerland. In his spy story *Ashenden*, which he published in 1928, Maugham described in his tiredly cynical way a view of Lucerne.

... It was true that the lake was absurd, the water was too blue, the mountains too showy, and its beauty, hitting you in the face, exasperated rather than thrilled, but all the same, there was something pleasing in the prospect, an artless candour ...

The Vorarlberg Question. At the end of the war, after the collapse of the Austrian monarchy, the Vorarlberg declared its right to self-determination and in a referendum voted overwhelmingly for union with Switzerland. The Austrian government sought to prevent this at the Paris Peace Conference. The Swiss had no wish for territorial expansion, though cultural and military arguments were advanced in some quarters in favour of a union. Great Britain was disposed to support the solution most favourable to Switzerland. However, the Supreme Allied Council, at the Peace of St Germain in 1919, finally decided to keep unchanged the old western frontier of Austria.

1919 The Société Suisse de Surveillance Économique (see 1915), regulating Swiss foreign trade under the Allied blockade, was abolished in July.

Swiss exports to the United Kingdom that year were the highest to any country. Trade contacts between Britain and Switzerland began to grow rapidly, and the British government appointed its first permanent British commercial diplomatic officer in Berne, J.R. Cahill.

The British engineering and shipbuilding company, Vickers Ltd, and Brown Boveri of Switzerland, came to an agreement on the use of Brown Boveri's patents and processes in the United Kingdom and the British Dominions. At the same time Vickers acquired shares in the Geneva engineering companies of Sécheron and of Picard-Pictet (both of whom had been war contractors to the British authorities), and opened an agency in Geneva. Vickers also subscribed for Sw. fr. 7m of new shares in Brown Boveri itself.

Lloyds became the first of the big British joint-stock banks to open an office in Switzerland in Zurich, to be followed by another in Geneva the following year.

Winterthur Swiss Insurance Company formed a joint company in London with Norwich Union, Norwich Winterthur Reinsurance Corporation.

Air transport was beginning, and a provisional Anglo-Swiss convention on air navigation was signed in Berne. Services, however, did not start until 1923.

The Swiss soprano Sophie Wyss came to Britain, where she became well known as a distinguished interpreter of the works of numerous contemporary British composers.

Sir Gordon Guggisberg, a Swiss-Canadian, was Governor of the Gold Coast.

A weekly journal for the Swiss community, *The Swiss Observer,* was launched in London. Dr Arnold Lätt was its first editor. *The Swiss Observer,* which subsequently became the property of the Federation of Swiss Societies, continued to be published until the end of 1984.

After the war, compulsory conscription in Britain was abolished. Winston Churchill wrote in his memoirs, *The World Crisis*: 'The idea of preserving a national militia on something like the Swiss system was certainly in the mind of the government; but contact with the constituencies swept it out of existence before it was even mooted.'

To help to make up the shortage of coal in Switzerland caused by a drastic diminution of German supplies, English coal for the first time arrived at Basel via Rotterdam.

With the opening up of the River Rhine after the war to international traffic, Basel began to become an important port of entry for British exports to Switzerland. There was already a British consulate there. In 1920 a British Chamber of Commerce in Switzerland was incorporated, with its head office in Basel and a branch in Lausanne (it was transferred to Zurich in 1963).

1920

Swiss trade with the United Kingdom was at an all-time high. Britain was again Switzerland's biggest export customer. However, the introduction of the McKenna duties on imported watches and movements had had such an adverse effect on his United Kingdom business that it caused Hans Wilsdorf (see 1903) to leave England and return to Switzerland. There he established Montres Rolex SA in Geneva.

The National Provincial Bank Ltd was the second large British bank to open an office in Switzerland, in Geneva. The same year Cunard, the British steamship company, established an office in Lucerne.

When the Allies decided, at the suggestion of President Wilson, to establish the seat of the League of Nations in Geneva, Britain supported the choice. But the Swiss government considered that Switzerland could not become a member of the League because its policy of neutrality would be incompatible with full membership. Long discussions took place. Finally, by 'The Declaration of London', Britain, together with other members of the Council of the League of Nations, recognised that the neutrality of Switzerland and the guarantee of its independence, which had entered into international

Hans Wilsdorf, who founded Rolex watches in England.

law by the treaties of 1815, were in the interests of world peace and therefore compatible with the Covenant of the League. Switzerland would be required to participate in any economic sanctions the League might decide to impose but not in any military sanctions. Switzerland thereafter joined the League.

The Swiss architect Theophil Schaerer (b. 1874) came to London, where he became a Fellow of the Royal Institute of British Architects.

Schaerer designed several important buildings in England and took part in the restoration of several historic properties, including Tunstall Hall and Leeds Castle.

In a lecture given at Oxford on intellectual relations between Switzerland and Great Britain, Dr. Arnold Lätt, the Swiss historian, said: 'I like to think that there is something English in the nature and in the character of the Genevans, and of the Swiss as a whole.'

In the aftermath of the war, twenty-three seasonal chaplaincies were reopened in British churches in Switzerland by the Colonial and Continental Church Society.

Among other British tourists in Switzerland that year were the writers Augustine Birrell, Frank Swinnerton and Beatrice and Sydney Webb, and the watercolourist Colin Bent Phillip (1855-1932).

1921

In London the Swiss Committee for Economic and Commercial Studies held a dinner attended by the presidents of the Zurich and Geneva Chambers of Commerce. The Swiss Minister, Charles Paravicini, stressed the Swiss desire for closer trade relations. Sir Joseph Broadbank, President of the Board of Trade, said that the free development of the Rhine route would be good business for London as well as Switzerland.

However, the wartime pent-up demand for goods having largely been satisfied, the value of Anglo-Swiss trade dropped sharply. At the same time the appreciation of the Swiss franc against sterling which had occurred since 1919/20 caused British tourists to curtail their stays in Switzerland and a number of British residents there to leave.

Pickfords Ltd organised a series of fifteen charabanc tours to Switzerland, transporting twenty-one passengers on each tour. The vehicles were made by the Swiss Saurer company. The first tour arrived at Vevey in May.

1922

Trade prospects were improving once more. In this year, and for the next four years, Britain was again Switzerland's biggest export market, taking, *inter alia*, more of Swiss exports of silk products and of chocolate than any other country.

A Marconi company was established in Berne in conjunction with the Marconi Wireless & Telegraph Company of London, to offer an overseas telegram service to several foreign countries. Much of the equipment for the radio station at Münchenbuchsee, and the training of operators, was provided by the British company.

One of the foremost English pioneers of skiing, Arnold Lunn, invented the modern slalom and organised the first competition (with double flags) in Mürren (Bernese Oberland).

The poet T.S. Eliot (1880-1965) came to Lausanne to take treatment and to convalesce from a break-down. There he wrote the final section of his poem *The Waste Land* – 'What the Thunder Said' – with its frequent references to mountains:

> The shouting and the crying
> Prison and palace, and reverberation
> Of thunder of spring over distant mountains

and its allusion to *Blick ins Chaos* by the naturalised Swiss poet, Hermann Hesse. Later that year Eliot spent some time in Lugano.

1923 Swiss import duties were still a problem for many British exporters. A 'popular initiative' by Swiss Socialists, calling for the reduction of Swiss customs duties and a reversion to the prewar tariff, was decisively rejected in a national referendum.

At a meeting in Berne, delegates from Anglo-Swiss Associations decided to form a federation, whose objects should be to help its members in the study of English and to encourage friendly relations between the English-speaking countries and Switzerland.

A party of British doctors, including the directors of four London hospitals, visited hospitals in Basel, Berne and Zurich.

The British Handley-Page Transport company began to run a weekly passenger air-service between Zurich-Basel, Paris and London, while the Ad Astra Air Transport Company of Zurich operated a mail service Zurich to London. (In 1931, Ad Astra merged with another Swiss company, Balair, to become Swissair.)

An English philanthropist, Sir Stanley Birkin, donated £20,000 towards the costs of Henry Spahlinger's institute at Carouge (Geneva), producing a new vaccine against tuberculosis.

Three British mountaineers, George Finch, P.G. Forster and R.H. Peto, made the first guideless ascent of the north face of the Dent d'Hérens.

OPPOSITE *The first ski ascent of the Eiger: Richardet and Amstutz just above the icefall. Photograph by Arnold Lunn.*

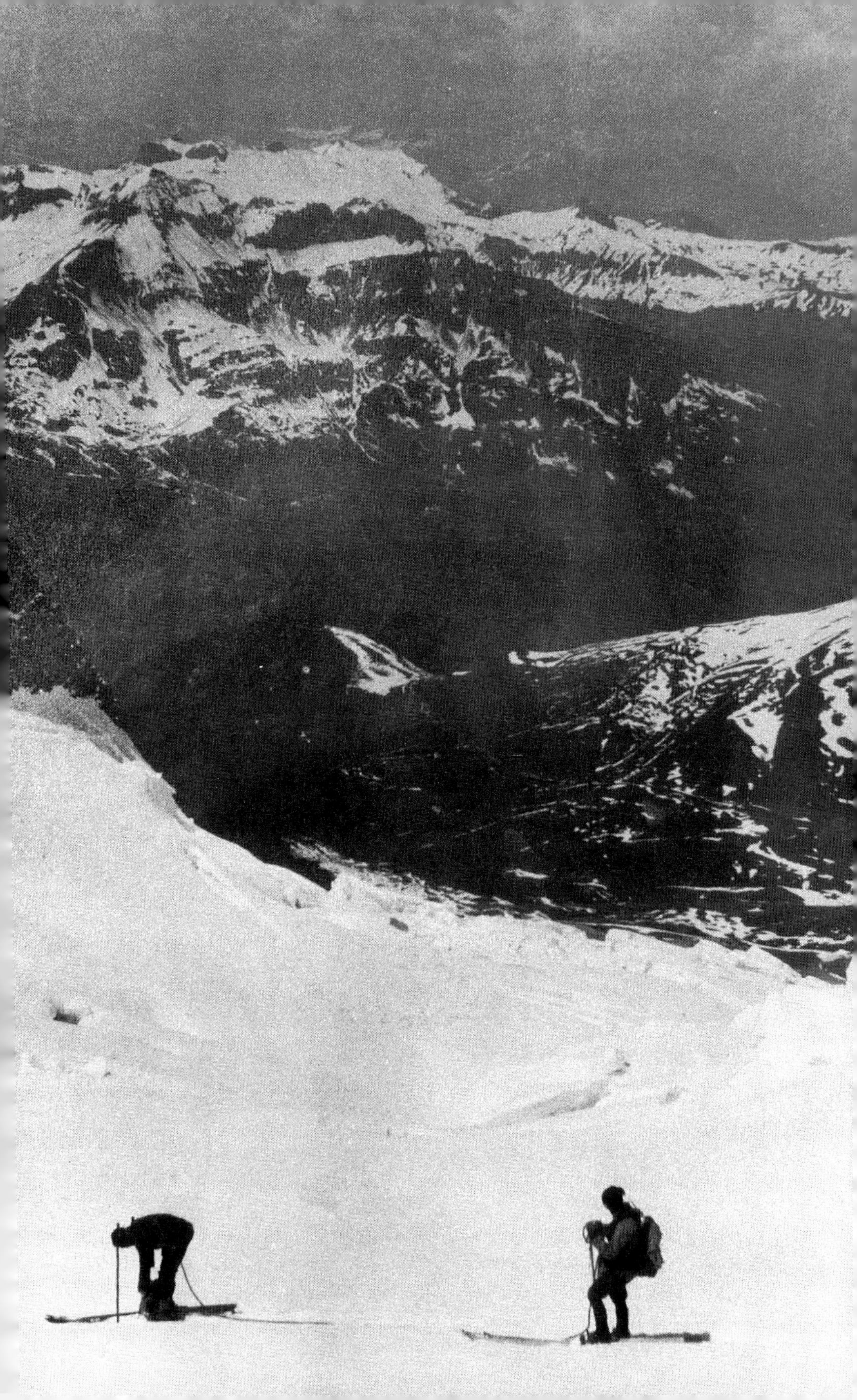

1924　In a magnificent pioneering adventure, Arnold Lunn (see 1922), with his friend Walter Amstutz, and two other Swiss, Willy Richardet and Fritz Ammacher, made the first ski ascent of the Eiger.

The same year, the Kandahar (K) Ski Club was founded in Mürren by Arnold Lunn and several British friends to encourage downhill ski-racing. A similar club on the Swiss side, and based on similar ideas, was founded by Walter Amstutz and two friends in Berne – the Swiss University Ski Club (SAS). It began to publish a year book, *Der Schneehase,* which was the counterpart in German of the *British Ski Year Book.*

In Davos, a ski marathon, 'The Parsenn Derby', was created by an English holidaymaker, F.S. Edlin. (When Edlin died, his ashes were scattered 'somewhere on the Parsenn' in accordance with his last wishes.)

An agreement was signed by the British Minister of Labour and a representative of the Swiss government for an exchange of hotel staff with a view to developing professional skills and knowledge of languages.

More Swiss companies were coming into the British market. The Zurich Insurance Group opened a London branch, while the cargo superintendents, La Société Suisse de Surveillance, were also established in London.

The air service between London and Switzerland was now operated by Imperial Airways and ran three times a week in summer.

A group of German-speaking Swiss in London founded their own Church, to run in parallel with the Swiss French-speaking Church which had held services since 1762. The German-speaking congregation first met in the church of St Anne and St Agnes in Gresham Street while the French-speaking Church continued to meet in Endell Street. The two Churches were united in 1938.

1925　The great era of skiing was in full swing. The first of the Anglo-Swiss university ski races was organised in Mürren by Walter Amstutz of Switzerland and Arnold Lunn of Great Britain.

The British were still revelling in the beauty of the Swiss mountains. The eminent climber Sir Claud Schuster was also at Mürren. He wrote:

'Patsy' Richardson and Jimmy Riddell on the slopes of Mürren

Suddenly there came into vision a great light from the Eiger. It passed behind that mountain, and threw up in strong relief the long line from the summit to the Mönch. Beyond it, as I knew well, was the risen moon . . . to us it was as if we gazed from without at the very battlements of heaven . . .

Schuster was a past president of the Alpine Club and of the Ski Club of Great Britain.

From August 1924 the British McKenna duties were not renewed on

Guido Reuge in an early Anglo-Swiss slalom

the list of imports on which they had first been imposed in 1915. This list included clocks and watches of great interest to Switzerland. The duties were, however, reimposed from July 1925. At the same time, Key Industry Duties were introduced on another important Swiss export, lace and embroideries, to protect Britain's own production in this area. In the months prior to July, there was a large influx of Swiss goods while importers built up stocks. As a result Swiss exports to the United Kingdom in 1925 were the highest for five years. United Kingdom imports into Switzerland also rose substantially.

Switzerland had again become important for the investment of foreign funds. British investment in Switzerland was increasing, though not on the scale of that from France and Germany.

The Swiss Foreign Minister, Giuseppe Motta, paid a visit to London, where he received a warm welcome from the British Foreign Secretary, Austen Chamberlain.

Austen Chamberlain also went to Switzerland, where he attended the Locarno conference.

Arnold Dolmetsch of Zurich, a Swiss immigrant in England, who was restoring many of the old harpsichords and other musical instruments in the British Museum, founded the Haslemere music festival, to be carried on later by his son Carl Dolmetsch (see also 1928).

At the Burlington House exhibition in London of the International Society of Artists, the Swiss section showed pictures by Ferdinand Hodler (1853-1913), the first time Hodler's work had been shown in Britain.

The MCC and Hampshire Cricket Club sent teams to play the boys of Zuoz school (Engadine), a Swiss establishment run on the model of an English public school.

Arnold Dolmetsch: portrait by H. Lambert.

1926 In *The Right Place: A Book of Pleasures* C.E. Montague described a modern journey through the Alps which differed markedly from that of John de Bremble some 800 years earlier (see 1188). He wrote:

> ... up to meet the bleaching chill that creeps in October from Göschenen down to Lucerne; and then the plunge into the tunnel's murmurous darkness under the very hub, the middle boss of all Europe, the rocky knot in which all her stone sinews are tied at their ends into one central bunch; and then the emergence, translating you out of a Teuton into a Latin world, from grizzled wintry tonelessness to burnished lustre, all the lingering opulence of sun-fed brown and yellow, purple, crimson and rose, Airolo, Bellinzona, Lugano ...

Since British importers had not yet been able to sell the large stocks of Swiss goods they had built up prior to the imposition of the McKenna and Key Industry duties in 1925, Swiss exports to the United Kingdom were down to Sw. fr. 300m. Imports into Switzerland of United Kingdom goods were just half that figure.

The first performance of British composer William Walton's (1902-82) overture, 'Portsmouth Point', was given in Zurich.

Dr W.A.B. Coolidge, mountaineer, writer and expert on Alpine photography, died in Grindelwald. The death occurred also of Henri-Edouard Naville (b.1844) of Geneva. An Egyptologist, he directed several digs for the Egypt Exploration Fund, making several important finds. He worked closely with British colleagues.

1927 The United Kingdom lost to Germany its place as the largest overseas market for Swiss goods.

Two English girls' public schools were founded in Switzerland, St George's College at Clarens, and Chatelard School at Les Avants, both near Montreux.

An article in the London *Times* identified Morgins as one of the few remaining resorts where 'English' skating was still practised, by a club called 'The Bears'.

Alpine Pastures, a painting generally considered to be the masterpiece of the Engadine artist Giovanni Segantini (1858-99), was exhibited in London.

1928 Colonel Sir Harold Mitchell (1900-83), one-time vice-chairman of the Conservative Party, won the first 'Inferno' ski race from the top

Competitors in the first 'Inferno' race, 1928, from the top of the Schilthorn to Lauterbrunnen (Bernese Oberland).

of the Schilthorn to Lauterbrunnen (Bernese Oberland) – the longest downhill ski race in the world. (Today the race is extraordinarily popular, some 1,500 competitors taking part on a piste which has been extended from the original nine kilometres to fourteen kilometres.)

In the first outstanding ski expedition by a British lady, Miss Maud Cairney made the first winter ascent of the Gabelhorn with two guides. The same year, another lady, Dorothy Pilley, together with Ivor Richards, climbed the north ridge of the Dent Blanche for the first time.

The Val de Travers Asphalt Paving Company, founded by J.W. Pattison, a former director of the Neuchâtel Asphalt Co. (see 1913), had obtained a concession from the canton of Neuchâtel and was paving many of the streets of London with Swiss asphalt.

The Dolmetsch Foundation was established by Arnold and Carl Dolmetsch (see 1925), devoted to reviving the music of the sixteenth, seventeenth and eighteenth centuries, while a Dolmetsch Collection of Early Musical Instruments was brought together at Haslemere.

Death of Adolphe Appia (b. 1862), Swiss scenic designer whose innovations in the use of light in stage and theatre production were

The Anglo-Swiss Ladies Race, Mürren, 1928.

followed all over Europe. In England Edward Gordon Craig became his most articulate disciple.

1929   British tourism to Switzerland was again increasing. Some 35% of all Swiss earnings from tourism was estimated to come from British visitors.

In March the Imperial Airways India service was routed via Basel.

Imports of British goods into Switzerland were down on the previous year. The Swiss correspondent of the London *Economist* complained of the lack of interest that British industrialists generally were showing in the Swiss market, 'where they advertise very little and send only a few commercial agents'.

Henri Dreyfus of Basel (1881-1944) was awarded the British Perkin Medal for his contribution to developments in the chemical industry.

The Swiss composer Arthur Honegger conducted his oratorio *Le Roi David* in Cambridge.

La beauté sur la terre, a novel by the Swiss writer Charles Ferdinand Ramuz (1878-1947) was published in an English translation as *Beauty on Earth*.

The importance of Switzerland as an international financial centre 1930
continued to grow. The United Kingdom was practically the only
European state not borrowing from Switzerland.

There were now British consulates in Switzerland at Basel, Berne,
Davos, Geneva, Lausanne, Lucerne, Lugano, Montreux, Neuchâtel,
St Moritz and Zurich.

A Swiss architect, Charles Frédéric de Steiger, came to England to
settle. Just before the Second World War Steiger designed and built
several of the biggest air-raid shelters in London.

Hans Renold (see 1879) merged his chain-making company with the
Coventry Chain Co., of Coventry, to form Renold Chains Ltd, with
head office at Wythenshawe near Manchester. This later became
Renold plc.

An Anglo-Swiss agreement on the double taxation of agency profits 1931
was signed in Berne.

In the early months of the year, following a heavy influx of foreign
funds seeking refuge in Switzerland, Swiss banks sought to discourage further inflows by allowing no interest on new deposits (see also
1971).

British tourists in Switzerland were fewer than usual; but a large
international Scout Jamboree was held in Kandersteg. Lord Baden-
Powell, the founder of world Scouting, who attended, wrote:

> Up here in the Swiss mountains, in the green valley of Kandersteg, one is
> very remote from the fuss and hurry of the world. Yet, from where I sit in
> the flower-decked balcony of this chalet, I can see the flags of twenty-two
> nations waving above the tents and camp fires of some three thousand young
> men gathered here.

Later in the year, in the increasingly difficult conditions brought on
by the world economic crisis, several Swiss banks were in trouble.
The Banque de Genèvè failed, involving the liquidation of two smaller banks as well.

In September, the United Kingdom came off the gold standard and
devalued the pound. The bank rate was raised to 6%, and the Sterling
Bloc was formed.

The suspension of sterling convertibility in Britain caused consternation in Switzerland where quite large sterling balances were held.

Lord Baden-Powell, 1916: portrait by Shirley Slocombe.

Sterling was withdrawn from Swiss banks, whose difficulties were further increased.

The British Chancellor of the Exchequer urged Britons to stay at home in order to save the pound. Amongst other things, this caused a collapse in the winter sports traffic between Great Britain and Switzerland. Several tour operators, and many Swiss hoteliers, found themselves in difficulties. Prices at many Swiss hotels were reduced by 10% to 20%.

Protectionist trade policies were adopted by both Britain and Switzerland. The Import Duties Act in Britain imposed a customs duty of 10% on most imports, later increased, for most goods, to 20%. Duties on a few items went higher still. At the same time the Ottawa Agreements, extending imperial preferences, and under which the Dominions were to help British industry by raising duties on manufactures from other countries, were also bad news for Swiss exporters.

1932

In Switzerland import quotas were introduced on a number of items and duties raised on others. Import compensation arrangements were also negotiated with several countries.

Anglo-Swiss trade was halved. Swiss exports to Britain suffered most. There were several failures in the Swiss embroidery and silk industries, both of which normally found their main outlets in the United Kingdom; and a number of Swiss watch factories closed down.

Sulzer Bros of Switzerland established a British company, Sulzer Bros (London) Ltd. In addition, in view of the increase in British import duties on their Swiss-made pumps, Sulzer began to make these in England in the factory of Hawthorne Davy & Co. of Leeds.

There were a number of political demonstrations in Geneva. When an anti-socialist demonstration turned into a riot, troops were called out and machine-gunned a crowd, killing three people. The *Economist* reported this incident as a 'fascist' rally and used the headline 'Butchery at Geneva'. It received a strong riposte from the President of the Geneva Chamber of Commerce who accused the journal of failing to understand the true nature of the Bolshevik menace to Swiss democracy and who said that the mob who caused the riot were maintained in Switzerland by the Soviet government under the guise of delegates to the League of Nations.

Owing to the continued world depression, unemployment in both Switzerland and Britain had risen sharply. In Switzerland it was 10.8% of the workforce. In the United Kingdom it had reached 21%, and about 3 million were out of work.

1933

In Switzerland tourists from Britain and elsewhere were still greatly down on earlier years. Railways and steamers reduced their fares, and hotels again lowered their prices.

314 Chronology 1933 – 1934

The Marconi company of London supplied a 15kw national broadcasting transmitter for use on Monte Ceneri for Italian-speaking Switzerland.

The rise in British tariffs against imports, and the abundance of unemployed labour in Britain, spurred more Swiss companies to begin making their products in the United Kingdom. Among the British subsidiaries of Swiss firms set up around this time were Bühler Bros (England) Ltd, Lindt (England) Ltd, Suchard Chocolates Ltd, Müller & Co. (England) Ltd, Winterthur Silks Ltd, Omega Watches and Zenith Watches (Great Britain) Ltd.

1934 The Swiss banking secrecy act was brought into force, primarily in order to protect the Swiss accounts of victims of Nazi Germany.

CIBA Laboratories was set up in the United Kingdom by CIBA of Switzerland to market pharmaceuticals in the United Kingdom.

Part of an Imperial Airways timetable, 1933.

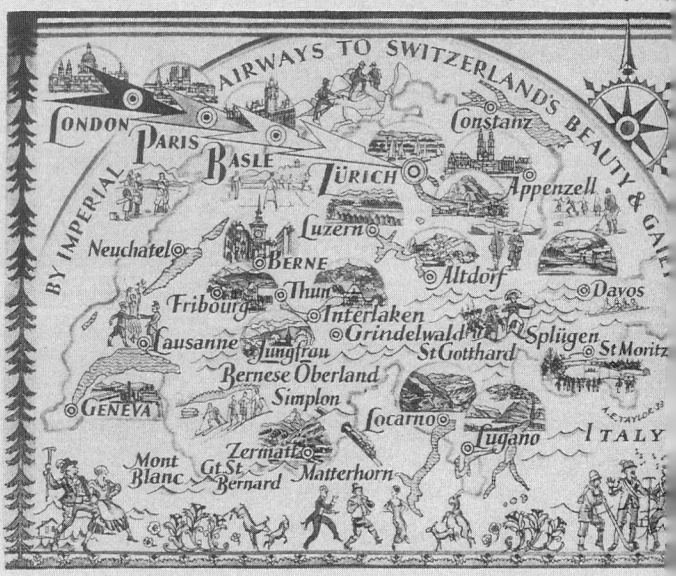

In order to overcome the United Kingdom tariff protection on its products, Senn & Co. Ltd of Basel, who had been selling ribbons to Britain since the mid-nineteenth century, decided to build a factory in Biddulph (Stoke-on-Trent). The United Kingdom subsidiary, Selectus Ltd, later took over a dyeworks in Luton.

An exhibition of the paintings of the artist Paul Klee (1879-1940) was held in London. (Of German origin, Klee was born in Switzerland, near Berne, and lived much of his life, and died, there.)

A translation of *Fragments d'un journal intime* by the Swiss writer Henri Frédéric Amiel (1821-81) was published in England.

1935

An air service to London by Swissair was begun. Together with Imperial Airways, both airlines ran a daily service in summer via Paris and Lille. The return fare London-Basel was £12.15s.; London-Zurich cost £13.16s.

The Georg Fischer steel works of Schaffhausen acquired the Britannia Iron & Steel Works Ltd of Bedford.

Another of the big British joint-stock banks set up in Switzerland. The Société Bancaire Barclays (Suisse) SA was constituted in Geneva. Barclays later opened an office in Zurich as well.

The official rate of exchange was Sw.fr. 15 to the pound. However, under a special scheme brought in by Swiss hotels, most of these accepted the pound sterling as Sw.fr. 16 during the tourist season.

The first ski-lift in Switzerland, built on the Bolgenschanze in Davos that year, was an immediate attraction for British and other skiers alike. It was followed within twelve months by more than a hundred ski-lifts all over the Alps.

The British climber Geoffrey Winthrop Young (see 1905), who had lost a leg in the First World War, made his last great ascent in Switzerland. With Marcus Heywood he climbed the Zinal Rothorn from Zermatt. In a bad fall on the descent, his life was saved by his Swiss guide, Joseph Knubel.

Unemployment had now increased to about 13.2% of the workforce in Switzerland, and had declined to about 14.3% in the United Kingdom.

1936

Switzerland abandoned the gold standard, and the Swiss franc was

A Swissair flight to London, 1935.

devalued by some 30%. Swiss import quotas were subsequently relaxed and some tariffs were reduced or abolished.

Dr Meyer, President of the Swiss Confederation and chief of the Federal Finance Department, said in a speech: 'The Swiss people will follow the example of the British and show the same coolness and discipline as the British did when the pound left gold.'

William de Vigier (b. 1912), a Swiss, founded the first Acrow company in Britain, which soon developed into a worldwide group specialising in engineering, steel, cranes and scaffolding.

1937   The devaluation of the Swiss franc had an almost immediate effect on British visitors to the winter sports in Switzerland. In January the number of British tourists in the Grindelwald area was up by about 70%, while the number of British 'visitor-nights' was some 50% higher.

In terms of value, Anglo-Swiss visible trade showed a great improvement (though part was due to the change in the Swiss franc-£ parity). Swiss purchases of cotton thread, cotton fabrics, shirts, motor vehicles, bicycles and coal all rose sharply (but British motor cars had only 2% of the total Swiss market). Swiss exports to Britain which showed significant increases included watches, machinery, tools, aluminium, dyes, silk fabrics and shoes.

The Swiss artist and painter of murals Hans Erni (b. 1909) spent the years 1937 and 1938 in London, where he was closely associated with Henry Moore, Ben Nicholson and Barbara Hepworth.

Roche Products Ltd (the United Kingdom subsidiary of Hoffmann-La Roche of Basel – see 1908) established its base in Welwyn Garden City. Designed by the leading Swiss architect Otto Salvisberg, the factory and offices were described by the *Architectural Journal* as 'The Building of the Year'.

The Swiss historian Jacob Burckhardt's classic work, *The Civilisation of the Renaissance in Italy*, was published in an English edition by Phaidon Press.

There were now two direct air services in summer between London-Basel and Zurich on weekdays, taking 3½ hours to Basel and a further 25 minutes to Zurich. There were also several air services with connexions to Switzerland via Paris. (Services were suspended on the outbreak of the war.)

1938

The cross-Channel and rail route London to Basel took 13 hours (compared with 14 hours 35 minutes in 1898).

The choral work, *The Vision of Isaiah*, by the Swiss composer Willy Burkhard (1900-55) had its first English performance in London. In reaction to some unfavourable notices given to it by several British critics, Ralph Vaughan Williams, then Britain's greatest living composer, wrote to *The Times* in its defence, saying that it was a 'deeply moving work which stood out amid a waste of arid note-spinning' that evening.[23]

The Swiss theologian Karl Barth, after his break with the Nazis, was invited to Aberdeen University to give a series of lectures on the Scottish Confession of Faith of 1560. Three universities – Aberdeen, Oxford and St Andrews – conferred on Barth the degree of Doctor *honoris causa*. (See also 1941.)

This was the year of the Munich crisis. Switzerland's attitude to Neville Chamberlain's ill-fated visits to Hitler at Berchtesgaden and Godesberg was one of apprehension – and disbelief that any satisfactory solution could come out of them.

As part of United Kingdom contingency planning in the event of a war with Germany, a draft war-trade agreement was sent to the British Legation in Berne in November, for discussion with the Swiss authorities. Switzerland would undertake not to export to Germany certain specific products it produced from imported raw materials and to limit, to amounts to be agreed, its exports of goods made wholly of Swiss materials. The United Kingdom was prepared to take from Switzerland quantities of certain specified goods.

1939 In March Erwin Matter of the Swiss government visited London for further discussions on the proposed war-trade agreement.

Charles Paravicini, Switzerland's most distinguished diplomatic representative to the Court of St James's up to that time, retired after twenty years at the Swiss Legation in London.

On the outbreak of war in Europe, the Swiss government made a formal declaration of neutrality to all the belligerent powers. The British government, in its reply, stated that it would respect Swiss neutrality 'as long as Switzerland herself shall use all the means in her power to maintain and defend a strict neutrality'.

For the duration of hostilities the Swiss government took over the protection of German and Italian interests in the United Kingdom and the Empire. Similarly, at Britain's request, the Swiss became the protecting power for British interests in Germany.

In November a Swiss economic mission led by Dr Hans Sulzer, head of the Swiss War Economic Organisation, and chairman of the board of directors of Sulzer Bros Ltd, came to London to negotiate on general trade and credit arrangements between Britain and Switzerland. Meanwhile, discussions on the war-trade agreement continued in Berne.

Two new products introduced by the Swiss pharmaceutical industry at this time, which were later to be used extensively by the British forces during the war, were DDT, developed by Dr Paul Müller of the Geigy company, and a Vitamin C compound, Redoxon, developed by Hoffmann-La Roche. In addition, Hoffmann-La Roche's subsidiary in England, Roche Products, increased its production of Vitamin B_1 by 300 times between 1939 and 1940, since the vitamin was needed to improve the nutritive properties of the British wartime flour.

The Geigy Company began making pigments and industrial chemicals in Great Britain; while the Nestlé Company began making Nescafé there.

In April a wartime agreement was concluded between the Swiss and British and, at first also, the French governments. A mixed Swiss-British-French Commission was set up in Berne to control the import and consumption of goods for which guarantees about their use were to be given by the Swiss. It was under the chairmanship of Dr M. Hotz, Director of Commerce at the Swiss Department of Economy.

1940

When France fell and Switzerland was surrounded by the Axis Powers, the Ministry of Economic Warfare in London proposed that the British economic blockade of enemy Europe should be extended to Switzerland and Switzerland treated on the same basis as Vichy France. The Foreign Office, however, argued successfully that as long as the Swiss government struggled to preserve some degree of independence, Britain should offer the encouragement of carefully regulated imports. The British Minister in Berne, David Kelly, protested that it would be unfair to class Switzerland with Vichy, 'a discredited clique . . . deriving their title from national pusillanimity. Whereas Switzerland was the oldest and most solidly established democracy in the world'.

When the possibility of a German invasion of Switzerland was very real, the Swiss President and Foreign Minister, Marcel Pilet-Golaz, made a speech to the nation which seemed to indicate that the country was preparing to come to an accommodation with the new Germany. The British government was in some doubt whether the Swiss would, in the event, blow up the railway tunnels through which the Germans were able to send supplies to Italy, or whether they would come to terms and allow the tunnels to be taken intact. The British Minister in Berne sought a secret meeting with the Swiss Commander-in-Chief, at which General Guisan gave his personal assurance that, should the Germans invade, the mines in the tunnels would be set off. The General said he would take entire responsibility. On David Kelly's advice, the British government accepted this assurance unreservedly.

In the autumn Professor Paul Keller came to London to make fresh arrangements for Swiss imports. Accommodation was reached on a specific list of goods and the war-trade schedules were considerably extended.

Unlike the First World War, when Anglo-Swiss trade had greatly increased, the physical isolation of Switzerland by the Axis Powers brought, from 1940 onwards, a sharp decline in trade between Britain and Switzerland.

However, some 35,000 Swiss Oerlikon guns and many millions of rounds of 20mm ammunition were manufactured in the United Kingdom during the war years.

1941 Unidentified aircraft frequently violated Swiss air space. After several incidents when bombs were dropped on Zurich and Basel, the Swiss protested strongly to the British government, alleging that the planes had been British. The British government replied that the evidence had been carefully examined but had been found inconclusive; they would nevertheless accept responsibility in view of the friendly relations between the two countries. The Swiss government expressed satisfaction at the amicable settlement of these incidents.

The Swiss were now economically dependent upon the supplies which the Axis Powers allowed them. In September the Swiss government signed a commercial agreement with Germany. The British Ministry of Economic Warfare announced that, in view of this, Britain would withdraw facilities for passing materials for Swiss industry through the blockade on all imports from overseas – with the exception of food, fodder and certain other goods destined for domestic consumption. It was emphasised that this was not an act of retaliation, but simply a recognition of a state of affairs which existed through no fault of the Swiss or of Britain.

In the light of the British attitude, the Swiss proposed a number of reciprocal concessions. By December the basis of a limited 'compensation agreement' had been agreed in principle. The British aim was first to obtain some Sw. fr. 2½m of Swiss goods a month (despite

German pressures on Switzerland) in return for allowing in monthly imports of a comparable value; second, to reduce Swiss trade with the Axis Powers, offering as an inducement the restoration of quotas which had been suspended since September.

Publication of the Swiss theologian Karl Barth's *Letter to Great Britain from Switzerland*. He had been invited to write it by some English clergy, to help maintain the link between Christians of the Anglo-Saxon world and those on the Continent from whom they were cut off by the war. In his letter, Barth condemned the earlier attempts at appeasement and strongly supported Britain's declaration of war and armed stand against the dictators. He urged all British Christians, with many arguments and references to the Bible, to oppose Hitler's Germany, as an unequivocal Christian duty, with all the means at their disposal.

On the 400th anniversary of the death of the Swiss physician Paracelsus (see c. 1518), a lecture on his doctrines and his influence on the reform of medicine was given at the Royal Society of Medicine in London.

1942　In February a high-level Swiss economic mission, headed again by Dr Hans Sulzer (see 1939), arrived in London to discuss the proposed compensation agreement, the revision of the war-trade agreement of 1940 and certain financial matters. They were welcomed by Lord Selborne, Minister of Economic Warfare. After eight months of negotiations, notes were exchanged to give effect to the compensation agreement, and an understanding on financial matters was reached with the Treasury. Allied pressure on individual Swiss firms dealing with Germany was suspended. However, the Swiss found it impossible to meet Allied demands which would have severely limited Swiss exports of war materials and certain types of machinery to the Axis powers.

Nine prominent Swiss journalists, invited to Britain as guests of the British government, were prevented from leaving Switzerland when the Vichy French government cancelled their transit visas through France.

1943　When the Germans occupied southern (Vichy) France, Axis pressure on Switzerland for more supplies was intensified. A jump in Swiss exports to Germany that summer led the British government to warn the Swiss Minister to London, Walter Thurnheer, that they might put pressure on Swiss firms who failed to restrain their exports to the Axis Powers. (The Allied 'Black List' already contained the names of over 1,000 Swiss companies.)

In September, the British government told the Swiss that the firm of Sulzer Bros would be put on the 'Black List' unless it signed a standard undertaking to restrict exports to the Axis countries to prewar levels. On the instructions of the Swiss government the company had to refuse, and consequently the Swiss government issued a formal decree forbidding Swiss firms from giving undertakings to any foreign government about their exports. Sulzer were put on the 'Black List', despite not being a manufacturer of arms or ammunition. Professor Keller (see 1940) came to London again and an agreement embodying new Swiss proposals was signed. It was agreed to de-list Sulzers against an undertaking on the company's behalf by the Swiss government.

Following the fall of Mussolini, there were mass escapes of prisoners of war from Italian prison camps, and hundreds of former British prisoners succeeded in reaching the Swiss frontier. Many came over the mountain passes into the Valais, some dying of exhaustion. Large numbers, struggling to make the glacier descents, were rescued by Swiss guides. (Later, an appreciable number of British servicemen interned in Switzerland, particularly airmen, were 'unofficially' helped by Swiss sympathisers to join secret escape routes through Vichy France.)

1944　The final form of undertaking about Sulzer Bros was agreed in March, and the firm was omitted from the new 'Black List'.

Later that year, following the decline of German power in Europe, the Swiss government was able to issue an embargo on the export of war material to belligerents.

The Swiss engineer Georges Roesch (1891-1969) joined Power Jets Ltd, which two years later became the National Gas Turbine Establishment. Roesch's work contributed largely towards the development of the gas turbine in Britain.

The novel by the Swiss writer Charles Ferdinand Ramuz (1878-1947), *Présence de la mort,* was published in an English translation as *The End of All Men.*

F.A. Voigt, writing in *The Nineteenth Century* magazine, expressed the view of many in Britain when he said:

Future generations will, perhaps, be grateful that in the Second World War, when Europe was being destroyed, there was a country called Switzerland, which remained neutral, not because she was inadequately conscious of wider and deeper issues, but because she was supremely conscious of them, and was, when disaster came to the world, ready for armed defence of a neutrality that meant not only the preservation of her own peace, but of the common heritage. . . . They will then see that in Switzerland a light, which elsewhere burns with flickering or murky flame or has been extinguished altogether, burns clear, bright and steady . . .

Death of Henri Dreyfus of Basel (see 1929), who left a large part of his fortune to British institutions concerned with the training of talented young chemists. After his death, his brother Camille Dreyfus (1878-1956) took over the direction of British Celanese Ltd (see 1916).

At Winston Churchill's meeting in October with Stalin in Moscow, Stalin proposed that Allied troops should be sent through Switzerland regardless of its neutrality, in order to attack the German forces in the rear. Churchill strongly opposed this suggestion, pointing out that it was not only impracticable but contrary to the political principles of the Western Allies. The idea was dropped.

On 3 December Winston Churchill wrote a minute to the Foreign Secretary

I put this down for the record. Of all the neutrals, Switzerland has the greatest right to distinction . . . She has been a democratic state, standing for freedom in self-defence among her mountains, and in thought, in spite of race, largely on our side.

In February Dingle Foot, Parliamentary Under-Secretary to the Ministry of Economic Warfare, visited Berne with an American official and negotiated with the Swiss government an agreement further restricting Swiss exports to Germany and German transit trade through Switzerland to Italy.

1945

In March, when General Karl Wolff, Commander of the German SS in Italy, put out secret peace feelers to the Allies, Lieutenant-General Sir Terence Airey and General Lemnitzer, the British and American Chiefs of Staff at Allied Headquarters at Caserta, arrived in Switzerland in disguise and had an exploratory meeting with him to make sure that he had authority to negotiate.

The Mönch and the Eiger, photographed by W.F. Donkin.

Slowly beginning to build up again, Swiss trade with the United Kingdom (imports plus exports) totalled less than Sw. fr. 60m.

In September Swissair resumed their Zurich-London air service.

Following a suggestion from Winston Churchill, the British military authorities asked Swiss publishers if they would send to Britain a selection of suitable books in German for the benefit of German prisoners of war, to help prepare them for their return to private life. The response was immediate and some thousands of Swiss books on various aspects of civil affairs were sent to prisoner of war camps throughout Britain.[24]

Returning to Switzerland after the war, Arnold Lunn wrote in his memoirs:

I walked to the terrace at Berne, and against the ebbing twilight I saw my beloved mountains, Wetterhorn, Eiger, Mönch and Jungfrau, serene and untroubled, untainted by the cruel and evil things against which we had been fighting, and still bearing witness to the eternal loveliness which man cannot mar, and which time cannot diminish. 'These, the great Alps, seen thus,' as Hilaire Belloc wrote in *The Path to Rome*, 'link one in some way to one's immortality.'

A major exhibition of the paintings of the artist Paul Klee (1879-1940) was held in the National Gallery in London.

Death of Sir Hans Vischer (b. 1876 in Basel). In 1900 Vischer had been sent to Northern Nigeria by the Church Missionary Society. He later joined the British Colonial Service and became an educational expert on Africa. He helped to found the International Institute for African Languages and Culture and also Africa House in London for African students.

Another member of the Vischer family, Marcus Vischer, who had for a time been vicar of Tenterden in Kent, took over as pastor of the English community in Basel. The chaplaincy was given permission to worship in the ancient St Nicholas's Chapel, a part of Basel Cathedral.

Warm political relations between Britain and Switzerland were quickly re-established after the war.

1946

On 17 September Winston Churchill chose Zurich to launch his first appeal after the war for Continental unity. In his famous speech 'The Tragedy of Europe', he made a strong plea for a United States of Europe. He talked of the 'vast quivering mass of tormented, hungry, careworn and bewildered human beings' waiting everywhere in

Winston Churchill after giving his historic speech in Zurich on the unity of Europe, 17 September 1946.

Europe in the remains of their cities and houses; but held out the hope of the peoples of Europe, 'rising to the heights of the soul and of the instinct and spirit of man', that a new Europe might be created from the ruins of the old – a new Europe which could give a sense of enlarged patriotism and common citizenship 'to the distracted peoples of this mighty continent'. Churchill also made a visit to Berne, where he was rapturously received by the crowds.

That summer the Churchills stayed for several weeks on holiday in a villa on the shores of Lake Léman, put at their disposal by a group of generous Swiss admirers.

Among others who holidayed in Switzerland in 1946 was Field-Marshal Lord Montgomery.

A three-year Anglo-Swiss monetary agreement was signed. Under the terms of the agreement Switzerland agreed to hold £15m in sterling, £10m which might be taken up in the first year and £5m in the second. A consequence of the agreement was the resumption of British tourist traffic to Switzerland; and, in addition, special consideration was to be given to Swiss requests for permission to export various products to the United Kingdom. The rate of exchange was fixed at Sw. fr. $17.35 = £1$.

British European Airways and Swissair opened daily air services London-Geneva.

After the book scheme (see 1945), the British authorities invited the Swiss government to send lecturers to talk to German prisoners of war in Britain, to help them prepare for private life again. Under the chairmanship of Federal Councillor M. Feldmann, an organisation was set up, Schweizerische Vortragsdienst, with Professor H. Zbinden as director, to provide several hundred lecturers from all walks of life. The expenses were shared between Britain and Switzerland.

The Society of Analytical Psychology was founded in London, to study and discuss the teachings and methods of the Swiss psychologist, Carl Gustav Jung (1875-1961). In the same year a British C.G. Jung Institute was opened.

In Switzerland a group of British got together and the British Residents' Association of Switzerland was founded in Lausanne; while the newly formed Swiss-British Society of Zurich held its inaugural dinner. Its president was Professor H. Straumann.

Ewiges England, a superbly comprehensive anthology of British poetry from Chaucer to Eliot, was published in Zurich in English text with German translations by Hans Fiest.

An important *Books of Switzerland* exhibition was held in London by Swiss publishers, under the auspices of the British Council in collaboration with Pro Helvetia. In his foreword to the exhibition catalogue John Masefield, the Poet Laureate and President of the National Book League, wrote:

Most English writers have thought tenderly and anxiously of Switzerland during these appalling years. They know how valiantly and at what cost the Swiss have preserved their freedom at a time when freedom seemed dying in Europe.

In Berne there was an exhibition of British books; and in Basel an Anglo-Swiss medical congress was organised.

The British conductor Sir Malcolm Sargent opened the Lucerne Festival with performances of 'Introduction and Allegro for Strings' by Edward Elgar and *The Perfect Fool* ballet music of Gustav Holst, while Benjamin Britten's new opera *Peter Grimes* had its first Swiss performance in Basel.

At Glyndebourne Opera House in Sussex, the Swiss conductor Ernest Ansermet (1883-1969) conducted the first English performance of Britten's *The Rape of Lucretia*. Ansermet gave many performances in England, particularly with his Orchestre de la Suisse Romande, and his records sold many thousands of copies there.

1947

In settlement of the year's deficit on the balance of payments between Switzerland and the sterling area, the United Kingdom transferred some £5m in gold to Switzerland.

An Anglo-Swiss agreement on the abolition of visas was concluded.

British tourists again began to pour into Switzerland. The number in 1946/7 was approximately 200,000. But Britain's postwar economic difficulties caused the government to put a ban on foreign travel between October 1947 and May 1948. This caused a setback for the Swiss tourist industry.

Charles Graves's *Switzerland Revisited* was published. Writing of his impressions of Switzerland soon after the end of the Second World War, he said:

Ernest Ansermet

The English are held in real esteem. The English language has become the smart language of Switzerland, thus supplanting the French. The respect for Great Britain in 1940 will last for centuries.

In June an exhibition in the Kunsthaus, Zurich, of the works of William Blake was seen by an estimated 11,000 people. It was the most successful exhibition the British Council had yet organised in Switzerland. It was accompanied by a representative collection of works by the Swiss artist who had done much to inspire Blake – Henry Fuseli (see 1779).

The Edinburgh-born artist and sculptor Eduardo Paolozzi (b. 1924) went to work for some years in Paris. He was influenced by the work he saw there of Swiss artists Alberto Giacometti and Paul Klee.

Part of Switzerland's gift to Princess Elizabeth on the occasion of her wedding that year was a month's holiday in Switzerland for a group of British schoolchildren.

A Swiss economic delegation, led by Hans Schaffner, Delegate for 1948
Trade Agreements, arrived in London for discussions within the
framework of the Anglo-Swiss monetary agreement of 1946. An
agreement was signed regulating the balance of payments between
Switzerland and the Sterling Area for the coming year. In order to try
to avoid a further outflow of gold payments from the United Kingdom to Switzerland, the Swiss agreed to increase their imports from,
and to control their exports to, the Sterling Area, and to continue to
hold a sterling balance of £15m.

The British Government announced the resumption of tourist allowances for holidays in Switzerland, to a maximum of £35 per adult
and £25 per child. However, because of high demand, the £5m set
aside for these allowances had to be rationed by monthly quotas.

British European Airways began a London-Zurich service.

The Swiss became the first Continental European country to embrace
the jet age, by ordering from Britain 75 de Havilland Vampire fighter
planes at a cost of £3.1m. An additional order was placed for ground
wireless installations and ammunition costing about £750,000. (See
also 1950 and 1954.)

After the last German prisoners of war had returned home from
Britain (see 1946), the former lecture centre of Wiston House was
reorganised into a more general study centre concerned with postwar problems. It was renamed Wilton Park, and numerous Swiss
continued to participate there with British and German lecturers.
Later, attendance was widened to include all countries in the Organisation for Economic Cooperation and Development (OECD).

The Anglo-Swiss Society was founded in London after a meeting
organised by Colonel Stuart Townend. The first president was the Rt
Hon Philip Noel-Baker, MP and the Swiss Minister in London was
made an honorary patron. At the inaugural dinner the following year
the speeches were broadcast by the BBC to Switzerland. (See also
1950.)

Following the Blake exhibition the previous year in Zurich, a Turner
exhibition of oil paintings and watercolours was opened in Berne by
the President of the Swiss Confederation, Dr Etter.

Several more Swiss companies opened manufacturing subsidiaries in
Britain in the years following the end of the war. They included

Hasler (Great Britain) Ltd at Croydon, Oerlikon Electrodes (GB) Ltd at Crawley and Volkart Bros (UK) Ltd in London. In the other direction, Imperial Chemical Industries Ltd established ICI (Switzerland) AG in Zurich.

A Swiss Folklore Festival was held in the Albert Hall in London in aid of the RAF Benevolent Fund. The following day Swiss singers and dancers from the cast performed at Buckingham Palace in honour of Queen Mary's eighty-first birthday.

At a concert in Zurich, the British composer Lennox Berkeley's *Stabat Mater* was performed for the first time. Also in Zurich, George Bernard Shaw's new play, *Buoyant Billions*, was given a polite but unenthusiastic reception at its world première.

As guests of a special Swiss committee, and with the help of the Swiss Red Cross, 250 British crippled ex-servicemen spent five weeks at Weggis on Lake Lucerne.

1949 Following negotiations in Berne and in London, the Anglo-Swiss monetary agreement was extended for twelve months until March 1950. The Swiss National Bank agreed to continue to hold up to £15m in sterling, and the British Government allocated a maximum of £4.6m for tourist allowances for Switzerland for the following year.

However, in the increasingly difficult economic situation in which Britain found herself after the war, and faced with another financial crisis, the £ sterling was devalued by about 30%.

Another English school, Aiglon College, was founded in Chesières-Villars (Vaud). There were by then approximately a dozen important English schools in Switzerland.

Field-Marshal Lord Montgomery was guest of the city of Zurich and found an enthusiastic welcome. Zurich was also host to the Lord Mayor of Manchester and to several Manchester journalists.

The Switzerland General Insurance Company was established in London.

A 'Welfare Office for Swiss Girls in Great Britain' was also established in London, largely to help the many Swiss 'au pairs'.

1950 The mid-century saw the first year in which the Swiss GNP per inhabitant (at $990) passed that of the United Kingdom. Between 1865 and 1950 income per head in Switzerland had been increasing at an average annual rate of 2.8% compared with about 1.3% in the United Kingdom.

Two new Anglo-Swiss governmental agreements were concluded. A new Anglo-Swiss trade and payments agreement was signed in Berne, while an agreement on air services was made in London.

Swiss trade with the United Kingdom (imports plus exports) had now recovered to Sw. fr. 500m. The trade balance had swung into Britain's favour.

Switzerland began to make Vampire fighter aircraft under licence from Great Britain (see also 1957); Brown Boveri & Co. Ltd. of Baden delivered an advanced gas-turbine locomotive to British Railways for trials.

Both the Swiss-British Society and the twenty-eight Anglo-Swiss Clubs in Switzerland extended honorary membership of their associations to members of the Anglo-Swiss Society in England. Later that year Professor H. Straumann from the Swiss-British Society of Zurich visited the Anglo-Swiss Society and gave a lecture at the Royal Society of Arts on 'What the Swiss and the British thought of each other some three hundred years ago'.

Several travel books on Switzerland were published in England. In his book *Swiss Enchantment* Monk Gibbon discussed the Swiss character:

Swiss character is a firm compound of realism and quite genuine idealism. The idealism never becomes woolly or Utopian; the realism, so far, has managed to avoid falling into that pit of unprincipled greed in which the unscrupulous pursuit of wealth tends to end. Deterioration threatens Switzerland just as it threatens all nations, but so long as she clings to her ancient virtues she is safer than most.

Death of Emile Jacques Dalcroze of Geneva (b. 1865), originator of eurhythmics or rhythmic dancing. He had many followers in Britain, some of whom founded the Dalcroze Society and the Dalcroze Teachers' Union. The ballet dancer Marie Rambert was one of his pupils.

A round of Anglo-Swiss official commercial negotiations made new arrangements to regulate trade for the next twelve months. They were mainly concerned with quotas for goods not yet placed on the 'open general licence' list. In view of the imbalance of trade the United Kingdom subsequently increased the quotas on Swiss goods such as watches, instruments and embroideries.

The Lord Mayor of London and Lady Lowson made an official visit to the Stadtpräsident of Zurich, Dr E. Landolt, and his council, in celebration of that city's 600th anniversary in the Swiss Confederation.

The Stadtmusik of Solothurn, consisting of some eighty wind players, gave a much-appreciated concert in London; while the Swiss singer Lisa Della Casa performed at the Glyndebourne Festival.

Sir Stafford Cripps, former British Chancellor of the Exchequer, died in Switzerland.

A 'Swiss Week', organised with the help of the Pro Helvetia Foundation, was held in Manchester.

Among education exchanges, the Universities of Neuchâtel and of Geneva awarded scholarships to British graduates, while several Swiss went on postgraduate courses to the United Kingdom with help from the British Council.

1952 On the death of King George VI, the President of the Swiss Confederation, Karl Kobelt, expressed to the Queen the wish of the Federal Council and the Swiss people to share in the mourning 'which has overtaken the land of our friends'.

Britain displaced the United States as Switzerland's second largest supplier of vehicles (coming after West Germany). The United Kingdom sent to Switzerland 5,673 vehicles worth Sw. fr. 33.6m (about £2.7m).

Two British Centurion tanks were sent to Switzerland for trials by the Swiss Federal Military Department.

The British De La Rue company formed a joint company with Giori in Lausanne, De La Rue Giori, to provide security printing installations.

An Anglo-Swiss Agreement on air transport (charter flights) was signed.

After the then Persian government denounced the Anglo-Persian Oil

Company's concession and diplomatic relations were broken off, the Swiss government took over the protection of British interests in Persia (now Iran).

An important exhibition of the works of the artist Graham Sutherland (1903–80) was organised by the British Council in Zurich.

In his book *Speaking of Switzerland,* published that year, Gavin de Beer remarked:

It is a curious thing that among the thousands of appreciations of Switzerland, its scenery, and what we can do in it with hands, feet, ice-axe and ski, the number of writers who have paused to think what it is that attracts them is small. Perhaps it is because the physical attraction is so great that the intellect is dimmed . . . 'Beautiful as a dream', wrote Byron of the view from the Col de Jaman, 'and now to me almost as indistinct.'

The British Legation in Berne was raised to the status of embassy. The Swiss Legation in London became an embassy in 1957.

1953

An Anglo-Swiss convention on social insurance was signed in Berne. It came into force the following year.

A British Festival Week was held in Zurich in June. Two London buses provided services in the city, and later did the same in Lucerne, St Gallen and Geneva.

At an exhibition of printed books and manuscripts at the British Museum, first editions of the Swiss writers Salomon Gessner, Pestalozzi, Lavater and Haller were shown; while an Arts Council exhibition in London of modern Swiss prints and drawings showed the work of Paul Klee, Max Bill, Oskar Dalvit, Max Hunziker and Max Truninger among others.

Returning members of the successful British Everest Expedition were greeted at Zurich airport by climbers from two Swiss 1952 expeditions to Everest. Sherpa Tensing was embraced by the celebrated Swiss guide Raymond Lambert, with whom Tensing had attempted Everest the previous year, reaching the highest point up to then.

A memorial to the Alpine writer Frank Smythe was unveiled in the Matterhorn Museum at Zermatt.

British composer Michael Tippett (b. 1905) had his 'Ritual Dances', from his opera *The Midsummer Marriage,* first performed in Basel by the Basel Kammerorchester conducted by Paul Sacher. In Zurich,

Comedy: *by Paul Klee, 1921.*

Schmid, the Tonhalle Orchestra gave the first performance in Switzerland of Vaughan Williams's Sixth Symphony.

1954 Another Anglo-Swiss trade agreement was signed in Berne. It provided for a greater flow of goods between the two countries for the following twelve months. Britain's strengthened balance of payments position enabled her to ease restrictions on imports. Switzerland was to send to the United Kingdom more ready-made clothing, shoes, sewing machines, electric blankets, cheese and grape juice, for which, and for a number of other products, quotas were raised by up to 75%.

A new Anglo-Swiss agreement on the double taxation of incomes was signed in London.

Negotiations between Swiss and United Kingdom delegations in London and in Berne, to review the working of the Anglo-Swiss air services agreement of 1950 and to consider possible amendments to Swissair's route schedule through Britain, ended inconclusively.

The Swiss Parliament approved the purchase of 100 British Venom fighters for the Swiss Air Force at a cost of Sw. fr. 115m.

The Old Vic Theatre Company visited the Zurich festival and performed

formed Shakespeare's *Hamlet*. The Boyd Neel Orchestra made an extensive tour of Switzerland, while a visit by the New English Consort and King's College Choir was organised by the Migros Cooperative Organisation. Michael Tippett's 'Divertimento on *Sellinger's Round*' for chamber orchestra was first performed by the Collegium Musicum of Zurich, and conducted by Paul Sacher, who had commissioned it.

Restoration of the fine organ in the church in Valère Castle, Sion (Valais), was completed. Identified in 1883 by the English organ specialist Arthur Hill as probably of late fourteenth-century origin, it had in recent years gradually become unusable. Restoration began as a result of the enthusiasm of an English music teacher from Eton who obtained permission to work on the organ during successive summer holidays in Sion, in support of which the local authorities provided funds and took over the final work. It is now the world's oldest playable organ.

Profession William Rappard, Professor of International Affairs at Geneva University, said in a speech in London at the City Swiss Club that he believed it was the art and the spirit of self-government which was really the bond between Britain and Switzerland.

After discussions between trade delegations in Berne, the British government agreed to increase their import quota on Swiss watches while the Swiss government increased their quota on imports of British tractors.

1955

The Swiss federal government's proposal to buy 100 British Centurion tanks for £14m was approved by the Swiss Parliament. The first six tanks were delivered within two months. (See also 1957.) Later that year a British Military Mission arrived in Berne to advise the Swiss Army on the use of the tanks.

Sulzer Bros of Switzerland began to deliver the diesels for nearly 1,400 main-line locomotives being made by Vickers-Armstrong for British Rail, making British Rail one of the largest operators of diesel locomotives in the world.

Arriving for a heads of government meeting in Geneva, the British Prime Minister, Sir Anthony Eden, replying to a speech of welcome from the Swiss President, Max Petitpierre, said . . . 'You [Swiss] have learned how to unite people of different creeds and races to

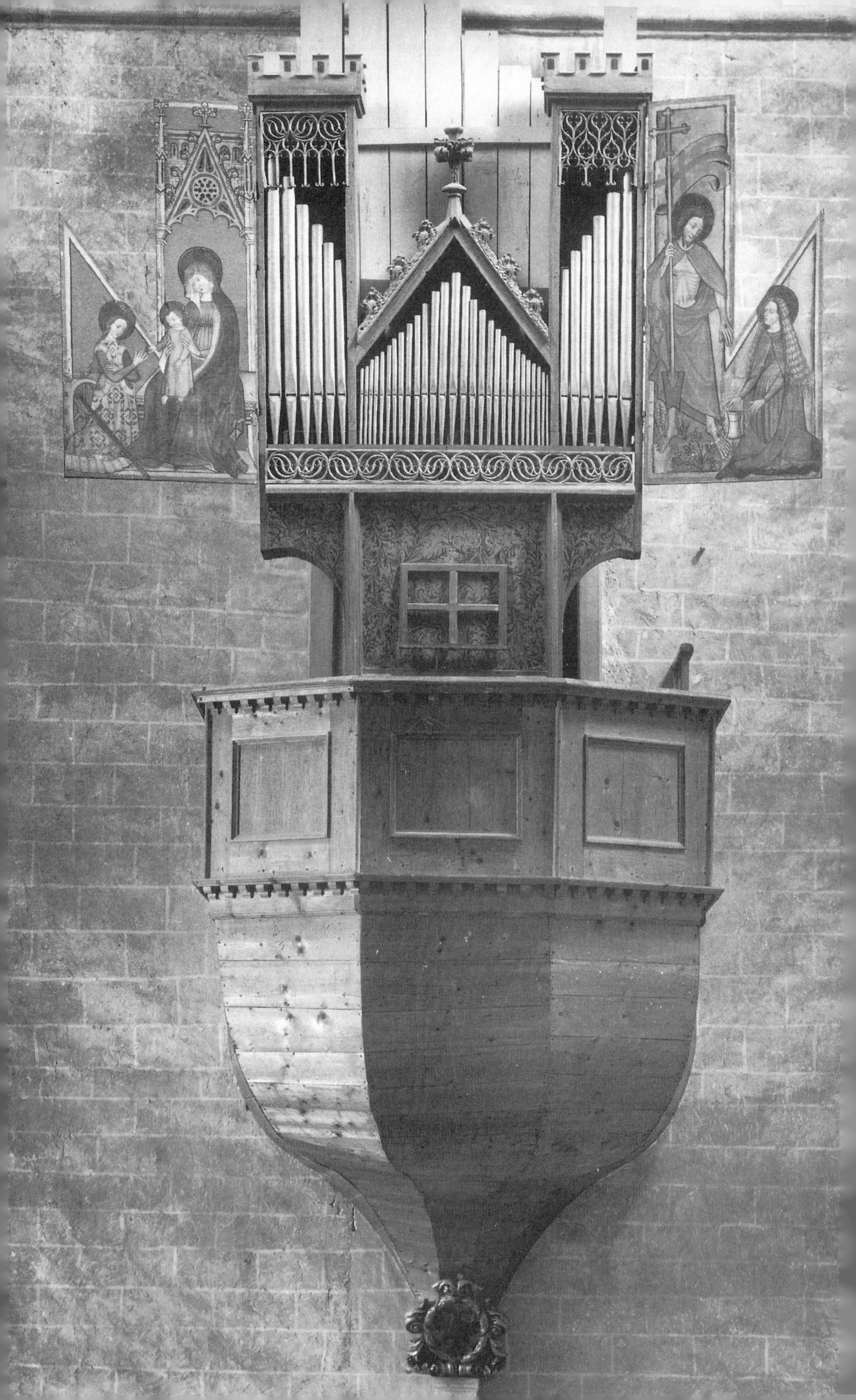

promote each other's peace and prosperity, and to show an example to the whole world.'

The Swiss National Tourist Office established a branch in London. It had previously used the office of Swiss Federal Railways.

Benjamin Britten, on another of his visits to Switzerland, went skiing with friends in Zermatt. While there he wrote an *Alpine Suite* for three recorders.

An exhibition of paintings by Angelica Kauffmann (see 1766) was held in London.

The annual British-Swiss inter-parliamentary ski races in Davos officially began (there had been informal races before then). The leading organiser on the Swiss side was the industrialist, René Bühler. The races enabled parliamentarians from both countries to meet for a week on the ski slopes in an atmosphere of friendship and informality.

1956

An Anglo-Swiss convention on the double taxation of the estates of deceased persons was signed in London.

On 6 November, at the height of the Suez crisis, and of the Hungarian uprising, when British and French troops were in Port Said and Soviet troops were in Budapest, the Swiss government launched a peace initiative. They appealed to the heads of government of Britain, France, the United States and the Soviet Union to hold a summit conference in Switzerland and offered their help in organising it. Although the suggestion was not taken up, the sincerity of the Swiss government's offer of good offices was generally recognised.

After the Suez crisis the Swiss took over the protection of British interests in Egypt.

Among 1956 musical events: the Swiss composer Frank Martin's opera *Der Sturm*, with its libretto based on Shakespeare's *The Tempest*, had its first performance; the British composer Michael Tippett, wrote 'Bonny at Morn', a Northumbrian folksong, set for unison voices and recorders, for the tenth birthday of the International Pestalozzi Children's Village at Trogen in Switzerland; Benjamin Britten's ballet *The Prince of the Pagodas* was first produced, with some of the more exotic designs of John Piper inspired by Paul Klee.

OPPOSITE *The organ (1390) in the church in Valère Castle, Sion.*

Both Benjamin Britten and Yehudi Menuhin had been coming regularly to Switzerland for some years. In 1956, partly at Britten's suggestion, Yehudi Menuhin began his annual summer music festival in Saanen Church near Gstaad.

A guide book, *Switzerland on £25*, published in London, showed how it was well possible to spend ten days in Switzerland in reasonable comfort, seeing much of the country, with all accommodation, meals, local travel and incidentals costing no more than £25. The rate of exchange was Sw. fr. 12 to the pound.

1957 The Swiss government signed a contract to buy 20 de Havilland Vampire jet training aircraft from Britain.

The Swiss government also placed an order with Vickers Armstrong (Engineers) Ltd for another 100 Centurion tanks (see 1955), and for 10 armoured recovery vehicles.

Four vertical storage pumps, among the largest of their type in the world, were supplied and installed at the Central Electricity Generating Board's Ffestiniog energy storage station by Sulzer Bros of Switzerland.

Anglo-Swiss trade reached the highest level since 1920. British imports into Switzerland were valued at Sw. fr. 450m, while Swiss exports to the United Kingdom totalled Sw. fr. 366m.

A visit to Switzerland by the London Festival Ballet was an outstanding success; while at Geneva some 2,000 people attended an outdoor performance of *As You Like It* by the Cambridge University Marlowe Society. In England the Swiss composer Frank Martin's oratorio *Golgotha* received its first performance by Sir Malcolm Sargent and the BBC Symphony Orchestra.

To note the arrival of the 250th Swiss child from Rapperswil to come to London in recent years on an exchange scheme, the young people of Rapperswil presented the Duke of Cornwall with a two-year-old fallow deer.

Four Swiss newspaper editors, René Baum, Peter Dürrenmatt, Jean Heer and Dr Stutzer made a visit to Britain.

1958 Following their purchase of British tanks, an order for 100 British Hawker Hunter turbo-jet fighters was placed by the Swiss government, at a cost of £13m. In addition, the Swiss decided to build under

Benjamin Britten: cartoon by Low.

licence in Switzerland British Armstrong Siddeley jet engines to power Swiss P16 fighter aircraft which were also to be built locally. However, few were completed.

The British Paymaster-General, Reginald Maudling, arrived in Berne for discussions with Swiss ministers on Switzerland's attitude towards the proposed European Free Trade Area (see also 1959).

For the first time in the history of Rhine navigation, a British company opened a regular passenger steamship service between London and Basel.

British merchant bankers Kleinwort Benson opened a Swiss subsidiary in Geneva; and among several other British banks to establish a

Some of the British military equipment ordered by the Swiss government since the end of the Second World War: ABOVE *Mark II Bloodhound missile (1961);* BELOW *Hawker Hunter (1958).*

ABOVE *Rapier Missile System (1980);* BELOW *Centurion tank (1953).*

Swiss presence in the next few years were Samuel Montagu and Warburgs, both in Zurich.

The Swiss-British Society of Berne was formed. Its first president was Dr Rudolf Stamm, Professsor of English Literature at the University of Berne, and a distinguished Shakespeare scholar (see also 1962).

1959 At the end of 1958, despite strenuous efforts by Britain and Switzerland and other Western European countries outside the Common Market, the endeavour to create, in close connexion with the European Economic Community (EEC), a purely economic European free-trade area had broken down. After considerable discussion and heart-searching, Switzerland joined the United Kingdom and five other countries in the launching of EFTA (European Free Trade Association) – see also 1972.

The British composer Benjamin Britten was commissioned by the University of Basel to write a cantata in honour of the 500th anniversary of the University's foundation, with a Latin text compiled from the charter of the University and from older orations in praise of Basel. *Cantata Academica (Carmen Basiliense)* was first performed in Basel in June 1960, under the direction of Paul Sacher.

An exhibition of the work of the British sculptor Lynn Chadwick (b. 1914) was held in Zurich.

Swiss trade with the United Kingdom (imports plus exports) exceeded Sw. fr. 1bn.

1960 Swiss firms were particularly active in the British market. Zurich Life Assurance company formed a subsidiary in London. They had had an alliance with Bedford Insurance company since 1933.

The Swiss Nestlé Group took over the old-established British food company, Crosse & Blackwell. This increased Nestlé's manufacturing capacity in the United Kingdom by the addition of six factories, including the largest fish-canning factory in the country.

In the British-Cypriot agreements establishing the Republic of Cyprus, it was provided that each party might, if necessary, ask the Swiss government to appoint an expert for determining the exact boundary of the United Kingdom sovereign base areas.

A new Central English Library in Zurich was opened by the British Ambassador. It was set up by the British Council with help from leading banks, insurance companies and industrial enterprises in Switzerland.

T. S. Eliot's play *The Elder Statesman* received its first performance in Zurich.

Death of the eminent Swiss pianist and conductor, Edwin Fischer (b. 1889), who gave many concerts in England.

Green Henry (Der Grüne Heinrich) by Gottfried Keller (1819-90), perhaps one of the greatest masterpieces of fiction by a Swiss writer, was finally published in London in its first complete English translation.

The benefits of Britain's and Switzerland's membership of the European Free Trade Area began to be felt, and Anglo-Swiss trade began to increase rapidly.

1961

An agreement for a Swiss government loan of Sw. fr. 215m (about £17.7m) to the British government was signed in Berne. The rate of interest was 3% and the loan was repayable not later than 31 December 1964.

The Swiss government decided to buy Bloodhound guided missiles from the Bristol Aircraft Co. of Britain, to the value of about £25m.

A fact-finding mission from the British Export Council for Europe, led by Sir James Hutchison, President of the Association of British Chambers of Commerce, visited Switzerland to seek ways of stimulating British trade with Switzerland. The visit coincided with a 'British Week' which was held in Basel.

A Pestalozzi Children's Village (see 1805) was initiated at Sedlescombe, Sussex, by British charitable interests.

In the Festival Hall in London, an 'Anglo-Swiss' concert given by the Lucerne Festival Strings, under the baton of Rudolf Baumgartner, played works by Purcell and 'Variations for Oboe and Strings' by the Swiss composer Rudolf Kelterborn. Heinz Holliger was the soloist.

Swiss television began a monthly programme of events in Britain entitled 'England Mosiak'.

According to the publication *Overseas Students in Britain, 1960/61*,

Switzerland was credited with having 1,000 students a year in private colleges in Britain – the highest number from any European country (see also 1973).

1962 It was a fruitful year for cultural relations. At the Lausanne spring festival, the Royal Ballet made its first visit to French-speaking Switzerland. At the Zurich festival, the Royal Shakespeare Company gave performances of *The Hollow Crown,* while the Old Vic Company staged *Romeo and Juliet.* At the Tonhalle, Zurich, one of the soloists was the British pianist Clifford Curzon. The Welsh soprano Gwyneth Jones performed for the season at the Zurich Opera House. (She later went to live in Switzerland.) Sir John Barbirolli conducted a concert at the Montreux festival. The Stadtmusik of Solothurn, under Dr Franz Königshofer, made its second appearance in London together with yodellers and alphorn, and the Musica Lausanne Ensemble gave a concert in the Wigmore Hall in London.

The Swiss dramatist Max Frisch's play *Andorra* was published in London in an English translation.

The Swiss-British Society of Basel was founded. Its first president was again Professor Dr Rudolf Stamm (see 1958), then Professor of English at the University of Basel.

A 'British Fortnight' was held in Geneva, complete with fashion shows, bagpipers, London policemen, a London bus, and the recorded chimes of Big Ben.

Turegum Versicherungen, Swiss re-insurers and a member of the Zurich Group, formed Turegum Insurance in London.

The British Chamber of Commerce in Switzerland changed its statutes to allow Swiss nationals to vote and to join the Council, and changed its name to the British-Swiss Chamber of Commerce. It was the first British Chamber in Europe to make changes of this kind.

1963 An Anglo-Swiss Cooperation Agreement on the peaceful uses of atomic energy was concluded.

A British Industrial Fair and a 'British Fortnight' was opened in Zurich by F. J. Erroll, President of the British Board of Trade. Sponsored by the Federation of British Industries, the Export Council for Europe and other British organisations, some 800 British firms took part. About 62,000 people visited the Industrial Fair. The Lord

Mayor of London, Sir Ralph Perring, presented a silver cup to the Zurich Municipal Council on the occasion of his visit during the 'British Fortnight'.

The first performance of Benjamin Britten's *Cantata Misericordium* took place in Geneva, conducted by Ernest Ansermet.

A play, *Die Physiker*, by the Swiss dramatist Friedrich Dürrenmatt (b. 1921), was produced in London under the title *The Physicists*.

Educational exchanges between Britain and Switzerland continued, in particular under the Young Research Workers' Interchange Scheme and the Foreign University Interchange Scheme, both sponsored by the British Council.

In a book published by the New Helvetic Society, *Switzerland, Present and Future*, Eric Mettler wrote of his upbringing among the Swiss business community of St Gallen.

As children we grew up with an Anglo-Saxon horizon without being conscious of it. All educated adults not only spoke German and French but also made jokes in English, read Galsworthy, and in addition to the creations of French haute couture, appreciated the advantages of British tweed and smoking pipes.

A visit to Switzerland by the Welsh Miners' Choir had an excellent reception.

Unilever (Schweiz) AG was established in Zurich by the Unilever Group.

The newly constructed ski-station on the summit of th Schilthorn (Bernese Oberland) was chosen for the main centre of action for the film of Ian Fleming's James Bond novel *On Her Majesty's Secret Service*.

Globe Air of Switzerland took delivery of its third Handley-Page Herald turbo-powered transport plane ordered from Britain.

1964

With pressure again on sterling, the Swiss National Bank extended to the Bank of England currency swap facilities to the equivalent value of $120m.

During the British balance of payments crisis the United Kingdom imposed, as an emergency measure, a 15% surcharge on British imports. Annoyed at this seeming violation of the EFTA agreement, Swiss exporters and the Swiss press strongly criticised the British government's measure. In reaction, a British Minister spoke of Swiss bankers as 'the Gnomes of Zurich'. ('Gnomes' was a word invented by the sixteenth-century Swiss doctor, Paracelsus, to denote a race of diminutive spirits fabled to inhabit the interior of the earth and to be the guardians of its treasures.)

The year saw a low point in Anglo-Swiss relations. In a spate of press articles about the Swiss, Lord Arran wrote that they 'washed everything but themselves'; and a speaker on a BBC satirical programme maintained that 'if Switzerland did not exist it would not have been necessary to invent it'.

International direct dialling from the United Kingdom to Switzerland was introduced by the British Post Office (see also 1966).

A new edition was published of *Modern Forms of Government* by Michael Stewart, British Foreign Secretary in the Labour Government of Harold Wilson. In it, Stewart wrote:

The unique characteristic of Switzerland is that she has adopted a form of politics and a way of life which sets a limit to the capacities of the human spirit, both for good and evil: it is a limit which mankind as a whole is not prepared to accept.

1965 The United Kingdom accepted the offer of a loan of $40m from the Swiss National Bank.

Britain's economic difficulties, which had sparked off the show of bad feelings between the Swiss and the British the previous year, found at least one sympathetic Swiss observer in J. R. de Salis, the former Professor of History at the Federal Institute of Technology in Zurich. Writing in *Die Weltwoche*, de Salis commented:

It is well known that Zurich's banking policy so exasperated a British minister concerned with economic affairs that he was betrayed into hostile remarks about our bankers . . . To the British, this emergency measure [the 15% import surcharge] was not primarily an infringement of the EFTA agreement, but a bitter necessity in defending sterling. When the Swiss of all people, who got rich during the war, cast reproaches at Britain, which was bled white and has still not recovered from the over-exertions of the war, the British call to mind their unhappy memories of Switzerland's wartime attitude. When the British call us 'gnomes' they mean to say that we are the last people to have any moral right to criticize the British import surcharge. There is a note of disappointed love, greater than in those of others, in comments from Britain . . .

An Anglo-Swiss Treaty for Conciliation, Judicial Settlement and Arbitration was signed in London. Under the treaty, a standing Anglo-Swiss conciliation commission was to be set up to consider disputes, with ultimate recourse if necessary to the International Court of Justice. This was the first bilateral agreement of this type signed by the British government.

Swiss trade with the United Kingdom (imports plus exports) exceeded Sw. fr. 2bn, having doubled in five years.

An exhibition at the Tate Gallery of the works of the Swiss sculptor Alberto Giacometti was a major event of the season in London.

A monument to Winston Churchill by the Swiss sculptor G. Piquet was unveiled near Oberhofen Castle on Lake Thun by Randolph Churchill. It was erected with money raised by public subscription.

The number of Swiss nationals registered as living in the United Kingdom was 13,885. To help look after their needs, there were thirty-five Swiss societies, clubs and institutes, which were grouped into a Federation of Swiss Societies in the United Kingdom.

A protocol was signed by British and Swiss representatives, amending the Anglo-Swiss double-taxation agreement of 1954.

1966

This was the last year that the rate of exchange between the Swiss franc and sterling was over Sw. fr. 12 to the pound.

The British merchant bank Singer & Friedlander opened a subsidiary in Zurich.

The Swiss Post Office ordered the supply and installation of two UHF television transmitters from Pye Ltd of the United Kingdom. They also introduced direct dialling from Switzerland to the United Kingdom (see 1964).

On the initiative of Max Petitpierre, a former President of the Swiss Confederation, and of the Swiss-British Society, a Swiss Winston Churchill Foundation was established in Zurich, together with a Churchill Memorial Library.

Among cultural events was a major exhibition in Basel of the work of the British sculptor Barbara Hepworth. The New Philharmonia Orchestra, the Royal Philharmonic, the Melos Ensemble and the National Youth Orchestra all performed in Switzerland. In London an exhibition showed the work of the Swiss artist Max Bill (b. 1908).

Seated Man: *Alberto Giacometti, 1949*.

That year the number of British visitors in Switzerland was at a postwar peak of over 700,000.

In May the United Kingdom repaid £28m of Swiss debt. 1967

Anglo-Swiss banking connexions were reinforced as the Union Bank of Switzerland opened an office in London; and Switzerland's largest life insurance company, Swiss Life Insurance and Pension Company, opened a branch there too.

The British merchant bank J. Henry Schroder opened a subsidiary in Zurich, and the British electronics company, Plessey, formed Plessey Verkaufs AG in Zurich.

Following the merger of the Swiss companies Sandoz of Basel and Wander of Berne, Sandoz took over responsibility for the manufacture of Ovaltine in the United Kingdom.

Sulzer Bros of Switzerland supplied to the RAF establishment at Farnborough the complete test-centre for the British version of the Anglo-French supersonic Concorde airliner.

In November the pound sterling was devalued by 14.3%. Following this, the big three Swiss banks, the Union Bank of Switzerland, Credit Suisse and the Swiss Bank Corporation, put a total of Sw. fr. 450m (£37.5m) at the disposal of the Bank of England in the form of a one-year credit at 5½% interest. To a large extent this loan was a repatriation of funds which had been withdrawn from London by Arab holders during the earlier turmoil in the Middle East and which had found their way to Switzerland.

At a dinner given by the Anglo-Swiss Society in London, Dr Jakob Burckhardt, President of the Swiss Federal Institute of Technology, called for cooperation in big scientific projects in Europe, such as the Centre for Nuclear Research in Geneva, as one means of combating the brain drain to the United States. Professor P. M. S. Blackett, President of the Royal Society, strongly endorsed Dr Burckhardt's views. Dr Burckhardt likened the brain drain of the 1960s to the blood drain of mercenaries from Switzerland during the Middle Ages.

The Swiss Finance Ministry ordered from the British Royal Mint 1968 45m cupro-nickel coins to replace some of the silver coins still in circulation in Switzerland.

The Swiss Centre was opened in Leicester Square, London, providing facilities for several Swiss restaurants, shops, offices, the Swiss Bank Corporation and the Swiss National Tourist Office. Kuoni Travel of Switzerland established a subsidiary, Kuoni-Travel Ltd, in the United Kingdom.

The expansion of banking links continued. Bank Julius Baer & Co. of Zurich opened an office in London (see also 1970), while the British merchant bank N. M. Rothschild & Sons opened a subsidiary in Zurich, and the British Bank of the Middle East opened one in Geneva.

The rate of exchange for sterling had deteriorated to an average of Sw. fr. 10.33 to the pound. This had an inevitable effect on the flow of British visitors to Swiss resorts. However, British tourists spent about Sw. fr. 200m in Switzerland.

Among Anglo-Swiss cultural events, the Bristol Old Vic played Shakespeare's *Hamlet* and *Measure for Measure* to full houses in Zurich; while an exhibition of the works of Swiss artist Richard P. Lohse (b. 1902) was held in London.

In a tour organised by the Swiss National Tourist Office, the Sherlock Holmes Society of London and the Conan Doyle Foundation in Switzerland staged a re-enactment of the 'fatal' struggle between Conan Doyle's hero Sherlock Holmes and his great opponent Professor Moriarty, at the Reichenbach Falls (see 1891). The part of Sherlock Holmes was played by Sir Paul Gore-Booth, then Permanent Under-Secretary of State at the Foreign and Commonwealth Office.

1969 The total value of loans floated in the Swiss capital market by British companies and other organisations was then estimated at about Sw. fr. 1.5bn.

Britain repaid to Switzerland the last instalment of the $40m credit which has been extended by the Swiss National Bank in 1965.

Swiss trade with the United Kingdom (imports plus exports) exceeded Sw. fr. 3bn for the first time. Over 36,000 British cars were sold in the Swiss market against 27,400 in 1968. British car manufacturers now had over 15% of the Swiss car market.

More British banks opened offices in Switzerland. The Standard Chartered Bank of London established a subsidiary in it own name in Zurich, as did both Keyser Ullmann and Grindlays Bank in Geneva.

Sherlock Holmes and Professor Moriarty at the Reichenbach Falls

The Swiss Re-insurance Company of Zurich opened a new British subsidiary. It had been trading with the United Kingdom since 1863.

The British brewery group, Bass International, formed Bass SA with local interests in Switzerland, in order to build a chain of British pubs there. The first, the Mr Pickwick, was opened in Geneva.

Two British minesweepers travelled up the Rhine to make an official visit to Basel.

A performance of Purcell's *The Fairy Queen* at the Lucerne Festival, with Benjamin Britten conducting a team of British soloists, the English Chamber Orchestra and the Lucerne Festival Choir, received an ovation lasting more than a quarter of an hour.

1970 A novel by the Swiss author Blaise Cendrars, *L'homme foudroyé*, was published in an English translation in London as *The Astonished Man*.

On the eve of an EFTA ministerial meeting in Geneva, the British Minister responsible for European Affairs, George Thomson, Chancellor of the Duchy of Lancaster, had talks with the Swiss government about possible membership of the European Economic Community.

Bank Julius Baer & Co. of Zurich, together with United Dominions Trust, established Julius Baer International Ltd in London, while the British merchant bank Guinness Mahon opened a subsidiary in Zurich.

Alusuisse of Zurich, the important aluminium group, acquired the British company High Duty Alloys Ltd; and the British Johnson Matthey precious metals group established Johnson Matthey & Brandenberger AG in Zurich.

The number of Swiss visitors to the United Kingdom was 186,000, spending just over £12m. British visitors to Switzerland totalled approximately 600,000.

1971 The British Prime Minster, Edward Heath, addressed a big audience in Zurich to commemorate the twenty-fifth anniversary of Winston Churchill's speech on European unity. He spoke from the spot from which Churchill had spoken in 1946.

There was an unprecedented inflow of money into Switzerland and the Swiss franc began to appreciate against almost all currencies. The sterling rate was down to Sw. fr. 10.05 to the pound. In order to protect the Swiss franc from speculative pressure, the Swiss National Bank forbade the granting of any interest on foreign funds entering Switzerland after 31 July.

Swiss trade with the United Kingdom (imports plus exports) had doubled in six years, and now exceeded Sw. fr. 4bn.

The Oerlikon-Bührle group of Zurich took over the British Manufacture and Research Co. Ltd of Grantham. The company had been formed in 1938 by Hispano Suiza (Suisse) SA of Geneva, and supplied the 20mm cannon needed for Spitfires and Hurricanes during the war.

CIBA-Geigy (UK) Ltd was formed, following the merger of the parent companies in Basel. (In 1969 CIBA had taken full control of the British photographic company Ilford, which it had acquired jointly with ICI in 1967.) Alusuisse of Zurich set up two new companies in Britain, Alusuisse (UK) Ltd and Swiss Aluminium Mining (UK).

A stained glass window by the British artist Graham Sutherland (see 1952) was dedicated in the Anglican church of St Andrew's, Zurich.

The Kammermusiker of Zurich gave a memorable concert in London with the Swiss harpist Ursula Holliger as soloist.

The United Kingdom left the European Free Trade Area in which she had been partners with Switzerland to join the Common Market (EEC) with which Switzerland had already negotiated a special agreement.

1972

The United Kingdom's departure from EFTA while Switzerland remained meant that the frequent opportunities for Anglo-Swiss contacts using the EFTA forum would in future be no longer available. Attention was therefore turned to increasing the number of purely bilateral contacts between Britain and Switzerland. Federal Councillor Pierre Graber, head of the Département Politique in Berne, made the first official visit of a Swiss Foreign Minister to Britain for half a century.

The inflow of money into Switzerland continued at an embarassing rate for the federal government. Following the nil interest rate imposed on foreign funds the previous year, the Swiss National Bank imposed a negative interest rate of 8% on all foreign funds coming

354   Chronology 1972

Window by Graham Sutherland at St Andrew's Church, Zurich.

into Switzerland after 30 June, levied at 2% per quarter in advance. The pound slipped further to Sw. fr. 9.55 to the pound.

As part of further measures to protect the Swiss franc from too rapid an appreciation, the Swiss government later imposed restrictions on the sale to foreigners of Swiss, or Swiss franc designated, shares and bonds, and of Swiss property.

On the other hand, there was a further large outflow of funds from the United Kingdom. The British government's decisions to take some pressure off sterling by floating the pound took the Swiss capital markets by surprise. The Swiss view finally was that it was the most sensible thing to do.

Credit Suisse of Zurich opened a branch office in London. They had had a representative office since 1954 and a joint company with the American First Boston Corporation there since 1966.

Two Swiss former bank employees were arraigned before an investigating magistrate under the Swiss banking secrecy act for having allegedly divulged to British officials details of accounts held in Switzerland by United Kingdom residents in contravention of British exchange control regulations.

The Swiss government bought 30 second-hand Hawker Hunter aircraft from Britain.

Earl Mountbatten of Burma visited Berne to enlist Swiss support for the Atlantic World Colleges.

Returning the Swiss Foreign Minister's visit of the year before, Lord Home (then Sir Alec Douglas-Home), accompanied by Lady Home, made the first official visit of a British Foreign Secretary to Switzerland. (Several Foreign Secretaries had been to Switzerland before but either on holiday or to attend international meetings.)

1973

Other British ministers visiting Switzerland that year were Sir John Eden, Minister of Posts and Telecommunications, Mrs Margaret Thatcher, Minister of Education, and John Davies, Chancellor of the Duchy of Lancaster, who delivered the Churchill Memorial Lecture on 'Britain and Europe' at Zurich University.

The Swiss Parliament decided to buy another 30 refurbished Hawker Hunter aircraft from Britain.

Sir Alec Douglas-Home and Federal Councillor Pierre Graber at Berne Airport, 1973.

The Swiss franc was floated, and increased sharply in value against sterling. The rate over the year averaged Sw. fr. 8.25 to the pound.

The Swiss gross national product (GNP) per inhabitant (at $6,193) had now increased to double that of the United Kingdom (at $3,095).

A British charter plane bringing women and children to Basel on a day's outing crashed in a blizzard when trying to land. It was the worst disaster in Swiss aviation history, with 108 people killed.

Cultural events that year included a visit by the London Festival Ballet to the Lausanne Festival. In addition, the London Philharmonic Orchestra, the Amadeus Quartet, the English Chamber Orchestra, the British conductors Charles Groves and John Pritchard and the executants Julian Bream, Moura Lympany and John Lill all performed in Switzerland.

The private Swiss bank, Lombard Odier of Geneva, opened a securities office in London. Five years later, in 1978, they opened Lombard Odier International Portfolio Management Ltd.

A Swiss, Archbishop Bruno Heim, became Apostolic Delegate of the Holy See in London.

The continuing popularity of English as a language among the Swiss was indicated by the fact that over 11,000 English language teaching records and cassettes of BBC English by radio lessons were sold in Switzerland, the largest number sold in any country that year.

The Swiss pharmaceutical company Hoffmann-La Roche were required by the British government to reduce sharply the prices of their drugs Librium and Valium in the British market, and to make restitution for allegedly overcharging. They later came to an out of court settlement.

There was a marked increase in British interest in the Swiss market. At least thirty-five new British firms established themselves in Switzerland during 1973.

Swiss trade with the United Kingdom (imports plus exports) for the first time exceeded Sw. fr. 5bn. Imports from the United Kingdom were almost in balance with Swiss exports to the United Kingdom.

1974

Following a further sharp rise in the Swiss franc, caused by an inflow of petro-dollars and other funds, the Swiss National Bank reintroduced negative interest rates on foreign deposits at 12% per annum.

The Swiss tourist trade was badly affected by the rise in the Swiss franc and the number of British tourists visiting Switzerland declined by 38% compared with 1973.

Swiss companies were active in the British market. Brown Boveri & Co. of Baden took over the British instruments company George Kent Ltd, and the Union Bank of Switzerland established UBS Securities Ltd in London.

A number of British companies were finding that Switzerland offered a good base for European-wide activities. Lucas Industries of Britain opened a regional office in Lausanne.

The Duke of Edinburgh made two private visits to Switzerland, one to attend the World Driving Championships at Frauenfeld, the other to attend a meeting of the Trustees of the World Wild Life Fund in Lausanne.

Benjamin Britten's *Billy Budd* was performed at the Zurich Opera House by the Welsh National Opera Company; and his new opera, *Death in Venice*, received its first Swiss performance in Berne.

The annual general meeting of the Federation of Anglo-Swiss Clubs in Switzerland was held at Interlaken and was addressed by the British Ambassador.

1975 The increase in the number official bilateral contacts continued. The first official visit to Britain of a Swiss Minister of Justice was made by Federal Councillor Kurt Furgler, at the invitation of the Lord Chancellor. A return visit was subsequently made to Switzerland by Lord Hailsham.

The head of the Division of Commerce at the Swiss Ministry of Economics, Ambassador Paul Jolles, made an official visit to London.

The Swiss Chief of the General Staff, Commandant de Corps J. J. Vischer, came to England at the invitation of the British Chief of Staff.

The memorial to Winston Churchill on the shores of Lake Thun in Switzerland was re-dedicated by his daughter, Mary Soames. Her husband Sir Christopher Soames gave the Winston Churchill Foundation Memorial Lecture in Berne.

In a further effort to stem the unwanted inflow of money, the Swiss National Bank raised the negative interest rate on foreign deposits from 3% to 10% per quarter.

The trend toward closer links in the financial field gathered pace. National Westminster Bank took a majority shareholding in the previously Swiss-owned Handelsbank of Zurich. Other British banks to open in Switzerland at around this time (through their own offices or through take-overs) included Midland and Williams & Glyns, both in Zurich; Morgan Grenfell and Robert Fleming in Geneva; and Hill Samuel who took over the Swiss-owned Bank von Ernst & Cie in Berne.

Bally Shoes of Switzerland, who had first entered the British market in 1892, formed a new British company, Bally Group (UK) Ltd, as part of their development in the British market.

Exhibitions of the sculptures of Henry Moore and of Barbara Hepworth were held in Zurich, while an exhibition about the work of the English architect Inigo Jones (1573-1625) was held in Berne. In England, an important exhibition of the paintings of Henry Fuseli (see 1974) was given at the Tate Gallery, in conjunction with the Pro-Helvetia Foundation.

The British Chatelard school for girls at Les Avants, near Montreux, was closed after nearly fifty years (see 1927). The fall in the value of the pound had proved too much for British parents.

The Central English Library in Zurich run by the British Council, was forced to close too, but on grounds of government economy.

In a particularly informative book, *Switzerland,* published in London, Professor Christopher Hughes wrote:

Switzerland maintains an honourable position in many fields of activity, but it is generally agreed that in the field of government she holds a light to the world which justifies her independence and material comfort. This especially applies to the institution for which Switzerland is best known, that is to say to 'pure democracy' – the Referendum in all its various forms.

At the British-Swiss Interparliamentary Ski Race at Davos the British side fielded a strong team which included the Lords Carr, Hunt, Limerick, Lyell, Orrr-Ewing, Sandford and Selsdon, and from the Commons, Winston Churchill, Sir Philip Goodhart, Bryant Godman Irving, Michael Grylls, Cecil Parkinson and Sir Richard Thompson.

1976

Roy Hattersley, Minister of State at the Foreign and Commonwealth Office, made an official visit to Switzerland.

Exchanging the visit of the Chief of the Swiss General Staff to Britain the year before, Field Marshal Sir Michael (later Lord) Carver went to Switzerland.

The value of the pound against the Swiss franc continued its decline. The average rate of exchange was Sw. fr. 4.50 to the pound, but at one time in the autumn the rate slipped to below Sw. fr. 3.00 to the pound.

In a further effort to tighten up on the inflow of foreign money into the country, the Swiss government limited the amount of foreign bank notes that could be brought into Switzerland to the equivalent of Sw. fr. 20,000 (about £4,500) per person in any three-month period.

The number of Swiss visitors to the United Kingdom reached 263,000, spending in all about £41m.

In the field of cultural relations, the Hallé Orchestra, the Monteverdi Choir and the Royal Ballet all visited Switzerland, and an important

'Turner in Switzerland' exhibition was held in Zurich. This featured Turner's Swiss watercolours, many lent by the British Museum.

The number of British residents in Switzerland was estimated at approximately 25,000, of which over half lived around the Lake of Geneva. They included businessmen, bankers, engineers, teachers, writers, artists and musicians, personalities of the stage, screen, opera and motor racing, and many retired people.

Among some of the personalities who resided (or had resided) there were Julie Andrews, Valerie Hobson, Deborah Kerr, Petula Clark, David Niven, Roger Moore, James Galway, Jackie Stewart, the Australian Joan Sutherland and the late Noël Coward.

1977 Continuing the policy of increased bilateral contacts between Switzerland and Britain, the Swiss Minister of Economy, Federal Councillor Ernst Brugger, made an official visit to Britain as guest of the Secretary of State for Trade. He had talks with several British ministers and met members of the Anglo-Swiss Parliamentary Group at the House of Commons.

A new comprehensive double-taxation convention between the United Kingdom and Switzerland was signed in London. It replaced the 1954 convention (as amended in 1966 and 1974).

The adverse rate of exchange for the pound against the Swiss franc was responsible for further reducing the number of British tourists to Switzerland. Of the total number of foreign tourist nights spent in Switzerland in 1977, British tourists were responsible for only 3.9%.

The Lausanne based ADIA group acquired the Alfred Marks chain of temporary employment agencies in Britain, while the Swiss Volksbank of Berne opened a representative office in London (to become a full branch in 1985). Handelsbank NW of Zurich followed with a London office in 1979.

On the occasion of the Silver Jubilee of Queen Elizabeth II's succession to the throne, a Queen's Jubilee Fund was established in Switzerland. With the help of Swiss and British contributions, a trust was established to provide for student exchanges between the two countries.

The Sir Arthur Conan Doyle Foundation launched a scheme to exchange serving police officers between Scotland Yard and the canton of Vaud. Over the next ten years more than fifty exchanges were arranged.

The British consulate in Basel was closed on grounds of economy.

A group of senior Swiss industrialists and bankers visited Britain for three days at the invitation of the Secretary of State for Industry, Eric Varley. The aim was to promote Anglo-Swiss collaboration and, particularly, to encourage the visitors to invest in the United Kingdom. They saw, among others, the Prime Minster, the Chancellor of the Exchequer, the Governor of the Bank of England, the Head of the British Overseas Trade Board, the Presidents of the TUC and of the CBI and leading industrialists and officials. In addition, a day's seminar was held in Basel to encourage Swiss investment in Britain. Alan Williams, Minister of State at the United Kingdom Department of Industry, gave the keynote address. 1978

The State Secretary of the Swiss Federal Department of External Affairs, Ambassador Albert Weitnauer, made an official visit to London.

Total Anglo-Swiss trade was now running at over Sw. fr. 6bn. per annum. But, reflecting the firmness of the Swiss franc, the exchange rate for sterling reached an all-time low of Sw. fr. 2.93 to the pound on 26 September.

Swiss Aluminium Mining (UK) opened a new £2.3m fluorspar processing plant at Broadwood, County Durham.

The British film actor Sir Charles Chaplin died at his home in Switzerland.

The Swiss dramatist Herbert Meier (b. 1908) published his play *Bräker*, about the self-taught peasant of Toggenburg who wrote a striking commentary on the plays of Shakespeare (see 1762). *Bräker* dealt with the clash between the imaginative and the materialistic worlds, symbolised by the almost concurrent impact on eighteenth-century Switzerland of two English inventions – Shakespeare's plays with their prospect of cultural enrichment, and Hargreaves's spinning jenny with its threat of ruin for much of the Swiss cotton industry.

The government of the newly constituted canton of Jura obtained from the British Museum the loan of the ancient Bible of Moutier-Grandval, for display at an exhibition in Delémont to mark the 1979 independence celebrations of the canton. The bible, dating from the ninth century, had been sold to the British Museum at the end of the eighteenth century.

With the arrival of North Sea oil the pound strengthened and the Swiss france-sterling exchange rate was at last roughly stabilised. It averaged Sw. fr. 3.53 to the pound.

The Swiss Defence Ministry announced that Switzerland was to spend £32m on buying British anti-tank bombs, rocket-launchers and electronic equipment for its Hunter jet fighter aircraft (see 1958).

An aerobatic team from the Swiss Air Force gave a display at an Air Tattoo at Greenham Common airbase in Berkshire. They brought with them a de Havilland Venom fighter which had been built in Switzerland in the mid-fifties under licence from Britain, and presented it to the RAF Museum at Hendon.

Three British skiers and a Swiss guide were killed in an avalanche during a skiing tour near Andermatt, while six British climbers were rescued by helicopter from the north face of the Eiger, after having been on the mountain for nine days.

1980 The Queen came to Switzerland, accompanied by the Duke of Edinburgh, in the first state visit of a British sovereign to that country. She was the guest of the President of the Swiss Confederation, Georges-André Chevallaz, and of the Federal Council. The visit had been planned for four years. The Swiss press reported the visit extensively with such appreciative headlines as 'Overwhelming Welcome for Queen Elizabeth' and 'Immense Jubilant Crowds'. The Queen, in a message of thanks to the Federal Council, said 'I hope that our visit may have helped to strengthen still further the long friendship that has existed between our two countries.'

The Swiss government placed a contract with British Aerospace for the Rapier missile system. British Aerospace agreed to provide offsets for at least half of the total cost of £200m, involving agreements to manufacture or supply with over 165 Swiss companies.

The Swiss Foreign Minister, Federal Councillor Pierre Aubert, had talks in London with the British Foreign Secretary, Lord Carrington.

Anglo-Swiss trade in gross terms had now reached over Sw. fr. 8bn. Imports of British goods into Switzerland totalled 5.1bn, while Swiss

Queen Elizabeth with the Swiss Minister of Justice, Federal Councillor Kurt Furgler, Basel, May 1980.

exports to the United Kingdom were Sw. fr. 3.1bn. Excluding the special movements of precious metals and of diamonds (now generally heavy in the Anglo-Swiss figures) the British share of the Swiss import market was about 4.6%.

The Swiss Bank Corporation established Swiss Bank Corporation International Ltd in London; and the private bankers A. Sarasin & Cie of Basel opened a representative office in London.

Swiss (fixed) investment in the United Kingdom was now estimated to total approximately £1,394m. Switzerland was the second largest investor in the United Kingdom after the United States. British investment in Switzerland was estimated to total about £595m.

1981

Reflecting its new status as an oil currency, sterling strengthened further against the Swiss franc. In February, it reached a high point of Sw. fr. 4.62 to the pound.

Exhibitions of the work of the Swiss sculptor Alberto Giacometti were held in Manchester, Bristol and London.

An order for 35mm twin naval anti-aircraft guns was placed by the British Royal Navy with the Oerlikon-Bürhle Group of Zurich.

The Zurich *Tages Anzeiger* summed up the views of much of the Swiss press towards the hunger striker, Sands, in Northern Ireland when it said that the British government had no choice but to let Sands die. Compromising with terrorism was no way of mastering it.

Swiss visitors to the United Kingdom totalled 281,000, nearly a quarter down on the record figure of 365,000 who came the year before.

The Camerata Bern, led by Thomas Furi, gave an outstanding concert at the Queen Elizabeth Hall in London. It included Elgar's 'Serenade for Strings'. The Swiss oboist Heinz Holliger also gave another concert in London.

1982 The Swiss government took over the protection of British interests in Argentina after Argentina's invasion of the Falklands.

The private bankers Pictet & Cie of Geneva established Pictet Asset Management (UK) Ltd in London, while the Midland Bank took a 69% interest in Handelsfinanz of Geneva. British banks now owned around 10% of the assets of all foreign banks established in Switzerland.

Schindler Holding AG of Hergiswil, Switzerland extended their interests in the United Kingdom by taking over Keighley Lifts Ltd of Yorkshire.

A notable exhibition of the Swiss artist Jean Charles Tinguely's mechanical sculptures was held at the Tate Gallery.

1983 The British Secretary of State for Trade, Lord Cockfield, visited Switzerland at the invitation of Kurt Furgler, the new head of the Federal Ministry of Economy. They signed a joint declaration in favour of wider mutual recognition of tests and test certificates showing conformity with the technical regulations of the importing country.

Sir Antony Acland, Permanent Under-Secretary of State at the Foreign and Commonwealth Office, visited his opposite number in the Swiss Department of External Affairs, Raymond Probst.

Unemployment in Switzerland was 1% of the workforce. In the United Kingdom it was 12%.

The number of British visitors to Switzerland totalled some 695,000. The total number of Swiss visitors to Britain was 310,000.

It was announced that the Royal Bank of Scotland was to buy the Seattle-First National Bank (Switzerland) AG in Zurich and to rename it Williams & Glyn's Bank AG.

The Swiss conductor Charles Dutoit made his début at Covent Garden Opera House, conducting Gounod's *Faust*.

The last of the British-made Venom jet fighters was phased out of the Swiss Air Force after having been in service for nearly thirty years.

After months of painstaking work conducted through Swiss diplomatic intermediaries, talks between the British and Argentine governments, for the first time since the invasion of the Falklands, were arranged in Berne. They swiftly broke down.

1984

The Swiss Foreign Minister, Federal Councillor Pierre Aubert, visited London for talks with the Foreign Secretary, Sir Geoffrey Howe. He also called on the Prime Minister.

The British Minister of State for Trade, Paul Channon, made two visits to Switzerland, the first to see the Basel Trade Fair and to talk to the State Secretary at the Swiss Department of Economy, M. Sommaruga, the second to Berne for discussions with the Swiss Minister of Economy, Federal Councillor Kurt Furgler.

In an important year for Anglo-Swiss economic relations, it was announced that the Union Bank of Switzerland was to take a 29.9% interest in the large British stockbrokers and fund managers Phillips & Drew, this percentage to be increased to 100% when London Stock Exchange rules allowed in 1986.

In June a new Vitamin C plant was opened by Hoffmann-La Roche on their 124-acre site at Dalry, Ayrshire. The cost, at £150 million, was the largest single investment by Hoffmann-La Roche ever made.

Watches of Switzerland Ltd, retail agents for many major Swiss watch manufacturers, celebrated their diamond jubilee year. Their business had grown from one small office in 1924 to sixteen showrooms throughout the United Kingdom.

Jacobs-Suchard, the Swiss coffee and chocolate group, set up a trading company, SOPRA, in London.

Ferranti Computer Systems of Manchester were awarded a £6.25m Swiss contract which included the design of a flight databased management system for Geneva and Zurich airports. Brown Boveri of Switzerland were awarded an order by London Transport Authority for prototype electrical propulsion equipment for a new generation of underground trains.

The Migros Organisation in Zurich (Federation of Migros Cooperatives) opened a new English language school in Cambridge, to add to the several language schools they already owned and operated in England.

A symposium – 'Modern Swiss Literature: Unity and Diversity' – was held at the University of London Institute of Germanic Studies. The contributors included professors of literature from both Swiss and British Universities.

Towards the end of the year, 'The British and Swiss in the Alps', a historical exhibition of pictures, books and documents, was held at the Alpine Club Gallery in London, to mark the seventy-fifth anniversary of the Association of British Members of the Swiss Alpine Club.

To mark the 400th anniversary of the City of Westminster in 1985, the Swiss proposed to give to London a carillon (or glockenspiel) of twenty-five bells, one from each of the twenty-three Swiss cantons dedicated to the twenty-three wards of Westminster, one from the Swiss Confederation and one from the Principality of Liechtenstein. The offer was gladly accepted and the bells, commissioned by the Swiss National Tourist Office, were installed the following year on the Swiss Centre in Leicester Square.

Notes

1 *Switzerland, Present and Future*, Berne: New Helvetic Society, 1962.
2 *Switzerland Revisited*, London: Geoffrey Bles, 1947.
3 *The Second World War*, vol. 6, London: Cassell, 1948.
4 J.M. Clark, in *The Abbey of St Gall* (Cambridge, 1926), says that there was a continual stream of thousands of Irish pilgrims passing through St Gall on their journey to Rome; and G. Hartwell Jones, in *Celtic Britain and the Pilgrim Movement*, says that St Bernard (?996–?1081) described the influx of Irishmen in his time as 'a flood'.
5 Jerrold Northrop Moore, *Edward Elgar: A Creative Life*, Oxford, 1984.
6 Mentioned by G. Schirmer in his fascinating book *Die Schweiz im Spiegel englischer und amerikanischer Literatur* (Zurich, 1929).
7 The victorious Bernese troops reputedly marched back into Berne singing a 'Gugler-song', the text of which is given in A. Vieusseux's *History of Switzerland* (London, 1840).
8 Another treaty with the French, reinforcing the 1515 treaty, was signed in 1521. Garrett Mattingley, in his *Renaissance Diplomacy*, states that between March 1515 and December 1521 nearly fifty embassies went from France to Switzerland, several of them with three or more accredited ambassadors.
9 Sir Thomas More may have taken the name from that of the dynasty of Zapolyai, Voivodes of Transylvania, who in the early sixteenth century joined forces with the Turks against the Christians in order to obtain the throne of Hungary. But, according to Sir Arnold Lunn, a marginal note in the first edition of *Utopia*, 'Gens haud dissimilis Elvetiis', makes it clear that More was referring to the Swiss.
10 In his *English Social History*, G.M. Trevelyan says that the psalm for the day was at that time sung in the rhymed, metrical, version of Sternhold and Hopkins, and that this was known by one of his ancestors as the 'Geneva Jig'.
11 See Dr Michael Lynch's 'The Origins of Edinburgh's "Toun College": A Revision Article', *Innes Review*, 33 (1982).
12 It was Sir Henry Wotton who had earlier jokingly described an ambassador as 'an honest man sent abroad to lie for his country', a description which, though he explained it as a 'merriment', earned him the deep displeasure of James I, notwithstanding two apologies to the king. The explanation for John Parkhurst's assignment must have given Sir Henry wry amusement.
13 The legend of St Lucius was mentioned both by Aegidius Tschudi in his history of Switzerland (see 1653) and by the Venerable Bede in his *Ecclesiastical History of England*. However, later evidence suggests that it may have originated in confusion between 'Britain' and 'Britium' (Birtha) in Mesopotamia, where there was a second-century Christian king called Lucius Abgarus.

14 See Winston Churchill, *Marlborough: His Life and Times*, vol. 3, London: Harrap, 1936.

15 It was long thought that Loutherbourg, who came to England from France and was much admired in England (amongst other things he helped David Garrick transform the whole of the scenery at Drury Lane), was of Swiss origin. He had many Swiss affinities; but recent research has shown him to have originated from Strasbourg.

16 I am indebted to Mr Douglas Simmons, formerly company secretary of Cadbury-Schweppes plc, both for this information on Schweppe and for so kindly allowing me to use the results of his research into some other aspects of Anglo-Swiss relations in Schweppe's time.

17 One important reason why the Swiss did not want to declare Wickham *persona non grata*, despite the strong pressure from the French to do so, was that they had a potential hostage in the investments they had in London (see Edgar Bonjour, *Die Schweiz und Europa*, vol. 4, 1, 3). But this money was sequestrated in any case after the French invasion of Switzerland (see 1798).

18 See Guy de Meuron, *Le Regiment Meuron 1781-1816*, Lausanne: Le Forum Historique, 1982.

19 Some sources say that while the Powers were taking their time to come to a decision on joint action, Palmerston sent private advice to the Federal Party in Berne to act quickly, and that this advice was followed by General Dufour, who commanded the Federal troops and now pursued the military campaign at top speed. However, Ann Imlah, who has made a careful study of the period, says in *Britain and Switzerland 1845-60* (Longmans, 1966) that no evidence can be found to support this. It may be that Robert Peel said something to this effect in Berne on his own initiative. He was certainly aware that events were moving faster in Switzerland than the Powers may have realised. But if he reported what he said to London, there is no record of it in the Foreign Office papers that remain in the Public Record Office.

20 This was probably the last occasion on which the Swiss government pursued an active foreign policy.

21 More information on the Gattis, and on the activities of other immigrants from the Ticino, can be found in Pino Peduzzi's most interesting book, *Pionere Ticinese in Inghilterra* (Bellinzona, 1935).

22 Quoted by Sir Gavin de Beer in his encyclopedic *Travellers in Switzerland* (Oxford, 1949), which is a mine of information on notable British visitors to Switzerland, De Beer's books on Switzerland, and also Beat de Fischer's work (see note 24 below), have given me many useful leads into hitherto little-known aspects of Anglo- Swiss relations.

23 Mentioned in Ursula Vaughan Williams, *R.V.W.*, Oxford, 1964.

24 Mentioned in Beat de Fischer's comprehensive and splendidly produced *2,000 ans de présence suisse en Angleterre*, Lausanne: Delachaux et Niestlé, 1976.

Bibliography of Anglo-Swiss Relations

The literature of Anglo-Swiss relations is quite large. A list of every publication which contained material of interest in some way or other to those relations would take up a volume in itself. However, of the English writing much is descriptive and concerned mainly with the physical aspects of Switzerland, with travel and with sporting and humanist associations. With one or two notable exceptions there are markedly few detailed or comprehensive historical studies of even particular periods in Anglo-Swiss relations. Most of the sources for these are Swiss, mainly in German, some in French; and a number of invaluable and carefully documented pieces of research exist. But even in Switzerland, apart from two or three excellent short monographs by eminent Swiss historians, there appears to be no fullscale and comprehensive work dealing with all aspects and all periods of our relations.

The following bibliography mainly comprises a fairly wide selection of those works dealing specifically with the British-Swiss connexion or which contain useful background material about some noteworthy aspect of that connexion.

The bibliography is divided for convenience into four broad sections, there being, inevitably, some overlap (i.e. some books may deal with subjects in more than one section):

A   Historical, political, diplomatic and military
B   Geographical, descriptive, travellers, visitors, mountaineering and winter sports
C   Cultural, artistic, scientific and religious
D   Economic, commercial, industrial and financial

Under Section C a number of English literary works (both poetical and fictional) have been included which contain significant references to Switzerland; but since the choice is so wide the selection of what to include and what to omit has had to be somewhat arbitrary.

The bibliography does not include straightforward guide-books, except for a few which are of historical interest to Anglo-Swiss relations. Nor does it include literary works by British authors translated and published in Switzerland, or literary works by Swiss authors translated and published in the United Kingdom (again with a few historical exceptions).

A good many of the titles listed have been consulted in drawing up the chronology of Anglo-Swiss relations and the preceding introduction. Other sources used for these have included a number of volumes of the *Calendar of State Papers* additional to the important ones given in the bibliography, various series of official papers relating to Switzerland available at the Public Record Office in London (again in addition to some of the major ones listed in the bibliography), various standard biographical dictionaries and encyclopaedias, past files of *The Economist, The Times* and the *Neue Zürcher Zeitung,* and a number of early copies of the *Foreign Office List*.

For researchers interested in the more detailed aspects of certain periods of Anglo-Swiss relations there are a number of original sources available – official records, manuscripts, collections of papers, etc, not contained in this bibliography. Most of them can be found in government archives or in the major libraries both in Switzerland and in Britain; and details of many of them are given in the more specialised studies of Anglo-Swiss history which are listed in Section A below.

A: HISTORICAL, POLITICAL, DIPLOMATIC AND MILITARY

(Note: Bilateral agreements and treaties are listed in the Index).

Adams, Sir F. Ottiwell, and Cunningham, C. D., *The Swiss Confederation*, London: Macmillan, 1899.
Aglionby, William, 'An Account of My Negotiation in Suizzerland in the Years 1702, 1703, 1704 and 1705...', London: Public Record Office, SP96. 10X1K 3546.
Ammann, H., 'Ein englischer Streit um die schweizerische Neutralität', *Monatshefte für Politik und Kultur*, no. 14, 1934/5.
Baker, F. Grenfell, *The Model Republic: A History of the Rise and Progress of the Swiss People*, London: H. S. Nichols & Co, 1895.
Barbey, Frédéric, *Suisses hors de Suisse: Au service des rois et de la révolution*, Paris, 1914.
Batten, J. Minton, *John Dury*, Chicago: Univ. of Chicago Press, 1944.
Béguin, Pierre, *Le balcon sur l'Europe, 1939-45*, Neuchâtel, 1951.
Bell, Col. C. W. B., *The Armed Strength of Switzerland*, prepared in the War Office, London: HMSO, 1889.
Bell, H. C. F., *Lord Palmerston*, London: Longmans, Green, 1936.
Beller, E. A., 'The Negotiations of Sir Stephen Le Sieur', *English Historical Review*, vol. 40, Jan 1925.
Beltz, George F., *Memorials of the Most Noble Order of the Garter*, London: William Pickering, 1841.
Benson, A. C., and Esher, Visct (edd.), *The Letters of Queen Victoria*, London: John Murray, 1908.
Benziger, C., 'Die schweizerischen Vertreter im Ausland von 1798 bis 1925', *Schweizerisches Konsular-Bulletin*, no. 12, 1926.
Bergadani, Roberto, *Carlo Emanuele I, Duca di Savoia, 1562-1630*, Turin & Milan, 1932.
Bertrand, Pierre, *Genève et la Grande Bretagne, de John Knox à Oliver Cromwell*, Geneva: Éditions du Lancier, 1948.
Bertrand, Pierre, 'Genève et la Grande Bretagne avant la Révolution', *Tribune de Genève*, 17/18 June 1945.
Beza, Theodore, 'Un document inédit de l'époque de l'Escalade. La lettre de Théodore de Bèze et des pasteurs de l'église de Genève à la Reine Elizabeth d'Angleterre', ed. C. Bourgeaud, *Journal de Genève*, Geneva, 1903.
Beza, Theodore, *see also* Section C.
Bèze, Théodore de, *see* Beza.

Bickersteth, Edward, *The Present Crisis in Switzerland*, London, 1848.
Bindoff, S. T., Malcolm-Smith, E. F., and Webster, C.K., *British Diplomatic Representatives 1789-1852*, London: Royal Historical Society, 1934.
Bindschedler, Rudolf, *Die guten Dienste der Schweiz 1939-1945*, Thun, 1959.
Blum, Eugen, 'Das Regiment de Meuron in englischen Diensten', *Figurina Helvetica*, 1958.
Boccard, François, *Histoire du Valais*, Geneva, 1844.
Boesch, Paul, *Ein englischer Gesandter [Christopher Mont] incognito bei Joh. Stumpf*, Zurich, 1949.
Bonjour, Prof. Dr Edgar, *Die Schweiz und England: ein geschichtlicher Rückblick*, Berne: Verlag A. Francke, 1934.
Bonjour, Prof. Dr Edgar, *Englands Anteil an der Lösung des Neuenberger Konflikts, 1856/57*, Basel, 1943.
Bonjour, Prof. Dr Edgar, 'Englands Einwirkung auf Preussen zu Gunsten der Schweiz 1856/57', *Schweizer Beiträge zur allgemeinen Geschichte*, vol. 1, 1943.
Bonjour, Prof. Dr Edgar, *Swiss Neutrality: Its History and Meaning*, London: Allen & Unwin, 1946.
Bonjour, Prof. Dr Edgar, *L'affaire de Neuchâtel sur le plan européen*, Neuchâtel, 1956.
Bonjour, Prof. Dr Edgar, 'Johannes von Müllers Verhältnis zu England', *Schweizerische Zeitschrift für Geschichte*, vol. 6, 1956.
Bonjour, Prof. Dr Edgar, *Geschichte der schweizerischen Neutralität*, 2nd ed., 6 vols., Basel, 1965-70.
Bonjour, Prof. Dr Edgar, 'Neuorientierung der britischen Politik gegenüber der Schweiz' (in *Neue Zürcher Zeitung*, 5 Jan 1974. Reprinted in vol. 4 of Bonjour's book *Die Schweiz und Europa* – below).
Bonjour, Prof. Dr Edgar, *Die Schweiz und Europa*, 4 vols, Basel: Verlag Helbing & Lichtenhahn, 1958-76.
Bonjour, Prof. Dr Edgar, *Europäisches Gleichgewicht und schweizerische Neutralität*, Basel, 1946.
Bonjour, E., Offler, H. S., and Potter, G. R., *A Short History of Switzerland*, Oxford: Clarendon Press, 1952.
Bonjour, Felix, *Real Democracy in Operation: The Example of Switzerland*, London: Geo. Allen & Unwin, 1920.
Bonjour, Felix, *Presse suisse et politique étrangère*, Vevey, 1912.
Bonnant, Georges, and Gagnebin, B., *Les relations politiques entre l'Angleterre et Genève aux 17e & 18e siècles*, Geneva, 1937.
Boos, Ernst, *Die Schweizerkolonie in England nach Berufsgruppen*, Einsiedeln, 1966.
Borgeaud, Charles, *La Nouvelle Angleterre, berceau de la démocratie, et Genève: Pages d'histoire nationale*, Geneva, 1934.
Borgeaud, Charles, 'L'Angleterre et la neutralité de la Suisse', in *Festgabe für Max Huber*, Zurich, 28 December 1934.
Borgeaud, Charles, *Documents sur l'Escalade de Genève: Documents de Londres, P.R.O. 1602-3*, Soc. d'Histoire et d'Archéologie de Genève, 1903.

Borgeaud, Charles, *see also* Section C.
Bory, Jean-René, *Les Suisses au service étranger et leur Musée*, Lausanne: Ed. Courrier de la Cote, 1965.
Bourcart, Charles D., *William Wickham, Britischer Gesandte in der Schweiz (1794-97 und 1799) in seinen Beziehungen zu Basel*, Basel, 1908.
Bovay, E. H., *Le Canada et les Suisses, 1604-1974*, Fribourg, 1976.
Bruce, A. K., *Matthäus, Cardinal Schiner*, London, 1952.
Bryce, James, Viscount, *Modern Democracies*, 2 vols., London: Macmillan & Co., 1921.
Bucher, Béatrice, *Abraham Stanyan 1705-1714* . . . , Zurich, 1952.
Bucher, E., *Die Geschichte des Sonderbundkrieges*, Zurich, 1966.
Büchi, Albert, *Kardinal Matthäus Schiner als Staatsmann und Kirchenfürst: ein Beitrag zur allgemeinen und schweizerischen Geschichte von der Wende des 15./16. Jahrhunderts*, vol. 1, Zurich, 1923.
Büchi, Albert, *Korrespondenzen und Akten zur Geschichte des Kardinals Matthäus Schiner*, 2 vols., Basel: Quellen zur Schweizergeschichte, Neue Folge, 1920, 1925.
Büchi, Albert, *Le Cardinal Mathieu Schiner*, Neuchâtel, 1950.
Burckhardt, F., *Die schweizerische Emigration 1798-1801*, Basel, 1908.
Burckhardt-Burckhardt, Carl, *Aus dem Tagebuch einer Baslerin zur Zeit des Durchmarsches der Alliierten, Beiträge zur Vaterlandischen Geschichte*, vol. 14, Basel, 1896.
Bürkli, Adolf, 'Die Schweizer im Dienste der holländisch – ostindischen Kompagnie', *Neujahrsblatt der Feuerwerkergesellschaft*, Zurich, 1879.
Bürkli, Adolf, 'General Niklaus Franz Bachmann', *Neujahrsblatt der Feuerwerkergesellschaft*, Zurich, 1882.
Bürkli, Adolf, 'Das Schweizerregiment von Roll im englischen Dienste, 1795-1816', *Neujahrsblatt der Feuerwerkergesellschaft*, Zurich, 1893.
Bürkli, Adolf, 'Das Schweizerregiment von Wattenwill in englischen Diensten, 1801-1816', *Neujahrsblatt der Feuerwerkergesellschaft*, Zurich, 1894.
Burnand, A., 'Le Colonel Henri Bouquet, Vainqueur des Peaux-Rouges de l'Ohio', *Revue Historique Vaudois*, Lausanne, 1906.
Butler, Capt. Lewis W. G., *The Annals of The King's Royal Rifle Corps*, vol. 1, *The Royal Americans*, London, 1913.
Calendar of Close Rolls, Edward I, Edward II & Edward III, London, 1898, etc.
Calendar of State Papers, Henry VIII, Spanish, vol. 2; *Elizabeth, Foreign, 1586-1588; Milan, 1385-1618; Venetian, 1603-1621; Cromwell, Domestic, 1653-1656; Victoria, 1856, vol. 61*, London: HMSO, various dates.
Cambridge Modern History, The, 13 vols., Cambridge, 1902.
Cameron, C. F., *Switzerland*, Edinburgh: T. C. & E. C. Jack, c. 1914.
Chancellerie d'État, Neuchâtel, *Neuchâtel et la Suisse*, Neuchâtel, 1969.
Chapuis, Alfred, *La Suisse dans le monde*, Paris, 1940.
Chapuisat, J.-P., 'Au Service de deux Rois d'Angleterre au 13e siècle: Pierre de Champvent', *Revue Historique Vaudoise*, Lausanne, 1964.
Charrière, Louis de, *Les dynastes de Grandson*, Lausanne, 1866.

Chastonay, Paul de, *Le Cardinal Schiner*, Lausanne, 1943.
Chopard, Adrien, *Die Mission des englischen Gesandten Philibert Herwarth in der Schweiz, 1692-1702*, Berne, 1932.
Chopard, Adrien, 'Genève et les Anglais, 16e-18e siècles', *Bulletin de la Société d'Histoire et d'Archéologie de Genève*, vol. 7, Geneva, 1940.
Chotzen, Th. M., 'Yvain (Owen) de Galles in Alsace Lorraine and Switzerland', in *Bulletin of the Board of Celtic Studies*, 4, pt. 3, 1928.
Churchill, W. S., *Marlborough: His Life and Times*, vol. 3, London: G. G. Harrap, 1936.
Churchill, W. S., *The Second World War*, vol. 6, London: Cassell, 1948.
Clifford, E. Rowland, *A Knight of Great Renown: Othon de Grandson*, Chicago, 1961.
Collingwood, R. G., and Wright, R. P., *The Roman Inscriptions of Britain*, London: Oxford U.P., 1965.
Coolidge, W.A.B., 'Two Bishops of Sion in England', *English Historical Review*, vol. 1, no. 4, 1887.
Coolidge, W.A.B., 'Switzerland', in *Encyclopaedia Britannica*, vol. 26, Cambridge, 1911.
Coolidge, W.A.B., 'Some Links between English and Early Swiss History', in *English Historical Review*, vol. 2, 1887.
Coolidge, W.A.B., *La Haute-Engadine et la Bregaglia à travers les siècles: Histoire et Bibliographie*, 1894.
Coolidge, W.A.B., *see also* Section B.
Cotton, Julian James, 'His Majesty's Regiment de Meuron', in *Calcutta Review*, vol. 113, no. 234, 1903.
Coulton, G. G., *A Strong Army in a Free State: A Study of the Old English and Modern Swiss Militias*, London: Simpkin Marshall, 1900.
Cramer, Lucien Edouard, *Correspondance diplomatique de Pictet de Rochemont et de François d'Ivernois, Paris, Vienna, Turin, 1814-16*; Geneva & Paris, 1914.
Cramer, Lucien Edouard, 'La mission du conseiller Jean Maillet en Angleterre 1582-1583', *Bulletin de la Société d'Histoire et d'Archéologie de Genève*, vol. 3, 1906-13.
Croft, Sutton [Sir Arnold Lunn], *Was Switzerland Pro-German?*, London, 1914.
Daendliker, Karl, *A Short History of Switzerland*, London, 1899.
David, Heinrich, *Englands europäische Politik im neunzehnten Jahrhundert: von den französischen Revolutionskriegen bis zum Tode Palmerstons*, Berne and Leipzig, 1924.
Davidson, F. H. N., 'His Majesty's Regiment de Meuron', in *The Army Quarterly*, 33, London, 1936.
de Beer, Sir Gavin, 'Neuchâtel: refuge d'Anglais sous Napoléon', *Musée Neuchâtelois*, 3rd series, vol. 1, 1964.
de Beer, Sir Gavin, *see also* Sections B and C.
De Lolme, John Louis, *The Constitution of England*, London, 1775.
De Lolme, John Louis, *The British Empire in Europe*, London, 1787.

De Lolme, John Louis, 'An Essay Containing a Few Strictures on the Union of Scotland with England', in *History of the Union between England and Scotland,* ed. Daniel Defoe, London, 1786.
de Salis, Family of, *The de Salis Family in the British Commonwealth,* Bristol: John P. de Salis, 1959.
Dickinson, H. W., *Sir Samuel Morland: Diplomat and Inventor, 1625-1695,* The Newcomen Society, Cambridge: Heffer & Sons, 1970.
Dictionnaire géographique, historique et politique de la Suisse, 2 vols., 1775.
Dictionnaire historique et biographique de la Suisse [especially the article on 'Grande Bretagne'], Neuchâtel, 1921.
Dictionary of National Biography, Oxford, 1917.
Documents diplomatiques suisses, 1848-1945, Berne, 1979.
Droz, J., *Histoire diplomatique de 1648 à 1919,* Paris, 1952.
Dumont, Eugène-Louis, *Exercices de l'Arquebuse et de la Navigation, 1474-1974,* Geneva, 1974.
Du Pasquier, Armand, 'À propos du Régiment Meuron, d'après les Cleghorn Papers.', *Musée Neuchâtelois,* 1928.
Durrer, R., *Heinrich Angst,* Glarus, 1948.
Eckinger, K., *Lord Palmerston und der Schweizer Sonderbundskrieg,* Berlin: Diss., 1937.
Engel, Claire Éliane, 'The Young Pretender and Switzerland', *Scottish Historical Review, no. 102,* Glasgow, 1947.
Engel, Claire Éliane, 'Genève et l'Angleterre', in *Zeitschrift für Schweizergeschichte,* 26, 1946.
Engel, Claire Éliane, *La Suisse et ses amis,* Neuchâtel, 1943.
Engel, Claire Éliane, *see also* Sections B and C.
Ernst, Fritz, *Europäische Schweiz,* Zurich, 1961.
Ewald, A. C., *Life and Times of Prince Charles Edward Stuart,* London: Chatto & Windus, 1875.
Fahrni, Dieter, *An Outline History of Switzerland,* Zurich: Pro Helvetia, 1984.
Feller, Richard, *Geschichte Berns,* vol. 3, Berne, 1955.
Fetscherin, Wilhelm, *Johann Heinrich Hummel, Dekan zu Bern (1611-1674),* Berne, 1856.
Fills, Robert, *The Lawes and Statutes of Geneva. Translated from the French,* London: Rouland Hall, 1562.
Fischer, Béat de, *2,000 ans de présence suisse en Angleterre,* Lausanne: Delachaux et Niestlé, 1974.
Fischer, Béat de, *Suisses, Genevois, Neuchatêlois et Grisons en Grande Bretagne au 18e siècle, Revue Versailles,* nos. 33 & 34, 1968.
Flaad, Paul, *England und die Schweiz 1848-52,* Zurich, 1935.
Fleming, Oliver, 'Instructions for Oliver Fleming, Our Agent Resident with the Protestant Cantons in Switzerland', London: Public Record Office, SP 96. 3 X I K 3 546.
Foreign Office, 'British and Foreign State Papers', vol. 2, 1814-1815, London: F.C.O.

Foreign Office, 'Correspondence Relative to the Affairs of Switzerland, Presented to Both Houses of Parliament 1847-48', Parliamentary Papers 847 LXV.
Foreign Office, 'Foreign Office Documents: Switzerland, series FO 74, FO 100, FO 192, FO 371, FO 425', Kew, Surrey: Public Record Office.
Foreign Office, *Letters and Papers, Foreign and Domestic, Henry VIII, vols. 2 &3,* London: HMSO, 1864.
Foreign Office, 'State Papers, Foreign, Switzerland', series SP 96, SP 101, London: Public Record Office.
Foreign Office, 'State Papers, Foreign, Savoy', series SP 92, London: Public Record Office.
Foreign Office, 'State Papers, Foreign, Venice, series SP 99, London: Public Record Office.
Foreign Office, 'Treaty with the Protestant Cantons, 1690.', SP 108/538, London: Public Record Office.
Foreign Office, *see also* Calendar of State Papers.
Fox, Sir Frank, *Switzerland,* London: A. & C. Black, 1915.
Freeman, Edward, *History of the Norman Conquest of England,* vol. 4, Oxford, 1877.
Frei, Daniel, *Swiss Foreign Policy,* Zurich: Pro Helvetia, 1983.
Furrer, P., *Histoire du Valais,* Sion, 1873.
Gagnebin, Bernard, 'Un diplomate genevois à la cour d'Angleterre' au 17e siècle, *Le Mois Suisse,* 26 May 1941.
Gagnebin, Bernard, 'Oliver Cromwell, Genève et les Vaudois du Piémont, 1655-1656', *Bollettino della Società di Studi Valdesi,* no. 72, Sept 1939.
Gagnebin, Bernard, *Les relations entre Genève et l'Angleterre,* Zurich: Atlantis, 1946.
Galbreath, D. L., 'Les Grandsons d'Angleterre', in *Archives Héraldiques Suisses,* 41, 1927.
Ganter, Henri, *Histoire des régiments suisses au service d'Angleterre . . . ,* Geneva, 1901.
Gay, Hilaire, *Histoire du Valais,* Geneva, 1903.
(Geneva), *The Troubles of Geneva, with the Warres Which the Duke of Savoy Hath Made against It These Three Yeares Space . . . Truly Translated According to the French Copie, by W.P.,* printed for Thomas Nelson, London, 1591.
(Geneva), *Tableau historique et politique des deux dernières revolutions de Genève, par . . . [Sir F. d'Ivernois],* London, 1789.
(Geneva), *Un récit anglais de l'Escalade,* 1603; reprinted, with an introduction by Leonard Chester Jones, Geneva, 1930.
Genner, Lotti, *Die diplomatischen Beziehungen zwischen England und der Schweiz von 1870 bis 1890,* Basel, 1956.
Giddey, E., 'Quelques aspects de relations anglo-suisses à la fin du 18e siècle: Louis Braun et Hugh Cleghorn', *Revue d'Histoire Suisse,* vol. 29, 1949.
Giddey, E., 'J. F. Erskine et son Régiment Suisse', in *Schweizerische Zeitschrift für Geschichte,* 4, 1954.

Gilliard, Charles, *A History of Switzerland*, London: Geo. Allen & Unwin, 1955.
Gisi, Wilhelm, 'Die Beziehungen zwischen der Schweiz und England in den Jahren 1515-1517,' Zurich: *Archiv für Schweizergeschichte*, 15, 1866.
Gonzenbach, August von, *Der General Hans Ludwig von Erlach*, 2 vols., Berne, 1880, 1882.
Grande, Julian, *A Citizens' Army: The Swiss System*, London: Chatto & Windus, 1916.
Gribble, F., 'The Destiny of Switzerland', *Edinburgh Review*, vol. 217, 1913.
Grosse Schweizer: 110 Bildnisse zur eidgenössischen Geschichte und Kultur, Zurich: Atlantis Verlag, 1938.
Grote, George, *Seven Letters on the Recent Politics in Switzerland*, London, 1847.
Gutknecht, Else, *Die Diplomatie des Auslandes in der Schweiz während des Sonderbundes*, Zurich: Selnau, 1917.
Hagen, Karl, *Die auswärtige Politik der Eidgenossenschaft, vornehmlich Berns, in den Jahren 1610-1618*, Berne, 1865.
Haldane, R. B., *Army Reform and Other Addresses*, London: T. Fisher Unwin, 1907.
Haller, Albrecht von, *Historia Stirpium Helvetiae*, Berne, 1768.
Haller, Albrecht von, *Alfred, König der Angel-Sachsen*, Göttingen & Berne, 1773.
Haller, Albrecht von, *The Moderate Monarchy: or, Principles of the British Constitution, Described in a Narratory of the Life and Maxims of Alfred the Great and his Counsellors*, London, 1849.
Hamlyn, Michael, 'Citizen Army that Guards Swiss Neutrality', in *The Times*, 1 May 1976.
Hardie, F., *The Political Influence of Queen Victoria, 1861-1901*, London: O.U.P., 1935.
Harold, F., 'The Swiss Background of the Purrysburg Settlers', *Huguenot Society of South Carolina, Transactions, no. 39*.
Hatze, Margrit, *Die diplomatisch-politischen Beziehungen zwischen England und der Schweiz im Zeitalter der Restauration*, Basel, 1949.
Hauser, H., *Histoire diplomatique de l'Europe (1871-1914)*, Paris, 1929.
Heyst, A., 'Switzerland: A Pattern for Europe?', in *Contemporary Review*, 209, Dec 1966.
Hofer, Walther, *Neutrality as the Principle of Swiss Foreign Policy*, Zurich, 1957.
Hoffman, Ann, *Lives of the Tudor Age, 1485-1603*, London: Osprey Publishing, 1977.
Hoffmann, Georg, 'Die grossbritannische Schweizerlegion im Krimkrieg', *Zeitschrift für Schweizergeschichte*, no. 4, 1942.
Holzach, Ferdinand, *Über die politischen Beziehungen der Schweiz zu Oliver Cromwell*, Basel, 1905.
Horn, David Bayne, *British Diplomatic Representatives 1689-1789*, London: Royal Historical Society, 1952.

Horn, David Bayne, *Great Britain and Europe in the Eighteenth Century*, Oxford: Clarendon Press, 1967 [especially the chapter on 'Great Britain and Switzerland'].
Horn, David Bayne, *The British Diplomatic Service 1689-1789*, Oxford, 1961.
Hottinger, Marie Donald, *The Stories of Basel, Berne and Zurich*, London: Dent, 1933.
Howard, E. W., 'The Problem of Democracy and the Swiss Solution', in *Edinburgh Review*, vol. 218, 1913.
Hughes, Christopher J., *Switzerland*, in *Nations of the Modern World* series, London: Ernest Benn, 1973.
Hughes, Christopher J., *The Parliament of Switzerland*, London: Cassell, 1962.
Hughes, Christopher J., *The Federal Constitution of Switzerland*, Oxford, 1954.
Hughes, Christopher J., 'Britain Learns the Lesson of the Referendum', in *Contemporary Review*, no. 226, June 1975.
Hug, Lina, and Stead, R., *Switzerland*, in *Story of the Nations* series, London: T. Fisher Unwin, 1920.
Hürliman, Martin, *Grands hommes de la Suisse*, Lausanne: Payot, 1945.
Hutton, Edward, *Colonel Henry Bouquet*, Winchester, 1911.
Imlah, Ann G., *Britain and Switzerland, 1845-1860*, London: Longmans Green, 1966.
Ischer, Theophil, *Die Gesandtschaft der protestantischen Schweiz bei Cromwell und den General Staaten der Niederlande, 1652-54*, Berne, 1916.
Istria, Dora d', *Switzerland, the Pioneer of the Reformation*, Geneva, [?] 1858.
Jones, G. Hartwell, *Celtic Britain and the Pilgrim Movement*, Cymrodorion Society, 1912.
Junod, Louis, 'La Lettre de Gibbon sur le gouvernement de Berne', in *Miscellanea Gibboniana*, Lausanne, 1952.
Karmin, Otto, *Sir Francis D'Ivernois, 1757-1842*, Geneva, 1920.
Keate, George, *A Short Account of the Ancient History, Present Government and Laws of the Republic of Geneva*, London, 1761.
Keesings Contemporary Archives, London: Longman Group, various dates.
Keller, Hans Gustav, *Christoph von Graffenried und die Gründung von Neu-Bern in Nord-Carolina*, Berne, 1953.
Kelly, Sir David, *The Ruling Few*, London: Hollis & Carter, 1952.
Kern, Johann Conrad, *Souvenirs politiques*, ed. Charles Dubois, Paris, 1887.
Kilchenmann, F., *Die Mission des englischen Gesandten, Thomas Coxe, in der Schweiz, 1689-1692*, Zurich, 1914.
Kilchenmann, J. Eduard, *Schweizer Söldner im Dienste der englisch-ostindischen Kompagnie in der Mitte des 18. Jahrhunderts*, Göttingen, 1911.
Kingsford, C. L., *Sir Otho de Grandison*, London, 1909.
Kimche, J., *Spying for Peace*, London: Weidenfeld & Nicolson 1961.
Kläui, Hans, 'John Pell als englischer Gesandter in der Schweiz', *Neue Zürcher Zeitung*, 20 May 1954.
Kohn, Hans, *Der schweizerische Nationalgedanke*, Zurich, 1955; as *Nationalism and Liberty: The Swiss Example*, London, 1956.

Laing, Samuel, [the Elder], *Notes of a Traveller on the Social and Political State of . . . Switzerland . . . and Other Parts of Europe*, London, 1842.
Laing, Samuel [the Elder], *Observations on the Social and Political State of the European People in 1848 and 1849*, London, 1850.
Lane-Poole, Stanley, *Life of the Right Honourable Stratford Canning*, 2 vols., London, 1888.
Langer, W. C., *Report on the Reserve and Auxiliary Forces of England and the Militia of Switzerland*, Washington, 1903.
Lardner, Dionysius, *History of Switzerland*, 1832.
Lätt, Dr Arnold, *Le Cardinal Mathieu Schiner et ses relations avec l'Angleterre*, Lausanne, 1919.
Lätt, Dr Arnold, *Zwei Schweizer General-Gouverneure von Kanada*, Brugg, 1925.
Lätt, Dr Arnold, *Schweizer Offiziere als Indianerkrieger und Instruktoren der englischen leichten Infanterie*, Zurich, 1933.
Lätt, Dr Arnold, 'Schweizer in England im 17. Jahrhundert', *Zeitschrift für Schweizergeschichte*, 1931.
Lätt, Dr Arnold, *Zwei schweizer Diplomaten im Dienste Grossbritanniens*, Basel, 1923.
Lätt, Dr Arnold, *Relations between England and Zurich during the Reformation*, Zurich, 1904.
Lätt, Dr Arnold, *see also* Section C.
Lémonon, E., *L'Europe et la politique britannique (1882-1911)*, Paris, 1912.
Liebeskind, W. Amédée, *Un prélat médiéval; Ermenfroid, Evèque de Sion*, Geneva, 1961.
Lipton, M., 'The Jewish Question in Anglo-Swiss Diplomacy', in *Jewish History Society of England: Transactions*, vol. 10, 1921-23.
Lloyd, Henry D., *A Sovereign People: A Study of Swiss Democracy*, London: Page & Co, 1907.
Loosli, C.-A., *La Suisse et ses rapports avec l'étranger*, Neuchâtel, 1917.
Luck, J. Murray, *History of Switzerland*, California: Sposs Inc, 1985.
Luck, J. Murray (ed.), *Modern Switzerland*, California: Palo Alto, 1973.
Ludlow, Edmund, *Memoirs of E. Ludlow, Esq.*, Vivay, 1698; reprinted, London, 1771; rev. ed., ed. C. H. Firth, Oxford, 1894.
Luthy, I. C. E., 'Un Suisse, Gouverneur-Général du Canada: Sir Frederick Haldimand, 1777-1784', in *Versailles*, 1er et 2e trimestre, 1975.
MacCrackan, William Denison, *The Rise of the Swiss Republic: A History*, London, 1892.
Mackie, J. D., *The Early Tudors, 1485-1558*, in *The Oxford History of England*, Oxford: Clarendon Press, 1952.
Mandrot, Lieut-Colonel de, 'Le Colonel C. P. de Bosset', *Musée Neuchâtelois*, 1865.
Marsay, Count de, 'Lettre aux magnifiques seigneurs, sindics et conseil de la République de Genève, le 5 decembre, 1736', *Amtliche Sammlung der Ältern Eidg. Abschiede, série 1245-1798*, 6, 1.
Marshall, Sir Peter, 'La présence britannique à Genève', talk given in Geneva to Rencontres du Lundi, 1982.

Martin, P.E., 'The Swiss Confederation in the Middle Ages', in vol. 7 of *The Cambridge Medieval History*, Cambridge, 1932.
Martin, William, *Switzerland from Roman Times to the Present*, London: Elek, 1971.
Martin, William, *A History of Switzerland*, London: Grant Richards, 1931.
Martin, William, *La Suisse et l'Europe, 1813-1814*, Lausanne, 1931.
Massini, Rudolf, *Sir Luke Schaub, 1690-1758*, Basel, 1953.
Massini, Rudolf, 'Der Vertrag von Turin (1754) zwischen dem Königreich Sardinien und der Republik Genf nach englischen Dokumenten', in *Basler Zeitschrift für Geschichte und Altertumskunde*, 47, 1948.
Mattingly, Garrett, *Renaissance Diplomacy*, London: Jonathan Cape, 1955.
Mayers, Michael John, *The Jesuit and Sonderbund Contest in Switzerland*, London, 1847.
Mayers, Michael John, *Note Book on the Late Civil War in Switzerland*, London & Zurich, 1848.
Meier, Markus, *Die diplomatische Vertretung Englands in der Schweiz im 18. Jh. (1689-1789)*, Basel, 1952.
Meuron, Guy de, *Le Régiment Meuron, 1781-1816*, Lausanne: Le Forum Historique/Editions d'En bas, 1982.
Meuron, Théodore de, 'Charles-Daniel de Meuron et son régiment, *Musée Neuchâtelois*, 1880.
Meyer, R., *Die Politik Englands und die europäischen Kleinstaaten*, Lausanne, 1916.
Meyer, Wolfgang D., *Ein Trewhertzig Ermanung des durchleüchtigsten undt grossmächtigsten Konigs in Gross Britanien, Jacobi des Ersten, etc.*, Basel, 1609.
Monter, E. William, *Calvin's Geneva*, New York & London: John Wiley & Sons, 1967.
Moore, Aubrey, *Lecture and Papers on the History of the Reformation*, London, 1890.
Morier, Robert, *Memoirs and Letters of Sir Robert Morier*, ed. Mrs Rosslyn Wemyss, London: Edward Arnold, 1911.
Moser, Franz A., 'Die Haltung Englands gegenüber der Verletzung der schweizerischen Neutralität durch die Alliierten im dezember, 1813, *Zeitschrift für Schweizergeschichte*, 1934.
Muirhead, James F., 'British Representatives in Switzerland', *Contemporary Review*, vol. 130, 1926.
Mülinen, Wolfgang Friedrich von, *Die Ritter von Strätlingen*, Berne, 1903.
Nabholz, Hans, with Muralt, L. von, Feller, R., and Bonjour, E., *Geschichte der Schweiz*, Zurich, 1938.
Naef, Henri, 'L'Escalade de Genève: un événement européen', in *Bibliothèque d'Humanisme et Renaissance*, 17, 1955.
New Helvetic Society, *Switzerland, Present and Future*, Berne: Buri, 1962.
Oechsli, Prof. Dr Wilhelm, *England und die Schweiz*, Zurich, 1919.
Oechsli, Prof. Dr Wilhelm, *History of Switzerland, 1499-1914*, Cambridge, 1922.
Oechsli, Prof. Dr Wilhelm, *Die Zürcher Revolution von 1839 in englischen Gesandtschaftsberichten*, Zürcher Taschenbuch, 1904.

Oechsli, Prof. Dr Wilhelm, *Die Schweiz im 19. Jahrhundert*, 2 vols., Leipzig, 1903, 1913.
Oechsli, Prof. Dr Wilhelm, *Quellenbuch zur Schweizergeschichte*, Zurich, 1901.
Oederlin, Max, *Lord Robert Fitzgerald, britischer Gesandte in Bern, 1792-1794*, Zurich, 1916.
Parry, C., and Hopkins, C., *An Index of British Treaties, 1100-1968*, London: HMSO, 1970.
Peel, Robert, *France, Savoy and Switzerland: Speeches by Sir Robert Peel, 1860-61*, London: Hatchards, 1898.
Petipierre, Jacques, *Neuchâtel et la Confédération Suisse devant l'Europe*, Neuchâtel, 1957.
Petrie, Sir Charles, *Diplomatic History, 1713-1933*, London: Hollis & Carter, 1946.
Piaget, Arthur, *Othon de Grandson, sa vie et ses poésies: mémoires et documents*, Société d'Histoire de la Suisse, 3rd series, vol. 1, Lausanne, 1941.
Picot, Albert, *Le rayonnement international de Genève*, Neuchâtel, 1968.
Picot, Albert, *Souvenirs de quelques années difficiles de la République de Genève*, Geneva, 1963.
Picot, Henry Philip, *The British Interned in Switzerland*, London: Edward Arnold, 1919.
Pictet, Edmond, and Gillièron, Jean, *Les relations de l'Angleterre et la République de Genève sous Jacques I*, Geneva, 1936.
Planta, J., *History of the Helvetic Confederacy*, 2nd ed., 3 vols., London: John Stockdale, 1807.
Powell-Jones, John, 'Stratford Canning en Suisse', talk given in Berne to La Grande Société, 1984.
Powicke, Sir F. Maurice, *Henry III and the Lord Edward*, 2 vols., Oxford: Clarendon Press, 1947.
Powicke, Sir F. Maurice, *The Thirteenth Century, 1216-1307*, vol. in *The Oxford History of England*, Oxford, 1962.
Preston, Sir Jacob, 'Switzerland and the War', in *Contemporary Review*, Sept, 1916.
Preston, Sir Jacob, 'Switzerland and the War', in *Contemporary Review*, Feb 1917.
Previté-Orton, C. W., *The Early History of the House of Savoy, 1000-1233*, Cambridge, 1912.
Previté-Orton, C. W. (ed.), *The Shorter Cambridge Medieval History*, Cambridge, 1952.
Prud'homme, L. A., 'Les Meurons', in *Royal Society of Canada: Transactions*, vol. 34, 1940.
Quaglia, Lucien, *La Maison du Grand Saint Bernard, des origines aux temps actuels*, Martigny, 1972.
Radcliffe, Sir Charles Delmé, *A Territorial Army in Being*, London: John Murray, 1908.
Radcliffe, Sir Charles Delmé, 'The Swiss Militia System', in *Journal of the Royal United Service Institution*, vol. 51, 1909.

Rappard, William E., *Collective Security in Swiss Experience, 1291-1948*, London, 1948.
Rappard, William E., *The British Empire as Seen from Geneva*, London: British Universities League of Nations Society, 1931.
Raulich, Italo, *Storia di Carlo Emanuele I, Duca di Savoia, 1580-1598*, 2 vols., Milan, 1896, 1902.
Read, John Meredith, *Historic Studies in Vaud, Berne and Savoy, from Roman Times to Voltaire, Rousseau and Gibbon*, London, 1897.
'Reports from His Majesty's Representatives Abroad respecting the Institution known as the Referendum', London: Comd. 5522, Miscellaneous no. 3, 1911.
'Report from His Majesty's Minister at Berne respecting the Institution known as the Initiative in Switzerland', London: Comd. 5634, Miscellaneous no. 6, 1911.
Reymond, Maxime, 'Le Chevalier Othon de Grandson', in *Revue Historique Vaudoise*, Lausanne, 1920.
Reynold, Gonzague de, *La démocratie de la Suisse*, Berne, 1929.
Reynold, Gonzague de, 'The Position of Switzerland: Its Importance for British Policy', in *New Europe*, 12 Sept 1918.
Reynold, Gonzague de, *see also* Section C.
Rich, John R., 'Switzerland and Britain: Some Aspects of a Partnership', talk given to the City Swiss Club, London, March, 1987.
Ricklin, A., Haug H., and Binswanger H. C., *Handbuch der schweizerischen Aussenpolitik*, Berne: Verlag Paul Haupt, 1975.
Robertson, L. A., 'Relations of William III with the Swiss Protestants, 1689-1697', in *Royal Historical Society; Transactions*, 54, 12, 1929.
Rook, Clarence, *Switzerland: The Country and Its People*, London: Chatto & Windus, 1907.
Roquebrune, R. L. de, 'Les suisses au Canada' in *Journal de Genève*, 6 June 1966.
Rossier, Edmond, 'L'affaire de Savoie en 1860 et l'intervention anglaise', in *Revue Historique*, ed. 90, 1905.
Rothwell, H. (ed.), *English Historical Documents, vol. 3, 1189-1327*, London: Eyre & Spottiswoode, 1975.
Rovillain, – , 'L'Angleterre et les troubles de Genève en 1766-67', in *Zeitschrift für Schweizergeschichte*, 7, 1927.
Ruchat, Abraham, Stanyan, Abraham, *et al.*, *'L'état et les délices de la Suisse; ou, Description helvétique historique et géographique* . . . Amsterdam, 1730.
Rumbold, Sir Horace, *Recollections of a Diplomatist*, London: Edward Arnold, 1902.
Rumbold, Sir Horace, *Further Recollections of a Diplomatist*, London: Edward Arnold, 1903.
Russell, F. S., *The Armed Strength of Switzerland*, London: War Office, 1880.
St John, Sir Frederick, *Reminiscences of a Retired Diplomat*, London: Chapman & Hall, 1905.
Salis, Jean-Rudolf de, *Switzerland and Europe*, London: Oswald Wolff, 1971.

Salis, Jean-Rudolf de, *see also* Sections C & D.
Salway, Peter, *Roman Britain (Oxford History of England)*, Oxford, 1981.
Salzman, L. F., *Edward I*, London, 1968.
Sargent, Winthrop, *The Life of Major John André*, New York, 1871.
Schazmann, P.-E., *Frégates de Nelson et Foyers de Genève*, Lausanne, 1943.
Shib, Karl, *Geschichte der Stadt und Landschaft Schaffhausen*, Schaffhausen, 1972.
Schirmer. G., 'Englische Urteile über das schweizerische Heerwesen', *Schweizerische Monatshefte für Offiziere aller Waffen, 1891*.
Schneebeli, Hans, 'Schweizertruppen im Dienste Englands', *Figurina Helvetica*, 2, 1960.
Schneewind, W., *Die diplomatischen Beziehungen Englands mit der alten Eidgenossenschaft zur Zeit Elizabeths, Jakobs I und Karls I (1558-1649)*, Basel, 1950.
Schulthess, K., 'Gute Dienste und Vermittlung in der auswärtigen Politik der Schweiz, 1847-1917', *Wissen und Leben, 18, 1917*.
Seton-Watson, R. W., *Britain in Europe 1789-1916, A Survey of Foreign Policy*, Cambridge, 1938.
Seippel, Paul, *La Suisse au dix-neuvième siècle*, Lausanne: Payot, 1899-1901.
Siegfried, André, *Switzerland: A Democratic Way of Life*, London: Cape, 1950.
Silberschmidt, Max, *Winston Churchill, Leader der freien Welt*, Zurich, 1969.
Simonde de Sismondi, J. C. L., *Considérations sur Genève dans ses rapports avec l'Angleterre, et les États protestants*, London, 1814.
Singer, G., *Die Bedeutung der Schweiz für England während der ersten Koalitionskriege*, Zurich, 1956.
Smith, Elizabeth Malcolm, *British Diplomacy in the Eighteenth Century, 1700-1789*, London: Williams & Norgate, 1937.
Smith, Elizabeth Malcolm, *The Life of Stratford Canning*, London: Benn, 1933.
Smith, Elizabeth Malcolm, *Palmerston*, London: Duckworth, 1933.
Smith, Logan Pearsall, *The Life and Letters of Sir Henry Wotton*, Oxford: Clarendon Press, 1907.
Soloveytchik, George, *Switzerland in Perspective*, Oxford, 1954.
Soloveytchik, George, *see also* Section D.
Spitteler, Carl, *Unser Schweizer Standpunkt*, Zurich, 1915.
Spon, Isaac (Jacob), *Histoire de Genève*, 2 vols., Geneva, 1730.
Spon, Isaac (Jacob), *History of the City and State of Geneva, trans. from the French*, London: 1687.
Stadler, Peter, *Genf, die grossen Mächte und die Eidgenössischen Glaubensparteien, 1571-1584*, Zurich, 1952.
Staehelin, Ernst, 'Die Basler Schulden des englischen Gesandten', *Basler Nachrichten*, 28 March, 1966.
Staehelin, Felix, *Der jüngere Stuartprätendent und sein Aufenthalt in Basel, 1745-1746*, Basel, 1949.
Stanyan, Abraham, *An Account of Switzerland Written in the Year 1714*, London, 1714.

Stanyan, Abraham, *Proposition von Herren Stanyan, Extraordinari Envoyé der Königin von Gross Britannien . . . vorgetragen an die Herren Häupter und Räthe der drey . . . Pündten zu Chur den 12. febr. 1707 (Urging them to open their mountain passes to the Imperial troops)*, Coire,1707.

Stanyan, Abraham, *Mémoire de M. de Stanyan, envoyé extraordinaire de S. M. la Reine de Grande Bretagne vers les Louables Cantons Réformés, presenté le 25 juilliet, 1707, à Monsieur le Gouverneur et à Messieurs du Conseil d'État de la Souverainté de Neufchâtel et Valangin*, 1707.

Stehlin, Karl, 'Sir Oliver Fleming, englischer Gesandter in der Schweiz, 1629-1638', *Anzeiger für schweizerische Geschichte und Altertumskunde*, 1856.

Stehlin, Karl, *Über die diplomatischen Beziehungen Englands mit der Schweiz im 16. und 17. Jahrhundert*, Basel, 1860.

Steinberg, Jonathan, *Why Switzerland?*, Cambridge, 1976.

Stelling-Michaud, S., *La carrière diplomatique de François-Louis de Pesme, seigneur de Saint Saphorin*, Lyon, 1935.

Stelling-Michaud, S., *Les aventures de M. de Saint Saphorin sur le Danube, etc.*, Paris & Neuchâtel, 1935.

Stelling-Michaud, S., *St Saphorin et la Politique de la Suisse, 1700-1710*, Villette-les-Cully, 1935.

Stern, Alfred, 'Die reformierte Schweiz in ihren Beziehungen zu Karl I. von England', Zurich: *Jahrbuch für schweizerische Geschichte*, vol. 3, 1878.

Stern, Alfred, 'Sir Oliver Flemings Depeschen aus der Schweiz', *Anzeiger für schweizerische Geschichte*, 1878.

Stern, Alfred, 'Die Neutralität der Schweiz in englischer Beleuchtung bei Voraussicht des Weltkriegs', *Neue Schweizer Rundschau*, NF. 1, 1933/34.

Stern, Alfred, 'Oliver Cromwell und die evang. Kantone der Schweiz,' in *Sybels Histor. Zeitschrift,* new series, 4.

Stern, Alfred, *see also* Section C.

Stewart, Michael, *Modern Forms of Government*, London: Allen & Unwin, 3rd ed., 1964.

Stoughton, J., 'Die Verbindung zwischen Basel und England zur Zeit der Reformation', *Urkundenbuch der Stadt Aarau*.

Strässle, Léon E., *Die Entwicklung der Schweizerischen Neutralität*, Fribourg, 1951.

Straumann, H., 'George Grote und der Sonderbundskrieg', in *Zeitschrift für Schweizergeschichte*, 27, 1947.

Straumann, H., *see also* Section C.

Streiff, Eric, *Die Einflussnahme der europäischen Mächte auf die Entwicklungskämpfe in der Schweiz, 1839-1845*, Zurich, 1931.

Stubbs, William, *Seventeen Lectures on the Study of Medieval and Modern History*, Oxford, 1886.

Sweeney, J. N., *Switzerland in 1876*, London, 1877.

Switzerland, 1975, Berne: Kümmerli & Frey, 1975 and other annual issues.

Tessier [?], Antoine, *History of the Negotiation of the Ambassadors Sent to the Duke of Savoy by the Protestant Cantons of Switzerland, concerning the Vaudois. Translated from the French original in Switzerland*, London, 1690.

Thieme, Max, *'Die Ehescheidung Heinrichs VIII und die europäischen Universitäten'*, Juristische Studiengesellschaft Karlsruhe, Schriftreihe, vol. 13, 1957.
Thiersch, H. W. J., *Edmund Ludlow und seine Unglücksgefährten als Flüchtlinge an dem gastlichen Herde der Schweiz*, Basel, 1881.
Thürer, Georg, *Free and Swiss*, Oswald Wolff, 1970.
Thürer, Georg, *St Galler Geschichte*, St Gallen, 1972.
Toynbee, Arnold, *The War and the Neutrals*, Oxford, 1956.
Trevelyan, G. M., *English Social History*, London: Longmans, Green, 1944.
Trevelyan, G. M., *British History in the Nineteenth Century and After (1782-1919)*, London, 1937.
Tyler, J. E., *The British Army on the Continent 1904-1914*, London: E. Arnold & Co., 1938.
Tyrrell, Robert, 'The British-Swiss Legion: Enigma of the Crimean War', in *Blackwood's Magazine*, no. 328, August, 1980.
Uhl, Othmar, *Die diplomatisch – politischen Bezeihungen zwischen Grossbritannien und der Schweiz in den Jahrzehnten vor dem ersten Weltkrieg*, Basel: Verlag Helbing & Lichtenhahn, 1961.
Vallière, P. E. de, *Honneur et Fidélité: Histoire des Suisses au Service Etranger*, Paris: La Presse Française et Etrangère, 1940.
Vargas, Philippe de, *L'Affaire de Neuchâtel 1856-57: Les Négotiations Diplomatiques*, Lausanne, 1913.
Vaughan, Robert, *The Protectorate of Oliver Cromwell and the State of Europe . . . Illustrated in a Series of Letters between Dr John Pell, Sir Samuel Morland, Sir William Lockhart, Mr Secretary Thurloe, etc.*, 2 vols., London: Henry Colburn, 1838.
Vetter, Prof. Dr Theodore, *Relations between England and Zurich during the Reformation*, Zurich, 1904.
Vetter, Prof. Dr Theodore, *see also* Section C.
Vincent, J. M., *Switzerland at the Beginning of the Sixteenth Century*, Baltimore: John Hopkins Press, 1904.
Vieusseux, A., *The History of Switzerland, from the First Irruption of the Northern Tribes to the Present Time*, London, 1846.
Vögeli, Rudolf H., *Die schweizerische Regeneration von 1830 bis 1840 in der Beleuchtung englischer Gesandtschaftsberichte*, Zurich, 1924.
Vogelin, H. A., *Die Gründung des schweizerischen Bundesstaates im Urteil der Engländer*, Basel, 1952.
Wake, Isaac, *A Threefold Help to Politicall Observations, i. concerning the xiii Cantons of the Helviticall League*, London, 1655.
War Office, W.O. 32/47/6708, Public Record Office, Kew, Surrey.
Weck, R. de, *La représentation diplomatique de la Suisse*, Freiburg, 1911.
Wedgwood, C. V., *The Thirty Years' War*, London: Jonathan Cape, 1944.
Wegg, Jervis, *Richard Pace: A Tudor Diplomatist*, London: Methuen, 1932.
Wickham, William, *The Correspondence of the Rt. Hon. William Wickham from the Year 1794*, ed. by his grandson, 2 vols., London, 1870.
Wiegner, E., *Der britische Imperialismus: Eine kritische Betrachtung des Chamberlain – Programms*, Diss., Zurich, 1938.

Wilkinson, Maurice, 'British Diplomacy: The Sonderbund War, 1847,' in *Month,* June 1927.
Wilson, W. M., 'The Swiss (Constitutional) Model for Europe', in *Contemporary Review,* August, 1942.
Winchester, B., *The Swiss Republic,* London: 1891.
Wirz, Hans Georg, *Das Regiment de Sacconay,* Berne, 1922.
Wiskemann, Elizabeth, 'The Swiss Confederation and the War', in *Fortnightly Review,* April 1940.
Wiskemann, Elizabeth, *see also* Section C.
Wood, Herbert Fairlie, *The King's Royal Rifle Corps,* London: Hamish Hamilton, 1967.
Wurstemberger, L., *Peter der Zweite,* Berne, 1856.
Young, George Malcolm, *Victorian England,* London: Oxford U.P., 1936.
Zschokke, J. H. D., *The History of the Invasion of Switzerland by the French,* trans. John Aikin, London, 1803.
Zeerleder, A., 'Die politische und literarische Mission des englischen Gesandten Abraham Stanyan in der Schweiz von 1705 bis 1713'. *Berner Zeitschrift für Geschichte und Heimatkunde,* 1942.

B: GEOGRAPHICAL, DESCRIPTIVE, TRAVELLERS, VISITORS, MOUNTAINEERING AND WINTER SPORTS

Achard, Paul, *Hommes et chiens du Grand-Saint-Bernard,* Paris, 1937.
Adam of Usk, *Chronicon,* ed. E. M. Thompson, London, 1904.
Adeane, J. H. (ed.), *The Girlhood of Maria Josepha Holroyd,* London, 1897.
Addison, Joseph, *Remarks on Several Parts of Italy and Switzerland Made in 1701-1703,* London, 1705.
Agassiz, Lewis, *A Journey to Switzerland,* London, 1833.
Allbutt, Sir Thomas, 'On Davos as a Health Resort, in *The Lancet,* 2, 1877.
Alpine Club, *see* Mumm.
Alpine Journal, The, various editions from 1863; 'Alpine Centenary' in no. 295, 1958.
Amery, Hon, L. S., *Days of Fresh Air,* London: Jarrolds, 1939.
Amstutz, Dr Walter, 'Portrait of a Pioneer, Sir Arnold Lunn, 1888-1974' (The Arnold Lunn Memorial Lecture), Zurich: De Clivo Press, 1979.
Anderson, Patrick, *Over the Alps,* London: Rupert Hart-Davis, 1969.
Anonymous, *A Walk through Switzerland in September 1816,* London, 1818.
Anonymous, *A Tour to Great St Bernard and Round Mont Blanc,* London, 1827.
Anonymous, *A Tour in Switzerland,* Edinburgh, 1842.
Anonymous, *A Little Journey to Switzerland,* London: Cassell, 1910.
Ashby, Douglas, *Things Seen in Switzerland,* London: Seeley, Service, 1928.
Association of British Members of The Swiss Alpine Club, *Inauguration of the Cabane Britannia on the Klein Allalinhorn, Saas Fee,* 1913.
Aubert, Fernand, *Pictet de Rochemont en Angleterre, 1787,* Berne, 1917.
Austin, A., *Among the Mountains,* Edinburgh, 1871.

Avebury, John Lubbuck, Baron, *The Scenery of Switzerland and the Causes to Which It Is Due*, London: Macmillan, 1896.
Badrutt, Johannes, *Johannes Badrutt Wins His Bet*, Swiss National Tourist Office, Sept 1964.
Bagge, Henry, *Switzerland Revisited by an Artist and Author*, London, n.d.
Bagger, Eugene, *The Heathen Are Wrong: Autobiography*, London: Eyre & Spottiswoode, 1941.
Bailey, Sydney D., *A Guide to Switzerland for School Visits*, London & Glasgow, 1963.
Baillie, Marianne, *First Impressions of a Tour upon the Continent in the Summer of 1818*, London, 1819.
Baines, E., *A Visit to the Vaudois of Piedmont*, London, 1855.
Bakewell, Robert, *Travels ... in Switzerland and Auvergne in 1820, 1821 and 1822*, London, 1823.
Ball, J., *Introduction to the Alpine Guide*, new ed., London, 1870.
Bancroft, Squire, *Mr and Mrs Bancroft on and off the Stage*, London, 1888.
Barnard, G., *Switzerland, Scenes and Incidents*, London, 1843.
Barrow, J., *A Tour on the Continent*, London, 1853.
Barrow, J., *Expeditions on the Glaciers, Including an Ascent of Mont Blanc, Monte Rosa, Col du Géant*, London, 1864.
Barry, Martin, *Ascent to the Summit of Mont Blanc in 1834*, London, 1836.
Bartlett, William Henry, *see* Beattie.
Baxter, Rt. Hon. W. E., *Impressions of Central and Southern Europe*, London, 1850.
Baxter, Wynne E., *Quiet Resting Places in the Swiss Highlands: Evolène, Ferpècle, Arolla*, London, 1898.
Bayne-Powell, R., *Travellers in Eighteenth Century England*, London, 1951.
Beattie, William, *Switzerland*, illustrated by W. H. Bartlett, 2 vols., London, 1836.
Beattie, William, *The Waldenses*, illustrated by W. H. Bartlett and W. Brockedon, London, 1838.
Beaufoy, Mrs Mark, 'A Journey through the Oberland and to Chamonix', J. M. Thorinton, *Alpine Journal*, 1928.
Belloc, Hilaire, *The Path to Rome*, London: Allen & Unwin, 1902.
Benson, E. F., *Winter Sports in Switzerland*, London, 1913.
Bernard, P. P., *Rush to the Alps: The Evolution of Vacationing in Switzerland*, New York, 1978.
Bernard, R. B., *A Tour through Some Parts of France, Switzerland . . .*, London, 1815.
Berry, M., *Journals and Correspondence*, London, 1865.
Bianconi, Piero, *Lugano Nostra*, Città di Lugano, 1972.
Bill, A. F., *Davos as a Health Resort*, London, 1906.
Bithray, E., *Switzerland and Italy*, London, 1883.
Blackwell, Eardley J., *Switzerland in 1854*, London, 1855.
Blaikie, Thomas, *Journal de Thomas Blaikie: Excursions d'un botaniste écossais dans les Alpes et le Jura en 1775*, ed. L. Seylaz, Neuchâtel, 1935.

Boddington, Mary, *Slight Reminiscences of the Rhine, Switzerland and a Corner of Italy,* London, 1834.
Bolla, Plinio, *Svizzera Romanda e Svizzera Italiana,* Zurich, 1942.
Bonnard, Georges, and de Beer, Gavin, 'Gibbon: Journal de mon voyage dans quelques endroits de la Suisse, 1758', in *Miscellanea Gibboniana,* Lausanne, 1952.
Bonner, Miss, *A Visit to the St Bernard in May,* London, 1877.
Bonney, T. G., *The Alpine Regions of Switzerland and the Neighbouring Countries,* London & Cambridge, 1868.
Bonney, T. G., *Lake and Mountain Scenery from the Swiss Alps,* London, 1874.
Bonney, T. G., *see also* Walton, Section C.
Bonstetten, C. V. de, *Souvenirs,* Paris, 1831.
Bonstetten, C. V. de, *see also* Herking, Section C.
Boos, H., *Thomas und Felix Platter,* Leipzig, 1878.
Bourrit, Marc Théodore, *Description des Alpes Pennines et Rhétiennes,* Geneva, 1781.
Bourrit, Marc Théodore, *Itinéraire de Genève, Lausanne et Chamouni,* Geneva, 1808.
Bourrit, Marc Théodore, *Nouvelle description des glacières . . .,* Geneva, 1787.
Bray, Anna Eliza, *The Mountains and Lakes of Switzerland,* London, 1841.
Bremer, Frederika, *Two Years in Switzerland and Italy . . .* trans. Mary Howitt, London, 1861.
Breval, John Durant, *Remarks on Several Parts of Europe,* London, 1726.
Breval, John Durant, *Remarks on Several Parts of Europe, Collected on the Spot since the Year 1723,* London, 1738.
Bridges, G. W., *Alpine Sketches, Comprised in a Short Tour through Parts of Holland, Flanders, France, Savoy, Switzerland and Germany during the Summer of 1814,* London, 1814.
Brigg, W. A., *Iter Helveticum: Journal of a Visit in Switzerland during September 1886,* Keighley, 1887.
Brindley, Arthur, *Living in the Swiss Alps,* Oxford, 1968.
British Ski Year Book, The, various editions from 1905.
Brockedon, William, *Illustrations of the Passes of the Alps,* London, 1828.
Brockedon, William, *Journal of Excursions in the Alps,* London, 1833.
Brooke, M. L., and Brooke, W. M. A., *Winter Life in Switzerland,* London: Pitman; Zurich: Burgi & Co, 1912.
Brooks, Pamela, *The Consul and the Queen of Geneva,* private monograph.
Brown, P. Hume, *Early Travellers in Scotland,* Edinburgh, 1891.
Brown, Prof. T. Graham, *Brenva,* London: Dent, 1944
Browne, J. D. H., *Stories from Switzerland,* London, 1852.
Brydges, Sir Samuel Egerton, *The Lake of Geneva,* Geneva: 1832.
Brydges, Sir Samuel Egerton, *Letters from the Continent,* London, 1821.
Brydges, Sir Samuel Egerton, *Recollections of Foreign Travel,* London, 1825.
Buckingham, James Silk, *Belgium, the Rhine, Switzerland and Holland: An Autumnal Tour,* London, 1848.
Burnaby, Mrs Fred, *The High Alps in Winter,* London, 1883.

Burnet, Gilbert, *Some Letters Containing an Account of What Seems Most Remarkable in Switzerland, Italy, etc.*, London, 1686.
Butler, Samuel, *Alps and Sanctuaries of Piedmont and the Canton Ticino*, 2nd ed., London, 1882.
Byers, Samuel, *Switzerland and the Swiss*, London, 1875.
Byron, Lord, 'Journal from September 18-25, 1816', in *Letters and Journals*, ed. L. A. Marchand, London: John Murray, 1973-82.
Byron, Lord, *see also* Section C.
Cadby, Will, and Cadby, Carine, *Switzerland in Winter*, London: Mills & Boon, 1914.
Cadby, Will, and Cadby, Carine, *Switzerland in Summer*, London: Mills & Boon, 1922, 1923.
Candaux, Jean-Daniel, *Voyageurs européens à la découverte de Genève, 1685-1792*, Geneva, 1966.
Carne, John, *Letters from Switzerland and Italy during a Late Tour*, London, 1834.
Carr, Alfred, *Adventures with My Alpenstock and Knapsack, or, A Five Weeks' Tour in Switzerland in 1874*, London, 1875.
Chamberlain, Sir Joseph Austen, *Seen in Passing*, London: Cassell, 1937.
Chambers, William, *A Tour in Switzerland*, Edinburgh, 1842.
Chapman, F. S., *Memoirs of a Mountaineer*, London: Chatto & Windus, 1945.
Chappell, Kingsley, *Wander with Me in Switzerland*, London, 1956.
Chappuzeau, Samuel, *L'Europe vivante*, Geneva, 1667.
Cheever, George Barrell, *Wanderings of a Pilgrim in the Shadow of Mont Blanc and the Jungfrau Alp*, Glasgow & London, 1847.
Childe-Pemberton, W. S., *The Earl Bishop: Frederick Augustus Hervey*, London, 1925.
Clark, Ronald William, *The Early Alpine Guides*, London: Phoenix House, 1949.
Clark, Ronald William, *The Victorian Mountaineers*, London: Batsford, 1953.
Clark, Ronald William, *A Picture History of Mountaineering*, London: Hulton Press, 1956.
Clark, Ronald William, *Six Great Mountaineers (Whymper, Mummery, Collie, Leigh-Mallory, Young, Hunt)*, London: Hamish Hamilton, 1956.
Clark, Ronald William, *Great Moments in Mountaineering*, London: Phoenix House, 1956.
Clark, Ronald William, *The True Book about Mountaineering*, London: Frederick Muller, 1957.
Clark, Ronald William, *We Go to Switzerland*, London: G. Harrap, 1958.
Clark, Ronald William, *An Eccentric in the Alps: W. A. B. Coolidge*, London: Museum Press, 1959.
Clark, Ronald William, *The Day the Rope Broke*, London: Secker & Warburg, 1965.
Clark, Sydney A., *Switzerland on Ten Pounds*, London: Ivor Nicholson & Watson, 1937.

Clark, Andrew, *Tour in France, Italy and Switzerland during the Years 1840 and 1841*, London, 1843.
Clason, F. L., *The Case of Switzerland, Briefly Stated*, London, 1802.
Clifford, Lady de, *A Picturesque Tour through France, Switzerland . . .*, London, 1817.
Clinker, Charles, *An Unconventional Guide for Tourists*, London, 1880.
Clissold, F., *Narrative of an Ascent to the Summit of Mont Blanc*, London, 1823.
Clowes, George, *Forty-Six Days in Switzerland*, London, 1856.
Cobb, H., 'Switzerland and The English Skater', in *Cornhill Magazine*, no. 55, November 1923.
Cobden-Sanderson, Thomas J., *The Journals*, London: R. Cobden-Sanderson, 1926.
Cockburne, W., *An Authentic Account of the . . . Death of Lord Camelford, with an extract from His Lordship's Will*, London: Hatchard, 1804.
Coghlan, Francis, *Guide through Switzerland and Chamonix*, London, ?1838.
Colam, Lance, *Switzerland on £25*, London: Frederick Muller, 1956.
Cole, Mrs H. Warwick, *A Lady's Tour round Monte Rosa*, London, 1859.
Coleman, E. T, *Scenes from the Snowfields*, London: Longman & Co, 1859.
Collings, Henry, *Switzerland As I Saw It*, London, 1876.
Conway, William Martin, *Zermatt Pocket Book: A Guide to the Pennine Alps*, London, 1891.
Conway, William Martin, *Mountain Memories*, London: Cassell, 1920.
Conway, William Martin, *The Alps from End to End*, London, 1895.
Conway, William Martin, *Autobiography of a Mountain Climber*, London, 1920.
Conway, William Martin, with McCormick, A. D., *The Alps*, London: A. & C. Black, 1904.
Cook, Sir Theodore Andrea, *Notes on Tobogganing at St Moritz*, London, 1896.
Cook, Sir Theodore Andrea, *Ice Sports*, London: Ward Lock 1901.
Cook, Thomas, *Cook's Tourist Handbook to Switzerland*, London, 1874.
Coolidge, W. A. B., *Swiss Travel and Swiss Guide Books*, London: Longmans, Green, 1889.
Coolidge, W. A. B., *The Alps in Nature and History*, London: Methuen, 1908.
Coolidge, W. A. B., *Alpine Studies*, London: Longmans, Green, 1912.
Coryat, Thomas, *Coryat's Crudities*, London, 1611; Glasgow, 1903.
Coxe, Henry, *The Traveller's Guide in Switzerland*, London, 1816.
Coxe, William, *Sketches of the Natural, Civil and Political State of Swisserland*, London, 1779.
Coxe, William, *Travels in Switzerland, 1789*, 3 vols., London, 1789.
Cranston, Maurice William, *Introduction to Switzerland*, London: Chaterson, 1949.
Cunningham, C. D., and Abney, W. de W., *The Pioneers of the Alps*, London, 1858.
Cunningham, C. D., and Abney, W. de W., *Christian Almer's Führerbuch, 1856-1894*, London: Sampson Lowe, 1896.

de Beer, Sir Gavin, *Early Travellers in the Alps,* London: Sidgwick & Jackson, 1930.
de Beer, Sir Gavin, *Alps and Men,* London: Edward Arnold, 1932.
de Beer, Sir Gavin, *Escape to Switzerland,* London: Penguin Books, 1945.
de Beer, Sir Gavin, *Travellers in Switzerland,* Oxford, 1949.
de Beer, Sir Gavin, *Speaking of Switzerland,* London: Eyre & Spottiswoode, 1952.
de Beer, Sir Gavin, 'Die "Premières" des Wetterhörner', in *Die Alpen,* February & March 1949.
de Beer, Sir Gavin, 'Anglais au Pays de Vaud', in *Revue Historique Vaudoise,* June & December 1951 and September 1952.
d'Auvergne, Edmund B., *Switzerland in Sun and Snow,* London, 1912.
D'Egville, A. H., 'The Inferno Race', from *The British Ski Year Book,* 1928.
Dennis, John, *Views in Savoy, Switzerland and on the Rhine,* Hackney, ?1822.
Dent, Clinton T., *Above the Snow-Line,* London: Longmans, Green, 1885.
Dent, Clinton T. (ed), *Mountaineering, with Contributions from W. M. Conway, D. W. Freshfield, H. G. Willink and Others,* London: Longmans, Green, 1892.
Devonshire, Georgiana Cavendish, Duchess of, *Sketch of a Descriptive Journey through Switzerland,* London, 1816.
Devonshire, Georgiana Cavendish, Duchess of, *Memorandums of the Face of the Country in Switzerland,* London, 1799.
Dixon, W. Hepworth, *The Switzers,* London, 1872.
Domville-Fife, Charles W., *Things Seen in Switzerland in Winter,* London: Seeley, Service, 1925.
Downes, George, *Guide through Switzerland and Savoy,* Paris, 1828.
Dowsing, William, *Rambles in Switzerland,* London, 1869.
Doyle, Sir Arthur Conan, 'A Ski Tour in 1893', reprinted in *The British Ski Year Book,* 1924.
Doyle, Sir Arthur Conan, *Memories and Adventures,* London: Hodder & Stoughton, 1924.
Drummond, A. T. K., *Scenes and Impressions in Switzerland and the North of Italy,* Edinburgh, 1853.
Duff, David Skene, *Edward of Kent,* London: Stanley Paul, 1938.
Duff, David Skene, *Victoria Travels,* London: Frederick Muller, 1970.
Duff, Mountstuart E. Grant, *Notes from a Diary, 1851-1872,* London, 1897.
Durham, W. E., *Summer Holidays in the Alps,* London, 1916.
Ebel, Johann Gottfried, *Instructions pour un voyageur qui se propose de parcourir la Suisse de la manière la plus utile,* 2 vols., 1795.
Ebel, Johann Gottfried, *The Traveller's Guide through Switzerland, Translated from the German,* London, 1818.
Eberli, Henry, *Switzerland, Poetical and Pictorial,* Zurich, 1893.
Eckenstein, Oscar, and Eckenstein, Lorria, *The Alpine Portfolio: The Pennine Alps from the Simplon to the Great St. Bernard,* London, 1889.
Egli, Emil, *Swiss Life and Landscape,* trans. E. Brockett, London: Paul Elek, 1949.

Elton, Charles I., *An Account of Shelley's Visits to France, Switzerland and Savoy*, London, 1894.
Engel, Claire Éliane, *La littérature alpestre en France et en Angleterre aux 18ᵉ et 19ᵉ siècles*, Chambéry, 1930.
Engel, Claire Éliane, *Mountaineering in the Alps*, London: Geo. Allen & Unwin, 1971.
Engel, Claire Éliane, *A History of Mountaineering in the Alps*, London: Geo. Allen & Unwin, 1950.
Engel, Claire Éliane, *Alpinistes d'autrefois*, Neuchâtel & Paris, 1935.
Engel, Claire Éliane, *They Came to the Hills*, London: Geo. Allen & Unwin, 1952.
Engel, Claire Éliane, *see also* Section C.
Evelyn, John, '*The Diary of John Evelyn*, ed. William Bray, London, 1818.
Fabre, Dominique, *Suisse*, Paris: Editions du Seuil, 1970.
Fawcett, Edward Douglas, *The Zermatt Dialogues*, London: Macmillan, 1931.
Fellows, Charles, *A Narrative of an Ascent to the Summit of Mont Blanc*, London, 1827.
Ferguson, F., *Wanderings in France and Switzerland*, London, 1869.
Ferguson, Robert, *Swiss Men and Swiss Mountains*, London, 1854.
Finch, George Ingle, *The Making of a Mountaineer*, London: Arrowsmith, 1924.
Fink, P., 'Reiseerinnerungen an die Schweiz (Moryson and Coryat)', in *Wissen und Leben*, 1 and 15, 1914.
Finnemore, John, *Switzerland*, London: A. & C. Black, 1908.
Fitzsimons, Raymund, *The Baron of Piccadilly*, London: Geoffrey Bles, 1967.
Forbes, Sir John, *A Physician's Holiday: or, A Month in Switzerland in the Summer of 1848*, London, 1849.
Forbes, Prof. J. D., *Travels in the Alps of Savoy and Other Parts of the Pennine Chain*, Edinburgh & London, 1843.
Forbes, Prof. J. D., *Travels Through the Alps*, ed. W. A. B. Coolidge, London, 1900.
Forbes, Murray, *The Diary of a Traveller over Alps and Appenines*, London, 1824.
Forrest, Archibald, and Bagge, Henry, *Switzerland Revisited*, London: Francis Griffiths, 1915.
Forster, R. W. E., 'The Alps of Glarus', in *Peaks, Passes and Glaciers*, 1859.
Forster, R. W. E., 'From the Grütli to the Grimsel', in *Peaks, Passes and Glaciers*, 1862.
Fowler, W. Warde, *A Year with the Birds*, London, 1886.
Freshfield, Douglas, *Below the Snow Line*, London: Constable, 1923.
Freshfield, Mrs Henry, *Alpine Byways*, London, 1861.
Freshfield, Mrs Henry, *A Summer Tour in the Grisons*, London, 1862.
Furse, Dame Katherine, *Hearts and Pomegranates: A Story of Forty-Five Years, 1875-1920*, London: Peter Davies, 1940.
Galton, Francis (ed.), *Vacation Tourists and Notes of Travel in 1860*, Cambridge & London, 1861.

Gardenstone, Lord, *Travelling Memorandums*, Edinburgh, 1791-95.
Gaudin, A., *Switzerland in Miniature: A Description of the Grand Model of Switzerland, by Prof. Gaudin of Geneva Now Exhibiting at the Egyptian Hall, Piccadilly*, London, 1825.
Gaudin, J. F. T., *Flora Helvetica*, Zurich, 1828-33.
Gaze, Henry, *Switzerland: How to See It for Ten Guineas*, London, 1861.
George, Hereford Brooke, *The Oberland and Its Glaciers Explored and Illustrated with Ice-axe and Camera*, London, 1866.
Gibbon, Monk, *Swiss Enchantment*, London: Evans, 1950.
Giberne, A., *Among the Mountains, or, The Harcourts at Montreux*, London, 1864.
Gibson, Hon. Harry, *Tobogganing on Crooked Runs*, London, 1894.
Gibbs, Roger, *The Cresta Run, 1885-1985*, London: Henry Melland, 1985.
Gillman, P., and Haston, D., *Eiger Direct*, London: Collins, 1966.
Girdlestone, A. G., *The High Alps without Guides*, London, 1870.
Godwin, C. G., *Notes of a Ramble in Belgium, the Rhine and Switzerland*, London, 1846.
Grande, Julian, *The Bernese Oberland in Summer and Winter*, London: Nelson & Sons, 1911.
Grasser, Johann Jakob, *Frantzösische und Englische Schatzkammer*, Basel, 1610.
Graves, Charles, *Swiss Summer*, London: Nicholson & Watson, 1938.
Graves, Charles, *Switzerland Revisited*, London: Geoffrey Bles, 1947.
Gray, Robert, *Letters during the Course of a Tour through Germany, Switzerland and Italy*, London, 1790.
Green, John Richard, *Stray Studies*, London, 1870.
Green, Vivian H., *The Swiss Alps*, London: Batsford, 1961.
Greville, Charles, *The Greville Memoirs*, London, 1875.
Grey, Rowland, *In Sunny Switzerland*, London, 1884.
Greyerz, O. von, *Beat Ludwig von Muralt*, Frauenfeld, 1888.
Gribble, Francis Henry, *The Early Mountaineers*, London, 1899.
Gribble, Francis Henry, *The Story of Alpine Climbing*, London: Geo. Newnes, 1904.
Gribble, Francis Henry, *see also* Section C.
Grimm, Samuel Hieronymus, *Reise nach den Alpen*, Zurich, 1776.
Grose, Francis, *Antiquities of England and Wales*, London, 1787.
Grosley, Pierre Jean, *Londres*, Lausanne, 1770.
Gross, Jules, *L'Hospice du Grand Saint-Bernard*, Paris & Neuchâtel, 1935.
Hake, Ormond, *Tobogganing* (The Badminton Library), London, 1892.
Haller, Albrecht von, *Iter Helveticum Anni 1739*, Göttingen, 1740.
Haller, Albrecht von, *Die Alpen*, Berne, 1793.
Haller, Albrecht von, *A. Hallers Tagebücher seiner Reisen nach Deutschland, Holland und England, 1723-1727*, ed. E. Hintsche, St Gallen, 1948.
Haller, Albrecht von, *Albrecht Hallers Tagebuch seiner Studienreise nach London, Paris, Strasbourg und Basel, 1727-1728*, ed. E. Hintsche, Berne: Verlag Hans Huber, 1968.
Hardmeyer, J., *Locarno and Its Valleys*, London & Zurich, 1886.

Harrison, F., *Among the Mountains*, London, 1892.
Harrison, F., *My Alpine Jubilee*, London, 1908.
Hartmann, A., *Berner Oberland in Sage und Geschichte*, Berne, 1915.
Havergal, Frances Ridley, *Swiss Letters and Alpine Poems*, ed. J. M. Crane, London, 1881.
Hawes, B., *Narrative of a Ascent to the Summit of Mont Blanc, Made during the Summer of 1827 by Mr W. Hawes and Mr C. Fellows . . .* privately, *1828*.
Hayden, John, *A Sketch of a Tour in Switzerland*, London, 1859.
Headley, J. T., and Cheever, G. B., *Travels among Alpine Scenery*, London, 1855.
Heathman, W. G., *Switzerland in 1854-55: A Book of Travel, Men and Things*, London, 1855.
Heger, Thomas, *A Tour Through Part of the Netherlands, France and Switzerland in the Year 1817*, London, 1820.
Heidegger, Heinrich, *Handbuch für Reisende durch die Schweiz*, 1787-90.
Hentzner, Paulus, *Travels in England during the Reign of Queen Elizabeth*, London: Cassell, 1889.
Hering, George E., *The Mountains and Lakes of Switzerland, the Tyrol and Italy*, London, 1847.
Herold, J. C., *The Swiss without Halos*, New York, 1948.
Hervey, William, *Journals of the Hon. W. Hervey*, Bury St Edmunds, 1906.
Hewlett, R. W., *St Moritz as a Health Resort*, London, 1871.
Hinchliff, Thomas W., *Summer Months among the Alps*, London, 1857.
Hobhouse, John Cam, *Recollections of a Long Life*, London: John Murray, 1909.
Hoek, Henry, *The Parsenn*, trans. William and Margaret Lockett, London: Sir I. Pitman & Sons, 1933.
Hog, Roger, *Tour on the Continent in France, Switzerland and Italy*, London, 1824.
Hogg, Garry, *Switzerland*, London: Weidenfeld & Nicolson, 1962.
Hogg, John, *Letters from Abroad – to a Friend at Cambridge*, London, 1844.
Hogg, Thomas Jefferson, *Two Hundred and Nine Days, or, The Journal of a Traveller on the Continent*, 2 vols., London, 1827.
Hollis, Thomas, *Memoirs of Thomas Hollis, with Appendix Compiled by F. Blackburne*, 2 vols., London, 1780.
Holman, James, *The Narrative of a Journey Undertaken in the Years 1819, 1820 and 1821, through . . . Switzerland . . .*, London, 1822.
Hookham, Thomas, *A Walk through Switzerland in September 1816*, London, 1818.
Hotels Seiler, *Hotels Seiler, Zermatt, 1855-1930*, Zermatt, 1930.
Howell, James, *Instructions for Forreigne Travell*, London, 1642.
Hudson, Charles, and Kennedy, E. S., *Where There's a Will There's a Way*, London, 1855.
Hutton, R. H., *Holiday Rambles in Ordinary Places by a Wife and Her Husband*, London, 1877.
Inglis, H. D., *Switzerland, the South of France and the Pyrenees*, London, 1840.

Irving, R. L. G., *The Romance of Mountaineering*, London: Dent, 1935.
Irving, R. L. G., *A History of British Mountaineering*, London: Batsford, 1955.
Jackson, Eileen Montague, *Switzerland Calling*, London, 1927.
Jahrbuch des Schweizer Alpen Club, various editions since 1864.
Javelle, J. M. F. Emile, *Souvenirs d'un Alpiniste*, Lausanne, 1897.
Johnson, Anna C., *The Cottages of the Alps*, New York, 1860.
Jones, Revd Harry, *The Regular Swiss Round*, London, 1865.
Kasser, Hans (ed.), *Swiss Panorama*, Zurich: Artemis, 1974.
Kennedy, T.S., 'Zermatt and the Matterhorn in Winter', in *Alpine Journal*, 1863.
Klucker, Christian, *Adventures of an Alpine Guide*, London, 1932.
Knebworth, Anthony, Viscount, 'An Atheist in Heaven', in *The Kandahar Review*, 1933.
Knowles, A. C., *Adventures in the Alps*, London: Skeffington & Son, 1913.
Labarge, Margaret Wade, *Medieval Travellers*, London: Hamish Hamilton, 1982.
'A Lady', *The Cottages of the Alps: or, Life and Manners in Switzerland*, London, 1860.
La Farina, G., *La Svizzera storica ed artistica*, illus. W. H. Bartlett, Florence, 1842.
Lamprell, E. E., *A Fortnight in Switzerland for Five Guineas*, London, 1905.
Landseer, John, *Some Account of the Dogs and of the Pass of the Great Saint Bernard*, London, 1831.
Landseer, John, *Les Voyageurs en Suisse*, 3 vols, Paris, 1803.
Larden, Walter, *Recollections of an Old Mountaineer*, London: Edward Arnold, 1910.
Larden, Walter, *Inscriptions from Swiss Chalets*, London: Oxford U.P., 1913.
Lascelles, Rowley, *Sketch of a Descriptive Journey through Switzerland*, London, 1796.
Lascelles, Rowley, *A General Outline of the Swiss Landscapes*, London, 1812.
Lascelles, Rowley, *Journal of a Short Excursion among the Swiss Landscapes, Made in the Summer of the Year Ninety-Four*, London, 1803.
Lascelles, Rowley, *Sketch of a Tour in Switzerland*, London, 1797.
Lassels, Richard, *An Italian Voyage*, London, 1698.
Latrobe, C. J., *The Alpenstock: or, Sketches of Swiss Scenery and Manners 1825-26*, London, 1839.
Laughlin, Clara E., *Where It All Comes True in Italy and Switzerland*, London, 1929.
Le Blond, Mrs Aubrey, *True Tales of Mountain Adventure*, London: T. Fisher Unwin, 1903.
Le Blond, Mrs Aubrey, *The High Alps in Winter: or, Mountaineering in Search of Health*, London: Sampson, Low, 1883.
Le Blond, Mrs Aubrey, *My Home in the Alps*, London: Sampson Low, 1892.
Le Blond, Mrs Aubrey, *The Story of an Alpine Winter*, London: G. Bell & Sons, 1907.
Lee, E., *The Baths of the Engadine, St Moritz and Tarasp*, 2nd ed., London, 1870.

Le Gallais, M., *Chroniques du Mont Saint Bernard,* Tours, 1860.
Lemaistre, J. G., *Travels after the Peace of Amiens through Parts of France, Switzerland . . .,* London, 1806.
Le Mesurier, W. H., *An Impromptu Ascent of Mont Blanc,* London, 1882.
Leonhardi, John, *Account of the Grisons,* London, 1711.
Le Sage de la Colombière, Georges-Louis, *Remarques sur l'État Présent d'Angleterre,* Amsterdam, 1715.
Letts, Malcolm, *As the Foreigner Saw Us,* London: Methuen, 1935.
Liddiard, William, *A Three Months' Tour in Switzerland,* London, 1832.
Lithgow, William, *The Totall Discourse of the Rare Adventures and Painefull Peregrinations of Long Nineteen Years' Travayles,* London, 1632.
Lloyd, Francis, *The Physiography of the Upper Engadine,* London, 1881.
Lockett, W. G., *The British at Davos,* Davos Public Interests Association, 1920.
Lockett, W. G., *Robert Louis Stevenson at Davos,* London: Hurst & Blackett, 1934.
Loges, Chrétien de, *Essais historiques sur le Mont St Bernard,* Geneva, 1789.
Longman, William, and Trower, H., *Journal of Six Weeks' Adventures in Switzerland . . .,* London, 1856.
Longman, William, and Trower, H., *A Lecture on Switzerland,* London, 1857.
Luc, J. A. de, *Lettres physiques et morales sur les Montagnes,* The Hague, 1778.
Luc, J. A. de, *Relations de différents voyages dans les Alpes de Faucigny,* Maestricht, 1776.
Lunn, Sir Arnold, *The Englishman in the Alps,* Oxford, 1913.
Lunn, Sir Arnold, *The Alps,* London: Thornton Butterworth, 1914.
Lunn, Sir Arnold, *Alpine Skiing,* London: Methuen, 1921.
Lunn, Sir Arnold, *The Mountains of Youth,* London: Oxford U.P., 1925.
Lunn, Sir Arnold, *A History of Skiing,* London: Oxford U.P., 1927.
Lunn, Sir Arnold, *Switzerland: Her Topographical, Historical and Literary Landmarks,* London: Harrap, 1928.
Lunn, Sir Arnold, *Mountain Jubilee,* London: Eyre & Spottiswoode, 1943.
Lunn, Sir Arnold, *Switzerland and the English,* London: Eyre & Spottiswoode, 1944.
Lunn, Sir Arnold, *Mountains of Memory,* London: Hollis & Carter, 1948.
Lunn, Sir Arnold, *The Story of Skiing,* London: Eyre & Spottiswoode, 1952.
Lunn, Sir Arnold, *The Cradle of Switzerland,* London: Hollis & Carter, 1952.
Lunn, Sir Arnold, *Zermatt and the Valais,* London: Hollis & Carter, 1955.
Lunn, Sir Arnold, *A Century of Mountaineering (1857-1957),* London: Geo. Allen & Unwin, 1957.
Lunn, Sir Arnold, *The Swiss and their Mountains,* London: Geo. Allen & Unwin, 1963.
Lunn, Sir Arnold, *Matterhorn Centenary,* London: Geo. Allen & Unwin, 1965.
Lunn, Sir Arnold, *Unkilled for So Long: Memoirs,* London: Geo. Allen & Unwin, 1968.

Lunn, Sir Arnold, *The Kandahar Story*, London: Geo. Allen & Unwin, 1969.
Lunn, Sir Arnold, *The Bernese Oberland*, London: Geo. Allen & Unwin, 1973.
Lunn, Sir Arnold, *see also* Section C.
Lunn, Sir Arnold (ed.), *Oxford Mountaineering Essays*, London: Edward Arnold, 1912.
Lunn, Sir Arnold (ed.), *The Englishmen on Ski*, London: Museum Press, 1963.
Lunn, Brian, *Switchback: An Autobiography*, London: Eyre & Spottiswoode, 1948.
Lunn, Sir Henry, *Chapters from My Life*, London: Cassell, 1918.
Lunn, Sir Henry, *How to Visit Switzerland*, London: H. Marshall & Son, 1896.
Lunn, Peter, 'Through a Glass Darkly', in *The British Ski Year Book*, 1944.
Lytton, Hon. Neville, *Winter Sports* (The Lonsdale Library), London, 1930.
MacCrackan, W. D., *Romance Switzerland, Teutonic Switzerland*, Geneva, 1895.
MacGregor, John, *My Note Book: Switzerland*, London, 1837.
Mackintosh, Sir James, *Memoirs*, London, 1836.
MacNeven, W. J., *A Ramble through Swisserland in the Summer and Autumn of 1802*, Dublin, 1803.
Mais, S. P. B., *I return to Switzerland*, London: Christopher Johnson, 1948.
Malby, Reginald A., *With Camera and Rucksack in the Oberland and Valais*, London: Headley Bros, 1913.
Maler, Joshua, *see* Müller.
Marcet, William, *Principal Southern and Swiss Health Resorts*, London, 1883.
Margerie, Emmanuel de, *Three Stages in the Evolution of Alpine Geology: de Saussure-Studer-Heim*, London, 1964.
Marriott, Michael, *Car-Camping in Switzerland*, London: Harold Starke, 1965.
Marsh, Herbert, *Two Seasons in Switzerland*, London, 1895.
Martel, Peter, *An Account of the Glaciers of the Alps in Savoy*, London, 1744.
Martyn, Thomas, *Sketch of a Tour through Swisserland*, London, 1787.
Massie, James William, *Recollections of a Tour*, London, 1846.
Mathews, C. E., *The Annals of Mont Blanc*, London, 1898.
Mathews, William, *Lecture on the Glaciers of Switzerland (Delivered 1858)*, Tunbridge Wells: Hepworth, 1902.
Matthews, Henry, *The Diary of an Invalid: The Journal of a Tour in . . . Switzerland . . . in the Years 1817-1819*, London, 1820.
Meier, Mariann, *The Young Traveller's Switzerland*, London: Phoenix House, 1950.
Meister, Jakob Heinrich, *Letters Writtten during a Residence in England: Translated from the French*, London: T. N. Longman, 1799.
Meister, Jakob Heinrich, *Souvenirs de mes voyages en Angleterre*, Zurich: Orell, Gessner, Füssli, 1795.
Mercier, J. J., *Mountains and Lakes of Switzerland and Italy*, London, 1871.

Merian, Matthäus, the Elder, *Topographia Helvetiae*, Amsterdam, 1644.
Meyer, Paul, 'Aus den Wanderjahren eines Basler Studenten des 17. Jahrhundert', *Basler Jahrbuch*, 1915.
Miège, Guy, *The New State of England*, 2nd ed., London, 1693.
Mikes, George, *George Mikes Introduces Switzerland*, London: André Deutsch, 1977.
Mikes, George, *Switzerland for Beginners*, London: André Deutsch, 1962.
Milford, John, *Observations: Moral, Literary and Antiquarian Made During a Tour Through the Pyrenees, South of France, Switzerland . . .* London, 1818.
Minto, Lord, 'Zermatt and the Breithorn in 1830', in *Alpine Journal*, 16, 1892.
Monkswell, Mary, Lady, *A Victorian Diarist*, London, 1944.
Montague, C. E., *The Right Place*, London: Chatto & Windus, 1924.
Moore, A. W., *The Alps in 1864*, London, 1867.
Moore, A. W., The Development of Winter Sports in the Engadine', in *The British Ski Year Book*, 1942.
Moore, John, *A View of Society and Manners in France, Switzerland and Germany*, London, 1779.
Morf, C., *Les pionniers du Club Alpin: étude historique*, 1875.
Morgan, John Minter, *A Tour through Switzerland and Italy in the Year 1846-1847*, London, 1850.
Mortoft, Francis, *Being His Travels through France and Italy, 1658-1659*, ed. Malcolm Letts, London, 1928.
Moryson, Fynes, *An Itinerary . . . Containing His Ten Yeares Travell through . . . Germany, Bohemia, Switzerland . . . etc.*, London, 1617.
Mügge, Theodore, *Switzerland in 1847*, London, 1848.
Muirhead, James F., *A Wayfarer in Switzerland*, London: Methuen, 1926.
Müller, J. G. (ed.), 'Bekenntnisse merkwürdiger Männer von sich selbst', vol. 6, Josua Maler, Winterthur, 1810.
Mumm, A. L., 'Ruskin in the Alps', in *The Alpine Journal*, 32, 1919.
Mumm, A. L. (ed.), *The Alpine Club Register, 1857-1863; 1864-1876; 1877-1890*, 3 vols., London: E. Arnold, 1923-28.
Mummery, A. F., *My Climbs in the Alps and Caucasus*, London, 1895.
Muralt, Béat Louis de, *Lettres sur les Anglais et les Français 1725*, Berne, 1897.
Muralt, Béat Louis de, *Lettres sur les Anglois*, Zurich, 1725.
Muralt, Béat Louis de, *Letters Describing the Characters and Customs of the English and French Nations*, London, 1726.
Muralt, Béat Louis de, *see also* Greyerz.
Murray, John, *A Glance at Some of the Beauties and Sublimities of Switzerland*, London, 1829.
Murray, John, *A Handbook for Travellers in Switzerland and the Alps of Savoy and Piedmont*, London: John Murray, 1838.
Murrell, Jemima, *Miss Jemima's Swiss Journal*, London: Putnam, 1963.
Needham, John Turberville, *Observations des hauteurs faites avec le baromètre au mois d'Aoust 1751 sur une partie des Alpes*, Berne, 1760.
Noel, Baptist W., *Notes for a Tour in Switzerland, in the Summer of 1847*, London, 1848.

Noel, Gerard Thomas, *Arvendel, or, Sketches in Italy and Switzerland*, London, 1826.
Ober, P., *Picturesque Tour through the Oberland in the Canton of Berne*, London, 1823.
O'Conor, Matthew, *Picturesque and Historical Recollections during a Tour through . . Switzerland*, London, 1837.
Ogrizek, D., and Rufenacht, J. G., *The Winter Book of Switzerland*, Berne: Kümmerly & Frey, 1949.
Olivier, Lord., 'Praise of Aargau', in *Nation*, 20 Dec. 1928.
Oppenheim, Roy, *Die Entdeckung der Alpen*, Frauenfeld: Huber, 1974.
Ormsby, A., *Memoirs of a Family in Swisserland*, 4 vols., London, 1802.
Peaks, Passes and Glaciers: A Series of Excursions by Members of the Alpine Club, ed. J. Ball, London: Longman, 1859.
Peaks, Passes and Glaciers, 2nd series, ed. E. S. Kennedy, London, 1862.
Peaks, Passes and Glaciers, 3rd series, ed. A. E. Field, Sydney Spencer, *et al.*, London: Methuen, 1932.
Pennant, Thomas, *Tour on the Continent, 1765*, ed. Gavin de Beer for the Ray Society, London: 1948.
Pennington, Thomas, *Continental Excursions, or, Tours into France, Switzerland and Germany in 1782, 1787 and 1789*, London, 1809.
Peyer, Gustav, *Geschichte des Reisens in der Schweiz: Eine kulturgeschichtliche Studie*, Basel, 1885.
Phillips, Francis, *A Reading Party in Switzerland*, London, 1851.
Phillips, John Burton, *Continental Travel in 1802-3: The Story of an Escape*, Manchester, 1904.
Pictet, Marc Auguste, *Voyage de trois mois en Angleterre, en Écosse et en Irlande*, Geneva, 1802.
Pilley, Dorothy, *Climbing Days*, London, 1935.
Platter, Thomas, *Beschreibung der Reisen durch Frankreich, Spanien, England und die Niederlande (1595-1600)*, Basel, 1698.
Platter, Thomas, *Thomas Platter: Autobiography*, New York: P. Monroe, 1904.
Platter, Thomas, *Thomas Platters, des Jüngeren, Englandfahrt im Jahre 1599*, ed. Hans Hecht, Halle, 1929.
Platter, Thomas, *Thomas Platter's Travels in England, Translated into English with an Introduction by Clare Williams*, London: Jonathan Cape, 1937.
Plunket, Hon. Frederica, *Here and There among the Alps*, London, 1875.
Polidori, John William, *Sketches Illustrative of the Manners and Costumes of France, Switzerland . . .* London, 1821.
Polidori, John William, *The Diary of Dr John William Polidori, 1816*, London: Elkin Mathews, 1911.
Powys, Llewelyn, *Swiss Essays*, London: John Lane, 1947.
Quaglia, Lucien, *La Maison du Grand Saint Bernard, des origines aux temps actuels*, Martigny, 1972.
Queensberry, Marquess of, *The Spirit of the Matterhorn*, London, n.d.
Raffles, Thomas, *Letters During a Tour through Some Parts of France, Savoy, Switzerland, Germany and the Netherlands*, Liverpool, 1818.

Ramsay, Andrew Crombie, *The Old Glaciers of Switzerland and North Wales*, London, 1860.
Ramsay, Sir James, 'Recollections of the Engadine in 1872', in *Alpine Journal*, 34, 1921.
Randolph,–, *Observations on the Present State of . . . Switzerland*, London, 1784.
Rawnsley, Hardwicke D., *Flower-time in the Oberland*, Glasgow, 1904.
Ray, John, *Observations, Topographical, Moral and Physiological . . . Made in a Journey through Parts of the Low Countries, Germany, Italy and France*, London, 1673.
Ray, John, *Travels through the Low Countries, Germany, Italy and France*, London, 1738.
Read, M., 'Gibbon's Journal de mon voyage dans quelques endroits de la Suisse', in *Historic Studies*, London, 1895.
Rébuffat, Gaston, *Men and the Matterhorn*, London, 1967.
Reresby, Sir John, *Memoirs and Travels of Sir John Reresby*, ed. A Juatt, London, 1904.
Rey, Guido, *The Matterhorn*, Oxford: Basil Blackwell, 1946.
Richardson, E. C., *Ski-Running*, London, 1904.
Richardson, F., et aliae, *Swiss Notes by Five Ladies*, Leeds, 1875.
Rickman, E. S., *The Diary of a Solitaire: or A Sketch of a Pedestrian Excursion through Part of Switzerland*, London, 1835.
Riddell, James, *The Ski Runs of Switzerland*, London, 1957.
Robson-Scott, W. D., 'Josua Maler's Visit to England in 1551', in *Modern Language Review*, vol 45, July 1950.
Robson-Scott, W. D., *German Travellers in England, 1400-1800*, Oxford: Basil Blackwell, 1953.
Roby, J., *Seven Weeks in Belgium, Switzerland, Lombardy, Piedmont, Savoy . . .*, London, 1838.
Roget, François Frédéric, *Ski Runs in the High Alps*, London: T. Fisher Unwin, 1913.
Roget, Samuel Romilly, *Travels in the Last Two Centuries of Three Generations*, London: T. Fisher Unwin, 1921.
Roland de la Platière, Marie Jeanne, *Voyage en Suisse 1787, ed. collationée, annot. et accompagnée d'un aperçu sur les débuts touristiques feminins dans les Alpes par G. R. de Beer*, Neuchâtel, 1937.
Rook, Clarence, *Switzerland: The Country and Its People*, London: Chatto & Windus, 1907.
Roscoe, Thomas, *The Tourist in Switzerland and Italy*, London, 1830.
Rose, G., *Out for a Holiday with Cook's Excursion through Switzerland and Italy*, London, 1870.
Reverdin, Olivier, *Introducing Switzerland*, Lausanne: Swiss Office for the Development of Trade, 1964.
Russell, John, *Switzerland*, London: Batsford, 1950.
Rye, W. B., *England as Seen by Foreigners, in the Days of Elizabeth and James the First*, London, 1865.

Salisbury, F. S., *Rambles in the Vaudois Alps*, London: Dent, 1916.
Sansom, J., *Travels from Paris through Switzerland and Italy*, London, 1807.
Saussure, César de, *A Foreign View of England in the Reign of George I and George II*, Trans Mme van Muyden, London: John Murray, 1902.
Saussure, César de, *Lettres et voyages . . . en Angleterre 1725-9*, ed. B. van Muyden, Lausanne, 1903.
Saussure, H.-B. de., *Voyages dans les Alpes*, Neuchâtel, 1779.
Schazmann, P.-E., 'Le Duc de Kent', in *La Tribune de Genève*, 7 December, 1967.
Schæzmann, P.-E., *see also* Section C.
Scheuchzer, Johann Jacob, *Historiae Helveticae Naturalis Prolegomena . . . 1700*.
Scheuchzer, Johann Jacob, *Itinera per Helvetiae Alpinas Regiones*, Leiden, 1723.
Scheuchzer, Johann Jacob, *Nova Helvetiae Tabula Geographica (1713)*, facsimile ed. with text by Arthur Dürst, Zurich: De Clivo Press, 1971.
Schuster, Lord (Claud), *Peaks and Pleasant Pastures*, Oxford: Clarendon Press, 1911.
Schuster, Lord (Claud), *Men, Women and Mountains*, London: Ivor Nicholson & Watson, 1931.
Seligman, Gerald, *Snow Structures and Ski Fields*, London: Macmillan, 1936.
Sherlock, Martin, *Lettres d'un voyageur anglois*, London & ?Geneva, 1779.
Sherlock, Martin, *Nouvelles lettres d'un voyageur anglois*, London, 1780.
Sherwell, Markham, *Ascension du Docteur Edmund Clark et du Capitaine Markham Sherwill à la première sommité du Mont Blanc les 25, 26 et 27 Août, 1825*, Paris & Geneva, 1827.
Shoberl, Frederic, *Switzerland*, London, 1827.
Schuckburgh, Sir George Evelyn, *Observations Made in Savoy . . . Being an Examination of . . . de Luc's Rules Delivered in His 'Recherches sur les modifications de l'atmosphère'*, London, 1777.
Shuttleworth, R. J., 'Account of a Botanical Excursion in the Alps of the Canton of Valais', in *Magazine of Zoology and Botany*, 2, 1838.
Simond, Charles, *Les Étrangers Domiciliés en Suisse*, Lausanne, 1926.
Simond, Charles F., *A Pedaller Abroad . . . Cycling in and around Switzerland*, London, 1897.
Simond, Louis, *Switzerland, or A Journal of a Tour and Residence in that Country in the Years 1817, 1818, & 1819*, London, 1823.
Smith, Albert, *The Story of Mont Blanc*, London, 1853.
Smith, A. R., *A Handbook of Mr A. Smith's Ascent of Mont Blanc*, London, 1852.
Smith, Edward, *Foreign Visitors in England during the Last Three Centuries*, London, 1889.
Smith, John, *A Month in France and Switzerland*, London, 1825.
Smith, J. Adam, *Mountain Holidays*, London, 1946.
Smith, J. Denham, *A Voice from the Alps*, Dublin, 1854.
Smith, J. Manton, *Jottings on my Journeys in Switzerland*, London, 1896.
Smith, William, *Adventures with My Alpenstock and Carpet Bag*, Rochdale, 1864.

Smyth, Ethel, *Impressions That Remained*, London, 1919.
Smythe, Frank Sydney, *Climbs and Ski-Runs*, London & Edinburgh: Blackwood & Sons, 1929.
Smythe, Frank Sydney, *Again Switzerland*, London: Hodder & Stoughton, 1947.
Smythe, Frank Sydney, *Swiss Winter*, London, 1948.
Somerville, Mary, *Personal Recollections*, London 1874.
Southey, C., *Life and Correspondence of Robert Southey*, London, 1850.
Sowerby, J., 'A Tour in the Alps in 1800', in *Alpine Journal*, 7, 1874-76.
Spindler, R., *Die Alpen in der englischen Literatur und Kunst*, Leipzig, 1932.
Spitteler, Carl, *Der Gotthard,* Frauenfeld, 1897.
Staël-Holstein, Mme A. de, *Lettres sur l'Angleterre*, Paris, 1825.
Staël-Holstein, Mme A. de, *Letters on England*, London, 1830.
Stanhope, P. H., Earl, *Letters from Switzerland*, Karlsruhe, 1834.
Stapfer, Philipp August, *A Picturesque Tour through the Oberland in the Canton of Berne in Switzerland*, London, 1823.
Starke, Marianne, *Travels on the Continent*, London, 1820.
Stephen, Sir Leslie, *The Playground of Europe*, London: Longman, Green, 1871.
Stephen, Sir Leslie, *Life and Letters*, ed. F. W. Maitland, London, 1906.
Stevenson, Robert Louis, *Swiss Notes*, London, 1923.
Stevenson, Robert Louis, *Essays of Travel*, London: Chatto & Windus, 1905.
Story, A. Thomas, *Swiss Life in Town and Country*, London: Geo. Newnes, 1902.
Strutt, Elizabeth, *Domestic Residence in Switzerland*, London, 1842.
Stoye, J. W., *English Travellers Abroad, 1604-1667*, London, 1952.
Stubbs, W. (ed.), *Memorials of St Dunstan*, Rolls series 392, (Sigeric of Canterbury), London, 1874.
Studd, R. G., *A Fortnight in Switzerland*, London, 1951.
Sweeney, J. N., *Switzerland in 1876: A Lecture*, London, 1877.
Syers, Edgar, and Syers, Madge, *The Book of Winter Sports*, London, 1908.
Symonds, John Addington, and Symonds, Margaret, *Our Life in the Swiss Highlands*, London & Edinburgh: A. & C. Black, 1892.
Symonds, Margaret, *Out of the Past*, London, 1925.
Talfourd, Sir Thomas, *Vacation Rambles and Thoughts*, London, 1845.
Tennant, Charles, *A Tour through Parts of . . . Switzerland, . . . in the Years 1821-1822*, London, 1824.
Thompson, Jane Dee, *The Great St Bernard Pass and Hospice and the Life of Saint Bernard de Menthon*, London: Epworth Press, 1929.
Thompson, S., *Swiss Scenery*, London, 1866.
Thompson, William, *Two Journeys through Italy and Switzerland*, London, 1835.
Tissot, Victor, *Unknown Switzerland*, London, 1889.
Tollemache, Beatrix L., *Grisons Incidents in Olden Times*, London, 1891.
Töpffer, Rodolphe, *Premiers voyages en zig-zag*, Paris, 1844.
Töpffer, Rodolphe, *Nouveaux voyages en zig-zag,* Paris, 1854.

Töpffer, Rodolphe, *Derniers voyages en zig-zag*, Geneva, 1910.
Townend, Paul, *Swiss Venture*, London: Robert Hale, 1956.
Trench, Francis, *A Walk round Mont Blanc*, London, 1847.
Treves, Sir Frederick, *The Lake of Geneva*, London: Cassell, 1922.
Trollope, Thomas Adolphus, *Impressions of a Wanderer in Italy, Switzerland, etc.*, London, 1850.
Tschudi, F. von, *Sketches of Nature in the Alps, Translated from the German*, London, 1856.
Tuckett, Elizabeth, *How We Spent the Summer: or, A Voyage en ZigZag in Switzerland and Tyrol with Some Members of the Alpine Club*, London, 1864.
Tuckett, Francis Fox, *A Pioneer in the High Alps*, London, 1920.
Tuckett, Francis Fox, *Hochalpenstudien*, Leipzig, 1873-74.
Tyler, J. F., *The Alpine Passes: The Middle Ages*, London: Oxford U.P., 1930.
Tyndall, Prof. John, *The Glaciers of the Alps*, London, 1860.
Tyndall, Prof. John, *Mountaineering in 1861*, London, 1862.
Tyndall, Prof. John, *Hours of Exercise in the Alps*, London, 1871.
Vial, A. E. Lockington, *Alpine Glaciers*, London, 1952.
Vizard, John, *Narrative of a Tour Through France, Italy and Switzerland*, London, 1872.
Voltaire (François-Marie Arouet), *Letters on England*, trans. Leonard Tancock, London: Penguin, 1980.
Wäber, A., *Descriptions géographiques et récits de voyages et excursions en Suisse*, Berne, 1909.
Walker, J. Hubert, *Mountain Days in the Highlands and Alps*, London: E. Arnold, 1937.
Walker, J. Hubert, *Walking in the Alps*, Edinburgh & London: Oliver & Boyd, 1951.
Wall, Daniel, *Traveller's Guide through Switzerland* (a revision of *Ebel's Guide*), London, 1818.
Walpole, Horace, *Letters*, London, 1846.
Walter, L. Edna, *The Fascination of Switzerland*, London: A. & C. Black, 1912.
Walter, W., *Letters from the Continent*, Edinburgh, 1828.
Waring, Samuel Miller, *The Traveller's Fireside: A Series of Papers on Switzerland, the Alps, etc.*, London, 1819.
Watkins, Thomas, *Travels through Switzerland, Italy, Sicily, etc.*, London, 1794.
Webb, Frank, *Switzerland of the Swiss*, London, 1909.
Weston, Stephen, *A Trimester in France and Switzerland*, London, 1821.
Wherry, George, *Alpine Notes and the Climbing Foot*, Cambridge, 1896.
White, Walter, *To Mont Blanc and Back Again*, London, 1854.
White, Walter, *To Switzerland and Back*, Birmingham, 1870.
Whymper, Edward, *Scrambles amongst the Alps*, London, 1871.
Whymper, Edward, *The Ascent of the Matterhorn*, London, 1880.
Wilkinson, Joshua Lucock, *The Wanderer, or, Anecdotes and Incidents . . . of a Ramble on Foot through France, Germany, and Italy in 1791 and 1793*, London, 1798.

Wilkinson, Bishop T. E., *Twenty Years of Continental Work and Travel*, London, 1906.
Williams, Charles, *The Alps, Switzerland and the North of Italy*, London, 1854.
Williams, Helen Maria, *A Tour in Switzerland: A View of the Present State of Governments and Manners of Those Cantons*, London, 1798.
Williams, Helen Maria, *Eindrücke einer Engländerin auf ihrer Schweizerreise von 1794*, Sarnen, 1919.
Wills, Sir A., *Wanderings among the High Alps*, 2nd ed., London, 1858.
Wills, Sir A., *The Eagle's Nest*, London, 1860.
Wilson, Dr Claude, *Mountaineering*, London, 1893.
Wilson, Dr Claude, *An Epitome of Fifty Years' Climbing*, private distribution, 1933.
Wilson, Francesca M., *Strange Island*, London: Longmans, Green, 1955.
Wilson, Henry Schütz, *Alpine Ascents and Adventures*, London, 1878.
Windham, William, *An Account of the Glacieres or Ice Alps of Savoy*, London, 1744.
Winter, J. B., *From Switzerland to the Mediterranean on Foot*, London, 1922.
Wise, A. T. Tucker, *The Alpine Winter Cure, with Notes on Davos Platz, Wiesen, St Moritz and the Maloja*, London: Baillière, 1884.
Wood, Edith Elmer, *An Oberland Chalet*, London: T. Werner Laurie, 1911.
Wordsworth, Dorothy, *The Journals of Dorothy Wordsworth*, ed. Ernest de Selincourt, London: Macmillan, 1941.
Wordsworth, William, *Descriptive Sketches Taken during a Pedestrian Tour in the Italian, Grison, Swiss and Savoyard Alps*, London, 1793.
Wordsworth, William, *see also* Section C.
Wyttenbach, Jacob Samuel, *Instruction pour les voyageurs qui vont voir les glaciers et les Alpes du Canton de Berne*, 1787.
Yates, Mrs Ashton, *Letters Written during a Journey to Switzerland*, London, 1843.
Yeames, A. H. S., *The Grand Tour of an Elizabethan*, Papers of the British School at Rome, vol. 7., 1914 (Sir Edward Unton with Richard Smith).
Yeo, J. Burney, *Notes of a Season at St Moritz in the Upper Engadine and of a Visit to the Baths of Tarasp*, London, 1870.
Yosy, A., *Switzerland: As Now Divided into Nineteen Cantons*, London, 1815.
Young, Geoffrey Winthrop, *Mountain Craft*, London: Methuen, 1920.
Young, Geoffrey Winthrop, *On High Hills*, London: Methuen, 1927.
Young, Geoffrey Winthrop, *Mountains with a Difference*, London: Eyre & Spottiswoode, 1951.
Young, Geoffrey Winthrop, *see also* Section C.
Young, Eleanor, and Young, Geoffrey Winthrop, *In Praise of Mountains*, London: Frederick Muller, 1948.
Zincke, Revd F. Barham, *A Month in Switzerland*, London, 1873.
Zincke, Revd F. Barham, *Swiss Allmends and a Walk to See Them, Being a Second Month in Switzerland*, London, 1874.
Zincke, Revd F. Barham, *A Walk in the Grisons*, London, 1875.
Zschokke, H., 'Erinnerungen an Karl von Bonstetten', in *Prometheus für Licht und Recht*, Aarau, 1832-1833.

C: CULTURAL, ARTISTIC, SCIENTIFIC AND RELIGIOUS

Adamina, J., *Le réveil religieux dans le canton de Vaud*, Lausanne, 1893.
Agassiz, D., *Sir Francis Bourgeois*, Lausanne, 1937.
Alexander, William Lindsay, *Switzerland and the Swiss Churches*, Glasgow, 1846.
Amstutz, Walter (ed.), *Turner in Switzerland* (text by John Russell and Andrew Wilton), Zurich: De Clivo Press, 1976.
Armattoe, R. E. G., *The Swiss Contribution to Western Civilisation*, Dundalgan Press, 1944.
Arnold, Matthew, *The Poems of Matthew Arnold, 1840-1867*, Oxford, 1909.
Arnold, Matthew, *The Popular Education of France, with Notices of That of Holland and Switzerland*, London, 1861.
Arnold, Matthew, *Schools and Universities on the Continent*, London, 1868.
Arnold, Matthew, *Essays on Criticism*, London: Macmillan, 1889.
Arnold, Matthew, *Letters*, ed. G. H. E. Russell, London, 1895.
Arnold, Thomas, *Life and Correspondence*, ed. A. P. Stanley, London, 1844.
Amiel, Henri-Frédéric, *Amiel's Journal: The Journal Intime of Henri-Frédéric Amiel*, trans. H. Ward, London: Macmillan, 1933.
Bacon, Francis, *The Essays of Francis Bacon, Lord Verulam*, London: Dent, 1904.
Bainbridge, W., *Alpine Lyrics*, London, 1854.
Baker, E. P., 'St Oswald (of Northumbria) and his Church at Zug', in *Archaeologia*, vol. 93, 1949.
Baker, John R., *Abraham Trembley of Geneva, Scientist and Philosopher, 1710-1784*, London: Edward Arnold, 1952.
Barth, Karl, *A Letter to Great Britain from Switzerland*, trans. E. L.H. Gordon and George Hill, London: Sheldon Press, 1941.
Barwell, Louisa Mary, *Letters from Hofwyl on the Institutions of De Fellenberg*, London, 1842.
(Basel), *Die Matrikel der Universität Basel*, ed. H. G. Wackenagel, Basel, 1956.
Batey, Mavis, 'An English View of Switzerland: Swiss Cottages in Great Britain', in *Country Life*, 161, 17 Feb 1977.
Beck, Marcel, *Swiss Books through Five Centuries*, catalogue of the historical section of 'Books in Switzerland Exhibition' at the Suffolk Galleries, London, Zurich, 1946.
Becker, George, *La musique en Suisse*, Geneva, 1847.
Beddoes, Thomas Lovell, *The Letters*, ed. Edmund Gosse, London, 1894.
Beddoes, Thomas Lovell, *The Complete Works of Thomas Lovell Beddoes*, ed. Edmund Gosse, London: Fanfrolico Press, 1928.
Bell, C. F., and Girtin, Thomas, *The Drawings and Sketches of John Robert Cozens*, Walpole Society, 1934-35, Oxford, 1935.
Belloc, Hilaire, *see* Section B.
Bennet, Edward Armstrong, *Carl Gustav Jung*, London: Barrie & Rockliff, 1961.

Bertschinger, Max, *John Ruskin und die Schweiz*, Berne, 1943.
Betteridge, H. T., 'Notes on A. von Haller', in *Modern Language Review*, Jul-Oct 1951.
Bettex, Gustave, and Guillon, Edward, *Les Alpes suisses dans la littérature et dans l'art*, 1915.
Beza, Theodore, *The Judgement of a Most Reverend and Learned Man from Beyond the Seas concerning a Threefold Order of Bishops, Translated from the Latin by John Field*, 1580.
Beza, Theodore, *see also* Donaldson.
Bèze, Théodore de, *see* Beza.
Bibby, Cyril, *Scientist Extraordinary: The Life and Scientific Work of Thomas Henry Huxley (1825-1895)*, Oxford: Pergamon Press, 1972.
Bircher, Martin, and Straumann, H., *Shakespeare und die deutsche Schweiz bis zum Beginn des 19. Jahrhunderts*, Berne: Francke Verlag, 1971.
Blanke, Fritz, *Columban und Gallus, Urgeschichte des schweizerischen Christentums*, Zurich, 1940.
Bodley, Sir Thomas, *The Life of Sir Thomas Bodley . . . Written by Himselfe*, facsimile of the 1647 edition, Oxford: Bodleian Library, 1983.
Boesch, Emile, *Albrecht von Hallers Lebenslauf*, Berne, 1877.
Boesch, Paul, 'The Swiss Stained Glass Panels in Wragby (Nostell) Church', in *Yorks. Archeological Journal*, 32, pt. 128, 1936.
Bonnard, G. (ed.), *Le journal de Gibbon à Lausanne, 1763-1764*, Lausanne, 1945.
Booth, C., *The Salvation Army in Switzerland*, London, 1883.
Boswell, James, *Boswell on the Grand Tour: Germany and Switzerland, 1764*. London: Heinemann, 1953.
Bourgeaud, Charles, 'Cartwright and Melville at the University of Geneva', in *The American Historical Review*, vol. 5, 1900.
Bourgeaud, Charles, *Histoire de l'université de Genève: L'Académie de Calvin, 1559-1798*, Geneva: Georg, 1900.
Bourgeaud, Charles, 'Le 'vrai portrait' de John Knox', in *Bulletin de la Société de l'Histoire du Protestantisme français*, Geneva, 1935.
Bowden, John, *Karl Barth*, London: SCM Press, 1971.
Bowles, William Lisle, *The Sorrows of Switzerland: A Poem*, London & Bath, 1801.
Bowles, William Lisle, *The Poetical Works of William Lisle Bowles*, Edinburgh, 1855.
Bräker, Ulrich, *Das Shakespeare – Büchlein des armen Mannes im Toggenburg vom Jahr 1780 (Nach der Original-Handschrift mitgetheilt von Dr Ernst Götzinger – 'Etwas über William Shakespeares Schauspiele von einem armen ungelehrten Weltbürger, der das Glück genoss, denselben zu lesen: Anno 1780)*, Jahrbuch der deutschen Shakespeare-Gesellschaft. Jahrg. 12. 1877.
Bridges, John, Bishop of Oxford, *A Defence of Government Established in the Church of Englande . . . Answering Also to the Arguments of Calvin, Beza, etc.*, 1587.
Brontë, Charlotte, *The Professor*, London: J. M. Dent, 1910.

Brookner, Anita, *Hotel du Lac*, London: Jonathan Cape, 1984.
Brougham, Henry, Lord, *Third Report from the Select Committee on Education, etc.*, London, 1818.
Brown, H. F., *John Addington Symonds: A Biography*, London, 1895.
Browning, Robert, *Paracelsus*, London, 1835.
Browning, Robert, *La Saisiaz*, London, 1878.
Browning, Robert, *Letters of Robert Browning*, ed. T. L. Hood, London, 1933.
Brydges, Sir Samuel Egerton (ed.), *The Anglo-Genevan Critical Journal for 1831*, Geneva, 1831.
Buchanan, Mary, *The Children's Village: Pestalozzi*, London: Vail, 1951.
Budé, Eugène de, *Jean Diodati*, Lausanne, 1869.
Bullinger, Heinrich, *De Scripturae Sanctae Authoritate, Certitudine, Firmitate et Absoluta Perfectione, Deus Episcoporum . . .*, Zurich: Froschauer, 1538.
Bullinger, Heinrich, *The Christian State of Matrimonye: The Orygenall of Holy Wedlock: When, Where, How and of Whom it was Instituted and Ordeyned . . .* Myles Coverdale, 1541.
Bullinger, Heinrich, *Sermonum Decades*, Zurich: Froschauer, 1549.
Bullinger, Heinrich, *To the Reverende Fathers in Christe, D. Rob. Horne, Bishop of Winchester, D. Ed. Grindal, Bishop of London, etc., to Maister N. and M. . . . Whether It Be Mortall Sinne to Transgresse Civil Laws*, 1566.
Bullinger, Heinrich, *A Confutation of the Pope's Bull published More Than Two Yeres Agoe against Elizabeth the Most Gracious Queene of England, Fraunce and Ireland, and against the Noble Realme of England: Together with a Defence of the Sayd True Christian Queene, and of the Whole Realme of England*, London: John Day, 1572.
Bullinger, Heinrich, *Commonplaces of Christian Religion, Compendiously Written, by Master H. Bullinger, and Translated into English by Ionn Stockwood*, London, 1572.
Bullinger, Heinrich, *Fiftie Godlie and Learned Sermons, Divided into Five Decades, Conteyning the Chiefe and Principall Pointers of Christian Religion . . . Translated out of the Latin into English by H. I., Student in Divinitie*, 3 vols., London: Ralph Newberrie, 1577.
Bullinger, Heinrich, *Two Epystles, One of Henry Bullinger (Dated Feb. 18, 1548) Wyth the Consent of All the Learned Men of the Church of Tygury: Another of Johan. Calvyne, Chefe Preacher of the Church of Geneve: Whether It Be Lauful for a Chrysten Man to Communicate or Be Partaker of the Masse of the Papysts, without Offending God and Hys Neyghbour or Not*, London: Robt. Stoughton, 1548.
Bullinger, Heinrich, *The Decades of H. Bullinger*, Cambridge, 1849-52.
Burnet, Gilbert, *The History of the Reformation in the Church of England*, London, 1679; Oxford: Clarendon Press, 1865.
Burney, Charles, *The Present State of Music in France and Italy*, London, 1771.
Burney, Charles, *Music, Men and Manners in France and Italy, 1770*, ed. H. Edmund Poole, London: The Folio Society, 1969.
Burns, James H., *Scottish Churchmen and the Council of Basle*, Glasgow: Burns, 1962.

Byron, Lady, *What de Fellenberg Has Done for Education*, London, 1836.
Byron, Lord, *The Prisoner of Chillon and Other Poems*, London, 1816.
Byron, Lord, *Manfred: A Dramatic Poem*, London, 1817.
Byron, Lord, *Childe Harold's Pilgrimage*, London, 1819.
Byse, F., *John Milton on the Continent*, London, 1902.
Calvin, Jean, *The Answer and Judgment of Master Ionn Calvin . . . Touching the Book of England After He Had Perused the Same Translated Faithfully out of the Latin by Mr Whittingham (22 Jan. 1555)*, 1660.
Calvin, Jean, *The Answer and Judgment of Mr John Calvin . . . Concerning the English Book of Common Prayer After He Had Perus'd the Same. To . . . Mr John Knox and Mr William Whittingham . . ., (22 Jan. 1555)*, n.d.
Calvin, Jean, *Lettres Anglaises 1548-1561, textes choisis, transcrits et présentés par Albert-Marie Schmidt*, Paris, 1959.
Cameron, James Kerr, *The First Book of Discipline*, Edinburgh: The Saint Andrew Press, 1972.
Cameron, James Kerr, *Letters of John Johnston (c1565-1611) and Robert Howie (c1565-c1645)*, Edinburgh: Oliver & Boyd, 1963.
Cameron, James Kerr, 'The Swiss and the Covenant', in *The Scottish Tradition: Essays in Honour of R. G. Cant*, ed. G. W. S. Barrow, Scottish Academic Press, 1974.
Campbell, Thomas, *Poems*, London: Aldine ed., 1875.
Canning, Stratford (Viscount Stratford de Redcliffe), *Shadows of the Past, in Verse*, London: Macmillan, 1866.
Chaix, Paul, *Recherches sur l'imprimerie à Genève de 1550 à 1564*, Geneva: Librarie E. Droz, 1954.
Charleston, B. M., 'The English Linguistic Invasion of Switzerland', in *English Studies*, 40, August 1959.
Chesterfield, Earl of, *Letters to His Son*, London, 1774.
Chicoteau, Marcel, 'La Suisse alémanique et les pèlerins anglais de Joseph Addison à Wordsworth', in *Comparative Literary Studies*, 2, 1941.
Clark, J. M., *The Abbey of St Gall*, Cambridge, 1926.
Clark, W. S., 'Milton and the Villa Diodati', in *Review of English Studies*, 1935.
Clerc, Jean Louis, *L'Enchanteur Carabosse (J. J. Heidegger)*, Lausanne, 1942.
Coburg, Beatrice von, *Switzerland: Selected Publications about Switzerland Written in English*, Berne: Swiss National Library, 1972.
Cockburn, James, *Views to Illustrate the Route of the Simplon*, London, 1822.
Cockburn, James, *Swiss Scenery from the Drawings of Major Cockburn*, London, 1820.
Coleridge, Samuel Taylor, *The Poetical Works of S. T. Coleridge*, London: Pickering, 1829.
Collins, John Churton, *Voltaire, Montesquieu and Rousseau in England*, London: Everleigh Nash, 1908.
Collins, William, *The Poetical Works*, Glasgow, 1777.
Constant de Rebecque, Henri-Benjamin, *Le cahier rouge*, Paris, 1907.
Cook, Sir Edward Tyas, *Life of John Ruskin*, London: Geo. Allen, 1911.

Courtois, Louis Jean, *Le séjour de Rousseau en Angleterre*, Lausanne, 1911.
Courvoisier, Jacques, *Zwingli: A Reformed Theologian – Lectures*, London: Epworth Press, 1964.
Crivelli, Aldo, *Artisti Ticinesi in Europa*, Locarno, 1970.
Cross, J. W., *George Eliot's Life as Related in Her Letters and Journals*, Edinburgh & London, 1885.
Dale, William, *Tschudi, the Harpsichord Maker*, London: Constable, 1913.
Dangerfield, Elma, *Byron and the Romantics in Switzerland, 1816*, London: Ascent Books, 1978.
D'Arblay, Fanny Burney, Mme, *The Diary and Letters of Madame D'Arblay*, ed. Austin Dobson, London, 1904.
Davenant, Sir William, *The Works of Sir William D'Avenant, Kt . . . . .*, London, 1673.
Davis, Thomas Osborne, 'William Tell and the Genius of Switzerland', in *Poems*, Dublin, 1846.
Deakin, H. C., *The Deliverance of Switzerland: A Dramatic Poem*, London, 1830.
de Beer, Sir Gavin, 'Meshes of the Byronic Net in Switzerland', in *English Studies*, 43, October 1962.
Defoe, Daniel, *Robinson Crusoe*, London, 1719.
de Pange, Victor, *Mme de Staël and Her English Correspondents*, Oxford, 1955.
Devonshire, Georgiana Cavendish, Duchess of, *The Passage of the Mountain of Saint Gotthard: A Poem*, London: Prosper, 1802.
Dickens, Charles, *The Letters of Charles Dickens, Edited by His Sister-in-Law and His Eldest Daughter*, 3 vols., London: Chapman & Hall, 1880.
Dickens, Charles, *see also* Forster, House and Storey.
Dickens, Charles, and Collins, Wilkie, *No Thoroughfare: A Play*, London, 1867.
Dixon, R. W., *History of the Church of England*, London, 1878-1902 (vol. 3).
Donaldson, Gordon, *Lord Chancellor Glamis and Theodore Beza*, Miscellany of the Scottish Historical Society, vol. 8, 3rd series, Edinburgh, 1951.
Donner, Henry W., *Thomas Lovell Beddoes: The Making of a Poet*, Oxford: Blackwell, 1935.
Doumergue, Émile, *La Genève Calviniste*, Lausanne, 1905.
Doyle, Sir Arthur Conan, 'The Final Problem', in *The Memoirs of Sherlock Holmes*, London: G. Newnes, 1894.
Ducros, Louis, *Images of the Grand Tour . . . 1748-1810*, Geneva: Editions de Tricorne, 1985.
Dudley, Sir H. Bate, *Airs, Duets, Trios, Glees, Chorusses in the Opera of the Travellers in Switzerland*, London, 1794.
Du Pasquier, Louis Gustave, *Leonard Euler et ses amis*, Paris: Librairie Scientifique. J. Hermann, 1927.
Du Pasquier, Marcel, *La Suisse romande: terre d'acceuil et d'échanges*, Lausanne, 1965.
Duppa, Baldwin Francis, *Education of the Peasantry in England (on Mr de Fellenberg's Lines)*, London, 1834.

Durkan, John, and Kirk, James, *The University of Glasgow (1451-1577)*. Univ. of Glasgow Press, 1977.
Edgeworth, Maria, *see also* Hare.
Edgeworth Maria, and Edgeworth, Richard Lovell, *Practical Education*, 2 vols., London, 1798.
Egli, Prof. Emil, *Kirchengeschichte der Schweiz bis auf Karl den Grossen*, Zurich, 1893.
Egli, Prof. Emil, *Die christlichen Inschriften der Schweiz vom 4.-9. Jahrhundert*, Zurich, 1895.
Egli, Prof. Emil, *Schweizerische Reformationsgeschichte*, Zurich, 1910.
Egli, Prof. Emil, *Heinrich Bullingers Diarium der Jahre 1504-1574*, Zurich, 1904.
Eliot, George (Mary Ann Evans), *Middlemarch*, London, 1872.
Eliot, George, *see also* Cross.
Emblen, D. L., *Peter Mark Roget*, London: Longman, 1970.
Engel, Claire Éliane, 'George Keate et la Suisse', in *Zeitschrift für schweizerische Geschichte*, 1948.
Engel, Claire Éliane, *Byron et Shelley en Suisse et en Savoie*, Chambéry, 1930.
Engel, Claire Éliane, *John Strange et la Suisse*, Aarau, 1949.
'English Schoolmaster, An', *Hours in a Swiss Classroom*, London, 1870.
Escarpit, Robert, *L'Angleterre dans l'oeuvre de Mme de Staël*, Paris, 1934.
Ervine, St John G., *God's Soldier: General William Booth*, 2 vols., London: Heinemann, 1934.
Eyles, V. A., *Louis Albert Necker of Geneva and his geological map of Scotland*, Transactions of the Geological Society, Edinburgh, vol 14, 1948.
Farner, Oskar, *Die Kirchenpatrozien des Kantons Graubünden*, Munich, 1925.
Farner, Oskar, *Zwingli, the Reformer*, trans. D. G. Slar, London: Lutterworth Press, 1952.
Fatio de Duillier, Nicolas, *N. Facii Duillerii Neutonus Ecologa*, ?Ghent, 1728.
Federmann, Arnold, *Johann Heinrich Füssli, Dichter und Maler*, Zurich & Leipzig, 1927.
Feist, Hans, *Ewiges England: Dichtung aus sieben Jahrhunderten von Chaucer bis Eliot*, Zurich, Verlag Amstutz, Herdeg, 1944.
Finberg, A. J., *Life of Joseph Mallord William Turner R.A.*, Oxford, 1939.
Flecker, J. Elroy, *Some Letters from Abroad, 1910-15*, London, 1930.
Fleig, Hans, *Geleitwort zu Miltons 'Rede für die Pressfreiheit und gegen die Zensur'*, Basel, 1944.
Fleming, Ian, *On Her Majesty's Secret Service*, London: Jonathan Cape, 1963.
Flood, John L. (ed.), *Modern Swiss Literature: Unity and Diversity*, papers from a symposium held in London, March 1984, London: Oswald Wolff, 1985.
Forbes, Prof. J. D., *Biographical Account of L.-A. Necker*, Edinburgh, 1863.
Forsberg, Roberta J., *Mme de Staël and the English*, New York, 1967.
Forster, John, *Life of Dickens*, London, 1872-4.
Fosca, François, *Jean-Etienne Liotard*, Lausanne & Paris, 1956.
Friedrich, Dr Roger, 'An English School in the Swiss Alps: Aiglon College', in *Swiss Review of World Affairs*, February 1972.
Freshfield, D., *Horace-Bénédict de Saussure*, Geneva, 1924.

Frommel, G., *Protestantisme dans la Suisse romande,* Lausanne, 1900.
Froude, J. A., *The Influence of the Reformation on the Scottish Character,* Edinburgh, 1865.
Fry, Elizabeth, *Memoirs of the Life of Elizabeth Fry: Edited by Two of Her Daughters,* 2 vols., London, 1848.
Fueter, Edouard, *Grosse schweizer Forscher,* Zurich, 1941.
Funke, Otto, *Die Schweiz und die englische Literatur: ein Vortrag,* Berne, 1937.
Funke, Otto, *Switzerland and English Literature,* 2 vols., Berne: Franckl, 1938-40.
Furner, Oskar, *Zwingli, the Reformer: His Life and Work,* Hamden, Conn: Archon Books, 1968.
Fuseli, Henry, *see* Füssli, Johann Heinrich.
Füssli, Johann Heinrich, *Remarks on the Writings and Conduct of J.-J. Rousseau,* London: T. Cadell, 1767.
Füssli, Johann Heinrich, *Lectures on Painting, Delivered at the Royal Academy, March 1801,* London, 1801.
Füssli, Johann Heinrich, 'The Lectures of Henry Fuseli', in *Lectures on Painting by the Royal Academicians,* ed. R. N. Wornum, London, 1848.
Garrett, Christina H., *The Marian Exiles: A Study of the Origins of Elizabethan Puritanism,* Cambridge, 1938.
Gautter, Thomas, *Johannes von Müllers Begegnung mit England: Ein Beitrag zur Geschichte der Anglophilie im späten 18. Jahrhundert,* Basel, 1967.
Gelpke, E. F., *Die christliche Sagengeschichte der Schweiz,* Berne, 1862.
(Geneva), *The English Church in Geneva: 'Le Livre des Anglais 1555-1560' and Continuation from the Registers of the Council of State 1560-1814 and 1853,* Geneva: English Printing Office, 1881.
(Geneva), *An Apology for the English Dissenters: Several Letters from the Pastors of the Church of Geneva to the Archbishop of Canterbury, the Bishop of London and the University of Oxford, with Their Answers . . .,* London, 1707.
(Geneva), *The Geneva Ballad, to the Tune of Forty-Eight: A Satire against the Puritans,* London, 1674.
(Geneva), *An Answer to the Geneva Ballad (in Verse),* London, 1674.
Gessner, Salomon, *The Death of Abel,* (from the German by Mary Collyer), *'New Idylls', or Pastoral Poems,* (translated W. Hooper), with *'A Letter to M. Fuslin on Landscape Painting',* London: T. Heptinstall, 1797.
Gibbon, Edward, *Memoirs of My Life,* ed. from Mss., Georges A. Bonnard, London 1962; ed. Betty Radice, London: Penguin, 1984.
Gibbon, Edward, *Private Letters of Edward Gibbon (1753-1794),* ed. R. E. Prothero, London, 1896.
Giddey, Ernest, *'L'Angleterre dans la vie intellectuelle de la Suisse romande au 18e siècle,* Lausanne: Bibliothèque Historique Vaudoise, 1974.
Glover, Richard, *The Poetical Works of Richard Glover,* London, 1806.
Godley, A. D., *Second Strings: Poems,* London, 1902.
Goldsmith, Oliver, *The Traveller: or, A Prospect of Society,* London, 1765.
Good, James Isaac, *History of the Swiss Reformed Church since the Reformation,* Philadelphia, 1913.

Graf, Emil, *Die Aufnahme der englischen und amerikanischen Literatur in der deutschen Schweiz von 1800-1830,* Zurich, 1951.

Graham, J., 'Lavater's Physiognomy in England', in *Journal of the History of Ideas,* no. 22, October 1961.

Gray, Thomas, 'Three Letters from Gray to Carl von Bonstetten dated 1770', in F. von Matthieson, *Letters Written from Various Parts of the Continent,* 1799.

Gray, Thomas, *Letters of Thomas Gray,* London, 1819-21.

Green, John Alfred, *The Life and Work of Pestalozzi,* London, 1913.

Gribble, Francis, *The Lake of Geneva and Its Literary Landmarks,* London: A. & C. Black, 1909.

Grütter, Dr Max, *Der Bund: ein Rückblick bei Vollendung des Hundertsten Jahrganges, 1850-1950,* Berne, 1950.

Guggisberg, Kurt, *Philipp Emmanuel von Fellenberg und sein Erziehungsstaat,* Berne, 1953.

Gulley, Frank, *The Influence of Heinrich Bullinger and the Tigurine Tradition upon the English Church in the Sixteenth Century,* Nashville: Vanderbuilt Univ. Press, 1961.

Guyan, Walter, and Stieffl, Otto, *Schaffhauser Kulturgeschichte,* Schaffhausen: Verlag Alfred Meili, 1969.

Haldane, A., *Memoirs of the Lives of Robert Haldane of Airthrey and of His Brother James Alexander Haldane,* London, 1852.

Haldane, Robert, *Letter to M. J. J. Chenevière: Occasioned by His 'Summary of the Theological Controversies Which of Late Years Have Agitated the City of Geneva', Published in the Monthly Repository . . . ,* Edinburgh, 1824.

Haller, Albrecht von, *Gedichte,* ed. Ludwig Hirzel, Frauenfeld, 1882.

Hardy, C. F., *J. L. Agasse, peintre genevois (1767-1849),* Geneva, 1921.

Hardy, Thomas, 'Lausanne: In Gibbon's Old Garden', and 'Zermatt: To the Matterhorn', in *The Complete Poems . . . ,* ed. James Gibson, London: Macmillan, 1976.

Hare, A. J., *Life and Letters of Maria Edgeworth,* London, 1894.

Harraden, Beatrice, *Ships That Pass in the Night,* London, 1893.

Hausermann, H. W., *The Genevese Background: Studies of Shelley, Francis Danby, Maria Edgeworth, Ruskin, Meredith and Joseph Conrad in Geneva,* London, 1952.

Hay, Marie, *The Story of a Swiss Poet: A Study of Gottfried Keller's Life and Works,* Berne: Wyss, 1920.

Heidegger, Johann Jakob, *Heydegger's Letter (in Verse) to the Bishop of London (Concerning a Sermon Preached by the Latter Condemnatory of Masquerades),* London: S. N. Cox, 1724.

Heidegger, Johann Jakob, see also Clerc and Vetter.

Hemans, Felicia Dorothea, *The League of the Alps,* Boston, 1826.

Hemans, Felicia Dorothea, *The Works of Mrs Hemans,* London, 1839.

Henderson, G. D., *The Founding of Marischal College, Aberdeen,* Aberdeen University Studies, no. 123, Aberdeen, 1947.

Herking, Marie L., *Charles Victor de Bonstetten, 1745-1832: sa vie, ses oeuvres,* Lausanne, 1921.

Herzog, E., 'Internationale kirchliche Beziehungen der christkatholischen Kirche der Schweiz', in *Internationale kirchliche Zeitschrift*, Jan-Mar 1919.
Heugh, Hugh, *Notices of the State of Religion in Geneva and Belgium*, Glasgow, 1844.
Heyer, Théophile, *Notice sur la colonie anglaise établie à Genève de 1555 a 1560*, Societié d' Histoire et d'Archéologie de Genève, yol. 9, 1855.
Hingeston-Randolf, F. C., (ed.), *Register of John de Grandisson, Bishop of Exeter*, London: George Bell & Sons, 1894-99.
Holcroft, Thomas, *Lavater's Essays on Physiognomy*, London, 1885.
Holman, Henry, *Pestalozzi: An Account of His Life and Work*, London: Longmans, 1908.
Holzer, E., *Das Bild Englands in der deutschen Romantik*, (Diss.), Berne, 1951.
Hopkins, Gerard Manley, *Notebooks*, ed. H. House, Oxford, 1937.
Horizon, Swiss Number, vol. 13, London, Feb 1946.
House, M., and Storey, G. (edd.), *The Letters of Charles Dickens*, Pilgrim Edition, Oxford,: Clarendon Press, 1965.
Huchoun of the Awle Ryale, *Morte Athure*, ed. Erik Bjorkmann, Heidelberg, 1915.
Hume, David, *A Concise and Genuine Account of the Dispute between Mr Hume and Mr Rousseau . . .*, trans. J. B. A. Suard, London, 1766.
Hume Brown, P., *John Knox: A Biography*, London, 1895.
Hurstfield, Joel, (ed.), *The Reformation Crisis*, London, 1965.
Hutchison, Sidney C., *The History of the Royal Academy, 1768-1986*, London: Robert Royce, 1986.
Hutton, James, *Memoirs of James Hutton*, ed. Daniel Benham, London, 1856.
Huxley, Leonard, *Thomas Henry Huxley: Life and Letters*, London: Macmillan, 1900.
Jackson, S. M., *Huldreich Zwingli. The Reformer of German Switzerland, 1484-1531*, London: Putnam, 1901.
James, Henry, *Daisy Miller*, London: Macmillan, 1879.
James, Norman G. Brett, *The Charm of Switzerland: An Anthology*, London: Methuen, 1910.
Jones, H. Bence, *Life and Letters of Michael Faraday*, London, 1870.
Keate, George, *The Alps: A Poem*, London, 1763.
Keate, George, *An Epistle (in Verse) to Angelica Kauffmann*, London, 1781.
Keate, George, *The Poetical Works of George Keate*, London, 1781.
Keller, –, *La chanson de L'Escalade de Genève*, Geneva, 1931.
Keller, F., 'Bilder und Schriftzüge in den irischen Mss. der schweiz. Bibliotheken', in *Mitteilungen der Antiquar. Gesellschaft*, Zürich, 7, 1853.
Kelly, J. A., *England and the Englishman in German Literature of the Eighteenth Century*, New York, 1921.
Kelly, John, *The Life of John Dollond, F.R.S.*, London, 1808.
Kingdon, Robert M., *Geneva and the Consolidation of the French Protestant Movement, 1564-1572*, Geneva, 1967.
Kirk, James, *The Influence of Calvinism on the Scottish Reformation*, Recs. Scottish Church History Society, 18, 1974.
Kirk, James, *see also* Durkan.

Knowles, James Sheridan, *William Tell: A Play in Five Acts*, London, 1825.
Knowles, John, *The Life and Writings of Henry Fusely*, 3 vols., London, 1831.
Knox, John, *History of the Reformation in Scotland*, ed. W. C. Dickinson, 2 vols., London, 1949.
Koenig, E. G., *John Ruskin und die Schweiz*, Berne, 1943.
Kressner, Helmut, *Schweizer Ursprünge des anglikanischen Staatskirchentums*, Schriften des Vereins für Reformationsgesch., no. 170. Jahrg. 59, Gütersloh, 1953.
Kuhns, Oscar, *Switzerland: Its Scenery, History and Literary Associations*, New York, 1910.
Lamb, Sir W. R. M., *The Royal Academy*, London: Bell, 1951.
Landon, Letitia Elizabeth, 'The Castle of Chillon', in *Poetical Works*, London, 1839.
Lang, Paul, *Helvetic Bibliography of Works Written in English, 1580-1922*, London, 1923.
Lätt, Dr Arnold, *Intellectual Relations between Switzerland and Great Britain*, Delémont, 1920.
Lätt, Dr Arnold, 'Cultural Relations between Switzerland and England', in *Journal of the Royal Society of Arts*, 3 Sept 1946.
Liddiard, William, *The Legend of Einsidlin*, London, 1829.
Lindsay, J. M., *Gottfried Keller: Life and Works*, London: Oswald Wolff, 1968.
Locker-Lampson, Frederick, *Reminiscences of Tennyson in Switzerland*, London, 1869.
Löhrer, Alfred, 'Pestalozzi in England', in *Schweiz. Pädag. Zeitschrift*, June 1924.
Löhrer, Hans, *Die Schweiz im Spiegel englischer Literatur, 1849-1875*, Zurich, 1952.
Lory, G., *Voyage pittoresque de l'Oberland bernois*, Paris, 1852.
Luck, James Murray, *Science in Switzerland*, New York: Columbia U.P., 1967.
Lunn, Arnold, *Switzerland in English Prose and Poetry*, London: Eyre & Spottiswoode, 1947.
Lunn, Arnold, 'The Wordsworths and Switzerland', in *Alpine Journal*, May 1944.
Lupton, Lewis F., *A History of the Geneva Bible . . .*, 5 vols., London: Fauconberg Press, 1966-71.
Lütolf, Alois, *Die Glaubensboten der Schweiz vor St Gallus*, Lucerne, 1871.
Lynch, Dr Michael, 'The Origins of Edinburgh's "Toun College"', in *Innes Review*, 33, 1982.
McCrie, Thomas, *Andrew Melville*, Edinburgh: William Blackwood, 2nd ed., 1856.
Macdonald, Isobel Hay, *The Buried Self: A Background to the Poems of Matthew Arnold, 1848-51*, London: Peter Davies, 1949.
Mackenzie, William, *The Swiss Patriots, and Other Poems*, London, 1817.
Macphail, J.H., 'Blake and Switzerland: The Influence of Swiss Thinkers upon Him', in *Modern Language Review*, April 1943.

Maddison, R.E.W., *Life of the Honourable Robert Boyle, F.R.S.*, London: Taylor & Francis, 1969.
Mallett, Sir Bernard, *Mallet du Pan and the French Revolution*, London: Longmans, 1902.
Mallet-Dupan, Jacques François, *Mercure britannique . . .*, London, 1798.
Mangenel, Ernest, *Léman vu par les peintres*, Lausanne: Eds. Baconnière, 1945.
Marcou, J., *Life, Letters and Works of Jean Louis Rodolphe Agassiz*, New York, 1896.
Martin, Charles, *Les Protestants anglais réfugiés à Genève au temps de Calvin, 1555-1560*, Geneva, 1915.
Martin, Charles, *La famille Stafford à Genève: son conflit avec Calvin, 1556*, Geneva, 1917.
Mason, A.E.W., *Running Water*, London & Glasgow: Collins, 1910.
Mason, Eudo C., *The Mind of Henry Fuseli: Selections from His Writings*, London: Routledge & Kegan Paul, 1951.
Matile, G.-A., 'Saint Guillaume, ses autels, sa chapelle, son portrait', in *Musée Historique de Neuchâtel et Valangin*, 3.
Maugham, W. Somerset, *Ashenden*, London: Heinemann, 1928.
Maxfield, Mildred E., *Studies in Modern Romansch poetry in the Engadine*, Cambridge, Mass., 1938.
Maxwell, J.C., 'Wordsworth and the Subjugation of Switzerland', in *Modern Language Review*, no. 65, Jan 1970.
Mayo, Charles, *Memoir of Pestalozzi*, London, 1828.
Mayo, Elizabeth, *Lessons on Objects: As Given in a Pestalozzian School at Cheam, Surrey*, London, 1831.
Medwin, T., 'Hazlitt in Switzerland', in *Fraser's Magazine*, 19, 1839.
Melville, Andrew, 'Melville's Panegyric on Geneva', in *Epitaphum Jacobi Lindesii, Qui Obiit Genevae, 17 cal. Jul. 1580 (delitiae poet.scot. 2, 123)*, quoted in McCrie's *Life* of Andrew Melville, see above.
Melville, James, *Autobiography and Diary of James Melville*, Edinburgh: Woodrow Society, 1842.
Melville, Lewis, *Life and Letters of William Beckford*, London: Heinemann, 1910.
Meredith, George, *The Adventures of Harry Richmond*, London, 1871.
Meredith, George, *The Amazing Marriage*, London, 1895.
Merz, Walter, *Englische Flüchtlinge in Aarau, 1557-1559*, Berne, 1900.
Meyer, André, *English Churches in Switzerland*, Zeitschrift Archäologie und Kunstsgeschichte, vol. 29, 1972.
Meyer, Peter, *Art in Switzerland*, London: Nicholson & Watson, 1946.
Mihles, Samuel, *Dr A Haller's Physiology . . .*, London, 1754.
Milton, John, *Complete Poetry and Selected Prose*, ed. E.H. Visiak, London: The Nonesuch Press, 1948, including: 'Ad Carolum Diodatum: Elegia Prima', 1626; 'Ad Carolum Diodatum: Elegia Sexta', 1629; 'Canzone: Diodati (e te'l dirò. . .)', c. 1630; 'On the Late Massacher in Piemont', 1655.
Montgomery, James, *The Wanderer of Switzerland*, London, 1806.
More, L. T., *Isaac Newton*, London: Constable, 1962.

More, Sir Thomas, *De Optimo Reipublicae Statu, deque Nova Insula Utopia*, 3rd ed., Basel, 1518.
More, Sir Thomas, *The Utopia of Sir Thomas More*, London: G. Bell & Sons, 1910.
Morell, J.R., *A Scientific Guide to Switzerland*, London, 1867.
Morland, Sir Samuel, *History of the Evangelical Churches of the Valleys of Piemont . . . etc.*, London, 1658.
Mosheim, Johann Lorenz von, *An Ecclesiastical History*, vol. 6, London, 1811.
Murray, Hugh, *The Swiss Emigrants: A Tale*, London, 1804.
Natan, Alex. (ed.), *Swiss Men of Letters: Twelve Literary Essays*, London: Oswald Wolff, 1970.
Nazelle, J., *Isaac Casaubon: sa vie et son temps (1559-1614)*, Paris, 1897.
Needham, John Turberville, *Observations des hauteurs faites avec le baromètre au mois d'Aoust 1751 sur une partie des Alpes*, Berne, 1760.
Nicolson, Hon. Sir Harold, *Benjamin Constant*, London: Constable, 1949.
Noel, Baptist Wrothesley, *The History of the Formation of the Free Church of the Canton of Vaud*, YMCA lectures, London, 1848.
Oppé, A.P., *Francis Towne, Landscape Painter*, Walpole Society, 8, Oxford, 1920.
Osborn, Annie M., *Rousseau and Burke: A Study of the Idea of Liberty in Eighteenth Century Political Thought*, London: Oxford U.P., 1940.
Owen, John, *Travels into Different Parts of Europe in the Years 1791 and 1792*, London, 1796.
Owen, John, *History of the Origin . . . of the British and Foreign Bible Society*, London, 1816.
Pagel, Walter, *Paracelsus: An Introduction to Philosophical Medicine in the Era of the Renaissance*, Basel & New York, 1958.
Pange, Comtesse J. de, *Le mystérieux voyage de Necker en Angleterre, 1766*, Paris, 1948.
Pange, Victor de, *Madame de Staël and Her English Correspondents*, Oxford, 1955.
Pange, Victor de, *Madame de Staël et le Duc de Wellington: 'Correspondance Inédite', 1815-1817*, Paris, 1962.
Pange, Victor de, 'Le rêve anglais de Mme de Staël', in *Versailles*, nos. 31 & 32, 1967.
Parker Society (Revd Hastings Robinson, ed.), *Original Letters Relative to the English Reformation, Written during the Reign of King Henry VIII, King Edward VI and Queen Mary, Chiefly from the Archives of Zurich; Epistolae Tigurinae in Translation*, Cambridge, 1846.
Parker Society (Revd Hastings Robinson, ed.), *The Zurich Letters: The Correspondence of Several English Bishops and Others, with Some of the Helvetical Reformers, during the Reign of Queen Elizabeth*, Cambridge, 1842-45.
Pattison, M., *Isaac Casaubon, 1559-1614*, London, 1875.
Pearson, Scott, *Thomas Cartwright and Elizabethan Puritanism*, Cambridge, 1925.

Percy, Lord Eustace, *John Knox,* London: Hodder & Stoughton, 1937.
Pestalozzi, Johann Heinrich, *Letters on Early Education: Addressed to J.P. Greaves,* London, 1827.
Pevsner, Nikolaus, *The Englishness of English Art,* London: Penguin, 1984.
Piaget, Arthur, *Othon de Grandson,* Lausanne, 1951.
Pianzola, Maurice, *Genève et ses peintres,* Geneva: Bonvent, n.d.
Pictet, Marc-Auguste, with Maurice, F.G., and Pictet, C., *Bibliothèque Britannique,* Geneva, various issues from 1796 to 1816.
Pictet, Marc-Auguste, with Maurice, F.G., and Pictet, C., *Bibliothèque Universelle des sciences, belles lettres, et arts* (successor to the *Bibliothèque Britannique*), Geneva, various issues 1816-35.
Pinloche, Auguste, *Pestalozzi and the Foundation of the Modern Elementary School,* London, 1892.
Pons, J., *L'éducation en Angleterre entre 1750 et 1800: aperçu sur l'influence pédagogique de J.J. Rousseau en Angleterre,* Paris, 1919.
Potter, G.R., *Zwingli and Calvin: The Reformation Crisis,* ed. Joel Hurstfield, London, 1965.
Potter, G.R., *Ulrich Zwingli,* London Historical Society, 1977.
Potter, G.R., *see also* Bonjour in Section A.
Pressland, Arthur J., *Education and Social Welfare in Switzerland: To commemorate the Pestalozzi Centenary,* London, 1927.
Private Schools in Switzerland, Swiss National Tourist Office, 1950.
Rambert, Eugène, *Alexandre Calame: sa vie et son oeuvre,* Paris, 1884.
Reed, Bertha, *The Influence of Solomon Gessner upon English Literature,* Philadelphia: Univ. of Pennsylvania, 1905.
Reverdin, Olivier, *Isaac Casaubon et Genève de 1596 à 1614,* Geneva, 1961.
Reynold, Gonzague de, *Histoire littéraire de la Suisse au 18e siècle,* Lausanne, 1912.
Reynolds, Ernest Edwin, *Baden-Powell: A Biography of Lord Baden-Powell of Gilwell,* Oxford, 1942.
Riedtmann, Oskar, *William Lisle Bowles* (Diss.), Basel, 1940.
Richardson, Samuel, *Sir Charles Grandison,* London, 1753.
Roche, Eugenius, 'William Tell: A Tragedy', in *The Dramatic Appelant,* vol. 1, London, 1808.
Roddier, H., *J.J. Rousseau en Angleterre au 18ème siècle,* Paris, 1950.
Rogers, Samuel, *The Alps at Daybreak: Poems,* London, 1814.
Rouquet, Jean André, *L'état des arts en Angleterre,* Paris, 1755; as *The Present State of the Arts in England,* London: J. Nourse, 1755.
Rousseau, Jean-Jacques, *Émile,* Amsterdam, 1762.
Rousseau, Jean-Jacques, *La nouvelle Héloïse,* Paris, 1764.
Rousseau, Jean-Jacques, *Les Confessions,* Geneva, 1782.
Rousseau, Jean-Jacques, *A Defence of Mr Rousseau against the Aspersions of Mr Hume, Mons. Voltaire and Their Associates,* London, 1766.
Royal Society, The, *The Record of the Royal Society for the Promotion of Natural Knowledge,* London, 1940.
Rudler, Gustave, *La jeunesse de Benjamin Constant, 1767-1794,* Paris, 1909.

Ruskin, John, *Modern Painters,* London, 1843-60.
Ruskin, John, *Sesame and the Lilies,* 2nd ed., London, 1865.
Ruskin, John, *Praeterita,* Orpington, 1885–1900.
Russell, John, *see* Amstutz.
Ruthrich, Albert, and Reverdin, Claude, *L'église suisse de Londres 1762-1952,* London, n.d.
Sager, Walter de, 'The Abbey of St. Gall and Its Library', in *The Connoisseur,* Feb 1968 and Oct 1968.
Salis, J.R. de, *Sismondi: la vie et l'oeuvre d'un cosmopolite philosophe, 1773-1842,* 2 vols., Paris, 1932.
Sandby, William, *The History of the Royal Academy of Arts,* London, 1862.
Schazmann, P.-E., *Charles Dickens in Switzerland,* Swiss National Tourist Office, 1972.
Schindler, Dr Johannes, *Das Bild des Engländers in der Kunst – und Volksliteratur der deutschen Schweiz von 1798-1848,* Zurich, 1950.
Schirmer, Dr Gustav, *Die Schweiz im Spiegel englischer und amerikanischer Literatur bis 1848,* Zurich, 1929.
Schirmer, Dr Gustav, 'Englischer Dichter über die Schweiz', in *Neue Zürcher Zeitung,* nos. 235-240, Aug 1905.
Schirmer, Dr Gustav, 'Charles Dickens und die Schweiz', in *Neue Zürcher Zeitung,* 5 & 8 March, 1912.
Schirmer, Dr Gustav, 'Englische Frauen und die Schweiz', in *Schule und Leben,* May, July, Sept, 1915.
Schmid, Walter, *Romantic Switzerland, Mirrored in the Literature and Graphic Art of the Eighteenth and Nineteenth Centuries,* Zurich, 1952.
Schroeter, Joachim, *Swiss Contributions to Science,* New York, 1960.
Schun, Willi, *Schweizer Musik der Gegenwart,* Zurich, 1948.
Schultess-Rechberg, Givon, *Heinrich Bullinger,* Halle, 1904.
'Schweizer Buch und England, Das', in *Atlantis* special number, no. 4, Zurich, April 1946.
Scott, Sir Walter, *Anne of Geierstein,* Edinburgh, 1829.
Scott, Sir Walter, 'War Song of the Royal Edinburgh Light Dragoons', in vol. 4 of *The Poetical Works of Sir Walter Scott,* Edinburgh, 1861.
Scott, Sir Walter, 'The Battle of Sempach', in vol. 6 of *The Poetical Works . . .,* 1861.
Seebohm, Frederick, *The Oxford Reformers – Colet, Erasmus and More,* London: Dent (Everyman), 1914.
Shaw, George Bernard, *Arms and the Man,* London, 1898.
Shelley, Mary, *Frankenstein,* London, 1818.
Shelley, Percy Bysshe, *Lyrics and Shorter Poems* (including 'Mont Blanc'), London: Dent (Everyman), 1907.
Silber, Kate, *Pestalozzis Beziehungen zu England und Amerika,* Zurich, 1963.
Silber, Kate, *Pestalozzi: The Man and His Work,* London, Routledge & Kegan Paul, 1960.
Singer, Charles J., *A Short History of Medicine,* London: Oxford U.P., 1928.
Singer, Charles J., *Science, Medicine and History,* 2 vols. London: Oxford U.P., 1953.

Smith, John Pye, *A Vindication of Those Citizens of Geneva . . .*, Hackney, London, 1825.
Sorrell, Walter, *The Swiss*, London: Oswald Wolff, 1972.
Soubies, A., *Histoire de la musique en Suisse*, Paris, 1899.
'Switzerland in Literature', *Adam International Review*, 15, 1947.
Spender, E. Harold, *In Praise of Switzerland*, London: Constable, 1912.
Spindler, R., *Die Alpen in der englischen Literatur und Kunst*, Leipzig, 1932.
Spyri, Johanna, *Heidi*, London: Dent, 1909, and other editions.
Staël-Holstein, Mme A. de, *Dix années d'exil*, London, 1821.
Steiner, George, 'What Is Swiss?', in *The Times Literary Supplement*, 7 Dec 1984.
Stelling-Michaud, S. (ed.), *Le livre du recteur de l'Académie de Genève*, 2 vols., Geneva, 1959.
Stern, Alfred, *Briefe englischer Flüchtlinge in der Schweiz, 1663-1671*, Göttingen, 1874.
Stern, Alfred, *Die reformierte Schweiz in ihren Beziehungen zu Karl I. von England, William Laud, Erzbischof von Canterbury und den Covenanters*, Zurich, 1878.
Stoddart, Anna M., *Life of Paracelsus, 1493-1541*, London: John Murray, 1915.
Stoughton, J., *Die Verbindung zwischen Basel und England zur Zeit der Reformation*, Urkundenbuch der Stadt Basel, 11.
Stoye, Enid, *Vincent Bernard de Tscharner, 1728-1778: A Study of Swiss Culture in the late Eighteenth Century*, Fribourg: Imprimerie St Paul, 1954.
Straumann, Heinrich, 'Switzerland and the English Speaking World', in *English Studies Today*, Berne, 1961.
Straumann, Heinrich, *Byron and Switzerland*, Byron Foundation Lecture, Nottingham Univ., Nottingham, 1949.
Straumann, Heinrich, *Contexts of Literature: An Anglo-Swiss Approach*, Berne: Francke Verlag, 1973.
Straumann, Heinrich, 'Shakespeare und die Schweiz', in *Schweizer Theater-Jahrbuch*, 30, der Gesellschaft für Theaterkultur, Berne, 1964.
Straumann, Heinrich, *see also* Bircher.
Stroehlin, Ernest, *Jean Petitot et Jacques Bordier*, Geneva, 1905.
Stunt, Timothy, 'Geneva and British Evangelicals in the Early Nineteenth Century', in *Journal of Ecclesiastical History*, no. 32, Jan 1981.
Symonds, John Addington, *Vagabunduli Libellus: Sonnets*, London, 1884.
Tavel, Hans Christoph von, *Un siècle d'art suisse*, Banque Populaire Suisse, Skira, Geneva, 1969.
Tennyson, Alfred, Lord, *Works*, London: H.S. King & Co, 1877; *Poems and Plays*, London: Oxford U.P., 1953.
Tennyson, Alfred, Lord, *The Princess*, London: 1847.
Thackeray, W.M., 'On a Lazy Idle Boy', in *Roundabout Papers*, 1863; London: Smith, Elder, 1891.
Thieme, Ulrich, *Allgemeines Lexikon der bildenden Künstler*, Leipzig: Verlag E.A. Seemann, 1913.
Thomson, James, *The Poetical Works*, Edinburgh, 1883.

Thornbury, W., *Life of Joseph Mallord William Turner*, London, 1877.
Treneer, Anne, *Life of Sir Humphry Davy*, London: Methuen, 1963.
Trinder, Barrie, *John Fletcher: Vicar of Madeley during the Industrial Revolution*, Ironbridge Gorge Museum Trust, Telford, Salop., n.d.
Tscharner, V.B. de, 'Einige Nachrichten von den berühmten Engländern Young und Richardson aus einem Schreiben des Herrn Bernard Tscharner an den Präsidenten von Haller, übersetzt in *Neueste Sammlung vermischter Schriften*, vol. 3, Zurich, 1757.
Underwood, Brian, *Faith at the Frontiers*, London: Commonwealth and Continental Church Society, 1974.
Utz, H., 'Thomas Hollis' Bequest to the Library of Berne', in *English Studies*, 40, 1959.
Vetter, Prof. Dr Theodor, *Literarische Beziehungen zwischen England und der Schweiz im Reformationszeitalter*, Zurich, 1901.
Vetter, Prof. Dr Theodor, *Englische Flüchtlinge in Zürich während der ersten Hälfte des 16. Jahrhunderts*, Zurich, 1893.
Vetter, Prof. Dr Theodor, *Shakespeare und die deutsche Schweiz*, Jahrbuch der deutschen Shakespeare-Gesellschaft, 1912.
Vetter, Prof. Dr Theodor, *Rudolf Zwingli und Rudolf Gwalter, die Enkel des Reformators, und ihre Schicksäle in England*, Zurich, 1902.
Vetter, Prof. Dr Theodor, 'J.J. Bodmer und die englische Literatur', in *J.J. Bodmer: Denkschrift zum 200. Geburtstag*, Zurich, 1900.
Vetter, Prof. Dr Theodor, *John Ruskin und William Morris, Feinde und Förderer der Technik*, Zurich, 1912.
Vetter, Prof. Dr Theodor, *Relations between England and Zurich during the Reformation*, London: Elliot Stock, 1904.
Vetter, Prof. Dr Theodor, *Zürich als Vermittlerin englischer Literatur im achtzehnten Jahrhundert*, Zurich, 1891.
Vetter, Prof. Dr Theodor, *Johannes Hooper, Bischof von Gloucester und Worcester, und seine Beziehungen zu Bullinger und Zürich*, Zurich, 1891.
Vetter, Prof. Dr Theodor, *Johann Jakob Heidegger, ein Mitarbeiter G. F. Handels*, Zurich, 1902.
Vetter, Prof. Dr Theodor, *Die Kulturbedeutung Englands*, Zurich, 1915.
Vetter, Prof. Dr Theodor, *Der Spectator als Quelle der Diskurse der Mahlern*, Frauenfeld, 1887.
Voisine, Jacques, *J. J. Rousseau en Angleterre*, Paris, 1956.
Vreeland, Williamson U., *Étude sur les rapports littéraires entre Genève et l'Angleterre jusqu'à la publication de la Nouvelle Héloïse*, Geneva, 1901.
Waidson, Herbert Morgan, *Jeremias Gotthelf*, Oxford: Basil Blackwell, 1953.
Waidson, Herbert Morgan, 'Jeremias Gotthelf's Reception in Britain and America', Cambridge U.P. reprint from the *Modern Language Review*. 43, 1948, no. 2.
Waidson, Herbert Morgan (ed.), *An Anthology of Modern Swiss Literature*, London: Oswald Wolff, 1984.
Wälchli, Gottfried, *Frank Buchser, 1828–1890: Sein Leben und Werk*, Zurich & Leipzig, 1941.

Walther, Rudolf, the Elder, *Rudolf Gwalther's Reise nach England im Jahr 1537*, trans. P. Boesch, Zurich, 1947.
Walton, Elijah, *The Peaks and Valleys of the Alps*, London, 1867.
Walton, Elijah, *Clouds and Their Combinations*, London, 1873.
Walton, Elijah, *The Bernese Oberland*, London, 1874.
Walton, Elijah, *Alpine Vignettes*, London, 1882.
Walton, Elijah, *Flowers from the Upper Alps*, London, 1869.
Walton, Elijah, *see also* Bonney.
Waring, Samuel Miller, *see* Section B.
Welti, Manfred Edwin, *Der Basler Buchdruck und Britannien*, Basel, 1964.
White, Eric Walter, *Benjamin Britten*, London: Faber & Faber, 1970.
Wildi, Dr Max, *The British and the Swiss* (an essay), Zurich: Pro Helvetia, 1965.
Wildi, Dr Max, *Künstler und Gesellschaft in England, 1850–1900*, Zurich, 1949.
Wildi, Dr Max, *Von Englands geistigen Beständen: Ausgewählte Aufsätze*, Zurich, 1944.
Wildi, Dr Max, *Die Dramen von T.S. Eliot*, Zurich: Kultur-und staatswissenschaftliche Schriften, 1957.
Wildi, Dr Max, Anglo-Zurich Annals, 1500–1954, in *The Book of Zurich*, Edwin Arnst *et al.*, Zurich, 1959.
Wildi, Dr Max, Wordsworth and the Simplon Pass, in *English Studies*, 40, 1959.
Williams, Cicely, *A Church in the Alps: A Century of Zermatt and the English*, Commonwealth & Continental Church Society, 1970.
Williams, Helen Maria, *Poems*, London, 1786.
Wilson, Arthur, (1595-1652), *The Swisser: A Play in Five Acts*, Paris, 1904.
Wilton, Andrew, *William Pars: Journey through the Alps*, Zurich: De Clivo Press, 1979.
Wilton, Andrew, *see also* Amstutz.
Wiskemann, Elizabeth, *A Great Swiss Newspaper: The Story of the Neue Zürcher Zeitung*, London; Oxford U.P., 1959.
Wiskemann, Elizabeth, Contemporary Writing in Switzerland', in *Times Literary Supplement*, 4 Jul 1958.
Wolf, A., *A History of Science, Technology and Philosophy in the Sixteenth and Seventeenth Centuries*, London: Geo. Allen & Unwin, 1950.
Wolf, A., *A History of Science, Technology and Philosophy in the Eighteenth Century*, London: Allen & Unwin, 1938.
Wordsworth, William, *Poems, Including Lyrical Ballads*, London, 1815.
Wordsworth, William, *Memorials of a Tour on the Continent, 1820*, London, 1827.
Wyss, Johann David, *Der schweizerische Robinson*, Zurich, 1841.
Yonge, Charlotte M., 'The Battle of Sempach, 1397', in *A Book of Golden Deeds*, London, 1864.
Young, Geoffrey Winthrop, *Wind and Hill: Poems*, London: Smith, Elder, 1909.
(Zurich, Lake of), *By the Margin of Zurich's Fair Waters*, London, ? 1840.

Zwingli, Huldrych, *Selected Works of Huldrych Zwingli (1485-1531), the Reformer of Switzerland,* trans. L.A. McLouth, H. Preble and G.W. Gilmore, ed. Samuel M. Jackson, Philadelphia: Pennsylvania U.P., 1901.

Zwingli, Huldrych, *The Latin Works and Correspondence of Huldrych Zwingli,* ed. Samuel M. Jackson, New York & London: Putnam & Son, 1912.

Zwingli, Huldrych, *Zwingli and Bullinger: Selected Translations with Introduction and Notes,* ed. G. W. Bromiley, London; S.C.M. Press, 1953.

D: ECONOMIC, COMMERCIAL, INDUSTRIAL AND FINANCIAL

Allen, Cecil John, *Switzerland: Its Railways and Cableways, Mountain Roads and Lake Steamers,* London: Ian Allan 1947.

Andres, Ernest, *Les relations économiques entre la Suisse et la Grande Bretagne depuis la deuxième guerre mondiale,* Fribourg, 1957.

Arlettaz, Gérald, and Jequier, François, 'Les Rapports consulaires de la Confédération Suisse', in *Business History,* 23 November, 1981.

Aschinger, Franz E., 'Zurich as a Center of Finance', *Neue Zürcher Zeitung,* 1959.

Ashton, Robert, *The Disbursing Official under the Early Stuarts: The Cases of Sir William Russell and Philip Burlamachi,* Bulletin of the Institute of Historical Research. vol. 30, 1957.

Ashton, Robert, *The Crown and the Money Market 1603-1640,* Oxford, 1960.

Bagge, J. Picton, *General Report on the Economic Situation of Switzerland,* London: HMSO, 1922.

Bairoch, P., 'Le volume des exportations de la Suisse de 1851 à 1975', in *Revue Suisse d'Histoire,* no. 28, 1978.

'Banker, The', 'Foreign Banks in London', review in *The Banker,* vol. 132, Nov 1982.

Bäschlin, Conrad, *Die Blütezeit der ökonomischen Gesellschaft in Bern, 1759-1766,* Laupen, 1913.

Béguelin, J. P., *An International Comparison of Business: Some Empirical Findings, 1948-1980,* National Bank of Switzerland, Zurich, 1981.

Bergeron, Louis, 'Pourtalès et Cie (1753-1801): Apogée et déclin d'un capitalisme', in *Annales E.S.C.,* no. 2, March-April 1970.

Bergier, Jean-François, *Genève et l'économie européenne de la Renaissance,* Paris, 1963.

Bergier, Jean-François, *Naissance et croissance de la Suisse industrielle,* Berne, 1974.

Bergier, Jean-François, *Histoire économique de la Suisse,* Lausanne: Payot, 1982.

Bergier, Jean-François, *Problèmes de l'histoire économique de la Suisse;* 2 vols., Berne, 1968.

Bergier, Jean-François, L'industrializzione in un paese senza materie prime: il caso della Svizzera (1800-1850), in *Rassegna economica . . . del Banco di Napoli,* 25, 1971.

Bergier, Jean-François, 'Le trafic à travers les Alpes et les liaisons transalpines du haut Moyen Âge au 17ème siècle', in *Le Alpi e l'Europa*, vol. 3, Economia e transiti, Bari, 1975.

Biucchi, B., 'Schweizerische Textilunternehmen im Zeitalter der industriellen Revolution (1800-1830)', in *Festgabe Josef Schwarzfischer*, Fribourg, 1972.

Biucchi, B., 'The Industrial Revolution in Switzerland, 1700-1914, in vol. 4 of the *Fontana Economic History of Europe* (see Cipolla, C.M.).

Biucchi, B., *Profilo di storia economica e sociale della Svizzera*, Locarno, 1982.

Bleuler, Werner, *Studien über Aussenhandel und Handelspolitik der Schweiz*, Zurich, 1929.

Bodmer, Johann Georg, 'John George Bodmer: A Biographical Sketch', in *Quarterly Review of Machine Tools and Workshop Practice*, 1895.

Bodmer, Walter, *Schweizerische Industriegeschichte. Die Entwicklung der schweizerischen Textilwirtschaft im Rahmen der übrigen Industrien und Wirtschaftszweige*, Zurich, 1960.

Bodmer, Walter, *Der Einfluss der Refugianteneinwanderung von 1550-1700 auf die schweizerische Wirtschaft*, Zurich, 1946.

Boesch, Hans, 'Die Unternehmungen von Johann Conrad Fisher', *Neujahrsblatt* der Naturforschenden Gesellschaft, Schaffhausen, 1952.

Bowring, John, *Report on the Commerce and Manufactures of Switzerland*, London: Parliamentary Papers, 1836 [60] 45.

Brown Boveri & Co., *Seventy-Five Years: Brown Boveri, 1891-1966*, Baden, 1966.

Brownlie, D., *Johann Georg Bodmer . . .*, Transactions of the Newcomen Society, 1925-26, vol. 6.

Bryce, George, *The Hudson's Bay Company*, London: Sampson Low, 1900.

Buess, H., 'A Swiss Manufacturer Sees the Industrial Revolution in England', *British Journal of Industrial Medicine*, vol. 9, 1962.

Bürgin, A., *Geschichte des Geigy-Unternehmens von 1758 bis 1939*, Basel, 1958.

Burnley, Mr., 'Reports by Mr. Burnley, Her Majesty's Secretary of Legation, on the Manufactures and Commerce of Switzerland', Parliamentary Papers, 1859 [2570] 30; 1860 [2716] 66; 1861 [2838] 63; 1863 [3222] 80; 1864 [3392] 61.

Buxbaum, B., *J. G. Bodmer*, Beiträge zur Geschichte der Technik und Industrie, vol. 12, 1922.

Cahill, J. R., *General Report on the Economic Situation of Switzerland*, London: Dept of Trade, HMSO, 1921.

Carswell, John, *The South Sea Bubble*, London: Cresset Press, 1960.

Cérenville, Bernard de, *Le système continental et la Suisse, 1803-1813*, Lausanne, 1906.

Chapuis, Alfred and Droz, Edmund, *The Jaquet-Droz Automatons*, Neuchâtel, 1956.

Chapuisat, E., *Le commerce et l'industrie à Genève pendant la domination Française*, Geneva & Paris, 1908.

Cipolla, Carlo M., *Clocks and Culture, 1300-1700*, London: Collins, 1967.

Cipolla, Carlo M., *Storia economica dell 'Europa preindustriale*, Bologna, 1974.
Cipolla, Carlo M. (ed.), *The Fontana Economic History of Europe*, 6 vols., London: Collins, 1973.
Clapham, J. H., *An Economic History of Great Britain*, Cambridge, 1926.
Clavel-Respinger, Alexandre, and Clavel-Respinger, Fanny, *Das Buch vom Wenkenhof*, Basel, 1957.
Clerget, Pierre, *La Suisse au 20ème siècle: étude économique et sociale*, Paris, 1908.
Crossland, Norman, 'The Everlasting League: A Survey of Switzerland', in *The Economist*, 270, 3 February, 1979.
Cunningham, William, *The Growth of English Industry and Commerce*, part 1 *Modern Times: The Mercantile System*, Cambridge, 1925.
Davidovic, George, *The Structure of Cooperative Unions and Central Cooperative Organisations in Various Countries: 1. Great Britain; 2. Switzerland*, Ottawa, 1965.
Dawson, W. Harbutt, *Social Switzerland*, London: Chapman & Hall, 1897.
Dérobert, E., *La politique douanière de la Confédération Suisse*, Geneva, 1926.
Desbuissons, Léon, *La Vallée de Binn, Valais: étude géographique, géologique, minéralogique et pittoresque*, Lausanne, 1909.
Dickenson, H. W., 'Bodmers Technisches Werk', in *Neue Zürcher Zeitung*, 6 Dec, 1936.
Dickenson, H. W., *Diary of Johann Georg Bodmer*, Transactions of the Newcomen Society, 1928-30, vol. 10.
Dreyfus Foundation, *The Story of the Camille and Henry Dreyfus Foundation and the Men It Commemorates*, New York, n.d.
Edwards, Ronald, *Industrial Research in Switzerland: Its Institutional and Economic Background*, London: Pitman, 1950.
EFTA, *Changes in the Pattern of EFTA Foreign Direct Investment*, Geneva: EFTA, 1969.
Ehrenberg, R., *Capital and Finance in the Age of the Renaissance*, trans. H. M. Lucas, London: Jonathan Cape, 1928.
Escher, J. C., *J. C. Eschers Briefe aus England*, Zürcher Beiträge zur Wissenschaftlichen und geselligen Unterhaltung 1815-1816.
Escher-Wyss, 1805-1955: 150 Years of Development, Zurich, 1955.
Fehrenbach, F. R., *The Gnomes of Zurich*, London: Frewin, 1966.
Feldhaus, F. M., *Zwei technologische Reisen nach England, 1814 und 1825*, Geschichtsblätter für Technik und Gewerbe, vol. 5, 1918.
Fischer, Johann Conrad, *Johann Conrad Fischer, 1773-1854, Tagebücher*, Schaffhausen, 1951.
Franzero, Carlo Maria, *Il conte di Cavour e i suoi Banchieri Inglesi*, Turin: Editrice Teca, 1968.
Frey, E., *Die schweizerische Handelspolitik der letzten Jahrzehnte*, Leipzig, 1892.
Gannon, Margaret, 'The Basle Mission Trading Company and British Colonial Policy in the Gold Coast, 1918-1928', in *Journal of African History*, 24, no. 4, 1983.
Gasser, Prof. Christian, and Meyer, Dr Werner, *Der schweizerische Kapitalmarkt*, St Gallen, 1952.

Gaulis L., and Creux, R., *Swiss Hotel Pioneers,* Paudex: Editions de Fontainemore, Swiss National Tourist Office, 1976.
Geering, Dr Traugott, *Die Handelspolitik der Schweiz am Ausgang des 19. Jahrhunderts,* Berlin, 1902.
Gnade, R., *The Metallurgist Johann Conrad Fischer, 1773-1854, and His Relations with Britain,* Schaffhausen 1947.
Gonzenbach, A. von, *De la réforme du tarif anglais et de ses conséquences probables pour le commerce Suisse,* Zurich, 1846.
Gregory, Gene, 'The Swiss Way to Economic Stability', in *Contemporary Review,* 230. April 1977.
Greyerz, Christoph von, *The Quasi-Corporation: Some Aspects of Legal Personality in English and Swiss Law,* Berne, 1971.
Habakkuk, H. J., and Postan, M. (edd.), *The Cambridge Economic History of Europe,* Cambridge, 1965.
Halevy, Elie, *A History of the English People in 1815,* London: Penguin, 1937.
Hasler & Co., *Hasler, 1852-1952: Hundert Jahre Fernmeldetechnik und Präzisionsmechanik,* Berne, 1952.
Hauser, A., *Schweizerische Wirtschafts – und Sozialgeschichte, von den Anfängen bis zur Gegenwart,* Zurich, 1961.
Heaton, Herbert, *Economic History of Europe,* New York & London: Harper Bros., 1936.
Heckscher, E., *The Continental System,* Oxford, 1922.
Heer, Jean, *The First Hundred Years of Nestlé,* Rivaz, Switzerland, 1966.
Heilbronner, Robert L., *The Great Economists,* London: Eyre & Spottiswoode, 1955.
Helps, Sir Arthur, *The Life and Labours of Mr Brassey,* London: G. Bell & Sons, 1872.
Henderson, William Otto, *Britain and Industrial Europe, 1750-1870,* Liverpool: Liverpool University Press, 1954.
Henderson, William Otto, *The Industrialization of Europe: 1780-1914,* London: Thames & Hudson, 1969.
Henderson, William Otto, *J. C. Fischer and His Diary of Industrial England, 1814-1851,* London: Frank Cass, 1966.
Henderson, William Otto, *Industrial Britain under the Regency: The Diaries of Escher, Bodmer, May and de Gallois,* London: Frank Cass, 1968.
Herries, Mr, 'Report by Mr Herries, Her Majesty's Secretary of Legation, on the Manufactures and Commerce of Switzerland', Parly. Papers, 1857. [2444] 55.
Hill, C. P., *British Economic and Social History 1700-1982,* London: Edward Arnold, 1985.
Hirst, Francis Wrigley, *Adam Smith, 1723-1790,* London: Macmillan, 1904.
Hoffmann, Hanes, *Die Anfänge der Maschinenindustrie in der deutschen Schweiz, 1800-1875,* Zurich, 1962.
Homberger, N., *La politique commerciale de la Suisse durant la deuxième guerre mondiale,* Neuchâtel, 1972.
Huber, J. G., *Bilder aus der bernischen Wirtschaftsgeschichte,* Schweizerischer Bankverein, 1974.

Huber, L. H., and Menzi, Karl, *The Story of the Chemical Industry in Basle*, Lausanne: CIBA, 1959.
Hunold, Albert Conrad, *The Industrial Development of Switzerland*, Zurich, 1954.
Iklé, Dr Max, *Les relations financières de la Suisse avec l'étranger*, National Bank of Switzerland, 61st Report, 1968.
Iklé, Dr Max, 'Switzerland's Invisible Earnings: A Comparison with Britain', in *The Banker*, 120, Jan 1970.
Iklé, Dr Max, *Switzerland: An International Banking and Finance Center*, Stroudsberg, Pennsylvania, 1972.
Jackson, Stanley, *The Savoy*, London: Frederick Muller, 1964.
Jaquet, Eugène, and Chapuis, Alfred, *Technique and History of the Swiss Watch*, London: Spring Books, 1970.
Jenks, L. H., *The Migration of British Capital to 1875*, London: Jonathan Cape, 1938.
Jenny-Trümpy, A., *Die schweizerische Baumwollindustrie*, Zurich, 1909.
Johr, W. A., *Schweizerische Kreditanstalt (1856-1956)*, Zurich, 1956.
Judges, A. V., 'Philip Burlamachi: A Financier of the Thirty Years War', in *Economica*, vol. 6, 1926.
Körner, M., *Solidarités financières suisses au seizième siècle*, Lausanne, 1980.
Koss, Stephen E., *Sir John Brunner, Radical Plutocrat, 1942-1919*, Cambridge, 1970.
Landmann, Julius, *Die auswärtigen Kapitalanlagen aus dem Berner Staatsschatz im 18. Jahrhundert*, Jahrbuch für schweizerische Geschichte, vol. 28 (1903), vol. 29 (1904), Zurich.
Lätt, Dr Arnold, *The First Anglo-Swiss Trader*, Zurich, 1946.
Levy, René, *The Social Structure of Switzerland*, Pro Helvetia, 1984.
Lincke, B., *Die schweizerische Maschinenindustrie und ihre Entwicklung in wirtschaftlichen Beziehungen*, Frauenfeld, 1911.
Lipson, Ephraim, *Economic History of England*, London 1943.
Lloyd, Samuel, *The Lloyds of Birmingham*, Birmingham: Cornish, 1908.
Lomax, Sir John, *The Diplomatic Smuggler*, London: Arthur Barker, 1965.
Lüthy, Herbert, *La Banque Protestante en France de la révocation de l'Edit de Nantes à la Révolution*, Paris, 1959-61.
Marshall, John, *A Biographical Dictionary of Railway Engineers*, Newton Abbot: David & Charles, 1978.
Martin, C., *Essai sur la politique monétaire de Berne 1400-1798*, 2 vols., Lausanne, 1978-83.
Martin, Jean, *Étienne Dumont*, Neuchâtel, 1942.
Masnata, Albert, *L'émigration des industries suisses*, Lausanne, 1924.
Massingberd, Hugh Montgomery-, and Watkin, D. J., *The London Ritz*, London: Aurum Press, 1980.
Mathias, P., *The First Industrial Nation: An Economic History of Britain, 1700-1914*, London, 1969.
Medlicott, W. N., *The Economic Blockade*, London: HMSO, 1952.
Meier, Mariann, 'La Suisse à Londres', in *Le mois économique et financier*, May 1985.

Midgley, T., and Hamer, L., *John George Bodmer, Engineer and Inventor, 1786-1864: Exhibition Illustrating his Work whilst in Bolton, 1828-1843*, Bolton: Chadwick Museum, 1928.
Mitchell, V. R., *European Historical Statistics, 1750-1975*, London: Macmillan, 1981.
Monter, William Edward, *Swiss Investment in England, 1697-1720*, Revue Internationale d'Histoire de la Banque, no. 2, Geneva, 1969.
Montres Rolex S.A., *Hans Wilsdorf*, Geneva, n.d.
Mottet, Louis H. (ed.), *Les grandes heures des banquiers Suisses*, Neuchâtel: Delachaux and Niestlé, 1986.
Mousson, A., 'Lebensbild von Johann Caspar Escher im Felsenhof', in *31. Neujahrsblatt des Waisenhauses in Zürich*, 1868.
Nordman, Roger, and Heller, Paul, *La Suisse, notre aventure*, Lausanne: Payot, 1972.
Ochsenbein, H., *Die verlorene Wirtschaftsfreiheit 1914-1918: Methoden ausländischer Wirtschaftskontrollen über die Schweiz*, Berne, 1962.
Overseas Economic Surveys: Switzerland, Dept. of Trade, London: HMSO, various issues.
Overseas Trade Statistics of the United Kingdom, Dept. of Trade, London: HMSO, various issues.
Peduzzi, Pino, *Pioniere Ticinesi in Inghilterra: The Gatti Family 1780-1980*, Bellinzona 1985.
Peter, Charlotte, 'Hans Caspar Escher, 1775-1859', in *Schweizer Pioniere der Wirtschaft und Technik*, vol. 6, 1956.
Pirenne, H., *Economic and Social History of Medieval Europe*, New York, 1937.
Piuz, Anne Marie, *Recherches sur le commerce de Genève au 17ème siècle*, Paris: A. & J. Picard, 1964.
Pole, W. (ed.), *The Life of Sir William Fairbairn*, London, 1877.
Pollard, S., *Peaceful Conquest: The Industrialisation of Europe, 1760-1970*, Oxford, 1981.
Prevost, Sir Augustus, *History of Morris, Prevost & Co.*, London, privately printed, 1904.
Ramsay, G. D., *English Overseas Trade during the Centuries of Emergence*, London: Macmillan, 1957.
Rappard, William E., *La révolution industrielle et les origines de la protection légale du travail en Suisse*, Berne, 1914.
Rappard, William E., *L'évolution de la politique économique de la Suisse de 1848 à 1948*, Zurich, 1948.
Rappard, William E., *Conditions de la prospérité helvétique*, Zurich, 1957.
Rieder, Dr Albert, *Die Handelsbeziehungen Schweiz-Commonwealth seit dem zweiten Weltkrieg*, Winterthur, 1960.
Ritz, Marie-Louise, *César Ritz: Host to the World*, London: Harrap, 1938.
Ritzmann, F., *Die Schweizer Banken: Geschichte, Theorie, Statistik*, Berne, 1973.
Roche Products Ltd., *Roche in Britain: The First Seventy-Five Years, 1908-83*, Welwyn Garden City, 1983.
Rohner, K., *Die schweizerischen Wirtschaftvertretung im Ausland*, Berne, 1944.

Roll, Eric, *A History of Economic Thought*, London: Faber & Faber, 1935.
Ruegger, P., *Das britische Empire und die schweizerische Wirtschaft*, Weltwirtschaftliche Studien, Geneva, H.z. 1947.
Ruffieux, R., *La Suisse de l'entre-deux-guerres*, Lausanne, 1982.
Salis, J. R. de, 'Die getadelte Schweiz: Urteile des Auslands', in *Die Weltwoche*, 27 Aug 1965. Reprinted in de Salis, *Switzerland and Europe, see Section A*.
Sandoz Ltd., *Sandoz in England, 1911-1961*, Leeds, 1961.
Sarasin, A. E., *Portrait of the Swiss Banker*, talk given to the Anglo-Swiss Society, London, 6 Feb 1968.
Sayers, R. S., *Lloyds Bank in the History of English Banking*, Oxford, 1957.
Schärer, R., 'Trade Relations between Britain and Switzerland', in *Export*, Jul 1948.
Schaffner, Hans, *L'organisation de l'économie de guerre en Suisse*, Lausanne, 1942.
Schib, Karl (ed.), *Johann Conrad Fischer, 1773-1854: Tagebücher*, Schaffhausen, 1951.
Schlaepfer, R., *Die Ausländerfrage in der Schweiz vor dem ersten Weltkrieg*, Zurich, 1969.
Schlotte, W., *British Overseas Trade from 1700 to the 1930s*, trans. W.O. Henderson, Oxford: Basil Blackwell, 1952.
Schmidt, P. H., *Die Schweiz und die europäische Handelspolitik*, Zurich, 1914.
Schmidt, P. H., *Die schweizerischen Industrie im internationalen Konkurrenzkampf*, Zurich, 1915.
Schwarz, J., *Bruttoanlageinvestitionen in der Schweiz von 1850 bis 1914*, Berne, 1981.
Schweizer Pioniere der Wirtschaft und Technik, Zurich, 1956.
Schweizerische Kreditanstalt, *Schweizerische Wirtschaftszahlen*, Zurich, 1980.
Schweizerische Nationalbank, *Das schweizerische Bankwesen im Jahre 1975*, Zurich: Orell Fussli Verlag, 1975.
Scott, O. A., *General Report on the Economic Situation of Switzerland*, London: HMSO, 1924.
Selectus Ltd., *Fifty Years of Manufacture in Biddulph, 1936-1986*, Biddulph, Staffs., 1986.
Setchell, H. L., *General Report on the Economic Situation of Switzerland*, London: HMSO, 1936 and 1938.
Singer, Charles J. (ed.), *A History of Technology*, Oxford: Clarendon Press, 1954-58.
Société des Arts, *Incendies de Genève: préservatifs et notice historique*, Geneva, 1834. (The Société sent to England to report on what precautions against fire were taken there.)
Société Suisse de Surveillance Économique, *Rapport de la Société Suisse de Surveillance Économique*, Berne, 1920.
Soloveytchik, George, *Leu & Co., 1755-1955*, Zurich, 1955.
Sperling, R. A. C., *General Report on the Economic Situation of Switzerland*, London: HMSO, 1925.

Statistiques annuelles du commerce extérieur de la Suisse, Berne, various issues.
Stephenson, Robert, and Swinburne, H., *Bericht des vom Bundersrat einberufenen Experten, Herren R. Stephenson und H. Swinburne über den Bau von Eisenbahnen in der Schweiz,* Berne, 1850.
Stewart, D., *Biographical Memoir of Adam Smith,* London, 1811.
Stucki, Lorenz, *The Secret Empire,* New York: Herder & Herder, 1971.
'Swiss, A,' *Great Britain's Right to Tax Her Colonies Placed in the Clearest Light,* London, 1774.
Swiss Bank Corporation, *Swiss Merchant Bankers in London,* London, 1954.
'Swiss (Engineering) Achievements', supplement to *The Engineer,* 19 Jun 1959.
Tawney, R. H., 'The Continental Reformers: Calvin', chapter in *Religion and the Rise of Capitalism,* London: Pelican, 1938.
Taylor, F. S., *A History of Industrial Chemistry,* London: Heinemann, 1957.
'Treaty of Friendship, Commerce and Reciprocal Establishment between Her Majesty and the Swiss Confederation, signed at Berne, September 6, 1855', Parliamentary Papers, 1856 [2041] 61.
Tripp, Basil H., *Renold Chains: History of the Company and Rise of the Precision Chain Industry 1879-1955,* London: Allen & Unwin, 1956.
Tussaud, John Theodore, *The Romance of Madame Tussaud's,* London: Odhams Press, 1921.
Union Bank of Switzerland, *Switzerland in Figures,* Zurich, various issues.
Union Bank of Switzerland, *Switzerland Economic Survey, 1970,* Zurich, 1970.
Ure, Andrew, *The Cotton Manufacture of Great Britain,* London 1861.
Veyrassat-Herren, B., *Négociants et fabricants dans l'industrie cotonnière suisse 1760-1840, aux origines financières de l'industrialisation,* Lausanne, 1982.
Vignoles, K. H., *Charles Blacker Vignoles: Romantic Engineer,* Cambridge, 1982.
Vignoles, O. J., *Life of C. B. Vignoles, Soldier and Civil Engineer,* London, 1889.
Vogel, Otto, Johann Conrad Fischer und die englische Tempergiesserei, *Stahl und Eisen,* vol. 40, 1920.
Volmar, F., *Geschichte und Entwicklung der bernischen Eisenbahnpolitik, 1848-1902,* Schweizerische Blätter für Wirtschafts - und Sozialpolitik, 60, 1902.
Waldvogel, William, *Les relations économiques entre la Grande Bretagne et la Suisse,* Neuveville, 1922.
Waldvogel, William, *La Suisse et ses rapports avec la Grande Bretagne,* Schweizerisches Konsular-Bulletin, no. 6, 1923.
Walker, R. J. B., *Old Westminster Bridge,* Newton Abbot & London: David & Charles, 1979.
Wartmann, H., *Industrie und Handel der Schweiz im 19. Jahrhundert,* Berne, 1902.
Watches of Switzerland Ltd, *Experience of Time: The Story of Watches of Switzerland Ltd, 1924-1984,* Aylesbury, 1984.

Watts, John I., *The First Fifty Years of Brunner, Mond & Co.*, Northwich, Derby, 1923.
Watts, Stephen, *The Ritz*, London: Bodley Head, 1963.
Weissenbach, P., *Das Eisenbahnwesen der Schweiz*, Zurich, 1913.
Weisz, L., 'Johann Caspar Escher', in *Neue Zürcher Zeitung*, 10 March 1955.
Welter, Karl, *Die Exportgesellschaften und die assoziative Exportförderung in der Schweiz im 19. Jahrhundert*, Berne, 1915.
Wicks, John, 'Swiss Banks On the Up and Up', in *The Banker*, 134, Jul 1984.
Willatt, Morris, 'Why Switzerland Works', in *Management Today*, May 1975.
Willatt, Morris, 'Made in Switzerland', in *George Mikes Introduces Switzerland*, London: André Deutsch, 1977.
Wittmann, W., 'Die Take-off-Periode der schweizerischen Volkswirtschaft', in *Zeitschrift für die gesamte Staatswissenschaft*, 1963.

APPENDIX A

British Envoys to Switzerland

★ *On special missions*

1514-17	**Richard Pace,**★ Zurich	
1514	**William Knight,**★ Zurich	
1514	**Sir Richard Woodhouse,**★ Zurich	
1523	**Richard Pace,**★ Zurich	
1523	**William Knight,**★ Zurich	
1602	**Henry Lock,**★ Geneva	
1617	**Sir Isaac Wake,**★ Geneva & Berne	
1618	**Sir Henry Wotton,**★ Grisons	
1625	**Sir Isaac Wake,**★ Chur, Zurich, Berne, Geneva	
1626	**Sir Isaac Wake,**★ Berne & Zurich	
1627	**Sir Walter Montagu,**★ Geneva	
1628	**Sir Thomas Roe,**★ Geneva & Basel	
	Earl of Carlisle,★ Protestant cantons & Geneva	
1629-44	**Sir Oliver Fleming,** Switzerland, Grisons, Geneva	
1634	**Sir Basil Fielding,**★ Geneva	
1654-58	**Revd Dr John Pell,** Zurich	
1654-55	**John Durie,**★ Aarau	
1655-57	**Sir Samuel Morland,** Geneva	
1656	**Jean-Baptiste Stuppa,**★ Protestant cantons	
1689-92	**Thomas Coxe,** Switzerland	
1690-92	**Philibert de Hervart,** Geneva	
1692-1702	**Philibert de Hervart,** Switzerland	
1695-1710	**Gaspard Perrinet, Marquis d'Arsellières,** Geneva	
1702-05	**Dr William Aglionby,** Switzerland	
1705-14	**Abraham Stanyan,** Switzerland	
1707-14	**Abraham Stanyan,** Grisons	
1709-13	**Francis Manning,** Grisons (Chargé d'Affaires)	
1715-17	**James Dayrolle,** Geneva	
1716-22	**Francis Manning,** Switzerland	
1717-34	**Armand Louis de Saint Georges, Count de Marsay,**[1] Geneva (and Chargé d'Affaires, Switzerland, from 1722)	
1734-39	**Count de Marsay,** Switzerland & Grisons	
1739-62	**Count de Marsay,** Geneva	
1743-49	**John Burnaby,** Switzerland	
1743-50	**Jerome de Salis,** Grisons	
1749-62	**Arthur Villettes,** Switzerland	

1762 - 64   Robert Colebrooke, Switzerland
1763 - 67   James, Count Pictet,[2] Geneva
1765 - 69   William Norton, Switzerland
1769 - 76   Jean Gabriel Catt, Switzerland (Chargé d'Affaires)
1772 - 74   Isaac Pictet, Geneva
1776 - 92   Col Louis Béat Braun,[3] Switzerland & Geneva (Chargé d'Affaires)
1792 - 95   Lord Robert Fitzgerald, Switzerland & Geneva
1793   François-Pierre Pictet,★ Berne
1795 - 97   William Wickham, Switzerland
1797   James Talbot, Switzerland (Chargé d'Affaires)
1798 - 1814 Relations with Switzerland suspended
1798 - 99   William Wickham,★ Zurich
1799   John de Salis,★ Chur
1814 - 19   Stratford Canning, Switzerland
1815   Henry Unwin Addington, Chargé d'Affaires during Canning's absence in Vienna
1820 - 22   Edward Cromwell Disbrowe, Switzerland (Chargé d'Affaires)
1822 - 23   Henry Watkin William Wynn, Switzerland
1823 - 25   Charles Richard Vaughan, Switzerland
1825 - 26   Richard Pakenham, Switzerland (Chargé d'Affaires)
1826 - 32   Hon Algernon Percy, Switzerland
1832 - 47   David Richard Morier, Switzerland
1847 - 50   Robert Peel, Switzerland (Chargé d'Affaires)
Sep 1847   Rt Hon Gilbert Elliot, Earl of Minto,★ Switzerland
Dec 1847   Rt Hon Sir Stratford Canning,★ Switzerland
1850   Rear Admiral Sir Edmund Lyons, Bt., Switzerland
1850 - 51   Edward Herries, Switzerland (Chargé d'Affaires)
1851 - 52   Sir Arthur Magenis, Switzerland
1851   William Dougal Christie, Switzerland (Chargé d'Affaires)
1852 - 53   Sir Andrew Buchanan, Switzerland
1853   Sir Charles Murray, Switzerland
1854 - 58   George John R. Gordon, Switzerland
1858 - 66   Rear-Admiral E. A. J. Harris, Switzerland
1867   Lord Savile, Switzerland
1868   Alfred Guthrie Graham Bonar, Switzerland
1874   Edwin Corbett, Switzerland
1878   Sir Horace Rumbold, Switzerland
1879   Lord Vivian, Switzerland
1881   Sir F. Ottiwell Adams, Switzerland
1888   Sir Charles Scott, Switzerland
1893   Sir Frederick St John, Switzerland
1901   Sir William Conyngham Greene, Switzerland
1905   Sir George Bonham, Bt., Switzerland
1909   Sir Henry Bax-Ironside, Switzerland

1911	**Sir Esmé Howard,** Switzerland
1913	**Sir Evelyn Grant Duff,** Switzerland
1916	**Sir Horace Rumbold, Bt.,** Switzerland
1919	**Sir Odo Russell,** Switzerland
1922	**Sir Milne Cheetham,** Switzerland
1924	**Rowland A. G. Sperling,** Switzerland
1928	**Sir Claud Russell,** Switzerland
1933	**Sir H. W. Kennard,** Switzerland
1935	**Sir G. Warner,** Switzerland
1940	**Sir David Kelly,** Switzerland
1942	**Sir Clifford Norton,** Switzerland
1946	**Thomas M. Snow,** Switzerland
1950	**Sir Patrick Scrivener,** Switzerland
1953	**Sir Lionel Lamb,** Switzerland
1958	**Sir William Montagu-Pollock,** Switzerland
1960	**Sir Paul Grey,** Switzerland
1964	**Sir Robert Isaacson,** Switzerland
1968	**Henry A. F. Hohler,** Switerland
1970	**Eric A. Midgley,** Switzerland
1973	**Sir John Wraight,** Switzerland
1976	**Sir Alan Rothnie,** Switzerland
1979	**Sir Sydney Giffard,** Switzerland
1981	**John Powell-Jones,** Switzerland
1984	**John R. Rich,** Switzerland

1 Count de Marsay was a Hanoverian, with credentials from the Hanoverian chancery, but he dealt almost exclusively with British interests.
2 James Pictet's assignment ceased in 1767 because 'he had departed from that neutrality of behaviour so strongly recommended to him'.
3 Louis Braun was Swiss, as were Jerome de Salis, James and Isaac Pictet and, particularly during the seventeenth and eighteenth centuries, several secretaries of legation (e.g. Martin, Tronchin and Necker).

Swiss Envoys to Great Britain

★ *On special missions*

1062	**Bishop Ermenfried of Sion,**★ Papal Legate, acting for Vatican
1070	**Bishop Ermenfried of Sion**★
1513	**Mauritz Hurus of Zurich and Johann Stolz of Basel**★
1516	**Cardinal Matthias Schinner of Sion**★
1582	**Councillor Jean Maillet,**★ Special envoy of the Republic of Geneva
1589	**Jacques Lect,**★ Geneva

1596	**Michael Bäldi of Glarus,*** Protestant cantons
1602	**Jacques Anjorrant,*** Geneva
1615	**Hans Rudolf von Erlach,** Berne
1653-54	**Johann Jakob Stockar of Schaffhausen,** Protestant cantons
1655	**Hans Ulrich Gessner of Zurich,***
1709	**Peter de Salis,** Envoy of the Grisons
1730	Official agents were appointed by the canton of Berne to represent their interests in London for periods of four years at a time, until 1763.
1762-63	**Louis de Muralt of Berne,**
1814-15	**C. F. de Freudenreich,** Envoy Extraordinary of the Republic of Berne
1815-16	**A. E. de Haller,** Envoy of the Republics of Zurich and Berne
1817	**Alexandre Louis Prevost,** Commercial Agent of Switzerland
1842	**Jean Louis Prevost,** Consul and Commercial Agent
1853	**Johann Rapp,** Agent and Consul-General
1860	**Auguste de la Rive of Berne,*** Envoy Extraordinary on special diplomatic mission
1869	**Albert Streckheisen,** Agent and Consul-General
1876-96	**Henri Vernet,** Agent and Consul-General
1891-1902	**Dr Charles D. Bourcart,** First permanent diplomatic representative of Switzerland[1]
1902-19	**Dr Gaston Carlin,** Minister Plenipotentiary
1917	**Henri Martin,** Consul General and Commercial Attaché
1919-39	**Dr Charles R. Paravicini,** Minister Plenipotentiary
1939-44	**Walter Thurnheer,** Minister Plenipotentiary
1944-48	**Paul Rüegger,** Minister Plenipotentiary
1948-55	**Henri de Torrenté,** Minister Plenipotentiary
1955-63	**Armin Daeniker,** Ambassador[2]
1964-66	**Béat de Fischer-Reichenbach,** Ambassador
1967-68	**Olivier Long,** Ambassador
1968-70	**René Keller,** Ambassador
1970-76	**Albert Weitnauer,** Ambassador
1976-79	**Dr Ernesto Thalmann,** Ambassador
1980-84	**Claude Caillat,** Ambassador
1984	**François-Charles Pictet,** Ambassador

1 Dr Bourcart was Chargé d'Affaires in 1891. He was promoted to Minister Resident in 1896 and to Envoy Extraordinary and Minister Plenipotentiary in 1900.
2 The Swiss Legation in London was raised to the status of Embassy in 1957. The British Legation in Berne had been made an Embassy in 1953.

APPENDIX B

Foreign Trade between Switzerland and the United Kingdom
(in millions of Swiss francs)

and

Exchange Rates between Sterling and the Swiss Franc
(in Swiss francs to £1)

Year	Total Trade Both Ways	Swiss Exports to the U.K.	Swiss Imports from the U.K.	Sw. fr. to £1 Exch. Rate
1855	140	60	80	25.05
1885	151	99	52	25.42
1890	159	107	52	25.15
1895	178	131	47	25.40
1900	238	176	62	25.53
1905	242	175	67	25.39
1910	313	200	113	25.00
1915	467	355	113	25.80
1920	1,112	646	466	21.68
1925	649	422	227	24.98
1930	404	265	139	25.08
1935	154	78	76	15.08
1940	183	95	88	19.67
1945	54	32	22	17.31
1946	255	58	197	17.35
1947	440	117	323	17.35
1948	496	140	356	17.35
1949	434	158	276	15.90
1950	507	137	370	12.25
1951	628	229	399	12.24
1952	569	233	336	12.20
1953	587	246	341	12.19
1954	584	267	317	12.22
1955	639	303	336	12.23
1956	740	329	411	12.23
1957	816	366	450	12.24

1958	785	372	413	12.23
1959	1,031	414	617	12.14
1960	1,044	471	573	12.13
1961	1,191	510	681	12.10
1962	1,371	560	811	12.14
1963	1,572	645	927	12.10
1964	1,894	781	1,113	12.06
1965	2,059	901	1,158	12.10
1966	2,205	918	1,287	12.08
1967	2,505	1,131	1,374	11.87
1968	2,713	1,291	1,423	10.33
1969	3,216	1,383	1,833	10.31
1970	3,752	1,585	2,167	10.32
1971	4,059	1,719	2,340	10.05
1972	4,400	2,036	2,364	9.55
1973	4,516	2,276	2,240	8.25
1974	5,041	2,539	2,502	6.97
1975	4,155	2,050	2,105	5.72
1976	4,665	2,182	2,483	4.51
1977	5,548	2,400	3,148	4.19
1978	6,247	2,869	3,378	3.42
1979	6,846	3,091	3,755	3.53
1980	8,207	3,134	5,073	3.90
1981	6,886	3,428	3,458	3.96
1982	6,449	3,268	3,181	3.54
1983	6,785	3,482	3,303	3.18
1984	9,810	4,835	4,975	3.13

The figures for exports and imports in 1855 are estimates made at the time by the British Legation in Berne. The other figures are taken from *Jahresstatistik des Aussenhandels der Schweiz* and other official Swiss statistical sources.

Up to 1927, gold movements were included in Swiss statistics. Gold other than gold for banking purposes continued to be included until 1935 for exports and 1943 for imports.

After 1930, re-exports (though not direct transit trade) are included in both Swiss imports and exports.

Up to 1931 Eire was included in the Swiss statistics for the U.K.

Before 1955, Swiss statistics for the U.K. had included Cyprus, Malta and Gibraltar.

The trade statistics generally: The figures have, in recent years, been to some extent distorted by the inclusion of precious metals and precious and semi-precious stones (particularly the value of diamonds sent to Switzerland for cutting and subsequently re-exported). But the total figures demonstrate the general trends.

Exchange rates are yearly averages.

Index

Index

Note: One and two figures indicate page numbers in the Introduction
Other figures indicate dates in the Chronology

Aar, River, 1858
Aarau, 36; 1556, 1655, 1690
Aargau, canton, 1375, 1556, 1592, 1690, 1815
'A' Battery, HAC, 1912
Abauzit, Firmin, 64; 1698
Abbate, Michael, 1515
Aberdeen, Lord, 1844
Aberdeen University, 59; 1573, 1938
abolition of visas, 1947
Aboukir Bay, Battle of, 1798
Absolom, John, 1858
Achard, Jacques, 74; 1790
achromatic lens 65; 1783
Acland, Sir Antony, 1983
Acrow group, 73; 1936
Acton, Lord, 1917
Acton, Sir John, 1810
Adam, Michael, 1541
Adam brothers, 43; 1766
Adam of Usk, 1402
Adams, Franklin, 1876
Adams, Harry William, 1896
Ad Astra Air Transport Co, 1923
Addison, Joseph, 10, 51, 54; 1701, 1744
Adelboden, 1902, 1904
Adia Group, 1977
Adler Pass, 1908
admirals, Swiss, in British Service: Grandison, Sir Otho de, 40; 1337; Morier, William, 1801; Prevost, Thomas Jacques, 1811
Aegeler, 1903
Africa, British policy in, 1892, 1900
African Association, England, 1812
Agasse, Jacques-Laurent, 43; 1802
Agassiz, L, 1833
Agassiz, Louis, 65; 1873
Aglionby, William, 28
Agreements, Anglo-Swiss, see Anglo-Swiss Agreements

Aigle, 1904
Aiglon College, 1949
Ainsworth, William Harrison, 1846
Airey, Lieut-Gen Sir Terence, 1945
Air Force, Royal, 1914, 1940, 1948, 1967, 1979
Air Force, Swiss, 1954, 1979, 1983
Airolo, 54; 1926
air-raid shelters, 1930
air services: Ad Astra Co, 1923; Balair, 1923; BEA – British Airways, 1946, 1948; charter flights, 1952; Globe Air, 1964; Handley Page Co, 1923; Imperial Airways, 1924, 1929, 1935; Swissair, 1923, 1935, 1945, 1946, 1954
Aix-la-Chapelle, Treaty of, 1747
Alabama Arbitration, Geneva, 1868
Albany, Duchess of, 1754
Albert, Prince, 1837, 1851, 1852, 1856, 1864
Alcuin, 49, 800
Aldgitha, 36
Alemania, 7th C
Aletschhorn, The, 1859, 1863
Alexander II, Pope, 1062, 1070
Alfred Marks Bureau Ltd, 1977
Allalinhorn, The, 1856
Allied 'Blacklist', 1943, 1944
Allied blockade of enemy Europe, 1915, 1919
All Souls College, Oxford, 1569
Almer, Christian, 1858
Alphubell, The, 1861
Alpine climbers, see climbers
Alpine Club, London, 34; 1840, 1857, 1859, 1863, 1894, 1984
Alpine literature, see Bibliography
Alpine paintings 46; 1769, 1770, 1816, 1820, 1825, 1837, 1844, 1852, 1865, 1875, 1927; see also artists

440 *Index*

Alpine passes, 1596, 1626, 1705, 1810
Alpine Ski Club, London, 1908
Alpine Sports Ltd, 1909
Alps, The, 1, 5, 6, 33, 34, 45, 65; c650,
    1027, 1692, 1713, 1739, 1770, 1816,
    1817, 1859, 1861, 1881, 1902, 1905,
    1908, 1913, 1926, 1984
Altdorf, 1845, 1866, 1872, 1882
Alusuisse, group, 73, 81; 1970, 1971
Amadeus IV, Count of Savoy, 17; 1246
Amadeus V, Count of Savoy, 1285
Amadeus Quartet, 58; 1973
Amalgamated Dental Co. Ltd, 1911
America, Swiss with British forces in,
    15; 1749, 1756, 1765, 1778, 1780,
    1811, *see also* Canada
America, North, 1756, 1765, 1811,
    1822, 1850, 1854, 1868
American War of Independence, 1775,
    1780
Amery, L.S., 1894
Ames, E.L., 1856
Amiel, Henri Frédéric, 1935
Amiens, Peace of, 30; 1802
Ammacher, Fritz, 1924
Ampère, André, 67
Ampthill, Lord, 1907
Amstutz, Dr Walter, 1924, 1925
Anderegg, Melchior, 1864, 1888, 1894
Andermatt, 1845, 1866, 1872, 1873,
    1904, 1979
Anderson, Eustace, 1857
André, Major John, 1780
Andrews, Julie, 1976
Anglicanism, James I's plan to convert
    Venice to, 1618
Anglo-Dutch War, 23; 1653
Anglo-Persian Oil Co, 1909. 1952
Anglo-Saxons, 36; 929, 949, 1027
Anglo-Swiss Agreements: Treaty of
    Defensive Union, 25, 69; 1690,
    1692; Treaty of Friendship,
    Commerce & Reciprocal
    Establishment, 69; 1855, 1856, 1914;
    postal convention, 1868; double
    taxation (Canton of Vaud), 1872;
    extradition, 1874, 1880; trademark
    protection, 1880; arbitration, 1905;
    air navigation, 1919; exchange of
    hotel staff, 1924; double taxation
    (agency profits), 1931; war trade
    agreement, 1940; wartime
    compensation agreement, 1942;
    wartime agreement (Swiss exports to
    Germany), 1945; monetary
    agreement, 1946; abolition of visas,
    1947; supplementary monetary
    agreement, 1948; monetary
    agreement (extension), 1949; trade &
    payments, 1950; air services, 1950;
    air transport (charter flights), 1952;
    social insurance, 1953; trade
    agreement, 1954; double taxation
    (incomes), 1954; trade agreement
    (import quotas), 1955; double
    taxation (estates), 1956; Swiss loan,
    1961, 1965; atomic energy, 1963;
    conciliation & judicial settlement,
    1965; double taxation (protocol),
    1966; new double taxation
    convention, 1977; tests & test
    certificates, 1983
Anglo-Swiss Associations, 1923
Anglo-Swiss Clubs, 1950, 1974
Anglo-Swiss Condensed Milk Co, 73;
    1866, 1874
Anglo-Swiss Medical Congress, 1946
Anglo-Swiss Parliamentary Group, 32;
    1977
Anglo-Swiss Society, London, 1948,
    1950, 1967
Anglo-Swiss telephone service, 1912,
    1964, 1966
Anglo-Swiss trade contacts, early, 38,
    68, 69; 1398, 1541, c1542, 1548,
    1593, 1628, 1653, 1681, 1690, 1716,
    1842, 1843, 1844, 1851, 1852, 1855,
    1860, 1880, 1883, 1884, 1885
Anglo-Swiss trade figures (from 1885),
    see Annex on Foreign Trade
Anglo-Swiss University Ski Races, 1925
Angst, Sir Henry, 1911
Anjorrant, Jacques, 1602
Anne, Queen, 40, 59; 1708, 1709, 1710,
    1716
Ansermet, Ernest, 58; 1946, 1963
Anshelm, Valerius, 1487
anti-British feeling in Switzerland, 31;
    1732, 1892, 1896, 1899, 1900, 1901,
    1907
anti-Swiss feeling in Britain, 77; 1900,
    1964, 1965
Appenzell, 1699, 1785, c1865
Appia, Adlophe, 1928
Arbon, 7th C
Arbuthnot, Alexander, 59
archers, English, at Battle of Morat, 1476
Architectural Journal, The, 1937

Arlaud, Jacques-Antoine, 1721
Arlaud, Louis, 1790
Armada, Spanish, 1599
Armstrong Siddeley jet engines, 1958
Army reforms, British, 14; 1906
Army, Russian, 29; 1799
Army, Swiss, 17, 18, 29, 30; c1498, 1516, 1815, 1822, 1838, 1851, 1906, 1907, 1908, 1910, 1912, 1919; *see also* Militia system, Swiss
Arnold, Matthew, 54, 60, 62; 1848, 1858
Arnold, Dr Thomas, 60; 1829
Arolla, 1904
Arosa, 1904
Arquebuse, Exercice de l', 1682, 1771, 1912
Arran, 3rd Earl of, 1559
Arran, 8th Earl of, 1964
Arthur, King, 5th C, c1195
Arthur, Prince, 1868
artists, British: Absolom, John, 1858; Adams, H.W., 1896; Beaumont, Sir G., 45; 1783; Beverley, W.R., 1844; Blake, William, 43, 45; 1779, 1905, 1947, 1948; Bonington, R.P., 46; 1825; Boyce, George Price, 1844; Brooke, J.W., 1887; Burford, Robert, 1837, 1852; Callow, William, 47; 1844; Caro, Anthony, 48; Chadwick, Lynn, 1959; Cockburn, James P., 1816, 1820; Collingwood, W.G., 1887; Compton, Edward, 1875; Constable, John, 45, 52; 1779, 1797; Cotes, Francis, 42; Cozens, J.R., 45; 1776, 1803; Cromek, T.H., 46; 1830; Danby, Francis, 46; 1830; Foster, M.B., 1844; Fripp, G.A., 1844; Gainsborough, Thomas, 43; 1793; Garvey, Edmund, 1769; Girtin, Thomas, 45; Goodwin, Albert, 1903; Hepworth, Barbara, 48; 1937, 1966, 1975; Hilliard, Nicholas, 42; Hoare, Sir Richard Colt, 1785, 1810; Hockney, David, 48; Hodson, Samuel, 1887; Holland, James, 47; 1844; Holmes, Sir C., 1903; Jackson, John, 1819; Jackson, Samuel, 1858; Jackson, Samuel Philip, 1858; Jones, Owen, 1908; Kneller, Sir Godfrey, 42; 1695; Leader, B.W., 1872; Lear, Edward, 47; 1844; Lee, Sydney, 1896; Leitch, W.L., 47; 1844;

Lockhead, James, 1896; MacWhirter, John, 1887; Moore, Henry, 48; 1937, 1975; Muller, W.J., 47; 1844; Nicholson, Ben, 48; 1937; Paolozzi, Eduardo, 48; 1947; Pars, William, 45; 1770; Paterson, Emily M., 1887; Phillips, Philip, 1844; Piper, John, 1956; Reynolds, Sir Joshua, 43; 1766, 1793; Richardson, T.M., jnr, 1837; Riley, Bridget, 48; Ruskin, John, 34, 45, 47, 54; 1835, 1856; Sandby, Paul, 1807; Smith, John 'Warwick', 45; 1781; Smith, Thomas, 1796; Stubbs, George, 1802; Sutherland, Graham, 48; 1952, 1971; Sutherland, Thomas, 1803; Swete, Revd John, 1816; Towne, Francis, 45; 1781; Turner, J.M.W., 2, 45, 46; 1802, 1842, 1844, 1948, 1976; Van Dyck, Sir Anthony, 42; 1611, 1640; Wallis, G.A., 1788; Walton, Elijah, 1865; Waterlow, Sir Ernest, 1887; Willink, Henry George, 1883

artists, Swiss: Agasse, J.L., 43; 1802; Appia, Adolphe, 1928; Arlaud, J.A., 1721; Arlaud, Louis, 1790; Bill, Max, 48; 1953, 1966; Böcklin, Arnold, 45; Bordier, Jacques, 42; 1641; Bordier, Pierre, 42; 1641; Bourgeois, Sir P., 43; 1793; Brandoin, M.V., 1807; Buchser, Frank, 43; 1853, 1862; Calame, Alexander, 47; 1844; Chalon, A.E., 43; 1796; Chalon, J.T., 43; 1796; 'Corbusier, Le' (Edouard Jeanneret), 41; 1908; Dalvit, Oscar, 1953; Dassier, J.A., 1740; Dassier, Jean, 1731, 1740; Ducros, A.L.R., 45; 1785, 1840; Erni, Hans, 1937; Ferrière, François, 1802; Füssli, Heinrich (Henry Fuseli), 42, 43; 1766, 1779, 1947, 1975; Gessner, Hans-Konrad, 1797; Gessner, Salomon, 1797; Giacometti, Alberto, 41, 48; 1947, 1965, 1981; Gos, Albert, 1880; Grimm, S.H., 43; 1768; Hodler, Ferdinand, 1925; Holbein, Hans, the younger, 42; 1543; Hunziker, Max, 1953; Hurter, Johann Heinrich, 1779; Kauffmann, Angelica, 42; 1766, 1768, 1955; Klee, Paul, 48; 1934, 1945, 1947, 1953, 1956; Link, J.A., 47; Linck, J.P., 47; Liotard, J.E., 42; 1753, 1790; Lohse, R.P., 48; 1968; Lory,

artists, Swiss – cont.
   Gabriel, jnr, 47; Lory, Gabriel, snr, 47; Mayerne, Sir T. de, 1611, 1630, 1631; Merian, Matthias (the younger), 42; 1640; Morier, David, 1743; Moser, G.M., 42; 1768; Moser, Mary, 42; 1768; Mussard, Jean, 1760; Petitot, Jean, 42; 1630; Petitot, J.L., 42; 1630, 1650; Piquet, G., 1965; Schmutz, Johann, 42; 1695; Segantini, Giovanni 45; 1927; Taeuber-Arp, Sophie, 48; Tinguely, J.C., 48; 1982; Töpffer, A.W., 46; 1825; Töpffer, Rudolphe, 1823; Truninger, Max, 1953; Wäber (Webber), Heinrich, 1802; Wäber (Webber), Johann, 43; 1776, 1802; Witz, Konrad, 45; Wolf, Caspar, 46; Wolfensberger, J., 1839
Arts Council of Great Britain, 1953
asphalt, 71; 1875, 1913, 1928; *see also* Val de Travers
Aston, Mr, 1732
Athelstan, King, 36; 929, 949
Atlantic World Colleges, 1972
Aubert, Pierre, 1980, 1984
Aubert, watchmaker, 1862
Audermars, 1862
Augustus, Prince, 1791
Australia, Swiss project for colonisation of, 1731
Austria, 28; 1690, 1707, 1802, 1832, 1834, 1848, 1850, 1860, 1912, 1918
Austrian invasion of the Grisons, 1622
Austrian Succession, War of, 29; 1747
au pairs, Swiss, 1949
Avants, Les, 1904, 1927, 1975
Avigliana, 1246
Axenfels, 1904
Axenstein, 1904
Axis Powers, 16, 70; 1940, 1941, 1942, 1943

Bachmann, Gen., 1799, 1815
Bacon, Anthony, 36; 1580
Bacon, Sir Francis, 11; 1580
Bacon, Lady, 1580
Baden, 1592, 1654, 1891, 1901, 1974
Baden-Powell, Lord, 1931
Bad Ragaz, 1904
Badrutt, Johannes, 1864, 1885
Baedeker guide, first, 81
Bakewell, R., 1821
Balair, 1923
Bäldi, Michael, 1596
Bale, John, 1555, c1558
Ball, John, 34; 1840, 1856, 1859
Ballaigues, 1904
Bally Group, 73, 81; 1892, 1975
Bamert, Matthias, 58
Balmhorn, The, 1864
Bank Law of Paris, 1721
Bank of England, 1730, 1809, 1901, 1964, 1967, 1978; Governor of, 1978; Swiss Governors of, 40; 1738, 1901
banking secrecy, Swiss. 78, 79; 1934, 1972
banks and bankers, British: Bank of England, 1730, 1738, 1809, 1901, 1964, 1967, 1978; Barclays Bank, 76; 1935; Baring Bros, 75; 1815, 1914; British Bank of the Middle East, 1968; Coale's Bank, Robert, 1815; Cook & Son, Thomas, 1914; Coutts, 1886; Fleming, Robert, 1975; Grindlays Bank, 1969; Guinness Mahon & Co, 1970; Hambros, 1867; Hill Samuel & Co, 1975; Keyser-Ullman, 1969; Kleinwort Benson, 1958; Lloyds & Co, 1815; Lloyds Bank, 76; 1865, 1919; Midland Bank, 1975, 1982; Montagu, Samuel, 1958; Morgan, Grenfell & Co, 1975; National Provincial Bank, 76; 1920; National Westminster Bank, 1975; Rothschild & Sons, N.M., 1968, Royal Bank of Scotland, 1983; Schroder, J. Henry, 1967; Singer & Friedlander, 1966; Société Bancaire Barclays (Suisse) SA, 1935; Standard Chartered Bank, 1969; Warburg, S.G., 1958; United Dominions Trust, 1970; Williams & Glyns, 1975, 1983
banks and bankers, Swiss: Achard, Jacques, 74; 1790; Baer International Ltd, Julius, 1970; Bank in Winterthur, 1856; Bank Julius Baer & Co, 1968, 1970; Bank von Ernst & Cie, 1975; bankers in Basel, 75; 1815; bankers in Geneva, 74; 1703, 1733; Banque de Genève, 1931; Banque Marcuard & Cie, 1854; Buisson, 1703; Burlamaqui, Philip, 40, 74; 1624, 1639, 1652; Calendrini & Co, 74; 1652, 1655; Calendrini, Jean Louis, 1652; Cazenove, 74; Chauvet, Pierre, 1790; Coulon, Berthoud &

Co, 1848; Credit Suisse, 76, 77, 82; 1856, 1967, 1972; Falck, Louis, 1865; Favre, 1703; Fonblanque, J. & A, & Thelluson, 1762; Galland, Alfred, 1889; Galland & Cie, 1889; Gaussen, François, 75; 1738; Gaussen, Peter, 74; 1738; General Bank of Switzerland, 1854; Guiguer, Louis, 1652; Haldimand, A.F., & Sons, 40; 1765, 1809, 1813, 1826; Haldimand, Anthony Francis, 1765; Haldimand, William, 75; 1809, 1846; Handelsbank, NW, 1975, 1977; Handelsfinanz, 1982; Hentsch & Cie, 1816; Leu & Co, 74; 1754; Lombard Odier, 1867, 1973; Lullin, 74; 1703, 1790; Malacrida & Co, 74; 1702, 1709, 1721; Marcet, 1703; Moilliet, Jean Louis, 75; 1815; Moilliet, J.L. & Sons, 1815, 1865; Morris Prevost & Co, 1813, 1914; Müller & Co, 74; 1702, 1709, 1719/20, 1720, 1721; Müller, Samuel, 1652, 1702; Necker, Jacques, 1793; Perdriau, 1703; Pictet, 74; 1790; Pictet & Cie, 1982; Pourtalès, Jacques Louis, 74; 1795; Pourtalès & Cie, 74; 1795; Prevost, A.L. & Co, 1813, 1901; Prevost, Alexandre Louis 75; 1813, 1817; Prevost, Sir Augustus, 1901; Prevost, Jean Louis, 1813; Rapp & Coulon, 1848; Roveray, Antoine de, 1790; Saladin, 1703; Sarasin, A. & Cie, 1980; Sellon, Gaspard, 74; 1751; Swiss Bank Corporation, 76, 77, 82; 1856, 1898, 1967, 1968, 1980; Swiss National Bank, 1949, 1964, 1965, 1969, 1971, 1972, 1974, 1975; Swiss Volksbank, 76; 1977; Thelluson, Peter, 74; 1762; Turrettini, François, 1652; Union Bank of Switzerland, 76, 77, 82; 1856, 1967, 1974, 1984; Zachary, Long & Haldimand, 1765
Banquiers Fugger of Augsburg, 1515
Bard, castle of, 1246
Bardney in Windsey, 1485
Baring Bros, 75; 1815, 1914
Baronius, Cardinal, 51; 1614
Barrington, Richard, 34; 1858
Barrow, Isaac, 64; 1676
Barth, Karl, 31; 1938, 1941
Barton, Daniel, 1904
Barton, Mrs Daniel, 1904
Basel, city & canton, *passim*

Basel Kammerorchester, 1953
Basel University, Scottish students in, 1588; University, 57, 59; 1503, 1529, 1555, 1588, 1599, 1959, 1962
Bass SA, 1969
Bas Tube Co Ltd, Le, 1905
Baum, René, 1957
Baume & Mercier, 1862
Baumgartner, Rudolf, 1961
BBC, 1948, 1964, 1973
BBC Symphony Orchestra, 58; 1957
Bear Hotel, Grindelwald, 1892
Bears, The, skating club, 1927
Beatenberg, 1904
Beatenbucht, 6th C
Beattie, William, 1844
Beatus, 6th C
Beaufoy, Col Mark, 1787
Beaumont, Sir George, 45; 1783
Becker, Hugo, 1892
Beckford, William, 53; 1785
Beddoes, Thomas Lovell, 53, 54; 1835
Bede, The Venerable, 49; 1563
Bedford Insurance Co, 1960
Belalp, 1904
Belgrave Square, London, 40; 1826
Bell, Gertrude, 1902
Bellinzona, 1882, 1913, 1926
Belloc, Hilaire, 54; 1817, 1902, 1945
Bennett, Arnold, 54; 1908, 1910
Bentham, Jeremy, 51; 1829
Bentham, Thomas, 1555
Bergier, Jean-François, 71
Berkeley, Lennox, 57; 1948
Berne, city & canton, *passim*; Minster, 1901; Treasury, 1709, 1714, 1721, 1798; University, 1813, 1958
Bernese, The, 1375, 1607, 1618, 1660, 1668, 1685, 1707, 1709, 1710, 1719/20, 1720, 1721, 1723, 1730, 1743, 1749, 1751, 1763, 1788, 1793, 1798, 1821
Bernese investments in Britain, *see* Swiss investments in Britain
Bernese Oberland, 6thC, 1776, 1817, 1841, 1844, 1845, 1846, 1861, 1871, 1875, 1890, 1902, 1909, 1910
Bernese troops in British service, 1665, 1688, 1692, 1694, 1709, 1746, 1795, 1809
Bernoulli, Daniel, 64; 1738
Bernoulli, Jakob, 64; 1676
Bernoulli, Johann, 64, 65; 1676, 1689, 1697, 1748

Bernoulli, Nicolas, 64
Beverley, William Roxby, 1844
Bex, 1904
Beza, Theodore, 21, 37, 49; 1558, 1569, 1570, 1576, 1580, 1590, 1602, 1604, 1611
Bèze, Théodore de, *see* Beza, Theodore
Bible, The, 11
Bible, Alcuin's, 800
Bible, 'Breeches', *see* Bible Geneva
Bible, Coverdale's, 1535, 1555
Bible, Geneva, 21, 49; 1560, 1620
Bible of Moutier-Grandval, 1979
Bible, Romansch, 1718
Bible, Zurich, 21, 49; 1535
Bibliothèque Britannique, 53, 60; 1796, 1798, 1803, 1829
Bibliothèque Universelle, 1803, 1816, 1900
bicycles, British, 1937
Bienne, 1788, 1789, 1903; Lake, 1804
Bietschhorn, The, 1859
Bill, Max, 48; 1953, 1966
Billroth, C.A.T., 63; 1851
Binn, valley of, iron ore project, 1732
Birkin, Sir Stanley, 1923
Birmingham, 1815, 1826
Birrell, Augustine, 1920
Bitzius, Albert, 'Jeremias Gotthelf', 1866
Blackett, Prof P.M.S., 1967
Blackwell, Eardley, 1850
Blaikie, Thomas, 67; 1775
Blake, William, 43, 45; 1779, 1947, 1948
Blanche of Savoy, 1256
Blessington, Lady, 1839
Bloch, Ernest, 58
Bloodhound guided missiles, 1961
Blumer, Samuel, 56
Blümlisalp, The, 1861, 1908
Blunt, Wilfrid Scawen, 54; 1858
bob-sleighs, 1890; race, St Moritz, 1898
Böcklin, Arnold, 45
Bodensee, *see* Constance, Lake of
Bodleian Library, 1555
Bodley, John, 1555, 1582
Bodley, Thomas, 1555
Bodmer, Johann Georg, 12; 73; 1816, 1817, 1824, 1849
Bodmer, Johann Jakob, 51; 1725, 1744, 1762
Boer War, 31; 1899, 1900, 1907
Bolgenschanze, Davos, 1935
Bolton, Lancs, 1824

Bon, Anton, 1912
Bon, Anton Sebastian, 1912
Bonar, A.G., 1868
Bonham, Sir George, 1908
Boniface, Archbishop, 1236
Boniface, Count of Savoy, 1259
Boniface VIII, Pope, 1290
Bonington, Richard Parkes, 46; 1825
Bonstetten, Capt, 1689, 1694
Bonstetten, Charles Victor de, 9; 1767
Book of Geneva, 1558
books, Swiss, for German POWs in England, 1945, 1946
Books of Switzerland exhibition, London, 54; 1946
Booth, 'General' William, 1883
Booth, Miss, arrested in Neuchâtel, 1883
Bordier, Jacques, 42; 1641
Bordier, Pierre, 42; 1641
Borromini, Francesco, 41; 1667; influence of, on English architects, 1667
Borthwick, Sir John, 1555
Bosset, Charles-Philippe de, 1808
Boswell, James, 34, 38; 1764
Boulton, Watt & Co, 1826
Bouquet, Gen Henri, 15; 1756, 1765
Bourcart, Charles, 1891
Bourgeois, Sir Peter Francis, 43; 1793
Bourrit, Marc Théodore, 65
Boveri, Walter, 1891
Bowles, William Lisle, 54
Bowring, Sir John, 1836
Boyce, George Price, 1844
Boyd Neel Orchestra, 1954
Boyle, Robert, 37, 63, 64; 1639, 1676
BP (Schweiz) AG, 1909
Bracken, C., 1908
Braid, James, 63; 1843
Bräker, Ulrich, 1762, 1978
Brandoin, Michel-Vincent, 1807
Brandt, Louise, 1748
Brassey, Thomas, 71; 1853, 1867
Braun, Louis Beat, 1752, 1782
Breadalbane, Lord, 1810
Bream, Julian, 1973
Brehmenbühl, The, 1906
Breitenfels, J. von, 1759
Breithorn, The, Oberland, 1867
Breithorn, The, Valais, 1821, 1855
Breitinger, J.J., 51; 1725
Bremble, John de, 1188, 1926
Brescia, siege of, 1516
Brienz, 1839, 1863
Brierly, Prof, J.L., 53

Brig, 1639
Brisson, Alexander, 58; 1580
Bristol Aircraft Co, 1961
Bristol, 4th Earl of, *see* Hervey
Bristol hotels, 34; 1770
Bristol Old Vic Co, 1968
Britain, *passim*
Britannia Iron & Steel Works, 1935
British Aerospace plc, 1980
British and Swiss in the Alps, The, exhibition, London, 1984
British Army, Swiss supplies for, 1854
British Bank of the Middle East, 1968
British Celanese Ltd, 73; 1916, 1944
British Cellulose & Chemical Manufacturing Co Ltd, 1916
British Chamber of Commerce in Switzerland, 1920, 1962; *see also* British-Swiss Chamber of Commerce
British colonels in Switzerland, 1799, 1815, 1854
British colonial markets, 1846, 1855, 1875, 1887
British consuls & consulates in Switzerland, 35; 1846, 1856, 1872, 1891, 1893, 1899, 1902, 1903, 1904, 1907, 1911, 1917, 1930, 1977
British Council, 1946, 1947, 1951, 1952, 1960, 1963, 1975
British-Cypriot Agreements, 1960
British East India Company, 74; 1624, 1751, 1752, 1769, 1784, 1788, 1792
British European Airways, 1946, 1948
British Export Council, 1961
British ex-servicemen in Switzerland, 1948
British firms in Switzerland, number of, 1973
British & Foreign Bible Society, 1804
British government, *passim*
British government stock, 74; 1703, 1709, 1754, 1790, 1798
British interests, Swiss protection of, 33; 1952, 1956, 1982
British investment in Switzerland, 73, 76; 1853, 1856, 1867, 1875, 1913, 1919, 1925, 1973, 1981
British Manufacture and Research Co, 1971
British Merchandise Marks Act, 1887
British Military Commission, to Switzerland, 1907, 1908
British Military Mission, 1799, 1815, 1955

British Museum, London, 40, 53, 57; 1776, c1784, 1827, 1925, 1953, 1976, 1979
British Overseas Trade Board, 1978
British POWs in Germany, 1917; in Switzerland, 1918, 1943
British Railways, 1824, 1843, 1950, 1955
British reactions to Swiss scenery *(see also* British views on Switzerland and the Swiss): Arnold, Matthew, 1848, 1858; Arnold, Thomas, 1829; Baden-Powell, Lord, 1931; Belloc, Hilaire, 1902; Bennett, Arnold, 1908; Bremble, John de, 1188; Browning, Elizabeth Barrett, 1849; Canning, Stratford, 33; de Beer, Sir Gavin, 1952; Cavendish, Georgiana, Duchess of Devonshire, 1799; Dickens, Charles, 1845; Eliot, George, 1849; Eliot, T.S., 1922; Gibbon, Edward, 1755; Hardy, Revd J.F., 1861; Harrison, Frederic, 1908; Keynes, Lord, 1905; Lunn, Sir Arnold, 1902, 1945; Maugham, William Somerset, 1918; Montague, C.E., 1926; Pater, Walter, 1875; Ruskin, John, 45; 1835, 1861; Schuster, Lord, 1925; Shelley, Percy Bysshe, 1817; Smith, Richard, 1563; Stephen, Leslie, 1871; Tennyson, Alfred, Lord, 1846; Walpole, Horace, 1739; Wills, Sir Alfred, 1854
British Residents' Association of Switzerland, 1946
British residents in Switzerland, 35, 36, 38; 1555, 1556, 1660, 1739, 1773, 1787, 1816, 1854, 1855, 1888, 1900, 1910, 1976
British Ski Year Book, 1924
British subsidies and gifts to Switzerland, *see also* British investment in Switzerland, 17, 18, 21, 23; 1514, 1515, 1516, 1582, 1584, 1589, 1602, 1655, 1656, 1799
British-Swiss Chamber of Commerce, 1962
British-Swiss interparliamentary ski race, Davos, 32; 1956, 1976
British Syphon Mfg. Co, 73; c1865
British tariff system, dismantling of, 1860
British textile machinery, 71; 1800, 1805, 1834

446 *Index*

British tourists in Switzerland, 35; 1764, 1816, 1835, 1859, 1864, 1869, 1871, 1873, 1874, 1893, 1900, 1902, 1905, 1913, 1921, 1929, 1931, 1933, 1937, 1946, 1947, 1948, 1966, 1970, 1974,. 1983
British trademarks, Swiss imitation of, 1852
British trade unions, 9
British views on Switzerland and the Swiss (*see also* British reactions to Swiss scenery): Aberdeen, Lord, 1844; Addison, Joseph, 10; 1701; Agassiz, L., 1833; Arnold, Matthew, 54; Arran, Lord, 1964; Bacon, Sir Francis, 11; Bakewell, R., 1821; Bale, John, c1558; Bennett, Arnold, 1908; Blake, William, 43; Boswell, James, 1764; Bryce, Lord, 7; Burnet, Bishop, 1685; Burney, Dr Charles, 1770; Butler, George, 1869; Campbell, Thomas, 1844; Canning, Stratford, 30; Castlereagh, Lord, 12; 1822; Chamberlain, Sir Austen, 1911; Churchill, Sir Winston, 32; 1919, 1944; Clarendon, Lord, 1856; Coryat, Thomas, 59; Coxe, Archdeacon William, 7, 14; 1776, 1789; de Beer, Sir Gavin, 1952; Dickens, Charles, 1846; Duff, Sir E. Grant, 1914; Eden, Sir Anthony, 1955; Elizabeth I, Queen, 1602; Elizabeth II, Queen, 1980; Evelyn, John, 10, 13; 1646; Ferguson, Robert, 14; Fox, Charles, 1788; Fry, Elizabeth, 1839; Gibbon, Edward, 1755; Gibbon, Monk, 1950; Goldsmith, Oliver, 1756; Graves, Charles, 1947; Gray, Thomas, 1739; Greene, Sir W.C., 1901, 190'5; Grote, George, 1847; Haig, Field-Marshal Earl, 14; Hollis, Thomas, 1748; Hughes, Prof Christopher, 1975; Hutton, James, 1748; Hutton, R.H., 1867; Johnson, Dr Samuel, 10; Kelly, Sir David, 1940; Lawrence, D.H., 1913; Marlborough, Duke of, 28; Masefield, John, 1946; Moore, John, 1773; More, Sir Thomas, 1516; Moryson, Fynes, 1592; Nash, Thomas, 1594; Pace, Richard, 1523; Pell, John, 1654; Pope, Alexander, 1728; Radcliffe, Col Delmé, 14; 1906, 1909, 1910; Ray, John, 1665; Reresby, Sir John, 1654; Rumbold, Sir Horace, 58; 1866; Ruskin, John, 11, 12; 1856, 1869; Shelley, P.B., 1817; Smith, Adam, 10; Southey, Robert, 1817; Stanyan, Abraham, 1, 13; 1714; Steinberg, Jonathan, 1; Stevenson, Robert Louis. 1880; Stewart, Michael, 1964; Symonds, J.A., 1877; Voigt, F.A., 1944; Wake, Sir Isaac, 22; 1626; Wall, Daniel, 1819; Wilde, Oscar, 1899; Wordsworth, Dorothy, 1820; Wordsworth, William, 5
British Weeks and other promotions in Switzerland, 1953, 1961, 1962, 1963
Britten, Benjamin, 57; 1946, 1955, 1956, 1959, 1963, 1969, 1974
Broadbank, Sir Joseph, 1921
Broadwood, John, 56; 1740
Brooke, John William, 1887
Brooke, Stopford, 54
Brougham, Lord, 59; 1805, 1818
Broughton, 1660
Brown Boveri & Co Ltd, 71, 73, 80; 1871, 1891, 1900, 1906, 1919, 1950, 1974, 1984
Brown, Charles, 71; 1851, 1871
Brown, Charles Eugene, 71; 1871, 1885, 1886, 1891
Brown, Yeats, 1835
Browne, T.L. Murray, 1868
Browning, Elizabeth Barrett, 54; 1859
Browing, Robert, 54; 1835, 1883
Brown's Hotel, London, 1912
Brugger, Ernst, 1977
Brünig Pass, 6th C, 1796
Brunnen, 1814
Brunner, John, 73; 1873
Brunner, Johann Conrad, 1727
Brunner Mond, 73; 1873
Brunner, Revd John, 1873
'Brunner's glands', 1727
Bryce, Lord, 7
Buccleuch, 3rd Duke of, 33; 1764, 1766
Bucer, Martin, 1547
Buchser, Frank, 43; 1853, 1862
Buckingham, Duke of, 1628
Buckmaster & Moore, 77
Budé, Jacob, Gen, 1781
Bühler Bros, 80; 1933
Bühler, René, 1956
Buisson, 1703
Bull, John, 55; 1603

Bullinger, Heinrich, 21, 49; 1541, 1547, 1548, 1551, 1553, 1555, 1558, c1558, 1570, 1653
Bund, Der, 31; 1850
Buol, Christian, 1877
Burcher, John, 1536, 1541, 1542, 1548
Burckhardt, Jacob, 1872, 1937
Burckhardt, Dr Jakob, 1967
Burckhardt, Johann Ludwig, 1812
Burford, Robert, 1837, 1852
Burgdorf, Berne, 1768
Burghley, Lord, c1579
Bürgi, Jost, 63; 1632
Bürglen, Thurgau, 1652
Burgundy, 7th C, 18; 1476
Burke, Edmund, 1767
Burkhard, Willy, 58; 1938
Burlamachi, Philip *see* Burlamaqui
Burlamaqui, Jean-Jacques, 1748
Burlamaqui, Philip, 40, 74; 1624, 1637, 1639, 1652
Burnaby, John, 28; 1743, 1744
Burnand, Denys-Guerard, 1749
Burnand, Sir Francis, 1749
Burnet, Bishop Gilbert, 34; 1685, 1747
Burney, Dr Charles, 33, 56; 1766
Burney, Fanny, Mme d'Arblay, 1773
Burns, Robert, 1789, 1885
Butler, George, 1869
Butler, Samuel, 51, 54; 1725, 1881
Buttisholz, Battle of, 49; 1375, 1829
Byron, Lord, 34, 53, 54; 1787, 1816, 1817, 1826, 1840, 1908, 1952

cable cars, Swiss, 35
Cadbury-Schweppes plc, 1792, 1816
Cahill, J.R., 1919
Cairney, Miss Maud, 1928
Calame, Alexandre, 47; 1844
Calcutta, Swiss commandant of, c1784
Calendrini & Co, 74; 1652, 1653, 1655
Calendrini, Jean Louis, 1652
Callender, 1835
Callow, William, 47; 1844
Calvin, Jean, 18, 21, 49; 1476, 1555, 1556, 1558, 1564, 1589
Calvin's Academy, Geneva, 18, 36, 58, 59; 1564, 1569, 1583, 1590, 1593
Cambridge, 1516, 1767, 1929
Cambridge, Mass., 1873
Cambridge University, 38, 59, 64; 1547, 1551, 1570, 1572, 1812, 1957
camera lucida, 1816, 1833; obscura, 1833

Camerata Bern, 1981
Campbell, Thomas, 54; 1844
Canada, Swiss in, 1778, 1795, 1811, 1813, 1816; Swiss settlement in, 1668; *see also* America, North
Candolle, Alphonse de, 67
Candolle, Augustin Pyrame de, 67; 1841
Canning, George, 1814, 1827
Canning, Sir Stratford, 30, 31, 33, 54; 1814, 1815, 1816, 1847, 1848
Canterbury Cathedral, 1614
cantons, Swiss, 5, 7, 18, 22, 86; 1513, 1514, 1515, 1516, 1582, 1617, 1699, 1743, 1747, 1790, 1793, 1814, 1815, 1822, 1844, 1854, 1984; Catholic, 22, 23, 24, 30; 1656, 1716, 1847; German-speaking, 1911; Protestant, 22, 23, 25, 28, 29, 30, 65, 69, 74; 1589, 1596, 1626, 1628, 1652, 1653, 1654, 1655, 1656, 1668, 1690, 1847
Canute, King, 33; 1027
capital inflows into Switzerland, 1931, 1967, 1971, 1972, 1974, 1975, 1976
Carillon on the Swiss Centre, 1984
Carlton Hotel, London, 1906
Carmarthen, Marquess of, *see* Leeds, Duke of
Carne, John, 1826
Caro, Anthony, 48
Caroline, Princess of Wales, 1814
Carolinum, Zurich, 59; 1611
Carouge, Geneva, 1923
Carr, Lord, 1976
Carrington, Lord, 1980
Cartwright, Thomas, 1570
Carver, Field-Marshal Lord, 1976
Casaubon, Issac, 51; 1593, 1614
Castegna, Grisons, 1776
Castlereagh, Lord, 12; 1814, 1815, 1822, 1827
Castoni, Angelo, 1890
Catherine of Aragon, Queen, 18; 1529
Catholic monasteries, 1818
Catholic powers in Europe, 22; 1626
Catholics, Swiss, 1847
Cato by Joseph Addison, 1701, 1744
Caulfield, Vivian, 1910
Caux, 1895, 1904
Cavendish, Georgiana, Duchess of Devonshire, 1799
Cavour, Count, 1843
Cawley, William, 1660
Cazenove, 74
Cecil, Sir Robert, 1559

Ceduald, King, c689
Cendrars, Blaise, 1970
Central English Library, Zurich, 1960, 1975
Centurion tanks, British, 16; 1952, 1955, 1957
Cenwald of Worcester, 929
Cephalonia, 1808
CERN, Geneva, 67; 1967
Ceylon, Swiss military commander of, 1797
Chadwick, Lynn, 1959
Chalon, Alfred-Edouard, 43; 1796
Chalon, Jean-Jacques, 43; 1796
Chamber of Commerce, Geneva, 1921, 1932; Zurich, 1921
Chamberlain, Sir Austen, 1911, 1925
Chamberlain, Joseph, 70; 1901
Chamberlain, Neville, 16; 1938
Chambésy, 1816
Chamonix, 1741
Champéry, 1775, 1904
Champfèr, 1904
Champvent, Pierre de, 1256
Champvent, William de, 1262, 1290
Chandolin, 1904
Channel Islands, 1256, 1337
Channon, Paul, 1984
Chantry, Sir Francis, 1819
Chapelle Anglaise, Holy Trinity, Geneva, 1853
Chaplin, Sir Charles, 1978
Chapman, Robert, 1856
Chappuzeau, Samuel, 1662, 1667
charabanc tours to Switzerland, 1921
character of the British, 5-12; of the Swiss, 5-12, 79
Charing Cross, London, 1818; Charing Cross and Strand Electricity Supply Co, 1886; Hospital, 40
Charlemagne, Emperor, 49; 800
Charles I, King, 42, 63; 1611, 1630, 1634, 1639, 1640, 1653, 1660
Charles II, King, 14, 25, 38, 42; 1650, 1663, 1667, 1679
Charles V, Emperor, 1523
Charles, Prince, 1957
Charles the Bold, 1476
Charles Emmanuel I, Duke of Savoy, 21, 68; 1582, 1589, 1602, 1610, 1613, 1615, 1617, 1618, 1621, 1622, 1627, 1628
Charles Emmanuel II, Duke of Savoy, 23; 1654, 1655

Charles Stuart, the Young Pretender, 15; 1745, 1754
Charlotte, Queen, 42, 65; 1752, 1768, 1773, 1781
Château d'Oex, 1902, 1904, 1916
Chatelard School, 1927, 1975
Chaucer, Geoffrey, c1370, 1946
Chauvet, Pierre, 1790
Chaux-de-Fonds, La, 1862, 1903, 1905
Cheam School, Surrey, 60; 1819
cheese, English, exported to Switzerland, 68; 1541
cheese, Swiss, exported to Britain, 1842, 1846, 1954
Chelsea, London, 1822; Old Church, 1724
chemical and pharmaceutical industry, Swiss, 72, 79; 1855, 1914, 1929, 1939; products exported to Britain, 1909, 1914; British chemicals imported, 1909
Chesières-Villars, 1949
Chesterfield, Earl of, 33; 1740, 1746
Chevalier, Antoine-Rodolphe, 1551
Chevallaz, Georges-André, 1980
Chief(s) of staff: American, 1945; British, 1945, 1975, 1976; Swiss, 1910, 1940, 1975, 1976
Chillon, Castle of, Montreux, 1828
Chittagong, Swiss governor of, 1752
chocolate, Swiss, exported to Britain, 1883, 1903, 1909, 1922; Swiss-owned factories in London, 1883
Christie, Daniel Beat, 1788
Christie, John, 1788
Chur, Grisons, c650, 1516, 1648, 1685, 1710, 1718, 1766, 1799, 1804, 1861, 1904; Cathedral, 1685
Church Missionary Society, 1945
Church of England, 1; 1552, 1572, 1752
Church of Scotland, 21; 1558, see also Presbyterianism
churches, British, in Switzerland, 35; 1556, 1685, 1830, 1853, 1870, 1886, 1887, 1892, 1902, 1904, 1920, 1945, 1971
churches, Swiss in Britain, 39; 1762, 1794, 1814, 1855, 1924
Churchill, Randolph, 1965
Churchill, Sir Winston, 16, 32, 54; 1894, 1919, 1944, 1945, 1946, 1965, 1966, 1971; Churchill Foundation, 16; 1966, 1975; Memorial, Oberhofen, 16; 1965, 1975;

Memorial Lectures, 1973, 1975;
  Memorial Library, 1966
Churchill, Winston, 1976
CIBA-Geigy group, 67, 68, 72, 73, 79;
  1855, 1911, 1918, 1934, 1971
City Swiss Club, London, 1856, 1917,
  1954
Civil Service, Swiss, 86
civil war in Switzerland, *see* Sonderbund
  War
Clairmont, Claire, 1814, 1816
Clarendon, 1st Earl of, 1682
Clarendon, 4th Earl of, 1856
Clarendon family, 36
Clarens, 1904
Clark, Petula, 1976
Clavel, Alexandre, 72; 1855, 1916
Clavel-Dreyfus Group, 73; 1916
Clayton Aniline Co, 1911, 1918
Cleghorn, Prof, Hugh, 29; 1790, 1795
Clementi, Muzio, 1740
Clias, Heinrich, 15; 1822
climbers, British in Switzerland: Amery,
  L.S., 1894; Ames, E.L., 1856;
  Anderson, Eustace, 1857; Ball, John,
  34; 1840, 1856; Barrington, Richard,
  34; 1858; Beaufoy, Col Mark, 1787;
  Bell, Gertrude, 1902; Blackwell,
  Eardley, 1850; Bracken, C., 1908;
  Browne, T.L. Murray, 1868; Brown,
  Yeats, 1835; Cairney, Maude, 1928;
  Callender, 1835; Chapman, Robert,
  1856; Churchill, Sir Winston, 1894;
  Conway, Lord, 34; 1881; Coolidge,
  Dr W.A.B., 1926; Davies, J.
  Llewelyn, 1858; Douglas, Lord
  Francis, 1865; English Students from
  Fellenberg's School, 1842; Finch,
  George, 1923; Forster, P.G. 1923;
  Forbes, Prof J.D., 34; 1841, 1844;
  Girdlestone, Revd A.G., 1870;
  Hadow, Mr., 1865; Hardy, Revd
  J.F., 1857, 1861; Herschel, Sir John,
  1821; Hinchcliff, T.W., 1857;
  Hornby, Revd J.J., 1867; Hudson,
  Revd Charles, 1855, 1865; Kennedy,
  T.S., 1862; Keynes, Lord, 1905;
  Larden, Walter, 1903; Lewis-Lloyd,
  Emmeline, 1869; Lindsay, Scott,
  1908; Lunn, Sir Arnold, 34; 1909,
  1924, 1945; Malkin, A.T., 34; 1839;
  Mathews, William, 1859; Moore,
  A.W., 1862; Moore, W.A.M., 1909;
  Peto, R.H., 1923; Pilley, Dorothy,
  1928; Richards, Ivor, 1928;
  Richardson, E.C., 1906; Roget, Prof
  F.F., 6; 1909; Schuster, Lord, 34;
  1925; Smith, Albert Richard, 1852;
  Smythe, Frank, 34; 1953; Speer, S.
  Templeton, 34; 1835, 1849; Stephen,
  Sir Leslie, 1859, 1861, 1871;
  Stratton, Miss, 1869; Tuckett, F.F.,
  1859; Tyndall, Prof John, 34, 67;
  1858, 1862, 1868; Walker, Francis,
  1864; Walker, Frank, 1826; Walker,
  Lucy, 34; 1864; Whymper, Edward,
  34; 1861, 1865; Wigram, William,
  1862; Windham, William, 1741;
  Winkworth, Mr & Mrs, 1863; Wills,
  Alfred, 34; 1854; Wybergh, Cecil,
  1908; Young, Geoffrey Winthrop,
  34; 1905, 1935
Clinton, Col H., 1799
Clinton, Gen, 1780
Clive, Gen Lord, of India, 1751, 1757,
  1776
Clive, Lord (later 1st Earl of Powis),
  1751, 1757
Clockmakers' Company, London, 1854
clocks and watches, English, c1696,
  1742: Swiss, exported to Britain,
  1851, 1855, 1862, 1903, 1905, 1909,
  1915, 1920, 1925, 1932, 1937, 1951,
  1984
clothing, British, exported to
  Switzerland, 1937; Swiss (ready-
  made) exported to Britain, 1954
coal, British, exported to Switzerland,
  1919, 1937
Cobden, Richard, 34; 1836
Cockburn, Maj James, 1816, 1820
Cockfield, Lord, 1983
Col de la Dent Blanche, 1909
Col de la Faucille, 1835
Col d'Hérens, 1909
Col de Jaman, 1952
Coleridge, Samuel Taylor, 54; 1807
Colet, John, 1516
Collace, William, c1573
Colladon, Anne, 1679
Colladon, Jean-Daniel, 67
Colladon, Sir John, 63; 1631, 1658
Colladon, Sir Theodore, 63; 1679, 1708
Collegium Musicum of Zurich, 1954
Collingwood, William Gershon, 1887
Collins, Wilkie, 1846, 1867
Collins, William, 54
Cologny, 53; 1816

Colonial and Continental Church Soc, 1904, 1920
Colonial Governors, Swiss in the British Service: Bosset, Col Charles-Philippe, Gov, Cephalonia, 1808; Braun, Col Louis Beat, Gov, Chittagong, 1752; Frischmann, Col Daniel, Col-Comm, Madras, 1751; Guggisberg, Sir Gordon, Gov, Gold Coast, 1919; Haldimand, Gen Sir Frederick, Gov and C-in-C, Canada, 1778; Imthurn, Sir Edward, Gov, Fiji, 1846; Meuron, Maj-Gen Pierre Frédéric de, Mil Comm, Ceylon, 1797; Munzinger, Werner, Gov-Gen, Eastern Sudan, 1872; Polier, Col Antoine Louis, Commandant, Calcutta, c1784; Prevost, Gen Sir George, Gov-Gen, Canada, (British North America), 1811; Prevost, Maj-Gen, Augustin, Gov, East Florida, 1778; Prevost, Maj-Gen Jacques, Gov, Antigua, 1756; Watteville, Maj-Gen, Abraham de, Mil-Gov, Quebec, 1813
Columbanus, 36; 7th C
Common Market, *see* EEC
communications between Britain and Switzerland: air travel, 1919, 1923, 1924, 1929, 1935, 1945, 1946, 1948, 1950, 1951, 1952, 1954; letters, 1654, 1691; London-Basel sea route, 1920, 1921, 1958; telegraph, 1854; telephone, 1912, 1964, 1966; travel times, 990, c1549, 1835, 1898, 1938
Como, Lake, 1833
composers – British, Swiss, *see* musicians
Compton, Edward, 1875
Concorde airliner, 1967
condensed milk, Swiss, exported to Britain, 1866, 1909
conductors, British, Swiss, *see* musicians
Conference of London, 1856
Connaught, Duke of, 1864
Conod, Marc-Antoine, *see* Pellis
Conrad, Joseph, 54; 1873
Constable, John, 52; 1779, 1796, 1797
Constable, Sir Thomas, 67; 1784
Constance, Lake of, 36; 7th C, 1799, 1817, 1853
Constance, public baths at, 1516
Constant, Benjamin, 11, 53; 1786, 1816
Constant, Charles de, 1816
Constantinople, 1628, 1729, 1801

Conti, Prince de, 1699, 1707
Continental Protestant League, Cromwell's plan for a, 23, 28; 1653, 1654
Continental System, Napoleon's, 1810
Conway, Lord, of Allington, 34; 1881
Cook, Capt, James, 43; 1776
Cook, Thomas, 34; 1818, 1863
Cook, Thomas & Son, 1914
Coolidge, Dr W.A.B., 1926
Cooper, Anthony Ashley, 1711, 1744
'Corbusier, Le', Charles Edouard Jeanneret, 41; 1908
Cork, Earl of, 1639
Cornhill Magazine, 1878
Corrodi, August, 1885
Corsica, 1795
Coryat, Thomas, 59
Cotes, Francis, 42
cotton goods, British, exported to Switzerland, 1785, 1835, 1836, 1883, 1884, 1893, 1904, 1937; Swiss, exported to Britain, 71; 1835, 1836, 1893
Coucy, Enguerrand de, 1375
Coulon, Berthoud & Co, 1848
Council of Europe, 32
Couronne, Hôtel de la, Solothurn, 1764
Courtaulds Ltd, 73; 1916
Courvoisier, 1862
Covent Garden Opera, London, 1983
Coventry Chain Co, 1930
Coverdale, Miles, 1535, 1555
Coward, Noël, 1976
Cowper, William, 60
Coxe, Thomas, 1689, 1690
Coxe, Archdeacon William, 7, 14, 34; 1714, 1776, 1789
Cozens, John Robert, 45; 1776, 1803
Craig, Edward Gordon, 1928
Cramer, Gabriel, 64; c1726
Cranmer, Thomas, 21; 1537, 1555
Crauford, Col Robert, 1799
Credit Suisse, 76, 77, 82; 1856, 1967, 1972
Cresta Run, St Moritz, 34; 1885
cricket on skates, at St Moritz, 1896
Crimean War, 12; 1854
Cripps, Sir Stafford, 1951
Cromek, Thomas Hartley, 46; 1830
Cromwell, Oliver, 14, 23, 28, 65, 74; 1652, 1653, 1654, 1655, 1656, 1658
Cromwell, Richard, 1658
Crosse & Blackwell, 73; 1960
Croz, Michel, 1865

Cuenod, Hugues, 58
Cumberland, Duke of, 1743
Cunard Steamship Company, 1920
Curchod, Suzanne, 1755
curling in Switzerland, 1885, 1911
Curzon, Clifford, 1962
Cuthbert, 49
Cyprus, Republic of, 1960
Czarnikow Ltd, 1846

Dalcroze, Emile Jacques, 1897, 1950
Dalcroze Society, 1950
Dalry, Ayrshire, 1984
Dalvit, Oskar, 1953
Danby, Francis, 46; 1830
Dartrey, Lord, 1779
Darwin, Charles, 67; 1859, 1873
Dassier, Jacques Antoine, 1740
Dassier, Jean, 1731, 1740
d'Athée, Gerard, 1215
Davidson, John, 1555
Davies, John, 1973
Davies, J. Llewelyn, 1858
Davos, 32, 43, 54; 1867, 1869, 1877, 1880, 1888, 1891, 1896, 1903, 1904, 1915, 1924, 1930, 1935, 1956, 1976
Davy, Sir Humphry, 67; 1814, 1829
DDT, 1939
de Beer, Sir Gavin, 1952
Declaration of London, 1920
defence sales, British, to Switzerland, 16; 1948, 1952, 1954, 1955, 1957, 1958, 1961, 1972, 1973, 1979, 1980, 1983
Defoe, Daniel, 3, 48; 1719
de Grandson, *see* Grandson
de la Rive, Auguste, 1860
de la Rive family, 1814
De La Rue Co, The, 1952
Delémont, Jura, 1979
Delius, Frederick, 57; 1901
Della Casa, Lisa, 58; 1951
Delmé-Radcliffe, Col C., 14; 1906, 1908, 1910, 1912
Delolme (*or* de Lolme), John Louis, 53; 1769
de Montfort, Simon, Parliament of, 7
Dente Blanche, 1862, 1928
Dent d'Hérens, 1923
Denzler, Col, 1851
de Salis, *see* Salis de
de Trey & Co, 1911
Devereux Robert, 37; 1607
Deyverdun, Jacques-Georges, 1767
Diablerets, Les, 1904

Dickens, Charles, 54; 1762, 1809, 1845, 1846, 1853, 1863, 1867
Dickson, Col, 1854
Diesbach, Nicholas de, c1465
Digby, Sir Kenelm, 1648
Diodati, Charles, 23, 63; 1633
Diodati, Jean, 1639
Diodati, Theodore. 63; 1633
Diodati, Villa, 1816, 1840
Disentis, Grisons, Abbey of, 614
Disraeli, Benjamin, 34; 1826
Dolland, John, 65; 1783
Dolmetsch, Arnold, 57; 1894, 1925, 1928
Dolmetsch, Carl, 57; 1925, 1928
Dom, The, Valais, 1858
Domesday Book, 1086
Dorchester Hotel, London, 1912
Douglas, Lord Francis, 1865
Dover, Thomas Platter's arrival at, 1599
Doyle, Sir Arthur Conan, 54; 1891, 1895, 1900; Foundation, 1968, 1977
D'Oyly Carte, Richard, 1888
Dranmor (Ferdinand Schmidt), 1888
Dreyfus, Camille, 1916, 1944
Dreyfus, Henri, 1916, 1929, 1944
Dreyfuss, George, 1905
Driffield, V.C., 1867
Drummond, Henry, 1818
Drury Lane, London, 1766, 1792
Ducros, Abraham-Louis-Rudolphe, 45; 1776, 1785, 1810
Dufour, Gen, 1847
Dulwich, College, 43, 1793
Dumont, Pierre Etienne, 51; 1829
Dunant, Henri, 1863
Duns Scotus, 1503
Duppa, Francis, 1818
Dür, Hans, 1556
Durie, John, 1655
Dürrenmatt, Peter, 1957
Dutch East India Company, 1652, 1795
Dutoit, Charles, 58; 1983
Duval, Thomas, 1798
Dyestuffs Act of 1922, 1918
dyestuffs, Swiss, exported to Britain, 72; 1914, 1918, 1937

East Florida, Swiss governor of, 1778
Ebli, 1541
Ebnefluh, The, 1868
Economic Warfare, British Ministry of, 1940, 1941, 1942
Economist, The, 1929, 1932

Eden, Sir Anthony, 1955
Edgeworth, Maria, 51, 59; 1798, 1805, 1835
Edgeworth, Richard, 51, 59; 1798, 1805
Edict of Nantes, Revocation of, 1685
Edinburgh, 60; 1583, 1764; University, 11, 38, 59, 67; 1583, 1786, 1789, 1806
Edinburgh, HRH The Duke of, 1974
Edlin, F.S., 1924
education, Swiss and British compared, 58, 59, 60, 62
educational exchanges, Anglo-Swiss, 1951, 1963
educational system, Swiss, 58, 59, 60, 85
Edward I, King, 15, 17, 33; 1270, 1273, 1282, 1285, 1286, c1289, 1290
Edward III, King, 15; 1344, c1370, 1375
Edward IV, King, c1465, 1476
Edward VI, King, 21; 1548, c1549, 1551, 1552
Edward VII, King, 40; 1905, 1906
Edward, Prince, Duke of Kent, 1789, 1792
Edward, Prince, son of George III, 1781
Edward the Confessor, 1062
EEC, 32, 70, 77; 1959, 1970, 1972
EFTA, 32, 70; 1958, 1959, 1961, 1964, 1965, 1970, 1972
Eggishorn, The, 1839, 1904
Église Helvétique, L', London, 1762
Egypt, 1795, 1798, 1956
Egyptian Hall, Piccadilly, 1825, 1852
Eiger, 1858, 1924, 1925, 1945, 1979
Eigerjoch, 1859
Einsiedeln, 1799; Benedictine Abbey of, 36, 49; 949, 1755
Einstein, Albert, 62
Elba, 30; 1795, 1815
Eleanor of Provence, 1236, 13th C
Elgar, Lady, 43
Elgar, Sir Edward, 43; 1946, 1981
Eliot, George, 54; 1849
Eliot, Nicholas, 1537
Eliot, T.S., 54; 1922, 1946, 1960
Elliotson, Prof John, 63; 1831, 1843
Eliott, Gilbert, 2nd Earl of Minto, 1816, 1847
Elizabeth I, Queen, 14, 21, 63; 1551, 1556, 1558, 1572, 1582, c1592, 1584, 1589, 1596, 1599, 1602, 1604
Elizabeth II, Queen, 1947, 1952, 1977, 1980

Elouis, Joseph, 56; c1781
Elsighorn, The, 1902
Ely, Bishop of, 1572
embroideries, Swiss, exported to Britain, 79; 1835, 1880, 1925, 1932, 1951
Emery, B., 34; 1818, 1833, 1835
Engelberg, 1904
England, *passim*
English Arts and Crafts Movement, influence on Le Corbusier, 1908
English Barrow, Buttisholz, 1375
English Chamber Orchestra, 58; 1969, 1973
English Condensed Milk Co, 1874
English, high level of knowledge of, in Switzerland, 55; 1923, 1961, 1973
English literature, influence of, in Switzerland, 48, 49, 51, 52, 53, 55; 1725
Entlebuch, The, Lucerne, 1375
Episcopalianism, Zurich's influence on development of, in England, 21; 1558
Erasmus, 49; 1516, 1518, 1529
Eremita, 1685
Erlach, Albrecht von, 1640
Erlach, Benedict ab, 1590
Erlach, Hans Rudolf von, 1615
Erlach, Sigismund, d', 1688, 1689
Ermenfried of Sion, Bishop, 38; 1062, 1070
Erni, Hans, 1937
Erroll, F.J., 1963
Erskine, James Francis, 1775
Escalade, The, 21, 55; 1602, 1603, 1613
Escher, Albert, 1824
Escher, Hans Caspar, 38; 1805, 1824
Escher-Wyss, 71; 1805, 1836; *see also* Sulzer Brothers
Essex, 2nd Earl of, 37; 1596
Eton College, 60; 1905, 1954
Etter, Dr, 1948
Eugene, Prince, 1709
Eugster, Albert, 73; c1865, 1912
Eugster, Lieut-Col Oscar Lewis, 1912
Euler, Leonhard, 64; 1768, 1783
Eurobonds, 77
eurhythmics, 1897, 1950
Eusebius, c850
Evangelicalism in Switzerland, 1818
Evelyn, John, 10, 13, 33; 1646
Everest expeditions, Swiss, 1953; British, 1953
exchange rate, 70; 1931, 1935, 1936, 1946, 1949, 1956, 1966, 1968, 1971,

1972, 1973, 1976, 1977, 1978, 1979, 1981, *see also* App B
Exercice de l'Arquebuse, 1682, 1771, 1912
Exeter Cathedral, 1327
Export Council for Europe, 1963

Faden, William, 1776
Fagius, 1547
Fairbairn & Lillie, 1824
Falck, Louis, c1865
Falckner, 1541
Falklands, Invasion of the, 1982, 1984
Faraday, Michael, 67; 1814, 1841, 1845
Farrar, Percival, 1902
Fatio de Duillier, Nicholas, 64; 1686, 1689
Favre, banker, 1703
Federal Institute of Technology, Zurich, 85; 1965, 1967
Federation of British Industries, 1963
Federation of Swiss Societies in the UK, 1919, 1965
Feldmann, M., 1946
Fellenberg, Emmanuel von, 59, 60; 1818, 1866, 1867
Fellenberg's school, English students at, 1842
Ferguson, Robert, 14
Ferney, near Geneva, 1764, 1766, 1776
Ferranti Computer Systems, 1984
Ferrière, François, 1802
Fielding, Sir Basil, 1634
Fielding, Henry, 1743
Fiest, Hans, 1946
Financial News, 1900
Finch, George, 1923
Finhaut, 1904
finishing schools, British, in Switzerland, 62
Finsteraarhorn, 1857, 1858, 1902, 1909
Fischer, Beat de, 1691
Fischer, Edwin, 58; 1960
Fischer, Georg, Ltd, 71, 73, 81; 1804, 1905, 1935
Fischer, Johann Conrad, 1804, 1815, 1845
Fitzgerald, Lord Robert, 29; 1790, 1793, 1794
Flecker, James Elroy, 54; 1915
Fleming, Ian, 1963
Fleming, Sir Oliver, 22, 69; 1629, 1645
Fletcher, John, playwright, 49; c1518
Fletcher, John, (J. de la Fléchère), 1752

Flüelen, 1872
Fonblanque & Thellusson, J. & A., 1762
Foot, Dingle, 1945
Forbes, J.D., 34, 67; 1841, 1844
Foster, Miles Birket, 1844
Forster, P.G., 1923
Fox, Sir Charles, 1852
Fox, Charles James, 34; 1782, 1788
Fox, Gerald, 1891
Fox, Henderson & Co., 1852
Fox Talbot, William Henry, 47; 1833
Foxe, John, 21, 49; 1555, 1559
François I, King, 17; 1515
Frankfurt, 1541, 1549, 1556
Fraubrunnen, 1375
Frauenfeld, 1974
Frederick I, of Prussia, 1707
Frederick the Great, 1740, 1754
Frederick William II, of Prussia, 1795
Frederick William IV, of Prussia, 1848, 1852, 1856, 1857
Free trade movement in England, 1842
French confiscation of Swiss wealth, 1798
French hospital, London, 1798
French influence in Switzerland, 17, 23, 25, 28, 29; 1515, 1523, 1596, 1597, 1654, 1658, 1689, 1692, 1704, 1716, 1743, 1790, 1794, 1803
French Revolution, 29, 74; 1792, 1793, 1802, 1807
Freudenreich, C.F. de, 1814
Fribourg, 17; 1259, 1754, 1816, 1844, 1850; Treaty of, 1515
Fridolin, c650
Friedrichshafen, Zeppelin workshops, Germany, 1914
Fripp, George Arthur, 1844
Frisch, Max, 1962
Frischmann, Daniel, 1751
Fritz, Gaspard, 1770
Froben, Johannes, 1516, 1518
Froschauer, Christopher, 1535, 1541, 1548, c1549, 1550
Fry, Elizabeth, 59; 1818, 1839
Furgler, Kurt, 1975, 1983, 1984
Furi, Thomas, 1981
Furka pass, 1873
Füssli, Heinrich, *see* Fuseli, Henry
Fuseli, Henry, 42, 43; 1766, 1779, 1947, 1975

Gabelhorn, The, 1928
gaesati, Rhaetian, in England, 12

Gainsborough, Thomas, 43; 1793
Galland, Alfred, 1889
Galloway, Lord, 1694
Gallus, 36; 7th C
Galsworthy, John, 1963
Galway, James, 1976
Garrick, David, 1766, 1771
Garter, Order of the, 1344, 1375
Garvey, Edmund, 1769
Gaskell, Elizabeth, 54, 1864
Gatti, Sir John, 1911
Gatti family, 40; 1886
Gatti's Restaurant, London, 1917
Gaudin, Prof M.A., 1825
Gaussen, François, 1738
Gaussen, Peter, 74; 1738
Gazette de Lausanne, 1816
Geigy Co, 72; 1888, 1914, 1939, *see also* CIBA-Geigy group
General Bank of Switzerland, 1854
General Sozietät der Englischen Baumwollspinnerei, 1800
Geneva: airport, 1984; British community in, 36, 37, 38; 1555, 1556, 1560, 1564, c1573, 1685, c1732, 1739, 1741, 1770, 1771, 1773, 1787, 1816, 1821; churches in, 1719; city, republic and canton, *passim*; close relations with England, 18, 21; c1696, 1773, 1816; Consistory of, 1580; Council of, 1584, 1668, 1685, 1763, 1772; influence on Scottish Church, 21; 1558, c1579; influence on Scottish universities, 58, 59; 1583; revolution in, 1782, 1794; University of, 1794, 1951, 1954, *see also* Calvin's Academy
Geneva, Lake of, 1817, 1824, 1826, 1840, 1849, 1946
Geneva, 'Queen' of, 1904
Genevois, Société des, 1685, 1703
Gentleman's Magazine, The, 1750
Geological Society, London, 1806
George I, King, 25, 59, 63; 1716, 1718, 1721, 1723, 1727
George II, King, 42, 53, 56, 59, 63; 1713, 1721, 1739, 1740, 1742, 1743, 1745, 1747, 1749
George III, King, 12, 40, 43, 59, 63; 1763, 1767, 1768, 1772, 1781, 1782, 1793, 1795; Coronation crown of, 1769; court of, 1802
George V, King, 1918

George VI, King, 1952
German influence in Switzerland; British fears of, 1892, 1906, 1911, 1912, 1914; on Swiss army system, 1906, 1908, 1910, 1911, 1912
German PoWs in Britain, Swiss books and lectures for, 1945, 1946, 1948
Gesner, Conrad, 63
Gesner, Johann, 65
Gessner, Hans-Konrad, 1797
Gessner, Hans Ulrich, 1645
Gessner, Salomon, 52; 1758, 1776, 1797, 1953
Giacometti, Alberto, 41, 48; 1947, 1965, 1981
Gibbon, Edward, 53; 1755, 1767, 1783, 1785, 1787, 1789
Gibbon, Monk, 1950
Giessbach, 1841
Giori company, The, 1952
Gilby, Anthony, 1555, 1560
Gillespie, George, c1573
Girard, Père Jean-Baptiste, 60; 1850
Girdlestone, Revd A.G., 1870
Girtin, Thomas, 45
glaciers, 65, 67; 1690, 1741, 1755, 1857
Gladstone, William Ewart, 60; 1860
Gland, 1899
Glarus, canton, 56, 68; c650, 1690, 1893
Glasgow, 1715, 1917; Church Assembly, 1639; University, 59; 1555, 1569
Glenshiel, 1719
Gletsch, 1904
Gletscherhorn, The, 1867
Glion, 1904
Globe Air, 1964
Gloucester, Duke of (brother of George III), 1782, 1787, 1792
Glover, Richard, 54
Glyndebourne Opera House, Sussex, 1788, 1946, 1951
Godman Irving, Bryant, 1976
Godwin, Mary, *see* Shelley, Mary
Gold Coast, Swiss governor of, 1919
Gold Standard, Swiss off the, 1936; UK off, 1931
Goldman, Maj, 1912
Goldsmith, Oliver, 54; 1743, 1756, 1766
Goodhart, Sir Philip, 1976
Goodman, Christopher, 1555
Goodwin, Albert, 1903
Gordon, George John, 1856

Gore-Booth, Sir Paul, 1968
Gos, Albert, 1880
Göschenen, 1926
Gosse, Edmund, 54; 1883
Göttingen University, 63; 1749
Goumoëns, George, 1715
Graber, Pierre, 1972, 1973
Graffenried, Christophe de, 1710
Graffenried, Frédéric de, 1816
Grandson (later Grandison) family, 38; Catherine de Grandson, 1344; John de Grandison, 40; 1327; Sir Otes de Grandson, 15; 1256, 1270, 1282, 1289, 1300; Admiral Sir Otho de Grandson, 40; 1337; William, Seigneur de Grandson, 1256; William de Grandson, 1256, 1300, 1327
Grandson, Otto de, c1370
Grandson, Neuchâtel, 38
Grand Tour, The, 33; 1593, 1746, 1750
Grant-Duff, Sir Evelyn, 1914
Grasser, Johann Jakob, 1606
Grauhaupt, The, 1840
Graves, Charles, 16; 1947
Gray, Thomas, 54; 1739, 1767
Great Exhibition, London, 1851
Great St Bernard pass, c689, 990, 1027, 1188, 1246, 1802
Greaves, J.P., 59; 1817
Greenham Common, Berks, 1979
Greene, Sir W. Coyningham, 1901, 1905
Green Jackets, see King's Royal Rifle Corps
Greenwich Hospital (Painted Hall), 1667
Greenwich, Royal Naval College, 1822
Gregory, St, 36; 949
Greville, Charles, 1775
Grenville, Lord, 1773, 1794, 1799
Grey, Lady Jane, 21; 1548, 1553, 1556
Grey, Sir Edward, 1908, 1912
Grey, Sir Paul, 1960
Griffith ab Einion, Evan, 1375
Grilly, Jean de, 1256
Grimm, Samuel Hieronymus, 43; 1768
Grimsel Pass, 1909
Grimwald, Abbot, 800
Grindelwald, 1690, 1802, 1817, 1871, 1889, 1891, 1892, 1904, 1926, 1937
Grindlays Bank, 1969
Grisons, canton, 5, 12, 22, 29, 36, 74; c614, 1596, 1618, 1622, 1626, 1653, 1685, 1705, 1709, 1742, 1789, 1799; see also Rhaetia
Grob, Johann Georg, 1558

Grob, Johann, 1664
Gros-Claude watches, 1862
Grose, Francis, snr, 1769, 1789
Grose, Francis, jnr, 53; 1769, 1789
Gros Fiescherhorn, The, 1862, 1888
Gros Lauteraarhorn, The, 1888
Grosley, Piere Jean, 1770
Gross national product, British, 1950, 1973; Swiss, 1950, 1973
Grossmünster, Zurich, 1519
Grosvenor, Earl of, 40; 1826
Grote, George, 1837, 1847
Grove, Sir George, 1866
Groves, Charles, 1973
Grylls, Michael, 1976
Grynaeus, Professor Simon, 1529, 1588
Gryon, 1904
Gstaad, 57; 1904
Gstaad annual music festival, 1956
Gualter, Rudolf, 1537
Gualter, Rudolf, the younger, 1572
Guggisberg, Sir Gordon, 1919
'Guglers', The, 1375
Guiffardière, Revd Charles de la, 1781
Guiguer, Louis, 1652
Guillaume, St, 36; 1234
Guinness Mahon & Co., 1970
Guisan, General Henri, 16; 1940
Gümmenen, 17; 1259, 1282
Gunpowder Plot, 55; 1606
Guy's Hospital, London, 1789

Habsburg, Dukes of, 81; 1259, 1375
Hadow, Mr, 1865
Hadrian's Wall, 12
Haggard, Sir Henry Rider, 1872
Haig, General Sir Douglas, 14; 1906
Hailsham, Lord, 1975
Haldane, R.B., 1906
Haldane, Robert, 1818
Haldimand, A.F., & Sons, 40; 1765, 1809, 1813, 1826
Haldimand, Anthony Francis, 1765, 1778, 1809
Haldimand, Lieut-Gen, Sir F., 1756
Haldimand, William, 75; 1809, 1846
Hall, Rouland, 1560
Hallam, Henry, 1846
Hallé Orchestra, 58; 1976
Haller, A.E. de, 1814
Haller, Albrecht von, 52, 63; 1711, 1739, 1749, 1752, 1953
Halley, Edmund, 64
Hambros, Bank, 1867

456 *Index*

Hamilton, 8th Duke of, 1773
Hamilton, Sir William, 1810
Hamilton family, 36
Hampshire Cricket Club, 1925
Handegg Falls, 1844
Handel, George Frideric, 55; 1713, 1740
Handelsbank, NW, 1975, 1977
Handelsfinanz, 1982
Handley-Page Herald, 1964
Handley-Page Transport Co, 1923
Hardy, Revd J.F., 1857, 1861
Hardy, Thomas, 54; 1897
Hargreaves' spinning jenny, 1978
Harlech Castle, Wales, 1286
Harrison, Frederic, 1908
Harrow School, 60
Haskil, Clara, 58
Haslemere Music Festival, 57; 1925
Hasler group, 1948
Haslital, The, 1259
Hattersley, Roy, 1976
Hauenstein tunnel, Olten, 1853
Hawksmoor, Nicholas, 1667, 1738
Hawthorne Davey & Co, 1932
Haydn, Franz Joseph, 1730, 1740
Haymarket, Opera House, London, 1713
Hay, Sir James, Earl of Carlisle, 1628
Hazlitt, William, 54; 1824
Heath, Edward, 1971
Heer, Jean, 1957
Heer, Oswald, 67
Hegner, Otto, 58; 1889, 1893
Heidegger, Johann Jacob, 56; 1713
Heiden, 1904
Heim, Archbishop Bruno, 1973
Hemans, Felicia Dorothea, 54; 1825
Hemsley, Lord, 1898
Henri IV, King, 1610
Henry III, King, 17, 38; 1236, 1246, 1259
Henry VII, King, 1487
Henry VIII, King, 12, 14, 17, 18, 42; 1513, 1514, 1515, 1516, 1517, 1523, 1529, 1542, 1543, 1547
Henry, Prince of Wales, 55
Hentsch & Cie, 1816
Hepworth, Barbara, 48; 1937. 1966, 1975
Herschel, Sir John, 1821
Hervart, Philibert de, 1689, 1699
Hervey, Frederick, 4th Earl of Bristol, 34; 1770, 1776, 1799, 1810
Hesse, Hermann, 1922

Heywood, John, 1800, 1801
Heywood, Marcus, 1935
High Duty Alloys Ltd, 1970
Hilarius, c650
Hill, Arthur, 1954
Hill Samuel group, 1975
Hilles, Barnaby, c1548
Hilles, Richard, 1541, 1542, c1548
Hilliard, Nicholas, 42
Hinchliff, T.W., 1857
Hirzel, Gottlieb, 1851
Hispano Suiza (Suisse) SA, 1971
Hoare, Sir Richard Colt, 1785, 1810
Hobbes, Thomas, 51; 1679, 1762
Hobson, Valerie, 1976
Hockney, David, 48
Hodler, Ferdinand, 1925
Hodson, Samuel, 1887
Hoffmann, E.T.A., 55
Hoffmann, Fritz, 1908
Hoffmann-La Roche group, 73, 79; 1908, 1937, 1939, 1973, 1984
Hofwyl, Institute for boys at, 59; 1818, 1839, 1842
Hogg, Quintin, 1889
Holbein, Hans, the younger, 42; 1543
Holderbank group, 81
Holinshed, Raphael, 49; *Chronicles*, 1550
Holland, James, 47; 1844
Holliger, Heinz, 58; 1961, 1981
Holliger, Ursula, 1971
Hollis, Thomas, 1748
Holmes, Sir Charles, 1903
Holmes, Oliver Wendell, 1835
Holmes, Sherlock, 54; 1891, 1968
Holst, Gustav, 1946
Holy Alliance, 1827
Home, Lady, 1973
Home, Lord, (Sir Alec Douglas-), 1973
Honegger, Arthur, 41, 58; 1929
Honegger, Caspar, 1834
Hooker, Richard, 51; 1594
Hooker, Sir William, 67; 1814
Hooper, John, 18; 1547, 1551, 1552
Hopkins, Gerard Manley, 54; 1868
Horn, D.B., 28
Hornby, Revd, J.J., 1867
Hornchurch, Essex, 13th C
Horne, Robert, 1555
Hotel Belvedere, Davos, 1880
Hotel d'Angleterre, Geneva, 1816
Hotel Drei Könige, Basel, 1754
Hotel Gütsch, Lucerne, 1868
hotels, Swiss, 35, 81, 82; 1828, 1912,

1924, 1931, 1933, *see also* under individual names
Hotz, Dr M., 1940
Howe, Sir Geoffrey, 1984
Howie, Robert, 59; 1588
Huber, Hans, 1893
Hudson, Revd Charles, 1855, 1865
Hudson's Bay Company, 1816
Hughes, Christopher, 1975
Huguenots, French, 22; 1628, 1685
Hull, Yorkshire, 1917
Hume, David, 39, 51; 1580, 1766, 1767
Hume, David, poet, 1580
Hummel, Pastor J. H., 1640, 1660, 1663
Hundred Days of 1815, 17; 1815
Hundred Years' War, 15; 1375, 1444
Hungarian uprising, 1956
Hüningen, 30
Hunt, Lord, 1976
Hunter jet fighter aircraft, 16; 1958, 1972, 1973, 1979
Huntsman, Benjamin, 1804
Hunziker, Max, 1953
Hürliman, Dr Martin, 54
Hurter, Ferdinand, 73; 1867
Hurter, Johann Heinrich, 1779
Hurus, Mauritz, 1513
Huskisson, William, 1823
Hürzel, Peter, 1541
Hutchison, Sir James, 1961
Hutton, James, 1748
Hutton, R.H., 1867
Huxley, Prof T.H., 62, 67; 1857, 1889
Hyde, Edward, Lord Cornbury, 1682
hypnotism, *see* mesmerism

I.C.I. plc, 73; 1873, 1948, 1971
Ilford films, 73; 1971
Imperial Airways, 1924, 1929, 1935
Import Duties Act, British, 1932
import restrictions, British; duties, 1915, 1920, 1925, 1926, 1932, 1933, 1934; import surcharge, 1964, 1965; quotas, 1946, 1951, 1954, 1955
import restrictions, Swiss, 1893; duties, 1885, 1887, 1895, 1902, 1923; quotas, 1932, 1936, 1955
Imthurn, Sir Edward, 1846
Imthurn, Johann Conrad, 1846
India, Swiss in British service in, 15; 1751, 1752, 1757, 1769, 1781, c1784, 1788, 1794, 1797, 1799, 1854
Industrial Revolution, The, 71, 80; 1752
interchange schemes: foreign university, 1963; young research workers, 1963
Interlaken, 1690, 1838, 1849, 1882, 1904, 1906, 1916, 1974
International Exhibition of Painting, London, 43; 1862
International Parliamentary Union, 32
International Society of Artists, 1925
investment, *see under* British and Swiss
Ireland, 25; 1256, c1289, 1689, 1690, 1782
Irish and Anglo-Saxon monks in Switzerland: Columbanus, 36; 7th C; Eusebius, c850; Fridolin, c650; Gallus, 36; 7th C; Gregory, 36; 949; Guillaume, 36; 1234; Magnoald, 7th C; Marcus, c850; Moengal, 55; c850; Sigisbert, 36; c614; Theodore, 7th C
iron & steel, British, exported to Switzerland, 1835, 1909
Iselin, Johann-Jacob, 1794
Italy, 18, 31; 1246, 1615, 1618, 1626, 1705, 1799, 1867, 1915
Ivernois, Sir Francis d', 1782, 1794

'Jacconets' cloth, 1893, 1904
Jackson, Miss E.P., 1888
Jackson, John, 1819
Jackson, Samuel Philip, 1858
Jacobs-Suchard group, 81; 1912, 1933, 1984
Jacquet-Droz, Henri-Louis, 1775, 1787
James I, King, 21, 55, 63; 1593, 1604, 1606, 1609, 1610, 1611, 1613, 1615, 1617, 1618, 1621, 1622, 1624
James II, King, 25; 1682, 1688, 1689, 1716
James Edward, The Old Pretender, 15, 25; 1715, 1719
James, Henry, 54; 1878
James of St George, Master, 1260, 1286
James, Regent of Scotland, 1576
Jameson Raid, Transvaal, 1896
Jamestown, Virginia, 1607
Jardin Anglais, Geneva, 1854
Jenny, Melchior, 1681
Jesuits, Society of Jesus, 1606, 1818
Jewell, Bishop John, 51; 1555
John, King, 1215
Johnson & Cock, 1761
Johnson, Dr Samuel, 10; 1767
Johnson Matthey group, 73; 1761, 1970
Johnston, John, 59; 1590, 1615
Jolles, Paul, 1975
Jones, Gwyneth, 1962

Jones, Inigo, exhibition, Berne, 1975
Jones, Owen, 1908
Jonson, Ben, 49; c1518
Journal de Genève, 1901
journalists, British, arrest of, in Switzerland, 1915
Joyce, James, 1915
Julius II, Pope, 1513
Jung, Carl Gustav, 63; 1946
Jungfrau, The, 1835, 1849, 1856, 1858, 1863, 1888, 1945
Jungfraujoch, The, 1862
Jura, The, 29; 7th C, 1789, 1817, 1902, 1979
Justus, 6th C

Kammermusiker of Zurich, 1971
Kandahar Challenge Cup, 1911
Kandahar (K) Ski Club, 1924
Kandersteg, 1863, 1904, 1909, 1931
Kauffmann, Angelica, 42; 1766, 1768; exhibition, London, 1955
Keate, George, 54; 1756
Keighley Lifts Ltd, 1982
Keith, Lord, 37; 1719, 1754, 1762, 1764, 1766
Keith, George, 37; c1573
Keith, William, c1573
Keller, Gottfried, 57; 1901, 1960
Keller, Prof Paul, 1940, 1943
Kelly, Sir David, 1940
Kelterborn, Rudolf, 1961
Kemble, John Philip, 1823
Kennedy, T.S., 1862
Kent, Duke of (father of Queen Victoria), 37
Kent, Fair Maid of, 1344
Kent, George, Ltd, 1974
Kerr, Deborah, 1976
Kethe, William, 1555
Kew Gardens, London, 67; 1814
Keynes, Lord, 1905
Keyser Ullmann, 1969
Kingsmill, Andrew, 1569
King's College, Aberdeen, 59
King's College Choir, Cambridge, 1954
King's Royal Rifle Corps (60th Rifles), 16; 1756; *see also* Royal American Regiment
Kinnoull, Lord, 1729
Kirschberger, Emmanuel, 1688
Klee, Paul, 48; 1934, 1945, 1947, 1953, 1956
Klein Fiescherhorn, The, 1888

Klein Matterhorn, The, 1855
Klein Schreckhorn, The, 1857
Kleinwort Benson, Ltd, 1958
Klosters, 1909
Kneller, Sir Godfrey, 42; 1695
Knight, Dr William, 1514, 1523
Knocker, Edward, 1890
Knollys, Sir Francis, 1555
Knowles, James Sheridan, 54
Knox, John, 8, 21, 36; 1556, 1558, 1582, 1685
Knubel, Joseph, 1935
Kobelt, Karl, 1952
Königshofer, Dr Franz, 1962
Korsakov, Gen, 29; 1799
Kruger, President, 1896
Kulm Hotel, St Moritz, 1864
Kunsthaus, Zurich, 1947
Kuoni Travel Ltd, 1968

Labelye, Charles, 40; 1738, 1750
Lac Léman, *see* Geneva, Lake of
Ladies' Ski Club of Great Britain, 1907
Lake Champlain, Canada, 1811
lake steamers, early, in Switzerland, 35, 71, 81; 1817, 1824, 1826, 1836, 1868
Lambert, Raymond, 1953
Landsgemeinde, 7
Landis & Gyr group, 73, 81; 1912
Landolt, Dr E., 1951
Landon, Letitia Elizabeth, 54
Lanfranc, Archbishop, 1070
Langtry, Lillie, 1888
Lang watches, Geneva, 1862
Lansdowne, Lord, 1901
Larden, Walter, 1903
Latimer, Bishop Hugh, 1547, 1555, 1559
Latrobe, Charles Joseph, 1824
Lätt, Prof Arnold, 1916, 1919, 1920
Laud, Archbishop, 1639
Lausanne, 25, 33, 37, 74; 990, 1755, 1770, 1783, 1787, 1788, 1816, 1823, 1826, 1852, 1853, 1854, 1887, 1889, 1897, 1900, 1904, 1910, 1922, 1930, 1946, 1952, 1974, 1977; British colony in, 37, 38; 1770, 1783, 1854, 1946; Cathedral, 1270; Spring Festival, 1962, 1973; University, 1746
Lauterbrunnen, 1802, 1826, 1858, 1863, 1871, 1904, 1928
Lavater, Johann Caspar, 53; 1776, 1953
Law, John, 1721

Lawrence, D.H., 54; 1913
Lawson, James, 1583
Leader, Benjamin Williams, 1872
League of Augsburg, War of the, 25
League of Nations, 1868, 1904, 1920, 1932
Leake, Col William, 1815
Lear, Edward, 47; 1844
Le Blond, Mrs A., 1907
Lect, Jacques, 1589
Leeds Castle, Kent, 1920
Leeds, Duke of, 1790
Lee, Syndney, 1896
Leibnitz, or Leibniz, Gottfried Wilhelm, 64; 1689, 1748
Leicester Square, London, 1852
Leitch, William Leighton, 47; 1844
Lemnitzer, Gen, 1945
Lenk, 1908
Lennox, Duke of, 1582
Lentulus, Paulus, 63; c1592, 1597
Lenzerheide, 1909
Leo X, Pope, 17; 1516
Leopold III, Duke of Austria, 1375
Le Sieur, Stephen, 1609
Leslie, Sir John, 1796
Leu & Co, see Bank Leu
Leukerbad, 1863, 1904
Lever Bros, 1898, 1904
Lever, Thomas, 36; 1556
Lewis-Lloyd, Emmeline, 1869
Leysin, 1904, 1916
Librium, 1973
Liddiard, William, 54; 1832
Liechtenstein, Principality of, 1984
Lill, John, 1973
Limerick, Lord, 1976
Linck, Jean Antoine, 46
Linck, Jean Philippe, 46
Lindsay, David, 1555
Lindsay, James, c1573
Lindsay, Scott, 1908
Lindt (England) Ltd, 1933
Linth, River, c650
Liotard, Jean Etienne, 42; 1753, 1790
Lisle, John, 1660, 1663
Lister, Joseph, Lord, 63; 1851
Liverpool, 1828, 1860, 1865, 1917
Llewellyn, Evan, 1375
Lloyds Bank, 73, 76; 1865, 1919
Locarno, 1904; Conference, 1925
Locher of St. Gallen, 1702
Lock, Henry, 1602
Locke, John, 51; 1704, 1748, 1762

Lockett, W.G., 1891
Lockhead, James, 1896
Locle, Le, c1670, 1775
Lodge, Sir Oliver, 1910
Loèche-les-Bains, see Leukerbad
Lohse, Richard P., 48; 1968
Lombard Odier et Cie, 1867, 1973
London, 14, 34, 38, 39, 40, 43, 54, 71, 77; Chronology, passim; Lord Mayor of, 1606, 1951, 1963; Swiss comments on, 1693, 1770, 1789
London Festival Ballet, 1957, 1973
London Infant School Society, 60; 1817
London Philharmonic Orchestra, 58; 1973
London Protocol, 1852
London Stock Exchange, 77; 1732, 1733, 1984
London Symphony Orchestra, 58
Londonderry, Lord, see Castlereagh
Longworth, James, 1800, 1801
Lory, Gabriel, father & son, 46
Lötschenlüke Pass, 1909
Louis I, Count of Savoy, 1444
Louis I, Count of Vaud, 1285
Louis XI, King, 1476
Louis XII, King, 17; 1514, 1515
Louis XIV, King, 1694, 1699, 1707
Louis XVI, King, 1791, 1793
Louise, Princess, 1868
Loutherbourg, Sir Philip de, 1789
Love, Nicholas, 1660
Lowson, Lady, 1951
Luc, Jean André de, 65; 1773, 1787
Lucas Industries, 1974
Lucerne, Lake, 81; 1756, 1776, 1819, 1868, 1948
Lucerne, town and canton, 34; 5th C, 1375, 1863, 1866, 1868, 1893, 1900, 1902, 1903, 1904, 1913, 1918, 1920, 1926, 1930, 1946, 1953, 1969
Lucerne Festival, 1946, 1969; Choir, 1969; Strings, 1961
Lucius, St, 1685
Luddism, 1832
Ludlow, Edmund, 14, 23; 1660, 1665, 1698, 1791
Lugano, 1829, 1889, 1904, 1907, 1914, 1926, 1930
Luini, Bernardino, 1869
Lullin, bankers, 74; 1703
Lullin family, 1790
Lunn, Sir Arnold, 34, 35; 1902, 1908, 1922, 1924, 1925, 1945

460 Index

Lunn, Sir Henry, 1902, 1909
Lunn's tours, 1902
Lutry, 1757
Lyell, Lord, 1976
Lympany, Moura, 1973
Lysjoch, The, 1859
Lyskamm, The, Zermatt, 1861

Maag, Peter, 58
Macaulay, Thomas Babington, Lord, 1853
MacDonnell, Thomas, 1663
Machiavelli, Niccolo, 12, 13
machinery, Swiss, exported to Britain, 1851, 1909, 1937, 1942
machine tools, Swiss, 81
McKenna duties, *see* import restrictions
MacWhirter, John, 1887
Madeley, Shropshire, 1752
Maggi, Julius, 1890
Magna Carta, 32; 1215
Magnoald, 7th C
Mahon, Lord, 1773
Maillet, Councillor Jean, 1582
Maison Chapuis, 1840
Malacrida & Co, 74; 1702, 1709, 1721
Malden, Surrey, 1086
Maler (or Mahler), Josua, 1551
Malkin, A.T., 34; 1839
Mallet, David, 1739
Mallet, John Lewis, 1783
Mallet, Paul, 1781
Mallet du Pan, Jacques, 1783
Maloja, 1889, 1904
Malplaquet, Battle of, 1709
Malta, 1795, 1802, 1808
Malthus, Daniel, 51; 1764, 1767
Malthus, Revd Robert, 51; 1764, 1767, 1802
Manchester, 1824, 1849, 1893, 1917, 1951, 1981; Lord Mayor of, 1949; Chamber of Commerce, 1893
Mandel, Mr, 1732
Manners, Roger, 1596
Manners family, 36
Mansfield, Count, 1618
Marcet, Alexandre, 1789
Marcet, bankers, 1703
Marcombes, Isaac, 1639
Marconi Ltd, 1922, 1933
Marcus, Bishop, c850
Maria Theresa, Empress, 1740
Marian persecutions, 21, 51; 1555, 1556, 1558, 1564

Marignano, Battle of, 12, 18; 1515, 1516
Marlborough, 1st Duke of, 14, 28; 1694, 1706, 1709
Marsay, Count de, 1717
Martigny, 990, 1639, 1802, 1863
Martigny, Geoffrey de, 1215
Martin, Frank, 57, 58; 1956, 1957
Martin, Henri, 1917
Martyr, Peter, 1547
Mary I, Queen, 21; 1547, 1555, 1556, 1685
Mary, Queen (of George V), 1948
Masonic lodge, Geneva, 1789
Massawa, Eritrea, 1872
Masefield, John, 1946
Mathews, C.E., 1888
Matilda, Queen, 1070
Matter, Erwin, 1939
Matterhorn, The, 34; 1855, 1861, 1862, 1865, 1868, 1869, 1897
Matterhorn Museum, Zermatt, 1953
Matterhorngletscher, The, 1865
Matthews, William, 1859
Matthey, Edward, 1761
Matthey, Frédéric, 1816
Matthey, George, 73; 1761
Matthey, Simon, 1761
Maudling, Reginald, 1958
Maudsley, Son & Field, 1851
Maugham, W. Somerset, 54; 1918
Mauvine, 71; 1855
Maximilian, Emperor, 17, 18; 1513, 1515, 1516
May, Capt de, 1694
May, Col de, 1709
Mayerne, Sir Theodore Turquet de, 63; 1611, 1630, 1631
Mayo, Dr Charles, 60; 1819
Mazarin, Cardinal, 1655
Mazzini, Giuseppe, 1834
M.C.C., The, 1925
Mecca, Burckhardt's visit to, 1812
Mediation, Act of, 1803
Medico-Surgical Society, 1789
Meier, Herbert, 1978
Meiringen, 1796, 1890, 1891, 1904
Meister, Jakob Heinrich, 6, 38; 1789, 1792
Melos Ensemble, 58; 1966
Melville, Andrew, 21, 59; 1558, 1569, 1576
Menthon, Bernard de, 1027
Menuhin, Sir Yehudi, 57; 1956

Meredith, George, 54; 1861
Merian, Matthias, the younger, 42; 1640
Mesmer, Franz Anton, 63; 1831, 1843
mesmerism, 63; 1831, 1843
Methodism, 1752; 'Archbishop' of, 1717; Methodist preachers in London, 1770
Metternich, Prince, 1832, 1847
Mettler, Eric, 16; 1963
Meuron, Charles Daniel de, 1781, 1795, 1799, 1813; Regiment, 1799, 1808, 1813, 1816
Meuron, François-Henry de, 1813
Meuron, Pierre-Frédéric de, 1797
Meyer, Conrad Ferdinand, 1885
Meyer, Dr, 1936
Midland Bank, 1975, 1982
Miège, Guy, 1693
Migros Co-operative Organisation, 1954, 1984
Milan, 18; 1515, 1516, 1618
Milanese envoy in Zurich, 1514
Military Commission, British, to Switzerland, 1907, 1908
military manoeuvres: British, 1910; Swiss, 1879, 1910, 1912
militia system, Swiss, 13, 14, 16, 85
Milton, John, 23, 33, 51, 54, 63; 1633, 1639, 1652, 1655, 1725, 1779
Mitchell, Col Sir Harold, 1928
Mittelhorn, The, 1845
Moengal, 55; c850
Moilliet, J.L. & Sons, 1815, 1865
Moilliet, Jean Louis, 73, 75; 1815, 1865
Mönch, The, 1925, 1945
Mond, 72; 1873
monetary control, Swiss, 85
Monico family, 1890
Monkswell, Lady Mary, 1902
Mont, Ebel de, 1256
Montcaux, 1904
Mont Blanc, 1741, 1782, 1852; game, 1852; quadrille, 1852
Mont Cenis, c689, 1628
Mont Cenis line, 1867; tunnel, 1867
Montagu, Sir Walter, 1627
Montague, C.E., 1926
Montana, Valais, 1904, 1908, 1911
Montaubon, 1818
Monte Ceneri, 1933
Monte Rosa, 1894
Monte Rosa Hotel, Zermatt, 1855
Montesquieu, Charles Louis de, 52, 87
Monteverdi Choir, 58; 1976

Montgomery, Field-Marshal Lord, 1946, 1949
Montgomery, James, 54; 1805
Montmollin, Julie de, 1781
Montres Rolex SA, see Rolex watches
Montreux, 1828, 1889, 1930; Festival, 1962; first hotel at, 1828
Montreux-Clarens, 1904
Montreux-Territet, 1904
Moore, A.W., 1862
Moore, Henry, 48; 1937, 1975
Moore, John, 1773
Moore, Roger, 1976
Moore, W.A.M., 1909
Morat, 17; 1259, 1282; Battle of, 49; 1476, 1829; Lake, 1476
Moravian missions in England, 1748
More, Sir Thomas, 49; 1516, 1518
Morgan Grenfell & Co., 1975
Morges, Vaud, 1807
Morgins, 1909, 1927
Moriarty, Prof, 1968
Morier, David, 1743
Morier, David Richard, 1801, 1844, 1847
Morier, Isaac, 1801
Morier, William, 1801
Morland, Sir Samuel, 1655, 1658
Morris, Prevost & Co, 1813, 1914
Morryson, Fynes, 33; 1592
Moser, George Michael, 42; 1768
Moser, Mary, 42; 1768
Motiers, 1764
motor vehicles, British, exported to Switzerland, 1937, 1969
Motta, Giuseppe, 1925
Moulinié watches, Geneva, 1862
Mount Snowdon, 1888
mountaineers, British, see climbers, British
Mountbatten of Burma, Earl, 1972
Moutier-Grandval, 7th C, 1979
Mozart, W.A., 1785
Mühletal, 1804
Mulgrave, Maj-Gen Lord, 1799
Müller, Johannes von, 1776
Müller, Dr Paul, 1939
Müller, Samuel, 1652, 1702
Muller, William James, 47; 1844
Müller & Co, 74; 1702, 1709, 1719/20, 1721
Müller & Co (England) Ltd, 1933
Münchenbuchsee, 1922
Munich crisis, 1938

Münsterlingen, Convent of, 36
Munzinger, Werner, 1872
Muralt, Beat Ludwig de, 6, 11; 1725
Muralt, Louis de, 1763
Murray, Gen, 1706
Murray, John, 1787; 1838
Mürren, Bernese Oberland, 1869, 1904, 1909, 1916, 1922, 1924, 1925
Murten, *see* Morat
Musica Lausanne Ensemble, 1962
musicians, British: Barbirolli, Sir John, 1962; Berkeley, Lennox, 57; 1948; Bream, Julian, 1973; Britten, Benjamin, 57; 1946, 1955, 1956; Broadwood, John, pianomaker, 56; 1740; Burney, Dr Charles, 56; 1766, 1770; Bull, John, 55; 1603; Curzon, Clifford, 1962; Delius, Frederick, 57; 1901; Elgar, Sir Edward, 43; 1946, 1981; Grove, Sir George, 1866; Handel, George Frideric, 56; 1740; Hill, Arthur, 1954; Holst, Gustav, 1946; Jones, Gwyneth, 1962; Lill, John, 1973; Ludlow, Edmund, 15; 1665; Lympany, Moura, 1973; Menuhin, Sir Yehudi, 57; 1956; Parry, Sir Hubert, 1889; Pritchard, John, 1973; Purcell, Henry, 1969; Sargent, Sir Malcolm, 1946, 1957; Smyth, Dame Ethel, 1882; Sullivan, Sir Arthur, 1879; Tippet, Michael, 57; 1953, 1954, 1956; Vaughan Williams, Ralph, 58; 1938, 1953; Walton, William, 57; 1926
musicians, Swiss: Ansermet, Ernest, 58; 1946, 1963; Bamert, Matthias, 58; Baumgartner, Rudolf, 1961; Becker, Hugo, 1892; Bloch, Ernest, 58; Blumer, Samuel harpsichord maker, 56; Burkhard, Willy, 58; 1938; Cuenod, Hughes, 58; Dalcroze, Jacques, 1897, 1950; Della Casa, Lisa, 58; 1951; Dolmetsch, Arnold, 57; 1894, 1925, 1928; Dolmetsch, Carl, 57; 1925, 1928; Dutoit, Charles, 58; 1983; Elouis, Joseph, 56; c1781; Fischer, Edwin, 58; 1960; Furi, Thomas, 1981; Gaspard, Fritz, 1770; Haskil, Clara, 58; Hegner, Otto, 58; 1889, 1893; Holliger, Heinz, 58; 1961, 1981; Holliger, Ursula, 1971; Honegger, Arthur, 41, 58; 1929; Huber, Hans, 1893; Kelterborn, Rudolf, 1961; Königshofer, Dr Franz, 1962; Lauber, Joseph, 1899; Maag, Peter, 58; Martin, Frank, 57, 58; 1956, 1957; Notker, Balbulus, 55; Raff, Joachim (Swiss-born German), 56, 57; 1892; Rousseau, Jean-Jacques, 57; 1953, 1959; Sacher, Paul, 57; 1953, 1959; Schmid, Erich, 1953; Stalder, J.F. Xavier Stalder, 56; 1753; Thalberg, Sigismond (Swiss-born Austrian), 56, 57; 1871; Tschudi, Burkhard harpsichord-maker, 56; 1740; Wyss, Sophie, 58; 1919; Zeugheer, Jakob, 1865; Zopfi, Hans harpsichord-maker, 56
Mussard, Jean. 1760

Nägeli, Karl Wilhelm von, 67
nannies, British, 62
Napier, Col, 1888
Napier, John, 63; 1632
Napier, Robert, 1872
Napoleon I, 29, 30, 86; 1802, 1803, 1806, 1810, 1814, 1815
Napoleon III, 1838, 1856, 1860
Napoleonic Wars, 5, 15, 74; 1800, 1808, 1814, 1818
Nash, Thomas, 49; 1594
National Anthem, British, 55; 1603, 1861, 1897
National Covenant, Scottish, 22; 1639
National Gallery, London, 1903, 1945
National Provincial Bank, 76; 1920
National Westminster Bank, 1975
National Youth Orchestra, 58; 1966
NATO, 16
Naville, Henri-Edouard, 1926
Neale, J.M., 55
Necker, Jacques, 11; 1755, 1793
Necker, Louis Albert, 67; 1806
Nelson, Admiral Lord, 1798
Nemours, Duchess of, 1699, 1707
Nestlé, 73, 81; 1866, 1874, 1883, 1890, 1903, 1939, 1960
Netherlands, 16, 25, 28; 1653, 1690, 1702, 1707, 1715, 1719; Swiss troops for, 1743
Neuchâtel, 68, 74; 1234, 1398, c1670, 1699, 1707, 1731, 1754, 1762, 1795, 1799, 1848, 1852, 1856, 1857, 1863, 1875, 1883, 1904, 1928, 1930; Lake of, 1256, 1260; Neuchâtel question, 30; 1699, 1707, 1754, 1848, 1852, 1856, 1857; Scottish governor of, 1754; University of, 1951;

Neuchâtel Asphalt Co., 1875, 1913, 1928
Neue Zürcher Zeitung, 1827, 1914
Neuhausen, 1886, 1904
Neumühle, Zurich, 1824
Neville, Sir Richard, 1773
New Berne, North Carolina, 1710
New English Consort, 1954
New Geneva, Ireland, 1782
New Helvetic Society, 1916, 1963
New Philharmonia Orchestra, 58; 1966
New Weisstor, 1850
Newcastle, 1st Duke of, 28
Newton, Sir Isaac, 64, 65, 67; 1686, 1687, 1689, 1697, 1698, 1704, 1721, 1738, 1739, 1748
Ney, Gen Michel, 1802
Nice and Villefranche, 68, 69; 1628
Nicholson, Ben, 48; 1937
Niederwald, Valais, 1888
Nightingale, Florence, 1838
Nile, Battle of, 1798; River, 1812
Niven, David, 1976
Noel-Baker, Philip, 1948
North, Lord, 1775
North America, *see* America
Northern Ireland, 1981
Norton, William, 29
Norway, 16; 1886
Norwich Union group, 1919
Notker, Balbulus, 55
Notre Dame-la Neuve, Geneva, 1556
Nyon, 1590

Oberaarhorn, The, 1861
Oberaarjoch, The, 1826
Oberhofen, 16; 1965
Obrecht, Herman, 16
Ochsenbein, Ulrich, 1847
Odier, Dr Louis, 1789
Oecolampadius, 1529
Oerlikon-Bührle group, 71, 73, 80; 1871, 1885, 1891, 1940, 1948, 1971, 1981
Old Pretender, *see* James Edward
Old Vic Company, 1954, 1962
Olten, 1850, 1852, 1853, 1872
Omega watches, 1933
Oporinus, 1555, 1559
Orchestre de la Suisse Romande, 1946
Orell Gesner & Co, 1762
Orr-Ewing, Lord, 1976
Orsonnens, Protais d'Odet d', 1816
Osborne, Lady, 47; 1844

Oswald, King, 1485
Ottawa Agreements, 1932
Ouchy, 54; 1816, 1826
Ovaltine, 73; 1909, 1967
Owen, John, 1804
Owen, Robert, 59; 1805, 1818
Oxford, c1518; Reformers, 49; University, 38, 59; 1547, 1550, 1551, 1558, 1569, 1572, c1732, 1920, 1938

Pace, Richard, 18; 1514, 1515, 1516, 1517, 1523
Pagani family, 1890
Palliser, Arthur, 1915
Palmerston, Lord, 30, 31, 76; 1816, 1847, 1850, 1852
Palmerston, 2nd Lord, 45; 1770
Pantaleoni, Heinrich, 1559
Paracelsus (Theophrastus Bombastus von Hohenheim), 49, 63; c1518, 1835, 1941, 1964
Paravicini, Charles, 1921, 1939
Paris, 1721, 1794, 1802, 1818, 1834, 1863, 1923, 1935, 1938; Peace of, 1764; Peace Conference, 1918, Revolution, 1832
Parkhurst, Bishop John, 1555, 1572
Parkhurst, John, 1613
Parkinson, Cecil, 1976
Paolozzi, Eduardo, 48; 1947
Parry, Sir Hubert, 1889
Parsenn, 1924
Parsons, Sir Anthony, 41
Parsons steam turbine, 1900
Pars, William, 45; 1770
Partridge, Nicholas, 1537
Paschoup, Capt Jean-François, 1757
Pater, Walter, 1875
Paterson, Emily Murray, 1887
Patek Phillipe, Geneva, 1851
Pattison, J.W., 1928
Paul IV, Pope, 1559
Payerne, 1911
Pearson, Karl, 62
Peel, Sir Robert, 1847, 1860, 1904
Peel, Robert, 1847, 1860
Pell, Dr John, 23, 65; 1654, 1655
Pellis, 1800, 1801
Percy, Thomas, 51; 1725
Perdriau, bankers, 1703
Perkin, Sir William, 71; 1855
Perkin Medal, 1929
Perring, Sir Ralph, 1963

Perronet, Vincent, 40; 1717, 1752
Pestalozzi, Johann Heinrich, 59, 60; 1805, 1817, 1818, 1819, 1866, 1873, 1953
Pestalozzi children's villages, 1956, 1961
Peter, Daniel, 1883, 1903
Peter of Savoy, 38; 1236, 1256, 1259, 1260, 1262, 13th C
Peterson, William, 1536
Petitot, Jean Louis, 42; 1630, 1650
Petitot, Jean, the elder, 42; 1630, 1641
Petitpierre, Max, 1955, 1966
Peto, R.H., 1923
Pevsner, Sir Nikolaus, 43
Pfäfers, monastery of, 929
Pfister, Theodor, 1891
Phelps, John, 1660
Philibert I, Duke of Savoy, 1476
Philip I, Count of Savoy, 1273, 1282, 1286
Philip the Fair, 1285
Phillip, Colin Bent, 1920
Phillips, Philip, 1844
Phillips & Drew, 77; 1984
photographers, early British, in Switzerland, 47; 1796, 1816, 1833
Picard-Pictet Ltd, 1919
Piccard, Prof. Auguste, 41
Pickering & Co, 1852
Pickfords Ltd, 1921
Pictet, Armand-Jacques, 1846
Pictet, François, 74; c1732
Pictet, François Jules, 67
Pictet, François-Pierre, 1792
Pictet, Isaac, 1772, 1782
Pictet, Count James, 1763, 1772, 1782
Pictet, Louis, 'Pictet of Bengal', 1769
Pictet, Marc-Auguste, 53, 60, 65; 1787, 1791, 1792, 1796, 1798, 1803, 1826
Pictet & Cie, 1982; Pictet Asset Management, 1982
Pictet de Rochemont, Charles, 53; 1787, 1796, 1803, 1814
Pictet family, 67; 1790
Piedmont, 23; 1654, 1655, 1692, 1694
Pilatus, Mount, 1868
Pilet-Golaz, Marcel, 1940
Pilkington, James, 1555
Pilley, Dorothy, 1928
Pillichody, Colonel, 1799
Piper, John, 1956
Piquet, G., 1965
Pitt, Thomas, 2nd Baron Camelford, 1804
Pitt, William, the elder, 53
Pitt, William, the younger, 29; 1788, 1792-4
Pius V, Pope, 1572
Planta, Andreas Rudolf von, 1850
Planta, Joseph (I), 1752
Planta, Joseph (II), 40, 53; 1776, 1781
Planta, Joseph (III), 1827
Planta, Miss, 1781
Plassey, Battle of, 1757
Platter, Thomas, 38; 1599
Plattsburg, Battle of, 1813
Plessey Co, plc, The, 1967
Po, River, 5
police officers, Anglo-Swiss exchange of, 1977
Polidori, John, 1816
Polier, Col Antoine Louis, 1751, 1784
Polytechnic continental holidays, 1889
Pontresina, 54; 1864, 1879, 1904
Pope, Alexander, 51, 56; 1725, 1728, 1779
Portree, Isle of Skye, 1806
Pourtalès, Jacques-Louis, 74; 1795
Pourtalès & Cie, 74; 1795
Power Jets Ltd, 1944
Powys, Llewelyn, 54
Prayer Book, Edward VI's second, 1552
Presbyterianism, Geneva's influence on development of Scottish, 8, 21; 1558
Presta, 1875
Prevost, A.L. & Co, 74; 1813, 1901
Prevost, Alexandre Louis, 1813, 1817
Prevost, Maj-Gen Augustin, 1756, 1778, 1811
Prevost, Sir Augustus, 75; 1901
Prevost, Gen Sir George, 1811, 1813
Prevost, Maj-Gen., Jacques, 1756
Prevost, Jean-Louis, 1813, 1843
Prevost, Col Jean Marc, 1756
Prevost, Thomas Jacques, 1811
Prevost-Dassier, 1787
Prince of Wales (son of George I), 1718
Priors Inn, London, 13th C
prisoners of war: British in Switzerland, 1915-18; Swiss, 1814
Pritchard, John, 1973
Pro Helvetia Swiss Council for the Arts, 1946, 1951, 1975
Probst, Raymond, 1983
proportional representation, Swiss, 7, 10, 86
protectionism, British, 1932; Swiss, 69; 1932, *see also* import restrictions

Protestant League, Cromwell's plan for, *see* Continental Protestant League
Prussia, 1802, 1832, 1848, 1850, 1860
Public Schools Alpine Sports Club, 1909
pubs, British, in Switzerland, 1969
Pully, Lausanne, 1830
Purcell, Henry, 1961
Puritanism, English, 1569, 1570
Pury, David, 1731
Pury, Jean-Pierre, 1731
Purysberg, South Carolina, 1731
Pye Ltd, 1966

Quebec, Swiss in, 1668; Swiss military governor of, 1813
Queen's Jubilee Fund, in Switzerland, 1977

Raff, Joachim, 56, 57; 1892
Ragaz, St Gallen, 1852
railway engineers and contractors, early British, in Switzerland: Brassey, Thomas, 71; 1853, 1867; Brown, Charles, 71; 1871; Fox, Sir Charles, 1852; Fox, Henderson & Co, 1852; Pickering & Co, 1852; Stephenson, Robert, 71; 1850; Swinburne, Harold, 1850; Vignolles, Charles, 71; 1853; Vignolles, Henry, 1853; Williamson & Co, 1852
railway tunnels, Swiss, 1940
Rambert, Marie, 1950
Ramillies, Battle of, 15; 1706
Ramsay, Lieut-Col John, 1799
Ramsay, Sir William, 67
Ramsay Memorial Trust, 67
Ramus, Petrus, 1569
Ramuz, Charles Ferdinand, 8; 1929, 1944
Rapier missiles, British. 16; 1980
Rappard, Prof William, 1954
Rappenstein, 1541
Rapperswil, 1957
Rapp & Coulon, 1848
Ray, John, 65; 1665
Red Cross, 1863, 1916, 1948
Red River Colony, 1816
Reding, Aloys, 1802
Redoxon, 1939
referendums, Swiss, 7, 87; 1923, 1975
Reformation, The, 18, 36, 42, 49; 1547, 1576
refugees, religious, in Switzerland, 18, 21, 36; 1547, 1555, 1556, c1558, 1560, 1564, 1570; political, 30; 1834, 1850
Regeneration, period of Swiss, 30; 1832, 1844, 1848
Reichenbach, 1802
Reichenbach Falls, 54; 1891, 1968
Remedius, Bishop, of Chur, 800
Renold, Hans, 73; 1879, 1930
Renold plc, 73; 1930
Reresby, Sir John, 34; 1654
research, Swiss investment in, 84
Reynolds, Sir Joshua, 43; 1766, 1793
Rhaetia, 22; c614, 800, 1626
Rhine, River, 5, 68, 79; 7th C, c650, 1259, 1542, 1681, 1691, 1920, 1921, 1958, 1969; Falls, 1886
Richard, Daniel Jean, 1670
Richard, Earl of Cornwall, 17; 1259
Richard II, King, c1370, 1375
Richardet, Willy, 1924
Richards, Ivor, 1928
Richardson, C.W.R., 1903
Richardson, E.C., 1903, 1906
Richardson, Samuel, 52; 1747, 1753
Richardson, Thomas Miles, jnr, 1837
Richardsons Westgarth & Co Ltd, 1956
Richelieu, Cardinal, 1627
Richmond, 3rd Duke of, 1750
Richmond, 1599, 1769
Richmond family, 36
Ridley, Bishop Nicholas, 1547, 1555, 1559
Riffelalp, 1904
Riffelhorn, 1842
Rigi, 34; 1837, 1844, 1863; first inn on the, 34; railway, 1871
Riley, Bridget, 48
Ritz, César, 40, 81; 1888, 1906
Ritz Hotel, London, 1906
Robinson, Sir Thomas, 1747
Roe, Sir Thomas, 1628
Roesch, Georges, 1944
Rogers, John, 1535
Rogers, Samuel, 54
Roget, Prof F.F., 6; 1909, 1913
Roget, Dr Peter Mark, 53; 1852
Rolex watches, 73; 1903, 1920
Rolle, 1791
Rolle, Louis de, 1795
Romainmôtier, 7th C
Romans, The, 12, 13
Romansch (or Ladin), 5, 41; 1710, 1718
Rome, 33; c689, 1776, 1877
Römer, J.J., 1817

Rosenlaui, 1902
Rossetti, Christina, 54; 1865
Rossi, Councillor, 1890
Rotary watches, 1905
Rothschild, N.M., & Sons, 1968
Rougeat, Etienne, 1708
Rousseau, Jean-Jacques, 39, 41, 45, 51, 52, 56, 59; 1476, 1594, 1679, 1704, 1730, 1747, 1762, 1764, 1766, 1767, 1802, 1804, 1825, 1861, 1866, 1908
Roux, Claude, 1668
Roveray, Antoine de, 1790
Roverea, Col, 1799
Royal Academy, London, 40, 42, 43; 1796, 1802, 1880
Royal Academy of Music, London, 57
Royal Adelaide Gallery Restaurant, 1886
Royal American Regiment, 15; 1749, 1756
Royal Anthropological Society, 1846
Royal Astronomical Society, London, 1854
Royal Ballet, 58; 1962, 1976
Royal Bank of Scotland, 1983
Royal College of Physicians, 1724, 1852
Royal Dutch Shell group, 1906
Royal Exchange, London, 1640
Royal Mint, London, 1968
Royal Navy, British, 15; 1731, 1811, 1981
Royal Philharmonic Orchestra, 58; 1966
Royal Shakespeare Co, 1962
Royal Society of Arts, London, 40; 1950
Royal Society of Medicine, 1941
Royal Society, The, London, 40, 64, 67; 1686, 1713, 1724, c1726, 1738, 1739, 1743, 1752, 1768, 1773, 1776, 1791, 1841, 1852, 1857, 1967
Rudolf of Habsburg, 1282
Rugby School, 60; 1829
Rumbold, Sir Horace, 58; 1866
Runnymede, 32
Ruskin, John, 11, 34, 45, 47, 54; 1779, 1835, 1841, 1856, 1859, 1861, 1869, 1908
Russell, John, 46
Russell, Lord John, 1860
Russia, 1832, 1848, 1860
Rütimeyer, Karl Ludwig, 67
Rütli, 32
Rynk, Hermann, 1514, 1515
Rynk, William, 1514

Saanen, 1802

Saanen Church, near Gstaad, 1956
Saas-Fee, 1904, 1912
Saas-Grund, 1904
Sacconex, 1816
Sacher, Paul, 57; 1953, 1954, 1959
Säckingen, c650
Saconnay, Col Jean de, 1694
Sage, George-Louis le, 1715
St Andrew Undershaft, 1574
St Andrew's Church, Zurich, 1971
St Andrews University, 59; 1569, c1573, 1790, 1938
St Anne's Church, Soho, 1804
St Anne & St Agnes, London, 1924
St Beatenberg, 1909
St Bernard, Hospice of, 13th C; Order of, 13th C; dogs, 1852
St Gallen, Abbey of, 36, 49, 55; 7th C, c850; Roll of the Fraternity of, 929
St Gallen, town & canton, 36; 800, 929, 1690, 1800, 1804, 1815, 1852, 1903, 1953, 1963, 1970
St George's College, Clarens, 1927
St Gotthard pass, 81; 5th C, 1402, 1563, 1775, 1802, 1844, 1845, 1913
St Gotthard tunnel, 1873
St John of Jerusalem, Hospital of, England, 1300
St John, Sir Frederick, 1899
St Leger, Lord, 1773
St Lucia, Swiss governor of, 1811
St Martin's Church, Vevey, 1660
St Maurice, Valais, 17; 1246, 1692, 1825
St Moritz, 1866, 1876, 1879, 1885, 1890, 1891, 1896, 1898, 1904, 1912, 1930
St Nicholas' Chapel, Basel Cathedral, 1945
St Paul's Cathedral, London, 1667
St Peter's, Zermatt, 1870
St Pierre, Isle of, Lake Bienne, 1804
Saint Saphorin, Sir François de Pesme de, 1718
Ste Ursanne, monastery of, 7th C
Saladin (bankers), 1703
Salève, The, 1838
Salford, Lancs, 1879
Salis, Col de, 1795
Salis, Hercules von, 1618
Salis, J.R. de, 1965
Salis, Jerome de, 1742
Salis, John de, 1799
Salis, Peter de, 1709
Salvation Army, The, 1883

Index 467

Salvisberg, Otto, 1937
Samedan, 1904
Sampson, Thomas, 1560
Samuel Montagu & Co., 1958
Sandby, Paul, 1807
Sandford, Lord, 1976
Sandhurst, 1822
Sandoz group, 68, 72, 73, 79; 1909, 1911, 1914, 1918, 1967
Sandwich, Lord, 1747
Sandys, Archbishop, 1555, 1572
Santa Maria degli Angeli, Lugano, 1869
Santa Maria del Monte, 1829
Sarasin, A., & Cie, 1980
Sardinia, 1754, 1834, 1848
Sargent, Sir Malcolm, 1946, 1957
Saurer Co, 1921
Saussure, César de, 11; 1726, 1729
Saussure, Horace-Bénédict de, 34, 65; 1770, 1779, 1796
Saussure, de, family, 67
Savage, Canon, 1902
Savory Milln & Co, 77
Savoy, 21, 28, 29; 1256, 1285, 1444, 1615, 1617, 1622, 1655, 1754, 1834, 1860, 1867
Savoy Hotel, London, 38; 13th C, 1888, 1906
Schaerer, Theophil, 1920
Schaffhausen, 69; 1639, 1690, 1776, 1917, 1804, 1905
Schaffner, Hans, 1948
Schalch, Andrew, 40; 1716, 1804
Scharnachtal, Conrad de, c1465
Schaub, Sir Luke, 1721, 1745, 1751, 1754
Scheidegg, The, 1817
Schentius of Glarus, 1536
Scheuchzer, Johann Caspar, 65; 1724
Scheuchzer, Johann Jakob, 65; 1704, 1713, 1724, 1776
Schilthorn, The, 1839, 1928, 1963
Schindler Holding, 73, 81; 1982
Schinner, Cardinal Matthias, 17, 18; 1513, 1514, 1515, 1516, 1517
Schinznach, 1776, 1904
Schmid, Erich, 1953
Schmutz, Johann, 42; 1695
Schneehase, Der, 1924
Schreckhorn, The, 1861
Schroder, J. Henry, 1967
Schuster, Lord, 34; 1925
Schwarz, Martin, 1487
Schweizer-Bund, 1879
Schweizerhof Hotel, Neuhausen, 1886
Schweizerischer Kaufmännischer Verein, 1888
Schweizerische Vortragsdienst, 1946
Schweppe, Jacob, 73; 1792, 1816
Schweppe. J. & Co, 1792
Schwyz, canton, 81; 1375, 1820, 1834
Schwyzer, Christopher, 1574
Scotland, 5, 8, 22, 65, 67; 1300, 1559, 1564, 1569, c1573, 1576, 1582, 1583, 1588, 1590, 1639, 1681, 1690, 1715, 1719, 1789, 1806; Presbyterian government in, 21; 1558, 1576, 1639; use of Swiss troops in, 1715, 1719
Scotland Yard, London, 1977
Scott, Sir Walter, 49; 1829
Scottish National Orchestra, 58
'Scotus Dundonensis', *see* Young, Peter
Scout Jamboree, Kandersteg, 1931
Scrimgeour, Henry, 58; 1564
Scorye, Bishop John, 1555
Sécheron Ltd, 1919
Segantini, Giovanni, 45; 1927
Seiler, Alexander, 1855
Selborne, Lord, 1942
Selectus Ltd, 1934
Selkirk, Lord, 1816
Sellon, Gaspard, 74; 1751
Selsdon, Lord, 1976
Senn & Co Ltd, 1934
Seringapatam, Battle of, 1799
Sesiajoch, The, 1862
Seven Years' War, 15; 1756, 1764
Sforza, Maximilian, 1515
Shakespeare, William, 49, 51, 57; c1518, 1572, 1594, 1599, 1725, 1762, 1725, 1770, 1776, 1779, 1954, 1968, 1978
Shaw, George Bernard, 1948
Shell Co, Switzerland, 1906
Shelley, Mary, 53; 1814, 1816, 1818, 1840
Shelley, Percy Bysshe, 34, 53, 54; 1814, 1816, 1817, 1820, 1840
Sherlock, Mr, 1776
shoes, Swiss, exported to Britain, 68; 1541, 1854, 1937, 1954
Siddons, Mrs, 1823
Sierre, 1904
Sigeric, Archbishop, of Canterbury, 990
Sigisbert, 36; c614
silk goods, Swiss, exported to Britain, 68; 1593, 1823, 1842, 1909, 1922, 1923

468　*Index*

Simmler, Josias, 1653
Simnel, Lambert, 1487
Simplon Pass, 1639, 1790, 1844
Simplon Tunnel, 1905
Singer & Friedlander, 1966
Sion, 17; 1062, 1513, 1732, 1863, 1954
Sismondi, J.C. de, 39, 51, 53; 1792, 1803
Six Articles, Act of the, 1547
skating, 34; 1891, 1902; 'English', 1927
Ski Club of Great Britain, 1903
ski clubs and ski races: Alpine Ski Club, 1908; Anglo-Swiss University Ski Race, 1925; British Swiss Interparliamentary Ski Race, 1956, 1976; Davos English Ski Club, 1903; First modern slalom competition, 1922; 'Inferno' Ski Race, 1928; Kandahar Challenge Cup, 1911; Ladies' Ski Club of Great Britain, 1907; Parsenn Derby, 1924; Ski Club of Great Britain, 1903; Swiss University Ski Club, 1924
skiers, early British: Adams, Franklin, 1876; Bracken, C., 1908; Cairney, Maud, 1928; Caulfield, Vivian, 1910; Edlin, E.S., 1924; Farrer, Percival, 1902; Fox, Gerald, 1891, (first to ski in Grindelwald); Knocker, Edward, 1890, (first to ski in Meiringen); Larden, Walter, 1903; Le Blond, Mrs A., 1907; Lindsay, Scott, 1908; Lunn, Sir Arnold, 34; 1902, 1908, 1909, 1922, 1924, 1925; Lunn, Sir Henry, 1902, 1909; Mitchell, Col, Sir Harold, 1928; Moore, W.A.M., 1909; Napier, Col, 1888; Pilley, Dorothy, 1928; Richards, Ivor, 1928; Richardson, C.W.R., 1903; Richardson, E.C., 1903, 1906; Savage, Canon, 1902; Wybergh, Cecil, 1908
skiing, 34; 1876, 1890, 1891, 1902, 1903, 1907, 1911, 1925; marathon, 1924; ski-mountaineering, 34; 1906, 1908, 1909, 1924; racing, downhill, 34; 1911, 1924, 1928, 1956, 1976; ski-lifts, 35; 1935; ski technique, 1910; slalom, 1922
slate, Swiss, exported to Britain, 68; 1681
Sloane, Sir Hans, 65; 1724
Smith, Adam, 10, 33, 51; 1764, 1766, 1787, 1803

Smith, Albert Richard, 1852
Smith, John, 1824
Smith, John 'Warwick', 45; 1781
Smith, Richard, 1563
Smith, Thomas, 1796
Smith, William, 1842
Smith, Wilson, 1890
Smollett, Tobias George, 1743
Smyrna, Turkey, 1801, 1854
Smyth, Dame Ethel, 1882
Smythe, Frank, 1953
Soames, Sir Christopher, 1975
Soames, Lady (Mary), 1975
Société de Cellonit Dreyfus et Cie, 1916
Société de Physique et d'Histoire Naturelle de Genève, 1834
Société Suisse de Surveillance, La, 1924
Société Suisse de Surveillance Économique, La, 1915, 1919
Society of Analytical Pschology, London, 63; 1946
Society of Apothecries, 1611
Society of Chemical Industry, Basel, 1855; *see also* CIBA
Society for the Propagation of the Gospel in Foreign Parts, The, 1904
soda water, 1792
Soho, Swiss colony in, 1867
Solothurn, 1764, 1852, 1853, 1951, 1962
Somerset, Duke of, 1476
Somerset, Protector, 21
Somerville, John, 1584
Somerville, Mary, 1834
Somerville College, Oxford, 1834
Sommaruga, M., 1984
Sonderbund War, 30, 86; 1847, 1850
Sondrio, English seminar at, 1618
Sopra, London, 1984
South Africa, 1731, 1854, 1892, 1896, 1899, 1900
Southey, Robert, 54, 59; 1805, 1817
South Sea Bubble, 74; 1720, 1721
Spahlinger, Henry, 1923
Spain, 21; 1516, 1596; influence in Switzerland, 22; 1596; invasion of the Valtellina, 1618; Kings of, 18; 1516, 1582, 1597; Spanish troops in Scotland, 1719; Spanish Netherlands, 1596
Spanish Succession, War of the, 28, 74; 1702, 1707
Spectator, The, 10, 51; 1701, 1725, 1847
Speer, S. Templeton, 34; 1835, 1845

Spencer, Herbert, 51; 1853, 1861
Spiez, 1904
Spitfire aircraft, 1971
Spitteler, Carl, 30, 31; 1914
Spyri, Johanna, 3, 49; 1884
Stadtmusik of Solothurn, 1951, 1962
Staël, Mme de, 11, 41; 1755, 1793
Stäfa, Duke of Gloucester's money stamped on. at, 1782
Stafford, Lady Dorothy, 1555
Stafford, Sir William, 1555
Stalden, 1732
Stalder, Josef-Franz Xavier, 56; 1753
Stalin, Joseph, 1944
Stamm, Prof Dr Rudolf, 1958, 1962
Stämpfli, Jakob, 1868
Standard Chartered Bank, 1969
Stanhope, Charles, (later 3rd Earl Stanhope), 1764, 1771
Stanhope, Philip, 33; 1746
Stanhope family, 36
Stanyan, Abraham, 1, 13, 28; 1705, 1707, 1710, 1714, 1747
Stationers' Company, The, London, c1549
steamship service, London-Basel, 1958
Steele, Richard, 10; 1701
Steiger, Capt de, 1689
Steiger, Charles Frédéric de, 1930
Steiger, Niklaus de, 1793, 1799
Stephen, Sir Leslie, 1859, 1861, 1871
Stephenson, George, 1850
Stephenson, Robert, 71; 1850
Sterling Bloc formed, 1931
Stevenson, Robert Louis, 3, 54; 1880
Stewart, Jackie, 1976
Stewart, Lord, of Fulham, 1964
Stockar, Johann Jakob, 1653
Stockhorn, The, 1841
Stolz, Johann, 1513
Strahlegg Pass, Old, 1835
Strand, London, 40
Strälingen, Johann de, c1289
Stratton, Miss, 1869
Straumann, Prof H., 1946, 1950
Strela Pass, 1906
Stuppa, Jean-Baptiste, 1653, 1655, 1656
Stutzer, Dr, 1957
Sudan, Eastern, Swiss governor of, 1872
Suez Crisis, 1956
Suisse, Société des, London, 1703
Sullivan, Sir Arthur, 1879
Sulzberger, Col Jean, 1854
Sulzer, Dr Hans, 1939, 1942

Sulzer, Heinrich, 1849
Sulzer, Johann Jakob, 1849, 1851
Sulzer Brothers Ltd, 71, 73, 80; 1805, 1849, 1851, 1871, 1876, 1905, 1932, 1939, 1943, 1944, 1955, 1957, 1967; *see also* Escher-Wyss
Susa, 1246
Sutherland, Duke of, 1839
Sutherland, Graham, 48; 1952, 1971
Sutherland, Joan, 1976
Sutherland, Thomas, 1803
Suvorov, General, 1799
Suvretta House, St Moritz, 1912
Swete, Revd John, 1816
Swift, Jonathan, 1759
Swinburne, Harold, 1850
Swinnerton, Frank, 1920
Swiss, The, *passim*
Swissair, 82; 1923, 1935, 1945, 1946, 1954
Swiss Alpine Club, 1863; Association of British Members of, 1912, 1984
Swiss Aluminium Mining, 1971, 1978
Swiss Bank Corporation, 76, 77, 82; 1856, 1898, 1967, 1968, 1980
Swiss banking, modern, establishment of, 82; 1856
Swiss Brigade, 1854
Swiss-British Society, 1950, 1966; of Basel, 1962; Berne, 1958; of Zurich, 1946, 1950
Swiss Catholic Diet, Lucerne, 22
Swiss Centre, London, 1968, 1984
Swiss Civil War *see* Sonderbund War
Swiss colony in England, 38, 39, 40, 41; 1574, 1685, 1703, 1745, 1762, 1814, 1817, 1867, 1888, 1890, 1900, 1913, 1919, 1924, 1965
Swiss Committee for Economic and Commercial Studies, *see* Swiss Economic Council
Swiss Confederation, The, Intro, *passim*; 1513, 1516, 1596, 1648, 1689, 1803, 1814, 1843, 1848, 1850, 1855, 1951, 1984
Swiss consuls and consulates in Britain, 1817, 1828, 1846, 1917
Swiss Cottage, London, 1830
Swiss currency, unification of, 69; 1855, 1856
Swiss Economic Council, 1918, 1921
Swiss Export Company, 1860
Swiss federal army, reform of, 1816, *see also* Army, Swiss

470 Index

Swiss Federal Constitution of 1848, 1848, 1850
Swiss Federal Pact of 1815, 1814, 1844, 1847, 1848
Swiss Folklore Festival, London, 1948
Swiss franc, appreciation of, 70, 84; 1921, 1946, 1948, 1971, 1974, 1976, 1977, 1978; devaluation of, 1936, 1937; flotation of, 1973, *see also* exchange rate
Swiss in important public posts in Britain, 40
Swiss insurance, importance of, 8, 82
Swiss in the British Diplomatic Service: Angst, Sir Henry, 1911; Braun, Louis Beat, 1752; Grandson, Sir Otes de, 1282; Le Sieur, Stephen, 1609; Morier, Isaac, 1801; Munzinger, W., 1872; Peter of Savoy, 1236; Pictet, Armand Jacques, 1846; Pictet, François-Pierre, 1792; Pictet, Isaac, 1772; Pictet, Count James, 1763; Planta, Joseph, 1776; Planta, Joseph (II), 1827; St Saphorin, Sir F. de Pesme de, 1718; Salis, Jérome de, 1742; Salis, John de, 1799; Salis, Peter de, 1709; Saussure, César de, 1729; Schaub, Sir Luke, 1721, 1745, 1754; Stuppa, Jean-Baptiste, 1653, 1655, 1656; Trembley, Abraham, 1747; de Vuippens, Girard, 1290
Swiss investments in, and loans to Britain, *see also* banks and bankers and under names of individual Swiss firms: 2, 40, 41, 72-77; 1703, 1709, 1710, 1714, 1719/20, 1720, 1721, 1730, c1732, 1754, 1763, 1789, 1790, 1795, 1798, 1815, 1816, 1916, 1961, 1965, 1967, 1978, 1981, 1984
Swiss Legation in London, 1891, 1917, 1939, 1953
Swiss Life Insurance Co., 82; 1967
Swiss Locomotive and Machine Works, Winterthur, 71; 1871
Swiss Mercantile Society, London, 1888
Swiss mountain guides, 34; 1852, 1857, 1858, 1861, 1864, 1865, 1867, 1888. 1894. 1902, 1943
Swiss National Bank, 85; 1949, 1964, 1965, 1968, 1969, 1971, 1972, 1974, 1975
Swiss National Museum, 1558
Swiss National Tourist Office, London, 1955, 1968, 1984

Swiss neutrality, 12, 13, 16, 17, 28, 29, 30, 31, 32, 78; 1515, 1793, 1814, 1815, 1908, 1913, 1914, 1916, 1920, 1939, 1944
Swiss Observer, The, 1919
Swiss pipe, introduction of, into British military bands, 1741
Swiss political parties, 86
Swiss Post Office, 1966
Swiss property in Britain, sequestration and release of, 1798, 1816
Swiss railways, 35, 38, 71; 1850, 1852, 1853, 1854, 1856, 1893, 1933, 1955
Swiss Re-insurance Company, 1863, 1908, 1969
Swiss School of painting, 1810
Swiss Southeastern Railway, conflict between Swiss and British stockholders, 1856
Swiss students in Britain, 25; 1599, 1690, 1888, 1951, 1961, 1963
Swiss television, 1961
Swiss University Ski Club, 1924
Swiss views on Britain and the British: Barth, Karl, 31; 1941; Bodmer, J.G., 12; 1816; Bonstetten, C.V. de, 9; Chappuzeau, Samuel, 1667; Constant, Benjamin, 11; 1786; Fischer, J.C., 1815; Füssli (Fuseli), Heinrich, 42; Grasser, J.J., 1606; Grossley, Jean, 1770; Kobelt, Karl, 1952; Lätt, Dr Arnold, 1920; Meister, J.H., 6; 1789, 1792; Mettler, Eric, 16; 1963; Meyer, Dr, 1936; Miège, Guy, 1693; Muralt, B.L. de, 6, 11; 1725; Pictet, Marc Auguste, 60; Platter, Thomas, 1599; Rappard, Prof W., 1954; Roget, Prof F.F., 6; 1909, 1913; Salis, J.R. de, 1965; Saussure, César de, 11; 1726; Spitteler, Carl, 31; 1914; Staël, Mme de, 11; Töpffer, A.W., 47; writer in Geneva, 12
Swiss visitors to Britain, 38; 1970, 1976, 1981, 1983
Swiss Volksbank, 76; 1977
Switzerland, *passim*
Switzers, Church of the, London, 1721
Symonds, John Addington, 54; 1877

Taeuber-Arp, Sophie, 48
Tages Anzeiger, 1981
Talleyrand, Charles Maurice de, 1803
Tallichet, Edward, 1900
Tarasp, 1904

tariff reforms, British, 1823
Tate Gallery, London, 1965, 1975, 1982
Tavel, Hans Christoph von, 42
Tell, William, 3; 1756, 1767, 1832, 1844, 1845
Temple, Earl, 1782
Tensing, Sherpa, 1953
Tennyson, Alfred, Lord, 54; 1846
textiles, British, exported to Switzerland, 68, 69; 1398, 1541, 1716, 1835, 1893, 1904, 1909, 1937
textiles, Swiss, exported to Britain, 68, 71; 1593, 1835, 1909. 1937, 1951
Thackeray, W.M., 54; 1852, 1861
Thalberg, Sigismond, 56; 1871
Thatcher, Margaret, 32; 1973, 1984
Thellusson, Peter, 74; 1762
Theodor, 7th C
Théodule pass, 1821
Thirty Years' War, 21, 22, 74; 1618, 1648
Thoman, Caspar, 1599
Thomson, Lord, of Monifieth, 1970
Thomson, James, 51; 1730, 1739, 1744
Thompson, Sir Richard, 1976
Thun, 16; 1802, 1848, 1858, 1882, 1904
Thun, Lake, 6th C; 1799, 1975
Thunersee, *see* Thun, Lake
Thurgau, 1838
Thurloe, John, 1653
Thurnheer, Walter, 1943
Thusis, 1904
Ticino, 40, 54; 1810, 1874, 1881, 1886, 1890
Ticonderoga, Battle of, 1778
Times, The, 14, 31; 1850, 1927, 1938
Tinguely, Jean Charles, 48; 1982
Tippett, Michael, 57; 1953, 1954, 1956
Tobler Company, 1912
tobogganing, 34; 1876, 1877, 1885, 1902
Tocqueville, Alexis de, 68
Toggenburg, 1762, 1978
Tonhalle, Zurich, 1962; Orchestra, 1953
Töpffer, Adam Wolfgang, 46; 1825
Töpffer, Rudolphe, 1823
Tour-de-Peilz, La, 53; 1785
tourism and travel, costs of holidays in Switzerland: Cook's tours (21 days for £19.17.6), 1863; Emery's tours (14 days for 20 guineas), 1818; Emery's tours (14 days for £20), 1835; *Fortnight in Switzerland for £5.5.0, A*, 1905; Polytechnic tours (27 days for £5.19.0), 1889; *Switzerland on £25* (10 days), 1956
tourism and travel, tours to Switzerland: Thomas Cook's by stage-coach, 1863; B. Emery's by stage-coach, 1818, 1835; Polytechnic holidays, 1889; Lunn's tours, 1902; Pickford's by charabanc, 1921; Public School Alpine Sports Club tours, 1909
Tourneisen, J.J., 1769
Tournes-Rilliet, Jean de, 1789
Towne, Francis, 45; 1781
Townend, Col Stuart, 1948
tractors, British, exported to Switzerland, 1955
trade unions in Switzerland, 84
Tscharner, Vincent Bernard de, 1751
Tschingel pass, 1839
Tschudi, Aegidius, 1653
Tschudi, Burkhard, 56; 1740
Traheron, Bartholomew, 1537, 1548
Travers, 1875
Travies, Mr., 1801
Treaty of Alliance 1815, Swiss accession to the, 30; 1815
Trembley, Abraham, 65; 1743, 1747, 1750
Trento, Pace with Swiss troops at, 1516
Trey, César de, 1911
Trey, Emmanuel de, 1911
Truninger, Max, 1953
Tuckett, F.F., 1859
Turegum Insurance, 1962
Turin, 1613, 1617, 1622, 1627, 1754, 1782
Turner, J.M.W., 2, 45, 46; 1776, 1802, 1810, 1842, 1844, 1948, 1976
Turner, Richard, 1555
Turrettini, Jean Alphonse, c1732
Turrettini, François, 1652
Tussaud, Mme Marie, 39; 1802
Tyndale, William, 1535
Tyndall, Prof John, 34, 67; 1857, 1858, 1862, 1868

UBS Securities Ltd, 1974
Ulmis, Johannes ab, 1548
unemployment, British, 1933, 1936, 1983
unemployment, Swiss, 77; 1933, 1936, 1983
Unilever group, 1963, *see also* Lever
Union Bank of Switzerland, 76, 77, 82; 1856, 1967, 1974, 1984

Unione Ticinese, London, 1874
United Alkali Company, 1867
United Dominions Trust, 1970
United States of Europe, Churchill's speech in Zurich, 1946
universities, Swiss, 85
University College, London, 68; 1831
University of London Institute of Germanic Studies, 1984
Unterwalden, 10, 81; 1375
Unton, Sir Edward, 1563
Uri, canton of, 81; 1756
Uster factory, near Zurich, 1832
Utrecht, Treaty of, 1709

Valais, canton, 1062, 1246, 1732, 1810, 1855, 1868, 1943, 1954
Val de Travers, 1913; asphalt, 71
Val de Travers Asphalt Paving Co, 1928
Valère Castle, organ of, 1954
Valium, 1973
Vallorbe, 990
Vallotton, Benjamin, 1917
Valtellina, The, 22; 1618, 1622
Vampire fighter planes, 16; 1948, 1950, 1957
Vanbrugh, Sir John, 1667
Van Dyck, Sir Anthony, 42; 1611, 1640
Van Neck & Co, 1763
Varley, Eric, 1978
Vattel, Emmerich de, 52
Vaud, canton of, 17, 38, 85; 1236, 1256, 1262, 1290, 1618, 1721, 1723, 1783, 1815, 1833, 1872, 1977
Vaughan Williams, Ralph, 58; 1938, 1953
Venice, 22; 1523, 1618, 1622; agent in Zurich, 23
Venom jet fighter planes, 16; 1954, 1979, 1983
Verbier, 1904
Vevey, 54; 1660, 1665, 1698, 1785, 1802, 1844, 1852, 1878, 1904, 1908, 1921
Vickers group, 1919, 1955, 1957
Victor Amadeus II, Duke of Savoy, 1694
Victoria, Duchess of Kent, 1844
Victoria, Queen, 34, 37, 43; 1789, 1796, 1818, 1837, 1851, 1852, 1856, 1860, 1864, 1868, 1869, 1901
Victoria Hall, Geneva, 1904
Victoria hotels, 1868
Vienna, Treaty of, 1814, 1815, 1847, 1860

Vigier, William de, 73; 1936
Vignoles, Charles, 1853
Vignoles, Henry, 1853
Villa Diodati, see Diodati
Villa Rosemont, Lausanne, 1846
Villars, 1883, 1904, 1908, 1909
Villefranche, 69; 1628
Villettes, Arthur, 1751
Villmergen War, 23; 1656
Vinet, Alexandre, 1842
Vischer, Sir Hans, 1945
Vischer, Comdt. de Corps J.J., 1975
Vischer, Marcus, 1945
Vita Insurance Co., 82
vitamins, Swiss production of, 79; 1939, 1984
Vitznau, 1904
Vivian, Lord, 1881
Voigt, F.A., 1944
Volkart Bros Ltd, 1948
Voltaire, François Marie Arouet, 74; 1733, 1756, 1764, 1766, 1776, 1802
Vorarlberg question, The, 1918
Vuippens, Girard de, 1290
Vulliamy, Benjamin Louis, 1781, 1854
Vulliamy, Justin, 40; 1742, 1781, 1854

Wäber, Abraham, 1776
Wäber, Heinrich, 1802
Wäber, Johann, 43; 1776, 1802
Wagner, J.J., 1684
Wake, Sir Isaac, 22; 1617, 1618, 1626, 1629
Wake, Archbishop William, 1719, 1723
Waldensians, massacre of, 23; 1654, 1655, 1658
Wales, 23; 1256, 1286, 1767, 1768
Walker, Francis, 1864
Walker, Frank, 1826
Walker, Lucy, 34; 1864
Walkinshaw, Miss, 1754
Wall, Daniel, 1819
Wallis, George Augustus, 1788
Wallis, John, 64; 1655, 1676
Walpole, Horace, 1739
Walpole, Sir Robert, 28; 1739, 1740
Walsingham, Sir Francis, 1555, 1582, 1599
Walton, Elijah, 1865
Walton, William, 57; 1926
Wander, A., Ltd, 1909, 1967
War of American Independence, 1775, 1780
War of the League of Augsburg, 1690

Warburg S.G., & Co, 1958
Waring, Samuel Miller, 54
Wasenhorn, The, 1844
Washington, George, 1780
watchmaking industry, Swiss, 80, 81;
    1670, 1932; exports to Britain, 69;
    1855, 1909, 1915, 1920, 1937, 1951,
    1955; for colonial markets, 1887
Waterford, Ireland, New Geneva plan,
    1782
Waterloo, Battle of, 30; 1815
Waterlow, Sir Ernest, 1887
Waters, Arthur William, 1869
Watt, James, jnr., c1773
Watteville, Maj-Gen A.L.K. de, 1813
Watteville, Robert de, 1086
Watteville Regiment, 1813, 1816
Webb, Beatrice, 1920
Webb, Sydney, 1920
Webber, John, *see* Wäber, Johann
Wedgwood, Josiah, 1796
Wedgwood, Thomas, 47; 1796
Wedgwood pottery factory, 1802
Weggis, Lake Lucerne, 1948
Weisshorn, The, 1856
Weitnauer, Albert, 1978
Welfare Office for Swiss Girls in Great
    Britain, 1949
Wellesley, Lord, *see* Wellington, Duke of
Wellington, 1st Duke of, 1802, 1814
Welsh Miners' Choir, 1963
Welsh National Opera, 58; 1974
Weltwoche, Die, 1965
Wengen, 1817, 1904, 1911
Wengernalp, 54; 1816
Wertmuller, Brothers, 1593
Wesley, Charles, 1752
Wesley, John, 40; 1717, 1748, 1752
West Point, USA, 1780
Westminster, City of, 1911, 1984
Westminster Abbey, 1062, 1070, 1770
Westminster Bridge, 40; 1738, 1750
Westminster School, 60
Westphalia, Peace of, 1648
Wetterhorn, The, 1854, 1945
White, Gilbert, 43; 1768
Whitgift, Archbishop John, 1589
Whittingham, William, 1556, 1560,
    1685
Whymper, Edward, 34; 1861, 1865,
    1897
Wickham, William, 29; 1794, 1797,
    1799, 1816
Wieland, Christoph, 1762

Wigram, William, 1862
Wilde, Oscar, 54; 1899
Wildstrubel, The, 1908
Wilhelm II, Kaiser, 1912
Wille, Commandant de Corps, 1910
Willink, Henry, 1883
Wilkes, John, 1765
Wilkinson, Joshua, 1791
Wilkinson, Bishop T.E., 1887, 1902
William, Bishop of Winchester, 1236
William I, King, 38; 1070, 1086
William III, King, 12, 14, 25, 40, 59, 64;
    1662, 1665, 1679, 1688, 1689, 1690,
    1692, 1694, 1698, 1707, 1716
Williams, Alan, 1978
Williams, Capt Edward, RN, 1820
Williams, Helen Maria, 54
Williams, Lt Col, 1799
Williams & Glyns, 1975, 1983
Williamson & Co, 1852
Wills, Alfred, 34; 1854
Wilsdorf, Hans, 73; 1903, 1920
Wilsdorf & Davis, 1903, 1920
Wilson, Harold, 1964
Wilton, Andrew, 45
Wilton Park, 1948
Winchester, 1070; Statute of, 15
Windham, William, snr, 1741
Windham, William, jnr, 1741, 1788
Windsor, 1773; Treaty of, 1523
Winkworth, Mr & Mrs, 1863
winter holidays in Switzerland,
    development of, 34; 1861, 1864,
    1869, 1876, 1885, 1892, 1902, 1909
Winterthur, 1801, 1851, 1871
Winterthur Insurance Group, 82; 1919
Winterthur Silks Ltd, 1933
Witz, Konrad, 45
Wolf, Casper, 46
Wolf, Reginald, 49; c1549, 1550
Wolfe, General, James, 1778
Wolfensberger, J., 1839
Wolff, Gen Karl, 1945
Wolsey, Cardinal, 17; 1513, 1516
Woodward, John, 1704
Woolf, Virginia, 1859
woollen goods, British, exported to
    Switzerland, 68; 1541, 1823, 1835,
    1909; Swiss, exported to Britain,
    1909
Woolwich Arsenal, 40; 1716, 1804,
    1822
Wordsworth, William, 5, 34, 53; 1790,
    1807

Wotton, Sir Henry, 22, 33; 1593, 1597, 1622, 1626, 1639
Wraight, Sir John, 1974
Wren, Sir Christopher, 1667
Wulflingen, 1801
Wybergh, Cecil, 1908
Wyndham, H.P., 1768
Wyss, Johann David, 48
Wyss, Salomon, 1805
Wyss, Sophie, 58; 1919

Young, Edward, 1739, 1751
Young, Geoffrey Winthrop, 34; 1905, 1935
Young, Peter, 1564
YMCA, The, 1916
Yverdon, 59; 990, 1260, 1805, 1817; English castle builder at, 1286

Zachary, Long & Haldimand, 1765
Zapolites, The, 1516, 1518
Zbinden, Prof H., 1946
Zenith Watches Ltd, 1933
Zermatt, 1821, 1855, 1858, 1868, 1881, 1889, 1870, 1894, 1897, 1904, 1909, 1909, 1955
Zeugheer, Jakob, 1865
Zinal, 1909
Zinal Rothorn, The, 1935
Zollikofer of St Gallen, 1653
Zopfi, Hans, 56
Zug, 1485
Zuoz School, Engadine, 1925
Zurich, *passim*; Academy, 51; 1725; airport, 1984; 2nd Battle of, 29; 1799; Bible, 1535; Council of, 1551, 1754, 1782, 1963; English seminary at, 1555; Festival, 1962; 'Gnomes' of, 77; 1964, 1965; Lake of, 1782, 1799, 1844; Opera House, 1962, 1974; University, 59; 1973
Zurich Insurance group, 1924, 1960, 1962
Zwilchenbart, Emmanuel, 1828
Zwingli, Huldrych, 18, 21, 49, 59; 1503, 1518, 1519, 1529, 1530, 1537, 1547, 1555, 1572, 1611
Zwingli, Rudolf, 1572

SWITZERLAND